THE HEKT-416-689STORY

ILLUSTRATIONS BY KENKICHI SUGIMOTO

ILLUSTRATIONS BY KENKICHI SUGIMOTO

THE

HEIKÉ

STORY

EIJI YOSHIKAWA

Translated from the Japanese by
FUKI WOOYENAKA URAMATSU

CHARLES E. TUTTLE COMPANY

Rutland, Vermont & Tokyo, Japan

Originally published in Japan as Shin Heiké Monogatari

© *1956 by Alfred A. Knopf, Inc.*

Published by the Charles E. Tuttle Company, Inc.
of Rutland, Vermont & Tokyo, Japan
with editorial offices at
2-6 Suido 1-chome, Bunkyo-ku, Tokyo 112
by special arrangement with
Alfred A. Knopf, Inc., New York

ISBN 0-8048-1376-0

First Tuttle edition, 1956
Nineteenth printing, 1995

Printed in Japan

A NOTE ON

the Historical Background of

The Heiké Story

and on Its Author

WILL BE FOUND ON PAGE 623

THE HEIKÉ

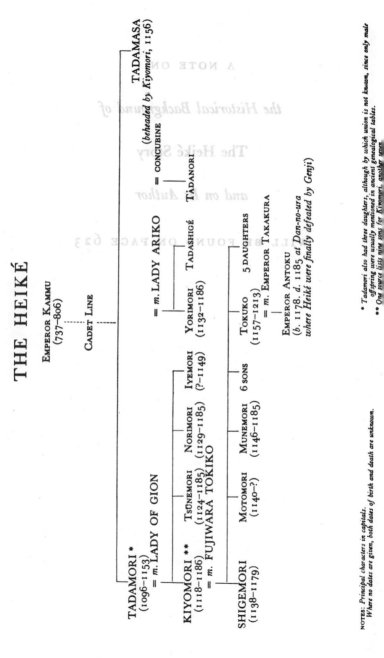

EMPEROR KAMMU
(737–806)

CADET LINE

TADAMASA
(beheaded by Kiyomori, 1156)

= CONCUBINE

TADANORI

= m. LADY ARIKO

YORIMORI
(1132–1186)

TADASHIGÉ

TADAMORI *
(1096–1153)
= m. LADY OF GION

IYEMORI
(?–1149)

NORIMORI
(1129–1185)

TSUNEMORI
(1124–1185)

KIYOMORI **
(1118–1186)
= m. FUJIWARA TOKIKO

MUNEMORI
(1146–1185)

6 SONS

MOTOMORI
(1140–?)

SHIGEMORI
(1138–1179)

TOKUKO
(1157–1213)
= m. EMPEROR TAKAKURA

5 DAUGHTERS

EMPEROR ANTOKU
(b. 1178. d. 1185 at Dan-no-ura
where Heiké were finally defeated by Genji)

NOTES: Principal characters in capitals.
Where no dates are given, both dates of birth and death are unknown.

* Tadamori also had three daughters, although by which union is not known, since only male offspring were usually mentioned in ancient genealogical tables.
** One source lists nine sons for Kiyomori, another seven.

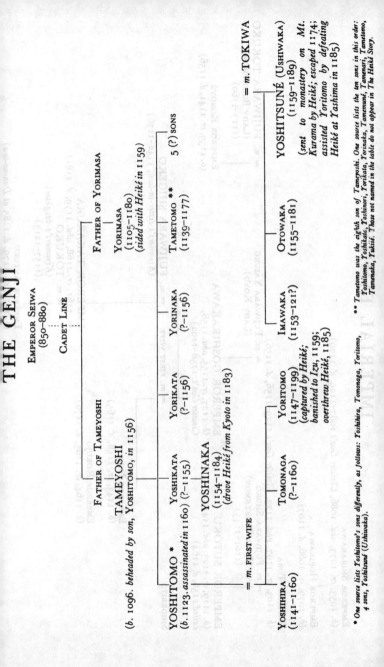

THE GENJI

EMPEROR SEIWA
(850–880)

CADET LINE

FATHER OF TAMEYOSHI

TAMEYOSHI
(b. 1096. beheaded by son, YOSHITOMO, in 1156)

FATHER OF YORIMASA

YORIMASA
(1105–1180)
(sided with Heiké in 1159)

YOSHITOMO *
(b. 1123. assassinated in 1160)

YOSHIKATA
(?–1155)

YORIKATA
(?–1156)

YORINAKA
(?–1156)

TAMETOMO **
(1139–1177)

5 (?) SONS

YOSHINAKA
(1154–1184)
(drove Heiké from Kyoto in 1183)

= m. FIRST WIFE

YOSHIHIRA
(1141–1160)

TOMONAGA
(?–1160)

YORITOMO
(1147–1199)
(captured by Heiké;
banished to Izu, 1159;
overthrew Heiké, 1185)

IMAWAKA
(1153–121?)

OTOWAKA
(1155–1181)

= m. TOKIWA

YOSHITSUNÉ (Ushiwaka)
(1159–1189)
(sent to monastery on Mt.
Kurama by Heiké; escaped 1174;
assisted Yoritomo by defeating
Heiké at Yashima in 1185)

* One source lists Yoshitomo's sons differently, as follows: Yoshihira, Tomonaga, Yoritomo,
4 sons, Yoshitsuné (Ushiwaka).

** Tametomo was the eighth son of Tameyoshi. One source lists the ten sons in this order:
Yoshitomo, Yoshikata, Yoshinori, Yorikata, Yorinaka, Tamemune, Tamenari, Tametomo,
Tamenaka, Yukiié. Those not named in the table do not appear in The Heiké Story.

IMPERIAL FAMILY

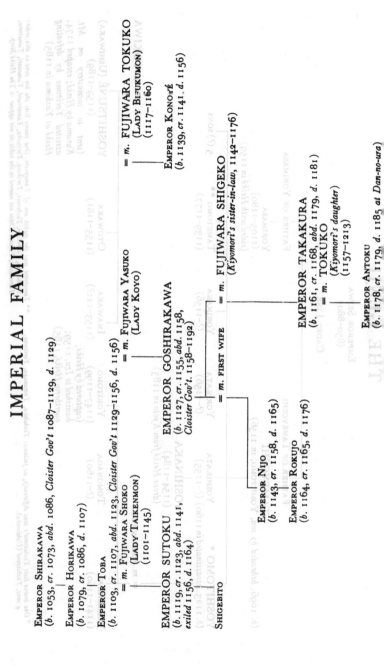

Emperor Shirakawa (b. 1053, cr. 1073, abd. 1086, *Cloister Gov't* 1087–1129, d. 1129)

Emperor Horikawa (b. 1079, cr. 1086, d. 1107)

Emperor Toba (b. 1103, cr. 1107, abd. 1123, *Cloister Gov't* 1129–1156, d. 1156)
= m. **Fujiwara Shoko** (Lady Taikenmon) (1101–1145)

Emperor Sutoku (b. 1119, cr. 1123, abd. 1141, exiled 1156, d. 1164)

Shigebito

= m. **Fujiwara Yasuko** (Lady Koyo)

Emperor Goshirakawa (b. 1127, cr. 1155, abd. 1158, *Cloister Gov't* 1158–1192)
= m. **first wife**

Emperor Nijo (b. 1143, cr. 1158, d. 1165)

Emperor Rokujo (b. 1164, cr. 1165, d. 1176)

= m. **Fujiwara Tokuko** (Lady Bifukumon) (1117–1160)

Emperor Konoé (b. 1139, cr. 1141, d. 1156)

= m. **Fujiwara Shigeko** (*Kiyomori's sister-in-law*, 1142–1176)

Emperor Takakura (b. 1161, cr. 1168, abd. 1179, d. 1181)
= m. **Tokuko** (*Kiyomori's daughter*) (1157–1213)

Emperor Antoku (b. 1178, cr. 1179, d. 1185 at *Dan-no-ura*)

THE FUJIWARA

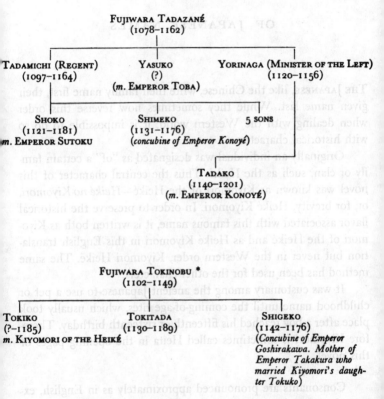

FUJIWARA TADAZANÉ
(1078–1162)

TADAMICHI (REGENT)　　YASUKO　　YORINAGA (MINISTER OF THE LEFT)
(1097–1164)　　　　　　(?)　　　　　(1120–1156)
　　　　　　　　　(m. EMPEROR TOBA)

SHOKO　　　　SHIMEKO　　　　5 SONS
(1121–1181)　(1131–1176)
(m. EMPEROR SUTOKU)　(concubine of Emperor Konoyé)

TADAKO
(1140–1201)
(m. EMPEROR KONOYÉ)

FUJIWARA TOKINOBU *
(1102–1149)

TOKIKO　　　　TOKITADA　　　　SHIGEKO
(?–1185)　　　(1130–1189)　　　(1142–1176)
(m. KIYOMORI OF THE HEIKÉ)　　(Concubine of Emperor
　　　　　　　　　　　　　　Goshirakawa. Mother of
　　　　　　　　　　　　　　Emperor Takakura who
　　　　　　　　　　　　　　married Kiyomori's daugh-
　　　　　　　　　　　　　　ter Tokuko)

* In history Tokinobu is known as a member of the Heiké clan. In The Heiké Story the author assumes he was a Fujiwara who
was disowned by his own clan after the Shrine Incident and that Tokinobu was formally made a member of the Heiké clan
after that.

NOTE ON THE

ORDER & PRONUNCIATION

OF JAPANESE NAMES

THE JAPANESE, like the Chinese, write their family name first, their given name last. While they sometimes now reverse this order when dealing with the Western world, it is impossible to do so with historical characters.

Originally an individual was designated as "of" a certain family or clan, such as the Heiké. Thus the central character of this novel was known as Kiyomori of the Heiké—*Heiké-no-Kiyomori*, or, for brevity, Heiké Kiyomori. In order to preserve the historical flavor associated with this famous name, it is written both as Kiyomori of the Heiké and as Heiké Kiyomori in this English translation but never in the Western order, Kiyomori Heiké. The same method has been used for the other characters.

It was customary among the ancient Japanese to use a pet or childhood name until the coming-of-age rites, which usually took place after a boy reached his fifteenth or sixteenth birthday. Therefore Kiyomori is sometimes called Heita in the opening pages of this novel.

Consonants are pronounced approximately as in English, except that *g* is always hard, as in Gilbert. Vowels are pronounced as in Italian and always sounded separately, never as diphthongs. Thus Heiké is pronounced *Heh-ee-keh*. There is no heavy penultimate accent as in English; it is safest to accent each syllable equally. The final *e* is always sounded, as in Italian.

CONTENTS

THE HEIKÉ STORY

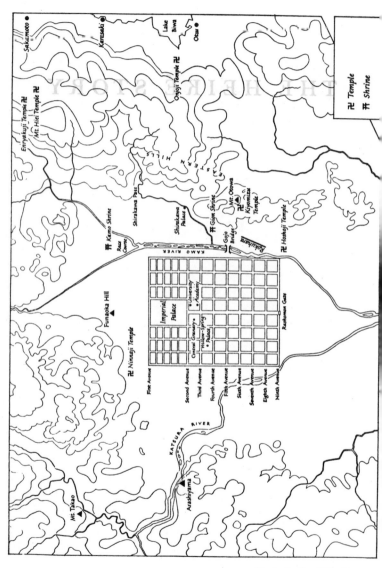

Kyoto in the 12th Century

Kyoto and its surroundings in the 12th Century

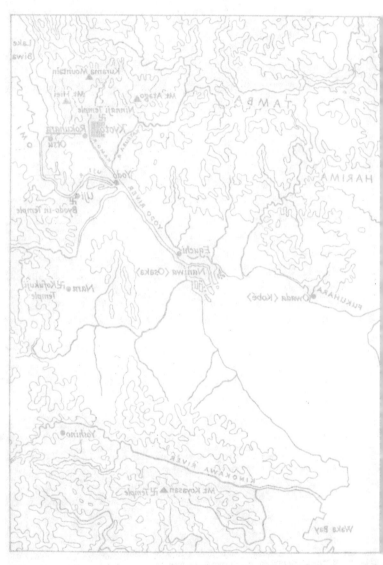

Kyoto and its surroundings in the 12th Century

CHAPTER I

THE MARKET-PLACE

And you, Heita, no more of that loitering and mooning along
the Shiokoji on your way back!" Heita Kiyomori heard
his father, Tadamori, shout after him as he set out on
his errand. He felt that voice pursuing him every step of the way.

He feared his father; his every word seemed to stick in the
back of Kiyomori's mind. The year before last, in 1135, Kiyomori
had accompanied his father and some men-at-arms for the first time
from Kyoto to Shikoku and then to Kyushu on an expedition
against the pirates of the Inland Sea. From April of that spring

5

until August they had hunted their quarry and, with the pirate chief and more than thirty of his henchmen in chains, returned to the capital triumphant, in an unforgettable march of victory. Yes, undoubtedly his father was a hero—despite everything!

Kiyomori's opinion of his father had changed after that. His fear of him, too. From boyhood Kiyomori had believed that indolence caused his father to shun people, that he lacked ambition, had no head for managing his worldly affairs, and clung to his poverty from pure obstinacy. This, however, was not the father he had observed for himself as a child, but the image impressed on Kiyomori's mind by his mother. As early as he could remember, their home at Imadegawa, in the purlieus of the capital, had been a miserable ruin; the leaking roofs had not been repaired for more than ten years; the untended gardens ran wild with weeds, and the decaying house been the scene of unending quarrels between his father and mother. And in spite of such disharmony, child after child was born to them—Heita Kiyomori, the eldest; Tsunemori, the second son; a third and even a fourth son. Tadamori, to whom the duties of a Palace official were distasteful, made no effort to put in an appearance at the Palace or the office of the Imperial Guards unless he was specially summoned. His sole revenues now were the crops from his manor in Isé, and except for occasional largess from the Palace, he received none of the emoluments of his rank.

Kiyomori was beginning to understand the reasons for those endless parental bickerings. His mother was a talkative woman—in the words of his father, one who talked "like oiled paper set on fire"—whose habitual complaint was: "At every word I say, you turn on me with grim looks. When have I ever seen you behave like a proper husband? I never knew you to behave as though you were the respected master of this house. There are laggards enough in this world, yet there must be few in this capital as lazy as you! Were you a state councillor or a court official, I could understand. Have you never taken thought for our poverty? You country-bred Heiké no doubt find this wretched penury suits you, but I, reared in this capital, and all my kinsmen come of the noble Fujiwara clan! Here, under this leaking roof, morning and night, yesterday and yet again today, I munch the same coarse fare. I shall not be at the moon-viewing and the imperial banquets when autumn comes, nor when spring returns shall I, in my festive robes, join the cherry-viewing at the Palace. I hardly know whether I am a woman or a badger as I go on like this day after day. . . . Ah, ill-starred woman that I am! Little did I dream that this was to be my fate!"

This would be only the prelude to an unquenchable stream of reproaches and complaints, if Tadamori did not silence her. And once this "oiled paper" was set on fire, what did she most bewail, crying to the heavens and calling upon the earth as witness? Even her son Kiyomori wearied of her complaints. He knew them each one. First, her husband, a sluggard, had never troubled his head about a livelihood. For years he had done nothing but stay at home —a good-for-nothing! Second of her complaints: because of his poverty, she had been obliged to forgo all exchanges of hospitality with her relatives, the Fujiwara; no longer could she attend the imperial entertainments or accept invitations to the banquets at the Court. Alas, she who had been born to grandeur and luxury had married a mere Heiké warrior and ruined her life. And she would end her laments with the cry: "Ah, had there only been no children! . . ." These words frightened Kiyomori as a child, harassed and saddened him unreasonably, so by the time he was sixteen or seventeen the grave look in his eyes often perplexed his mother.

Kiyomori wondered what she would have done if there had been no children. But this he knew: she regretted above all things her marriage to his father; were it possible she would even now leave him, make up the lost years by returning to that life of extravagant splendor; like her patrician kinswomen drive about in an ox-carriage, bathed in moonlight and garlanded with blossoms; dally with this captain or that courtier; exchange love lyrics with gallants, leading the life of those ladies told in the *Tales of Genji*. She could not die without fulfilling her destiny as a woman.

Over and over again the "oiled paper" thus took flame. And her young sons, hardly believing she could be their mother, watched her daily with mournful eyes.

7

Kiyomori, now nearly twenty, was indignant; if her sons were such a hindrance to her, why did she not leave them? As for his father, how could he endure all this in silence? Was Kiyomori to shout back at this woman in his stead? The bitch! Who, indeed, were the Fujiwara, those Fujiwara of whom she bragged without regard for his father's feelings? A fool—his father, who only dared to shout at his sons! The coward! See how people jeered at the Squint-Eyed One who married a beauty only to find her a shrew!

People seemed to think that children always sided with their mother, but in this house it was otherwise. The youngest, not yet weaned, and his third brother were still too young to take sides, but Tsunemori, old enough now to understand what went on, sometimes stared with hate in his eyes at their mother when she raved. At such times the brothers were ashamed of their father. He—a man—who seemed to live only to be abused by his wife, sat quietly listening to her tirades, his scarred eyelids drawn down over his crossed eyes, staring mutely at the clenched fists in his lap.

Kiyomori had to admit that his father was ugly—that pockmarked face, those eyes which had got him a nickname, this man in his forties and the prime of his years. . . . On the other hand, there was his beautiful mother, looking as though she were still in her twenties. Little wonder that those who saw her refused to believe she was the mother of four sons. Though she was reduced to penury, her toilette remained irreproachable. She showed no sign that she knew or cared when the retainers, unable to endure the sight of their misery, stole out to barter furtively for food, or tore the bamboo from the rotting hedges and planks from the floor for the kitchen fires, or the wailing children made water in their grimy clothes. She would repair in the morning to her boudoir, where not even her husband was allowed to set foot, lay out her gold-lacquered comb-cases and mirrors, and in the evening retire to her bath to polish her skin. She often startled the household by appearing in her richest finery, announcing that she was off to pay her respects to her relatives, the Nakamikado, and with the languid airs of a court lady would stroll to the nearest stable to hire a carriage and drive away on her calls.

8

"Fox-woman . . . bewitching fox-woman!" the retainers sneered when she was out of hearing. Even graying Mokunosuké, who had come as a boy to serve in the household, would stand with an inconsolable child weeping on his back and gaze with smoldering eyes after the departing mother. Later he could be heard walking the path round the stable in the dark, singing lullabies to his young charge. Tadamori, at such times, would usually be seen leaning against a post in the shadows, his eyes closed, silent, lost in thought.

Tsunemori had a scholarly bent; indifferent to what went on about him, he spent his days at his books. He and Kiyomori had enrolled at the Imperial Academy of Chinese Classics at an early age, though the latter after a time ceased to go. In spite of his father's urgings, Kiyomori felt there was nothing to be gained from reading Confucius, whose teachings seemed unrelated to the world that he saw around him or the life in his own home. Kiyomori usually idled about as his father did. Often, lying sprawled by his brother's desk, Kiyomori would chat about the horse-races at Kamo or gossip of the women in the neighborhood; or when his brother Tsunemori was disinclined to listen, would continue to lie there, staring vacantly at the ceiling, picking his nose. At other times he would rush to the archery range at the rear of the house to twang a bow, or abruptly dash off to the stable and later come home savagely whipping his mount, drenched with sweat. Seemingly, he acted only on impulses.

Kiyomori often reflected that his mother was queer; his father no less so; only Tsunemori seemed to be like other people. Even he, Kiyomori, the eldest and heir, also was odd. All in all, they were a strange lot, an ill-assorted family. Yet the Heiké of Isé were one of the few warrior families coming of a distinguished line. In the capital, where it was known that the Heiké traditions had come down through several generations, people prophesied that the family tree would send forth more and yet more branches and bring renown to that name. Kiyomori, however, was indifferent to such talk, aware only that he was young and carefree and full of a sense of well-being.

9

He knew the nature of the errand on which he was going, for he had read the letter entrusted to him. Kiyomori was on his way to borrow money of a relative, his uncle. This had happened often enough, and he was to see his father's only brother, Tadamasa, a member of the Imperial Guards, to whom Tadamori constantly turned with pleas for help.

At New Year's Kiyomori's mother had taken to bed with a cold; in her usual way she drove her husband to his wits' end by her vanity and reckless extravagance, demanding that the court physician attend her, calling for costly drugs, complaining that the bedclothes were heavy, and scolding that the food was not fit for an invalid.

The poverty that Tadamori was able to put out of mind blew on them overnight like an icy wind. Although his victory over the pirates two years ago had been rewarded with imperial gifts of gold and other favors, which relieved him of his money difficulties, this unforeseen good fortune had only led his wife to indulge in lavish spending. Tadamori believed there was enough to provide for his family for another year, until her illness exhausted what remained in less than three weeks and they were reduced to sipping thin rice gruel for their morning and evening meals.

Painfully composing another of his begging letters to his brother, Tadamori turned to his son. "Heita, forgive me for sending you again to your uncle. . . ." This was the errand on which he was to go. Kiyomori raged with a sense of injury—to be told not to loiter and moon again on the Shiokoji! Even a child deserved to have some diversions. Was he not twenty this spring? Yet he, a mere youth, was sent to borrow money. Kiyomori was filled with self-pity, reflecting as he walked that there could be nothing wrong in coveting a few pleasures.

"Again, Heita," Kiyomori's uncle exclaimed as he laid down the letter with disgust. When he gave his nephew the money the letter requested, Kiyomori's aunt appeared, and she stormed: "Why do you people not go and beg of your mother's kinsmen? Are they not all nobles of the Fujiwara clan?—the most honorable

Nakamikado—that dazzling galaxy of aristocrats! Doesn't your mother boast of them? Go, tell this to your father, too!"

Then began a tirade in which uncle and aunt proceeded to abuse Kiyomori's parents. What could be more humiliating than this—to have others so critical of his father and mother? Large tears rolled down his cheeks.

Kiyomori knew, none the less, that his uncle's life was no easy one. Although a system of Imperial Guards had been created, and more and more warriors were employed at the Court and the Cloister Palace, the Fujiwara aristocrats regarded the warriors as no better than slaves. They were valued only for their ferocity, likened to that of the hounds of Kishu and Tosa, and not permitted to rank with the courtiers who surrounded the imperial dais; their fiefs in the provinces were mainly barren mountain tracts or waste moors. The warriors were despised, condemned as though they were plebeians; without the honor due their calling, they subsisted precariously on the meager proceeds of their manors, and their poverty had passed into proverb.

The bitter winds in February were sometimes called the First East Winds, but the longing for spring somehow made them seem more piercing. Perhaps it was the gnawings of hunger that made Kiyomori shiver. Neither his uncle nor his aunt had asked him to stay and dine with them. It was better so, Kiyomori reflected; his one thought had been to escape from that house. Never, never again would he come on another such errand. Not even if he were reduced to beggary. How maddening to have wept, while they probably thought that his tears fell at the sight of the money. How galling! His eyelids were still swollen, and Kiyomori felt passers-by turn to stare at his tear-stained face.

This, however, was not why strangers turned to peer at him, but rather young Kiyomori's appearance—his wrinkled robe and grimy under-tunic. The ox-tenders and under-servants were more warmly clothed than he. Not even the waifs playing under the Rashomon Gate wore such rags. Had he not carried his long sword, for what would they take him—his mud-splattered sandals and

1 1

leather socks; the faded, peaked cap from which the lacquer had chipped, tipped rakishly to one side; this stocky figure with its hard muscles; a head slightly too large for the body; eyes, ears, and nose of generous proportions; the eyebrows—like two caterpillars—beneath which the narrow eyes slanted down at the outer corners, lending charm to a face that might otherwise look ferocious or even cruel; this odd-faced little fellow with fair skin and large, ruddy ears, which made the youthful features strangely attractive?

People in passing wondered who this young warrior could be, where he served as a Guard—remarked how he strode along with his arms folded. Kiyomori knew that this pose which he assumed only in the streets—never before his father—was frowned on by Tadamori, who thought it extremely unseemly for one of high birth. But this manner had become a habit with him on the streets —something Kiyomori had learned from the men who crowded the Shiokoji. He could not possibly go there today; money he had—that galling, borrowed cash! He trembled for himself. The magnetism of the Shiokoji tugged at all his senses. Weak of will, he felt he could never resist going there.

Arrived at the crossroads, he gave in. The warm wind blowing his way from the Shiokoji brought odors that tantalized him and mocked at his hesitation. There they were, the same ones, at it as usual—the old woman selling roasted pheasant legs and small sizzling birds on spits; next to her stall, a man with a large jug of wine, drunkenly singing and laughing uproariously as he served his customers; there, on the shady side of the market-place, the young orange-seller sitting forlornly with a basket of fruit in her lap; and there the peddler of clogs, the shoe-menders, father and son. There they were—more than a hundred small stalls, side by side, displaying dried fish, old clothes, and gaudy knickknacks with which these people sustained a bare living.

To Kiyomori each stall, each soul here seemed borne under by the crushing weight of the world; everyone here was a pitiful weed, trodden underfoot—a conglomeration of human lives putting down roots in this slime, living and letting live in the struggle to survive; and he was stirred by the fearful and magnificent courage communicated by the scene. The steam from boiling food and the smoke from roasting meats seemed to veil the secrets of that swarming crowd in mystery—the groups of street gamblers, the enticing smiles of the wantons who threaded their way through the throng, the loud wailing of infants, the drumbeats of the ballad-singers—all that medley of odors and sounds made his head reel. This was the paradise of the lowly, matching the cultivated pleasures of the aristocrats, the gay capital of the common folk. And this was the reason for Tadamori's stern warnings not to disgrace him by coming here.

But Kiyomori liked it here. He felt at home among these people. Even the Thieves' Market, whose stalls sometimes appeared under the giant nettle tree at the west corner of the market, kept him enthralled. Call them robbers and cutthroats—were they not amiable enough when they had sufficient to fill their bellies? Something was out of joint in a world that drove these men to steal. There were no scoundrels here—rather, they were to be found among the august clouds of Mount Hiei, at Onjoji Temple, and even in Nara, where they made the halls and towers of the Buddhist temples their fortresses—those many evil Buddhas in their robes of brocade and gold.

Nursing such thoughts, Kiyomori found himself in the midst of the jostling crowds; peering here, pausing there, he strolled about, heedless of the night coming on. Not a soul was to be seen under the nettle tree, but in the gathering twilight he made out the glow of tapers, bouquets of flowers and the quivering ascent of incense smoke. Soon dancing-girls and women of a lower order began to appear in groups, one after another, approaching the tree to worship.

The old story ran that long ago the mistress of a notorious brigand had lived on the spot where the nettle tree now grew. In time the superstitious came to believe that prayers offered here would cause a maiden's lover to dream of her, or bring a loathsome malady upon a hated rival. The brigand's death in prison on the 7th of February 988 caused a great stir, and from that time on, the ruffians of the market-place and women of various callings perpetuated his memory with offerings of incense and flowers on the seventh day of each month.

More than a hundred years had passed since this lawless character, the son of a courtier of the Fourth Rank, had gone about wildly burning, pillaging, and murdering, yet he was not forgotten by the common people, for his name seemed branded on their memories. His evil deeds had been the sensation of a period marking the peak of Fujiwara power and magnificence. To the common people the brigand's defiance of the established order was an expression of their secret antagonism, and instead of censuring his deeds they honored them. It was as though neither incense nor flowers would cease to be offered here while a single Fujiwara breathed; and others than the superstitious came to pray here.

"Something of that brigand is in my blood, too," Kiyomori mused; the glowing points of light under the tree began to look like beacons pointing the way to his own future, and he suddenly grew afraid Turning on his heel, he prepared to take flight.

"Well, Heita of Isé! Why the staring and for so long—these young women who come to pray under the nettle tree?"

In the dark Kiyomori could not tell who addressed him. In the next instant the stranger stepped forward and seized Kiyomori by the shoulders and shook him so violently that his head wobbled helplessly.

"Ah, you—Morito!"

"Who else but the warrior Morito? That you should forget me! What are you doing here and why the dazed look?"

"Eh, dazed? I didn't realize that. Are my eyes still swollen?"

"Ho, ho! So there's been a quarrel between your beauteous mother and the Squint-Eyed One, and you could not endure it at home?"

"No. My mother's ill."

Morito laughed coldly. "Ill?"

Morito had been his schoolmate at the Imperial Academy; though a year younger than Kiyomori, he had always seemed the elder even then, and mature. Kiyomori and the others had lagged

1 4

far behind Morito in their studies, and their teacher had predicted a brilliant career for this pupil.

Morito laughed again: "I mean no disrespect, but the lady, I assure you, suffers from attacks of self-love and capriciousness. There's no need to worry, my dear lad; instead, let us be off—for some wine."

"Eh—wine?"

"Certainly. The Lady of Gion's the mother of many sons, but she hasn't changed much from that lady of old. Come, stop fretting."

"Morito, who is this Lady of Gion?" Kiyomori stammered.

"Don't you know of your gracious mother's past?"

"No. And you do?"

"Hmm—if you wish, let me tell you. Come with me, anyway. Leave the Squint-Eyed One to his fate. These are troubled times, Heita. Why let your spirits grow hunchbacked in the springtime of your youth? I thought nothing could trouble you. Stop blubbering and behaving like that woman!"

So saying, Morito once more shook Kiyomori roughly, then strode ahead into the dark.

The room had no walls; thin wooden partitions separated it from the next room; an old strip of cloth took the place of curtains, and a piece of straw matting hung in the doorway. Not even a sound sleeper could sleep through the uproar in the next room— the thumping of hand-drums, the clashing of earthenware, and the obscene singing. A sudden thud as of a body falling shook the house; a loud burst of men's and women's voices raised in laughter followed.

"What! Where am I? Confound it, what time is it?" Kiyomori woke suddenly in great confusion. A woman lay sleeping beside him. There was no mistake about it—this was the brothel on Sixth Avenue. Morito had brought him here. What a fix! He must get home.

What lie could he tell them at home? He could see his father's furious look, hear his mother's nagging and the sound of his little brothers crying with hunger. Good! At least he had not spent all the money borrowed from his uncle. He would go now; Kiyomori sat up wide awake. Where was Morito—still carousing? He would see what all the noise was about.

He trod on the woman's dark hair as he stepped over her sleeping form and peered through a knothole, which let in a thin stream of light; some pine-oil lamps lighted an unfurnished room; straw mats covered the plank floor, and three or four evil-faced priests in clerics' robes, wearing long swords, held dancing-girls on their laps or were embracing them. A few empty wine-flasks lay rolling on the floor.

So Morito had gone, leaving him alone here!

Overcome by panic fear, Kiyomori pulled on his ragged outer robe, buckled on his sword, and in great agitation felt his way along a passage toward a door. In the darkness his fumbling foot struck a metal object that clanged loudly as he stepped outside.

At this sound the priests sprang out of their room, shouting: "Stop, stop! Who dares knock down my halberd and then leave? Wait, you little rascal, there!"

Kiyomori came to a halt, petrified. As he turned to look back, the cold glitter of a halberd flashed in his eyes. This was without doubt the cunning hand of one of those burly priests from Mount Hiei or Onjoji Temple. The challenge had come as swift as the hand of the God of Death. At once the fumes of the wine vanished, the memory of delights, the remorse, and Kiyomori, turning, fled with all his might into the night winds.

As he came in sight of his home, his heart sank. There was the crumbling, wattled-clay wall, covered here and there with dead grass, and the sagging roof of the main gate. What was he to do? What was he to say? Tonight he shrank from the mere thought of seeing his mother; he would rather face his father's wrath. Anger boiled up in Kiyomori; he could not endure the thought of hearing her voice; otherwise, he would have her plead with his father, would beg her forgiveness, and even seek her caresses. Where in the world could a son nurse more treacherous thoughts than he did tonight? Looking up at the wall, he felt sick at heart and aban-

doned. Sanguine and emotional, he was now assailed by a wild
tumult of thoughts that made his eyelids and temples twitch. If
only he had not heard of his mother's past! If only he had not
listened to that Morito!

Remorse overcame him—the memory of Morito, the carousing with those women. All the events of that drink-sodden evening
drifted back in snatches. More vividly than all these he recalled
that room in the brothel—the dark, tangled hair and the warm,
limp limbs. What did it matter whether she was a beauty or a hag?
He was twenty and had tasted for the first time of a strange, unforgettable sweetness, an ecstasy that flooded all his senses with
amazement. His mind kept revolving round a memory that smol-
dered hot in him. Did the scent of her body cling to his? The
thought held him back for an instant; then with one great leap
he cleared the wall. Never had he landed on the other side with
such a deep sense of guilt as tonight. He often came home this
way after his usual night escapades. He found himself in the familiar vegetable patch behind the stable.

"Oh, is it you, my young master, Heita?"

"Hmm—is it you, Old One?" Kiyomori quickly stood erect,
pushing back his tumbled hair. It was the aging retainer, Mokunosuké, who could make him feel almost as guilty as his father did.

Long before Kiyomori was born, Mokunosuké had come to
serve in this house; his two front teeth were now gone, and though
people gossiped about his spineless master and jeered at the poverty of the Heiké, loyal Mokunosuké alone sternly stood guard
over the dignity of his master's house, maintained its ceremonials,
and never relaxed from those offices he thought due from a retainer to his warrior lord.

"And you, my young master, what have you been doing with
yourself? There's not a single light to be seen on the roads at this
time of night," he said, stooping to pick up Kiyomori's worn cap;
as he handed it to Kiyomori, his eyes searched him, scenting something amiss.

"Could you have been brawling with those roistering monks
or been mixed in some bloody quarrel at the crossroads? Though

1 7

I begged the master to go to rest, he would not. Ah, well—welcome back, welcome back."

The narrowed eyes filled with relief, but Kiyomori shrank from the searching look bent on him. So his father was still awake! What of his mother? He quailed at the thought of what lay in store for him. Mokunosuké, without waiting for any questions, began: "Set your mind at rest, my young master, and quietly off to rest. Now to your bed."

"Is it all right, Old One, for me not to go to my father's apartments?"

"In the morning. Let this Old One come with you and add his excuses."

"But he must be furious at my tardy return."

"More than usual. He summoned me at sundown. He seemed beside himself and ordered me to 'go search for that rascal in the Shiokoji.' I patched things up as best I could."

"Yes, and what lie did you give him?"

"Remember, my young master, that it pained me to lie to him, but I told him that I ran to your uncle's, found you in bed with a pain in your stomach, and said that you would return as soon as it was day."

"I'm sorry, Old One, forgive me."

The blossoms of the plum tree by the stable gleamed icily against the dark night. The chilled scent of the blossoms suddenly stung Kiyomori's nostrils, and a spasm passed over his face. Hot tears spilled on Mokunosuké's shoulder as Kiyomori flung his arms round the old man, who stood rigid with foreboding. Under the brittle ribs of his old body, a great wave of feeling suddenly seemed to swell. The long-suppressed love of the stoic old man went out to meet Kiyomori's intense burst of emotion. Together they broke into loud weeping, clinging to each other, until they sank to the ground overcome.

"Oh, my young master, do you—do you so depend on me?"

"You are warm. Listen, Mokunosuké, only your old body seems warm to me. I am alone like the solitary crow abandoned to

1 8

the winter winds. My mother is what you know her to be. That father is not mine—Tadamori of the Heiké is not my father!"

"Eh! who has been saying such a thing?"

"For the first time I've heard the secret about my father! Morito of the Guards told me."

"Ah—that Morito!"

"Yes, Morito. Listen, he said: 'The Squint-Eyed One is not your real father. The Emperor Shirakawa sired you, and *you*, the son of an emperor, go about with an empty belly, in those rags and worn sandals. What a spectacle!' "

"Enough! Say no more," Mokunosuké cried, flinging up his arm as though to silence Kiyomori. But Kiyomori seized his wrist and wrenched it savagely.

"There is more—and you, Old One, know more of this! Why have you kept this from me so long?"

He glared at the old retainer. Mokunosuké, his wrist aching, cringed under that menacing look; the words seemed to be wrung from him as he said: "There, there, calm yourself. If that is so, then Mokunosuké must also speak, though I don't know what Morito of the Guards has been telling you."

"Listen, this is what he said: 'If you're not the son of the late Emperor Shirakawa, then without doubt you're the son of one of those vile priests from Gion. Whether you're the son of an emperor or the offspring of an evil priest, I make no mistake in telling you that you're not Tadamori's real son.' "

"What does that callow Morito know? A touch of learning has turned his head and he thinks all men are fools. As for him, people call him a wastrel. You are rash to believe that shallow-minded fellow, my young master."

"Then, Old One, tell me under oath whether I am an emperor's son or the seed of some debauched priest. Speak! I dare you to tell me!"

Kiyomori was determined that the old man should not protest ignorance. Actually, Mokunosuké was the only other party to this secret, and his candid face clearly showed that he knew it.

CHAPTER II

THE LADY OF GION

Kiyomori of the Heiké was born in 1118. His father, Tadamori, at that time was twenty-three. Although known as
the Squint-Eyed One, mocked at for his poverty, made
the laughing-stock of the common people, and looked down on by
other members of the Heiké clan, this had not always been so.
Tadamori's father had served three successive emperors, been high
in their favor as a shrewd and loyal attendant, and Tadamori had

grown up in the midst of palace splendors. When the Heiké warriors were called up to serve in the Imperial Guards, and gradually outnumbered the Genji warriors, Tadamori and his father became figures of importance. The Emperor Shirakawa chose them to remove Genji warriors from the Court; pitted the two against the powerful armed clergy, and installed father and son in the Court itself as a check on the influence of the Fujiwara courtiers.

Following his abdication, when he became known as the ex-Emperor Shirakawa, the aging monarch took the tonsure and retired to the Cloister Palace. There he established an administration independent of the central government, a Cloister Government, an anomaly which not only made it a rival of the regnant sovereign, but further sharpened the conflict between the Genji and Heiké clansmen.

After his father's death Tadamori succeeded to his father's position, and the ex-Emperor placed even greater trust in the modest Tadamori by appointing him his personal bodyguard. On the visits that the abdicated monarch made from his palace on West Third Avenue to Gion, on the other side of the Kamo River, he always summoned Tadamori and his retainer, Mokunosuké, to accompany him. These clandestine excursions at night were to visit his mistress, for though well in his sixties, he was endowed with unusual vitality, and his amorousness matched the vigor with which he conducted the affairs of his Cloister Government.

There was nothing unusual in the ex-Emperor's keeping a mistress; rather was it an established custom among the aristocrats then to court such women as won their fancy, and become their lovers without censure. There was a reason, however, for the monarch's keeping the identity of his mistress unknown, for she was a dancing-girl whose calling prevented her being admitted to the Palace and installed there. No one knew where and when the aging Emperor had first seen her, but there was gossip that she was a daughter of a nobleman, Nakamikado. Only four or five of the courtiers in attendance on the ex-Emperor knew that a house had been built in Gion, in a garden fenced about with cedar boards, and that the unknown beauty, whom they called the "Lady of

Gion," had gone to live there; they let it be said, however, that she was the mistress of a retired courtier, and living there for the sake of her health.

The Lady of Gion was she who later became Kiyomori's mother. There was no doubt of her having given birth to him. As for his father, she alone knew the secret and chose to keep it a riddle, causing her son to suffer for it twenty years later.

The night was black and the sough of leaves mingled with the sound of the autumn drizzle, setting up a chill murmur along the miry roads and rivulets and on the wooded hills. On this bleak night the ex-Emperor, accompanied by Tadamori and his retainer Mokunosuké, set out on a visit to Gion.

The drenched leaves suddenly gleamed balefully with a red glow that flashed between the trees, and the ex-Emperor crouched, trembling at what he saw.

"Ha! A demon!"

An apparition with a gigantic head appeared between the trees, baring a row of gleaming teeth.

"Strike, Tadamori! Strike!" came the ex-Emperor's anguished cry. Mokunosuké replied, but Tadamori ran forward silently with his halberd poised. The three were soon convulsed with laughter and resumed their way, for the specter was nothing more than a priest, wearing a hat of bunched straws, who had just lighted his oil-vessel as he made his way down the hill from Gion.

That night's adventure seemed to amuse the ex-Emperor inordinately. He was heard to repeat the tale of that encounter with the priest over and over again to his gentlemen-in-waiting, and at each retelling never failed to praise Tadamori's conduct, for had he been timid, would they not have had a dead priest on their hands? The idling courtiers, who prided themselves on their perspicacity, shook their heads among themselves: it was hard to accept his majesty's tale in its entirety. Had he not since that night ceased altogether in his visits to the Lady of Gion? And what was even more puzzling was his giving the lady to Tadamori for wife soon after. And Tadamori, since his marrigae to the lady, lost his zest for living. What was more, Tadamori was never heard to let fall a single word of that night's adventure. Was not all this baffling? There was even more room for speculation when less than nine months from the time Tadamori took the lady to Imadegawa, she gave birth to a son. So his majesty's tale of the priest on that rainy night was somewhat fanciful, a pretext, perhaps. . . .

Even the most curious dared not pursue their conjectures further. To do so was not in good taste among courtiers; moreover, such speculations, they knew, could raise grave issues, best avoided in the interests of self-preservation. The wise merely smiled knowingly.

At that time Mitsuto Endo, Morito's uncle, was a Guard at the Palace. Eighteen years later he told his nephew the story, introducing it with the remark: "Isn't Tadamori's eldest son, Heita Kiyomori, a schoolfellow of yours? I wonder if Tadamori still believes he was honored by the ex-Emperor when given the beloved, the Lady of Gion, for wife, and she soon after gave birth to that Kiyomori? If so, the poor fool! I met a fellow the other day who knew the Lady of Gion intimately. He must now be in his fifties, and lives in one of the temples near Gion, where he's known as the bawdy priest, Kakunen. He claims to be Kiyomori's real father."

"Eh!—is that the truth?"

Morito's interest was suddenly aroused by this revelation about his friend, for he had heard some loose gossip that Kiyomori was an emperor's son. Morito eagerly asked: "You say that the story comes from this Kakunen, who you believe is telling the truth?"

"It was over our wine, somewhere, when we were bragging about our exploits with women, that this Kakunen, whispering that he had never told any man this secret, let me hear it with these very ears."

"Extraordinary!"

"I was astounded, too. I can hardly believe that even a loose-living priest would go to such lengths to lie. Besides, the story hangs together. . . ."

Kakunen, at great length, had told Morito's uncle this tale: Kakunen had once had a glimpse of the Lady of Gion through a crack in the cedarwood fence and lusted after her. As she was his majesty's favorite, he found no way to approach her, and for some time had hovered about the enclosure, followed her about morning and evening whenever she went out, until one day chance brought about the consummation of his schemes, and he took her by violence.

Since the aging ex-Emperor came rarely, and Kakunen was a handsome novice of thirty, in a temple a stone's throw from her house, the Lady of Gion, after a brief period of indecision, was won over by the young priest's blandishments.

On that night of autumn rain, when it seemed least likely that the ex-Emperor would make a visit, Kakunen stole out to an assignation with the Lady of Gion, very nearly came face to face with his majesty, and was almost killed by his bodyguards. If Kakunen was not to be believed, then whose child was that born later under Tadamori's roof?

Mitsuto exacted a promise from his nephew that the story would not be repeated, and Morito kept it to himself until his chance meeting with the ragged and wretched-looking Kiyomori on the Shiokoji, when the secret became unbearable. Partly from the desire to rouse him, Morito invited Kiyomori to drink with him and imparted the story.

"Old One, I know it all now. There's no use in trying to hide it from me. Your own eyes saw everything that night twenty years ago. Is Morito lying, or does he tell the truth? No, I implore you, tell me whose son I am! Old One, I beseech you, tell me the truth, then I can think of the blood in these veins and of my destiny! I beseech you. . . . I beseech you!"

The voice in the shadow of the stable grew still. There was a sound of sobbing. Mokunosuké uttered no word. Above the eaves by the plum tree the eastern clouds were breaking and the winds of dawn struck them chill to the bone.

Mokunosuké sat motionless, his head sunk on his breast, like a figure carved from stone, and Kiyomori, breathing heavily, continued to stare fixedly at the old man. Only the steady pulsing of their hearts seemed to break the agonizing silence that hung over the frozen earth in the dawn.

Mokunosuké groaned deeply at the thought of the revelation he must make.

"I will speak, since you command me to, but first calm yourself." Then he began:

Twenty years ago, the year in which Kiyomori was born, on a black night of rain, Mokunosuké was a witness to an event. He was with his master, Tadamori, accompanying the ex-Emperor, and had seen what took place on the hill near Gion. Yet who would believe the truth about an encounter that had taken place twenty years ago? Even Mokunosuké himself doubted that Kiyomori would believe what he had to tell, for though there was some fact in what that troublesome Morito had said, and in the gossip that circulated —the rainy night, the priest, Tadamori's courage—Mokunosuké's was a different story. He had seen, that night at Gion, a priest make his hurried escape over the fence surrounding the house of the Lady of Gion. That night he was aware that all was not well between the ex-Emperor and his favorite. He had heard the lady weeping; Tadamori had been summoned within; his majesty's voice was heard raised in anger, and the ex-Emperor had returned to the Palace long before daybreak. All this had been quite unusual, beclouding the events of that night. The gossiping of the world at large, even when examined more closely, still threw no light on the truth. That same year the Lady of Gion was given in marriage to Tadamori, and at his home was delivered of a male child, an indisputable fact, which still gave no clue to the child's paternity. Yet when this child demanded so desperately to be told the truth, Mokunosuké stood firm in his belief that no breath of his own speculations should be added to the mystery concerning his master's son. To do so would be an act of disloyalty to his warrior lord.

Like a fretting child that has been soothed, but continues to sob, Kiyomori, locked in the arms of the old man, let himself be led to his room.

"Now sleep," said Mokunosuké. "Let me speak with the master in the morning; Mokunosuké will explain matters. Have no fears." As he would have done for his own child, Mokunosuké arranged the pillows and laid the coverlets over Kiyomori. Kneeling by his head, the old retainer said: "Now, now, let all your troubles be forgotten in dreams. Whoever you are, you are a man, after all. Take courage, you're no cripple with those fine limbs. Think of the heavens and the earth as your mother—your father. Doesn't that thought comfort you?"

"Old One, you bother me. Let me sleep and forget."

"Ah, well, then, this old heart too is at peace." Turning once more to look at Kiyomori's sleeping face, Mokunosuké bowed, stepped back out of the room between the screening curtains of the doorway, and departed.

Kiyomori had no idea of how long he had slept. Someone was shaking him and calling his name. He struggled to open his sleep-drugged eyes. The shadow cast by the raised shutter of the door showed that it was long past noon. Tsunemori stood by his bed; his nervous, chiseled features looked strained as he bent over him, repeating: "Come . . . you *must* come. Because of you, Father and Mother . . ."

"What—me? What of me?"

"The quarreling began this morning, and even the noon meal has been forgotten. There seems to be no end to it."

"Another of their quarrels? What's that to me?"

Yawning deliberately, Kiyomori stretched his arms and flexed them, saying defiantly: "Let me be. What have I to do with their quarrel?"

Tsunemori implored: "That won't do, you're the reason for it. Listen to our brothers whimpering and crying with hunger!"

"Where is Mokunosuké?"

"He was called to Father's apartments a short while ago, and Mother seems to be taking him to task."

"Well then, I'll go," Kiyomori replied, springing out of bed and throwing a scornful look at his timid brother. "Give me my robes—my robes."

"You have them on."

2 6

"Oh, so I slept in them, did I?" Kiyomori remarked, drawing the remainder of the previous night's money from his sash. Thrusting some money at Tsunemori, he said: "Get the little ones something to eat. Tell young Heiroku to go for you."

Tsunemori drew back. "We can't do that, it will annoy Mother so, and then—"

"Who cares? I'm doing this!"

"But even you—"

"You fool! Am I not the eldest, and haven't I a right to give a few orders?"

Flinging some money into his brother's lap, Kiyomori left the room. His footsteps thudded across the veranda. At the well near the kitchen he gulped down large draughts of freshly drawn water; he next bathed his face, wiping it on the sleeve of his draggled robe, then started slowly across the courtyard.

Tadamori's apartments, in a wing as decayed as the main house itself, were on the other side of the inner court. Kiyomori stepped up onto the rotting veranda, his heart thumping wildly. Gliding from behind the folding shutters, he said: "Forgive me for being late last night. I did what you asked me to."

The instant his shadow fell across the threshold, there was silence, and three pairs of eyes were turned on him. Mokunosuké's eyes fell immediately; Kiyomori too averted his eyes from the old retainer; neither could endure to meet the other's eyes. Forcing himself to appear cool, Kiyomori approached his parents with a defiant air and unceremoniously thrust some money at them.

"Here is the money borrowed from my uncle—not all of it, though. I spent some last night when I met a friend, and I gave Tsunemori a little just now to buy food for the children, who are crying with hunger. This is the rest. . . ."

Before he could finish speaking, an awful change came over Tadamori's face, as though shame, self-pity and consuming rage struggled within him. He glanced at the small handful of money, and the scarred eyelids looked uglier than ever, contorted in an effort to hold back his tears.

"Heita! Take that away! What do you mean by flinging down

that money before you have even made your salutations?" hissed Yasuko, sitting erect and severe beside her husband, and with a withering side-glance at Kiyomori. (So this was she who had been called the Lady of Gion, who was given in marriage to Tadamori by the Nakamikado as though she had been their daughter!)

As Kiyomori's eyes came to rest on her profile, something flared up in him and made him tremble. "What did you say, Mother? If you had no need for that money, why did you send me to borrow it as though I were a beggar?"

"Silence! When did I send you on such an errand? That was your father's doing!"

"But isn't the money for this penniless family? Don't you have any use for money?"

"No," said Yasuko, shaking her head decidedly, "I need no such miserable help." The flush on her face made her glow, belying her thirty-odd years.

Kiyomori's large ears crimsoned; a threatening look appeared in his eyes; the clenched hands in his lap twitched spasmodically as though he were about to spring up and strike her.

"Then, Mother, you have no need for food from now on—tomorrow?"

"No, Kiyomori, I am not satisfied with mere food. . . . Ah, so you've come, too, Tsunemori? Then listen, the two of you. I am sorry for you, but today I am at long last permitted to leave Tadamori. We are no longer husband and wife. It is customary for the sons to remain with their father. This is the last you will see of me." Laughing lightly, she continued: "Your regrets will vanish more swiftly than the mists. You have always sided with your father, whom you believe to have been wronged."

Kiyomori started. He looked at his mother more closely. She was supposed to be ill, and yet she was fully clothed. As was her custom, she had painted her face carefully; her hair was perfumed; her eyebrows delicately painted in; her outer cloak, gay enough for a girl in her twenties, was draped about her. What was this? Not just another of the usual quarrels. Her habitual threat had been that she would leave them—forever—and both her husband and her sons had grown accustomed to these intimidations of hers, but never before had she appeared so calm and thus dressed for travel.

Tadamori had the air of having acquiesced to her. Kiyomori was overcome with consternation. He hated this mother, yet he was dismayed by the thought that she was his own flesh and blood. Turning to Tadamori, he faltered:

"Father, is this true—what my mother says?"

"It is so. You have all put up with this for so long, but this is true and it is best for you all."

Kiyomori choked. "Why—but why?" He heard his brother strangle back a sob. "But this must not happen, Father, with all these children. . . ."

The childish-sounding appeal seemed to amuse Tadamori, who smiled in spite of himself. "Heita, it is all right and for the best."

"What's 'all right'? What will happen to all of us?"

"Yasuko will be happy. As for all of you—this seems best. There is no need to fuss. Don't be anxious."

"But Tsunemori tells me that I am the reason for all this. If I've been at fault, let me try to make amends." Turning to his mother, Kiyomori pleaded: "What of my poor brothers? I promise, Mother, to do what will please you. Only think this over once more!"

As he spoke, Kiyomori was puzzled and chagrined by the strength of his feeling for his mother. Mokunosuké and Tsunemori were weeping aloud. Bewildered, Kiyomori too broke into tears, though Tadamori and Yasuko sat there cold and unmoved.

Tadamori then broke in sharply: "Stop, enough of your tears! Until now I endured everything for the sake of my sons, but now I have roused myself from my dreams. Fool that I was! These twenty years I, Tadamori of the Heiké, let a woman order me about and let the years pass in one agony. I have been a fool! I can hardly blame you, Heita, for your foolishness," and he laughed bitterly.

At this sardonic sound Yasuko, who sat arrogantly erect, flushed deeply and retorted: "What do you mean by laughing? You

2 9

mock me! Laugh as much as you like, jeer at me. Were his majesty alive today, even *you* would not dare to humiliate me like this! Remember that his majesty appointed the Nakamikado as my foster parents!"

Tadamori continued to laugh. "One of these days I shall pay my respects to the Nakamikado who honored the humble Tadamori with this lady for these many years."

Yasuko flashed her vindictive eyes on Tadamori and, with a vehemence intended to brand her words on his memory, said: "And did you not see to it that I bore child after child? Has there been a single day when you tried to give me any pleasure? Twenty years—and in spite of my loathing, the love of my children kept me here! These two—Heita and Mokunosuké, were they not gossiping maliciously of me by the stable at dawn? And were they not talking disrespectfully of his late majesty, saying that the Lady of Gion had a secret lover—some evil priest? And this old Mokunosuké, claiming that he saw it all, and the two wondering who of the three men was Heita's real father! I saw and heard them babbling insanely, and I've made up my mind that I will not endure another day in this house! What reason have I to stay here, when even my own son has turned against me?"

"Enough, enough!" cried Tadamori. "Have we not talked of this all morning? Didn't you get Mokunosuké to come here and abuse him to your heart's content? This is all useless—stop!"

"Then testify for me!"

"But didn't I say just awhile ago that Heita Kiyomori was your son and mine?"

"Heita, did you hear that?" Yasuko said, turning her harsh eyes on Mokunosuké. "And did *you* hear, you with your idle scandals! No one can deny that I was favored by his majesty, but what scoundrel has been telling you an old tale of twenty years ago? Tadamori denies it, and old Mokunosuké pretends innocence. Surely, Heita, you would not lie to your mother?"

"No, it is I and only I, Mother. . . . I *must* know who is my real father."

"Didn't your estimable father just tell you?"

"That was out of pity. Though I'm told who is my father, I will continue to honor this man as my real father. I refuse to let you go until I'm told," Kiyomori cried, seizing the sleeve of Yasuko's robe and pressing it against his tear-swollen eyes, entreating her: "Speak, you know! Whose son am I?"

"He has gone mad, this child!"

"Mad I may be, but because of you this man, my father, has spent these twenty long years in solitude, wasting his youth! You monstrous fox-woman!"

"What do you mean by this—to your mother?"

"You may be my mother, but you enrage me beyond words! You are foul and unclean, and I loathe you!"

"And what do you expect me to do now?"

"Let me strike you! My father won't—he hasn't dared to raise his hand against you these twenty years!"

"The gods will punish you, Heita!"

"How?"

"In those bygone days, my body was beloved for a time by his majesty himself. Had I remained at Court, I would have been honored there, yet I lowered myself by coming to this ridiculous house! And to think that you dare to raise your hand against me—this is treason to his majesty himself! I could not forgive even my own son!"

Kiyomori's deafening cry filled the room. "You fool! What if it was his majesty!" With all his strength, he struck a resounding blow on his mother's cheek and saw her fall.

"The young master has taken leave of his senses!"

"Ho, you there! Come, the young master is possessed by a demon!"

"See how he raves! Help!"

"Hurry!"

And a great commotion swept over the household.

Impoverished though he was, Tadamori had once held a governorship in the provinces, and in his own right as a Heiké held a post in the Imperial Guards at the Cloister Palace. Though subsisting close to starvation now, he insisted on keeping a retinue of some fifteen or sixteen retainers, one of them Mokunosuké's son, the steward, Heiroku.

Heiroku knew that his father had been called to his master's apartments that morning, and, fearing for his father's safety, had crouched by the hedge near the courtyard. At the sound of screams and loud voices he leaped to his feet, calling loudly for the other retainers, and darted straight across the inner court, realizing as he ran that the uproar had lasted but a few moments.

Yasuko lay face down on the ground as though she had fallen from the porch. Her plum-colored cloak, her white, green, and multicolored robes lay in a tangled heap about her streaming hair, and she made no attempt to rise. Kiyomori stood with his shoulders heaving, while his father held a tight grip on his wrist. Tsunemori and Mokunosuké, with looks of relief and bewilderment, appeared uncertain what they should do next.

At the sound of hurrying feet, Yasuko, who had lain motionless, raised her head, shrieking: "You there, call a carriage! Send a runner to my parents to tell them of this! Oh, shameful deed. . . ."

A servant ran off to fetch a carriage from a near-by stable, and another ran all the way to the Nakamikado mansion on Sixth Avenue. Tadamori watched the scene dispassionately as the servants hastened to carry out her orders.

The carriage was now on its way, and Yasuko half-swooning was carried away by one of the retainers to the gate. For a time her high-pitched, tearful voice mingled with the sound of Tsunemori's and his younger brothers' weeping. Tadamori stood motionless, as though bracing himself against these sounds.

"Heita!" As he spoke, Tadamori loosened his hold on his son's wrist. Freed from the vise-like grip, the swollen artery released a great spurt of blood, which rushed tumultuously through Kiyomori's whole body. The veins in his temples throbbed and he broke into weeping, unashamed, like a forsaken child.

Tadamori drew the tear-streaked face to his breast; rubbing his cheek against his son's rough hair, he said: "I have triumphed at last! I have now won my victory over that woman. Heita, forgive me. I was a coward to let you strike her. I am a failure as a father, but I will see to it that you do not suffer any more. You shall see me restore the name of Tadamori of the Heiké. Do not reproach me with your tears. Stop reproaching me with them."

"Father—I understand how you feel."

"You still call me 'Father'?"

"I do. Let me call you 'Father,' my father!"

The crescent moon gleamed sharply. Through the rising purple mist came the faint sound of Mokunosuké singing lullabies.

CHAPTER III

THE HORSE-RACE

In the spacious grounds of East Third Avenue in Kyoto stood the Cloister Palace, to which the emperors retired upon abdication. Since the time of the ex-Emperor Shirakawa, however, this imperial retreat had become the seat of a Cloister Government whose elaborate administration rivaled the Eight Departments and Twelve Offices of the Court itself. And it was thus that the small capital held two governments. But when May brought the green burgeoning of willow trees and the scent of fresh soil to Kyoto, few

3 4

remembered that this was the center of the country's political life, for it was transformed into a metropolis of pleasure, the capital of the fashionable and the City of Love, where court nobles and officers of the Cloister Palace surrendered themselves to spring, put aside their duties, and abandoned themselves to gaiety—not that this did not happen at other seasons of the year, but that this was more marked in spring—for what courtier could endure the disgrace of not composing a few verses to the spring?

One morning in late April, each pebble and stone in the Kamo River glinted, burnished by the rains of the past night, and the sun, gleaming on the crest of the Eastern Hills, told of the fullness and richness of spring.

The ex-Emperor's carriage rolled out resplendent through the Cherry Gate, beneath blossoming festoons of a drooping cherry tree. Gentlemen-in-waiting and attendants took their places with noisy excitement, matching their steps to the slow progress of the bullock that drew the royal corriage on its way.

"See, his majesty enjoys these outings," passers-by exclaimed. "Now that it is almost May, he probably goes to Kamo to see the trial races for the horses that have just arrived from the provinces."

An ox, dappled black and white, drew the carriage, whose shafts were wound with bunting. The only occupant of the carriage was a sallow-skinned aristocrat, still in his mid-thirties; flat-cheeked, with small, deep-set eyes and a taciturn look set off by compressed lips, the ex-Emperor Toba.

Men and women in passing paused to peer up at him, while the ex-Emperor gazed back intently as though the street scene interested him.

Only his eyes moved to and fro, and sometimes, as though amused by what he saw, the corners of his eyes drooped in a half-smile. People followed that glance and smiled back at him in understanding.

Near the paddock by the racecourse, the cherry blossoms were at their height. Under the noon sun the sensuous perfume of flowers mingled with the hot fragrance of new grass and was wafted along on each puff of wind.

"So you've seen that jet four-year-old too? Of the forty or fifty colts sent up from the provinces, there's not one to match him! Seeing him, I can hardly contain myself." Wataru of the Genji, his eyes riveted to the paddock rails, kept repeating this. A number of colts were huddled by the rails where they had been tethered.

Wataru continued half to himself: "I'd give anything to ride him. I know just how it would feel to be astride him. What a beauty—that line from his hoofs to his croup!"

The youths sat under a large cherry tree near the paddock, hugging their knees. Of the two Sato Yoshikiyo was indifferent and did little more than smile faintly in response.

"Doesn't it seem so to you, Yoshikiyo?" Wataru asked.

"How—what do you mean?"

"Think what it would be like to come riding in victorious along this sunlit Kamo, waving your whip to a thunder of applause!"

"Never thought of it."

"Never?"

"I'd be even less interested if I'd picked the winner. What use is there in a good horse if the rider doesn't care?"

"You sound as though you were lying and not merely modest. There's no reason why *you* couldn't ride him—in fact, either of us can, since we're Guards at the Palace."

Yoshikiyo laughed. "You're talking of something else, Wataru."

"Of what, then?"

"Aren't you thinking of the Kamo races in May—*the* races?"

Wataru quickly replied: "Naturally, all these colts were picked for that event."

"But"—Yoshikiyo shrugged—"I'm *not* interested in horseracing. Accompanying his majesty on horseback is entirely another thing."

"Yes, but what of the day you go into battle?"

"I can only pray that that day will not come. There are too many disturbing things these days for us warriors to think about."

"Hmm . . ." mused Wataru, turning troubled eyes on his

3 6

friend, "I never expected to hear anything like this from the lips of the famous Yoshikiyo of the Guards. What ails you, eh?"

"Nothing at all," replied Yoshikiyo.

"In love?"

"Not that I've not had some affairs—but it's my wife," Yoshikiyo said. "She gives me no reason for complaint, but I must tell you—a few days ago she gave birth to a jewel of a child, and I too have become a father!"

"That's not unusual. When we warriors marry, we start families, have children. . . ."

"Quite right, and what a number! Yet what troubles me most is that we have so little pity or love for those who bear our children."

Wataru laughed aloud at this. "Something's the matter with you!" he said, and lapsed into silence, fixing his gaze on the paddock, where he now saw Heita Kiyomori and Morito sauntering. The two seemed to recognize the couple under the tree. Kiyomori's ruddy face broke into a smile, which displayed his even, white teeth. Wataru raised his hand, and beckoned to them, knowing that Kiyomori would share his enthusiasm.

Quickly leaving his companion, Kiyomori approached with a greeting and soon found a seat between the two, who once had been his schoolmates at the Imperial Academy. Wataru was five years his senior, Yoshikiyo two. Morito, who had not joined them, was also one of this intimate group. Between these youths in their twenties there was a strong bond of friendship which came of an awareness that they held the future in their strong young hands, a consciousness of secret hopes and dreams shared.

The Imperial Academy had been set up exclusively for the education of the nobility and scions of the Fujiwara clan, but, as time went on, the attendance of warriors' sons above the Fifth Rank was permitted. In their studies as well as in the treatment accorded them, discrimination between the offspring of the nobles and the warriors, however, led to constant friction. The young patricians sneered that the barbarous sons of impecunious warriors had little to gain from books, while the warriors' sons quietly fumed with

thoughts of future revenge, and their feuding reflected the seeth-
ing, subterranean conflict now growing between their elders.

Kiyomori was typical of the unpolished, indigent, and un-
lettered warrior youth, and for that reason despised by the young
aristocrats. He was well liked, however, by the young men of his
own class. For those who left the academy there was a university,
but the sons of warriors were excluded from it on the pretext that
their future lay in training as men-at-arms, so Kiyomori and his
friends were among those who, on leaving the academy, enrolled
with the Department of Military Affairs and eventually were assigned to guard the Cloister Palace.

For Kiyomori, whose father shunned society and whose
mother had neglected him, the Guards provided a convenient and
easy occupation for indulging his indolent and aimless habits, and
his fellow Guards rarely saw him report for duty. Following Yasuko's departure, however, Tadamori was a changed man and made
up his mind to start his life anew. To Kiyomori he confided: "I
am still in my forties, we must make a new beginning."

And soon after this, Tadamori once more resumed his duties
at Court.

"Isn't Morito coming? I thought I saw him with you."

Looking round, Kiyomori replied: "He's somewhere about—
shall I call him?"

Wataru quickly interposed: "No, don't bother him. He seems
anxious to avoid me these days. But, Heita, have you seen that four-
year-old? What do you think of him—splendid, isn't he?"

Kiyomori snorted, drawing down the corners of his full mouth,
then slowly shook his head. "That black one? Not that one—he's
no good."

"Eh? Why—that fine colt?"

"No matter how fine, those four white fetlocks bring bad
luck."

Wataru was taken aback at this reply, which drew his attention
to the white markings on the colt. Whether in the stirrup or appraising a horse at sight, Wataru was confident that he was as good
a judge of horseflesh as any. Four white fetlocks had always been

regarded as a bad omen in even a chestnut or bay, and Wataru had failed to notice this. Though he quickly concealed his chagrin, he was a little nettled to have Kiyomori, who was younger, give him a lesson in the fine points of a horse; he was also aware that Yoshikiyo sat near by, grinning.

Wataru laughed. "So those white fetlocks are no good—and what of warriors who are cross-eyed, pock-marked, and red-nosed, are they, too, no good?"

Kiyomori bristled. "Now, now, why draw comparisons between horses and my father? That's going a bit far—"

But Wataru broke in. "So even *you* are superstitious like those bloodless aristocrats who live in those sunless Palace rooms, talking of things that 'pollute,' things that are 'unclean,' things that are of 'good omen,' of 'bad omen'—forever preoccupied with silly fears, while we young ones who have sprung from the good sunlit earth would not own to such superstitions! Ill-omened—some aristocrat long ago must have owned such a horse and had his insolent chin bitten, or was pitched off his horse and had his thigh bones cracked! That's where the superstition must have started."

Wataru continued doggedly: "Let me tell you about Tameyoshi of the Genji, who was chief of the Police Commission in 1130, when the monks of Mount Hiei rioted. He went to suppress that uprising on a chestnut with four white fetlocks, and everyone knew it was his favorite horse. Then again, the year before last, I swear it was a bay with white fetlocks that came off victorious in the race between the Palace horses and those of Lady Taikenmon."

"Yes, yes, I know. I was casting no slurs at that fine colt by being superstitious," Kiyomori replied.

"I had hoped to get a name for myself by riding that horse at the Kamo races," Wataru explained.

"So *that* was what made you lose your temper?"

"I wasn't angry, I only wanted to make fun of superstitions. I can see how a superstition might even be in my favor. It's possible they'll not find anyone willing to ride him."

Kiyomori made no reply. For one so sanguine, he was at times curiously sensitive about trifles. Perceiving that he was in no mood for further talk, Wataru turned to Yoshikiyo, only to find him completely oblivious of the conversation and absorbed in watching an occasional white petal come fluttering and floating to earth.

"Ah, there's the imperial carriage!"

"Oh, his majesty looks this way!" All three instinctively leaped to their feet and started running in the direction of the paddock, where crowds thronged to meet the arriving carriage.

Like no other epoch that preceded it, this age gave itself up entirely to pleasure and gambling, poetry tournaments, the blending of perfumes and incense, pageants, miming, dice-games, outings at the four seasons to view the beauties of nature, cockfighting and archery matches. Earlier, court circles regarded seasonal excursions and poetry parties as the natural complement to living; yet never had men at large regarded all things as its playthings as during this new age which sought to transmute even its religion and politics into exquisite pastimes—all, with the exception of war. At the word "war," both high and low trembled, for the seeds of conflict were now sown far and wide: among the powerful armed clergy; to the east; to the west, where the pirates of the Inland Sea periodically made their forays; and close at hand in the very capital itself, where the Court and the Palace were at odds with each other. Lately it was openly rumored that the Genji and Heiké in distant provinces were mobilizing their soldiers, and that a storm was brewing.

People were uneasy. Something ominous permeated the air itself. Still, in the midst of that foreboding and effeteness, a feverish hunger for pleasure seemed to consume everyone, and the crowded Kamo racecourse was one sign of it. According to the old chronicles, horseracing became a royal sport about the year 701, indulged in by Guards on the grounds of the Imperial Palace during the May Festival. In these troubled times, however, horseracing was no longer confined to the course at Kamo in May, but took place in shrine compounds, on the estates of the courtiers and noblemen who entertained the Emperor or the ex-Emperor and their ladies, on the broad stretch of Second Avenue, or were even improvised at imperial picnics. As races were held on straight courses, wide enough for ten horses to run abreast, it was even possible to have contests on any of the main avenues of Kyoto.

One sovereign, it was also written, was so carried away by his fever for horseracing that he set aside twenty of his manors in the provinces for the breeding of racehorses, and in the capital itself ordered the building of lavish stables requiring an army of grooms and attendants to maintain them. The late monarch as well as his son, the present ex-Emperor, were no less addicted to this sport, and the royal visit today to Kamo was to select a horse, in anticipation of the races in May, from all the thoroughbreds sent from numerous stud farms in the provinces.

"Is Tadamori here?" the ex-Emperor inquired, ignoring the courtiers around him. "I see no exceptional ones today. What do you think?"

Tadamori, who stood modestly apart, merely raised his head to reply: "Your majesty, there is just one."

"Just one—that black colt from the manor at Shimotsuké?"

"Yes, your majesty."

"The one I have been watching for some time—the colt tethered to that post? Yet these gentlemen and horse-fanciers all warn me against him; they say those four white fetlocks bring bad luck."

"A common saying, your majesty, but not worth considering—" Tadamori began, regretting his habit of plain speaking. "Of all these horses, I see none equal to that colt; that fine head, that eye and the sweep of the tail."

The monarch hesitated. He was anxious to have the black colt taken to his stables and trained for the May races, at which he hoped to win against the Emperor's horses. But, like his courtiers, he also was superstitious.

"If your majesty wishes, I will take the colt to my stable and keep him until the day of the races," Tadamori ventured, recalling his own impulsive words and the effect they had had on the assembled noblemen.

"That should do no harm. Take him and be sure of his training until the races," Toba replied.

The story of the black colt spread throughout the Cloister Palace, where many of the courtiers were ill-disposed toward Tadamori. Though a mere warrior, he was permitted near the imperial dais, the only warrior singled out for such honor, and the jealous courtiers resented him. They feared that the Squint-Eyed One would usurp their privileges, and distrusted him, believing that Tadamori knew the secret of ingratiating himself with the ex-Emperor. In spite of the years that Tadamori had held aloof from the Palace and refused invitations to the seasonal entertainments and observances, the ex-Emperor's regard for him had not diminished. Not only did Tadamori continue to receive tokens of the abdicated monarch's attachment, but further honor was shown him by Toba's eagerness to accept Tadamori's opinions as final. Tadamori's reinstatement at the Palace once more roused the suspicions and distrust of the courtiers.

On returning home, Tadamori stood by the black colt stroking its nose, saying: "Ah, what pettiness! Nothing has changed in that old pond where those courtiers croak."

"Father, there's no way to live in this capital except by ignoring the slander. Just laugh at the fools."

"Heita! Back already?"

"I saw you leave the Palace and followed you, since I'm not on duty tonight."

"Heita, never show your resentment."

"No, but I'm waiting for my revenge, and I haven't forgotten your words about starting a new life. We *are* much happier here at home now."

"I'm afraid you've been lonely since your mother left."

"Remember, Father, we promised not to talk of that. . . . Now about that colt—"

"Hmm—a fine horse. Better exercise him morning and evening."

"I have that in mind. To tell you the truth, Wataru of the Genji who is with me in the Guards, tells me he wants to train the colt. He's been begging me to ask you to obtain his majesty's consent, for he wants to ride that colt in the Kamo races."

Tadamori thought for a moment and then said: "Wataru—but don't you want to ride him yourself? You, rather than Wataru?"

"Those four white fetlocks—if it were not for them—" Kiyomori hesitated, drawing his thick brows into a nervous frown that startled his father. Tadamori was surprised by the discovery that this careless son of his had ideas of his own.

"I'm sure Wataru can be trusted. I can't say how his majesty will feel about this, but I shall ask—that is, if you still have no intention of riding the colt yourself," Tadamori said, a little disappointed. Calling some retainers, he gave them directions for the feeding and grooming of the four-year-old, and shortly after went to his rooms, now empty of his wife and her reproaches. Resting in the lamplight, he called his young sons to him and played with them, as had now become his habit.

Several days later Tadamori told Wataru himself of the ex-Emperor's consent, and later instructed Kiyomori to take the colt to Wataru's home. Leading the horse by its reins, Kiyomori started on his way to Iris Lane on Ninth Avenue. Passers-by turned to remark: "A magnificent horse—for the Court or the Palace?" But Kiyomori spoke to no one, glad to be rid of an ill-omened horse.

Wataru was expecting Kiyomori and was cleaning out the stable when his friend arrived. He was beside himself with joy.

"It's almost dark. I'm sorry my wife hasn't returned yet, but you must stay and drink with me. This is an occasion to celebrate. We shall drink to it in imperial wine!"

Kiyomori stayed until the lamps were lit and the wine made him tingle to his fingertips. Looking round, he found himself comparing his surroundings with his own home, and noted that the house had little in the way of furnishings, but was exquisitely clean. The polished beams gave out a dark gleam; comfort pervaded the air; a sheen lay over everything—undoubtedly the industry of the young wife whom Wataru had married at the end of the past year. Kiyomori was envious. He listened to Wataru and his praises of his wife. When he finally left, Wataru accompanied him to the gate, one like that of any other warrior's house with its

thatched roof and wattled-clay wall, and there came face to face
with Wataru's wife. On seeing the departing guest, she quickly
drew off her outer cloak and bowed. Kiyomori was conscious of
the scent in her hair and sleeves. With difficulty he stammered out
his greetings as Wataru presented his wife.

"You're back just in time. Heita, this is my wife, Kesa-Gozen,
who once served at Court," Wataru said eagerly, stopping to tell
her of the black colt in the stable.

Although this was his friend's wife, Kiyomori felt shy and awkward. Aware of his flushed cheeks, he unsteadily resumed his way
along the now dark Iris Lane. Kesa-Gozen's face haunted him.
Was it possible that so lovely a woman really existed? Her image
hovered before him as he walked on. A new star had bloomed for
him in the spring skies above him. . . . Then an arm suddenly
reached round and gripped him silently. A highwayman! People
talked about being attacked at this crossroad at night! Kiyomori's
hand slid to his sword.

"Don't be alarmed, Heita. Come with me to the house we
visited that other night." There was a low laugh at Kiyomori's ear.
It was Morito. Kiyomori could hardly believe his ears. What was
Morito doing in this deserted quarter of Kyoto, his face muffled
up like a brigand's?

"Surely, you'll come along to that house on Sixth Avenue?"
Morito persisted. Kiyomori's thoughts leaped at the proposal, but
a sudden distrust of this fellow made him hesitate.

"Come, I saw you this evening on your way to Wataru's, and
I followed you," Morito added, as he began to lead the way. His
suspicions allayed, Kiyomori followed him, drawn by something
compelling in Morito, and soon felt that good luck had waylaid
him.

In the house of call near the Palace they drank recklessly, and
caroused as they had done that other night. When he was alone
at last with one of the women, Kiyomori, a little bolder than at
his last visit, ventured to ask:

"Where is my friend? Where does he sleep?"

The woman tittered. "He never spends his nights here."

"Has he gone home then?"

The woman appeared sleepy and too tired to reply. "He's always like that. How should I know what he does?" she said, flinging her arms round Kiyomori's neck.

Kiyomori struggled free. "I'm leaving, too! That Morito is playing some trick on me!"

Kiyomori quickly left the house, but the gentle ghost of Iris Lane no longer walked with him.

The following day Morito did not report for duty at the Guards, nor did he appear for several days, and Kiyomori brooded over this. Now, whenever he arrived at the Palace, it was Kesa-Gozen's husband, Wataru, who always greeted him eagerly whenever they met in the Palace corridors, and with a look that bespoke his happiness.

At the servants' gate of the Nakamikado mansion on Sixth Avenue, a cluster of women peddlers, balancing baskets or boxes of silk cords, flowers, and cakes on their heads, peered into the premises laughing and chattering noisily.

"We want nothing, nothing today, you wenches!"

"Come, buy some cakes for the May Festival!"

"We're too busy with work for the feast tonight. We're dizzy with work! Come tonight, tonight. . . ."

"You fools! You vulgar slaves!" the peddlers jeered.

A steward suddenly appeared at a door, bawling and scolding at the backs of the under-servants. "Here, here! Enough of that chaffing with those women! Who has charge of the bathhouse today? The lady's impatient. The steam in the bath isn't hot enough!"

At the sound of the bellowing, two menservants separated themselves from the group and fled toward the east wing. The fire for the bath had turned to ashes. They scurried about in great agitation, gathering twigs and faggots to start the fire.

One of Yasuko's maids appeared on the veranda; wrinkling

her nose and blinking at the smoke, she called out: "Here, what are you doing there! You careless slaves, what if my lady takes cold?"

The bathhouse with its low ceiling and latticed floor was quite dark. The naked bodies of the two women gleamed through the steam, dripping with perspiration.

"Ruriko, what lovely little breasts—like small cherries!"

"You embarrass me, aunt, don't stare at me so."

"I couldn't help thinking of the days when my skin was fair like yours," Yasuko mused.

"But you're so lovely even now."

"Yes?—" said Yasuko, looking long at her own breasts.

Ruriko's words were not all flattery, but Yasuko, cupping her breasts in her hands, felt that they had lost their firmness. The tips were stained dark like the seeds of an apricot. She had borne four sons and realized that the springs of her youthfulness were running dry. She stared at the small white scars on one breast where Kiyomori in a fit of temper had bitten her when he was two or three years old.

Anger suddenly welled up in her at the thought of Kiyomori, who had struck her so cruelly—and with a retainer there! Had he not once nursed at these breasts? Was this how sons treated their mother? Were this so, then how unrewarding to be a mother! He seemed to think that he had grown to manhood without her care! Resentment filled Yasuko as she sat there motionless, her fingers curled round her breasts.

Ruriko soon left the bathhouse. She was the niece of the mistress of the mansion. It was customary for young girls to be given in marriage by the time they were thirteen or fourteen, but Ruriko, who looked more than her sixteen years, was not even affianced. Rumors were that her father, Fujiwara Tamenari, a governor in one of the provinces, was too occupied with his duties to arrange a match. It was also said, however, that he had often disobeyed the orders of the central government, and at the request of the Minister of the Left, a relative who considered his dissident cousin dangerous, had been assigned to a distant post.

Ruriko herself seemed unconcerned about her unmarried state and found that the days passed pleasantly enough. Ever since Yasuko arrived and took possession of the apartments of the east wing, Ruriko spent most of her time there, leaving her own rooms in the west wing unoccupied. She often spent the night in the east wing or took her baths with Yasuko, who passed her time gossiping with the young girl, initiating her in the use of cosmetics, airing her views on love affairs, or instructing her in the secrets of appraising men. Ruriko soon came to admire the older woman and became warmly attached to her.

The master of this mansion was one Iyenari, a good-natured nobleman in his fifties, who, on retiring from a government post, indulged a passion for cockfighting. Being childless, he had considered adopting his wife's niece, Ruriko, but a most disconcerting situation had arisen in February—Yasuko's unexpected arrival. He sounded her out on her plans for departure, but Yasuko expressed no intention of returning to Imadegawa. He appealed to her maternal feelings by reminding her of her four children, but Yasuko appeared quite indifferent to them. To shake her self-confidence he hinted that though she was still enchanting at thirty-eight, she could hardly expect to remarry. But Yasuko was deaf to such insinuations and behaved as though she had returned to the parental roof permanently. She took possession of the best rooms in the house, ordered baths in the morning, spent long hours over her toilette in the evening, and proceeded to realize for herself her notions of a high-born lady's life.

She never hesitated to use the carriages whenever she wished, ordered the servants about at her whim, while they gossiped slyly in the servants' quarters about the strange men who visited her apartments at night. If Iyenari was so tactless as to express his displeasure at her conduct, Yasuko flew into a rage, forcing him to take back his words, and assumed the haughty airs of a royal mistress, never letting Iyenari forget that she had once been the late Emperor's favorite and arrogantly telling him to hold his tongue.

Iyenari had had his fill of such reminders. He ceased to remind Yasuko of the past, when she was Ruriko's age and he had arranged

the liaison between her and the amorous Emperor, for she remembered too well that the monarch in return had seen to Iyenari's
promotion at Court, had rewarded him generously with additional
acres to his manor, and lavished many other gifts on him. Yasuko
had long looked upon Iyenari's wealth as in part her own, and
even after her marriage to Tadamori often came to the Nakamikado to demand whatever she wished.

A misfortune of his own making had returned to plague
Iyenari. Lately his palate for pleasure had become dulled. Yasuko,
on the other hand, was full of gaiety as an unending stream of
visitors came to call on her in the east wing, stayed to play dice-
games, burned incense, and practiced on various musical instruments. Even Iyenari's old friend at cockfights deserted him for
Yasuko and was now one of her intimates.

Iyenari's mansion, like the fashionable dwellings of other
aristocrats, was a spacious building with an east and a west wing.
A long, covered gallery, running the entire length of the main
house, connected the two wings, from which roofed passages pro-
jected at right angles to form the sides of an inner court. Elegant
enclosed pavilions at the end of the passages commanded a full
view of the court, its miniature landscape of island, lake, and flowing stream.

Yasuko's influence over Ruriko troubled Iyenari, for the young
girl was now a complete captive to the older woman's charms and
spent all her time in the east wing—some distance from the family apartments on the opposite side of the court. Iyenari cease-
lessly cautioned Ruriko not to spend so much time there, warning
her that nothing good would come of these visits. But his authority in his own house had collapsed. He ordered the servants to
keep a watch on Ruriko, but in vain, for they now went about
in fear of Yasuko.

So this was why even the stout-hearted warrior Tadamori
had withered in his youth, Iyenari reflected wryly. This was why
Tadamori had been called eccentric; and this was the doubtful
legacy that the late Emperor had bequeathed him. Iyenari saw his

hair turning gray in the brief space of two months, and marveled at Tadamori, who had endured this burden for twenty years.

Ruriko had spent another night in the east wing, and Iyenari was beside himself this morning with helpless rage. He had just finished arranging some irises in a vase, placed a helmet adorned with wistarias on a helmet-stand, prepared the sweet-flag wine and set out the cups with which to toast the May Festival, and then sent a servant to fetch Ruriko, only to be told that she and Yasuko were in the bathhouse—had been there for some time.

He turned accusingly to his wife and complained: "Now you shall see what happens to her one of these days! We shall have another Yasuko on our hands, mark my words!" But the sight of the azure skies and the brilliant sunlight quickly made him regret his petulance. "Ah, let us forget all this, for today is the Fifth of May!" he exclaimed. "Bring me my court robes; it's about time for me to go," he said, though he rose listlessly as he spoke.

Today was the day of the Kamo races. By now the paddocks were surely boiling over with the surging throngs. Iyenari, as in previous years, was a member of the committee in charge of the festivities following the races. He toyed with the idea of a feigned illness, thought better of it, put on his ceremonial robes, and placed the flower-decked helmet on his head. While his wife secured its cords under his lifted chin, he gave some orders to a servant.

"Bring out the carriage—the new one, mind you!"

The messenger hurried off to the servants' quarters, but soon was back with the news that the ladies only awhile ago had driven off in the elegant new carriage!

"The imbeciles!" Iyenari roared at the messenger. What ever made them take the new carriage? Not a word to him! Ruriko should have known better! Even that young woman seemed to have lost all respect for her uncle and aunt! Was it possible that even she had been ensnared by the feigned love of that mere tenant?

Iyenari was both angry and sorry for himself. There was nothing he could do now but take the old carriage. He concealed his unhappy countenance behind its shutters as it rolled through the main gate.

Soon, in the distance, beneath the clouds of dust, he glimpsed the massed crowds thronging the Kamo course. Between the verdant young foliage he caught the flash of red and white bunting, the rippling of colored pennants, the clusters of the "sacred tree" tied to the starting-post; then gradually the entrance to the racecourse came into view, milling with jostling humanity.

His carriage was now caught in a tangle of vehicles. Who could believe there were so many carriages? He had never realized that such a variety existed in the capital. Amazing! Suddenly he sat up, cursing roundly to himself. There was his very own, his new carriage just crossing his path with a fine flourish of whips! Curses on that mare—that old female whom no one could saddle!

The ceremony announcing the day's entries had just ended. From the royal box, the nineteen-year-old Emperor Sutoku, his Fujiwara consort at his side, glanced round him smiling. The ex-Emperor Toba was also there, surrounded by court ladies and other attendants, who stood throughout for the opening ritual. When they took their seats, an excited hum rose as the company exchanged lively comments on the jockeys and horses.

The grounds were dotted with numerous tents for the grooms, the musicians in the band, and physicians dispatched to care for the usual casualties.

Each leaf on the trees of the near-by Kamo Shrine scintillated in the breeze. The music of the orchestra drifted on the wind over the heads of the crowds. On the green turf near the paddock gate, where a pennant waved, impatient racehorses threw the grooms into a frenzy. Now and again a long roar of mirth swept the stands as a spirited steed, the bit between its teeth, sent a groom sprawling, or a colt, being tried for its pace, stood with its feet planted, relieving itself in front of the imperial pavilion. In the royal box the Emperor and ex-Emperor smiled with amusement, while waves of laughter passed over the flower-bedecked rows of patricians. Here, rank on rank, the ostentation and elegance of the Court and Palace were displayed in the many-shaped headdresses and the rainbow-colored robes. The younger courtiers affected the fashion of lightly powdered faces, painted eyebrows, and rouged cheeks and exhaled the scent of the rare perfumes they carried in their sleeves. In one of the pavilions courtiers in helmets decked with wistaria made a wide splash of purple, scenting the air with the fragrance of flowers.

This was the day of the Kamo races; no less was it a tournament of fashion and extravagance in which the Court and the Palace sought to outdo each other. And all unseen to the beholder, this was the tilting-field in the rivalry between the Emperor and the abdicated monarch. Though occupying the same box, son and father rarely spoke to each other. Theirs was an estrangement of many years, and the gulf between them had only widened with the passing of time. Behind their estrangement lay a grotesque history.

Emperor Sutoku was the ex-Emperor Toba's first-born son by his consort, Fujiwara Shoko, who had been a maid-in-waiting at the Cloister Palace at the time Shirakawa had abdicated and taken the tonsure. The ex-Emperor Shirakawa's attentions to young Shoko were so ardent that the courtiers whispered among themselves that the notoriously amorous monarch's devotion was more than paternal. Shoko, chosen after a few years to be the Emperor Toba's concubine, was soon elevated to be his consort, the Empress. Reluctant to sever his relations with Shoko even after she had become his son's wife, the ex-Emperor Shirakawa continued to visit her in secret. The young Emperor Toba was ignorant of the intrigue until his Empress gave birth to the Crown Prince. It was then swiftly rumored at Court that the Emperor had been quite indifferent to the first cries of the newborn infant, convinced that the child was not his own but his father's.

The ex-Emperor's unnatural conduct and treachery poisoned Toba's youth, leaving a wound that refused to heal, and his bitter disavowals of his son Sutoku, who now reigned, created rancors and recriminations which threatened to set off a holocaust between the heads of the two governments. Yet how urbanely was it concealed today in the perfumed elegance of the Kamo races! Who could believe that these flower-embowered ranks, these powdered, effeminate figures, absorbed in the pursuit of pleasure, were fuel for the terrible conflagration lying in store for them?

"See how his majesty smiles!"

"The Emperor now stands. He watches with such interest!"

Such were the remarks exchanged between the courtiers whose eyes were on the racecourse, but whose inward vision hovered around the two rulers, constantly aware of the bitter hatred coiled in the hearts of those two.

Event followed event until noon. Dust rose high over the parched racecourse.

"You seem dazed, Wataru. What's the matter?" Kiyomori inquired of his friend, whom he found standing idly at one side of the warriors' pavilion.

The black four-year-old with the white fetlocks, in which Wataru had placed so much hope, was not on the list. Puzzled by this omission, Kiyomori had waited since the start of the races for a chance to speak to Wataru, who shrank from his questions and replied dejectedly:

"This morning, while it was still dark, I made the mistake of taking the black colt from the stables here and giving him a run. . . . It was fate—just bad luck."

"What happened?"

"The carpenters who were here yesterday setting up the stands must have left some nails about, for the colt stepped on one and got it in his right hind hoof. I wish it had been I that was spiked!"

"Hmm—" was Kiyomori's only reply as the jockeys' superstition flashed across his mind. Wataru would only jeer at it again. But Kiyomori's next words were immeasurably comforting to Wataru.

"Don't lose heart, Wataru. There will be other races in which he can compete. There's Ninna-ji this autumn. He's good enough to win anywhere. Why hurry him?"

"Umm. . . . I'll enter him this autumn!" Wataru exclaimed.

Kiyomori began to chuckle. "Why such regret? Have you bet heavily on this colt?"

"No, sheer obstinacy. They've all been telling me that this colt would bring bad luck."

"Did you go through the 'whip ritual'?" Kiyomori inquired.

"The 'whip ritual'? I'll have none of that! Pure superstition! Why should these riders who have priests mumble incantations over their whips expect to win? I thought I would open their eyes."

While Wataru spoke, Kiyomori's eyes wandered. To the roll of drums, two horses and their riders streaked away from the starting-post in a curl of dust, but he was not looking at them. His eyes swept over the massed heads in the main pavilion. Between the throngs of men and women he caught a glimpse of his mother. Among all those elegantly dressed women, his mother stood out breath-takingly lovely in her gorgeous robes.

The eyes of the crowd were fixed hard on the course, but his mother's glance was turned toward him. Their eyes met. She beckoned to him with her eyes, but Kiyomori stared back at her coldly. She continued to smile, cajoling and pleading, as though amused by a sulking child, then turned to speak to Ruriko, who stood beside her. At the same moment a thunder of applause shook the air. A flourish of drums rolled at the goal post, where a crimson flag waved to signal that the Palace horses had won the day. A chorus of voices burst into a victory song, which rose and swelled around the ex-Emperor's pavilion.

Wataru muttered a few words and left. Kiyomori also turned to go. He pushed his way through the crowds in the direction of the main stand. Yasuko's eyes, like an angler's line, seemed to draw him in closer and closer to her. As he drew near her, her eyes asked: "And did you come, after all?"

Kiyomori, making his way toward his mother, felt only hatred for her. All his hate and rage were in the look that he gave her as he approached the pavilion where she sat. As he became conscious of the many women around him, he suddenly felt awkward and shy, and waves of red dyed his cheeks and large ears.

"You amusing child!" Yasuko laughed as she studied her son's discomfiture. "What makes you so shy? Am I not after all your mother? Come here to me."

In her voice were all those accents of love which only a mother knows how to employ. But it was not his mother who had caused him to blush. To him she was not a woman, but the embodiment of beauty—a beauty that he hated and yet prized above everything. With a sensation of hurling himself over an invisible barrier, Kiyomori came close to her. It was neither strange nor unnatural to be close beside her like this, he thought, but his glance wandered vaguely as if seeking refuge from the eyes turned on him.

Yasuko observed his uneasiness and quickly concluded that Ruriko was the cause of his discomfiture. She stole a side look at one and then at the other and, turning to Ruriko, whispered: "This is my son, Heita Kiyomori, of whom I spoke one day."

To Kiyomori she then said: "When you were three or four years old, you visited the Nakamikado with whom Ruriko is now staying."

In spite of Yasuko's efforts to put him at his ease, Kiyomori remained silent. His pounding heart made him flush more deeply. Ruriko saw this and turned crimson. Her eyelids fluttered and drooped as though she faced a glare, and an audible sigh escaped from her lips.

Kiyomori felt a familiar, nauseating sensation come over him as he stood beside his mother. (Beautiful and deceitful, that she was!) He felt impelled to question her once more. Was he the son of an emperor or of a debauched priest? Who was his real father? An insupportable grief over her unchasteness seemed to goad him to seek an answer. To him she now seemed more sullied than all the common whores and courtesans in the capital.

In a period of grossly unrestrained relations between the sexes, Kiyomori realized that he expected of his mother a chastity that he had no reason to demand. Yet as her child, her son, he had wanted to believe that she was the purest of women, the noblest, the archetype of love itself. From those infant years when he had nursed at her breast, he had gazed up at this ideal—his mother;

throughout his boyhood, the figure had not changed, until with Morito's revelation she was transformed into a soiled lump of flesh. Utterly revolted, Kiyomori felt her uncleanness to be also his; until that time he had been happy in the thought that the blood of Tadamori of the Heiké and a chaste mother ran in his veins, but now he felt only a self-loathing.

On that night when he met Morito and was told of his mother's past, Kiyomori in rage and despair cast his youth and innocence to a whore. The contempt for his mother was that which he now felt for himself. He loathed his own flesh and his blood; the only thing that held him back from a course of lust and dissipation was Tadamori, this man who was not his real father, the Squint-Eyed One whose great love and forbearance he could not bring himself to spurn. Tadamori's love alone made Kiyomori vow that he would be a worthy son and keep watch over his unruly passions.

The sight of his mother was enough to make Kiyomori forget his resolutions. He wondered if this turbulent blood was all that he had got from her.

Yasuko was disappointed and annoyed. Kiyomori showed no signs of relenting toward her. She had expected him to come to her with tears. She was also irritated by his indifference to Ruriko and his studied absorption in the sights around them.

"Heita, what makes you hesitate so? Are you afraid that Tadamori will hear of this?" she finally asked.

"Yes—my father is here and I fear he will see us."

"Does that matter? Though Tadamori and I have separated, you are still my son, aren't you? I know how lonely and miserable you and your little brothers are without me."

"No!" Kiyomori quickly retorted. "My brothers, the horses in the stable, and all are well and happy. No one ever speaks of you!"

Yasuko laughed quickly to conceal the change that came over her face, and, for some reason that Kiyomori could not make out, seized his wrist and clung to it.

"And you—you have never wanted to see me?"

Kiyomori struggled. "Let me go. My father is looking this way. He sees us. Let me go!"

"Heita!" Yasuko exclaimed, giving him an arch smile. "Tadamori is not your father, though I am your real mother. What makes you so partial to him? You must come to see me, Heita, for I often long for a sight of you. And Ruriko will be good company for you, too."

Kiyomori once more struggled to free his wrist, certain that his father had seen him by now.

Beyond the tumult of the crowds and the dust writhing over the course, the sun paled, marking the end of the races and the long day. The Emperor and the ex-Emperor left their pavilion, followed by their attendants, and turned their steps toward the Kamo Shrine, where, to the accompaniment of sacred music, priests performed the rites of lustration. Once more the assemblage repaired to the pavilion, there to drink a toast to the winners and to watch the jockeys receive the royal congratulations.

The formal presentation of trophies took place in the autumn at a court banquet, when the winners claimed their stakes—placer gold, rolls of silk, and rare incense. At the nightlong feasting, warriors and courtiers alike drank freely of the abundant wine. Victor and vanquished alike danced and sang. Victory was the beginning of defeat, defeat the beginning of victory. This was the natural law, the ever-revolving Buddhist Wheel of Life. To the courtiers flushed with wine, life was pleasure, and pleasure life. What was victory, or what defeat? Had not the Fujiwara prospered for three hundred years, and had not success and even more success been theirs for generations?

This day of the Kamo races was only an interlude in the long pursuit of pleasure. Above the cherry trees, thick with leaf, rose the moon. The Emperor's coach and the ex-Emperor's carriage rolled away from the course, followed by those of the courtiers and officials.

Tadamori left the Palace late that night, in a happy mood, for the ex-Emperor had been in good humor all day. Mokunosuké usually came to meet his master, bringing him his horse, but tonight Tadamori found Kiyomori waiting for him at the Guard Office.

"Where is Mokunosuké?" he asked.

"He was here tonight, but I sent him home and told him I would wait for you," Kiyomori replied.

As he climbed to his saddle, Tadamori remarked: "So you waited for me. You look tired, Heita."

Kiyomori grasped the leading reins and looked up at his father in the starlight. Should he or should he not tell? He must speak, though the telling might hurt his father. Kiyomori had sent Mokunosuké home and waited for this chance to be alone with his father. If Tadamori had not seen him that afternoon, it would be better to say nothing, he thought. He was certain, however, that his father had seen him even at that distance. His father would never bring up the matter, for it was like him to keep his loneliness and sorrows to himself. Why should he let a shadow be cast over his father again? Pondering thus to himself, Kiyomori found that the horse had led him almost to Imadegawa, and decided to speak to his father after all.

"Father, did you know that my mother was at the races?"

"So it seemed."

"I did not really want to see her again, but she called to me so that I finally went to her."

"You did?" said Tadamori, narrowing his eyes and scrutinizing his son. He did not seem displeased, so Kiyomori continued half apologetically:

"She looked as young as ever, decked out like a shrine virgin or a lady-in-waiting. But I had no tears for her. I could not feel that she was my mother."

"I'm sorry to hear that, Heita," was Tadamori's quiet reply.

"Why, Father?"

"There's nothing so pitiful as a motherless child, Heita. That you should see her and yet force yourself to disown your mother was most callous."

"I am *your* son. I can get along without a mother!" Kiyomori said hotly.

The figure on horseback shook his head. "You are wrong, Heita. If anyone has hardened your heart, then the fault is mine, for I have let my children look upon our incessant quarrels in a loveless home. It was I that let your mother appear unsightly to you. It was my fault. It is unnatural for a son to feel as you do. Be frank, Heita, if you wish to see your mother, go and visit her."

"How can that woman be my mother? She has been unfaithful to her husband, and does not love her children, and thinks of nothing but satisfying her whims!" Kiyomori protested.

"You must not speak of her as I have been prone to do, Heita. You have little reason to say such things of her. You and she are forever mother and child. Love that forgives all is the truest love and will surely bring you together."

Kiyomori did not answer. He could not understand his father. Was it because his father was too profound, or was he himself still too young to understand?

When they reached their home, Mokunosuké, Heiroku, and the other retainers met them at the gate. Lights flickered over the unkempt garden and the modest clean-swept, wooden stoop of the house. This simple, harmonious, and well-ordered life had not been theirs until three months ago. Kiyomori wondered what reason he had to regret his mother's going. There was no room for loneliness now, and why could his father not believe this?

CHAPTER IV

A LADY IN THE MOONLIGHT

That year, in mid-August, Wataru of the Genji invited some ten of his closest friends in the Guards to come and share a large jar of wine with him and view the moonlight in his garden. His friends, however, knew that there was another reason for the invitation. In the autumn the Emperor and the ex-Emperor were going on a pilgrimage to the Ninna-ji Temple. They were also attending the races which would be held in the temple compound. The official date of this event had already been announced—the 23rd of September—and the Guards knew that Wataru was waiting impatiently for a chance to prove himself and the black four-year-old with the white fetlocks.

"It's to drink to his success," Wataru's friends told each other. One of them jokingly added: "He's afraid to appear stingy, since it's customary for riders to give a large party for relatives and friends after the 'whip ritual' has been performed. Wataru has no love for these priests. He scoffs at those 'holy Buddhas,' as he calls them, saying he doesn't need their help. So instead of all the prayers and incantations, and a big banquet, he calls this a moon-viewing party!" The remark was greeted with much laughter.

Another Guard said: "Listen, you know how he feels about his young wife, Kesa-Gozen, who once served at Court. He is so infatuated with her that even on night duty all his thoughts are at home. We once asked to meet her, but all he would do was smile and say she was his 'secret love' and not to be seen, and so forth. I think he wants us to meet her tonight."

Thus talking and chaffing among themselves, the guests arrived at Wataru's house, where the gate stood wide open in welcome and the paving stones had been freshened with a sprinkling of water. Gathered in Wataru's guest-room, the young men fell silent and remained subdued while trays of food were brought in. It was not until the wine arrived that they once more were at their ease and talked and joked among themselves.

Heita Kiyomori and Sato Yoshikiyo were also there. Kiyomori noticed that Morito was not present, and was about to ask about him, but thought better of it. He had recently sensed that Wataru and Morito were uneasy in each other's company. No one else seemed to notice this, but Kiyomori often wondered if he was imagining this, for he found himself on his guard with Morito since the latter had told him the strange secret concerning his birth. Morito's behavior troubled Kiyomori. He feared for Morito, in whom, he knew, a keen mind battled with violent primitive lusts. Furthermore, he had observed the furtive look that came into Morito's eyes whenever he and Wataru were together. This look contrasted oddly with Morito's habitual swaggering. Nowadays, too, Morito went about with bloodshot eyes and haggard cheeks, and

Kiyomori had concluded that he was nervously fatigued, from either excessive studying or else heavy drinking and dissipation. He concluded that Wataru disliked Morito and had not invited him.

The wine was passed around and the young warriors were now at their ease. "Come, host," they called, "isn't it time for her to appear? Stop tantalizing us!"

Wataru was pressing wine on Yoshikiyo, who sat with his cup untouched.

Lifting his cup at last, Yoshikiyo addressed Wataru: "I once attended a poetry contest at the Palace when a lady named Kesa-Gozen was applauded for her poems, so she is not entirely unknown to me. Now that she is the mistress of a household, I doubt that she has opportunities for composing verse. A pity that such talent should be lost to us! You must have her attend the poetry parties, Wataru, for we crude warriors most lack an appreciation of literary accomplishments and, what is more, despise them. . . . Might I then say that this warrior and his poet wife are like a graceful painting—the pine and the chrysanthemum—a most felicitous wedding? These men envy you. Can you blame them for being so jealous?"

Yoshikiyo laughed heartily. The wine made him expansive and less somber than usual. The guests grew boisterous, clamoring: "Yoshikiyo, talking of poetry again? Whenever that fellow opens his mouth, our wine grows cold!"

"Come, come, good host, bring out the real thing!"

"Quickly let her appear before us—your friends!"

They boistrously entreated and demanded that Wataru bring out his wife, until he finally asked: "Shall I call dancing-girls to entertain us in my humble home?"

"No, no! Let us have a glimpse of the lady—Kesa-Gozen—she who is lovelier than all the famous dancing-girls in this capital!"

Wataru, laughing, begged for mercy, protesting: "She is shy— she will not leave the kitchen, where she warms the wine for my guests and busies herself with pleasing them. I fear she will not come and let these lamps shine on her."

"Let us see the light in your kitchen, rather than the autumn

moon," the guests shouted. One of them staggered to his feet and
made for the kitchen, but Wataru sprang after him and dragged
him back with promises to fetch his wife. The guests continued
to badger Wataru, who was quite sober now; assuring them that he
would present her fittingly as a warrior's wife, he begged them to
wait a little longer and left the room. When he reappeared, he
seated himself on the veranda which faced the garden, saying:

"The black colt that you know was entrusted to me now shows
every sign of being a winner. I now look forward to entering him
in the Ninna-ji races when the Emperor makes his pilgrimage, and
hope to celebrate that occasion with you. Now tell me what you
think of the colt."

Wataru's guests grew silent. They knew how Wataru had labored over the horse's training, even staking his reputation on it.
No one complained that he had broken the promise made awhile
ago, and they called out together: "Let's see him!"

Following his example, they seated themselves on the veranda
facing on a small inner garden. The August moon shed enough
brilliance for them to see the horse. Wataru faced the garden and
called to someone.

Clop, clop, clop rang out the hoofs as the horse drew near.
Crickets stopped chirring. The bushes near a bamboo fence stirred;
dew rolled down among the leaves with a sound like the scattering
of pearls. The garden gate swung open and a woman appeared, leading the colt by its reins. Noiselessly she stepped through the moonlight and then stopped in the middle of the garden.

The guests drew in their breath and made no sound—surprised, delighted, and amazed.

There stood the horse in the moonlight. His coat shone like
jet, like the wet plumes of a raven. A noble beast with fine legs and
magnificent muscles. There was no comparing him now with the
colt of the spring. His long tail almost swept the earth, and the four
white fetlocks gleamed as though he trod snow.

The guests, however, were not watching the horse, but the
figure that stood silently bowing to them. This, then, was Kesa-
Gozen?

She did not appear shy. A smile hovered on her lips as she turned to face the rearing horse, quieting it until it stood motionless.

Was it a trick of moonlight that made her look like the Kannon in the Dream Hall? Her fingers gleamed white to their very tips, and her long hair was as glossy as the horse's coat.

"Ah," Kiyomori sighed to himself, "I would have a wife, too, were there another such as she in this world!" He swallowed hard and then blushed furiously at the sound he made in his throat.

Night after night of moonlight succeeded one another. In the hills and on the plains the deer mated and squirrels danced among the wild grapevines. All the beasts of the fields seemed to be moonstruck.

Kiyomori, sitting at home, was restive. He watched his brother poring over his books by the light of a small lamp suspended near the old desk their mother had left behind, and itched to make fun of him. Here he was—eighteen—and not a thought of women in his head! He sighed for this sorry brother of his. There was nothing in the poor fellow's books that Kiyomori did not know. He watched Tsunemori. He had succumbed, Kiyomori thought, like so many other warrior youths these days, to the fad of borrowing books from the libraries of the Imperial Academy and the university—those Confucian classics in their Sung bindings from China, which had moldered undisturbed for some two hundred years on dusty shelves. What could Tsunemori possibly find interesting in Confucius' *Analects* or the *Four Books*? He himself had pretended to listen and slept through those lectures expounding the Great Sage's teachings. The Confucian precepts were just ornaments, aimed only to promote the interests of the privileged, admonishing as they did the warriors and the common people to obey their superiors. By what authority had Confucius defined those codes governing the conduct of men? What had Confucius enjoyed in his lifetime, or what great deeds had he done? Had bloodshed ceased in China because of him?—thieves become honest men?—or liars reformed? Even the venerable sage had once been worsted in an argument with a notorious criminal and been reduced to human stature.

"Foolish brother!" Kiyomori finally said. "Why fill your dull brains with such nonsense? . . . There's a paneled screen at the Court, covered with paintings of wise men and the sages; people believe that merely sitting in that room with those images will fill one with wisdom. So you, too, propose to stuff that head of yours with the likenesses of sages? Utter foolishness! We're not aristocrats! They feed us, and when they order us, must we not instantly go out and kill even those who have done us no harm? Are we not completely at their mercy? Leave those books—have done with them!"

Kiyomori was sprawled on his back in the doorway; the upper half of his body lay in the room, and his legs were thrust out over the edge of the veranda. Mosquitoes hummed about him as he lay in the shadows, gazing at Tsunemori absorbed in his books. Kiyomori was annoyed and fumed inwardly; his father had long since gone to bed, all the servants were asleep, and yet Tsunemori insisted on staying up late. He had irritably refused to accompany Kiyomori on one of his nocturnal prowls. He was a nuisance, this young brother of his, so unlike himself in temperament, though they had the same mother. Disturbing thoughts began to trickle through Kiyomori's mind, like the persistent drip of rain through a leaking roof. He wondered if the difference lay in not having had the same father. This thought made him forget his fear of Tadamori and the constraint he felt with his brother, and he yawned deliberately, muttering to himself: "Well, I'll go now. A fine moonlight night, too." He raised himself suddenly from his supine position and let one foot slide down on the dew-soaked sandals under the veranda.

"Where are you going?"

"I am trying to decide," Kiyomori replied.

"But at this hour?"

"Some of us Guards promised to meet Wataru on a moonlight night when he would take his colt out for exercise."

Tsunemori was incredulous. "What? Exercise a horse so late?"

"It's not unusual for riders to try out their horses secretly before the races."

"You're lying!"

"What?" cried Kiyomori angrily, staring at the bright halo around the lamp.

Tsunemori quickly left his desk and came to his brother and whispered: "Greet Mother for me. Will you take this?"

Kiyomori gasped as he felt of the letter that his brother thrust into the breast of his robe.

"You have her permission to visit her, don't you? I long to see her too. She left Father, but she is still our mother. I'll wait until my time comes to see her. Tell her so for me. . . . It's all in that letter."

Tears rolled down Tsunemori's cheeks. Kiyomori saw how each drop caught the glitter of moonlight. Ridiculous! What reason had he to pursue that mother of his? Softened, however, by the sight of his brother's tears, Kiyomori said gently:

"You're wrong, Tsunemori. I'm going to keep my promise to Wataru."

"Don't try to deceive me," Tsunemori insisted, "there are visitors who've told Father they saw you near the Nakamikado mansion."

"No! Who has been telling such fantastic tales?"

"Fujiwara Tokinobu. He is one of the few courtiers whom Father trusts, and I don't doubt his word," Tsunemori replied.

"So that old man has been coming round these days, has he?"

"There are matters that cannot be discussed at the Palace, and that is why he comes here."

Kiyomori scratched his head. "Caught! If so many people know, I might as well confess. I'll take your letter to Mother, Tsunemori. I tell you, however, that Father said I should go to see her if I wished."

"Then let me come with you!" cried Tsunemori.

"You idiot!" Kiyomori burst out, disconcerted. "Have you no consideration for Father? There's no need to tell him about my night escapades, though, and remember—not a word to Mokuno-suké!"

Kiyomori made his exit over the wall. His brother's tearful face seemed to float before him, but he soon forgot it. Above him spread the Milky Way. The night winds cooled his feverish limbs. Where was he going? He did not know. What had caused his restlessness tonight? Whatever it was, it made him dreamy, drove him to madness, to tears, left him sleepless, until he felt desperate. He believed in some Supreme Being, as did those Buddhists who preached the virtuous life. He wondered and agonized about the man from whom he had inherited this wild blood of his. Was this a strain of madness which had passed to him from his mother or the late Emperor? If so, was he responsible for his acts? He hadn't the courage to go alone to the brothel on Sixth Avenue, but if Morito were here now, he would go instantly to those women, to any woman, or even to a fox in the shape of a woman in the moonlight. Anything—anyone who could still this thing which raged in him like a wild beast. Any illusion that would quiet it, lay it to rest. . . . . To touch some woman . . . to meet one now by chance.

Kiyomori walked on in a sort of delirium. He did not know how he got there, but he stood outside the walls of the Nakamikado mansion. No use—he was a coward! The wall here was much higher than the one at home. He knew that his mother's apartments were in the east wing. He recalled her words at the Kamo races— "Come to see me. . . . Ruriko will be good company."— Ruriko, far too pretty and superior for a mere dreamy warrior youth. There was no reason, however, why he should not try to see her on the excuse of visiting his mother. It was not love that made him seek her out, but his dreams.

Each time he came here, his courage evaporated. He blamed his timidity and grew discouraged at the sorry figure he made. Standing there in his old robes and worn sandals, there passed through his heated imagination those many tales he heard daily about the courtiers—the aristocrat who could lightly abduct a princess, bear her away to the open fields where the tall grass waved and the *hagi* flower bloomed, while away the night with her until the moon grew pale in the dawn, and dew jeweled her eyelids, then steal back with her unseen. Kiyomori thought of the courtiers who casually dropped love-letters in the halls of the Palace where ladies-in-waiting passed, and waited for night to bring the touch of sinuous tresses and hot lips. . . . He wondered why fate had not decreed such things for him. . . . He was a coward! If only he could put away that cringing thing in him!

Tonight he was determined to go through with it. He now stood on top of the wall, but again grew irresolute. Wild visions rioted through his heated brain. Wait! A cool wind blew on his sweating body. Through his mad fancying he remembered Mokunosuké's words: "Whoever you are, you are a man after all. You are no cripple with those fine limbs." Whether he was the son of an emperor or the child of an intrigue, was he not a child of the heavens and the earth? What he wrestled with now were his own lusts!

He suddenly wanted to laugh at himself on his high perch. He gazed up at the Milky Way flung across the heavens. Not bad—not bad at all to be alone like this under that vast autumn sky!

What was that? Again!

In the distance a tongue of flame licked at the sky. He stared in the direction of a roof that lay inside the city walls. Nothing unusual—just another fire. Fires were no longer rare these days. As the red glow spread, he thought of the numberless common folk, huddled in miserable sleep while the frivolous aristocrats ruled in pampered luxury; the two governments plotted against each other, and the ruthless armed clergy rioted. Those flames, leaping so hungrily at the sky, were the tongues of the starving masses, the common people for whom there was no redress and whose only means of protest lay in firing the objects of their hate. He recalled the more recent conflagrations: the Bifuku Gate, the West Quarter, the High Chancellor's villa. How the downtrodden and the criminals, whose very existence depended upon the prosperity of the Fujiwara, had gloated under a rain of ashes and sparks at the sight of the destruction!

Kiyomori jumped down from the wall—on the outer side—and started off at a run in the direction of the confused noises that now filled the streets.

The long, uninterrupted autumn rains caused a great deal of grumbling, but this year neither the Kamo nor the Katsura River flooded its banks. The foliage on the Northern Hills was already beginning to turn.

The pilgrimage to the Ninna-ji Temple was only ten days away, and the Guards at the Palace were busy with preparations for that event. Though still unsure of himself, Kiyomori was pleased by his new duties. The Sixth Rank had been conferred on him; he was now a Guard officer, an outrider for the imperial carriage, and determined to perform his duties faultlessly. He stayed late at the Palace and returned home nightly, too hungry and weary for idle dreaming.

On the 14th of September, shortly before midnight, there was a sound of feet hurrying toward Kiyomori's room. It was Heiroku, the steward, who called out that a messenger had arrived on horseback from the Palace. The young master was to put on his armor and report immediately.

What was this sudden summons? Kiyomori leaped out of bed. He was not, however, unduly surprised. Tsunemori's teeth chattered with excitement, and the words came tumbling out of his mouth: "What is it—war?"

"I don't know. Anything can happen these days."

"Could the monks of Mount Hiei or Kofukuji have marched on the capital with their mercenaries to petition the authorities again?"

Kiyomori opened his armor chest and pulled out his corselet, greaves, and armor tassets. As he started putting them on, he called to Tsunemori:

"Go to Father's apartments. With Mother gone, there's no one to help him with his armor."

"Mokunosuké is there with him. Shall I get mine?"

Kiyomori smiled in spite of himself. "You stay here and keep the little ones from crying."

There was a great clatter and angry shouts all round the house. The retainers were bringing the horses from the stable, bearing arms and pine torches from the storehouses, and frenziedly cursing at each other. In the open yard where the retainers usually assembled, Tadamori sat astride his horse. When Kiyomori appeared, he ordered Mokunosuké to open the gates, put spur to his horse, and was gone. Sixteen or seventeen retainers, carrying halberds, filed out at a run, hurrying to overtake Tadamori.

Nothing disturbed the sleeping streets, and Tadamori ordered his men to keep a watch out for fires. The gates on all sides of the Palace wall were barred, an anticlimax to all this feverish arming, and they went on to the Guard Office, where the gates stood open. Between the trees they saw lights in the main building of the Palace and sensed that something unusual had happened. There was a message for Tadamori: his majesty's aide wished to have a word with him. Tadamori rode through the inner gate and then disappeared into the Palace.

Kiyomori, meanwhile, arrived at the Guard Office. Leaving his horse with a retainer, he shouldered his way through the dense crowd of Guards and armed men who surrounded the building, hoping to catch in the babble of voices some explanation for the summons.

"You never can tell about people. It was only last month that we Guards met at Wataru's house in Iris Lane."

Faces—faces—faces. Nothing but excited faces and excited talk.

"Yes, I was there that night. We were quite drunk and badgered Wataru into letting us see the moon in his kitchen instead of the moon in his garden. . . ."

"It was just like Wataru to introduce his wife in the graceful way he did."

"Even the light of the moon seemed too harsh for her as she turned her unsmiling face toward us."

"She was all elegance, like a white peony, though she had just come from her kitchen. . . ."

"Like a spray of pear blossoms in spring!"

"Ah, how pitiful! How pitiful, indeed!"

With more show of feeling than was usual among the Guards, one of them lamented: "Though she was another man's wife, I do say she was lovely beyond words. And that Kesa-Gozen murdered. . . ."

Kiyomori could not believe his ears. Kesa-Gozen dead? Murdered? Her image in his heart was so real that he refused to believe she was dead. The unspeakable worst had happened to her. He felt he had more words in praise of her beauty than any man there. But she was another man's wife and he had believed he did wrong in even thinking of her. Now that everyone spoke of her, he no longer was afraid of admitting to himself that he had adored her. Roughly he pushed his way through the crowd as though bent on business that concerned him alone.

"Is it true? Is there no mistake about it? The murderer—who is the murderer?" Kiyomori demanded.

Someone spoke to him. "The master calls you."

Kiyomori turned and hurried toward the inner gate, where his father waited. He did not recognize his father in the man who spoke.

"Post yourself at the foot of Kurama Road, near First Avenue," Tadamori commanded; "watch out for every man that passes. Consider every man suspect. Leave no one unsearched. Don't let the murderer escape. He may be disguised, but there's no mistaking him."

Kiyomori could not wait further. "Who is this man I am to capture?" he interrupted breathlessly.

"A warrior, Endo Morito."

"What! Morito killed Kesa-Gozen?"

"Yes, he," Tadamori replied heavily. "He has disgraced the name of the Imperial Guards—and of all things, because of an infatuation for another man's wife."

At that moment Morito's uncle, Endo Mitsuto, came rapidly

through the inner gate, his eyes averted and his face sickly. He slipped by quickly as if eager to escape, but every eye scrutinized him as though he were the murderer's accomplice.

Armed retainers, other than his own, now gathered round Tadamori. He had conferred with his majesty's aide and was now prepared to give the men an account of the events of that night.

Kesa-Gozen had been murdered early that night of the 14th, about the Dog Hour (eight o'clock). The place: her own home in Iris Lane. Her husband was away at that time.

Morito, who had had a nodding acquaintance with Kesa-Gozen's mother, either before her daughter left the Court to be married or soon after her marriage to Wataru, it was never known exactly when, fell wildly in love with Kesa-Gozen.

People believed that Morito's exceptional gifts as a scholar, widely recognized, would win him an imperial grant and enable him to enter the university, where he would attain to the highest honors conferred there. Lately, however, his fellow students and friends in the Guards had begun to look askance at him and avoid him, for Morito had for some time been acting strangely.

Ardent and persevering by nature, Morito was not only a scholar, but an eloquent speaker, daring, and confident to the point of condescending to all his acquaintances. In matters pertaining to amours, he was more than self-assured, and when carried away by his passions, he was a formidable man with his magnificent physique—a madman, deaf to all reason.

His one-sided love affair with Kesa-Gozen, the headlong infatuation of a man not to be turned from his purpose, was her doom. He passionately importuned her, until she grew afraid; intimidated her by insinuating that Wataru would pay the price for her resistance, until his threats finally determined the course she would take. She secretly made up her mind that she would meet his challenge with one of her own.

Morito, desperate and on the brink of losing his mind, demanded a final answer from her, and Kesa-Gozen was prepared to give it. She lucidly considered the consequences of the promise she would give him, and this is what she said:

"There is no choice for me now. Hide yourself, on the night of the 14th, in my husband's bedroom, at the Dog Hour. Earlier in the evening I shall see that he bathes and washes his hair, ply him with wine, and then see him to bed. While he lives, there is no way in which I can meet your wishes. I shall wait for you in another part of the house while you go through with it. My husband is deadly with a sword; therefore, creep quietly to his pillow, feel for his wet hair, and then with one blow strike off his head. Be sure you strike clean."

Morito feverishly assented. Early on the night of the 14th he did exactly as he was told. He had no trouble whatever and felt no need to examine the head that he grasped by its damp locks. None the less he stepped out on the veranda to look at the head by the light of the moon.

He screamed. Froze. The head of his beloved dangled from his hand.

In that one horrid cry torn from the depth of his being were mingled his shame, his grief, his despair, and the agony of the mortal wound he had dealt himself. He sank numb to the floor. At that instant the colt in the stable neighed shrilly, pawed wildly, and would not stop neighing.

Morito finally rose to his feet. Moaning incoherently in the direction of the dark room, he took the cold thing, clammy with its wet hair and fresh blood, and drew it close to him under his arm, then leaped to the garden, cleared the hedge and bushes in a bound, and vanished into darkness like a malevolent ghost.

Tadamori recounted what so far was known of the murder, adding: "This crime involves not only one woman and a warrior. It casts a shadow over the Palace and puts a stain on the honor of the warriors of the Imperial Guards. It will be to our further shame if the murderer is tried by the Criminal Court and sentenced by the courtiers. It is our responsibility to capture the murderer. Set up guards at the twelve city gates; post watches at all the crossroads of Ninth Avenue, and we shall surely trap the criminal."

The mass of dark figures listened tensely and acknowledged

the orders with a movement of their heads. Kiyomori nodded and tasted the salt tears that fell on his lips. He suddenly saw his secret love for Kesa-Gozen for what it was and her loveliness in a new light. Had he been drawn to Iris Lane like Morito, he too might well have done the same! Maniac or fool, which was he? Which Morito? His heart sank at the thought of capturing Morito single-handed, but the sight of the men excitedly streaming out of the gate in the early dawn brought his courage back, and Kiyomori rode off into the mist to his post on Kurama Road, his eyes hard and glinting.

The story of Kesa-Gozen's death soon reached every ear in Kyoto. It was talked about everywhere. Strangers, as well as those who knew her, tenderly mourned for her, denouncing Morito as a ghoul—a raving madman. Him they could never forgive, they said, and loathed him the more because he had once shown such promise. But more than the curiosity, the horror, and the pity that Kesa-Gozen's death aroused was the realization of how lightly most men and women regarded a woman's fidelity. There were few who were not profoundly moved, and who did not shudder at the thought of what she had done to preserve her womanliness.

The common folk of the Shiokoji grieved for her. Even the harlots of Sixth Avenue, who nightly hawked their bodies for a living, wiped the tears from their tawdry painted faces in pity, and not a few of them mingled discreetly with the crowds at Kesa-Gozen's funeral to leave nosegays for the dead one.

The courtiers, and the highborn ladies, too, were moved by the tale of Kesa-Gozen, though many appraised it cynically, for in the sheltered decadence of their lives what was a woman's virtue but an elegant commodity, a graceful pawn, casually bestowed and lightly withdrawn, for the pleasure of men? What then, they said, was so noble in Kesa-Gozen, who had defended her honor with her life? Was it not the natural timidity of a woman that drove her to this extremity? There were some who said with a shrug that a woman's whim to die in her husband's stead at the hands of a crazed lover was scarcely a matter for the courtiers to fuss over, that if the affair was to be regarded seriously at all, it was a sign of corruption in the Guards. What had happened to the Guards these days, these warriors who were assigned to keep watch at the Palace or sent as messengers between the Palace and the Court? If there were profligates there, Morito certainly was not the only one! What else could one expect of those warriors? Hadn't several days passed since Kesa-Gozen's funeral without the Guards having captured the murderer? This was inexcusable! Who could rely on these warriors in times of danger if they were incapable of even catching one madman?

Malicious gossip soon spread, and charges were brought against Tadamori by the courtiers. The responsibility for that crime was his. What led him to wait so assiduously on his majesty? Was he not the chief of the Guard Office? Was it not he who had urged his majesty to choose that ill-omened colt with the white fetlocks? And he that induced Kesa-Gozen's husband to take it? Tadamori undoubtedly was the cause of all this mischief! Was it not a heinous offense even to jest about a taboo? Was he not guilty of blasphemy?

Tadamori's offense was reviewed by the courtiers and there was even talk of a trial. This turn of affairs alarmed the ex-Emperor. He realized that he alone was to blame for this malicious outburst against the unworldly Tadamori. Not only had he honored him but he had loved and trusted this warrior as he did no other man.

To the courtiers' charges the ex-Emperor replied: "It is only a few days until we leave for Ninna-ji Temple. . . . As for Morito's capture—let us consider that for discussion later on. As for these charges that Tadamori is responsible for allowing Wataru to take that ill-omened colt—since it was I that consented to it, it would amount to bringing those charges against me." Toba laughed wryly as he sought to pacify the courtiers, who ceased to press their charges against Tadamori, though not for long.

Word went out from the Palace that watchers at the crossroads of the capital would be withdrawn the following day. The Guards who had been on duty now for seven days were both alarmed and crestfallen. Where had Morito gone, carrying Kesa-Gozen's head? Had the earth opened and swallowed him, or had he done away with himself?

It looked as though Morito's whereabouts would end in mystery. Since that calamitous night, no one had seen him or anyone remotely resembling him. The Police Commission sent their secret agents to comb the environs of Kyoto, but there still were no clues to be found.

Tonight was to be the last when sentinels would be stationed at the crossroads of Kyoto.

"There's something suspicious about the Palace inside the Northwest Gate. Not only is his uncle on duty there, but he must still have some old acquaintances there. . . ."

Kiyomori, who overheard this conversation, was startled. He was guarding First Avenue with sixteen or seventeen of his housemen, a number of them in disguise.

Right enough! He had not thought of searching his immediate surroundings, and Morito had once been a Guard at the Northwest Gate before coming to the Cloister Palace. The Northwest Gate was not far off. He swelled with pride at the thought of how he would succeed. Passing his halberd to his other hand, he beckoned to Heiroku, who stood at a distance to his rear, shouting:

"Get Mokunosuké to come here. I'm off to the Northwest Gate. Stand guard here. The watches end tonight."

Mokunosuké appeared. "To the Northwest Gate? My young master, what business do you have there?"

"Old man, I smell a rat over there."

Mokunosuké, knitting his brows, shook his head slowly. "Better not. It will do you no good when they hear you've been carrying your search into the palace of a princess."

"Why should that matter? I don't suspect her."

"You would be wise to watch your step. You know how a trivial matter can lead to serious results in affairs concerning the Court and the Palace."

"I shall go, nevertheless. They tell me their Guards are laughing at us and vowing they will get our man. This is my chance to catch Morito. I'm certain Morito is praying that if he is caught, it will be I that gets him!"

Flushed to the ears by wild visions of success, Kiyomori stole a sidelong look at skeptical Mokunosuké. "When Morito finds he is cornered, he will think of me. I even feel that he's expecting me! Mokunosuké, when my father comes, tell him where I've gone."

The Northwest Gate was only a short distance away, and to allay Mokunosuké's fears, Kiyomori started out on foot, leaving his halberd behind.

The Imperial Palace stood in the north center of the city in a rectangular enclosure, about one mile by three quarters, containing various residential apartments, ceremonial halls, and the many departments of state. Immediately outside the enclosure were numerous small palaces and mansions of the nobility, as well as the university, which adjoined the South Gate. There were twelve gates to the enclosure and two additional side-gates—the Northeast Gate and the Northwest Gate, the latter entrance leading to the palace where Kesa-Gozen had once served.

Kiyomori felt there was sufficient reason to investigate this quarter. It was quite possible that both the outlaw and those who sheltered him would consider this spot immune from search. At this thought Kiyomori broke into a run. As he entered the wide, clean avenue flanked with pine trees, he heard shouts and repeated orders to stop. With an air of annoyance, Kiyomori looked back.

"I? . . ."

The Guards here were also on watch, he realized. He walked back deliberately toward a group of them.

"Go back! Get out!" the Guards bawled, blocking Kiyomori's path, not even troubling to ask his name.

Kiyomori stubbornly insisted: "I *will* pass! I come on urgent business." He raised his eyebrows. "Needless to say, I serve his majesty the ex-Emperor Toba. Why should I wish to disturb her highness?" he blustered, turning an angry red. The Guards thought him a belligerent little fellow, and the situation was fast getting out of hand; it was Kiyomori against some sixteen or seventeen Guards, when an elderly warrior, possibly a senior officer, appeared on his rounds and stood for a moment observing the altercation. Then he approached Kiyomori from the rear, struck him a resounding blow on his corselet, and addressed him as though he were a child:

"So, it's you, Heita? What's this spluttering? What's this all about—this impertinence?"

"Ah. . . ." Memories of that bleak wind in February, that sad, sad day, the gnawing of his empty stomach, and that galling money suddenly flashed across Kiyomori's mind. "Is it you, uncle? Indeed! And this is your force? I thought I recognized some of your retainers among them."

More than at the ridiculous figure he felt he presented, Kiyomori boiled with rage at the thought that these men had deliberately insulted him by pretending not to recognize him. He could never think of this uncle—nor his aunt—without seeing coins in his mind's eye; he had gone countless times to their residence at Horikawa to borrow money; listened to them abuse his parents; endured their criticisms and unending complaints. He reflected sourly how he must always seem like a penniless imp to this uncle. It was his fate to be always treated with contempt and dismissed as a fellow with a warped disposition.

"Come, Heita, what do you mean by 'indeed'? We haven't seen you at Horikawa for some time—not that your visits were ever welcome. . . . Your neglect, I must say, gives me pleasure."

Kiyomori wilted. He had been arrogantly asserting himself in the name of the Palace Guards and now he was ready to crawl into a hole. Putting away his pride and rancor, Kiyomori meekly appealed: "Is it—quite impossible?"

His uncle, meanwhile, obtained from his men a brief account of what had happened and guessed what Kiyomori was after.

"Impossible! Absolutely! What do you mean by resisting? You are exactly like that obstinate father of yours. Why do you have to take after that indigent father of yours? Get on home!" he roared.

Just then Tadamasa noticed a courtier's carriage coming out by the Northwest Gate and loped away in great haste, just in time to deliver a deep bow as the carriage rolled past.

Kiyomori turned and started walking back. This had been unavoidable. He thought he heard the Guards laughing behind his back. Then he began to wonder whose carriage it was that he had just seen. As he looked round, he saw an ox approaching. The setting sun blazed on the lacquered body and shafts of a flamboyant lady's carriage, embellished with patterns in metalwork of silver and gold. The bamboo blinds were half-drawn. It was not the Princess's carriage, nor could the occupant be seen, but a young ox-tender walked beside the carriage, switching at the flies. Kiyomori came to a halt in the shade of a cedar tree and waited for the carriage to pass him. As it rolled by, he boldly stared up into it.

"Oh! . . ."

He thought he heard a voice. A blind was rolled up and the ox-boy ordered to stop. Someone leaned out and called his name.

"Mother!" Kiyomori replied impulsively, and leaped onto one of the shafts. "Was this the carriage that just came out by the Northwest Gate? Was it you, Mother?"

"Why, what do you mean by all these questions? You never seem glad to see me whenever we meet."

Yasuko wore the robes of a court lady and, as usual, was elegantly made up. Decked out in her gay robes, she seemed even younger and lovelier than Kiyomori had ever remembered her to be—at home, at the Kamo races.

"Your uncle, Tadamasa, was at the gate just a moment ago, waiting to greet me as I left. He said nothing about you, but didn't I see you talking together?"

"Has my uncle lately begun to pay his respects to you and shown himself friendlier?"

Yasuko laughed. "How you amuse me! You haven't answered any of my questions, and do nothing but try to cross-examine me. Your uncle has changed considerably. He is most courteous to me."

"He—and my aunt—who used to speak so ill of you?"

"Now, Heita, do you begin to understand why I hated being poor? Her highness has taken a fancy to me, and I go regularly to take part in the dancing at her palace. Your uncle now behaves like

7 8

a proper retainer toward me, for he knows he must humor me if he expects to come up in the world."

So that was it! Kiyomori spat at the feet of the ox. How like his uncle! As for his mother's visits to the palace at the Northwest Gate—she had probably had the Nakamikado use their influence at Court, and was making good use of her talents as a dancing-girl. Fit counterpart to that uncle! Whenever Kiyomori met his mother, he felt that his father, Tadamori, the man who was not his real father, was more his own flesh and blood than she.

Kiyomori suddenly felt disappointed, bitter, and sad. The sight of his mother made him wretched. The flies buzzing about the ox kept stinging his face and irritating him, so he left her abruptly. But Yasuko called him back in great agitation, and with an arch look said:

"Heita, wasn't there something else you wanted to ask me?"

Kiyomori started violently. He thought he saw a figure hiding in the carriage, looked more closely, and saw Ruriko.

"Heita, have you nothing more to tell me?" Yasuko asked, laughing. "Ruriko," she then said, "won't you give this to Heita?"

Ruriko drew back in confusion, concealing her face behind Yasuko's shoulder. Yasuko drew out a large orchid-chrysanthemum and held it out to Kiyomori: "Her highness, the Princess, gave this to Ruriko, who wishes you to have it, Heita. Go write some verses on this flower and bring them to me at the Nakamikado mansion —some exquisite lines that will win Ruriko's heart."

Kiyomori stood in a daze as he watched the carriage slowly disappear in the distance. So his mother now planned to revenge herself on Tadamori by using Ruriko to lure him from his father! Kiyomori found he had absent-mindedly crushed the flower and stripped it of all its petals. Using the stalk for a switch, he walked back to his post at the crossroads.

Two horses and a man were waiting for him there. Kiyomori felt low in spirits. Mokunosuké, who had anxiously waited for him, seemed dejected.

"Where are all the others? Have they gone home already?"

"We had our orders to discontinue the watches from tonight. What of your search at the Northwest Gate?"

"Useless, I should not have gone. Where is my father?"

"Let us talk on our way back. Come, get on your horse."

Mokunosuké saw Kiyomori mount and next climbed into his own saddle.

"Back to the Palace, Old One?"

"No, home to Imadegawa."

Kiyomori was surprised. The Guards were supposed to assemble tonight at the Guard Office, where his father would speak to them. Tadamori was also to report to his majesty and his aide for further instructions.

"Mokunosuké, has something happened to my father?"

"I understand he has decided to resign from his position at the Palace."

"Is this true? Is it because we have not succeeded in arresting Morito?"

"He is too much a man to let criticism of that sort trouble him. The courtiers are maligning him. He can't endure facing those unjust and ambiguous charges they bring against him. . . . I didn't have the heart to ask him anything more."

"Does this mean he goes into seclusion again?" Kiyomori felt like saying: "Poverty again!" His armor suddenly seemed to weigh him down.

Mokunosuké mumbled half to himself: "Oh, why is fate so harsh to him? The times are wrong, the world is evil! . . . Fortune *must* smile on him some time!"

Kiyomori hardly knew his own voice as it suddenly rang out clear and challenging like a battle cry:

"Here am I, Old One! Was it not you who once said I was child of the heavens and earth, that I was no cripple with these fine limbs? Here he is—that one! What is fate, that we should wait upon it?"

CHAPTER V

"THE TRODDEN WEED"

HIS brothers came out to meet him, and Kiyomori saw their shadowy figures under the sagging gateway as he dismounted; Tsunemori, who carried three-year-old Norimori on his back, called out: "Welcome home, brother! Father's back already."

"Hmm. . . . With all of us gone for seven days, the little ones must have missed us."

"Yes, I had trouble with Norimori, who kept crying for

Mother," Tsunemori began, but stopped short at the look on Kiyomori's face. "Oh, yes, Father wished to see you the moment you got back."

"Oh? Well, then I'll go in this way. Old One, take my horse," Kiyomori said. Handing the reins to Mokunosuké, he started across the courtyard toward the light that burned in his father's rooms.

Smoke rose briskly from the kitchen fires. The retainers, who had returned earlier in the evening, were still in their armor, preparing the evening meal for the large household—cooking rice, chopping wood, and bringing in potatoes and other vegetables from the kitchen plot. As with most warriors' households where there were few women to help and poverty prevented their hiring underservants, master and retainers alike did the farming, tended the horses, and worked in the kitchen as well.

"Ah, so you're back, Heita! My thanks for your labors."

"Father, you must be tired after your duties of the past week, and you must feel it the more for our not having captured Morito."

"We've done everything possible and have nothing to regret. Morito is not one to be caught so easily."

"Could he have killed himself, Father?"

"I doubt it. His was no light offense, and I cannot believe that he would take his own life. . . . And, Heita, there's something I want you to do."

"Is it urgent?"

"Yes, take one of the colts to the city and sell him for whatever price you can get; then buy as much wine as you can."

"One of the colts! Do you really mean it?"

"Mmm. . . . See how much wine you can get."

"But, Father, there'd be more than all of us can finish in three days! This is too humiliating—I can't go! What could be more humiliating for a warrior than to be forced to sell his horse?"

"That's why I send you. Go, and live down that shame. Sell him at any price—the sooner, the better."

Kiyomori quickly left his father and went to the stable. Three of the seven colts there were their most prized possessions. He carefully looked over the remaining four. Dumb creatures that they were, there was not one among them that he did not love! Had they not all been with him and his father on that dangerous campaign in the west the year before last and faced death with them? What countless times he had fondled them!

He knew that horse-fairs were sometimes held near the market-place, so Kiyomori went to the house of a horse-dealer whom he knew, sold the colt, and purchased wine. Three large jars were loaded onto a handcart, and Kiyomori helped the wine-merchant bring the cart back to Imadegawa.

The evening meal was late, but the autumn night was long for such feasting as was rarely seen in a warrior's house. Summoning all his retainers to the spacious room in the main house, Tadamori unsealed the jars of wine, ordered casks of salted fish and pickles to be brought, usually stored for emergencies, and called in all the retainers to drink.

"I know you are all tired after your seven days' watch. By rights you should be drinking wine at the Palace tonight, but my failure prevents me from setting foot inside its gates. I have re-signed my post. Let me try to make amends to you in this way. A day will surely come when your loyalty will be rewarded. This wine —the best I can offer you—is in token of my gratitude to you, my men. Come, drink all you can. Let us drink all night, and sing to fortify our warrior hearts!"

The candles flickered in the night wind as the retainers sat with bowed heads, silent. They knew that wine flowed copiously to the accompaniment of music at the nightly banquets of the nobles, but occasions when a retainer could taste wine were rare. Tonight their very vitals groaned at the aroma, and their hearts grew full at the thought of Tadamori's regard for them.

And Tadamori said: "How this garden suits our poverty—the wild luxuriance of its autumn flowers! Come, drink, all! Fill up your cups, fill up your cups!"

The men held up their wine-cups. At the Palace, Tadamori had the reputation of being a lusty drinker, and Kiyomori, lifting his vessel, began:

"Father, tonight I shall drink at least half as much as you!"

8 3

"Well and good—only keep away from the houses on Sixth Avenue!"

Tadamori's reply drew a loud burst of laughter, in which he joined with unusual heartiness. Kiyomori colored with chagrin. How had such tales reached his father's ear? Who of these men had been making the rounds of the bawdyhouses on Sixth Avenue? It was useless to protest, and to draw attention from himself he called to one of the men:

"Heiroku, Heiroku, give us a song—one of the ballads popular in the capital now!"

"You sing, young master, one of those tunes picked up in the neighborhood of Sixth Avenue!"

"Enough of such jokes!"

A voice from the other end of the room launched into a popular ballad; one by one the men joined in; hands clapped in time; someone beat out the rhythm on a wine-jar. Some rose to dance, others broke into new songs. Wildly they sang as they drank, and as they grew more boisterous, a few began to rail:

"Time and again those courtiers have plotted against our master, and now they try to break the bond between him and his majesty by saying he failed to capture Morito!"

"What? Fool! Haven't they succeeded? Hasn't our master resigned from his post?"

"Why should he be blamed? Why did our master resign so meekly? . . . This is too much! Those aristocrats—my blood boils when I think of them! What does his majesty think of all this?"

"If he trusts and loves our master, why doesn't he put down the plots and intrigues against him? Can't he see that the jealousy of the courtiers is bringing slow death to our master?"

"Yes, though his majesty rules, he has no power over those courtiers who surround him, and our master refuses to let his majesty be distressed because of him."

"They know that too well, those aristocrats!"

"Doesn't the master himself admit that though he ranks with the courtiers, he is despised for being a warrior?"

"Then why does his majesty allow it? Let me ask the Emperor

himself! I will bawl this question until it reaches his ears in the Palace!"

"Madmen! Fools!"

The retainers fell silent, but continued to shake their heads angrily. Pretending not to hear them, Kiyomori watched them, and finally rose to join a group. Throwing out his arms, he embraced the heads on either side of him.

"Here—you warriors—why this moaning and complaining? Have you no more sense than toads or vipers? Our time hasn't come. Have you no patience? Are we not the 'trodden weed' still? The time is not yet here for us to raise our heads. Must you still complain?"

The strong odor of heated bodies and the fumes of the wine filled his nostrils as he held the men close. He felt tears of bitterness fall hot on his knees. As a mother bird draws its young close under her wing, so did Kiyomori, exulting, draw his men to him and, calling for more wine, drained his cup in one draught.

The stalled beast turned loose in the fields to fend for itself reverts in time to its wild state. Man's barbarous nature asserts itself even more swiftly, and this was true of Morito, whose transformation back to savagery seemed to come overnight.

"Should I go on living? Am I better off dead? What am I to do with this self? They still pursue me—give me no time to think. . . . I must rest, and yet they keep following. I stop to take breath, and they still—" "I—I—I," he repeated to himself, not realizing that that self with which he identified himself no longer existed.

On that night when he escaped from the house in Iris Lane and mysteriously eluded his pursuers, Morito could not remember which way his feet took him. He slept in the open, hid himself in hollow trees, and ate whatever he could find in his wild flight. His clothes were now in tatters, his bare feet caked with blood and mud, and his eyes gleamed like those of some wild beast.

This was the man of letters, the gifted Morito, for whom there had been such high hopes. Who could find in this shape the scholar, the proud Morito? Who could believe that this was he

8 5

who looked down on his fellow men with scorn? Yet the shape still breathed, walked, and moved. That which lived merely existed.

His ears were now sharpened to every bird cry, and the sight of rabbits and deer no longer startled him. He felt himself one with the birds and beasts of this wild solitude. But the slightest sound of men approaching made his hair bristle. There they were—coming! Taking a fresh hold on the round object that he carried, Morito would stand frozen for an instant, his bloodshot eyes wild, searching this way and that.

A sleeve of his outer robe was torn off to make a wrapping for the thing he held tight to him. It was the head of Kesa-Gozen. He had not laid it down for even a moment since that night. The blood had seeped through and dried hard until, drenched with dew and stained with earth, it looked like lacquer. More than a fortnight had passed since Morito had fled, and the head now gave out the odor of putrefaction. But he clung to it day and night, and when he drowsed, he seemed to see Kesa-Gozen once more in the flesh.

Nothing about her had changed. He heard the silken rustle of her garments as she drew near and whispered to him. He breathed her fragrance, felt the warmth of her body as she leaned toward him. Though spiders spun webs around his pillow of dead leaves, and pale sunless fungi grew about his head, they seemed less real than the fantasies that visited him in his delirium.

Once more they were boy and girl, hovering like butterflies over the flowerbeds of the Palace gardens. Then he saw himself as the pitiful youth, lovelorn to madness—to death. And in his dreams he moaned: "O Kesa-Gozen, why will you not look on me? There is no one to deliver me from this torment but you, O heartless one! Why did you marry Wataru? Pity me! Give me but one night by your side. Let me once steal this forbidden blossom, then let this offense, more grievous than all the Ten Sins, cast me down to the bottomless, fiery pits of hell, for what agony can exceed this which I now endure?"

And in his fevered dreams he saw her closed eyes and sought her lips with his own. Between the folds of her tumbled robes he glimpsed her pale limbs, the curve of her naked breasts; reaching out for her, he would find her **no longer** there, and the dream would dissolve, leaving him tortured with thirst for her. Awake once more he would break into an agony of weeping, until all nature at midnight seemed to lament with him.

It was still dark when Morito, worn by tears and a night of haunted dreams, awoke. Rising, he staggered and stumbled on blindly, not knowing where he was, when all his nerves tingled suddenly in response to curious new sensations. An icy current seemed to thunder through his brain and a wild roaring filled his ears, echoing and re-echoing in his head.

The Narutaki Rapids—on the road to Takao with its maples!

Dawn had come, and a pale moon hung in the sky. Morito looked about him, filling his eyes with the crimson of maples all over the hillside. Never had the morning light seemed so crystal clear. He was sane once more. Then the events of that night—the 14th of September—came back to him vividly as though he once more stood at the scene. The thundering of the Narutaki Rapids and the baying of waters suddenly sounded like the terrible lamentations of a despairing mother—Wataru's hoarse cries of hate, the mocking laughter of his fellow Guards, and the angry cries of people.

Facing the rapids, Morito cried out as though in reply: "Let me die! . . . I cannot face the world alive!"

Swaying, he clung to a boulder and looked down into the boiling current, and as he gazed he spied a group of stonecutters making their way from the opposite shore, leaping from rock to rock as they approached in his direction. Like a flash Morito turned and took flight, swiftly clambering to the crest of a hill.

Arrived at the top, he placed the bundle he carried on the ground, then fell heavily to his knees, struggling for breath. Sweat poured down his body, and he rubbed his hairy chest, panting.

Die he must, now that he had regained his senses, he thought.

"Forgive me, my beloved," he then cried, lifting his hands in prayer. One by one he whispered the names of those he knew, entreating their pardon, then took the wrapping from the head.

"Now look at Morito, who will atone with his own life," he

8 7

whispered. "Look once more at the world, for I, too, will soon be dust."

Numbly he stared at what he saw. The hair, matted with blood into lacquerlike strands, clung stiffly to the cheeks and forehead.

"Ah, my beloved, can this be you?"

The head resembled nothing more than a large clump of clay. As the sky filled with light, he saw how the flesh had shrunk under the tangled lattice of hair; the bones jutted out, and the skin was mottled. The ears had shriveled and looked like dried mussels; the eyes seemed carved from blue wax stained white. Nowhere could he discover the features he had once adored.

And he prayed: "Dai-nichi Nyorai, Dai-nichi Nyorai!" ("Great Illuminator!")

From the death mask before him his eyes traveled heavenward. In front of him rose the sun like a ball of fire. The roofs of the capital, the Eastern Hills, and the spired pagodas lay shrouded in mist, and all he could see was the immense, flaming wheel of light. Then he suddenly remembered. . . .

The hermitage—more exactly speaking, a modest villa, where the Abbot Kakuyu frequently stayed—stood in a pocket of the Togano-o Hills, on the road to Takao, just where the Narutaki Rapids flow to join the Kiyotaki Rapids. Although he was Abbot of the Togano-o Temple, he spent much of his time at Toba, and people of the region were accustomed to call him the Abbot of Toba—Toba Sojo. He had once been the Abbot of Enryakuji Temple on Mount Hiei, but in these times when monks carried arms and went about firing and plundering, Toba Sojo was often heard to say that he made a poor figure of a monk, since he had no stomach for fighting.

The Abbot's life, too, was unusual. Instead of having lay monks live with him at the villa, he had a young soldier and three menservants to attend him, and to the curious who inquired with some surprise whether the occupant of the villa was a priest or a layman, the Abbot gravely explained that the servants were not his but those of a person of high rank from Kyoto, who was visiting him.

Now in his seventies, the Abbot was one of the many sons of a brilliant and wayward courtier, renowned in his day as the author of a chronicle. Kakuyu, though he inherited a considerable fortune, entered holy orders when quite young, but soon found the life little to his liking. In time—to the neglect of his ecclesiastical duties—he began indulging his taste for painting. Scroll after scroll appeared from his brush, pungent with wit and full of satirical fun. Never had their like yet been seen, for his eye, turned critically upon the troubled scene about him, saw men in the likeness of animals—apes and hares, racing; badgers in priests' vestments; frogs prancing about in coronets—and his brush pictured the evils of the clergy, the extravagant absurdities of the aristocrats, their fantastic superstitions, the struggle for power in officialdom, and all the follies and evils of humankind.

The Abbot was hard at his painting one day when his servant announced a guest. Putting aside his brush and inkstone, Toba Sojo turned to receive the caller, a youthful Guard from the Cloister Palace, Sato Yoshikiyo.

"I envy you your life, your reverence. Whenever I come to visit you, I am convinced that man's life was meant to be lived close to nature."

"Why envy me?" Toba Sojo replied. "I can't see why you don't choose the life that you most desire."

"More easily said than done, your reverence."

"Is that so? He who lives in the mountains yearns for the city, and the city-dweller would rather live in the mountains," the Abbot chuckled, "and nothing is ever to one's liking. . . ."

"Oh, your reverence, there go your pictures—the wind!"

"Those scraps of paper? Never mind them. And now, have you come up here to see the maples and to compose a poem or two?"

"No, your reverence, I am on my way to Ninna-ji Temple on matters that have to do with the imperial pilgrimage."

"Yes? It's amazing how his majesty doesn't tire of all this

horseracing. I shouldn't be surprised if the human race turns into a horde of evils running neck and neck, and the Guards become a herd of wild horses, runaway colts, and vicious stallions. A frightening thought indeed!"

Toba Sojo turned abruptly to call in the direction of a room at the rear of the villa: "Boy, are the persimmons I asked for ready? Bring some fruit to our guest."

There was no reply, but a faint murmur of voices could be heard at the back of the house. Then a youth who appeared from round the corner of the house approached the veranda. Some stonecutters who lived in the vicinity, he said, had come in terror to report that since morning they had seen a strange, wild-looking man wandering barefooted in the near-by hills; a sleeve of his robe was missing. They had stealthily observed his movements, followed him, and seen him disappear into the dense growth among the hills where he buried some large object that he apparently cherished. At the approach of the stonecutters, the creature had vanished like a bird into the depth of the forest on Takao.

"And what of it?" the Abbot exclaimed. "Why trouble yourself with such a trifle? Are you thinking of pursuing the man?"

"Nno—not exactly, but the stonecutters are talking excitedly about capturing him. They think he's a brigand."

"Let him be, let him be. These are hard times and even a brigand must live. He will be fed when they get him to jail, but what of his wife and children? Isn't that so, Yoshikiyo?"

Yoshikiyo appeared to be struck by a thought and was gazing at the clouded crest of Takao with an abstracted look. He was about to reply, seemed to think better of it, and apologized instead for his long stay and quickly left the villa.

A persimmon that the birds had left uneaten hung golden red under the autumn sky, and the sound of stonecutters' chisels echoed icily among the clouds of the peak.

CHAPTER VI

THE BOY WITH A GAMECOCK

Frost had already fallen, and the screeching of shrike could be heard. Yellow and white chrysanthemums that flourished like weeds by the wayside were beginning to shrivel. A certain bleakness already hung in the air.

". . . Let me see. Is it likely for a nobleman to be living on the fringe of the city in surroundings sprawling with the huts of the common people?"

It was a sunny October day, warm as spring, when Kiyomori wandered about Seventh Avenue with a letter from his father to a government official, Fujiwara Tokinobu. His father had sent him to the Central Granary, where Tokinobu was employed. On arriving there, Kiyomori had been told by a clerk that the gentleman had left a short while ago for the Education Department to look up some old records. Advised to seek him in the library, Kiyomori, once more on foot, set out for the Education Department, a few steps from both the Imperial Academy and the Central Granary. There, however, he was told that Tokinobu had left, but the clerk ventured the information that the gentleman had gone home and gave him Tokinobu's address, on Seventh Avenue, so Kiyomori had turned his steps thither.

Kiyomori was appalled by the muddy roads and the squalor of the surroundings in which he found himself. He saw nothing that resembled a mansion. There were no imposing gates or stately buildings, that harmonious blending of T'ang and native architecture which one saw in the central part of the capital, occupied for centuries by government offices, the palaces of the nobility, and the mansions of the great families. This district on the fringe of the capital and the quarters behind the broad avenues were little more than open fields with scattered settlements, where clogmakers, armorers, papermakers, tanners, and dyers pursued their calling. The last autumn rains had flooded the streets into shallows and rivulets in which street urchins set snares for snipe, or fished for carp that fattened on the excrement thrown out on the roads.

Kiyomori stopped to look about him, wondering whether he should make some inquiries, when he saw a knot of people crowding excitedly around something.

There was a noisy cackling—a cockfight! Before he knew it, Kiyomori found himself one of the crowd. From the veranda of a near-by house, apparently that of a trainer of gamecocks, the trainer's wife, an old woman, and some children craned to see what was going on. Some passers-by were being pressed to stand as witnesses by the hard-faced trainer, whose assistant stood behind with a basket containing his prize fighting-cock. A young lad had challenged the trainer, who was haggling loudly over the amount of the wager.

"Coins—nothing less than coins! No small stake's going to make up for injuries to my bird! I'll fight you for money. Boy, did you bring some money?"

"Ah-eee—money suits me," replied the lad, who seemed to

be only fourteen or fifteen years old. He was small, but the bold look he gave the trainer matched the defiant look of the gamecock he held under his arm; he gave the trainer a dimpled smile of scorn. "How much? How much will you bet?"

"Good! How's this?" the trainer offered, counting some money into a small basket, in which the boy placed an equal number of coins.

"Ready?" Still holding his struggling bird tight under his arm, the lad squatted, measuring off the distance between himself and his opponent's bird.

"Wait, wait! Some people still want to bet. Now, don't be so impatient, boy." The trainer turned to the spectators and eyed each one, taunting in half-jocular tones: "Come now, there's not much sport in merely looking on. What about a little betting— just a little?"

A rapid chinking of coins followed. Just then the referee and his stakeholder appeared. There were enough people now to bet on the trainer's bird, but few willing to risk anything on the lad's.

"Here, I'll make up the rest for the boy!" Kiyomori cried, startled by the sound of his own voice. He drew out some money. There was just enough.

"Ready?" signaled the referee. The eyes of the crowd were instantly riveted in grim silence to a spot on the ground.

"Boy, what's the name of your bird?"

"Lion, trainer. What's yours?"

"You don't know? Black Diamond—off we go!"

"Wait! The referee gives the signal."

"Impudence, you sound like a professional!"

Both birds craned at each other with outstretched necks. The judge gave the sign, and the cocks flew at each other. Pebbles rattled and bloodstained feathers began to fly. The fight was on.

An old man gazed round at the circle of faces with evident enjoyment, ignoring the cockfight. He wore the robes of a priest and straw sandals; a young manservant attended the priest, who stood resting his chin on the head of his cane.

". . . Ah, the Abbot of Toba!" Kiyomori was dismayed,

cockfights were illegal and the Abbot also disapproved of street gambling; it would never do to be seen by him; he often came to the Palace. But Kiyomori, anxious about his money, was reluctant to leave and attempted to conceal himself behind a man next to him.

A shout went up. The fight was over. Sweeping up his winnings and hugging his bird to him, the young lad brushed past Kiyomori on winged feet and vanished.

Kiyomori was about to leave with an innocent air when he was stopped short by someone calling him: "Young man—Kiyomori of the Heiké—where are you off to?"

"Ah—your reverence!"

The Abbot's voice held no reproof. "Wasn't this most enjoyable? I also was sure that lad's bird would win, and he did."

Greatly relieved and emboldened, Kiyomori said: "Your reverence, did you bet on the fight?"

The Abbot laughed heartily. "No, I'm a poor one for such things."

"But you guessed right, didn't you?"

"No, I'm hardly a judge of gamecocks. That trainer's bird is old like me; that lad's young like you. There was no question as to which would win, but you've been cheated of your winnings by that—stakeholder, as they seem to call him."

"Your reverence is the reason for that. Had you not been here, I would have picked a quarrel with that fellow."

"No, no, that would have been a mistake. You would have lost after all; don't you see that that fellow is the trainer's accomplice? No, maybe it's just as well that you don't understand. And by the way, how is your father? I hear he has resigned and gone into seclusion."

"Yes, your reverence. He is well. He dislikes getting involved in those Palace affairs."

"I quite understand how he feels. Tell him from me to take care of his health."

"Thank you," said Kiyomori as he started to leave. "Oh,

9 4

your reverence, do you know whether Tokinobu of the Central Granary lives in this neighborhood?"

"You mean Tokinobu formerly of the Military Department? Boy," said the Abbot, turning to his servant, "do you know?" The servant replied that he did, and directed Kiyomori to follow the canal along Seventh Avenue to an old shrine to the Medicine God. The mansion was on the other side of a bamboo grove in the shrine compound, he said, adding in gratuitous detail—that Tokinobu, because of his close connections with the Heiké, not only was considered odd, but was poor into the bargain; something of a scholar, and therefore queer—certainly ill-suited for the Military Department, and even now considered rather eccentric at the Central Granary. The mansion, he concluded, would very likely prove to be something of a surprise.

"Hmm—" mused the Abbot, "something like your father, I should say. So there are aristocrats who resemble your father. Young man, tell your father that it's getting too cold for me in the hills at Togano-o, and that I shall soon be wintering at my hermitage in Toba, where I shall continue to paint. Ask him to visit me once in a while." And so saying, the Abbot turned and went on his way.

Kiyomori walked on past the bamboo grove near the shrine until he found himself outside a wattled wall running, it appeared, the entire length of a block. The decrepit gate took Kiyomori by surprise, for it compared very poorly even with the one at home. He almost feared to call out lest the tottering structure collapse, but there was no need to hallo for he spied a crack in it wide enough to crawl through. He decided, however, to make his presence known in the usual manner by calling out loudly several times. Soon he heard footsteps. The gate creaked and groaned on its hinges as though someone was opening it with great difficulty, and the face of a young boy suddenly peered through.

"Oh? . . ." The lad stared at Kiyomori round-eyed.

Kiyomori's face broke into a friendly smile of recognition. They had met a short while ago. But the boy abruptly left Kiyo-

9 5

mori where he was standing, clattered off in great agitation, and disappeared.

A spring that bubbled up in the compound of the shrine to the Medicine God flowed along an artificial bed beneath the enclosing wall of the estate and through the courtyard. Like a length of silk, it looped and wound its way through the garden, past the east wing of Tokinobu's mansion, round a grove of trees and through a bamboo thicket, until it disappeared under the wall on the other side of the grounds. The mansion appeared to have been a former imperial villa and lacked nothing in the beauty of its surroundings; the main house and the wings, however, were in a state of disrepair rare even outside the capital. But the garden had been carefully preserved in all its former elegance and seemed to reflect the gracious spirit of its present owner. Every inch of the garden was neat and swept clean.

Not even an under-servant appeared, so Kiyomori peered in and spied two young girls at the lower end of the garden washing clothes in the stream. Their long sleeves were looped back out of the way, and the hems of their outer tunics were tucked up, revealing their white ankles. He was certain that they were the daughters of the house and suddenly felt pleased at the errand that had brought him here.

If they were sisters, then the boy was undoubtedly their brother. The younger of the two still wore her hair knotted on her head in child-fashion; Kiyomori was curious how old the other might be.

They were dyeing thread for weaving. Near by was a dyeing vat and long skeins of silk were strung to dry between the balustrades of the house and a crimson maple tree. He was uncertain how he should address them, and afraid he might startle them, but then the younger of the two girls suddenly looked up and saw him. She whispered something in the other's ear; the two sprang up, dropped what they were doing, and fled toward one of the wings of the house.

Though left quite alone now with the waterfowl floating in

the stream, Kiyomori was not annoyed. He decided that this was an opportune moment for washing his hands in the stream and straightening the cap on his head.

"Well, Kiyomori, how are you? Come in, come in," said a voice that Kiyomori recognized as one he had heard many times in his own home. Kiyomori bowed low in the direction of a covered gallery from which the voice came.

When Tokinobu had shown him into a sparsely furnished but immaculately clean room, Kiyomori delivered the letter from his father.

"Ah—thank you," said Tokinobu, taking it with an air of already knowing what the letter contained. "Isn't this the first time you've been here?"

Kiyomori responded punctiliously to Tokinobu's small talk with the sensation of facing an examiner at the academy. It was not so much Tokinobu's rather pedantic air, but his preoccupation with thoughts of his elder daughter that made itself felt in his conversation. Kiyomori regarded Tokinobu's unkempt beard and his high aquiline nose with distaste, but his thoughts were elsewhere, busy with entrancing imaginings. He soon realized that he was being received with a hospitality which a mere messenger hardly deserved. Wine was served and trays of food were brought in. In spite of his unpolished manners, Kiyomori's sensibilities could throb as delicately as harp-strings in a faint movement of air. He was unperceptive neither of what his father had lately had in mind nor of the train of thought that now occupied Tokinobu. Kiyomori, who appeared rather reserved at first, not from any need to be cautious, but because it was his nature to reserve judgment, resettled himself comfortably on the kneeling-cushion, resolving to put off his constraint. He would drink liberally, give his host an opportunity to observe his young guest, while Kiyomori would see for himself whether Tokinobu's daughter was pretty or not. She appeared from time to time and then withdrew tantalizingly; she finally came in and seated herself near her father. She was mature and, though not beautiful, fair-skinned and oval-faced; Kiyomori also noted with relief that her nose was not aquiline like her father's. She was obviously her father's favorite.

"This is Tokiko, the elder of the two you saw in the garden," said Tokinobu, introducing her. "Eh?—the younger, Shigeko, is still a child, and I doubt she will come even if I call her." Though he smiled genially, weariness and age showed in the eyes glowing with the effects of wine. He began to reminisce about Tokiko's mother, whose death left him, like Tadamori, to rear his children alone. As the wine loosened his tongue, Tokinobu tearfully confessed that he had not been able to come to terms with the world, and had failed to give his daughters the usual joys of a carefree girlhood. With an involuntary side-look at Tokiko, he added: "She is nineteen, almost twenty, and yet she can hardly utter a word before guests."

Nineteen! Kiyomori was dismayed. She was old! But he reflected that it was hardly her fault that she was still unmarried, for his father, Tadamori, was in part responsible for this. He thought of his father and the unrelenting hostility of the Palace courtiers. They had plotted for several years to oust Tadamori from his favored position, until his failure to apprehend Morito provided them with the long-sought chance to hound him from the Palace in disgrace.

Kiyomori recalled what his father had recently told him about Tokinobu, and felt impelled to reconsider his opinions about Tokiko. Tokinobu had been indirectly involved in Tadamori's unfortunate relations with the Palace courtiers, and the role that he had played had affected him and his daughters adversely. Their childhood had in many ways resembled Kiyomori's, and he understood now how greatly indebted his father was to Tokinobu.

To understand the circumstances leading to Tadamori's retirement from the Palace, it will be necessary to go back to March 1131, when Kiyomori was fifteen. At that time the great temple of Sanju-Sangen-Do with its one thousand images of Buddha was completed and the entire capital participated in an elaborate dedication ceremony. On that occasion the ex-Emperor Toba not only presented Tadamori with additional manors, but gave him the rank of a courtier, an unprecedented honor to a warrior, which so affronted the court nobles that they agreed to assassinate Tadamori on the night of a Palace banquet at which he was to appear. Fear more than jealousy was at the bottom of this plot.

An anonymous letter tossed into Tadamori's house on the eve of the banquet warned him of an attempt on his life. On receiving the message, Tadamori had smiled coolly, saying that he would meet the challenge as a warrior, and on the night of the banquet he appeared at the Palace carrying his sword. There, in sight of the suspicious courtiers, he drew out his blade to test its edge against his topknot. The steel, glinting like ice in the light of the candles, filled the watchful courtiers with misgivings. A State Minister, who was passing along one of the open galleries of the Palace just then, noticed two suspicious-looking figures, fully armed, crouching in a corner of the inner court, and called out to them; an officer of the Sixth Rank soon arrived to challenge the intruders, and received the reply: "We are trusted housemen of Tadamori of the Heiké. We have been warned that harm might come to our master. We shall leave only at the risk of our lives."

The courtiers, who soon heard of this, were dismayed. On the following day, led by a Minister, they demanded that Tadamori be punished for appearing at the Palace armed and accompanied by his soldiers. The ex-Emperor, troubled, summoned Tadamori for an explanation. With suitable expressions of regret, Tadamori calmly produced the sword, unsheathed it, and showed that it was only a blade of bamboo painted silver. His house men, he said, had only acted as all loyal retainers would to their liege lord. The monarch commended Tadamori for his wisdom, but his enemies at Court grew even more uneasy with every token of the ruler's regard for Tadamori, and when they heard that it was Tokinobu who had warned Tadamori of their plot, they hounded him from the Court. Tokinobu, already well along in years, soon found all opportunities to advancement closed.

"Look out, there's another puddle!" young Tokitada shouted excitedly, waving his flaming torch at Kiyomori's feet as they groped their way past a bamboo grove.

Kiyomori was intoxicated—completely overcome with drink. Though he professed himself able to find his way home, Tokinobu had been dubious, and at Tokiko's insistence sent the boy to accompany Kiyomori as far as the footpath on Seventh Avenue.

By the time Kiyomori was ready to leave, Tokiko had been far from retiring; she had talked and laughed, and Kiyomori thought he perceived a certain warmth in the glances she gave him. But, alas, she was nineteen! This bothered him; she was more like an elder sister. He wondered whether it was because he compared her with Ruriko. None the less, he decided to tell his father that Tokiko's appearance and disposition pleased him perfectly. What had really captured his fancy was Tokiko's sixteen-year-old brother, Tokitada.

"Ho, Lion," Kiyomori teased.

Waving his torch back and forth in glee, Tokitada shot back: "What, you lackey!"

"Oh? No lackey, but a young warrior."

"A young warrior is only an overgrown lackey!"

"So, my young blade, didn't I find you on the street at a cockfight?"

"And you, gambling! Guilty, too! Now what has my father been telling you?"

Kiyomori laughed. "Here's another one just like me, you droll one!"

"Another what?"

"Another young toad."

"A young toad is a tadpole. I'll bring Lion to peck at you."

"I give up, I give up," Kiyomori protested. "Give me your hand—here's the path—pledge a lifelong friendship!"

The wintry gusts from the Northern Hills swept the dead leaves before them unmercifully, hurling them against the miserable huddle of huts Kiyomori had seen that afternoon. Blown and twisted by the wind, Kiyomori vanished into the night, while a small figure on the footpath waved to him with a torch.

It was customary for Tadamori's sons to appear every morning before their father and to salute him formally. Even Norimori, the youngest, was there to receive his father's greetings, delivered with grave courtesy. And it was usual for Tadamori to say a few cheering words to his motherless sons, who welcomed the ritual as they did the daily rising of the sun.

Kiyomori recounted the happenings of the previous day:

"The honorable Tokinobu sent no reply to your letter. I could not find him at the Central Granary, so I went to his home. In fact, I had some difficulty finding my way around that district and barely succeeded in finding him. He was most hospitable, and I didn't get away until quite late, and he sent you his greetings."

Kiyomori then went on to relate how he had met Toba Sojo.

"So the Abbot seems content with drawing. . . . He is of noble birth, and had he wished might have distinguished himself among his peers," Tadamori mused, as though secretly ashamed of his present inactivity.

"That's his nature; a most unusual person," Kiyomori replied curtly, feeling that his father's remark was somewhat beside the point, for he had fully expected his father to inquire at length about Tokinobu and his daughter Tokiko. Contrary to his expectations, Tadamori had nothing to say that even broached the subject of a match. Instead he said: "And, by the way, I hear that his majesty will soon leave on a pilgrimage to Anrakuju-in Temple."

"Yes, his majesty leaves on the morning of October 15 for the dedication of the Great Hall. I hear he will spend two or three nights at the Detached Palace at Takeda," Kiyomori replied.

"You must be busy at the Guard Office. I'm sure you haven't neglected your duties since I resigned, and I hope you are exerting yourself doubly in serving his majesty."

"I do, Father, but the warriors there are dissatisfied. They now have you as an excuse for airing their grievances. They haven't forgotten how the Court treated Yoshiiyé of the Genji, who spent several years quelling uprisings in the northeast. Though he was successful, the supreme council ruled that he had done this entirely on his own and refused to recompense him, so that Yoshiiyé was obliged to sell his house and lands; even then he was barely able to pay off his soldiers. Even you, Father, know that your last campaign in the west—brilliant as it was—was rewarded so meagerly that there was barely enough to share with our men. All that came of it was this—this same poverty of ours."

"That is the warrior's fate."

"And is it right for the aristocrats to withhold all privilege from the warrior and see that he remains forever under their heel? We know that that is their intention, but every warrior is anxious about the future."

"That does not matter, for we do not serve them, but his majesty."

"But they have the power of life or death over us and can act in the name of the throne, which they also serve. We have no direct appeal to his majesty. What, then, are we to do? That's why the warriors have become disheartened. You must after all come back to the Palace."

"The time hasn't come yet. They are better off without me just now."

"And there's talk that Tameyoshi of the Genji, who has been under a cloud for some time, is in favor again at the Palace. There are rumors, too, that Yorinaga, the Minister of the Left, has interceded for him with his majesty. All this gossip has been disquieting."

"Heita, you'll be late. You should arrive at your duties early. And remember, you have the pilgrimage before you."

"Forgive me if I have offended you," Kiyomori said, sensing that he had somehow displeased his father, in whom he perceived a firmness and purposefulness which he lacked before.

The Detached Palace at Takeda, south of the capital, was a favorite retreat of the ex-Emperor Toba, who found the view across the Kamo and Katsura rivers so pleasing that he had ordered the Anrakuju-in Temple to be built here. As the time of the dedication drew near, the sovereign expressed a desire for a three-storied pagoda for the temple group, and invited Nakamikado Iyenari, now retired from the active life of the Court, to join the pilgrimage, directing him to draw up plans for the pagoda and to supervise its construction.

An unending line of noblemen's carriages, processions of priests in their vestments, and crowds of inquisitive sightseers from all over the countryside made their way to the temple, where the destitute swarmed like flies to receive alms. Numberless Guards were posted along the route; and on the banks of the rivers, around the hamlet of Takeda, and wherever they camped, great bonfires lighted up the sky at night.

The ex-Emperor's stay lasted two days. Toward evening of the second day a chill rain fell and the scene, which had been alive with people, became strangely still. The Great Hall loomed through the darkness in all its magnificence, shimmering dreamlike in the reflected light of the many watch-fires.

The Guards were settling at last to a late evening meal in their temporary shelters. An allotment of imperial wine had been distributed among them on the previous day, but they had all been too busy to taste it. Some Guards were drying their hunting cloaks at the fires; others had already taken off their armor and were passing around wine-cups and attacking their food.

One Guard remarked: "It may be just gossip, but Wataru of the Genji didn't come for the dedication."

"Wataru? Oh, you mean Kesa-Gozen's husband. What's become of him?"

"Hmm . . . just before we started, he quite suddenly went to take leave of the Minister of the Left, who, it appears, urged him to reconsider his decision, but Wataru handed in his resignation to the Palace aide and hasn't been seen since in the capital."

"Oh, what did he mean by that?"

"Doubtless, consumed by hate for Morito, who murdered his wife, he's gone off to find him and take his revenge. He has been saying that he no longer can endure being pointed out as the husband of the murdered woman."

"There's no telling when Morito will be found. Wataru can hardly be blamed for feeling as he does. Seems to me, though, that Morito is fated to sin and to live out his span tortured with remorse."

"People have been saying that they've seen him in the hills of Takao or around Kumano. In fact, there have been any number of such stories, so he must be alive."

While the Guards talked among themselves, the gleam of lights between the trees at the farther end of the Palace showed that the ex-Emperor's entourage—the courtiers, priests, and ladies-in-waiting—were probably whiling away the hours with a poetry contest; from the sovereign's apartments, however, came no strains of music; darkness lay around it, and only the rain showed white.

"Is Yoshikiyo here? Has anyone seen Sato Yoshikiyo?" Kiyomori's face suddenly appeared out of the night, round-eyed and anxious. Several Guards called to him, urging him to stop and share their wine, but Kiyomori shook his head and continued anxiously: "No time for that now. I'm not quite certain of this, but I heard that one of Yoshikiyo's housemen was taken into custody by the Police Commissioner's men at noon. Some brawl at the Rashomon Gate. I just got word and I'm afraid Yoshikiyo hasn't heard of this. I can't find him, but if any of you know where he is, tell him."

Though his easygoing ways were frowned on by everyone at the Palace, Kiyomori's wholehearted concern for his comrades-in-arms made him popular among the Guards, and at times like this they were more than eager to assist him.

"What! At the Rashomon Gate? He's in for trouble now. The sooner we let him know, the better."

Kiyomori's anxiety was contagious and the Guards sprang to their feet. Four or five men hurried off in different directions through the rain.

CHAPTER VII

A WARRIOR TAKES HIS FAREWELL

Yoshikiyo could not be found. He was not in the Guard quarters. Someone suggested that he might be with Lord Tokudaiji's retinue, delayed by some unexpected duties, and that he might already have received the bad news about his retainer. One of the Guards asked: "Hasn't he turned up yet? I wonder what's keeping him."

"Are you sure that Yoshikiyo has heard of this? Surely, he's not such a coward that he's going to leave his retainer in the lurch?"

"We'd better try to send him word of this."

The Guards stood about, anxious and perplexed, hardly tasting their wine, and annoyed at Yoshikiyo's failure to appear. They were impatient for good reason.

"Whatever's happened, it won't be easy to get Tameyoshi's men to release him. . . . What can Yoshikiyo be doing?"

The men were tired and despite their anxiety some were already asleep; others dozed, and the rest were already befuddled by the wine.

Yoshikiyo finally appeared outside one of the huts. "Greetings, all of you! I've put you to a great deal of trouble, but I shall be off now. I should be back by dawn, at the latest—in time to join you on the return journey. Don't be too anxious on my account." Yoshikiyo wore his riding cloak and was leading his horse. His only companion was a lad, bearing a lighted torch.

The Guards stared at Yoshikiyo's composure in astonishment. A warrior—with a talent for writing verse—behaving like this in a crisis, their looks of contempt implied.

"Eh, so you expect to bring your retainer back by morning, Yoshikiyo? Do you realize whom you'll be dealing with?"

Kiyomori alone remonstrated with Yoshikiyo for his foolhardiness. Didn't he realize, he asked, that Tameyoshi, former chief of the Genji Guards, had nothing good to say of the warriors who had replaced his own men at the Palace? He was if anything their worst enemy, always on the lookout to find fault with the Heiké Guards. Yoshikiyo had better think things over. Tameyoshi's ill will was notorious and there was no predicting what pitfalls were in store for Yoshikiyo. It was dangerous to go alone and attempt to negotiate with Tameyoshi. If he was going alone, they would all go with him in the name of the Guards and be ready to meet force with force.

"Come, all of you," cried Kiyomori, "we'll go with Yoshikiyo and rescue his man!"

A few shouted: "Here's fun!" and crowded outside noisily, relishing the thought of a skirmish and eager for blood. Some twenty soldiers now surrounded Yoshikiyo with cries of "Off we go, now! Off we go!"

Yoshikiyo did not move, but threw out his arms to restrain them.

"Wait, you're acting like children over a matter of no importance. Remember, you each have your duties here and we want no disturbances during this pilgrimage. Since my messenger caused all this trouble, I'm the one to go and negotiate for him. Just make it appear as though nothing has happened."

Calming the Guards, Yoshikiyo turned away from Kiyomori abruptly as though irked by the fuss; and ordering his young groom to hold his torch high, spurred his horse into the darkness and rain.

Earlier that day, Yoshikiyo had sent his trusted retainer Gengo with some poems addressed to some ladies who served Lady Taikenmon, the Emperor's mother and ex-consort of the abdicated Emperor Toba. Lady Bifukumon, for whom Toba had put away Lady Taikenmon, accompanied Toba on the pilgrimage, and Yoshikiyo, a member of the imperial suite, could not help being reminded that Lady Taikenmon now lived in lonely retirement with few friends to visit her. He had therefore gathered some poems he had written during the lavish two-day tour, addressed them to several poetess friends in Lady Taikenmon's household, and sent them by Gengo to the capital. It was immaterial to Yoshikiyo whether Gengo had got into trouble on his way to or from the capital, for his thoughts sped like arrows to Tameyoshi's mansion. Although he seemed untroubled to Kiyomori and the other Guards, Yoshikiyo knew too well the reputation of the man he was about to meet. Gengo, his beloved retainer, was in danger, and if there was need for it he was ready to give his own life for him. He urged on his horse, praying that no harm would come to Gengo before he reached him.

It was almost midnight and the rain had cleared. The moon glowed fitfully through a veil of clouds and shone eerily on the roof of the mansion and the ghostly gateway. Tameyoshi, about to retire for the night, heard loud knocks at the gate, and the night watchman remonstrating angrily. Tameyoshi went himself to see what was amiss, found Yoshikiyo, led him to a room facing an inner court, and there by the dim light of a lamp listened to his story.

Yoshikiyo found Tameyoshi not at all the dreaded person that rumors made him out to be. Circumstances were against him, and Tameyoshi, the grandson of a famous chieftain, was no more than the head of a warrior household. Still in his early forties, Tameyoshi of the Genji was pleasing of manner and amenable to reason.

"Certainly, I quite understand. I shall look into this matter immediately. There is too much talk nowadays of skirmishes between my men and the Guards. if your messenger is being held without cause, there shall be no delay in releasing him. Ho, there, Yoshitomo!" Tameyoshi called across the court to a room on the other side. Yoshitomo, his eldest son, soon appeared and knelt on the veranda at a respectful distance, courteously inquiring what was wanted. Yoshikiyo looked at the youth approvingly—a good son.

After a few words with his father, Yoshitomo departed to summon the housemen and servants and to question them; in a short time he reappeared and knelt outside in the garden.

"I have brought the honorable Yoshikiyo's messenger and one of our soldiers, who challenged him."

Gengo's face was swollen as though he had been badly beaten. He burst into tears at the unexpected sight of his master.

"Whose prisoner are you?" Tameyoshi demanded.

"Your son's, the honorable Yoshikata's."

"The reason for your arrest?"

Yoshitomo answered for the prisoner, explaining what had happened toward noon that day. Gengo, he said, was stopped at the Rashomon Gate and questioned by Yoshikata's soldiers for carrying what appeared to be an official document. Gengo had refused to hand over the scroll, insisting that it was sent by certain ladies to his master, and had added that the soldiers could not in any case read them.

"And then?"

Yoshitomo resumed: "I was told that Yuigoro snatched the scroll from Gengo and trampled on it, and Gengo then attacked him in a rage, crying that his master had been insulted. The other soldiers at the Rashomon Gate then rushed at Gengo, thrashed him soundly, and threw him into jail."

"So. Call Yoshikata," Tameyoshi ordered.

A youth, barely twenty, soon appeared. Tameyoshi rebuked him for the misconduct of the soldiers in his charge and, as he finished speaking, suddenly rose and kicked his son, who toppled from the veranda to the garden. Turning to Yoshikiyo, Tameyoshi then said: "I now leave you to deal as you will with this soldier and my son. I blame myself for what has happened and will go myself to Lady Taikenmon's palace to offer apologies. I deeply regret what has happened to your retainer. It was most unfortunate, and I beg you not to hold this against me, but will try to forget this matter."

Surprised and relieved by this unforeseen settlement of the affair, Yoshikiyo begged Tameyoshi to be lenient with Yoshikata and his soldier and then departed with Gengo from the mansion where he had expected to meet with the worst.

There was no denying that Tameyoshi came of distinguished forebears, Yoshikiyo reflected admiringly, for breeding like his was not to be found among common warriors. He was dogged, however, by foreboding. Tameyoshi was biding his time; it was apparent that the man had not forgotten how his grandfather had endured a lifetime of humiliation at the hands of the aristocrats, and that Tameyoshi waited grimly for some chance to take his revenge.

Around him the capital lay muffled in sleep. The moon drifted serenely through a curtain of clouds. And though no dirges came to his ears, Yoshikiyo was certain that such tranquillity would not be for long.

Kiyomori and Tokiko were married in December of that year. "Well, will you marry her?" Tadamori had asked Kiyomori, who flushed deeply at this query and merely replied: "Oh—"

There was no need for further words between these two who understood each other so well.

For three nights in succession, as was the custom, Kiyomori made his way in secret to the mansion near the shrine to the Medicine God to woo his future wife. Through the cold that nipped at his ears and over the sodden roads he went full of joy. The mansion was darkened in sleep, save for one small light streaming out into the night from under the lifted shutter of Tokiko's room. It was the symbol of love beckoning to him from the far end of the universe, filling Kiyomori with visions more stirring than his most impassioned dreams. And to those two, parting at dawn, something more profound than passion seemed to transform the crowing of cocks and the frosted boughs and dissolve the world in poetry.

In the ordinary course, Tokiko would have come to the house at Imadegawa as Kiyomori's bride, but Tokinobu's more spacious mansion became the young couple's home. Friends of both families agreed that the alliance between a penurious warrior's house and an impoverished nobleman's was eminently fitting.

As his share for the wedding feast Tokitada killed and dressed his prize gamecock, the one he had long concealed from his father, and offered it to Kiyomori.

"What! You killed your treasured gamecock for tonight?"

Tokitada merely grinned.

Kiyomori was speechless with amazement. He feared only his father, but the spirited temper of this mere boy chilled him. What unplumbed depths was he yet to discover in the lad's sister, his newly won wife?

In the following spring, 1138, Tokiko knew she was with child and told her husband. Kiyomori heard her in silence, flushed with dismay. Compunctions at the memory of the one night spent in the arms of a woman on Sixth Avenue assailed him and mingled with the realization that at twenty-one he had become a father.

". . . Are you not glad?" Tokiko hesitated

Fearing he had hurt her, Kiyomori quickly replied: "Happy —yes, but we're warriors, and it must be a son." Had he been a nobleman, he might have prayed that the child would be a girl who would grow in matchless beauty to win favor as an imperial concubine, but such thoughts did not occur to him. Not even the vague stirrings of parental love moved him.

Winter rolled round once more. On a morning in November after a heavy fall of snow, when the lying-in room lay deep in drifts, the cry of a newborn infant was heard. Tokiko's attendants hurried to the young father and congratulated him on the son born to him. Exulting, Kiyomori could only pace the hall between the lying-in room and his own.

"Old One—get out my horse, my horse!"

Mokunosuké, who with a number of other housemen from Imadegawa had accompanied Kiyomori to his new home, appeared. "My young master, how happy you must be!"

"Relieved—merely relieved!"

"Are you going to the shrine now to offer thanks?"

"No, I must see my father at Imadegawa before anything else. Old One, the snow is deep . . . you must stay here."

Kiyomori rode out through the gateway. As he approached the bamboo grove, he heard loud shouts from behind. It was his wife's brother, Tokitada, calling: "I'll go part of the way with you; the bamboos block the road," as he overtook Kiyomori's horse. Weighted with snow, the bamboos leaned over heavily to the ground and blotted out the road. Tokitada whipped out his dagger, slashed at the snow-laden branches one by one, leaping ahead like a hare, and looking back now and again with a look of triumph.

"Thank you, that will do," Kiyomori cried, watching the nimble, quick-witted lad with awe. His thoughts suddenly returned to the child born that morning and a warmth, the awakening of a father's love, flooded over him. That son—there was no doubt of it—was his very own by Tokiko!

As far as he could see, the roofs of Kyoto and the Eastern and Western Hills girdling the capital lay deep in snow. The solitary figure, galloping over the roads, startled occasional passers-by to curiosity and alarm. Kiyomori reached the gates of Imadegawa and soon was face to face with his father, to whom he announced breathlessly: "Born at last—a son!"

"So he's come . . ." Tadamori replied, his eyes filling as he spoke.

Kiyomori could scarcely hold back his own tears as he gazed at the man whom he honored more than a father. Some strange fate had brought them together. They faced an uncertain future, for the portents of trouble were now unmistakable. In the past three years alone numerous mansions had been burned to the ground. The powerful monasteries fought among themselves with increasing violence, destroying temples and pagodas, and marched on the capital with their mercenaries to underline their demands of the authorities. And, in the meantime, the birth of Emperor Sutoku's son, the Heir Apparent, fanned the hostility between the Court and the Cloister Government, for the abdicated Toba had proclaimed his infant son by Lady Bifukumon the Crown Prince and successor to the throne.

Mounting disturbances throughout the country and general unrest caused the cloistered Toba to send for Tadamori, imploring him to take a post at the Palace once more. And Tadamori, at the time his grandson was born, finally consented, accepting the Fifth Rank and a position in the Justice Department. Kiyomori was also promoted at the ex-Emperor's wish, and the star of the Heiké seemed to be rising.

Though the jealous courtiers did not oppose Tadamori's reinstatement, they soon intrigued to bring charges of treason against him. There had been gossip that Tadamori was secretly paying court to the daughter of a Fujiwara nobleman, Ariko, a lady-in-waiting at the Palace, who later became wet-nurse to the Heir Apparent. Tadamori's enemies were certain that his affair with one who served Toba's rival would bring a sentence of death against him. But the ex-Emperor had known for some time of the affair, and, unknown to the courtiers, encouraged and sanctioned the marriage by which Tadamori already had two sons.

Toba Sojo, who had spent a lifetime laughing at the world through his drawings, died in the autumn of 1140, full of years. As he lay dying, he said: "Though I am a monk, let there be no monkish rites for me when I am dead. I have lived too long mocking at abbots, bishops, and priests with tails peeping from under their vestments. To bury me with solemn chants and prayers would indeed be the supreme jest."

Under the thatched roof of the hermitage the Abbot now lay deaf to the sound of the falling leaves and the subdued murmurs of mourners, exchanging tales of his past and his oddities. His chief mourner, a high-ranking courtier, saw that the simplest rites were performed at the funeral, to which both the Emperor and the ex-Emperor sent their deputies; courtiers, arriving in their carriages, threaded their way on foot with the humble folk from the hamlet of Toba to the hermitage in the hills.

"The honorable Yoshitomo—this is most unexpected!"

Sato Yoshikiyo left his companion to address Tameyoshi's eldest son, Yoshitomo of the Genji, who quickly stepped to the side of the road and greeted Yoshikiyo with great courtesy: "I was not quite sure whether it was you or not, since I met you only once that night . . ." he began.

"I fear it was an intrusion to have come so late that night on the matter of my retainer. I have not seen your father since then, but I renew my apologies to him," Yoshikiyo replied.

"No, the fault lay with us, I am ashamed to confess. Have you come to pay your last respects to the Abbot?"

"Ours was a slight acquaintance, but if it were possible to see him again, I would gladly go in pursuit of him," said Yoshikiyo. Recalling his companion, he quickly introduced him. "This is Kiyomori of the Heiké. Have you never met before?"

"Ah? Possibly we have."

Yoshikiyo watched the unconcealed pleasure with which the two young warriors greeted each other, and it suddenly occurred to him that this chance encounter was somehow significant. A Heiké soldier and an officer of the Police Commission—a Heiké and a Genji!

"I shall soon be on my way east to settle in Kamakura—to my fiefs, where so many of my clansmen are. You must not fail to visit me if ever you are in those parts," Yoshitomo said on parting.

Yoshikiyo, ever reticent, seemed more silent than usual today. Such taciturn natures did not attract Kiyomori. They walked on in silence until they reached a crossroad, where Kiyomori took his leave. Yoshikiyo then asked: "Are you on your way home?"

"Yes, the roads in that district are deserted at night and my wife and son anxiously await my return. My greatest joy these days is to see my son."

"How old is he?"

"Just two."

"How winsome he must be! There's no way to explain the tenderness one feels for a child. . . . You must hurry to him now."

And they parted in the dusk.

A month later, on the 15th of October, Yoshikiyo vanished.

Kiyomori, incredulous, made inquiries among his friends and acquaintances about what had happened and was told that on the day before his disappearance, Yoshikiyo had left the Guard Office with a cousin slightly older than he. The two had gone home, discussing the emptiness of human existence, and had parted with promises to meet the following morning. That night the cousin suddenly fell ill and died, and Yoshikiyo, who went to meet his cousin the following morning, stood outside his cousin's house and heard the sorrowing cries of the young wife, the aging mother, and the young children. There and then he discovered he could not grieve with them, for it came to him that death, the inescapable fate of all men, was after all a daily occurrence, a platitude repeated once more before his own eyes. Yoshikiyo thereupon left his cousin's house for the Palace, where he handed in his resignation and without a word to his fellow Guards went home. His abrupt departure puzzled Palace circles; there seemed to be no explanation for his strange behavior, for Yoshikiyo stood high in the ex-Emperor's regard as a gifted poet, and there had ever been talk that Yoshikiyo would soon be promoted to the Police Commission.

Later, when he arrived home, Yoshikiyo appeared distraught, and the servants listened anxiously to his young wife's weeping in an inner room where Yoshikiyo was closeted with her for some time. When he reappeared, it was with an air of forced calm, but when his much-petted four-year-old daughter ran and clung to him, Yoshikiyo savagely thrust her from him, telling himself as he did so that he must forget all human ties if he were to take leave of the world and enter holy orders. He then drew out his dagger, sheared off his topknot, and flung it at the ancestral tablets in the family oratory before fleeing from the imploring cries of his household.

Ten days later it became known that Yoshikiyo had taken the vows of priesthood and assumed the Buddhist name of Saigyo. There were some who had even seen him near the temples of the Eastern Hills.

Kiyomori listened perplexed to his father-in-law's remark: "It is difficult to believe that one so young, so gifted, could have made this decision on mere impulse. It is possible that Yoshikiyo has chosen to follow a more positive and higher way of life." Kiyomori thought of obtaining a more satisfactory explanation from his father, but soon forgot even this, for more disturbing than the disappearance of his friends were those events which marched on him one by one; he now felt the quickening of a powerful vision within him.

CHAPTER VIII

COMET OVER THE CAPITAL

In December 1141, though it surprised no one, the twenty-two-year-old Emperor Sutoku was suddenly dethroned, and the three-year-old-son of the ex-Emperor Toba and Lady Bifuku-mon was declared ruler and duly installed.

In mid-January, less than a month later, a young monk walked alone through the leafless woods of the Eastern Hills, gathering twigs broken off by the heavy fall of snow. Few would have recognized him as Yoshikiyo of the Guards, though his monk's robes sat ill on him.

"Ah, is it you?"

Saigyo stopped at the sound of someone hailing him. "You— Gengo?"

"You were not at your hermitage, nor could they tell me at the temple where you were. I thought you might have gone down to the capital and was on my way there to look for you. What are you doing?"

Saigyo smiled brightly. "I came out to gather fagots, but this silent valley and my thoughts kept me so occupied that I find the sun going down."

"Fagots?—Alas, gathering fagots!" With this Gengo quickly seized the bundle of sticks from his former master, inquiring as he did so whether Saigyo was on his way back to his hermitage.

"Has something urgent brought you?" Saigyo asked.

Gengo quickly replied: "All is well with your family. I have disposed of the house, the waiting-women and the horses. The titles to your manors have been relinquished."

"I am indeed grateful. I cannot tell you how thankful I am that this has been done."

"Your relatives, too, seem to have given up hope that you will ever change your mind, and the mistress will very soon go with your daughter to live with her parents."

"So—they have finally given me up? That makes me deeply happy."

Yoshikiyo's brows cleared as he spoke. His last anxious thoughts had been for his wife and child.

They had now reached Saigyo's frail shelter, a comfortless hut behind the main temple. Saigyo gathered together some poems that lay scattered on a small table, put away his inkstone, and set about whittling kindling with a dagger, while Gengo washed at a near-by stream the provisions he had brought and set a pot of gruel to cook on the hearth.

In spite of Saigyo's repeated prohibitions, Gengo, his former retainer, visited him from time to time, insisting that he would come even on pain of death.

Their supper ready, Saigyo and Gengo, like fellow monks and equals, sat down beside the hearth. Even when they were through eating, they talked on.

Soon after his master's departure, Gengo had formally announced his intention of becoming a monk, and though he had not yet taken the tonsure, he had chosen the Buddhist name Saiju and looked forward to joining Saigyo in his retreat. Yoshikiyo, however, would not consent to Gengo's taking the vows and, to test him further, advised him to wait another year or two.

"I had almost forgotten this," Gengo said, placing a letter before Saigyo.

The letter, delivered by a messenger from Lady Taikenmon, was written in a lady's flowing hand and difficult to read because of the many messages and poems that crowded the page. Saigyo held it up to the fire, wrinkling his brows in an effort to decipher it. When he had read the letter through, he said nothing, but stared at the flickering flames on the hearth.

Several of his poetess friends who waited on Lady Taikenmon had written to him with news of themselves and their mistress. Lady Taikenmon, one wrote, was lonely and had on several occasions expressed her ardent desire to enter a nunnery. This was understandable, Saigyo reflected. The step now appeared inevitable. Her son, Sutoku, had been dethroned and her future too had become uncertain. Saigyo reflected that she, who had been acclaimed one of the famous beauties of her day, was now in her early forties. Deeply as he pitied her, he wondered what would become of his friends who served her. If they did not follow their mistress to a nunnery, where would they find safety from the upheavals he foresaw?

Gengo broke the silence. "Have you heard about Morito?"

Saigyo, who was dreamily contemplating the beauty of the white ashes and glowing embers, looked up suddenly. "Morito?" he asked, as though trying to recapture some faraway memory.

"His name was removed in December from the official list of

criminals. A traveler lately from Kumano in Kishu told me that Morito is now a monk, the same Morito who killed Kesa-Gozen five years ago and disappeared. He has taken the name Mongaku, and this past autumn vowed to do penance for one hundred days by bathing in the sacred waters of the Nachi Falls."

"Ah, Morito! . . . There's nothing like the falls at Nachi for chastising the flesh, and no way to salvation except by good works."

"This traveler told me he went to the Nachi Falls to see what this mad monk was like and found Mongaku, all in white, a coarse straw rope about his waist, praying hoarsely as he bathed in the lashing waters—a sight to freeze anyone's blood! Mongaku it seems lost consciousness several times and would have drowned were it not for the caretaker at the falls. I was told that his hair and beard almost conceal his face and sunken eyes, and that he seems hardly human."

"So that's what happened to him." Plucking a burning brand from the fire, Saigyo began tracing some words in the ashes of the hearth.

A note of sympathy crept into Gengo's voice as he repeated the story of Morito's self-flagellations. Gengo had been one of those who most bitterly condemned Morito, and listening dispassionately to Gengo's account, Saigyo thought he detected in Gengo a certain reluctance to commit himself to a lifetime with a recluse who warmed himself at the quietly rustling fire. How was Gengo to know, Saigyo reflected, that this unheroic existence imposed even greater torment than the icy lashings of the Nachi Falls in its thousand-foot leap? How was Gengo to realize that Saigyo had not slept a single night undisturbed since he had fled his home for the Eastern Hills, that his sleep was haunted by the cries of his beloved daughter from whom he had torn himself.

Who knew that during the day, when he went about his tasks of drawing water and chopping wood as he composed verses, the sighing of the wind in the treetops of the valleys below and the pines surrounding the temple sounded to him like the mourning of his young wife, and so troubled his nights that sleep no longer visited him? Never again would Saigyo find peace. He had wrenched asunder the living boughs of the tree that was his life. Remorse and compassion for his loved ones would dog him to the end of his days. In the waters of the Nachi Falls, Morito was ridding himself of those worldly passions and torments which were man's natural lot, and seeking regeneration in the sacred waters. They both sought freedom from those ambitions and desires which eternally torture men.

In the ashes on the hearth Saigyo traced and retraced the word, "pity." He had yet to learn to accept life with all its good and evils, to love life in all its manifestations by becoming one with nature. And for this he had abandoned home, wife, and child in that city of conflict. He had fled to save his own life, not for any grandiose dream of redeeming mankind; neither had he taken the vows with thoughts of chanting sutras to Buddha; nor did he aspire to the brocaded ranks of the high prelates. Only by surrendering to nature could he best cherish his own life, learn how man should live, and therein find peace. And if any priest accused him of taking the vows out of self-love, not to purify the world and bring salvation to men, Saigyo was ready to admit that these charges were true and that he deserved to be reviled and spat upon as a false priest. Yet, if driven to answer for himself, he was prepared to declare that he who had not learned to love his own life could not love mankind, and that what he sought now was to love that life which was his. Gifts he had none to preach salvation or the precepts of Buddha; all that he asked was to be left to exist as humbly as the butterflies and birds.

The following morning—the 19th of January—Saigyo left his hermitage for the Fourth Avenue in the capital. Snow was falling and he was tempted to turn back, but the thought of the letter Gengo had brought made him go on. He had not seen his friends for some time, and who knew what changes were in store for them? He crossed a bridge on which the snow lay deep and turned his steps in the direction of Lady Taikenmon's palace. At one of the crossroads of the capital he found that a crowd had gathered in spite of the storm. There were cries of: "They're sending off the exiles!"

"A couple of prisoners!"

"Husband and wife, who are they? What was their crime?"

Saigyo attempted to turn off on another road, but it too was choked with people and horses. Officers of the Police Commission stood ready to suppress signs of violence from some soldiers who seemed to be retainers of a person of rank.

"Look, barebacked! Too cruel—and they such gentle folk!" sobbed some women, craning above the crowd, and quickly concealing their faces in their sleeves.

Some lower officials with bamboo staves now appeared and roughly warned away the crowd, crying: "Back, back! Clear the road!" With peremptory orders they began pushing back the people. From the gateway of a mansion emerged two unsaddled horses on whose backs a man and a woman were roped to each. An official led the procession, bearing a sign inscribed: "Moriyuki of the Genji and his wife, Shimako, ordered banished to the land of Tosa for acting under orders from Lady Taikenmon and invoking the death-curse against His Majesty's Consort, Lady Bifukumon."

Saigyo knew the white-haired Moriyuki and his wife, old and trusted retainers to Lady Taikenmon. Shocked by what was happening to them, Saigyo could not restrain a cry of grief. The sound caused the crowd to surge toward the pair with cries of: "Farewell, Honorable Moriyuki, a sad farewell! May good health always be yours!" The people kept pace with the advancing horses as though reluctant to see the pair go. Then the watchful officials began laying about them with their bamboo staves, shouting angrily: "Here, you common folk, how dare you come near!"

Saigyo was not easily intimidated; agile enough to dodge the flailing staves, he let himself be carried along with the crowd, but in the excitement of the moment he slipped in the snow. The hoofs of an official's horse struck him as he fell, and Saigyo lost consciousness. When he came to himself, he still lay in the mud-streaked snow. Crowd and horses had vanished. Around him was a midnight silence and the swirling snow, blotting out all trace of what had happened awhile ago as though in a dream.

Saigyo did not make his intended visit to Lady Taikenmon that day.

There were rumors that the charges of witchcraft were true, others that they were false, that the affair was a plot. The truth was never known. Outwardly, Kyoto was the same Capital of Peace and Tranquillity, though currents of unrest ran turbulently beneath it.

Not long after, the ex-Emperor Toba took the tonsure and his first consort, Lady Taikenmon, became a nun at the Ninna-ji Temple. Saigyo heard of this from her gentlewomen, who wrote that the lady at the age of forty-two had had her head shaved and taken leave of the world.

From his hermitage Saigyo watched spring approaching to the sound of bird-calls.

The great bridge of Gojo was completed; it spanned the Kamo River, linking the capital on its eastern side with the flanks of the Eastern Hills. A few years before, a certain monk, Kakuyo, appealed to the populace for support, soliciting their hard-earned pennies for its construction; he himself took part in the building of the bridge, carried stones, helped dig its foundations, and lived in a small hut on the banks of the river until the bridge was finished.

Of him the common folk said: "Though there are monks and priests who go about firing one another's temples and monasteries, here, at least, is one holy man."

With the building of the bridge, the capital spread toward the southern part of Kyoto, as far as the hill on which Kiyomizu Temple stood. What had once been a waste of tall grass and woods was soon cleared as the site for an imposing mansion. As the building progressed, people were curious as to who the owner might be, but no one seemed to know.

Early in the summer of 1145, even before the plaster had dried on its walls, members of the family and numerous housemen arrived, and it soon came to light that the master was Kiyomori of the Heiké, himself, the newly appointed chief of the government's Central Office.

Turning to his wife, Tokiko, Kiyomori asked proudly: "Now tell me what you think of the house, though it can hardly compare with your father's."

Tokiko, now the mother of three, rejoiced with her husband over their new home. With their seven-year-old son, Shigemori, they inspected the house, passing from room to room, fragrant with fresh wood, and along the galleries.

"Your father," Kiyomori resumed, "who is even odder than mine, says he prefers his ancient house to this one and refuses to come here to live with us. Ah, well, if he likes it where he is, he might as well stay there. I had to wait eight years for this."

It was barely eight years since their marriage, and neither Kiyomori nor Tokiko had dreamed that they would so soon have a home of their own. Looking back over those years, Kiyomori often wondered how he had accomplished this. How brief and unreal those years of privation now seemed. Their housemen, waiting-women, and under-servants had increased tenfold, and there were more than a dozen horses in the stable.

Tadamori, his father, had also prospered, and occupied a high post in the Justice Department; he also had fiefs in the provinces of Tajima, Bizen, and Harima.

Tameyoshi of the Genji also had retrieved his fortunes. Kyoto swarmed with fresh contingents of soldiers from the east, all vassals from Tameyoshi's domains in Bando. His sons, now high-ranking officials, each maintained his own men-at-arms, and the military prestige of the Genji proclaimed them as one of the great families of the capital.

The nobility, however viewed the increasing wealth of the warriors and their growing power with alarm. There was no denying that the dangers which beset the existing order made this change inevitable, and that the ruling class must look to the warriors for protection, for the authority of the throne was now threatened from without and within. The last restraining influence on the Cloistered Emperor (Toba) and his son, the abdicated Sutoku, was gone, now that Lady Taikenmon had retired to a nunnery, and the enmity of the two former rulers had come into the open. Court circles foresaw a struggle for power. Factions already divided the Court, and plots and intrigues succeeded one another in rapid confusion. And, to add to the prevailing unrest, the militant clergy of Mount Hiei and Nara, in defiance of decrees from the throne, threatened to make war upon each other. To Tadamori and Kiyomori of the Heiké, and to Tameyoshi of the Genji was given the task of suppressing the fighting monks and guarding the throne.

On the hot summer nights of July 1146, troubled faces all over the capital were turned up at the sky, where a fiery body trailed its luminous tail.

"A comet! Every night, too. . . ."

"There to the northwest—see that huge comet!"

"Something's about to happen—nothing good, at that."

People in the capital were now sure that the apparition in the heavens was a portent of disaster, for there were ominous reports at this time that the monks of Nara had got together a vast army and were preparing to declare war on a rival monastery. Messengers on horseback began arriving morning and evening from Nara, and Tameyoshi was ordered to Uji with his troops.

Consternation shook the Court. Geomancers and astrologers were summoned to say whether the sign in the heavens was for good or evil. Priests recited prayers and incantations to ward off misfortune.

Not long after, on the 25th of August, news reached the Court from Ninna-ji Temple that Lady Taikenmon had passed from this world at the age of forty-five.

In the following year the monks of Nara challenged the monasteries of Mount Hiei in battle, and Kiyomizu Temple was destroyed by fire. In this same year, 1147, when he was thirty, Kiyomori of the Heiké was promoted to the Fourth Rank and given the title of Lord Aki. As the governor of a province he received all the honors and stipends attached to the post. For Kiyomori the long-awaited day in which he was to test out his secret dreams had arrived.

CHAPTER IX

MONK SOLDIERS OF THE
HOLY MOUNTAIN

The Holy Mountain they called it—Mount Hiei rising above its foothills beyond the upper currents of the Kamo River, visible throughout the year from every crossroad of the capital, not too distant, nor yet too close. From daybreak to sunset the city's inhabitants could lift their weary eyes to exclaim: "Ah! there can be no such suffering and such hate as consumes us here. . . ." Here where men snarled and bit, deceived and fawned on one another, and gave blow for blow, men refused to believe that the mountain was just another dwelling-place for men, for if that hill of salvation were like this city of evil, where then were men to place their faith, or where find peace?

They insisted: "Ah no, there alone burns the light of Truth daily." In this city, consumed by the lust for blood, the common people only asked that they might look up to that light and cling to the belief that the Buddha saw all things—judged the just man just, and the good man good.

A thread of a new moon hung in the sky. On the steep path to Shimei Peak a figure like a pain-twisted ape tottered and wove its way upward. It was an aged sage, clinging to his pilgrim's staff. The shape finally emerged on a rocky crest. Below him yawned a black chasm and about him spread the wide evening sky, under which he, trembling, came to his knees.

"*Na—namu*. . . ."

Tears coursed down his cheeks as he clasped his hands in prayer, and he lifted up his voice and wept, addressing the universe.

"*Namu amida butsu* (Mercy, Amida Buddha) . . . *namu Amida* . . . *namu* . . . *Amida—bu—*" he moaned. "Mercy . . . have mercy on me!" Prostrating himself, he cried aloud: "Blind to my folly, I tried to bring salvation to men and cannot even save myself. Which way am I to turn? Knowledge has only brought me darkness. Learning has set me far from the path of truth. I have lived in vain. This Holy Mountain is the very seat of evil. I fear to live any longer. I dare not live any more on this mountain. Merciful Buddha, if your promises are true, grant me a sign that there is a paradise, and that man can attain to it—then let me die."

Long he wept and in broken syllables reproached himself and grieved.

In his youth he had tasted deeply of the world's bitterness and sorrows, and, praying that he might become a holy man to relieve suffering mankind, he had dedicated himself to the life on Mount Hiei. For more than forty years, almost the full span of a man's life, he had worn the garments of an ascetic, practiced all manner of austerities, and mortified his flesh. For seven years, barefooted, he had made the rounds of the temples of the peak and valleys by day, until his feet bled, and meditated through the nights, then immured himself for years in the darkness of a treasure-house to pore over the Buddhist sutras until his sight grew dim. Then he traveled throughout the land, engaging with scholars of other sects in religious debates until he was acclaimed as the wisest sage of his day. In his declining years he was made the Abbot of a monastery, the recognized authority on the Four Doctrines of the Tendai sect of Mount Hiei. Yet no disciples came to sit at his feet in his monastery in the hills, for the temples of Mount Hiei had yearly grown more magnificent; their sanctuary lights shone even more brilliantly in their innermost shrines; their granaries overflowed with the abundance from manors in many provinces to sustain more than ten thousand monks, scholars, disciples, novices, and numberless slaves, and the prosperity of the Tendai sect only brought him utter despair.

"Though the first father of these monasteries, Saicho, labored here to the day of his death, my learning can do no good, I have no more strength to live. . . . Woe is me! Though Buddha comes to meet me after death, of what use will it be? You ravens among these hills, come feed on my flesh for your day's meat!" And with this the aged monk staggered to his feet and in the next instant cast himself down into the gorge.

In the early dawn, long before the hour for morning services, a cry that seemed to echo among the clouds above Mount Hiei startled the monks from their sleep.

"The bell in the Great Lecture Hall calls! Come to the Lecture Hall!"

The deep booming of the bell still trembled in the air as the monks hurriedly threw their priests' robes over their armor, fastened on long swords, and seized their halberds. Up they crowded from the monasteries in the hills, like clouds boiling through the gorges, the aged monks clinging to their pilgrim staffs. A few stars still straggled in the late June night. Masking their faces in silken scarves or the sleeves of their robes, old and young priests, shod with straw sandals, hurried up the slopes. Cupping their hands, they hallooed over the darkened roofs of the monasteries and dormitories: "Come to the Great Hall! The bell sounds for a general assembly." Like warriors mustering for battle, they excitedly asked one another why they were being summoned.

A monk suddenly came to a halt in a clump of grass on the defile below Shimei Peak. "Ya, ya! A corpse—an old man, too! To which monastery does this priest belong, I wonder." A bloody figure lay among the boulders, its face battered beyond recognition; several monks stood round staring down at it, when one of them quickly stepped forward to examine a rosary twined around the dead man's wrist and exclaimed: "Ah! the Abbot Jitsugyo, who has been ailing for so long at his monastery. No mistake—it's he."

"What! That venerable sage?"

"No doubt about it. Take a good look."

"How could he have got killed? He must have missed his footing on Shimei Peak."

"I doubt it. He has suffered from palsy for so long, and probably in despair hurried his own death."

"That could not be the only reason. Those who have seen him lately say that to every man he met he had been cursing the rottenness and the depravity of our Tendai priesthood."

"He was always dissatisfied—a man who never smiled. Years of poor health must have caused this. Poor soul—poor soul!"

"Well, what can we do now, for the assembly bell still calls us?"

"Death would have come sooner or later to the sick man. Now that he's dead, this is no time for us to worry about a corpse —the general meeting may be for orders to march down the mountain. We can take care of his funeral later. We must get on to the assembly. Come, on to the Lecture Hall!"

Turning away from the dead man, the monks hurried on.

Group after group of armed priests went by with hasty side-glances at the body.

The sun was rising. Near the dead sage's face a dew-laden gentian stirred in the breeze. His mouth gaped, revealing a single tooth, and for the first time he seemed to smile at the mountain.

A single beam, one hundred and ten feet long, supported the front porch of the Great Lecture Hall. At the foot of the wide staircase leading up to the hall, a hulking monk crouched on a stone and faced the assemblage. Over his coarse-woven armor he wore his vestments. The long sleeves of his flowing robe half-concealed his face, and he held a spear. Some eight or nine monks, young and old, stood on the porch above and gazed down over the massed heads.

One of the priests was concluding a long and fiery address: ". . . This may seem a trivial affair, but actually it is a serious matter, for it reflects upon the prestige of our Church. Not only does the affair leave us open to the contempt of our rival sects, but it is a threat to the very existence of our order on Mount Hiei, the guardian of the state. Brethren, whatever you think, the gist of our argument leaves us only two choices. Are we or are we not to make an armed protest? I ask for the unreserved opinions of all who are gathered here."

The general assembly had been called to acquaint the monks with an incident that had occurred a few weeks before in early June at the annual religious festival at Gion. At the height of the sacred celebrations the monks had been drawn into a fracas with two soldiers. The monks, it was true, were somewhat the worse for drink as were the two warriors, so both parties were equally open to blame. None the less, the affair could not be ignored, he said, for the warriors not only had given the monks and the Gion priests a beating, but had wounded some other monks who had come to intervene, and then escaped. The populace had witnessed the brawl, and blood had been spilled on consecrated ground. The priesthood had been openly insulted. Was the Church to overlook such an affair and let these warriors go unpunished? The matter had been referred to the Justice Department and the Police Commission, and the offenders tracked down and identified. It was found that both warriors served at the Cloister Palace; one was a retainer of Kiyomori, Lord Aki, and the other was his brother-in-law, Tokitada. The priests of Gion had demanded repeatedly that the culprits be handed over to them, but Lord Aki had merely laughed and ignored the injunctions. Warrants for their arrest had been filed with the Justice Department, but its chief, Tadamori (Kiyomori's father), had ignored them. The ecclesiastical authorities had finally sent a delegation in the name of Mount Hiei to the ex-Emperor and the Regent, demanding Tadamori's and Kiyomori's impeachment; they had, however, received nothing but evasive answers—an insult to the Church!

This was the outrageous state of affairs, and the priesthood had lost all patience. Both the Court and the Palace, moreover, were growing indifferent to the authority of Mount Hiei. Did not these monasteries to the north of the capital guard the "demon entrance" to ward off malignant influences? Was it not by imperial decree that the Tendai monastery had been established on Mount Hiei? Was it not the Emperor himself who more than three hundred years ago ordered the building of the Komponchudo on the mountain, so that the holy flame of peace might burn for unending ages in the main sanctuary?

"Shall Tadamori and Kiyomori be allowed to trample underfoot the dignity of the Tendai Church? Shall even the ex-Emperor and the Regent shamelessly disregard the authority of our priesthood? They scorn our past and have nothing but contempt for us!"

The priest flung up his clenched fist as he ended his impassioned speech. A shudder passed over the muffled assemblage in front of the Great Hall; then a violent roar escaped from their lips:

"To the capital! Down to the capital!"

"An armed protest! An armed protest! Justice shall be done!"

Once more that day the great bell sounded for the march down the mountain. Borne on the shoulders of priests, the Sacred

Shrine came to rest before the Komponchudo, where the deities were invoked and a solemn declaration to march on the capital read to the thousands who crowded the great temple plaza.

Angry murmurs were exchanged: "It is some time now since we visited the Cloister Palace and the Court. It is only right to visit them with the Sacred Shrine and emblems from time to time and to remind them we are not to be scorned. This is a heaven-sent chance to put fear into the hearts of those warriors."

The June sun beat down mercilessly; to the sound of cicadas droning a march on all sides, the Sacred Shrine made its descent from the mountain. A great host followed after, moving forward as relentlessly as a landslide.

The armed protests of Mount Hiei's priesthood were not rare and thousands of monks marched on the Court or the Regent's house to press their demands, usually succeeding in making themselves heard, for no man dared incur the anger of the deities by defying the priests. In the presence of the Shrine even the Emperor descended from his dais to prostrate himself.

CHAPTER X

THE HERETIC

Tadamori and Kiyomori—father and son—may not be important, but these warriors at the Palace of late have begun to borrow the majesty of the tiger. It's time we plucked them out like weeds, or they'll cause trouble later on."

"No, it's the whole Cloister Palace that is slighting us."

"You mean that dispute over the manor at Kagashirayama?"

"That's it. We've had no answer to our demands on that matter."

"That manor naturally comes under our jurisdiction. When the monk who held tenure over Kagashirayama died, the Palace assumed that the land reverted to his majesty."

"A high-handed attempt at unlawful seizure. . . ."

"The Cloister Palace is where we should go!"

"We should visit it more often, or else they'll get into bad habits!"

By evening several thousand armed monks with the Sacred Shrine had poured down the mountainside, and like thunderclouds bore down on the capital from the north, following the banks of the Kamo River in the twilight to a position not far from the city gates. As darkness fell they tramped to an ominous chanting of sutras, and their blazing torches seemed to scorch the earth and set the clouds on fire.

In every village and hamlet along the marchers' route, terror seized the inhabitants as though the God of Evil himself were marching through; not a soul could be seen. In their hovels of boards, mothers clutched their children to them, hid their faces, and stopped up their ears, waiting for the terrible invaders to pass on.

At Gion the Sacred Shrine was installed in the temple sanctuary, where the monks set up watches, and through the night the light from their fires made the hot vapors of the Eastern Hills burn with a spectral glare.

The novelty of possessing a new home, and his own interest in building, provided Kiyomori with continuous pleasure. Since settling at Rokuhara, he was never content unless carpenters were constantly altering and making additions to the house. A rivulet that flowed down from the hills behind Kiyomizu Temple and past his estate reminded Kiyomori of the stream that flowed through the court of his father-in-law's mansion, and Kiyomori was taken with the idea of having the stream deflected through his garden. He spoke of this to his wife, who said:

"Yes, if we can have a stream flowing through the garden, then my sister and I can do some dyeing. I'll hire a weaving-girl and design some new patterns in unusual colors; then you and the children shall have some very special clothes."

Not only was Tokiko a skilled weaver, but as a young girl she had once been a maid-in-waiting at the Court, where she had seen and handled the rich brocades and embroideries of the imperial wardrobe.

"Good! I can watch you and your sister at your dyeing, as I did on that first day I saw you."

Kiyomori grew enthusiastic over the plan and had men start immediately on the work. By summer it was completed.

"Now, with the stream running through the garden, there will be fireflies about. I must get my father to come and see this," said Kiyomori.

On the same night that Tadamori and Ariko, Kiyomori's stepmother, were visiting Rokuhara, the monks from Mount Hiei arrived in the capital.

Ariko and Tokiko, who were about the same age and could almost be taken for sisters, seemed to find much pleasure in each other's company, and the sight of them with his three grandchildren playing about them gladdened Tadamori, who sat and sipped his wine in a pleasantly reflective mood. He enjoyed the thought that this once easygoing and heedless son of his was now not only a trusted court official, but Lord Aki, the master of a new mansion. For Kiyomori, mellowed with wine, life seemed to have reached its ripest moment.

"Had Tsunemori only come with you, he might have played his flute for us," he remarked.

"Do you enjoy listening to the flute?" Ariko replied. "If you have one, let me play something for you."

Kiyomori turned to Tokiko and asked her to bring his flute.

Tadamori sat and watched the fireflies weaving over the stream; as he slowly drank his wine, he listened to Ariko play, and soon was leaning against a post, dozing. Tadamori suddenly sat up, awake; someone was running in by the front gate and racing toward the enclosure by the stables. There was a shout, and he could hear the retainers in their quarters stirring excitedly.

"They've come!"

Tokitada, Tokiko's brother, appeared in the room in great agitation, crying out that the monks of Mount Hiei had arrived in the capital. Behind him crouched Kiyomori's retainer, Heiroku.

From their blanched faces it was clear that they both knew the serious nature of this announcement.

Ariko's eyes sought Tadamori's as she put down her flute.

"A pity this had to happen tonight," Kiyomori murmured to himself, and then turned to his father with a smile. "So they've come at last!"

Now wide-awake, Tadamori sat up erect, remarking quietly: "So they've come, have they? We'll have to go out and face the tempest. Those monks from Mount Hiei are as inevitable as thunderstorms in summer and gales in the autumn. In all likelihood this house will be blown away like leaves before a whirlwind."

"I realize it," Kiyomori replied, "and I can only bow to the will of heaven, but not to the will of these men. I can always build again upon the ruins of this house."

"If your mind is made up, then far be it from me to counsel you otherwise, Kiyomori, but if you're prepared to lose your home, then I'm ready to give up my son. Should you fall in the fight, I still have another son, Tsunemori, and after him a grandson, Shigemori."

"Father, there's no need to be anxious. I pray that the monks will come here first, for I fear what may happen if they decide to march on the Cloister Palace."

"His majesty has been warned to make no concessions to Mount Hiei this time, or they'll otherwise make a practice of harassing him. He has already refused to hand over the Kagashirayama manor to Mount Hiei."

"That is undoubtedly the real reason for this armed protest and not that affair at Gion. Tokitada's brawl with those monks was a commonplace and not anything they would ordinarily take seriously."

At these words Tokitada and Heiroku, who had withdrawn to the hall, came forward.

"No, brother, it is true that I gave several a beating. They found fault with Heiroku for some small misdemeanor, ordered him to prostrate himself in apology, demanded the name of his master, and finally insulted us in language no warrior would put up with, so I went at them. If you hand me over to the monks, there should be no trouble at all. Let me give myself up to those men at Gion. Forgive me for what I've done."

"Wait, wait, Tokitada, where are you off to?" Kiyomori demanded.

"I must be the reason for this serious disturbance," cried Tokitada.

"Didn't I tell you to leave this matter to me? Have you taken leave of your senses? Haven't I already said that I would face the consequences? And you—Heiroku—mind you, I'll settle this affair singlehanded. If there is need for it, my father is here to help. Understand, Heiroku, that if I intend to use you as a scapegoat, there's no need for me to repeat that I'm prepared to take the consequences. I seem to hear thousands of voices—the voices of the common folk in the market-place—urging me to go forward and do what must be done. . . . More is at stake now than my life. On me turns the future of the warriors. Let's not quibble longer, lest this rare opportunity slip through my fingers."

In the pained silence that followed, the retainers could be heard arming themselves in readiness for Kiyomori's orders.

"Father, will you stay a little longer?"

Tsunemori's arrival on horseback, accompanied by several retainers and horses, brought Tadamori to his feet.

"No, this has been a most refreshing evening. . . . And, Kiyomori, the worst may yet happen, so I suggest that you send the women and children to a safe place before morning."

With such words of caution, Tadamori unhurriedly made his way out to the courtyard and mounted his horse. Kiyomori saw Ariko into her litter, then climbed into his saddle, saying that he would go with them part of the way. With his brother riding beside him, Kiyomori slowly led the party out by the gate.

Fireflies clustered on their saddles and were caught in their sleeves. A flutter of wind set numberless small insects whirling into eddies of brightness.

As the procession of twenty arrived at the Gojo Bridge, Kiyomori glanced back over his shoulder and saw how the watch-fires of near-by Gion lit up the sky balefully.

Morning. The capital looked strange. Every house was shut-tered, not a soul was abroad. The great avenues were deserted as at midnight. Now and then a warrior clattered by. Ten horses, twenty horses went past; then three or four, led by soldiers, pro-ceeded in the direction of the Court; officials hurried by to their duties at the Palace.

"I wish to have a word with Kiyomori, Lord Aki. I am Tada-masa of the Heiké. Where is he on duty?"

All eight gates of the Cloister Palace were crowded with war-riors in full armor. Tadamasa, Kiyomori's uncle, had slipped away unaccompanied from the Court and come seeking his nephew.

A warrior stopped to reply: "Lord Aki may not have come yet. There's a rumor that the monks will attack his residence be-fore they march on either the Court or the Palace."

"Ah, I see, he's more concerned for the safety of his own property than the Palace. Sounds very like him. I shall be off to Rokuhara, then."

Tadamasa turned his horse's head east and galloped off to-ward Gojo Bridge. As he neared it, he noticed a figure on horse-back coming toward him. The horse ambled, swinging its tail comfortably.

"Ho! Uncle, and where are you off to?" Kiyomori called out as Tadamasa sped past.

Tadamasa reined in his horse sharply and wheeled to a stop. As Kiyomori came toward him, he burst out angrily:

"Ha, so it's you, Kiyomori! Mind that speech of yours! What do you mean by 'where are you off to'? As soon as I heard that more than two thousand monks had arrived from Mount Hiei, my first thought was for you. Alas, I said, here you were at long last rid of your poverty, able to build yourself a mansion, and the end so soon in sight. I was sorry for you, and felt for you as only an uncle can for his nephew. I was sure I could help you, and was on my way to you at top speed."

"That—was most kind of you," said Kiyomori laughing airily, though he politely inclined his head, "but, uncle, don't you realize with whom we are dealing? No one, not even his majesty, dares to oppose those who come with the sacred emblem. No matter how much help you offer, we are helpless against these monks from Mount Hiei. Unless you have come to view the ruins of my house, your words, to say the least, are comical. I realize you meant this most kindly."

"Hmm—I now understand. I met your father at dawn at the Justice Department and he seemed to think as you do. In fact, the two of you are exactly alike. . . . So neither of you cares what happens. You're completely indifferent to what happens."

"My father speaks for himself, and I for myself. There's nothing odd in keeping cool. On the contrary, what's the matter with you? These armed petitions aren't anything unusual."

"Enough. The more you chatter, the more I realize that you and your father are cowards."

Tadamasa, unwilling to admit that this nephew of his was now a man, persisted in his habit of bullying Kiyomori as though he were the same ragged youth of ten years ago. Kiyomori, on the other hand, tolerated Tadamasa only because he was his father's brother. He knew no one he disliked more thoroughly. Lately, he had noticed a certain apprehensiveness in Tadamasa and sensed that Tadamori's promotion to the Justice Department, as well as his new title and rank, were somehow unnerving to his uncle, though Tadamasa had no reason to envy them since he had recently received an important post at Court.

"Come, get down, Kiyomori, get down and listen to what I have to say."

"No, I'm on my way to see to the defense of the Palace, and this is no time for me to be loitering."

"And you who should be among the first at the Palace— what do you mean by ambling along at this hour as though reluctant to be on your way?" said Tadamasa, hurriedly dismounting and seizing Kiyomori's stirrup.

"Now what do you want?" Kiyomori asked impatiently, dismounting reluctantly, and seating himself under one of the pine trees along the highway.

"Now listen to me. If you refuse, from this very day I renounce all the sacred ties of blood between us," Tadamasa declared.

"Now what do you mean by that?"

"You are completely blinded by love of your wife. Tokiko has you dancing at her will."

"Do you speak of my wife?"

"Who but Tokiko? You have let her talk you into causing this disaster, fatuous husband that you are! I've never known such stupidity as yours. Why don't you hand over Tokitada to the authorities of Mount Hiei?"

"Ah, just a moment, I don't quite understand. Are you saying that since Tokitada is my wife's brother, I have listened to Tokiko's pleadings and that I am therefore responsible for this serious situation?"

"That may be it. I don't need to ask you, since that much is obvious to me, your uncle:"

"So that's it, and that's how it appears to you?"

"Swear to me here and now that you will give up Tokitada and your houseman Heiroku while you remain a prisoner in your own house and await judgment. I, in the meanwhile, will ride at once to Gion and speak to the monks myself. They will then have no reason for pressing their demands, and we shall avert a calamity."

"I refuse."

"What!"

"Let them tear me limb from limb before I hand over those two."

"Why do you refuse? Of what value are the lives of those two compared with their majesties' peace of mind?"

"Tokitada and Heiroku are not alone guilty. Should misfortune visit the Court, that can only be the result of its continued abuses. If the Palace is attacked, that can only be the result of misgovernment. I can hardly be held responsible for the outcome."

"Are you mad, Kiyomori? Those shameless words of yours!"

"No more shameless than those you've been spitting out until now. My wife is very dear to me, but she doesn't make up my mind for me."

"Very well, very well. . . . I've said enough. Let come what may! I've also heard you say something that can't be overlooked. Whatever happens to their majesties is no concern of yours?"

"That I did say, undoubtedly."

"You traitor! You base one!"

"Indeed?"

"The gods will surely rain down punishment on that impious head of yours! What a monster to have for a nephew! . . . No, I shan't risk my position at Court because of you. I wash my hands of you, Kiyomori!"

"Why, what a temper you're in!"

"You and Tadamori—the pair of you—spurn my offers of help. Wait and see, you will regret this. . . . No, I've no reason to be concerned further for you. Tell your father this: from this moment, I, Tadamasa, renounce all claim to being a member of the Heiké clan."

Uncertainty, death itself stalking the capital, led Tadamasa in a moment of panic to repudiate all ties with the Heiké. Kiyomori, however, listened to his uncle's outburst with a smile, as though this were just a tiff before breakfast.

Kiyomori watched Tadamasa and his horse until they vanished in the distance in a swirl of dust, then rose and untethered his mount; as he settled himself in his saddle, two figures sprang out from between the trees and seized his horse's reins from either side.

"Ho, you—Tokitada and Heiroku? You were slow in returning, so I came on ahead. What now? What of Tokiko and the children?"

"We have done as you ordered. They are safe at Anryakuju-in Temple, and you need have no fears for them."

"Good! As long as the women and children are safe, Mokuno-suké can see to the house at Rokuhara. I have nothing more on my mind now. Good work!"

At this, Tokitada and Heiroku hid their faces against their forearms and wept, begging Kiyomori to forgive them; they cried that they knew no way of making amends; not only had they brought down the wrath of Mount Hiei, but their folly had sown discord among the Heiké, they said.

"Here, enough of this blubbering, I'm off—" Kiyomori said, spurring his horse to a gallop.

Shaken off, the two stared after Kiyomori with the dust blowing in their faces, then followed after him at a run.

Three priests, the leaders of the monks from Mount Hiei, stalked out of the Cloister Palace, raging. From their furious looks it was plain that their demands had been rejected. They stopped at the gatehouse to reclaim their spears, swung them under their arms with a flourish and called to twelve underlings as they marched out of the gates.

It was usual for the monks to send their representatives to the government to present their demands, and if refused they invariably brought the Sacred Shrine and holy emblems into the capital and terrorized the authorities into acquiescing, for not even the civil powers dared oppose the Shrine.

Today Mount Hiei had demanded the persons of Lord Aki's brother-in-law, Tokitada, and the retainer Heiroku. In conjunction with this, the monks once more pressed their claim to the Kagashirayama manor, but the ex-Emperor had refused.

A wave of excitement passed through the ranks of the warriors. There were cries of: "Here comes Lord Aki, Kiyomori of the Heiké!"

The Guards cheered as Kiyomori appeared with his usual jaunty air. Smiling broadly to either side of him as he rode between the armed ranks, Kiyomori sensed a sudden rise in the soldiers' spirits. Sweat poured down his face, and his large ears seemed to quiver. Following him came the crestfallen Tokitada and Heiroku, odd contrast to the debonair figure on horseback.

Palace secretaries, officials, and courtiers with drawn faces crowded the dais-room, where the Cloistered Emperor waited for Kiyomori.

Kiyomori knelt. "Your majesty, though Mount Hiei's real demand is for the Kagashirayama manor, it is my housemen who caused the monks to come here. I alone am responsible for this. Permit me, therefore, to deal with Mount Hiei as I see fit."

The Cloistered Emperor consented; there were no protests from the frightened courtiers, no questions how Kiyomori would induce the orderly withdrawal of the monks to Mount Hiei. Kiyomori made obeisance and withdrew.

His men watched him from a distance, talking among themselves. "We can expect nothing from those weak-kneed courtiers, but his lordship will surely have a plan."

Until now Kiyomori's every move had been followed closely by those around him and there had been considerable speculation as to what step he would next take. His refusal to give up Tokitada and Heiroku to the monks won the complete approval of his soldiers, who regarded him with respectful affection. Kiyomori was one whom any soldier felt he could talk to man to man. There was nothing which distinguished Kiyomori from other warriors in respect of courage or skill with arms, but his quick sympathy for the poor and downtrodden and his readiness to defend them made him popular with his men; that and the curious faculty he possessed of communicating his own gaiety. Wherever he went, his generously proportioned face—the eyebrows like caterpillars, the down-slanting eyes, the large nose, the full lips, the youthful ruddy cheeks and round chin, and those heavy-lobed ears which quivered whenever he laughed—caused merriment.

The owner of these features came out by an inner gate and started across the Palace plaza. He was soon surrounded by warriors who pressed on him with cries of: "Kiyomori of the Heiké, what came of the talks?"

"Is there to be an imperial decree?"

"What happened, and what does his majesty say?"

Question after question was flung at him rapidly. Mopping

his heated brow, Kiyomori pulled up the helmet slung at his back, set it on his head, and tied the cords under his chin.

"Now, now, there's no need to worry. I go straight to Gion to stop their marching with the Shrine."

"Stop them?"

"Here, leave it to his lordship to do that!"

"But those monks fear nothing; they scorn us as less than the dust under their feet, and last night showed they're thirsty for our blood. Should you go there, sir, there's no telling what they'll do. . . ."

"That's true, but I'm taking Tokitada and Heiroku with me. Much as I regret it, I shall have to turn them over to the monks and try to reach an agreement."

"Eh? Then you *will* give them up, after all, to the monks?"

"I have no choice."

"What a thing to do! So his majesty expects the warriors to take the brunt of it after all?"

"Come, stop this useless arguing. But remember that it was I who proposed this solution, not his majesty. Now let me be off to halt them before they leave Gion. If happily I return alive, there'll be a tale to tell. Now each man of you to his post."

With Tokitada and Heiroku following him, Kiyomori rode away on the dazzling sunlit highway, parched white with heat. Every leaf and blade drooped under the blazing sun. The guards stared, speechless, after the three as though they were the ghosts of the dead walking at noon.

From the stone staircase of one of the temples in Gion, the three leaders who had returned from the Cloister Palace harangued two thousand monks, gathered to hear the outcome of the negotiations.

" . . . We find no sincerity in his majesty. Both petitions have been thrust back at us. There's no hope that even the matter of the Kagashirayama manor will be settled. There's nothing left for us but to march on the Palace with the Sacred Shrine to bring his majesty to his senses."

A mad roar went up: "To the Palace, then! Chastise them!" and with this the multitude began assembling their weapons and surged toward the sanctuary where the Sacred Shrine rested amid tapers burning like myriads of stars and clouds of incense which all but enveloped the groves of Gion. To the massed chanting of sutras, the measured clanging of gongs, and to drums, throbbing like savage alarms to war, the great army got under way, and the air pulsed as though charged with some diabolic influence. Borne at last on the shoulders of white-robed priests, and shimmering blindingly with encrustments of gold, slowly, slowly swaying, the Sacred Shrine made its way down the hill onto the great highway.

A figure suddenly darted out in front of the oncoming shrine and held up a hand. "Wait, you infernal priests!" On his head was a black helmet of iron, bare of insignia; he was incased in black armor, wore straw sandals, and held up a long bow. Not far behind him were Tokitada and Heiroku, unarmed, their faces set hard like masks.

"I, Lord Aki, Kiyomori of the Heiké, demand that you hear me. Among all you evil ones there must be at least one who will listen to reason."

To the advancing host, he looked like Asura, the God of War, hewn out of jet, with yawning jaws from which issued a torrent of sound.

Astounded by the temerity of this fellow and his words, the monks shouted: "Whew! . . . Kiyomori!" Then a mad roaring broke loose. "Slash him to bits for the festival of blood!"

The leaders who walked ahead showed no surprise and brought the marchers to a stop, restraining them. "Let him speak. Let no one touch him. Let us first hear what he has to say."

The Shrine-bearers pushed back the angry crowd, crying: "No man shall come near the Shrine and defile it! Beware of the sacred emblem!"

Kiyomori stood his ground, still shouting hoarsely: "That which you demand, I now give you. Here are Tokitada and Heiroku—take them! Remember, however, they're still alive."

The wary looks of the leaders changed to mocking smiles at

Kiyomori's words. Kiyomori took another deep breath and continued: "That affair at Gion brought on this. See me, O you gods! And you, Buddha, unstop your ears! Hear what I have to say. Both sides are guilty, for were they not intoxicated? Has it not always been said that both parties to a quarrel are in the wrong? I, Kiyomori, therefore, give up these two whom I love to Mount Hiei, and in return demand a hearing of this sacred object, the symbol of your godhead!"

Rumblings of laughter greeted Kiyomori's words. "Look at him, Kiyomori, Lord Aki! How he raves! He's mad!"

Kiyomori's body was contorted in an effort to make himself heard. Sweat poured down his cheeks and chin and from behind his ears, like water bubbling on hot iron.

"Mad or not, listen further to what I have to say. Let this god hear me, too! Whether it is a divinity or Buddha himself, it is a curse, a delusion, and the cause of suffering to men! It is no more than an object of idolatry! Has it not deceived men for centuries and led them astray, this abomination from Mount Hiei? But Kiyomori is not deceived. Hear me, therefore, you cursed godhead, and beware!"

Consternation spread through the monks as Kiyomori fitted an arrow to his bow; it creaked as he arched it like the full moon; then he aimed straight at the Shrine.

One of the leaders leaped forward shrieking: "Alas! A curse on you, blasphemer! You shall die foaming blood!"

"Die? Then so be it."

The bowstring twanged, the arrow hissed and pierced the very center of the Shrine. From two thousand throats came a frenzied roar. The white-robed priests sprang to their feet, shouting rapidly to one another, and the air was suddenly filled with wails, angry shrieks, cries of anguish, the screams of half-demented men, moans, and bestial howls.

Never had the Shrine been thus desecrated! Never had any man raised a hand against it, for had he dared, he would have been struck dead instantly, foaming blood. Yet there stood Kiyomori, nor did blood gush from his mouth. The emptiness of the myth had been exposed in broad daylight, and the priests stripped of all authority. Aghast, the leaders quickly sought to turn the mob's disillusionment into fury by urging them on to violence.

"Don't let that madman escape!"

The massed body of monks broke loose. Kiyomori vanished in an onrush of flashing spears, dust, and flailing staves. Not far off, Tokitada and Heiroku were soon engulfed by the mob and lost to sight.

Kiyomori's bowstring snapped; he laid about him with his bow, felling three or four of his opponents, and fighting on as though possessed. But the odds were against him, for he had no other weapon.

"Don't kill him! Get him alive!" The monks baited him as though he were a boar at bay. The leaders clamored hoarsely: "Catch him! Beat him down! We'll drag him back alive to Mount Hiei!"

"Capture him alive, alive!" they cried. They could hold him for ransom in their future talks with the Palace, or else punish this arch-rebel as an example to the people of Mount Hiei's authority.

The unwieldy mob moved clumsily, and in the hand-to-hand fighting Kiyomori wrenched a halberd from one of the monks. With it he hacked at arms and legs until he drew blood, and saw six or seven wounded or dead sprawl to the ground. He caught glimpses of Tokitada and Heiroku not far off, dodging in their attempts to get to him. Fragments of their anxious cries reached him, and he called back to them: "Don't yield! Keep up your courage! The same sun looks down on all of us!"

All this took place in a matter of moments. Meanwhile the outcry and commotion attracted the common folk in the vicinity. In a short while a dense crowd had gathered noisily at the scene. One of them picked up a stone and shouted: "Don't let the wolves of Mount Hiei devour you!" There were loud cries of: "You good-for-nothing hirelings!" "You cursed monks!" The jeering mass was clamoring: "At those greedy, evil priests!" as they snatched up fragments of rock and stones, which they hurled at the churning monks. A howl of indignation was followed by another volley of

stones. Just then a black column of smoke shot up from among
the trees of Gion. Another column, then another, and yet another
followed. At this sight the monks wavered and then began to fall
back in confusion. Calling to one another that they had been ambushed, the battling monks turned about in full retreat. Forgotten
now was the inviolability of the Shrine in the panic; it careened
wildly at a sharp angle above the heads of the dissolving mass,
borne on the shoulders of the priests as they fled madly toward
Gion.

Kiyomori stood on a slope of the Eastern Hills and gazed
down into the distance, laughing aloud. "There they all go! Astounding!" His black armor lay on the ground where he had
thrown it and he stood stripped to the waist, mopping the sweat
from his body. Ridiculous! And he burst once more into laughter.
Not he, but the two thousand had retreated! He had planned to
escape when the arrow pierced the Shrine, and given Tokitada and
Heiroku strict orders to do the same, thirsty as they were for a fight
to the death. ("No dog's death for either of you. Don't mind appearances, just get away.") They had agreed to meet each other
on the hill behind Kiyomizu Temple.

Kiyomori was puzzled by the monks' retreat. That rain of
stones had no doubt taken them by surprise, but it must have
been the sight of the smoke that had sent them into a rout. He
stared at the smoke which turned the sun a blood-red, and was
musing over the cause of the fires, when he saw Tokitada making
his way up the hill alone.

"Ah, you're safe!"

"Well, here you are, Tokitada, but where's Heiroku?"

"Heiroku got away from that bloodthirsty crowd, too."

"Will he join us here later?"

"I met him at Todoroki Bridge, watching the smoke and saying that he was sure his father had something to do with it. He
then went off at a run toward Gion. He'll surely come later."

"So, that's it. Mokunosuké's not one to be sitting idle at
Rokuhara. That Old One has been up to something—setting fire
to the seats of their trousers!"

He was right in his guess. Mokunosuké, as the senior retainer left in charge of the house at Rokuhara with twenty younger retainers, was unable to endure the thought that Kiyomori was perhaps risking his life for Heiroku, and early that day, after seeing his mistress and her household go into hiding, had quietly laid plans of his own and sent off the remaining retainers to the foot of the Eastern Hills to conceal themselves. Little did he guess that Kiyomori would make the daring gesture that he did. Mokunosuké had schemed to set fire to the temples and shrines of Gion if the monks marched on the Palace or came to attack Rokuhara. A fortunate combination of events, however, had been even more effective.

Mokunosuké and Heiroku finally ascended the hill in search of Kiyomori; face to face with each other once more and safe, their hearts overflowed with gratitude. They lifted their hands in prayer to the crimson sun, as the tears coursed down Kiyomori's cheeks. To himself, Kiyomori whispered: "Truly, the heavens and the earth were with me, and the protecting spirits of my forefathers took pity on this weakling and shielded him."

Still half-clothed, Kiyomori seated himself on a rock ledge and cheerfully resumed: "Now, all of you, our troubles for the day are over; after this comes tomorrow, the day after, and the days that follow after—then retribution."

"That will surely come," Mokunosuké replied, frowning, "and it will be no laughing matter then."

"Ho, let a hundred such come, and I shall be victorious, for I have two allies."

"What do you mean by that?" Mokunosuké ventured.

"One is my father at Imadegawa, the other the miracle from heaven—the rain of stones. Surely, Old One, you saw them— those men who sprang up from nowhere and rained down stones on those monks?"

The voices of approaching men interrupted Kiyomori. Tokitada quickly peered round the corner of a rock into the defile below. The others reached for their armor and weapons. Motioning for silence, Mokunosuké quickly assured Kiyomori that the men were in all likelihood the other retainers coming to meet him. Kiyomori's housemen soon appeared, and from them he obtained an account of how they had stolen into Gion and surprised the enemy by setting fire to the huts and small outbuildings there. Relieved to hear that they had spared the temples and shrines, Kiyomori commended Mokunosuké for his shrewd maneuver.

"Old One, you are as wise as you are old. Had it been I, I would have razed all the temples and shrines at Gion." At this the old retainer shook his head deprecatingly.

"No, no. This I learned from my lord, Tadamori, who on that night of the banquet when the court nobles lay in wait to murder him, carried a bamboo sword simulating a blade of great renown, and foiled his enemies. Today's feint was no more than a poor attempt to imitate your father."

The old man's modest words swiftly brought the Squint-Eyed One to Kiyomori's mind. For a moment he sat silent with lowered gaze as though something had crossed his mind; then looking up, Kiyomori said: "Old One, let us now go down to Rokuhara and there await orders from the Palace. I have accomplished what I set out to do. I feel light of heart now and have no regrets. I shall in all humbleness await judgment. What do you say, Tokitada?"

Springing to his feet, Kiyomori drew on his leather corselet, and with his retainers followed the course of the stream flowing down to Rokuhara.

"So the son of the Squint-Eyed One, Kiyomori, did it, did he? What a thing to do!"

Kiyomori's defiance of Mount Hiei convulsed the entire capital, but an ill-concealed satisfaction underlay popular astonishment. Even the courtiers had nothing ill to say of Kiyomori, while the rival monasteries of related sects held up Mount Hiei for ridicule. As the shock of surprise subsided and fears of retaliation from the monks died away, people began to speculate on how the authorities would deal with Kiyomori.

The Cloistered Emperor, Toba, received repeated threats

from Mount Hiei, and the Regent and state ministers met daily to consider the forceful demands of the priesthood. Toba, who held the real reins of power, attended the state conferences, giving no sign that he commended or censured Kiyomori's act, and listened closely to all that was said. Throughout the discussions, the Minister of the Left, Yorinaga, insisted that Kiyomori should receive the death penalty, arguing that this alone would instill the fear of the gods in the people and appease the authorities on Mount Hiei.

Dignified of bearing and graced with many of the attributes of a courtier, Yorinaga was not only a scholar well versed in the Chinese classics and Buddhist literature, but a compelling speaker, whose arguments were hard to refute. When crossed, however, his violent temper and arrogance made him a man to be feared by even his peers, for he respected neither person nor rank if he were thwarted.

"It is true," Yorinaga said, "that this is not the first time Mount Hiei has come with its armed petitions, but Lord Aki's act cannot be regarded as a just reprisal. What he has done is nothing less than sacrilege. He has flouted the gods and sinned against Buddha, and to overlook his deed is to acquit a criminal and pave the way to insurrection. I doubt that the priesthood will view this affair lightly. No one welcomes the thought of insubordination, which will lead to civil unrest, and for the public good I refuse to listen to any pleas to spare Kiyomori."

There was a murmur of dissent among some of the ministers, but Yorinaga quickly cowed them into silence. "Do I hear some unreasonable expressions to the contrary? Let me hear these opinions. Let us discuss them here."

Only by the expression of his eyes, closely searching the faces of each of his courtiers, did the Cloistered Emperor betray his anxiety. Not even he dared contradict Yorinaga. There was one, none the less, who objected: Shinzei, a high-ranking courtier, claiming descent from an influential Fujiwara minister, and a member of the southern branch of that clan. Though a Fujiwara,

Shinzei had never been popular among his powerful relatives at Court and for many years had been relegated to positions of obscurity. Not until he was in his sixties did he succeed in obtaining a post of any significance at the Cloister Palace, and this, court gossips related, was due to his wife, Lady Kii, a lady-in-waiting to Lady Bifukumon. As a state councilor, Shinzei's duties entailed the drafting and proclaiming of imperial decrees. His abilities were of no mean order, for he had early established a reputation as a scholar, the equal of any at Court, and Yorinaga himself had been one of his disciples.

At the last of the imperial conferences it was Shinzei who said to Yorinaga: "How very convincing your arguments sound! Doesn't it seem to you, sir, that you argue the case for Mount Hiei? Three rulers—Shirakawa, Horikawa, and Toba—recognized the necessity for putting a check on the clergy of Mount Hiei, yet none succeeded. We cannot say that Kiyomori has. He nevertheless has opened the way toward bringing them to their senses. Has he not shown the priesthood that the Court is not to be intimidated by their arrogance and their show of force?"

Shinzei spoke with the assurance of one who knew the Cloistered Emperor's mind; he was also aware that both the ruling class and the common people had no sympathy for the monks and upheld Kiyomori. He then pleaded: "What he did appears unpardonable, yet we must remember that his majesty and the courtiers gave Kiyomori complete freedom to deal with the monks as he saw fit. If Kiyomori overstepped the bounds of the authority given him and deserves punishment, then let those who approved his request likewise share his guilt. It is true that he desecrated the Sacred Shrine, yet were it a true emblem of the gods and of Buddha, would it have been so vulnerable? Rather can it be said that Kiyomori's deed swept away the clouds of deception and helped men renew their belief in heavenly beings. Has that assault upon the sacred emblem brought the gods and Buddha falling to earth, or called down darkness on the world?"

Discreet laughter greeted Shinzei's words. Yorinaga smiled

wryly and pursed his wide mouth as his eyes came to rest on the Cloistered Emperor's look of agreement. This concluded the last of the imperial conclaves. A proclamation was made, ordering Kiyomori to pay a fine in copper, and news of Kiyomori's light penalty spread rapidly throughout the capital. The common people and mercenaries rejoiced with the Heiké clansmen. Genji warriors heard the report sullenly. Indignation and grudging admiration moved the leaders on Mount Hiei to admit among themselves that they had met an adversary to be reckoned with later on. Torn by internal dissensions and threatened from without by attacks from the monasteries of other sects, the monks of Mount Hiei after a few veiled threats on the civil authorities were mollified when the rulers ceded to them the Kagashirayama estates.

Tameyoshi of the Genji was a favorite of the Minister of the Left, Yorinaga, whose father before him had always been partial to the Genji, and Yorinaga had invited Tameyoshi to his residence one evening for a talk.

"Tameyoshi, you have not yet had enough to drink," Yorinaga said. "We have to admit that State Councilor Shinzei has the upper hand this time. Time will bring more favorable winds our way. This has been an unavoidable setback for you. It also appears that his majesty all along has supported Kiyomori."

Yorinaga had drunk heavily and a mood of despondence had come over him. "His majesty, the Cloistered Emperor, is too partial to Tadamori and Kiyomori of the Heiké. Compared with them you have not been very successful, but wait, one of these days I shall see that the Genji come into their own."

This promise was one Yorinaga had made Tameyoshi for several years, and in pressing for Kiyomori's indictment he had hoped to put a check on the Heiké for good.

"Sir," Tameyoshi said, "let us forget all this. I shall gratefully accept duty in some distant province immediately, for I have no further ambitions."

This was not the first time that Tameyoshi had declined Yorinaga's offers of support, for there were certain disadvantages in taking the Minister's proffered help. Tameyoshi, on the other hand, had hoped to be sent to northern Japan, where many Genji clansmen had settled in his grandfather's time, but his requests had been turned down each time by the Fujiwara courtiers, who feared to send him any distance from the capital, and induced Tameyoshi to stay in Kyoto, where they could keep him under their eye.

[The Heretic]

hand, had hoped to be intimately allied when the new Genji
clansmen had settled in... ...Tower... ...requests
had be... ...down... ...who
feared... ...distance from... ...duced
Tameyo... ...Kyoto, wh... ...ked... ...under
their ev...

CHAPTER XI

FOXES AND A LUTE

ime hung heavily on Kiyomori's hands. After paying an
indemnity in copper, he was ordered suspended from his
official duties for a year. During that time of retirement
the sensation he had created died down. His offense, nevertheless,
also affected his near kin: Kiyomori's father was suspended from
his office for one hundred days; as a member of the Fujiwara family, Tokinobu, Kiyomori's father-in-law, forfeited indefinitely the
right to the name and protection of the Fujiwara.

Kiyomori repeatedly exploded in wrath to his brother-in-law Tokitada: "It's just as well. You and your good father may as well call yourselves Heiké. The Fujiwara are not the only family in existence."

Had his sentence been more severe, Kiyomori would still have had little reason to complain, but the precautions taken by the Fujiwara aristocrats seemed to have touched a sore spot. "They've shown what cowards they are in attempting to protect themselves. They're wary; they're afraid that anyone bearing the Fujiwara name and related to one as crude as I might bring misfortune upon them. Yet they were secretly pleased by what I did. This is an insult more painful to endure than the sentence they've given me. Tokitada, don't ever forget this."

Tokitada's sprightliness lightened the gloom of Kiyomori's secluded life; he provided a responsive listener for Kiyomori's confidences; more daring than Kiyomori, he also had bookish leanings, which Kiyomori lacked; possessed of a retentive memory, Tokitada's discernment often left Kiyomori speechless.

Kiyomori was strolling listlessly to the stables to look over his horses when he heard the cheering twang of bowstrings and turned his steps toward the archery range. An arrow hissed by and transfixed the center of the target with a sharp snap.

"Well done!" Kiyomori cried. Two figures swung round and faced him smiling: Shigemori, his ten-year-old son, and Tokitada, who was giving him lessons in archery.

"What do you think of Shigemori's shooting?" Kiyomori queried.

"As you see, he does very well, but—he doesn't seem quite able to shoot straight, nor to have enough strength. Temperament, probably."

"He's still young, Tokitada, and his bow is small."

"There's no denying that. A man's character, however, shows in his shots. Did you never hear of Tameyoshi's youngest son?"

"I believe I have."

"That lad whom Tameyoshi found so headstrong—I saw him at an archery match when he was eleven. He had a powerful bow even then and shot an arrow so deep into a mound of earth that two men together could not pull it out. Yes, he finally became completely unmanageable and caused his father a great deal of trouble."

Kiyomori laughed aloud. "Tokitada, you must be speaking of yourself."

"I? No, no, I've given up cockfighting, and haven't been in a brawl since that time at Gion. That taught me a lesson."

"No need to give up so soon, Tokitada. I hear that the Nara monasteries are again rioting, though Mount Hiei has given us no trouble since. I fear that one arrow hasn't been enough to cure them of their fighting."

"And that reminds me that at the end of last August, Tame-yoshi of the Genji took his soldiers down to Uji and succeeded in turning back several thousand armed monks who were on their way to the capital. Since then the Court, I hear, has shown him much favor."

Kiyomori's envious look drove Tokitada on to greater volu-bility. "I also hear that the Minister Yorinaga is encouraging the Genji and plans to appoint Tameyoshi chief of the Guards while you and your father wait out the term of your penalty."

Kiyomori's slight frown betrayed nothing of his feelings, but the quiet surface of his days was ruffled. Just then Heiroku, the re-tainer, appeared to announce that Oshimaro, the armor-maker, was waiting to see the master. Kiyomori, who welcomed any visi-tor who would relieve the tedium of his days, quickly turned back to the house.

"I have come, sir, on the matter of the armor you ordered," the humpbacked old armor-maker said gruffly. His armor was said to be unequaled. Every strand of the armor-threading and each metal plate was assembled with matchless skill. Kiyomori, who had heard that the crotchety old man demanded astonishingly high prices and was particular about his customers, had ordered a suit of armor with a design of cherry blossoms worked into it. The armor was almost finished.

"The leather has been dyed to your order, sir, the plating

finished—the thongs, leather camail, and greaves—everything is ready, except the foxskins you promised me. Now what do you wish me to do about that, sir?"

The old man used the skin of a freshly killed fox to reinforce vital points in the armor; Kiyomori, when ordering his armor, had promised two skins on whatever day the armor-maker named. The fur was to line the shoulder-guards, the skirt of the cuirass, and the underarm pieces. There was a secret to boiling the glue with which the uncured skins were attached to the armor; the glue required more than two days of slow simmering over embers and was then applied immediately to the skins, which, if they were not ready at hand, meant that the glue would have to be thrown out.

"I don't know how many days I have waited for you to appear, nor how many times the glue has gone to waste," the old man grumbled accusingly. "If any common skins suit you, it would be quite easy. If you are satisfied with such armor, there are plenty of armor-makers to please you, and you might as well order yours elsewhere."

"No, no! I'm sorry. Don't be angry—I beg you not to be so angry, my good man," Kiyomori remonstrated. "I sent my housemen out hunting several times, and each time they came back with badgers and hares, but no foxes. This time I shall go myself. Now —let me see, hadn't we better set a day?"

"And leave me again in the lurch?"

"Hmm—no, not this time."

"I don't mean to boast, but you must understand I can't leave the boiling of the glue to an apprentice or my wife. There's a secret to regulating the fire, stirring the glue, and watching the pot come to a boil, and I must spend two nights and days with my soul in the task, watching that pot. Then—no skins! The glue thickens and has to be thrown out. You can understand what a rage I am in by then."

"No, this time there'll be no mistake about it. What about the evening of the day after tomorrow? Just about dusk when the lamps are lit, I shall come without fail to your house and deliver the skins to you myself."

"You mean *you* will do that?"

"I would not leave it to anyone else now."

"What if you go back on this promise of yours?"

"I'll pay a fine in copper or anything else you ask for."

The old man shook with laughter and slapped his thigh. "Good! You are after all Lord Aki, who shot at the Shrine. I take you at your word. I'll go home and start right away on the glue, and look for you at dusk of the day after tomorrow."

On the following day Kiyomori took his favorite bow from its case, restrung it, and then went down a passage to look for his wife. A maidservant said that her mistress was busy in the weaving-house and offered to fetch her, but Kiyomori waved her aside. "If she's in the weaving-house, don't call her, just get out my hunting clothes."

Wearing his leather hunting trousers, a quiver slung at his back, and bow in hand, Kiyomori stopped at the weaving-house which had been built at his wife's wishes. There were two looms, space for dyeing vats, and embroidery stands.

Tokiko sat at her loom while her children played happily about her. She was proud of her accomplishment and enjoyed clothing her family in cloths of unusual design, for which she had often been complimented.

"Why—why so suddenly?" she said, leaving her loom. "Who is going with you?"

"I'm going alone. It's better for me to remain as inconspicuous as possible just now."

"Surely you should have at least one of the young serving-lads go with you."

"No, I shan't be going to the hills, and I should be back by sundown. What of that length of cloth you were going to send Shinzei's wife?"

"It has been dyed and the embroidery finished. Wouldn't you like to look at it?"

"Never mind, it won't be necessary since I have no eye for such things," Kiyomori replied, and departed by a rear gate.

Kiyomori had heard indirectly that Shinzei alone had spoken

in his defense. Since then he had come to regard Shinzei as an ally and recently became friendly with him. When Tokiko suggested sending one of her finest cloths to Shinzei's wife, Lady Kii, Kiyomori had warmly agreed to the plan.

Kiyomori had often heard that foxes were seen inside the capital as well as beyond the city gates, but now as he looked about him he saw nothing but the silvery plumes of tall grasses stretching across the autumn fields. He spent the whole day walking through the fields, and at evening turned home footsore and empty-handed.

The next day it drizzled fitfully, but by noon the skies cleared. Tokitada, who had heard about Kiyomori's lack of success, urged him to remain at home, and made preparations to go with Heiroku.

But Kiyomori protested: "Oh no, when I saw you and Shigemori practicing with your bows yesterday, I suddenly felt a longing for mine—a kind of fretting for it from long idleness, I suppose."

As soon as Tokitada and Heiroku left, Kiyomori himself set out. This time he scoured the region outside the northern gates of the capital until sundown. He walked through the tall wet grass until his trousers were soaked through and his clothes damp to the armpits. He floundered over boggy ground, through waterfilled hollows, and over hillocks thick with *hagi* blooms, until a pale mist began to descend over the scene. A faint rose still stained the western sky, and a sickle of a moon hung in the indigo above him.

"Not a fox in sight—only birds winging their way home—and yet they say that the barking of foxes can be heard on these autumn nights," Kiyomori muttered.

In the distance he caught the gleam of a light in a field-watcher's hut. He pictured to himself the glue bubbling in the armor-maker's house, and the thought of disappointing Oshimaro made him feel a little desperate. He regretted his rash promise to bring two live foxes to the armor-maker at sundown.

The fields about him were now bathed in a deep blue light. As he turned to retrace his steps, there was a quick scuffling at his feet in the thick undergrowth; something crossed his path with a bound and vanished. Kiyomori instantly fitted an arrow to his bow, when another shadow slipped almost between his feet and disappeared with a rustle. At once he set out in pursuit of a vanishing tail; following it from grass-clump to grass-clump, he suddenly came on a fox squatting rigidly in a hollow; its eyes were fastened in paralyzed fascination on Kiyomori's arrow. He drew his bow. There was a low snarl and a disagreeable odor assailed his nostrils. He looked closely and saw more than one fox; two furry bodies were huddled together there. A pair of fiercely gleaming eyes were now turned on him. An old fox with a brindled tail bristled at him. The vixen, half-concealed by her mate, crouched with her claws showing, snarling deep in her throat as she watched the hand on the bow with terrified eyes. She was scrawnier than the fox, more like a wolf; the bones of her shoulders jutted out, her fur was lusterless, and her belly stuck to her ribs. Kiyomori looked again more sharply and saw how she shielded a young cub under her. They might have escaped to safety had it not been for her young, Kiyomori thought. Three—what luck! For an instant he considered which to shoot first. The full-drawn bow creaked. A phosphorescent glow seemed to emanate from the trapped pair, and they gave out a weird moan. The fox crouched threateningly, with desperate courage, while the vixen arched itself more closely round the cub.

Kiyomori's arm suddenly felt nerveless. "Ah, you pitiful, pitiful creatures! Beautiful family! Nobler far than stupid men . . ." he cried softly to himself. What was he doing here with his arrow? Cornering these creatures? Armor—an armor to brag about! Save his dignity before that armor-maker because of a promise? Foolish . . . foolish! If the old man jeered at him, why should it matter any more; a common suit of armor would do as well! Armor did not make a man, nor did it signify valor.

"Dumb creatures that you are, how magnificent! Sorrow, love —parental love incarnate! Were I that old fox—what if Tokiko and Shigemori were trapped like this? Even the beast can rise above itself—could I as much?"

Kiyomori swung his bow round and let his arrow fly at a single star that shone in the darkened sky.

A movement like a gust stirred the grass at his feet, and then all grew still. He looked down; the foxes were gone.

On his way home Kiyomori stopped outside the ragged hedge of the armor-maker's house. He shouted at the humpbacked figure moving across the path of light cast by a small lamp: "Good man, good man, I want no foxskins for my armor! Use anything you like. I'll explain later on. Come tomorrow and penalize me in whatever way you will."

The pungent odor of boiling glue rose in the air as a humped shadow came out on the veranda with a steaming caldron. "What! You don't want your armor? What did you mean by that promise of yours? I tell you I've stayed up for two days and nights like a fool, boiling this glue! So you shot at the Shrine as a joke, did you? So I was mistaken in Lord Aki! Do you think I will make armor for anyone that has made a fool of me? I refuse—I absolutely refuse to do any work for you!—Here, you wild dogs, come and eat this stuff!"

The vessel of hot glue suddenly flew through the air and dropped at Kiyomori's feet. Steam and the smell of glue choked him and he turned on his heel and made his way home glumly.

Soon after, in November, the ban against Kiyomori was lifted, and he returned to his duties at the Palace. A few days before this happened, however, a visitor appeared at the servants' gate, begging tearfully for a word with the master.

"I have no right to ask to see Lord Aki, but . . ."

Oshimaro, the armor-maker, was shown into the house. His humped back was bent over even farther, and he refused to look up. "My lord, I beg you to forget my hasty words that day—the caprice of a foolish old master craftsman—" Beads of sweat broke out on the old man's wrinkled brow.

"And what is the trouble now, good man?" Kiyomori laughed, as he asked for an explanation of the visit.

"In a fit of temper I threw a caldron of glue at you, sir, and called you names, but I overheard one of your retainers telling about your unsuccessful hunting trip that day and I was overcome with shame when I heard what you did out of compassion for mere animals. As a master armor-maker, I beg you to let me make you a new suit of armor. Not only must a warrior be strong with his bow, but he must have a heart full of pity like yours for all living creatures. One who makes armor for such a warrior cannot but put his heart and soul into his task.—To tell you the truth, sir, I have brought the armor you ordered with me today. Will you not look at it and allow me to present it to you?"

There was no trace of condescension in Oshimaro's manner now; no words in praise of his own handiwork. The look of delight in Kiyomori's face seemed to be sufficient reward for him and he soon hobbled off.

Kiyomori basked in his regained freedom. One evening upon his return home, he stepped into his wife's room, and there found a lute he had never seen before. Tokiko explained that the lute was a gift from Lady Kii, who had sent it by a priest that same afternoon. She went on to relate that the priest had stayed for a while to talk and congratulated her repeatedly on having such a fine husband. Tokiko had protested, she said, with smiles, but curious as to the reasons for such praise of Lord Aki, she had pressed Lady Kii's messenger to talk further and discovered that Oshimaro, the armor-maker, had gone about telling people of Kiyomori and the foxes. The story had finally reached Shinzei; moved by this account of Kiyomori's compassion, Shinzei had brought out a treasured lute that had been his mother's, and had asked his friend the priest to take it to Kiyomori as a token of his regard. The priest then told Tokiko that the foxes were messengers of the Goddess of Mercy and Love, and that by sparing the foxes Kiyomori had gained merit. Shinzei, the priest added, had also expressed his belief in the goodness of Lord Aki. After his rambling talk the priest had left with a blessing on the lady of the house and her husband.

Kiyomori took up the lute, turned it over several times on his lap to examine it.

"A very fine lute," he finally remarked.

Tokiko replied: "There must be a signature on it somewhere."

"Here—"

"It says 'Wind in the Fields.' "

The lute was embellished with a design of wild flowers in gold lacquer, and a poem by Shinzei to his dead mother was inscribed in the intricate pattern.

"Tokiko, can you play this?"

"Tokitada is an even more accomplished musician than I, I'm sure."

"Eh, I didn't know that Tokitada had such talent. Well then, let me play you something. For all my unpolished ways you may not believe it, but when I was only eight, I took part in the singing and dancing of the sacred dramas at Gion. My mother, the Lady of Gion, loved such showy affairs."

As he spoke, Kiyomori felt a twinge at the heart. Where was she now—his mother, that fox-woman, she who could not even compare with that noble vixen? Would that she were alive, and unhurt. Surely she could no longer be beautiful—she must now be in her forties. Where was she now? Had some man wounded and abandoned her in a corner of the world? . . . Kiyomori was at a loss to explain the emotions that welled up from unknown depths and seemed to flood over him. His heart ached. As though to still the pain, he pressed the lute to him and hummed softly, running a finger down the four strings in a tinkling cascade of sound.

"Now what is that tune?" Tokiko laughed.

"Oh, you may not recognize it. It is—it is the 'Song of a Mortal' from the *Manyoshu*," he joked solemnly, though his lashes glistened moistly as he spoke.

CHAPTER XII

THE DEAD SPEAK

Fujiwara Tsunemuné, a courtier of the Third Rank, was a young man of considerable accomplishments. Though a nobleman, he was not altogether effete, for the society of which he was a member was not only the hub of politics, but the center of the intellectual life of his day, and of the younger courtiers he seemed to concentrate in himself all the outward excellences of a triumphant aristocracy. Fastidious and elegant in appearance, as he was in manner and address, Tsunemuné had the tastes of a scholar and a wide reading of the classics; an accomplished writer of verse, a skilled player of the aristocratic game of football, and a talented musician, he possessed above all an awareness of the fluctuating currents in court life.

On a day that Tsunemuné had accepted a court chamberlain's invitation to attend a game of football, the Regent Tadamichi's secretary appeared in one of the imperial pavilions and quietly informed Tsunemuné that the Regent wished to speak to him. Tsunemuné accompanied the secretary to an arbor-house set apart on an islet surrounded by waterlilies.

It was early summer—June of the year 1149. The child-Emperor Konoye was to celebrate his eleventh birthday soon, and his advisers were preparing for his enthronement. The question of selecting a consort for him had become urgent, for it was only fitting that the young ruler should attend the Great Thanksgiving Service at his crowning with the future empress. The Cloistered Emperor Toba had for some time given the matter careful thought; rumors had already spread as to where the choice might fall, and every acceptable branch of the Fujiwara with marriageable daughters was fiilled with the hope that this supreme honor might come its way. The choice was to be made in utmost secrecy and with every consideration of how it might affect the delicate balance of politics. History had shown that an ill-advised choice could embroil the Court in plots and even plunge the country into war.

At no time did the duties of his office weigh more heavily on the Regent than now. For many months he had given the problem painstaking thought and he had finally arrived at a decision. Considered in every possible light, his selection of Tadako, the daughter of the Minister of the Left, seemed unassailable; though only eleven—scarcely more than a child—her natural gifts and already exquisite beauty destined her, he believed, for that high role which he had in mind for her. One obstacle, however, stood in the way of making the choice known. Tadako was his brother Yorinaga's foster-daughter. No love was lost between brothers so dissimilar in character, and Tadamichi, unwilling to swallow

his pride, hesitated to acquaint Yorinaga with a choice to which
the Cloistered Emperor had already given his consent. It disquieted him to think of the truculence with which Yorinaga was
certain to receive this highly welcome announcement, and in his
perplexity it occurred to him to send Tsunemuné as his deputy,
this courtier whose tact and patience could be trusted to smooth
down any awkwardness that might arise. The football game, therefore, presented Tadamichi with a chance to call Tsunemuné to
him and divulge his plan.

Tsunemuné listened to the Regent with elation. The task
pleased him by its importance. It also opened up to him the possibilities of furthering his position at Court. And after setting a
day on which he would return with Yorinaga's answer, Tsunemuné departed.

Tsunemuné's meeting with Yorinaga began unpropitiously.
The Minister ventured no comment beyond a guarded "So Tadako is asked to become the empress?" This was followed by a
wry smile. After some desultory talk Tsunemuné's oblique attempts to elicit a reply were rewarded.

At length Yorinaga asked: "Is this urgent? Does this call for
an immediate answer?"

Assured that this was the Cloistered Emperor's desire,
Yorinaga pressed Tsunemuné for the reasons that prevented the
Regent from coming in person. Explanations that state affairs kept
Tadamichi at Court did not satisfy him, but Yorinaga finally said:
"I have no objections to Tadako's being made the empress, but I
exact a promise that she will be proclaimed the consort at the Emperor's crowning; I will not have her installed at Court as a mere
concubine. I must otherwise refuse. There must be absolute assurances that she will be made the empress."

Yorinaga's answer was laid before the Cloistered Emperor
and the Regent and accepted. Tadako shortly after was admitted
to the Court. Before many months had elapsed, however, the
Regent was dismayed when the Cloistered Emperor commanded
him to replace Tadako by another, the nineteen-year-old Shimeko,
a favorite of Lady Bifukumon, who had for a number of years seen

to the training and upbringing of this maid-in-waiting, planning that the young girl, whom she had come to love as her own daughter, should become her son Konoyé's consort. On learning that Tadako had been chosen without consulting her wishes, Lady Bifukumon bitterly chided her husband, the Cloistered Emperor, and prevailed on him to yield to her demands.

Yorinaga's rage and mortification when he heard this were extreme. He saw his chances for power and honor slipping away. Determined that his will should prevail over even that of the Cloistered Emperor, he turned to his father for support.

Fujiwara Tadazané, Yorinaga's father, was seventy-two years of age and for some years had lived in retirement at his villa in Byodo-in at Uji. As the oldest of the Fujiwara courtiers, he still wielded an influence that was not inconsiderable, for not only was he related to the imperial house on his mother's side, but one of his daughters had been the Cloistered Emperor's first consort. His career had been an enviable one. He had served two successive rulers with honor, and had occupied some of the highest posts in the government. Even in retirement he enjoyed the pomp and ceremony befitting one of great eminence, and notables from the capital continued to visit him at his villa. Tadazané, despite all the qualities that made him a successful courtier, possessed a weakness which seemed to negate all that he stood for; he loved his youngest son, Yorinaga, to a fault, and by some curious discordance of temperaments was bitterly hostile to his eldest, Tadamichi, the Regent.

Yorinaga's sudden arrival at the villa in Uji caused Tadazané's thin eyelids to twitch under the white brows. He listened to his son in silence. But the sight of his son's misery and dejection finally made him draw up his thin frame, as though he were summoning up his last reserves of strength, and he said at last: "Come, you must not let this disturb you too much. I am not too far gone in years that I cannot intercede with his majesty for you. I will go myself and see that matters are set right. Today I shall make an exception and ride alongside you to the capital."

Matters were not so easy as Tadazané had expected. On one

pretext or another he was refused an audience with the Cloistered Emperor; his letters were returned unanswered; a fortnight
went by and he found he had made no headway. At last, at the
courtier Tsunemune's urgings, Tadazané agreed to a meeting with
the Regent, from whom Tsunemuné obtained the promise of an
audience. Still another month went by with no sign of the promised meeting; until, utterly worn and heartsick, Tadazané returned
to Uji.

Winter came. December and the year were drawing to a close.
Only a few days remained before the entire Court suspended its
customary occupations for the elaborate ceremonials ushering in
the New Year, when Yorinaga once more appeared at Uji, distraught. Shimeko had been formally admitted to the Court, and
the last opportunity for pressing Tadako's claim, he said, was slipping away.

Tadazané roused his housemen and servants at dawn. The
oxen's breath hung like white wreaths in the morning air as Tadazané's carriage rumbled over the frozen road to Kyoto. It was not
until nightfall that he reached the Palace courtyard, where only the
Guards' watch-fires shed any light. Pelting hail sprayed upward
from the cavernous eaves; shutters were rolled back and doors
thrown open to admit Tadazané. He was conducted to an anteroom, and there he waited, utter despair in every line of his face.
He had come prepared to wait until death itself intervened. The
icy hours dragged by in a bitter contest of wills: pride, love, vain-
glory, infatuation. The monarch at last relented and appeared.
Besieged by the tears and entreaties of aging Tadazané, he was
forced to give in.

On New Year's Day, Tadako was proclaimed the Empress-
elect, and in March she stood crowned beside the child-Emperor.

The Regent, who found the torrid heat in July intolerable,
retired to his villa outside Kyoto and was rarely seen at Court.
Yorinaga, however, was indefatigable, concentrating his tireless
energies on the numerous minutiæ of his office. His brisk appearances in the various departments of the government struck terror

into the hearts of the minor officials and left the courtiers exhausted and more languid than ever. As a close relative of the young Empress, Yorinaga was aware of the exalted position he now occupied, and he applied himself diligently to the affairs of government, fully confident of the fruits he would gather from his labors. As the adviser to the boy-Emperor he now displaced in fact, if not in name, the Regent, his own brother, and a faction was now developing in his train. The preference he gave the Genji over the Heiké at Court also was evident. He had recently dispatched Tameyoshi of the Genji instead of Kiyomori to negotiate with the fighting monks of Nara when they threatened to march on the capital with their armed thousands.

Tadazané, long past the age for active duty, once more appeared at Court, where he now served as an honorary minister; all his efforts were now spent in support of Yorinaga; secretly determined that nothing should be left undone, Tadazané intimated to the Cloistered Emperor that Tadamichi's health and abilities made him unsuitable for carrying out the duties of a regent. But when he heard that Tadamichi refused to resign out of fear that Yorinaga would cause strife and bloodshed, Tadazané in rage went to the archives of the Imperial Academy, where the family records and the great seal of the Fujiwara were kept. These he removed and placed in Yorinaga's keeping to signify that he disowned his eldest son, Tadamichi, and he appointed Yorinaga as his heir and successor.

In 1151 the boy-Emperor Konoyé became thirteen. At about this time he began to have trouble with his eyes, which he constantly kept covered with pads of red silk. The Regent, Tadamichi, for whom the young ruler had developed a strong attachment, found a skilled physician, one lately returned from China, and sent him to attend the Emperor. The Emperor's increasing distress touched Tadamichi, who visited him often and sought by kind words to console him. The spectacle of this frail boy, immured from birth in sunless palace rooms, prisoner to his sovereign position, the victim and pawn of savage rivalries that surrounded him, moved Tadamichi to deep pity. He could not help thinking how the young ruler's life was far from a happy one. Hedged about by rigid court rituals, what did he know of the abandon and joys of a carefree boyhood? When had he ever played in the winter snows; whistled in the springtime when every tree broke into blossom; splashed like the water imps in the summer rivers, and basked under the hot sun; or climbed the hills in autumn and shouted from their tops until his lungs were stretched to bursting? It was doubtful, however, that Tadamichi ever reflected that he himself was one of those who had helped create this pallid figure of pathos.

On the 24th of July 1155, the Emperor Konoyé died in his seventeenth year. His reign had lasted less than five years. The people mourned for him. His father, the Cloistered Emperor, was struck down with grief, and Lady Bifukumon was inconsolable.

Soon after the boy-Emperor's death a strange tale was brought to Lady Bifukumon by one of her ladies-in-waiting, Lady Kii, the wife of Councilor Shinzei. She had heard a chilling story from one of her serving-women, who said she had heard it from a wandering friar. The Emperor Konoyé had died unnaturally. Some persons unknown had invoked the death-curse against him and brought about his untimely end. Almost a year before, she was told, the friar had himself seen the evil rites performed in a lonely shrine on Mount Atago. Lady Bifukumon was horrified and distraught by what Lady Kii told her, and ordered her to send at once for a medium—Yasura of Shin-kumano Shrine.

The medium arrived and for a long while was wrapped in meditation. Suddenly a violent trembling came over her; she shook free her long hair as the spirit of the dead Emperor took possession of her and spoke through her mouth: " . . . A spell was cast over me. Spikes were hammered into the Tengu Demon's image in Mount Atago Shrine. I was blinded by them. They caused me to die. Ah . . . woe is me!" When the voice ceased, Yasura fell to the floor and lay unconscious. Lady Bifukumon shrieked loudly in horror and, clutching wildly at her robes, abandoned herself to a paroxysm of weeping so violent that her distressed gentlewomen grew afraid and called loudly for water and restoratives as they carried her away to her bedchamber.

The medium meanwhile came to herself and departed as though nothing unusual had happened, clasping in her arms a cloth bundle in which were the various paraphernalia of her profession and some gifts that Lady Kii had given her. As Yasura stepped out by one of the rear gates, she paused to peer into her bundle and with a pleased air drew from it an appetizing morsel that smelled like roasted duck meat; greedily stuffing it into her mouth, she turned to go home, thoughtfully chewing, when she noticed some dogs following her, and stooped to sweep up some stones to fling at them. One of the missiles struck the wheel of a passing cart; the young workman pulling it came to a stop and hailed Yasura familiarly:

"Well, Yasura, on your way home?"

The medium approached him with a coy air and stopped to chat in low tones, sharing with him another tidbit from her bundle. When they had finished eating, he helped her onto his cart and once more continued in the direction of Shin-kumano Shrine.

Two years earlier, in January 1153, Kiyomori's father, Tadamori of the Heiké, died suddenly after a few weeks of illness brought on by a cold. He was then fifty-eight. In the last years of his life Tadamori had accomplished little, for those years also marked Yorinaga's rise to power and his open favoring of Tameyoshi of the Genji and his sons. It was not likely that any Heiké would forget that it was Yorinaga who had once demanded the death penalty for Kiyomori in the trial following the desecration of the Sacred Shrine, and it also stood to reason that the Minister would give the Heiké no quarter. Yet Kiyomori showed no sign of resenting Yorinaga's partiality for the Genji. Utterly bereft, Kiyomori felt in his loneliness that the supporting pillar of his life had been torn away. And before he had time to recover from his grief, Kiyomori found new anxieties crowding on him. Not only did he have numerous sons of his own, but the guardianship of his younger brothers and half-brothers was now his. As the young chieftain of the clan, he had much to learn, for the future of the Heiké was in his hands.

Shortly after the boy-Emperor's death, Councilor Shinzei summoned Kiyomori to him. Kiyomori, after Tadamori's death, had come to regard Shinzei, his senior in age and rank, as a friend and a source of solace and strength. Not only did he consider the Councilor his benefactor, the man to whom he owed his life, but he counted on Shinzei as the single protecting influence between the Heiké and Yorinaga, the Minister of the Left. He was certain that Yorinaga, with all his singleness of purpose, was no match for the shrewd Councilor, for Shinzei was inscrutable and let no man into his thoughts. There were depths in him that no one had yet dared to explore; he excelled in the discharge of the delicate functions of his office—no easy task for most men—demanding no recognition and quietly persevering in his duties year after year.

In the privacy of Shinzei's office Kiyomori was entrusted with a curious and secret mission.

"Grave issues are involved. This is urgent. Any indiscretion on your part may rouse the suspicions of Yorinaga and Tameyoshi of the Genji—to your undoing. Wait until sundown, then send out your men one by one," Shinzei said, repeating his warning.

That night a band of some fifty warriors left the capital and started toward the hills northwest of Kyoto, a good distance beyond the city gates. They were soon making their way swiftly up the slopes of Mount Atago, converging on one of the crags, where they met to take counsel. Shortly afterward they were again on their way, in search of Jomyo, chief priest of Mount Atago. Arrived at his gates, they pounded loudly, calling for admittance.

"We come from the Cloister Palace, soldiers of Kiyomori of the Heiké, Lord Aki. We have reports that someone has tampered with the Tengu Demon in the main shrine here and brought the death-curse on the late Emperor. The Cloistered

Emperor orders Lord Aki to make a search and obtain evidence.
Lead us to the shrine. Refuse, and you will be guilty of resisting
an imperial order!"

A sound of confused movements arose within; then Jomyo
himself appeared and spoke to Kiyomori. "If you come on his
majesty's business, you bear papers. Permit me to see them."

"Ho, you there, kneel!"

As Jomyo came to his knees, Kiyomori thrust the official
writ at him.

"There is no mistake about it—I cannot refuse. The doors
will be opened immediately. This way, your lordship." Calling
for more torches, Jomyo led the way toward the shrine. His
shadow loomed up gigantic against the sanctuary doors. A key
grated harshly in the lock. Great tongues of flame undulated eerily, lighting up the cavernous interior, and there in front of
Kiyomori towered an image of the Tengu Demon, a spike pro-
truding from either eye.

"What—spikes!" Kiyomori gasped, as did Jomyo and the
others who craned over their shoulders.

There was nothing more to do. Kiyomori had seen that for
which he had been sent. It was uncanny and the sight made his
flesh creep. He had always scoffed at stories of witchcraft, but
this—! A cold shiver ran down his spine.

"Good. This shall be reported at once." Kiyomori turned
away, shaken by what he had seen. The doors were secured and
Kiyomori's seal affixed. Ordering the greater part of his soldiers
to stay behind on guard, Kiyomori rode that same night back to
Kyoto and to Shinzei.

For an instant Shinzei's eyes seemed to bulge from their
sockets as Kiyomori related what he had seen; then he relapsed
into his usual composure, remarking: "As I thought. . . ."

It was Lady Bifukumon who had urged the Cloistered Emperor to send Kiyomori and his soldiers to Mount Atago, and
who carefully imparted her belief that Yorinaga and his father
had caused the young Emperor's death by witchcraft. She furthermore warned him against these two, whom she said had de-

signs on the throne. In due course two hermits appeared at the Palace as witnesses and described the evil rites they had seen performed by some wandering friars. Where these friars had gone no one knew, for they had vanished like the summer clouds, they said. And not long after, Yorinaga and his father were forbidden the Cloister Palace.

In the meantime the question of selecting a new emperor had become urgent, and Yorinaga and his father were mystified when they found themselves barred from the high councils. The reason for their sudden fall from grace soon became clear to them, but when they declared their innocence in letters to the Cloistered Emperor, their pleas for a hearing came back unanswered through Councilor Shinzei's office. Nothing they did seemed to soften Toba's displeasure.

Between the lattices of one of the Palace windows an official watched father and son enter their carriages and drive away for the last time. Shinzei smiled sardonically; had they known, they would have watched their steps more closely; Yorinaga had never had cause to suspect that this silent figure, hunched over his desk for years, was his bitterest enemy. Nor did the Minister know that this man's wife, Lady Kii, was Lady Bifukumon's confidante.

Shinzei broke into soundless laughter. "See, my fine demons —doesn't it hurt? A spike in the right eye and one in the left? Who is to tell you that it was I, Shinzei, who did this?"

CHAPTER XIII

THE WILLOW-SPRING PALACE

For close to fourteen years the existence of a certain man had almost been forgotten. This was the ex-Emperor Su-toku, who, forced to abdicate when he was twenty-three, had gone to live at the Palace of the Willow Spring with only a small retinue. Those years were spent in the practice of various religious devotions in his private chapel, in reading, and the writing of poetry. It was also his habit to stroll unaccompanied through the Palace park and to rest in the shade of a giant willow tree that grew beside a bubbling spring. This spring, renowned for the sweetness and purity of its waters, had been there even before Kyoto had been founded, people said, and in times long forgotten a willow tree had sprung up beside it. The waters of the Willow Spring, as it came to be called, were kept only for the ex-Emperor's table, and a caretaker lived in a small lodge near by.

As he stood under the giant willow one day, Sutoku called to the guardian of the spring: "I thirst—bring me water."

The caretaker quickly appeared, carrying a newly baked clay bowl, which he filled with the sparkling water.

"Sweetness itself—like the dew from heaven," the ex-Emperor said, handing back the empty vessel and seating himself on a stone in the willow tree's shade. The caretaker brought a freshly woven reed mat, which he spread for his visitor.

Then Sutoku said: "You seem contented, caretaker. How long is it since you came here?"

"I have watched for fourteen years over this spring, your majesty, for I was with your housemen when you came to live here."

"Fourteen years! And what did you do before that?"

"My father was a court musician and taught me from childhood to play on the flute and flageolet; at ten I was sent to the Palace Academy of Music, and when I was fourteen I performed for the first time before your majesty. It was an honor I shall never forget. Then came your abdication at the end of that year."

"Then you and your father before you are not of the common people, for there are only four families in this capital admitted to that calling."

"My father was Abé Torihiko, a musician of the Sixth Rank."

"And your name?"

"I—" the caretaker bowed low—"I am called Asatori."

Sutoku's eyes settled in wonder on the bowed head before him. "What made you leave your calling—your father—to become a mere caretaker of this spring?"

Asatori shook his head in denial. "No, this is no menial task, sir, for water is the very source of life, and to guard this spring which quenches your majesty's thirst is no mean calling. My father long ago gave your majesty lessons on various instruments, and was a favorite of Lady Bifukumon. Though musicians, we are needy folk, so when the time came to celebrate my coming of age, some of your robes were sent to me for a gift; these were made into my ceremonial suit, so I was turned out like a fine young gentleman. I shall remember that for the rest of my life!"

"Oh, did such a thing ever happen?"

"Your majesty would not recall such favors to your humble subjects, but my father never forgot them. When the time of your abdication came, I shall never forget how he said: 'Asatori, it will not be possible for me to follow his majesty, but you are only a pupil at the academy and may go wherever you choose. Follow his majesty and serve him loyally in my stead. I have other sons to carry on our name and our calling.' He then gave me a flute as a parting gift, and I came with you here and have watched over this spring ever since."

Sutoku, who had been listening closely with bent head and closed eyes, looked up, smiling faintly as Asatori ended his narration. "Your flute—do you have it here with you now?"

"It is put away carefully in a case made from a strip of one of the robes your majesty sent me, and has become a keepsake from my father."

"Keepsake? But your father must still be living."

"No, that flute is now a memento. My father is no longer in this world, and, since it was his last wish that I stay with you, I shall remain here until the sources of this spring run dry."

"Ah—" sighed Sutoku heavily as he rose to his feet. His mother, Lady Taikenmon, too, was dead. How fleeting was man and all things of this world, he mused. "One of these nights when the moon is full, you shall play to me on your flute. How cool this air! Asatori, I shall come again soon."

Asatori's eyes followed Sutoku as he vanished among the trees. This chance meeting and the artless moments of talk with one whom he otherwise dared not approach filled him with delight. Through the summer nights Asatori waited for the moon to grow full, recalling Sutoku's promise to listen to him on his flute.

About this time people who passed the Willow-Spring Palace began to notice with curiosity how numerous litters and carriages arrived at the long-neglected Palace. There were rumors that the young Emperor Konoyé had not long to live, and that the dethroned Sutoku's son, Prince Shigebito, the Cloistered Emperor Toba's grandson, would ascend the throne. Among the many visitors who came to call on the ex-Emperor were Yorinaga and his father, Tadazané, who until now had ignored Sutoku's existence. They came with repeated assurances that good things were in store for him, that his son was all but crowned. And the prospect of renewed prosperity and the resurrection of his hopes led Sutoku to forget his promise to the caretaker of the Willow Spring.

Asatori gazed forlornly at the full moon and waited for the monarch, who did not come. He watched the coming and going of litters and carriages, and grew anxious, for the Willow Spring lost its sparkle and grew muddy—portent of some upheaval in nature, or the forerunner of calamity.

Popular expectations were disappointed when in October the Cloistered Emperor's fourth son, Sutoku's younger brother, was proclaimed Emperor and invested as Goshirakawa. Sutoku was overwhelmed. His own son, who stood in direct line of succession, had been passed over. Lady Bifukumon, he felt certain, had played no small part in influencing the Cloistered Emperor's choice, and he, Sutoku, had been singled out for her ill will. There was little consolation to be found in Yorinaga's words: "Patience—and yet more patience. Your time will yet come."

The new reign opened in April 1156. By summer of that same year the rule of the Cloister Government, which had lasted uninterrupted for twenty-seven years, was over. Toba died at the Detached Palace of Anrakuju-in Temple on the night of July 2. News of his approaching end reached the capital that same afternoon, and a vast flurry ensued as litters and carriages jostled one another in their haste to reach the hamlet of Takeda, on whose outskirts the temple stood. In the tangled concourse of fast-trotting animals and shouting, sweating men, one carriage forced its way through and rolled swiftly onward. Behind the drawn blinds of his tossing carriage, Sutoku concealed a face drawn with grief.

Carriages were drawn up, inside as well as outside the Palace gates. There was no room to spare even in the wide enclosure fronting the Palace, so crowded was it with men-at-arms, attendants, and litters. A hush hung like a pall over everything. No aides came to meet Sutoku's carriage, and his grooms were obliged to call out loudly to announce his arrival. Sutoku feverishly rolled up a blind, crying sharply to his grooms: "Let me down, let me down, I say!"

Even as his carriage rolled in by the gateway, the solemn booming of temple and pagoda bells had ceased. He caught the sound of intaken breaths and the murmur: "His majesty's eyes are now closing—" Sutoku saw the quick movement of men dropping to their knees, the lifting of hands in prayer, and he was overcome with grief. It was not a monarch who was dying, but his own father! Those long years of bitterness—the estrangement —one last meeting would be enough to wipe away that.

"Let me down, I say! What's this senseless confusion? Pull up at the door—hurry!"

At the sound of that frenzied command, the grooms wrenched the carriage round and forced a way through the welter of vehicles. As the carriage pulled up at the portico, a wheel struck a litter that stood by, crushing it with a harsh rending sound. At this, Akanori of the Genji and several other warriors who stood on guard at the door leaped forward cursing.

Livid, Sutoku cried out in his anger: "Out of my way, insolent ones! Can you not see who I am? How dare you interfere!"

Akanori advanced with a threatening air. "Now that I see who you are, I have even more reason to forbid you to come any farther. I have orders not to admit you. Back! Back!"

Beside himself, Sutoku now leaned out of his carriage. "What,

you petty official! I am here to see his majesty, my father, yet
no one comes to meet me, and they dare to send mere soldiers
to carry out their orders!"

"My orders are from Korekata, Captain of the Right, who
serves his majesty. A warrior must do his duty. You shall not go
a step farther!"

"I'll have no dealings with you wretches. . . ." Trembling
with rage, Sutoku prepared to step down from his carriage when
the Guards charged at the carriage and thrust it back; Sutoku's
grooms leaped on the soldiers to grapple with them; at the im-
pact the carriage lurched; Sutoku, clutching for a blind, was
thrown to the ground between the carriage shafts. A blind came
away in his hand as he fell and crashed heavily across the shafts,
lacerating Akanori's cheek, from which the blood suddenly oozed.

Those in the Palace were quickly told that the ex-Emperor
Sutoku had gone mad, wounded a Guard, and was now on his
way to the inner apartments. Korekata, the Captain of the Right,
who was sitting beside Councilor Shinzei when the news of the
scuffle was brought to him, started from his seat. A frightened
scream from one of the ladies-in-waiting made him fly down the
long corridors. As he approached the entrance, a shaft of light
from one of the anterooms lit up a pillar in the hall, and there
he came face to face with Sutoku. His face was a pale mask; his
eyes stared unseeing; his sleeve was torn, and his hair straggled
wildly across his forehead.

The captain's hands shot out in a gesture of refusal. "Sir—
you may not enter," he cried, blocking the way. "You must not
be seen in your present condition. I beg you to leave very quietly."

Sutoku seemed not to understand and brushed Korekata's
arms aside roughly. "Out of the way! I must see him now—at
once!"

"Sir, can you not understand that you may not see him?"

"I—I don't understand—Korekata! What is wrong in my
wanting to see my dying father? You are a fiend to interfere!
Out—out of my way!"

Korekata's voice rose to a shout as he restrained the distraught Sutoku. "You are mad, I tell you! Whatever you say, you shall not see him!"

Sutoku suddenly broke into a terrible sobbing as he struggled to shake off the captain's restraining arms, but the latter called some Guards, who soon dragged Sutoku away weeping and struggling and forced him into his carriage.

The luminous interior of the Temple was swallowed up in billows of incense; in mournful unison gongs sounded a dirge; one thousand priests bowed their heads silently as the spirit of Toba departed from this world.

Before the short summer night was over, a rumor swept through the Palace at Takeda like a gathering wave. The whisper went from ear to ear: The ex-Emperor is forming a conspiracy. . . . Incredible? There had been signs of it beforehand—a report from the Guard Office confirmed it. The Tanaka Villa, on the opposite bank of the river from the Detached Palace, where Sutoku was staying, was suspect. Since the Hour of the Boar (ten o'clock) a meeting appeared to have been held there. From another source in the capital came a report that on the previous afternoon, horses and carts piled with weapons were seen making their way at irregular intervals to the Willow-Spring Palace. Eyewitnesses recounted seeing frightened groups of women and children, with household goods, hurrying at midday toward the Northern and Eastern Hills. The avenues of the capital were as deserted as a city of death at midnight. . . .

Yorinaga's disappearance from among the mourners in the death-chamber left no room for doubt. Not only he, but Tsunemuné, Tadazané, and others known to be in sympathy with Sutoku were missing. It was clear that a plot was under way.

Until the seventh day of strict mourning was over, the gates of the Detached Palace and the Tanaka Villa were closed to all comers, nor was anyone seen to go out. When night came, however, figures in various disguises crept out from either side to reconnoiter.

On the second day of mourning Yorinaga left the courtiers surrounding the bier with the excuse that urgent matters recalled him to Uji. As he settled back in his carriage, he raged: "There they sit at the wake, whispering of plots, shedding tears while their eyes search each other suspiciously, concealing their treachery behind a solemn show of chanting priests! Who can abide drowning in that sea of mock tears?"

Under cover of darkness Yorinaga's carriage made its way from the Detached Palace to the Tanaka Villa, where he stole in to meet the ex-Emperor Sutoku.

"Never has such a thing been heard of—a son forbidden to see his dying father! I know too well how you suffer. Even now I left the new Emperor surrounded by Lady Bifukumon and those evil ones. Never has the throne been the prey of more evil advisers," said Yorinaga, lifting his eyes to Sutoku's.

At Yorinaga's words something flared up in Sutoku's brooding eyes. "Yorinaga—Yorinaga, you are the only man I dare trust!" Sutoku cried. The tears poured down his cheeks unchecked.

"I—my son—we are the rightful heirs to the throne, and yet we have been thrust aside—buried alive. The people expect me to ascend the throne once more. . . . Yorinaga, is this not so?"

Yorinaga's eyes were closed, as though he was meditating. The answer was ready. He had kept it for some time in his own breast. Who was to tell Sutoku that the words issuing from his own lips were no more than the substance of Yorinaga's own ambitions?

Sighing loudly, Yorinaga finally spoke. "It is all a matter of time. When your majesty decides that the time has come, that will be the moment decreed by the gods. To reject that which the gods offer is to anger them. There have been other monarchs who regained the throne, and what reason have you to hesitate?"

Yorinaga was supremely confident. Not only did he have the time-honored *Book of Stratagems* by heart, but he was certain, too, of his hold over Tameyoshi of the Genji.

That night Yorinaga revealed the plot by which Sutoku was to regain the throne. From the Palace across the river came

courtiers and officers who had received their instructions from
Yorinaga. The conspirators conferred all night and into the next
day, setting the stage for a war, and as the assembling of troops
here would excite suspicion and hamper their movements, Yorinaga soon left for Uji to pursue the next step in his plans.

At sunrise the great temple bells boomed. The seven days
of mourning were over. All day long until sundown the bells
sounded, and the unending chant of sutras mingled oddly with
the whinnying of horses. The gates of Tanaka Villa, however,
remained closed. Sutoku did not appear even at sundown for
the rites marking the end of strict mourning, and Councilor Norinaga heard the murmurs against Sutoku grow louder. Fearing that
the rumored plot was true, he quickly took horse to the bedside of
his ailing brother, a high-ranking court officer, to ask for advice.

Painfully rousing himself, Norinaga's brother said: "As you
can see, I am in no condition to seek an audience with the ex-
Emperor and to dissuade him. I doubt even then that there would
be any use. It may be too late, but I advise you to return quickly
and urge his majesty to take the tonsure at once; that at least will
insure his personal safety. We ourselves will not be able to escape
this disaster."

On arriving back at Tanaka Villa, Norinaga was alarmed at
finding Sutoku and his entourage hurriedly preparing to leave for
the Shirakawa Palace, near the capital. At once he sought to dissuade the ex-Emperor.

"Your majesty, it will be unseemly for you to leave before the
forty-nine days of lesser mourning are over. Moreover, there are
rumors that you are conspiring against the throne, and your departure at this time will only confirm what people are saying. . . ."

But Sutoku, smiling, waved Norinaga aside, saying that he
had been warned in secret that his life was in danger. While he
was speaking, troops of heavily armed warriors arrived to escort
him, and Norinaga was ordered to accompany the suite. Late that
starless night of July 9 began the slow march for Shirakawa.

Torches were not lighted as the procession started on its way to the creak and grind of heavy carriage wheels and the clanging of arms in the dark.

Soon after the ex-Emperor left the Willow-Spring Palace, a band of armed warriors arrived there and took possession of it. Asatori, the caretaker, watched them, dismayed. Their horses fouled the white-sanded courtyard, and soldiers made free with the Palace, stalking roughshod through the great halls and chambers, looting the storehouses for food, and even breaking into the women's quarters, from which came the frightened screams of the occupants. When, however, the soldiers, shouting coarsely, stripped to bathe in the Willow Spring, and drank from the well-bucket, Asatori could no longer contain himself.

"Sirs—if you please, you will not use this spring."

"What's this? What do you mean by that, you wretch?" they bellowed, taking no more notice of him than if he were a scarecrow.

"This is the Willow Spring, which is only for his majesty's use. There is a well over there—and a stream. I beg you not to come here."

"And who are you to give orders?"

"I am the caretaker of the Willow Spring."

"Caretaker? Oh, so you watch this spring, eh?"

"It is my task to care for this spring and keep its waters clean. I guard this spring with my life."

The soldiers roared with laughter at Asatori's reply.

"Nonsense! Enough rain falls in the capital to fill your spring. I dare say his majesty doesn't drink so much as the Great Dragon and dry up this spring!"

"You are rude fellows. Who are you and who let you come here to make such disorder?"

"Disorder? Who is disorderly? We were sent here to guard the Palace. Our orders are from the Minister of the Left. Go ask the Minister himself."

"Do you mean Yorinaga, the Minister?"

"Yorinaga or whatever's his name—that's neither here nor

there, nor any business of ours. When the war starts there'll be no
Palace or Willow Spring, for that matter. Here's our chance to
turn out the storehouses and fill our bellies!"

Asatori reluctantly turned away. The sunlight glinting on their
halberds and swords made him tremble. This was no time to argue
with these churlish soldiers, who would fall on him without hesitation. There was nothing he could do except watch them from
afar. Soon he saw one of the warriors climb a tree and shade his
eyes, staring intently into the grounds of the Takamatsu Palace, a
short distance away. Something he saw caused the soldier to
scramble down in haste and three soldiers to leap to their horses
and gallop off.

Asatori leaned back against the trunk of the giant willow, full
of anxious thoughts for his master, the ex-Emperor. If war broke
out, what had he, Asatori, a humble caretaker, to give but his loyalty—his life? There was nothing he could do but stay and guard
the spring.

A summer breeze played among the long fringes of the willow; a green thread tossed gently to and fro, caressing Asatori's
cheek.

"There are not enough soldiers, not even enough for his majesty's protection," Councilor Shinzei remarked to the Regent.

Only the night before, there had been great excitement and
indignation when Lady Bifukumon's ladies-in-waiting had
screamed at discovering an owl-like figure hunched in the top of
a large hazel tree outside the window of their boudoir. Guards had
come running at the outcry and shot down with their strong-bows
some poor wretch—a young priest who confessed to watching the
ladies at their toilette.

"Something must be done," Shinzei said. "It is in times like
this that the warriors are most apt to be hatching plots. Is it not
about time to have those captains whom his late majesty recom-
mended set up here for our greater safety?"

The Regent did not reply at once. "It may be necessary. . . ."
If he seemed to hesitate, it was because his brother Yorinaga was

known to be one of Sutoku's supporters, and the Regent knew he must soon declare on which side he stood. Then he continued: "Councilor Shinzei, which captains do you suggest as bodyguards to the Emperor?"

"That—that was decided by his late majesty shortly before his decease. A list was drawn up and approved by him."

"I was not told that such a list had been made."

"It most certainly exists."

"When? Who has it now?"

"While his majesty was alive it was entrusted to the Captain of the Bodyguard of the Left and Fujiwara Mitsunaga. Following his majesty's decease, the document was given to Korekata, Captain of the Right, for safekeeping. I had intended to have Lady Bifukumon herself see it when the mourning period was over. His late majesty's wishes must be carried out exactly. Shall I suggest an audience with the Emperor?"

Tadamichi did not demur. "As I have said before, I have no objections whatever."

"The captain shall be told, as well as Lady Bifukumon."

On the fifth day after the Cloistered Emperor's death, Lady Bifukumon and the Emperor's advisers met to discuss the contents of the will. Though not so intended, the meeting was in fact a war council. Fearing a warriors' revolt after his death, Toba had taken the precaution of drawing up a list of ten Genji and Heiké captains as bodyguards to the new Emperor and Lady Bifukumon. Yoshitomo of the Genji, Tameyoshi's son, had been named chief of the ten captains.

One name, however, was conspicuously missing from the roll.

"Why has Lord Aki, Kiyomori of the Heiké, been omitted?" Shinzei interposed evenly, his eyes turned expectantly on Lady Bifukumon. "Tadamori of the Heiké was a familiar figure at the Court. His widow, Kiyomori's stepmother, Lady Ariko of Harima, I understand was once wet-nurse to the Crown Prince. His late majesty, I am sure, did not forget this."

Kiyomori was not entirely unknown to Lady Bifukumon, who had often heard Lady Kii speak of him, and she quickly replied:

"True, I was with his late majesty when he drew up this list. I was consulted on this same matter on another occasion, and his majesty seemed to feel that Kiyomori was to be trusted, but he also feared that Kiyomori's stepmother might enlist his sympathies on behalf of Prince Shigebito. That was why Kiyomori's name was omitted. He did say, however, that if Kiyomori had no commitments elsewhere, he should be appointed when the need arose. Yes—now I remember distinctly that those were his words."

Shinzei seized on Lady Bifukumon's words to conclude: "We have no reason to believe that Kiyomori is committed elsewhere. We must also remember that after the Gion affair, Yorinaga made himself Kiyomori's bitterest foe. There were slandering tales, too, which made even his majesty turn against Kiyomori for a time. It would be a great pity now to omit Kiyomori deliberately. And you, sir?" Shinzei said, motioning to Tadamichi. "What is your opinion?"

"At no time have I had any objections to Lord Aki. I bear him no ill will, neither do I wish to see him ignored."

"Shall we, then, include him—Kiyomori?"

"It appears advisable."

Another name was added to the roster of bodyguards for the Emperor Goshirakawa. All eleven captains were the heads of influential families, maintaining levies from their manorial estates. On the following day, the 8th of July, troops began arriving at Anrakuju-in Temple in such numbers that the grounds overflowed with soldiers. First to appear was Yoshitomo of the Genji and his soldiers, followed by the other captains and their men-at-arms. Last to arrive was a young warrior on horseback, and his contingent of two hundred horsemen. At the registering-office he announced his identity in a clear ringing voice:

"This is I—second son of Lord Aki, Kiyomori of the Heiké—Motomori of Aki, officer of the Fourth Rank, aged seventeen. My father received the imperial summons; mustering orders have gone out to all vassals in his domains and to those who have ancient ties with our house. He will arrive later with his troops. I have come in advance in his stead."

Those who turned to look saw a clear-eyed lad in leather armor dyed a deep blue and stippled in a fine pattern of saffron. He carried a full quiver of black-feathered arrows, and wore the cap of his rank; a helmet was slung at his back.

An exclamation of surprise escaped from some elderly warriors: "Oh! Is it possible that Kiyomori already has such a fine son?" Motomori's bearing reminded them not only of Kiyomori himself, but of the grandfather, Tadamori, and of the swift passing of the years.

CHAPTER XIV

THE RED BANNER OF THE HEIKÉ

Rokuhara, where Kiyomori had come to live so many years
ago, was no longer an isolated settlement on the edge of
Kyoto, but a small town swarming with the Heiké clan.
Kiyomori's eldest son, Shigemori, who had come here as a child,
was now eighteen. The lonely waste of field and swamps, across
which an occasional funeral and priests passed on their way to
Toribeno and the Kiyomizu Temple, had undergone a startling
change after the Gojo Bridge was built. The marshland had been

drained and the narrow twisting paths had given way to tree-lined roads. Wattled walls sprang up to enclose large dwelling-houses with great curving roofs; massive gates were interspersed among small houses that crowded one another in ever-increasing numbers. The larger residences, outcrops of Kiyomori's mansion, were occupied by members of his family and their retainers. A two-storied gate to admit horsemen led to Kiyomori's new and spacious mansion, whose grounds sloped down to the Kamo River. Ridge upon ridge extended out from the main roof until the central building was lost in a maze of roofs.

For two days warriors had been arriving on horseback from Kiyomori's distant fiefs and crowding the estate. Later arrivals were forced to bivouac in the open under the trees along the river, and still more troops kept rolling in like a tide. Many had come by forced marches or by riding day and night.

From Rokuhara, Motomori and his soldiers could be seen following the course of the river in a southerly direction; wild shouts and cheers were heard as the red banner of the Heiké floated above him and the heads of the slowly vanishing horsemen.

"What's that—the shouting?" Kiyomori turned to ask those about him.

"The honorable Motomori is now passing along the opposite bank of the river on his way to Uji."

"Ah, so that's it," Kiyomori replied shortly. Seven men were with him: Tokitada, his brother-in-law, now an under-secretary at the Court; his brother Tsunemori; Mokunosuké, his old retainer, and one of his sons; and three clansmen from Isé.

". . . A total of six hundred." Tokitada had just finished reading the list of warriors who had already arrived. "I expect there will be more by tomorrow morning at the latest, but so far six hundred and eighty-eight are accounted for."

Kiyomori asked Tokitada to read off the list of volunteers once more. The large room where they sat had wide corridors crossing one another on all four sides. One of Tokiko's serving-girls waited hesitantly in sight of the room and peered at the group anxiously.

"My lord," she finally ventured, "my mistress has sent me in great haste—"

"What does she want?" Kiyomori demanded impatiently.

"The honorable Motomori is passing along the river now and my lady begs you to watch him."

"What's this?"

"My lady wishes you to see him starting out on his first campaign."

"I have no time for such things. Tell the mistress that Motomori has not started on any cherry-viewing jaunt."

"Yes, my lord."

"Tell her to prepare herself with tears and weeping for that time when they send home his head."

The serving-girl fled as though she had been rebuked, and vanished down a passageway, suppressing her sobs.

Kiyomori's eyes followed the disappearing figure, and remarked dryly: "They don't know, these women—the savagery of war—they've never seen it. There's enough fighting going on all the time to the west and east, but it hasn't happened here for centuries. None of you know what war is. You're getting your first taste of it, and it won't be easy for any of us here."

A heavy silence met Kiyomori's words, for each man had been secretly thinking of the eagerness he felt for the coming conflict, when Kiyomori's remark suddenly reminded them of the grimness of war—the clashing of arms, the fighting, the flames, the greed for honors. What were they but the empty dreams of fools? Better was it for them to think once more of their wives, their children, and of the useless regrets that would follow.

A young serving-lad sat beside Kiyomori keeping the air gently in motion with a large fan. Kiyomori sat cross-legged on a kneeling-cushion. The heat bothered him. He had taken off his armor and thrown it down in front of him. He sat in his white under-tunic; the collar of the tunic was open and from time to time he exposed his chest to the cooling movements of the fan.

If there were some who regarded the captain's rough and ready ways as virile, there were others who looked at them askance

—and Tokiko was one of them. Kiyomori could almost hear her saying: "Really, that's just why the courtiers misunderstand you, and Tameyoshi of the Genji and Yoshitomo say you're rude. With all our sons at the Court now, it's about time you stopped behaving like that Heita of Isé who used to loiter in the market-place!" Only his wife and stepmother dared to remonstrate with him, and Kiyomori, usually gentle and compliant with them as he was apt to be with most women, would listen to Tokiko submissively and promise to mend his ways. But it was doubtful that he took her rebukes quite seriously, for as soon as she was out of sight, he forgot his promises, and there were reasons that he should.

He was now thirty-nine and in his prime—a toughened, experienced warrior—and the future was still before him. What it held he could not guess. It was not clear to him yet just what part he would play in it. What fired him now was a consuming desire to act. The despised warrior was now ready to gamble on this one chance. He knew well what this meant—life, wife, children, and home. And he was unwilling to act impulsively on a single summons from the throne. He had acknowledged the order by sending Motomori with two hundred soldiers, but still showed no sign that he himself was ready to go. This was the 10th of July, and he watched the sun slowly slope to its setting.

To many the question of whether to take up arms for the Emperor Goshirakawa or to support Sutoku presented a dilemma, but to Kiyomori the issue was clear. He had never intended to side with Sutoku. He had seen from its start that the movement to support the ex-Emperor was no more than a conspiracy with Yorinaga behind it. Yorinaga expected no aid of him any more than Kiyomori expected to gain anything by taking sides with Yorinaga. They were long-declared foes. Kiyomori also had heard that his uncle Tadamasa was among the first to join the conspirators, but this had not moved Kiyomori to throw in his lot with the Emperor. By declaring himself on Goshirakawa's side, Kiyomori knew he would be risking the lives not only of his family at Rokuhara, but of Heiké all over the country. A false step at this moment would cast unnumbered women, children, and the aged into an inferno. This thought alone made him hesitate. By sending Motomori he could consider his duty done and bide his time. But the clamor of a powerful inner voice insisted that *the moment* had arrived and tempted him to throw all caution aside. Another such chance he was sure would not come to him. This chance was the key to his future.

And while he hesitated the memory of a curious incident kept recurring to him. It took place in the year following his father Tadamori's death, when Kiyomori was on his way to Kumano Shrine. On the trip by water from Isé to Kishu, a large sea-bass had floundered on board and caused the boatmen to exclaim excitedly that the fish was an augury of good fortune for the Heiké. Kiyomori was told that the deity of Kumano Shrine had sent this sign because of his piety. Kiyomori, though he scoffed at superstitions, was not quite willing to disbelieve what was told him. It pleased him to think that this had happened when he was on his way to offer prayers for his father, though what followed was scarcely a fulfilment of the prophecy, for Yorinaga soon after came into power.

But Kiyomori now asked himself whether the Emperor's summons was after all the chance augured by the god at Kumano Shrine. It was apparent that the conflict between the Emperor and Sutoku was no more than the plotting of court factions against each other, the clashing of overweening ambitions, a base struggle for power. Who was he to cast in his lot beside theirs in a struggle of evils? Ambitions he had, a goal, a dream. As the chief of the Heiké he had to see that the thriving clan grew and prospered further, and that the warrior class ended the rule of the Fujiwara barons.

Toward dusk Tokitada received word that Yorimori, Kiyomori's step-brother, was arriving with sixty soldiers. He hastened to tell Kiyomori, who he knew had been anxiously awaiting this news since the previous day. Kiyomori was beginning his evening meal, but he quickly finished it, directing Tokitada meanwhile to send Yorimori to him. Kiyomori had doubted that his stepmother, Lady Ariko, would send her son to join him, for he was barely twenty and under no obligation to come to Kiyomori's assistance. Had she urged Yorimori to support the ex-Emperor Sutoku, Kiyomori would have had to look on her and his half-brother as enemies, and the thought had pained him.

"Oh, here you are, Yorimori!" Kiyomori's brows cleared; his face lighted up with relief and unconcealed pleasure.

Yorimori, who seemed to fear that he had incurred Kiyomori's displeasure by his tardiness, made elaborate obeisance. "Though I have arrived much later than the others, I beg you not to put it down to cowardice."

"Nonsense! As you can see for yourself, I haven't even started. . . . Our good mother's feelings aside, I have been anxiously waiting for you to appear. Tell me what she said to you."

"She gave me no instructions, she only said that I was to obey you implicitly."

"Did she say which side would come out victorious?"

"She wept, and said that she believed that the ex-Emperor had not intended matters to come to this."

"Good!" In that instant Kiyomori made up his mind. His stepmother, who had once been a member of the ex-Emperor's household, believed there was little hope for Sutoku's cause. Kiyomori was inclined to rely on her judgment.

"Tokitada, see that the soldiers are fed and get plenty of sleep. We leave in the morning between two and three."

Kiyomori was soon asleep, but toward midnight he was up and calling his three brothers and his son Shigemori to take part in drinking the ceremonial wine that Tokiko poured for them. Tokiko helped Kiyomori with his armor. The sword that Tadamori had given him hung at his side. Yorimori wore another of the prized Heiké swords.

The story now reverts to the time of Tadamori's death, the 15th of January 1153, three years earlier. Tadamori, fifty-eight at the time, was survived by six sons—Kiyomori, Tsunemori, Norimori and Iyemori, by his first wife, the Lady of Gion, and Yorimori and Tadashigé by his second wife, Ariko. He was chief of the

Justice Department then and enjoyed a measure of prosperity he had never before known. The years of grinding poverty during which he had reared his sons made him take thought of how he might insure the fortunes of his house, and it was an open secret that he had amassed considerable wealth by shrewd trading with the pirates and smugglers who brought quantities of precious merchandise from China into the port of Bingo, one of his southern feudatories.

When Tadamori's slight cold turned for the worse and there seemed to be little hope for his recovery, Tsunemori came to Kiyomori with tears in his eyes, entreating him: "Let me bring Mother here to see Father for the last time."

"Mother? What do you mean by 'Mother'?"

Kiyomori pretended not to understand. Ariko, their stepmother, had constantly been at Tadamori's bedside nursing him. It was not she of whom Tsunemori spoke, but the Lady of Gion. Tsunemori, Kiyomori thought impatiently, had not changed much from that softhearted brother of his youth, though he was now a court official, a married man with a family. This reminder of his mother sent an angry surge of blood through Kiyomori.

"Even if we felt that that was the right thing to do, we've no idea of how Father feels. Forget about her, forget her, Tsunemori!"

Tears flowed down Tsunemori's cheeks. "I cannot. . . . Father has never forgotten her. When our stepmother was not there, he asked me several times what could have happened to her."

"Is this true, Tsunemori?"

"It couldn't be otherwise, for she was after all the mother of his four sons."

"That being so, it would be awkward with our stepmother here."

"She goes out every morning while it is dark to the temple to pray for Father's recovery. We could have her come then."

"Do you know where she is now and what she is doing? I've heard nothing of her since she left us—whether she's alive or dead."

"If you won't be angry with me, I shall bring her in the morning very quietly before it is light."

"So you know where she is, and you've seen her from time to time?"

Tsunemori was silent.

"Here, why don't you answer me? How can I tell whether she lives near here or at a distance?"

Kiyomori's voice rose to a shout. The thought that Tsunemori sometimes saw the mother whom he refused to acknowledge gave him a jealous pang. He had an impulse to strike Tsunemori in the face with his clenched fist.

Tsunemori, prostrating himself, implored: "This is all I shall ever ask of you!"

Kiyomori spat out his answer: "Do as you please! I'll have nothing to do with this. It all depends on Father."

Ever since Tadamori's condition had seemed to grow worse, Ariko went in her litter daily before dawn to Kiyomizu Temple, undaunted by snow or rain. This morning Tsunemori saw her litter start out on the frosted road, and when Ariko was safely out of sight, Tsunemori held out his hand to someone hiding in the shadow of one of the doors and led the figure to his father's sickroom. Kiyomori, who slept in the next room, was awakened by voices and the sound of stifled weeping.

". . . It makes me happy to see you once more. You, too, have had much unhappiness. Our sons are now grown. I have no anxieties for them, but I am troubled for you. I have not fulfilled my promise to his late majesty, if I have neglected you. That has troubled me all these years. If only I could be sure that you will find happiness and contentment in the years to come . . ."

Kiyomori, who caught fragments of what his father was saying, was infuriated. He also felt hurt at being ignored. Though he did not doubt his dying father's sincerity, he wondered if it was possible for his father to have grieved all those years for his mother —that vain, heartless woman who had given Tadamori nothing but trouble, and had abandoned her children.

It was soon time for Ariko to be back, and Tsunemori, his

arm about his mother's shoulders, led the weeping Lady of Gion away by a rear gate. Kiyomori heard her leave and leaped from his bed. He sped down the passage to get a glimpse of her through a hedge, then burst into tears at what met his eyes. His once beautiful mother was now like flowers that frost has touched. Her face was heavily powdered, but he noticed that her cheeks sagged; her hair had lost its brightness. He rapidly counted up in his mind—fifty. She was now fifty! A woman at fifty—and he wondered what she did for a living. Recalling his sick father's words, he suddenly felt grateful for Tsunemori's solicitude for their mother.

"Come, put on your cloak. You must not grieve like this, for it will make you ill. I shall go with you as far as your gate. Wrap your cloak around you and conceal your face so people will not notice us."

When the two were out of sight, Kiyomori went to his father's bedside and sat down. For a while he watched his father's face, and then with a great effort whispered: "Father, are you satisfied now?"

A silence intervened; then Tadamori's eyelids slowly quivered open. "You, Kiyomori?"

He settled back into silence once more. "That box—over there . . ." he said at last. His fingers fumbled in the box and he finally brought out a fan, which he handed to Kiyomori without a word. After a time he spoke again: "Have no doubt. You are the son of the late Emperor. He gave me this fan on the last trip on which I accompanied him. It is by right yours."

That day Tadamori, feeling that his end had come, called his sons to him and gave each a memento. To Kiyomori he left a suit of leather armor, an heirloom, and one of the famous swords of the Heiké. To Yorimori, the eldest of his sons by Ariko, he presented one other prized blade of the Heiké. And this he did out of his regard for Ariko.

Some time after Tadamori's death, when Kiyomori was alone, he unfolded the fan and found a poem inscribed on it. The opening lines were in his father's hand, but the closing stanza was in a script Kiyomori did not recognize, but which Mokunosuké later assured him was the Emperor Shirakawa's. It ran: "Tadamori shall care for it until it becomes a great sheltering tree." The meaning was clear to Kiyomori. He was the Emperor Shirakawa's son given to Tadamori to rear as his own. The riddle of his birth was now answered, but Kiyomori felt nothing beyond a piercing regret that he was not Tadamori's real son. Never again did he look at the fan, which was laid away in a box and forgotten.

On the 11th of July, Kiyomori and his troops left Rokuhara before dawn for the Takamatsu Palace and arrived there at sunrise. After registering they went to their several posts. Kiyomori, running his eyes along the list of names in the register, found that Yoshitomo of the Genji had also been assigned here.

The red banner of the Heiké now waved beside the white standard of the Genji, and by nightfall the scorching flames of war reached the capital.

ordering Tameyoshi to come at once to assist the wellborn
Sutoku, and from Tadayuki, Yorinaga's father, it came soon after
urging Tameyoshi know that Yorinaga's will attempt to restore
Sutoku to the throne rested solely on Yorinaga's confidence in the
Genji. Yorinaga counted on Tameyoshi's warriors as the core
.... and .... including .... of Nara and
men-at-arms from Kendai .... that .... sent to
him, Tameyoshi .... Emperor,
ordering him to return to .... as a way to stamp
out the revolt.

Tameyoshi, other .... in favor of ....
agon of the .... built .... at the .... leader-
ing the .... estate .... no ....
The .... had a ....
ordinary .... contact .... on ....
.... are
Tameyoshi is ....
as chief .... he Imperial .... Palace ....
pan him of our ....

The malifference that existed between Yoshitomo and his
brothers was not unnatural. Not only was he their half-brother,
but at twenty-three he had left Kyoto for eastern Japan to live
among the Genji at Kamakura, and in that time distinguished
himself as a warrior with .... a chieftain in his own
right. If ivy was mixed with the brothers' accusations that Yoshitomo betrayed Sutoku of obligations. He owed his entire position
of strength to those in faction .... by .... position
of the Omuda, and yet he had unhesitatingly joined the Emperor's
cause.

CHAPTER XV

THE WHITE BANNER OF THE GENJI

Every man in his lifetime seems fated to meet at least one or
two misfortunes of devastating proportions, or so it appeared to Tameyoshi of the Genji, who for several days
did nothing but sigh heavily. His eyes were bloodshot and his hair
seemed to have turned whiter. He was sixty and faced with a decision more momentous than any he had ever encountered. Yorinaga, to whom Tameyoshi owed many favors, had sent a message

ordering Tameyoshi to ride at once to assist the ex-Emperor Sutoku, and from Tadazané, Yorinaga's father, had come similar urgings. Tameyoshi knew that Yorinaga's rash attempt to restore Sutoku to the throne rested solely on Yorinaga's confidence in the Genji. Yorinaga counted on Tameyoshi's warriors as the core around which he would gather the fighting monks of Nara and men-at-arms from his feudatories. At the time Yorinaga sent for him, Tameyoshi had also received a summons from the Emperor, ordering him to report at once with his son Yoshitomo to stamp out the revolt.

Tameyoshi's other six sons had never seen their father in such agony of mind and begged to be taken into his confidence, swearing that they would stand with him in whatever decision he made. They were filled with resentment against Yoshitomo, who had not consulted with any of them, and complained bitterly:

"He has no love for his own flesh and blood, nor does he care for our clan. He is only greedy for honors, jealous of his position as chief of the imperial bodyguard. What does he care whether we join him or not?"

The indifference that existed between Yoshitomo and his brothers was not unnatural. Not only was he their half-brother, but at twenty-three he had left Kyoto for eastern Japan to live among the Genji at Kamakura, and in that time distinguished himself as a warrior, winning recognition as a chieftain in his own right. Envy was mixed with the brothers' accusations that Yoshitomo lacked a sense of obligation. He owed his rising position to Yorinaga, at whose invitation he had replaced Kiyomori as chief of the Guards, and yet he had unhesitatingly joined the Emperor's cause.

"What have you decided, Father?"

"We can't delay much longer."

"For the last two days, our soldiers have been arriving from all parts of the country. They crowd the streets from here to Horikawa. There's hardly room for bedding them and yet they keep coming. They're getting impatient for you to start, and there are rumors that they'll take matters into their own hands and go off on their own."

Thus pressed by his sons, Tameyoshi was forced to answer: "Patience, a little more patience. To tell the truth, the idea of siding with the ex-Emperor Sutoku is distasteful to me. Neither do I have any desire to answer the summons from the Court. These are my real feelings now. I see no way clear to me. Remember this, however: we must protect the women and the children. Tell that to our soldiers. If there are any that want to fight, let them join whichever side they please."

An angry outburst met Tameyoshi's words. Were the Genji to remain spectators in this war and be laughed at, his sons asked. Words were easier than deeds. Would the Genji all over the country be content to stay neutral? It was all very well for Tameyoshi to say he would not take sides, but how did he expect to escape the tide of war? What assurance had he that he and his property would be spared the flames? Would the blood-crazed soldiers on either side respect his neutrality? Was it not more likely that contempt for his cowardice would result in his being made a target for both sides, and would not his own soldiers become victims of the warring parties?

Tameyoshi, listening to these arguments, felt the points were well made. His eyes had not been closed to the tragic outcome, and his anguish deepened the furrows in his brows and cheek. "It is indeed as you say. Let us consider, however—if we side with the ex-Emperor, then Yoshitomo, my son, is our enemy. If we take up arms for the Emperor Goshirakawa, I shall be guilty of rank ingratitude to our benefactor, Yorinaga. Neither choice will save us from that hell—war. I, Tameyoshi, who have upheld the honor of the Genji, am now forced to lay down my arms. Were it possible, I would take the tonsure and escape into hiding. . . . Come, let us wait another night. Give me just one more night to decide."

Tameyoshi's sons were unsatisfied, but they ceased to press him further because of his evident torment.

Though another messenger arrived from Yorinaga, Tameyoshi

sent back the reply that he was too ill to appear; and to a letter from his son Yoshitomo he curtly answered that no response was to be expected. Rereading his son's letter, however, Tameyoshi's eyes filled.

Yoshitomo wrote: "There cannot be two rulers. Whatever the claims of the ex-Emperor, my duty lies with the Emperor. I can do no less than be loyal to him. I beg you, my father, and my brothers, to take up arms for him and come quickly. I understand your feelings. I know there are many obligations that make it painful for you to arrive at a decision, yet there is no choice but to support our cause. I weep to think that we of the same clan, bound by ties of blood, may yet take up arms against each other. Should the ex-Emperor's troops interfere with your coming, I will myself come out to meet you and give you escort. Your ungrateful son is most anxious for you, my aging father. Make this hard decision now, and let us see your standard raised beside those who fight for our Emperor. Your other sons will rally to you in this crisis."

Tameyoshi's heart filled with pride. This was unmistakably his own son speaking. He felt his indecision begin to give way when the Councilor Norinaga appeared once more with a last appeal from Yorinaga. Tameyoshi parried for time: "Tell them that Tameyoshi is too old and feeble."

Norinaga, however, was insistent and refused to take this for a reply. "I understand too well how you feel. Is it possible, however, that Tameyoshi of the Genji, who owes much to the Minister, is now turned ingrate? Does he now refuse and welcome the defeat of the ex-Emperor?"

Once more Tameyoshi protested: "In spite of their urgings, I can only say that I am too infirm to be of any use."

"It will be enough to say that you are on our side. There will be no war-councils until you come. They are willing to wait until you arrive."

Haggard, Tameyoshi fell silent, staring at Norinaga with hollow eyes. He finally said: "Last night I had a dream—an evil one. In it I saw eight suits of the Genji armor. A great whirlwind suddenly arose and tore them to tatters, and I awoke. I now see that this war means nothing good to our house. Disaster now hangs over the Genji. . . ."

"It astonishes me that a warrior like you puts his faith in dreams. How can you expect me to take back this for an answer? I dare not leave until you give me a definite reply. You put me in a very difficult position; I shall stay here if need be until dawn."

Tameyoshi suddenly realized that they had been conversing in the dark; someone was heard to say: "I have brought lights, sir. May I come in?" Presently a tall heavily built youth of about eighteen entered with lighted candles, which he set in tall stands. As he started to leave, Tameyoshi stopped him. "Wait, Tametomo, wait!" Turning to Norinaga, Tameyoshi said: "You may have heard of this son who had such a reputation for wildness even as a boy. He is the youngest of my eight sons and the only one who makes a good fighting man. The others are indifferent soldiers by comparison, but Tametomo is fit to go in my place. If he is acceptable—and if he consents—I send him in my stead. Does this suit you, Tametomo?"

The youth eagerly replied: "Let me go, if you wish it."

Although Lady Bifukumon's favorite, Shimeko, did not become the empress, she remained at Court in attendance upon the boy-Emperor Konoyé, and following his death remained there, though with a considerably smaller number of servants to wait on her. Among those she insisted on keeping with her was a young serving-maid, Tokiwa. Tokiwa had been chosen at fifteen from among hundreds of beautiful candidates to enter Shimeko's service. She had not been long at the Court when Yoshitomo of the Genji, captured by her loveliness, secretly made her his mistress, and at twenty she already had two sons by him. Shimeko, who had grown deeply attached to Tokiwa, forgave her for an alliance which Lady Bifukumon would frown on, and that Tokiwa might not be separated from her children, offered her and her aged mother the use of a small house inside the grounds of the Court. Lady Shimeko knew, however, that a time would come when Tokiwa's secret could no longer be hidden and Tokiwa would be obliged to give up Yoshitomo of the Genji, Yorinaga's favorite, or else leave the Court.

As relations between the Court and the ex-Emperor grew more strained, war seemed inevitable, and Yoshitomo feared to visit Tokiwa. On one of his stolen visits to her he said: "Wipe away your tears, my dear one. You needn't fear that I shall abandon you if a war comes. Do you believe that I would let these two little ones become my enemies?" Laughing tenderly, he pushed back a strand of hair from her wet cheek and tucked it behind a small ear, into which he continued to whisper: "Tell no one, but if war breaks out, I shall not hesitate to take my men and go to the support of the Emperor. What I owe to the Minister, Yorinaga, will mean nothing if the throne summons me. I am not the Minister's vassal. Whichever side my father and brothers choose, I am on the side of his majesty. No longer need you fear angering Lady Bifukumon because of me, for now you can proudly say that Yoshitomo, your lover, is one of the Emperor's own men."

Cupping his hands around Tokiwa's face, he drew it to him, and laid his mouth on her lips, which now trembled into a smile. Heedless of the infant that slept at her breast, he gathered her to him, mingling his tears with hers.

Panic reigned in the capital as rumors of war spread. Frightened inhabitants, carrying the sick, streamed out of the city for the hills with whatever small possessions they could take. Tokiwa's fears and anxiety, however, seemed insignificant beside the news that Yoshitomo was the first to join the Emperor's forces. Her heart swelled with the knowledge that he was true to her, that the banner he carried was also the pledge of their love. Now she could proudly own to all the world that she was his. She could hardly wait to carry the news to her mother, and hurried through her evening tasks; then lightly veiling her face in her summer cloak, she slipped away to her home. Her steps quickened unconsciously with imaginings that she heard her children's cries until she reached her gate. Then as her hand reached for the latch, she was startled by someone addressing her:

"Isn't this the lady Tokiwa?"

"Who is it?" she replied cautiously, and turned in fear to face a figure in armor.

"Yoshitomo of the Genji sent me."

"Yes?"

"I have a message for you. There will be fighting in the capital by morning. You are to leave the capital immediately."

"Yes, I came to speak to my mother of it."

"How are your children?"

"Both are well."

"How old are they?"

"The elder is three; the younger is only an infant of a few months."

"Then . . ." The man mumbled his words. "Their names?"

"Imawaka, and the baby is—" Tokiwa, suddenly grew suspicious and looked more closely at the man, who fled abruptly. Before he was out of sight, ten of Yoshitomo's retainers appeared, saying that they had been sent to escort her, and without further ceremony entered her house and began assembling her belongings in preparation for leaving. From them she could gather nothing of the identity of the stranger who had just accosted her.

Toward midnight Tameyoshi's retainer Magoroku returned to report that Tokiwa was leaving the capital that same night with her two children.

"Are you preparing to leave, sir? As soon as you have made up your mind—"

An expression of bitterness spread over Tameyoshi's face and was lost in the deep furrows and wrinkles, which soon assumed the shape of a smile.

"I have made up my mind. I must not go on like this, for the young will not listen to reason. There is neither right nor wrong for them, for they feel they must test their limbs, and I told them to do as they pleased." And Tameyoshi suddenly roared with laughter.

"Are they alone going to join the ex-Emperor?"

"What am I to do alone here with this old carcass of mine? Do you believe I can refuse to go to his aid? This is my fate, the lot of the warrior. There must be no hesitation in answering his summons, and I am ready to go. Yoshitomo has decided. He has cast his lot with the Emperor, and there is no turning back for him now."

"So it appears."

"It's just as well. He has chosen the path he will follow. . . . Get me my armor, Magoroku."

The days of silence and inertia now broken, Tameyoshi prepared himself to meet the supreme test of his declining years. To Councilor Norinaga, who still waited, Tameyoshi now gave his reply.

Eight suits of armor, treasures of the Genji handed down from generation to generation, were brought and Tameyoshi gave one to each of his sons, ordering one to be delivered that same night to Yoshitomo.

On the morning that Tameyoshi set out for the palace at Shirakawa with his sons and soldiers to join Sutoku's troops, Kiyomori also reported for duty at the Court.

Only a week had elapsed since the death of the Cloistered Emperor. There were now many courtiers and officials, malingerers, who refused to take part in the approaching struggle and barricaded themselves inside their mansions. Councilor Norinaga, after taking Tameyoshi's reply to the ex-Emperor, fled Shirakawa for one of the monasteries outside Kyoto and took the tonsure. Tsunemuné of the Fujiwara, who accompanied Yorinaga to Uji, vanished shortly afterward, and many others refused to answer the summons from the Court.

Motomori, Kiyomori's son, who left Kyoto on the morning of the 10th, took up his position on the Uji Road by noon. The peremptory temper of his men and the ring of authority in their voices showed that they were aware of their new importance. Travelers on their way to Kyoto from outlying districts, ignorant of developments in the capital, were ordered to turn back. Courtiers and officers attempting to escape from the capital were forced to retrace their steps.

"Ya, ya! Who comes here?"

"Some nobleman—by his carriage."

"Careful now, he has a large retinue with him."

A wicker coach followed by a carriage ornamented with fine metalwork was approaching. Some twenty armed soldiers accompanied them.

"Halt, you there!" Motomori's soldiers shouted, barring the road. They had heard that Yorinaga might be returning to Kyoto by this route and were certain that this was he. The occupants of the vehicles, however, proved to be two courtiers who produced documents to show that they had gone to Uji on private matters. Yorinaga, in the meantime, had made his way to the capital in a litter by another route and was already safe at his headquarters at Shirakawa.

Motomori and his men were disappointed at not apprehending the Minister Yorinaga. The sun was setting, and they had set about feeding their horses and preparing their evening meal, when they saw some ten horsemen and thirty foot-soldiers hurrying toward them from Uji. Motomori quickly rode out to meet them.

"Halt! Where are you from and which way are you going?"

The horsemen instantly came to a standstill, and the foot-soldiers drew up behind them. A splendid figure in black leather armor and horned helmet lowered his head in greeting. "We come from the near-by district in response to news of disturbances in the capital. Who bars our way?"

Motomori replied: "We have orders to guard this road. Those who go to the aid of the Court will pass, but all others may not proceed. I am the grandson of Tadamori of the Heiké, second son of Kiyomori, Lord Aki; Motomori, officer of Aki, aged seventeen!"

Motomori's soldiers advanced with their bows drawn, when the stranger announced that he was Chikaharu of the Genji, on his way to the ex-Emperor Sutoku. A shouting arose and the whizzing of arrows began to fill the air. Chikaharu and the ten horsemen suddenly charged with heads lowered on their horses' manes, their swords drawn, spears leveled. Failing light and the dust, curling up in clouds from under the galloping hoofs, combined to obscure the oncoming horses, and Motomori's troops retreated hastily to a near-by shrine to regroup themselves. Looking down from the knoll on which he stood, Motomori rallied his soldiers: "You men of Isé—there are not more than forty-five of them. With five or six of you to their one, we can force them to surrender."

Motomori's troops rushed to the assault once more and this time succeeded in wounding or killing several of their opponents and capturing the rest. But Chikaharu fought on alone to the last, until the thrust of a grapnel-spear unhorsed him. Then Motomori was soon on his way to the capital with his prisoners.

As Motomori prepared to leave the Court for the Uji Road, he was detained for a brief ceremony in which a higher rank was conferred on him.

Early next morning, when Kiyomori finally appeared at the Court, he was received eagerly and with congratulations on Motomori's success in capturing Chikaharu of the Genji alive. Flushed with pride and smiling broadly, Kiyomori made a round of calls on his fellow captains to make known his arrival and to offer apologies for his tardiness. Last of all he greeted Yoshitomo.

"Ah, Kiyomori of the Heiké!"

"And you, Yoshitomo of the Genji!"

Their eyes met. A silence ensued as each recalled their first meeting one autumn afternoon long ago at Toba Sojo's funeral. Yoshikiyo Sato had made the introduction. Yoshitomo had then spoken of going to Kamakura. Yoshikiyo soon after had fled his home, taken the tonsure, and become the wandering monk poet Saigyo. Sixteen years had gone by, though it seemed to have happened only yesterday. Many changes had taken place in the capital since then. Some of their youthful companions were now dead or had left Kyoto. Neither had dreamed of meeting again thus—comrades in the cause of the Emperor. They were rivals, too—Genji and Heiké—but a common purpose now bound them as brothers-in-arms.

"I was anxious about you," Yoshitomo began, "for there were

any number of rumors concerning you. I am greatly relieved that you've come after all to join us here."

"I sent my son with some of my troops and stayed behind to attend to the mobilizing of my men. My apologies for this delay."

"But you must be pleased to know how your son has already distinguished himself."

Kiyomori laughed deprecatingly. "And to think that these young ones are making out better than their elders—stealing our triumphs!"

"I envy you,, Yoshitomo said, "for your house is not divided against itself as mine is."

The smile vanished from Kiyomori's lips. In his elation over Motomori it had not occurred to him what this fratricidal war must mean to Yoshitomo. The unaccustomed weight of his armor made Kiyomori feel even more ill at ease; he groped in his mind for words of sympathy that somehow refused to come, stared awkwardly before him, then with a few abrupt words, turned and left.

Yoshitomo winced at the blunt, unsympathetic back suddenly turned on him.

That same day the Court moved to the Imperial Palace at the north center of the capital, where the headquarters of the Emperor's forces was established. On Yoshitomo's advice it was decided that the first blow would be struck that night by a surprise attack on the palace at Shirakawa, where Yorinaga's reinforcements could not be expected to arrive earlier than noon of the following day. This move, Yoshitomo maintained, would forestall a three-column attack on the Imperial Palace itself.

In the meantime Tameyoshi and his sons with their horse and foot militia arrived at Shirakawa, where they found the ex-Emperor and his advisers in a frenzy of anxiety. News of Chikaharu's capture on the previous evening increased the disquiet over the failure of Yorinaga's other troops to arrive from outlying provinces. Yorinaga had counted on three thousand horse and foot to arrive in time for a combined attack on the capital, and no more than sixteen or seventeen hundred had yet reported in. Nor could he expect the monks from Nara and Yoshino, who had promised aid, to come for another twenty-four hours. The fevered atmosphere heightened that night as Yorinaga looked out across the Kamo River and saw the glow in the western sky change to dense columns of smoke. Before long, messengers arrived with the news that the Willow-Spring Palace, where part of Yorinaga's troops were garrisoned, was in flames. Although the Minister ordered an auxiliary force to be sent there, Tameyoshi of the Genji and Tadamasa (Kiyomori's uncle) prevailed on him to desist, pointing out the wisdom of further strengthening the defenses of the Shirakawa Palace.

Tadamasa and his three hundred horse and foot, to which were added a hundred of Yorinaga's own forces, took up their post at the eastern gate of the Palace, facing the foothills of Mount Hiei. On the opposite side of the Palace, overlooking the Kamo River, Tameyoshi stationed himself and his well-appointed forces at the main western gate. His youngest son, Tametomo, and an additional one hundred mounted and foot-soldiers, commanded a smaller gate of the same wall.

Yorinaga, who inspected the defenses of the Palace, could not suppress his dismay at the paucity of his troops, though Tameyoshi's presence, he assured himself, was almost as good as ten thousand. Yorinaga's spirits rose, however, when he saw Tametomo and his twenty-eight mounted soldiers. They had been trained in the arts of war in Kyushu, where Tametomo's fame as a fighter had become legendary. He eyed the youth with curiosity. Tametomo stood a head taller than the tallest around him. He wore heavy armor threaded with white lacings, under it a dark-blue tunic, and carried a long sword in a scabbard of bearskin. One of his soldiers carried his iron helmet. This was the notorious Tametomo, who as a wild, headstrong lad had caused his father much trouble, and at thirteen had finally been sent to his kinsmen in Kyushu; there, at only seventeen, he had gained a name as a fearless warrior and was acclaimed as one of the local chieftains.

Yorinaga approached Tametomo to obtain his views on strategy, and was told: "We cannot expect to win unless we make a night attack. Tonight is not too soon. I am rather surprised by the hesitation to do so."

"A tactic that would occur to even the most inexperienced soldier"—Yorinaga smiled—"and we have already prepared for that."

"That being so," Tametomo continued, "we must cripple the enemy in the capital on both flanks and from the rear by flame, and then throw in our troops from the front. We can thus trap the enemy and at the same time make the best use of our inferior numbers."

"What if your brother Yoshitomo attacks first?"

"I'll send an arrow through his helmet and force him to turn tail."

"Kiyomori of the Heiké, I hear, is in the field."

"There's nothing to brushing aside his troops and making straight for the Palace and taking the Emperor prisoner. This is the moment to strike. Now—before dawn."

"A daring bit of strategy, I dare say," Yorinaga said smiling scornfully, "and good enough, I imagine, when ten or twenty horses are engaging in one of your local skirmishes down in Kyushu, where I hear you have quite a name, but you must realize that our operations here are not on such a petty scale. I fear, Tametomo, that your opinion carries little weight with us here."

Sullen-faced, Tametomo returned to his post, and there lay down on his large shield to find sleep until dawn.

"The enemy have attacked!"

"The enemy have crossed the river!"

Shouts and cries rang out shortly before dawn of the 12th. There was confusion in the Palace, the clangor of arms and the neighing of horses. Bowmen, who lined the walls of Shirakawa Palace, were already aiming their shafts at the approaching enemy.

Yoshitomo, at the head of more than a thousand mounted warriors and foot soldiers, arrived on the right bank of the Kamo River, opposite Shirakawa, and was preparing to ford it, when he saw dawn whitening the shoulder of Mount Hiei. Realizing the disadvantage of advancing with the rising sun full in their faces, he turned back and led his troops downstream a short distance before fording the river; then began a slow march northward until he reached a point just out of reach of the enemy's arrows.

Tameyoshi of the Genji ordered the south and west gates to be opened and was about to ride forth when Tametomo galloped out ahead of him shouting: "Let me be first to the attack!" He was pursued by his elder brother, Yorikata, protesting Tametomo's right to be the first in the field. Tametomo forthwith, impatiently calling out that he did not care, made off toward the western gate by the river.

In the half-light of the dawn Yorikata galloped toward the enemy line and challenged them: "Who comes there, Genji or Heiké? This is I, Yorikata, fourth son of Tameyoshi of the Genji!"

One of Yoshitomo's soldiers replied to the challenge, giving his name and rank as retainer of Yoshitomo, Lord Shimotsuké. Demanding that the general himself appear, Yorikata sent two arrows flying in rapid succession close to where Yoshitomo sat astride his horse. He saw two horsemen succumb to his shafts, and then turned to go back, when an arrow glanced off his helmet. Without more ado, Yorikata galloped back to his cheering comrades.

Roused to fury by the sight of his wounded soldiers, Yoshitomo started in pursuit of Yorikata, vowing he would chastise his brother for his insolence, but his soldiers restrained him by force.

Kiyomori, meanwhile, rode upstream along the left bank with more than eight hundred horses to a point north of Shirakawa Palace and waited for Yoshitomo to open the attack. As the sun rose and the heavy mist over the river lifted, he saw how Yoshitomo's troops were deployed. Though neither side showed any movement, Kiyomori's heart began to drum wildly. Savage shouts and cries rose from either side in a barbaric crescendo. Between the dispersing mist, he saw how the distance between the opposing lines narrowed imperceptibly. Suddenly fifty horsemen detached themselves from Kiyomori's troops and advanced to the river-bank opposite the gate guarded by Tametomo. Three warriors then rode forward, demanding the name of him who stood at the gate, announcing themselves as retainers of Kiyomori of the Heiké.

A strong young voice rang out above the rushing sounds of the river:

"This is I, Tametomo, Tameyoshi's son. I have no arrows to spare for such as you. Even your leader, Kiyomori of the Heiké, is a sorry match for me. Go back and tell him to come."

As three arrows whistled past Tametomo in unison, his carelessly aimed shaft climbed through the air with a weird whine and pierced clear through the chest of one warrior and lodged in the shoulder-piece of a second. The riderless horse reared, whinnying madly; horsemen to the rear quickly came forward in a phalanx, their bows set, to give cover to the two warriors and their wildly plunging mounts, while a rain of arrows came from the enemy.

The ground shook and rumbled under Kiyomori; his horse, nostrils aquiver, suddenly trembled and tossed its mane. "What's that?" he demanded sharply. The crowding of mounted soldiers around him kept him from reining round his horse, when a warrior galloped up to Kiyomori shouting:

"Itoroku has fallen! Tametomo shot him. Your lordship, you'll be his next target if you don't get beyond the range of his arrows."

"What, Itoroku fallen? Why should we fear Tameyoshi's youngest son?"

"Your lordship, see for yourself—this arrow!"

From his shoulder-piece the warrior drew out an oversized shaft and handed it to Kiyomori. It was a polished length of bamboo of three years' growth, tipped with iron sharpened to a chisel edge, and fletched with pheasant.

"I see—a wicked-looking one, fit for bringing down demons. Good reason that the men fear him."

Kiyomori examined the arrow interestedly, then abruptly said: "There's no reason why we should attack this gate. I had no orders to do so and only chose this at random. If we find this somewhat forbidding, we'll try the North Gate. To the North Gate!"

As the order went out, Kiyomori's troops made a concerted move to the north, but Kiyomori's eldest son, Shigemori, who heard the command, cried out:

"What folly! Folly, indeed, to choose the North Gate, because of Tametomo's arrows. A shame on us who are under orders from the Emperor!"

Calling to some thirty horsemen about him, Shigemori impetuously started toward the enemy.

"Stop him! Bring him back!" Kiyomori cried in alarm to those around him, "only a madman would be rash enough to face that bow and risk his life!"

Even at a distance Shigemori presented a fine target for his enemies, for he wore that day a tunic of red brocade under his armor and carried a sheaf of twenty-four arrows in his quiver. The warriors restrained him with some difficulty, for Shigemori, protesting loudly and scornfully at his father's cowardice, struggled to escape, until one of his men said: "Let me go in your stead and face Tametomo himself." The soldier was off before his comrades could restrain him, and there were shouts of "Come back, come back!" But Koreyuki, looking back over his shoulder, replied: "I ask no one to come with me, nor do I wish any of you to follow me. Just watch!"

Accompanied by two foot-soldiers, he forded the river. Tametomo came out to meet Koreyuki, but, seeing him hesitate, retired inside his gate and closed it. When he was within shooting distance of the gate, Koreyuki loudly challenged Tametomo, who finally rode out, smiling scornfully, and replied: "Welcome, foolhardy one! I am Tametomo. You shall release the first arrow at me. The second is mine."

Before he even finished speaking, Koreyuki's arrow pierced the left tasset of Tametomo's armor. As he watched Koreyuki hurriedly fitting another arrow to his bow, Tametomo released his own, which dug through the thickest part of his opponent's thigh and lodged in his saddle, pinning the rider there for an instant. Koreyuki's soldiers quickly ran forward as he pitched backward and fell from his horse, and, hoisting him to their shoulders, ran back to their lines as fast as their legs would carry them.

The riderless mount, covered with blood, galloped wildly back and forth along the riverbank, then made its way downstream in the direction of Yoshitomo's lines. Some of Yoshitomo's soldiers ran out to meet the fear-crazed horse, lest it plunge among their troops and cause a stampede. There were shouts of "Catch him, catch him, step on his bridle!" until they had finally caught it; then they found a stirrup filled with blood, and a giant arrowhead embedded in the saddle.

"Here, is this really an arrowhead? Who owns such a powerful bow?"

"That must be Tametomo of the Genji."

One of Yoshitomo's retainers led the horse to where his master was, and said: "Sir, just look at this! I've heard of such arrows, but I never believed I would ever see anything like this."

Yoshitomo, however, did not appear surprised. A wry smile appeared on his lips as though he pitied Masakiyo for his timidity. "Come, Tametomo is not a man yet and cannot draw such a strong bow. This looks to me like a clever trick to frighten us. Masakiyo, the troops will be divided into two companies, of which one will attack Tametomo's gate."

Masakiyo, accompanied by two hundred foot-soldiers, rode toward a gate in the western wall, and in the accustomed manner challenged Tametomo, who appeared at once.

"So it's you, Masakiyo, a retainer to Lord Yoshitomo. Have you come to offer yourself as a mark?"

Masakiyo quailed for an instant, but mustered up courage to call out defiantly: "I am one of the Emperor's loyal followers. My duty is to kill traitors!" And with these words he released an arrow, then quickly made his way back to his men. The arrow pierced the neck-piece of Tametomo's helmet. Plucking it out, Tametomo dashed it to the ground and cried out: "So you dare insult me, Masakiyo? Let me catch you with these bare hands so I can look at your face and see who you are."

With this, Tametomo started in pursuit of Masakiyo, who, uttering a yell of terror, fled before him. Tametomo, his bow under one arm, his other arm waving, continued to gallop after Masakiyo until the frantic cries of his soldiers made him wheel abruptly and return to his post.

Yoshitomo, who looked on from a distance, saw his brother retreat and ordered five of his best warriors to ride out and engage him, saying: "Tametomo's bow is good in a sea fight, but his horsemanship is weak compared with ours."

The sun was now high in the sky, and the summer trees were filled with the droning of cicadas.

Tametomo turned at the sound of cries behind him and made a rush at the approaching horsemen, who gave way before him. One figure on a coal-black stallion, whose appearance proclaimed him to be a general, stood in his path. He wore a horned helmet and the armor of the Genji.

"This is I, Yoshitomo of the Genji, who come in the Emperor's name. Who are you to raise your sword against rightful authority? If you are of the same clan, lay down your arms and disperse your men. I warn you for your own sake."

Tametomo stared full at his brother's face and cried out: "Let me tell you who I am. I am the son of Tameyoshi of the Genji, who sprang to the call of his liege lord, and I am he who will stay with his father in life and in death. I am not so ungrateful as to forget my own father for love of fame. I'm no cur, and I, Tametomo, will fight any dog or whoever calls himself my enemy."

"You dare say that to me, Tametomo?"

"I do. I have itched many days to tell you this."

"Do you, my brother, dare fight me? Do you refuse to acknowledge the authority of the Emperor? If you revere him and honor the ways of virtue, then lay down that bow and prostrate yourself before me."

"I may be wrong in fighting a brother, but is it right for you to raise your hand against your own father?"

. . .

2 1 6

The tree-lined road along the western and northern walls of the Hoshogon-in Temple between Shirakawa and the Kamo was the scene of the bloodiest fighting that day. Across the road a stream twisted its way through the flat landscape, broken only by a grove encircling the roofs and spires of the Shichikatsu-ji Temple, and beyond it rose the foothills of Mount Hiei, and here the two armies fought each other with a copious spilling of blood, and even at sunset the slaughter went on. Between the clouds of dust which partly concealed the foe, Tametomo sometimes caught sight of his brother, Yoshitomo, recognizable in his Genji armor, and was tempted time and again to send his arrows at that soldierly figure. Implausible as it seemed, Tametomo was tempted to believe that a secret compact existed between his father and Yoshitomo and that the victors would sue for mercy for the vanquished. Tametomo did not use his bow unless challenged, and saw that his brother did the same. Yoshitomo's soldiers, however, were not afraid of Tametomo's deadly bow and attacked one after another so boldly that there was no way of telling who was friend or foe.

Though twenty-three of Tametomo's best horsemen were killed and the rest wounded, fifty-three of Yoshitomo's finest men were cut off in death and some eighty maimed, and the battlefield was piled with the bodies of the dead and flowed with their blood while the struggle went on. Believing that the odds were against Yoshitomo, Tametomo called to his men:

"I'll frighten the general with a shaft and, when the enemy begins to fall back, plunge in and scatter his troops."

Tametomo locked his fingers around his heavy bow and arched it.

"Ah, is it safe, sir? What if—"

"Easy enough, my arm remembers its skill."

Tametomo aimed his shaft at the star in Yoshitomo's helmet. Clouds of dust and the flourishing of weapons obscured his view, but he drew a deep breath and released an arrow. He watched it as it sped toward that distant speck in Yoshitomo's helmet, scraped the mark, and traveled on until it embedded itself in one of the pillars of the temple gate. When Yoshitomo saw this he grasped his reins and rode furiously at Tametomo, crying: "A poor hand, indeed, for one who has no rivals in Kyushu!"

"No, no, you may be an enemy, yet my heart tells me you are my brother, and I only shot at the star in your helmet. If you want me to, I can do better," Tametomo replied.

Tametomo, now filled with rage, set another arrow to his bow, when one of Yoshitomo's retainers, fearing for his master's safety, rushed forward with his lance aimed at the legs of Tametomo's horse. An ugly, strangling sound was heard; blood and dust mingled as the soldier fell, skewered through the throat by Tametomo's shaft.

Both armies had now drawn close together in a hand-to-hand struggle to the death. Tametomo's lieutenant fell, and only a few of his Kyushu soldiers were still alive, for Tametomo's feats with his bow were no match for Yoshitomo's superior numbers. It suddenly became dark, though a few hours still remained before nightfall, and through black clouds of smoke the sun could be seen suspended like a copper disk in the western sky.

A short while before, Yoshitomo had sent a messenger to the Imperial Palace, saying: "As matters now stand, victory is in the balance. I cannot vouch for what will happen if the enemy's reinforcements arrive tonight; the conflict may spread to the capital itself. We can win only by setting fire to the Palace at Shirakawa. Much as I shrink from desecrating the holy buildings close by and seeing them needlessly reduced to ashes, to spare the citizens of the capital a like fate I beg for orders to proceed. If the command is to continue fighting, that shall be done."

The reply came back that Yoshitomo should act as he thought fit. His soldiers thereupon chose a building to the leeward of Shirakawa Palace and set fire to it. There had been no rain for several days, and everything was as dry as tinder; a brisk west wind soon helped the flame spread to the stables and servants' quarters to the south of the Palace, and in no time the north section was also wrapped in smoke.

"They've done it! I feared that more than Yoshitomo's sol-

2 1 8

diers. He knows how to win." Tametomo stood still on the field where his fallen comrades lay about him, and stared at the flames lapping at the sky, and laughed in his despair. "He is fearless, but I fear for my aging father. We must find a way to retreat in safety."

Gathering the remainder of his warriors round him, Tametomo galloped off in a shower of arrows.

Tameyoshi and his five other sons successfully defended the west and south walls of the Palace all day, but Tadamasa, who guarded the east wall, had to call for help several times when the enemy broke through. He had all but lost the will to fight, for defeat seemed inevitable. Flames leaped across the walls and spread relentlessly from tree to tree, advancing on the Palace itself and wrapping it in thick smoke.

diers. He knows how to win." Tametomo stood still on the field
where his fallen comrades lay about him, and stared at the flames
lapping at the sky, and replied slowly. "He is fearless, but
I fear for my aging eyes...... Let us part at last in safety."

Catherine, the reins......

tomo escaped of the showed ...... The other sons successfully defended the
we ...... the Palace ...... but Tadamasa, who
go ...... several times when the
cl ...... the will to fight, for de-
fe ...... as towers and spread
rele ...... on the Palace itself and
wrap ......

CHAPTER XVI

SWORDS AND ARROWS

The war-cries of the soldiers and the whistling of arrows
approached the gates like a storm. Cries of despair rang
through the Palacé halls, and the sound of running feet
echoed along the galleries.

"For your lives—for **your lives**—now!"

"His majesty! He must escape. . . ."

"The enemy are at the gates! No time must be lost! Now is
the time to fly or the flames will overtake us!"

Iyehiro and his son burst into the apartments where the ex-Emperor Sutoku and his dazed attendants sat immobilized with fear.

"To the small gate at the south—we can get through there. Fly now!"

Yorinaga, roused from his stupor, cried out: "Iyehiro, Iyehiro, save us!"

The end of a balustrade, running the length of the apartments, suddenly took flame and soon was a blazing framework from which choking smoke billowed downward, enveloping those below it and their horses in strangling fumes. The ex-Emperor Sutoku, who was hurriedly lifted to his horse, clung to his saddle, helpless to control the rearing animal, until a secretary sprang up behind him and spurred the horse toward a gate. Yorinaga followed close behind, a courtier riding pillion. The maze of buildings on the north side of the Palace were now a roaring, burning mass; flames consumed tree after tree and showered down sparks. The searing blast soon caused a whirlwind, which blew men and horses hither and thither.

The ex-Emperor Sutoku galloped north of Shirakawa, while other horses and foot-soldiers straggled after him in confusion, until they were left far behind.

As Yorinaga galloped out by one of the small gates, he gave a hideous cry and plunged from his saddle, dragging his companion with him. Other riders drew up to see what had happened and found Yorinaga writhing in agony, an arrow through his neck; blood spurted from the wound, rapidly staining his pale-blue hunting tunic.

"Quickly—pull out the arrow!" the courtiers cried to one another, but no one moved until an aide approached them.

"We have no time to lose! If the enemy finds us, it will be the end of us," he cried, and, kneeling, he drew out the arrow, stanched the blood, and got two officials to carry Yorinaga away to a peasant's hut near by and there left him.

The ex-Emperor Sutoku, meanwhile, escaped to the foot of the Eastern Hills, where he abandoned his horse and, accompanied by Tameyoshi of the Genji, Tadamasa, and several courtiers, painfully made his way on foot over the wild hillside. Tired and footsore, Sutoku presently cried that he was thirsty. His troubled followers, however, could find no water, for their path lay along a ridge, and the extended drought had dried up the springs. Then they heard a voice calling from behind.

"Here, here is water for his majesty. I have brought him water."

Sutoku's followers were astonished to see a man breaking his way through the thick undergrowth and clambering toward them. It was Asatori, the caretaker of the Willow Spring, who prostrated himself before Sutoku.

"Here is water from the Willow Spring itself, your majesty," Asatori said, holding out a length of green bamboo with trembling hands.

Sutoku stared at Asatori in astonishment: "The caretaker of the Willow Spring!"

Asatori bowed.

". . . Asatori!"

"Your majesty, the bamboo may have tainted this water, but this is from the same spring from which you have drunk these fourteen years."

"But how—what made you come all that way with water for me?"

"It seems like a dream now, but only the day before yesterday the Emperor's troops surrounded the Willow-Spring Palace and there was fighting there. Though I was determined to stay and guard the spring, the flames drove me away."

Asatori spoke rapidly, for he saw how the ex-Emperor's attendants were anxious to be on their way.

"Asatori, I shall drink this water which you brought in the goodness of your heart. . . ." Lifting the section of bamboo to his lips, the ex-Emperor drank deeply. "This is most refreshing. Sweet as the dew from heaven!" he said, handing back the container, not quite empty. "Keep the rest yet, for it is too precious to throw away."

Night came, but there was no rest for the fugitives, for the Emperor's troops were now scattered throughout the hills in search of them. Too tired to care any longer what happened, Sutoku begged his followers to leave him, telling each one to find his way to safety. But Tameyoshi, tears in his eyes, admonished him: "We cannot leave you here, sir. You must try to bear this a few days longer. It wrings my heart to see you exposed to such hardships. I believe we can find our way to the road which leads down to Omi. Once there, we can decide what we shall do to recover our losses."

Even before their disastrous retreat, Tameyoshi had discussed a plan with Yorinaga, but the Minister had confidently waved it aside. Tameyoshi had planned, should the coup fail, to reach the eastern side of Mount Hiei and cross Lake Biwa to Omi, on the opposite shore. There he was sure he could find refuge with other Genji clansmen. He was certain that they would rally to him in sufficient numbers for a retaliatory attack. Failing this, he had thoughts of going farther east to the Kanto Plain in the region of Sagami, where numerous branches of the Genji had settled, and of there gathering an army that would finally restore Sutoku to the throne. All this Tameyoshi recounted to the ex-Emperor, but Sutoku confessed he had lost all hope and wished for nothing more than to be left with two followers, while the others escaped to safety.

The ten who had accompanied Sutoku in his flight accepted their dismissal. Last to leave were Tameyoshi and Tadamasa, who set out separately for Mount Hiei before dawn.

The two officials who stayed behind with the ex-Emperor now urged the safety of going farther into the hills, but the tired Sutoku hung back. A sudden rustling in the undergrowth startled the three, and a voice was heard:

"Your majesty, allow me to carry you on my back and go part of the way with you, for the path is dark and the way grows steeper."

"Asatori! What made you come again? Why haven't you gone with the rest?"

"I, too, must go into hiding, but let me serve you a few days longer."

Asatori stooped and offered to carry Sutoku on his back.

A heavy mist hung over the peaks, but in the distance the sky over the City of Peace and Tranquillity still glowed a sullen red from the fires consuming part of the capital. Toward dawn, while Sutoku slept, Asatori disappeared. He returned later with some food that he said he had begged from a hermit who lived near by.

Iyehiro, who had kept watch all night, now said: "It will not be possible to cook anything here for fear the smoke will be seen by our enemies. Just before dawn I thought I heard soldiers' voices right above us. His majesty apparently wishes to take the tonsure, but there is no one here to perform the rites. Can you find us an old litter so we can carry him until we find a priest?"

Taking Mitsuhiro with him, Asatori led the way down to a hamlet, and was back soon with an old dilapidated litter.

Both Iyehiro and Mitsuhiro then took off their armor and other accouterments, tucked back their sleeves, and looped up their tunics to make themselves appear as much like servants as they could. That day they carried Sutoku down through the hills toward the capital. News that the fighting was over brought refugees straggling back from the hills and near-by hamlets, and the litter mingled inconspicuously with groups of old and young who were returning to their homes in the capital.

Iyehiro and Mitsuhiro, unused to their task, staggered and tottered over the dust-laden roads, streaming with perspiration, in search of Lady Awa's mansion. When they reached it they found the gates barred and no sign of life within. From there they went on to the house of Councilor Norinaga and found the mansion deserted, for Norinaga, a passer-by told them, had taken the tonsure just before the war began and no one knew where he had gone. Next they knocked at the gate of a gentlewoman who had served in Sutoku's household, but no one appeared; all they saw was a kitten curled up under a hedge. From east to west they crossed the capital, seeking refuge, and found none. Now and again they passed great houses from which came the sounds of the victors rejoicing. Twilight had set in when Iyehiro recalled a small temple where they might find admittance; once more they shouldered their burden and made their way there. They found an old priest, a relative of one of Iyehiro's housemen, who served Sutoku a bowl of millet porridge and later shaved his head by the dim light of a lamp.

The following day Iyehiro and Mitsuhiro took Sutoku to Ninna-ji Temple, where his younger brother was Abbot. The Abbot was away, and his servants refused to admit them until, at Sutoku's insistence, they were allowed to find shelter in one of the outhouses. Here Sutoku's two companions finally took leave of their master, and each departed for some unknown destination in a distant province.

With the firing of the palace at Shirakawa began the destruction by flame of the mansions of those who had sided with the ex-Emperor. For four days and nights the air of the capital was acrid with smoke. On the second night, however, a drizzle set in, and on the third day a heavy rain fell. That night a boat piled with firewood floated down the Katsura River and waited at the river mouth for the wind and rain to subside. Several shivering figures, half-concealed by rush mats, huddled wet and miserable at the bottom of the boat, and from time to time there were groans from one who lay prone on the planks.

"Have we reached Uji yet? . . . How much longer will it be?" Yorinaga asked in a bare whisper.

The dying Yorinaga's last prayer was to see his father in Uji once more.

Nothing more eventful than the beady-eyed stares of cormorants along the riverbank interrupted the slow progress toward Uji. From time to time Yorinaga groaned as an attendant held down the struggling man and applied burning wormwood to the wound in his throat. The treatment had so far stanched the blood and, in the summer heat, kept maggots from breeding in the open wound. Incense smoke and the fumes of wormwood drifted on the air, while Yorinaga, roused from his stupor, wept with pain.

When they finally arrived at Uji, they were told that Tada-zané had fled to Nara. Then began Yorinaga's slow progress in a wooden litter to the Kofukuji Temple in Nara, where he arrived on the night of July 14. The groves of Kasuga Shrine and Sarusawa Pond were wrapped in mist. Not a single light shone from the monasteries round about.

The two courtiers who attended Yorinaga knocked on the gates of the Kofukuji Temple. Answering calls were heard inside, and some warriors and a priest, fully armed, appeared. After a whispered colloquy Toshinari alone was conducted within. Yori-naga's father was still awake and soon appeared. Toshinari quickly told him what had happened and of how Yorinaga had been brought here. But reports of Yorinaga's ignominious defeat had already reached Tadazané. Except for the slight tremor of his white-bearded chin he betrayed no emotion, no sign that he welcomed this son whom he loved so blindly.

At last he said: "Alas, Toshinari, to think that your master has come to such an end! There is no use in our meeting in these unhappy circumstances. Toshinari, I say to you, take him away where no one will see or hear him."

As he finished speaking, Tadazané's thin frame was convulsed with weeping. By sheltering his son he would bring Yorinaga's wife, his children, and his relatives under a ban that would lead to certain death.

Toshinari withdrew from the house in deep dejection. The litter still stood where he had left it in the obscuring mist. He stooped to the moaning Yorinaga and quietly recounted his talk with Tadazané.

"What!—my father?"

The litter lurched as Yorinaga struggled to a sitting position. There were a few muffled words, then a guttural sound. The litter gave another lurch, and a hollow silence followed. Toshinari and his companion called to Yorinaga, but there was no reply. When they looked in they found him dead. He had bitten off his tongue. Fearing discovery, the two carried the litter while it was still dark down Nara Hill and out into a field where they dug a pit into which they lowered the litter with Yorinaga in it. And before filling in the grave, Toshinari cut off his topknot and threw it in after the dead man to signify that he had renounced the world. Several of his companions followed his example, and then they took leave of each other and went their separate ways.

The capital quickly resumed its customary activities, though the relentless hunt for traitors continued unabated. Travelers, ignorant of recent events, arriving by any of the seven main approaches to Kyoto, were alarmed to find the barriers heavily guarded and the city under martial law. As soon as it was known that Sutoku had taken the tonsure and that Yorinaga had died of his wound, certain rumors began to circulate throughout the capital with a curious persistence. It was said that all who gave themselves up at once to the authorities would be regarded as unwilling participants in the revolt and pardoned; that the other leaders would receive light sentences. These promises, issuing from an unknown source and unconfirmed by any official proclamation, lured many courtiers and high officials out of hiding. Soldiers as well as others of Yorinaga's following surrendered daily by the score and were thrown into jail, whence the cries of prisoners put to the torture by fire and water escaped over the high walls.

Korekata, Captain of the Bodyguard of the Right, was appointed chief judge and presided at the trials, for which voluminous records had been compiled. Many a courtier and officer grew pale when the evidence produced in court not only convicted rebels, but in retrospect cast suspicion on those who had connived at the death of Konoyé, the boy-Emperor.

It was now clear that the intelligence deftly guiding and shaping state affairs was Councilor Shinzei, the exemplary, taciturn official, who for so many years had effaced himself and escaped Yorinaga's eye, and emerged at long last in a position close to the throne. It was Shinzei who ordered the unrelenting search for traitors; to him could have been traced the rumors of amnesty; and when the time came for drawing up a list of honors, Shinzei was deferred to in the naming of recipients.

To Yoshitomo had fallen, many said, the most coveted prize of all, the post of Master of the Imperial Stables—an unheard-of honor for a warrior; there were others, however, who believed that Kiyomori had acquired the more significant honor: the governorship of the province of Harima and the title Lord Harima, for the domain facing on the Inland Sea had once been his father's and many of the Heiké had settled there. That a tacit understanding might exist between Shinzei and Kiyomori occurred to a few who were aware of the close friendship between them. Shinzei, they knew, courted the good will of the warriors as much as Kiyomori ardently sought a powerful friend at Court for the Heiké.

Before Kiyomori had time to put off his armor for a night's sleep, he was ordered to take three hundred soldiers, cross Mount Hiei, and go to the towns of Otsu and Sakamoto on Lake Biwa in search of Tameyoshi and his sons and arrest them. Secret agents reported that Tameyoshi was hiding in a temple on the other side of Mount Hiei and was waiting to cross the lake to escape east by the Tokaido highway. But a careful search of Mii-dera Temple and its environs yielded nothing; nor was there any trace of the fugitives in Otsu or the small fishing settlements between it and Sakamoto, so Kiyomori turned his search to Izumi Crossing, on the estate of one of the near-by monasteries. The small settlement, to whose teahouses the monks went for their dissipations, was a landing-place for vessels plying back and forth across the lake, and the bawdyhouses buzzed with excitement when Kiyomori and his troopers arrived to surround it in a house-to-house search. The headman and brothel-keepers were summoned and questioned by Kiyomori. Then a garrulous, elderly woman appeared, offering some information.

"Now, I can't say whether it was Tameyoshi or not, but a fisherman told me that early this morning six or seven warriors in very fine armor were taken across the lake to Omi."

While Kiyomori was questioning the woman, a gong began to sound an alarm, and wild shouts were heard at the approach to the village. News of Kiyomori's arrival had reached the monastery and the monks had armed and descended in a body to expel the trespassers. By the time Kiyomori reached the scene, he found his soldiers engaged in a fierce fight with the monks. Arrows whistled through the air as the monks fell upon Kiyomori's soldiers with their powerful halberds. Kiyomori quickly drew his bow and was taking aim at a heavily built monk when the latter threw up his hands with a shout.

"Ya! Is it you, Kiyomori of the Heiké? Wait, Lord Harima! If it's you, I'll pick no quarrel with you here!"

"What, you refuse to fight? What cowardly priest is this?"

"I am Abbot Jisso of this near-by monastery."

"What?"

"Have you forgotten that we met eight or nine summers ago —in June—at the foot of Gion Hill when we marched on the capital with the Sacred Shrine? There was only one warrior who dared to defy us and shot at the sacred emblem. Surely you haven't forgotten that day!"

"That was I, Kiyomori of the Heiké."

"That one arrow turned us back. We swore then that we would some day have our revenge. There were others, however, who secretly admired you, and I was one of them."

"And then?"

"I swore that I would try to meet you some day, certain that you would be interesting to talk to."

"Wherever you say. At any time that pleases you."

"Yes, but what's the reason for this disturbance?"

"No harm was intended. I have orders to capture Tameyoshi. This was entirely unavoidable."

"Withdraw your men at once. We'll meet some other day."

"As you say. I'm ashamed to admit it, but we've made a mistake."

Disgruntled by their failure to capture Tameyoshi, and raging at the monks' attack on them, Kiyomori's men withdrew only after they had set fire to the villagers' huts.

After twenty days nearly every person of account had been captured and imprisoned, except for two—Tameyoshi of the Genji and Tadamasa of the Heiké, Kiyomori's uncle.

As he rode back to Rokuhara, Kiyomori consoled himself with thoughts of shedding his armor for a steaming bath, and after that, sleep. He had just crossed Gojo Bridge when an ill-kempt figure in priest's robes, his face masked by a scarf and almost completely concealed by a wide pilgrim's hat, darted toward Kiyomori from the shade of the trees.

"Ah, Lord Harima, wait! Wait!"

The man cast away his pilgrim's staff as he threw himself at Kiyomori and clung to a stirrup. "I—it is I, Lord Harima, your uncle!"

"What?" Kiyomori started in astonishment and quickly ordered his soldiers to stand back. He reined in his horse and stared blankly at the ragged figure, scarcely able to believe his ears. "Leave me here. Get over there in the shade and wait," he ordered his men.

The priest collapsed against Kiyomori's stirrup, weeping: "Oh, my nephew, this is your uncle, Tadamasa. Save me! . . . I implore you, my own flesh and blood, to have mercy. I came to you, my last hope, Lord Harima, my own nephew, spare me! Oh, spare me!"

"Here, let go! Kiyomori has no uncle. You have no reason to call me your nephew."

"What do you mean—you? Am I not your father's brother?"

"Didn't Tadamasa of the Heiké, in that summer nine years ago when I went out to meet the monks from Mount Hiei, fear for his safety and renounce all blood-ties with the Heiké?"

"Ah, but that was so many years ago. . . ."

"You had no pride then, neither do you now."

"I was mistaken. . . . I made the greatest mistake of my life when I let the Minister Yorinaga draw me into that conspiracy. I take back those words disclaiming all ties with the Heiké."

"Too late for regrets. I accept no excuses. You're a common criminal—a traitor."

"Do you mean that you're willing to see me captured and executed?"

"Why don't you plead with the throne? I'll have nothing to do with you. My orders are to arrest all rebels. My duty is to hand you over to the authorities."

"You're heartless! . . . Ah—"

"Out of my sight! Go wherever you will! Go, otherwise you shall be made a prisoner."

"No, no! I have hidden many days in the hills with scarcely anything to eat, and I have barely dragged myself here by escaping the watches at the crossroads. If I go elsewhere, I shall surely be caught by other soldiers. . . . Yes, you, Lord Harima, shall punish me by striking off my head!"

"Why choose me for your executioner? Why not surrender yourself to the authorities? If that is distasteful to you, then take your own life like a true warrior."

"I shall do neither. I came here seeking mercy of my own nephew. If he refuses me, then no appeal to either heaven or earth can save me. I choose to have that nephew behead me. That's my last wish. Come, Lord Harima, strike! Strike off my head!"

Here was this impossible uncle of his, Kiyomori thought. Tadamasa, however, knew Kiyomori. He had known him from the time he was a sniveling youngster, as a wretched, poverty-stricken youth. He also knew how easily his nephew was moved to pity, and Tadamasa was ready to take advantage of this. He was sure that Kiyomori would not have the heart to turn against him. Tadamasa was certain that his tears would get him off lightly. And it was as Tadamasa had surmised, for Kiyomori felt completely helpless, as though he were the victim and not his uncle.

That same night he lodged Tadamasa in one of the houses at Rokuhara and the following evening paid a visit to Shinzei in secret. Kiyomori, who appeared buoyant even in the strenuous days following the fighting, now seemed listless and worn. Something was weighing on his mind, and he stared vacantly at the lights in Shinzei's guest chamber, waiting for Shinzei to appear.

CHAPTER XVII

THE RIVER OF BLOOD

Both Kiyomori and his host were flushed with the wine that Lady Kii poured for them. After they had tossed off several cups to celebrate their victory, Lady Kii, anticipating an exchange of confidences between the two men, dismissed the servants and waited on them herself.

"Behead him you must. There's nothing else to do except to behead him. You'll never be much of a man if you're soft-hearted," Shinzei repeated, taunting Kiyomori for his lack of spirit. "You're troubled by the thought that Tadamasa is your uncle, but didn't he disclaim blood-ties with you?"

"Yes, he feared the consequences of that affair of the Sacred Shrine, and that same morning renounced all kinship with me."

"Then he has no claims on you."

"But there are—"

Shinzei's bloodshot eyes held Kiyomori's as he continued: "Blood-ties—but I thought that the late Emperor Shirakawa was your real father, not Tadamori of the Heiké."

"Yes, that I learned from my father at the time he died. Though I may be the Emperor Shirakawa's son, what did he ever do for me? Tadamori was more than a father to me. How can I ever forget him? Tadamasa is his brother, and I cannot endure the thought of making him my prisoner, much less beheading him."

Shinzei laughed. "You are much too good-natured." Turning to his wife, he said: "Was there ever anyone with such senseless scruples?"

Lady Kii replied: "I'm afraid I don't quite understand. What is it that troubles him so?"

"Well, listen. Kiyomori comes here to me moping, and when I inquire what troubles him so, he tells me he is ready to give up his new title and lands that Tadamasa of the Heiké may go free."

"Dear me, so Tadamasa of the Heiké came to you because you are his nephew?"

"He hides him and then after much painful thought comes to me, begging me to intercede for Tadamasa at Court. I have been reproving him for a fool. Now what do you make of this?"

"I hardly know what to say—"

"Even you, a woman, who have had to perform many a distasteful task in secret to meet the wishes of Lady Bifukumon and of his late majesty, must smile at this womanish shrinking of a chief of the Heiké—this Lord Harima."

"This is too much, Shinzei—making me an object for ridicule. As I have just said, I have made up my mind."

"Do I still see traces of dejection and irresolution in you? You seem lively enough, but I detect signs that you're still troubled."

"Nothing—nothing more serious than the petty qualms common to doltish youths. I find it difficult to harden myself to this. . . ."

"It is entirely another matter in your case. Tadamasa is a rebel, and you are merely carrying out the commands of the throne. He no longer has any claims on you. No ties of blood exist between you."

"That I know. It shall be done. I no longer hesitate."

"It would be folly to spare him; you may only bring misfortune on yourself. Who can say that if he goes free, he will not rally the Heiké in other parts of the country and bring an army against you?"

"True. I have shown myself a coward. If the throne orders it, it shall be done tomorrow."

"The sooner the better, for if it becomes known that you gave him sanctuary, there's no telling what will happen to you and all the Heiké."

"You are undoubtedly right."

His irresolution gone, Kiyomori left Shinzei's mansion. A cool wind blew on his fevered cheeks, but a nauseating dizziness suddenly overcame him, causing him to reel in his saddle. The thought of what was expected of him made Kiyomori's head swim with horror. His whole being shrank from the thought of decapitating his uncle. A deep melancholy came over him, and he shook his head and beat on his temples with his clenched fists in desperation. A born coward. . . . Much as he detested Tadamasa, he saw no escape from this thing.

Tadamasa awoke late in the morning in a dim, barely furnished room in the servants' quarters. He found a medicinal bath prepared for him on his arrival, and later had gorged on a supper of gruel; assuring himself that his life was safe, he had slept soundly. He finished his morning meal with zest, and his thoughts then turned to his sons, who had been scattered during the fighting. Where were they now? Had they been captured or killed, he wondered.

"Is Tadamasa of the Heiké here?"

Startled from his musings, Tadamasa stared at the personable warrior in his early thirties who walked in. There was something familiar about him, and yet Tadamasa saw no resemblance between him and Kiyomori.

A note of bravado crept into Tadamasa's voice as he replied: "I am he. Who are you?"

"Tokitada, under-secretary at the Court."

"Ah, Lady Harima's brother. Contrary to my expectations, Lord Harima most generously gave me refuge. I commend myself to you, sir."

"So I understand. The warrior must be worthy of his name to the very end. If you care to shave or arrange your hair, I will wait a few moments for you."

"Wait for me? Am I to be taken elsewhere?"

"That will be at four o'clock this afternoon. I have been sent to put you in bonds."

"Eh? Bind me? Who gave such orders?"

"Lord Harima himself."

"Impossible! Call Lord Harima! Tell him I must speak with him."

"It will do you no good. We received an injunction from the Court this morning, and have orders to behead you by four o'clock this afternoon."

"Eh—!" As Tadamasa rose unsteadily to his feet, protesting: "N-n-nonsense! Impossible!" Tokitada leaped at him and both men crashed to the floor struggling. Some warriors who were waiting outside quickly crowded into the room with ropes and secured Tadamasa.

"Call my nephew! Bring him here—Lord Harima! What does he mean by deceiving a helpless old man?" shrieked Tadamasa, but the door was nailed to and a guard placed outside, while Tokitada quickly departed.

Kiyomori spent the morning alone in his apartments; he reminded himself of Shinzei's words, but his heart remained heavy.

"Brother, it has been accomplished."

"Ah, is it you, Tokitada? What has he been snarling?"

"He clamored most vexingly. An odious old man for one so near his end."

"Had I known this would happen, I would have shown no pity and had him bound on the spot. He would then have got off lightly."

"Not so. You must remember that this is Tadamasa of the Heiké. There is no question of his guilt."

"Have you seen the warrant that just arrived from the Court?"

"Yes, I have seen it. The execution takes place today at four, on the riverbank, a short distance from Gojo Bridge."

"To think that I agonized all night over Tadamasa, and now the order is to behead his three sons as well! Those are Shinzei's wishes."

"No worse than what we went through during the fighting when our sandals were soaking with blood."

"That was quite another matter. Different altogether."

"This, too, is war. What makes you think that the execution ground is not also a battlefield?"

Tokitada's bluntness was more heartening than Shinzei's specious reasoning and quieted Kiyomori's distrust of himself. "For a nap, then. It's still several hours until four. Tokitada, hand me that box over there."

Kiyomori lay staring at the summer sky; from under the curving eaves he saw how the clouds raced across the face of the sun, throwing the world into abrupt shadow and then into dazzling light.

Public executions had become a daily occurrence since the war's end, but the common folk showed no sign of tiring of the spectacle. A motley crowd now swarmed on both banks of the Kamo above Gojo Bridge. Arriving officials, who viewed the executions as a salutary warning to the rabble, made no move to drive off the multitudes who kept coming in spite of the lowering skies. Fierce gusts whipped at the black and white strips of screening drapery marking off the execution ground and threatened to tear them away; a few heavy drops of rain fell.

Three youths sat submissively in a kneeling position on rush mats placed at equal distances apart on the edge of the river. Near by, a coroner dispatched by the Imperial Guards, and jail officers who had completed the necessary arrangements waited for Kiyomori and Tokitada to appear. Their arrival soon created a stir among the gaping crowds. Kiyomori dismounted and walked down toward the river, exchanging civilities with the waiting officials; following him came Tokitada, flanked by warrior escorts and leading Tadamasa on a rope. The prisoner was ordered to take his position on a fourth mat. Suddenly the three youths started to their feet crying: "Father!" The rope that bound each prisoner was secured to a stake, and jerked the three violently backward or threw them sideways to the ground as they sprang up. The sight of his sons caused Tadamasa to assume a fittingly paternal air and he admonished them:

"Calm yourselves. We must be resigned. This is a bitter moment for me; none the less, I am thankful for this unlooked-for chance to see you all once more. This was decreed by our *karma*."

Tadamasa's voice, now hoarse from noisily resisting his captors, rose to a rasping shout. "Listen, my sons—this is but the warriors' lot that brings us to die here like this, yet we have not fallen so low as that beast, that ingrate, Kiyomori! What wrong did we commit in being loyal to our sovereign lord? We never forgot his favors. . . . Look at him there, the same Kiyomori I knew of old. *There* is an ingrate, if ever there was one! What reason have we to feel shame?"

Tadamasa glared at Kiyomori, who was now seated at a table. Kiyomori glared back and said nothing; his eyes fell at the sight of one so close to death; the color drained from his cheeks, leaving him ashen.

Tadamori suddenly lashed out at Kiyomori. "Yeh, Kiyomori! If you have ears to hear, then listen! Have you already forgotten those faraway days when Tadamori was penniless and could scarcely feed you even the most niggardly gruel, and sent you many a time to me to borrow money?"

Kiyomori remained silent.

"Do you remember how you came to me on those bitter winter days in your ragged robes, like a beggar, with your tales of woe? Have you forgotten that you wept as you wolfed down the cold food I gave you out of pity? How I laugh to think that that starving devil is now the great Lord Harima! Let bygones be bygones, but what's this—betraying your uncle, who befriended you in your youth? So you call yourself a man who have bartered my head for more favors from the Court?"

"You fall short of even the brutes! Answer me—you—if you can!"

". . . ."

"I thought not. How can you? So you intend to behead me—your benefactor—your father's own brother? . . . Perhaps it was fated by my *karma*. So be it, then. I'll recite no prayers, but say the name of Tadamori over and over as I wait for the stroke."

Tadamasa's voice rose to a hideous shriek: "Here, now, strike!"

The clouds overhead grew thicker, casting a heavy murk over the scene. There was no sun by which to tell the hour. Thunder mumbled at a distance; the surface of the river grew choppy as a cold wind tore along the river front hurling sand and spume before it, and flinging the screening drapery to the ground. Though hardened to executions, the officials huddled in a group as though cowering from Tadamasa's rantings. The sharp sting of raindrops, however, seemed to rouse them.

"Four o'clock, Lord Harima—perhaps even past the hour."

"Oh?" Kiyomori received the announcement with a dazed air. With great effort he came to his feet. As he stood up, Tadamasa's eyes rolled upward and then sideways, following Kiyomori as he moved toward him.

"Tokitada—the sword."

Tokitada, who followed a step behind, unsheathed it. His eyes sought Kiyomori's white face with a look that said: "Which one?"

"That end."

A youth's face shot round at Kiyomori's pointed finger. Kiyomori glanced away quickly.

"Hurry, Tokitada—don't flinch," Kiyomori urged.

"This is nothing," Tokitada murmured. As he spoke, an odd sound like the squelch of a wet cloth struck the ears of the onlookers. In that same moment the sword flashed and dripped blood.

"Ah, Naganori, they've done for you!" Tadamasa cried. Another head fell with the same curdling sound.

"Tadatsuna! Ah, Tadatsuna!"

The cry mingled with the rumble of thunder overhead. Tadamasa's voice trembled to a shriek as the sword descended for the third time, but in a fumbling stroke. Tokitada suddenly looked up dazed and searched the faces about him with a numbed stare.

"Here, Tokitada, what's happened to you?"

"Water—give me water before I finish the last. Everything went black; my hands lost their nerve. . . ."

"Coward! The blood's sickened you. . . . Here, let me do it."

Kiyomori's temper flared. He strode the few steps up to Tadamasa and stared coldly at the face turned up to him. He felt drained of all feeling and seemed to float in a white void. The core of his brain was like ice, so cold that it seared him. The sound of a short laugh startled him, until he realized it came from his own lips as he stood over Tadamasa, gripping his sword.

"Tadamasa of the Heiké, is there anything more that you wish to say? I'm to give you the death blow."

"Hmm—see if you can," Tadamasa hissed defiantly, throwing back his head as though to stave off the last moment. Instead of exposing the nape of his neck, he sat up rigidly, arching his chest. "I never did like you—not even as a child, Kiyomori—you! I now understand why; it was a premonition of this."

"I believe you; nor have I ever detested anyone as I do you."

"As snow to ink—so unlike are we, uncle and nephew. You win. I die at your hands and nothing could be more galling than this."

"Bitter as this may be to you, this, too, is war."

"Not war, but fate. Your turn comes next, Kiyomori."

"No need to wait for that. Now, are you ready?"

"Don't hurry. One word more."

"What's that? What more have you to say?"

"Truly, the resemblance is unmistakable. There's no mistaking the spawn of that evil priest."

"What priest? What?"

"Your sire."

"Whomsoever I resemble, I had no other father but Tadamori."

"Come, come, Tadamori's first wife, the Lady of Gion, herself told me that you were not his son, nor that of the Emperor Shirakawa. The truth is that she had you by that debauched priest who was her lover . . ." Tadamasa babbled on.

"A curse on you foul-mouthed . . . die!" Kiyomori swung his sword. It flashed white, cutting clean through Tadamasa's neck.

Splattered with blood, Kiyomori stood motionless, his dripping sword at rest.

Lightning flashes darted before his unseeing eyes. Thunder crashed. The cloth screen flapped wildly. The ground under his feet seemed to roll.

"You fool! The more fool!"

"Madman! Brute!"

"You fiend!"

"You demon incarnate!"

This was not the voice of the thunder, but the howls of the crowd, their rage unleashed by the hateful sight of one who had put his four kinsmen to the sword. A shower of stones fell about Kiyomori, but he made an attempt to escape. A heavier rain of missiles struck his armor, his face and hands, from which blood now trickled. The cries of the multitude were drowned in a crescendo of roars. Kiyomori's attendants galloped into the crowd, which quickly melted away before the drawn swords. But Kiyomori continued to stand stonily near the four headless corpses. The rain now swept in white sheets over the lone figure; blue-white lightning flashed obliquely across the lifted pagodas on the Eastern Hills. Yet he stood motionless in the drenching rain, his sword drooping before him.

"My lord . . . my lord."

"The officials have left, sir."

"The crowd has dispersed."

"Your duty has been accomplished with no mishaps."

"It is time for you to leave, sir."

Kiyomori's soldiers crowded about him anxiously, impatient to be off, but he turned away from them and climbed the embankment; in the softly falling rain he lifted his eyes toward a break in the clouds and murmured a prayer. Then he called quietly: "Tokitada, Tokitada!"

The troubled faces of Tokitada and the soldiers cleared at the sound of Kiyomori's usual level tones. A rainbow arched the evening sky. An evil dream seemed to have dissolved, and Tokitada came forward leading Kiyomori's horse.

Taking the reins from him, Kiyomori spoke over his shoulder: "Stay here, Tokitada, with four or five of our men. Take the four bodies with care to the burning-ground at Toribeno. I shall go home and keep vigil tonight. I leave the interment to you."

That night Shinzei received Tadamasa's head. Korekata, the Captain of the Right, brought the four heads from Rokuhara to the waiting Shinzei, who inspected them by candlelight.

"Very well." He nodded, and listened to an account of the execution, of Tadamasa's last moments, of Kiyomori's conduct, and of the delays.

Shinzei suddenly laughed aloud, slapping his thigh.

"So that was what happened, and there are exceptions to the saying that the condemned die penitent. There are not too many like Tadamasa who die bitterly protesting their entrance into paradise. As for Kiyomori—a white-livered fellow. It's a wonder that he fought as he did at Shirakawa."

On the following day Shinzei summoned Yoshitomo and in his usual deliberate manner said: "Sir—Master of the Imperial Stables, Lord Harima brought in his uncle's head last night. A most exemplary act. . . . And, by the way, have you had any reports of one who has shown himself an even more dangerous rebel than Tadamasa? I mean Tameyoshi of the Genji, who directed operations against us."

The courteous, ingratiating tones chilled Yoshitomo to the heart. He turned pale.

"Sir, a careful search is being made—no trace of him and his sons has yet been found."

"His majesty is kept informed of your diligence in rounding up the traitors, you understand."

"Everything is being done to further the search, and I am sure they will be captured, but—"

"But what?"

Yoshitomo's head drooped. Shinzei gave him a quizzical look from under his brows.

For three days and nights Tameyoshi, his sons, and their three retainers hid in a temple in the hills between Shirakawa and Lake Biwa. The caretaker there received them kindly, and they were able to get food and sleep and a chance to dress their wounds as they made plans to find a boat that would carry them across the lake in their flight eastward. But during that time, as ill chance would have it, an old ailment, rheumatism, crippled Tameyoshi and kept him in bed in a small room of the dilapidated temple. And as the defeated warrior lay there, there passed through his mind the long parade of his sixty years, tinged with regrets and loneliness, for he had had his full share of sorrows.

In the meantime, one of his sons and Magoroku, a retainer, went down to Otsu to see about hiring a boat, while Tametomo and the rest kept a sharp lookout for their pursuers.

The two, Yorikata and Magoroku, were soon back with the news that they had found a fisherman willing to ferry them by stealth across the lake. That night, the 17th of July, the fugitives cautiously made their way to the appointed spot, the giant pine tree at Karasaki. On arriving there they were dismayed to find no sign of the boat. As they peered through the dark, they suddenly saw a blaze of torches coming toward them with a clatter of hoofs and shouts.

"We are trapped!" Tametomo cried, and, quickly ordering Magoroku to escape with Tameyoshi to the hills, prepared the others to make a stand until the two had reached safety.

Half-carrying and dragging Tameyoshi, Magoroku at last reached a temple in the hills. There a priest to whom Magoroku told his desperate tale gave them shelter. But at daybreak Magoroku, still fearing pursuit, bore Tameyoshi on his back and made his way through a valley of Mount Hiei, until they came to a temple in Kurodani.

Broken in body and spirit, Tameyoshi confessed to Magoroku that he held out no hope of rallying an army even though he succeeded in reaching eastern Japan.

"Nothing remains to me now, Magoroku, except to take the tonsure and surrender to my son, Yoshitomo," he said.

When Tameyoshi's sons finally rejoined him, they found to their sorrow that he had already received the tonsure at the hands of a priest. And they wept. "Now are we robbed of all purpose. What is there left for us to look forward to?"

But Tameyoshi replied: "Not so, my sons, you cannot stay with me forever. A time comes when the fledglings must leave their nest for the endless blue that stretches before them." And he shed bitter tears at the thought that he had no more consoling words than these for his sons.

Magoroku, who had been sent to the capital with a letter from Tameyoshi to Yoshitomo, returned, saying that Yoshitomo had shown great joy on reading the message. Eager for more news of his son, Tameyoshi inquired whether Magoroku had also spoken with Yoshitomo, and was told:

"He was not at his house, and thinking I might find him at the lady Tokiwa's, I went there. I was fortunate to find him, still in his armor, and dandling his children on his lap."

"And you found him playing with my grandchildren? So he knows now what it is to be a father. There were two, were there not?"

"Yes—and it appeared that they look for another very soon, and because of it his lordship was deeply concerned for his lady."

"Ah, they tell me she is a pleasing young woman. He alone of us all is fortunate."

Tameyoshi's sons watched their father with silent frowns as he read Yoshitomo's letter to himself:

"I await your coming. My retainers will meet you at the edge of the woods on this side of the Kamo. You need not be anxious. I am prepared to forfeit all the honors that have come to me that I may plead for you with his majesty."

His sons, however, were unwilling that Tameyoshi should leave them and surrender himself to Yoshitomo, and Tametomo said:

"My father, is there no way in which to dissuade you? Who knows whether Yoshitomo is to be trusted or not? I feel you are in danger. Stay with us."

"Whatever you may say, Tametomo, I cannot believe that Yoshitomo would deceive me. Contemptible as I may appear, I do not go because my own life is precious to me, but to seek pardon for all of you—that, and because this is the only way in which he, too, will find peace of mind."

Tametomo shook his head. "It is only natural for you to think so. What son would wish to see his father put to death? Yet, were he such a monster as to allow it, no amount of worldly success would lay the pangs of remorse from which he would suffer ever after. On the other hand, consider how the Emperor betrayed his own brother, the ex-Emperor; the Regent his own brother, Yorinaga."

Tameyoshi pondered these words, but was not persuaded. "I have already sent Magoroku with a message to Yoshitomo. Others in the capital must know by now where we are. Were I to reach Kamakura and then fail to raise an army, I should in the end have to sue for peace with my life. There seems to be no choice for me other than this."

On the following day Tameyoshi, leaning on Magoroku, made his way down to the Kamo. Loath to see him depart, his sons followed him until they were close to the capital, believing they would never see their father again.

Tameyoshi paused to look back, saying: "My sons, we are now near the capital. It is time for us to part—there must be an end to our farewells."

And Tameyoshi's sons lifted up their voices and wept.

A litter waited for Tameyoshi at the edge of the wood by the Kamo, and that evening he was carried to Yoshitomo's mansion, where three serving-women received him and saw to it that he bathed, brought him fresh garments and medicaments and all manner of foods, so that he wanted nothing.

That night he slept soundly, untroubled by insects and the fear of wild beasts.

Tameyoshi's first thought on awaking was that he was safe under his son's roof. It was not until noon, however, that he saw Yoshitomo, who came to him secretly. Less than three weeks had elapsed since they last met, but to them it seemed as though many years had gone by in that time. Tameyoshi and Yoshitomo wept quietly when they came face to face.

". . . My father, forgive me for the pain I have given you."

"Forgive? Yoshitomo, your father is guilty of high treason. I have no right to be here. Treat me as you would a criminal."

"My heart breaks to have you say this."

"No, no, Yoshitomo, I am an old man and resigned to my

fate. This only I beg of you—to spare your brothers, the guiltless women, and the children. Let me be punished in their stead."

"It is for me to give up all I have to save you, my father."

"But, remember, there are many at Court who think differently. Take no rash step that will endanger your life. I only ask that you, my eldest, succeed to the chieftainship and preserve our name," Tameyoshi pleaded.

That night Yoshitomo, concealed in his ox-carriage, drove to Shinzei's residence. Shinzei was not at home. He had for some time been extremely busy and was not expected to return from the Court that night, his servants said. The next night Yoshitomo went again and was fortunate in having Shinzei receive him.

When Yoshitomo had finished speaking, Shinzei replied coldly:

"What! You ask that Tameyoshi's life be spared? Even I can do nothing for you. It is, moreover, most indiscreet of you to come to me on this matter. It would be more to the point if you presented your appeal in person to the courtiers."

Yoshitomo, however, did not lose heart. A general, Masasada, a former Minister of the Right, he knew was a man of wide sympathies, trusted in higher circles of the Court, and in the confidence of the Emperor. To him Yoshitomo went one night and was received with kindness. None the less, the general was not inclined to optimism.

". . . Yes, I feel that I understand what you are going through. But in these troubled times I can give you no assurances that the Court will even consider your appeal, though I shall see what can be done by adding a few words myself," Masasada said warmly.

At the next meeting of the Court councilors, Masasada himself presented Yoshitomo's appeal. Not only did he plead that Tameyoshi's life be spared in exchange for Yoshitomo's recently acquired honors, but he went on to say: ". . . The taking of one life will lead to the taking of another, and another, until even a hundred will not suffice, says an ancient adage. Tameyoshi sided with our enemies from a sense of loyalty. He is an old man and past sixty, an old soldier racked by infirmities. His grandfather was a warrior of great valor who subdued the enemies of the imperial house in the farthest marches, and there are many who still remember his exploits. To condemn Tameyoshi to death will surely kindle the hatred of those who remember his grandfather. As we judge, so also shall we be judged. It grieves and alarms me to think that harsh measures carried out in the name of the throne will only add to those barbarities we already see around us. Are not mercy and an all-embracing love the substance of the imperial prerogative?"

Someone laughed. It was Shinzei.

"What's over is over. Today is today. The task of government is to deal with the present. Sir, you give us fair words, but are you not aware of what is happening around us today?" he asked.

"If we spare Tameyoshi, how then are we to deal with the pretender to the throne—Sutoku? If instead of sentencing him to death we banish Tameyoshi, who can say that he will not marshal an army in the far provinces and once more march against us? Did Kiyomori hesitate to put his uncle to the sword? Is it just to make an exception of Tameyoshi and his sons?"

A malicious smile played over Shinzei's features all the while he spoke and watched Masasada.

"The Police Commissioner tells me that Lord Yoshitomo has given Tameyoshi asylum. Strange and improbable as this sounds, if proved true, this would be a flagrant violation of an imperial decree. Indeed, the honorable gentleman proposes that we be lenient when I already consider him deserving of the death penalty."

Shinzei flung out his last words savagely. Since the end of the war his authority had increasingly come to the fore, and the general realized that he had no chance of winning out against Shinzei.

Masasada later summoned Yoshitomo and told him of what had taken place at the council. "I advise you to act with great discretion, otherwise you may expect the other captains to attack you in your own house."

Tortured by remorse, Yoshitomo reproached himself for not casting his lot with his father's. His trusted retainers Masakiyo and Jiro soon saw what was going on in their master's mind. Not only they but the other retainers who had shared Yoshitomo's triumphs grew fearful at the thought of what might happen to him. It was likely that he would not only be ordered to behead his own father, but be stripped of all his honors and outlawed.

After two wakeful nights Yoshitomo called Masakiyo and Jiro to him and spoke with them.

Toward evening of that same day Masakiyo and Jiro brought a litter outside Tameyoshi's room and said: "There has been very disturbing talk about you, and our master is troubled for your safety. He has neither slept nor taken food these several days in his anxiety. There are some unbelievably malevolent persons at the Court. Because of them it seems advisable for you to go into hiding somewhere in the Eastern Hills, and we are to accompany you."

Tameyoshi rose to go with them, and turning in the direction of Yoshitomo's room, he raised his clasped hands. "Truly, it has been said that there are no treasures more precious than one's children. Only my son would go to such lengths in his solicitude for me. Such magnanimity cannot be forgotten. I shall remember this to the end of my days," Tameyoshi repeated again and again with tears.

Toward dusk Tameyoshi's litter was carried out by a rear gate and borne through the oncoming night. The bearers seemed to follow a road other than that leading to the Eastern Hills; and when they finally were outside the capital in an open field, Tameyoshi found that several of Yoshitomo's housemen had arrived and were waiting with an ox-carriage.

Masakiyo nudged Jiro, who frowned and waved him off, muttering:

". . . You do it. I cannot."

Masakiyo shrank away irresolute and called to the litter-bearers: "Aah—you there, set down the litter. . . . Sir, we are now outside the city and still have some distance to go; will you not take the carriage now?" And he came close to the litter. He drew back to give Tameyoshi room to step out, tightening his grip on his sword as he waited. Jiro suddenly spoke from behind and nudged the hand on the hilt.

"Masakiyo, a word with you. . . ." As he spoke, Jiro walked a few paces ahead of the litter and turned to Masakiyo, who joined him. "Here—not by trickery, I tell you. He is, after all, the master's father and it does not seem right."

"Well then, what?"

"Why not tell him everything? Let him then say his prayers. Even though he meets his end out in this desolate waste, he is after all Tameyoshi of the Genji and deserves to die as a fine warrior should."

"You are right, quite right. But that makes it all the harder. You do it."

"Not for anything! That is beyond me. You are the one for it."

After this whispered colloquy, Masakiyo turned back to Tameyoshi and told him why he had been brought here.

Tameyoshi received the disclosure quietly. "So." As he seated himself on the ground, he said with deep feeling: "Why did not my son tell me this himself? I can understand his reluctance, but a father's love encompasses much." Tameyoshi's tears fell as he continued: "Did—did he not know that a father's love can rise even above this? All those many years since he left his mother's breast and played at my knees, did he not even then come to know every corner of this heart?—Ah, Yoshitomo, that alone grieves me. Our lives are like foam on the stream, yet are we not father and son, linked to each other by ties from another life? Why could you not open your heart to me? I have fallen, indeed, yet not so low as to seek anything for myself when I came to you. Since this was

2 4 9

fated by the gods, why could we not have spent a last evening together, lamenting this and opening our hearts to each other before parting?"

When he ended, Tameyoshi settled himself more firmly on the ground and wept no more, as though the tears of a lifetime had been spent. Composing himself further, he clasped his hands and recited a prayer. Then he turned to Masakiyo and whispered in tones as gentle as the rustling of his monk's robe: "Masakiyo, strike."

Yoshitomo soon after presented his father's head to the authorities at the Court. Though Tameyoshi's head was not dishonored by exposure in public, the common people cursed Yoshitomo more bitterly than they did Kiyomori. With the exception of the youngest, Tameyoshi's other sons were soon after captured and executed. Tametomo, who escaped to Kyushu, was later brought back a prisoner to the capital. There the tendons of his arms were severed before his banishment to the island of Oshima in the east.

CHAPTER XVIII

SONG ON A FLUTE

Offerings of incense, flowers, and small piles of stones began to mark the roadside and bridges where so many warriors had lately fallen in battle. They were left there by pious common folk who took no part in the conflict. Crones with infants strapped on their backs, housewives returning from market, potters on their way to the city once more to hawk their wares, peddlers of rush mats, nuns, and even an occasional ox-tender paused to offer prayers for the nameless dead.

"Ah, you pitiful dead, and more pitiful discord! Can these, indeed, be tokens of the goodness at the heart of men? Good, good!"

A hulking figure in a wide hat of plaited bamboo and tattered monk's robes stood at a crossroad muttering to himself as he stared round him at the flowers and incense near some charred ruins. He appeared to be in his early forties and shouldered a pack such as itinerant priests carry; he leaned on a pilgrim's staff; a rosary was wound round a hairy wrist. His head was not shaven and his hair hung in unkempt profusion about his travel-stained face; his worn straw sandals were caked with mud. The stern look on his face made him seem more terrible than any monk from Mount Hiei. As he moved away, striding rapidly through the streets of the capital, the sight of the ruins he passed seemed to move him deeply and he prayed aloud lustily: "*Namu Amida-butsu, namu Amida-butsu. . . .*"

"There he goes, the priest with the loud voice!"

"Shaggy-headed one, O shaggy-headed demon!"

"Priest-man, priest-man, where are you going?" chanted the street urchins who recognized him.

The ragged figure turned and grinned good-naturedly, exposing a red mouth through his shaggy beard.

"Shaggy one, give us some cakes!"

"Rice cakes, please!"

"Pennies will do!" the children continued to shout, running after him.

"Nothing now. Next time, next time." The figure waved, turning a corner with long strides.

In a short while he was standing before the gates of Councilor Shinzei's mansion, where he stopped to rub his beads and pray. Then striding boldly in by the gateway, he hurried past the carriage-house, planted himself at the entrance porch, and hallooed loudly.

"This is I—Mongaku—from the Togano-o Hills, north of the capital. I came here yesterday and the day before. I must have speech today with the honorable Councilor; I have somewhat to tell him. Someone go tell him I am here."

Mongaku's thundering voice seemed to have penetrated to the inner rooms of the spacious residence; some frightened servants hurried off toward the master's apartments, and others came out of the servants' quarters. Then three young warriors and the chief steward appeared. They greeted Mongaku with great courtesy. Then one of them said: "I regret to tell you that the master is detained at the Court and has not yet returned. We have no idea when he will be back, for he is so busy with matters of state."

"Oh?—On my way here I stopped at the Guard Office, and the register showed that he left the Court last night at the Hour of the Cock (six p.m.). He *should* be at home.—Why does he shun me? Is he not busy with restoring public peace and setting the minds of the people at rest? I have not come for any idle chatting, but to share some anxious thoughts and to give him advice. I therefore ask that my message be carried to him."

"Yes, yes. I shall see that he is told another day."

"Not some other day! I beg to see him now. Enough of these transparent lies! Go tell him now."

"But today—"

"Now—today! It shall not be tomorrow, for every day means so many more lives lost. In the name of peace—this is most urgent. If you refuse, I shall bellow to him from here."

Mongaku showed no sign of budging even an inch. Removing his pilgrim's pack, he sat down on the ground.

Councilor Shinzei and his wife, Lady Kii, were entertaining a friend in the Spring Pavilion, where the cook had been called to prepare a special dish before them as they sipped their wine.

"Tch—a nuisance!" Shinzei remarked testily with a quick glance at his guest's litter.

"Let me see what it is," said his son, Naganori, rising.

Shinzei whispered in his son's ear: "If it is that troublesome priest Mongaku, who has been sending written protests to the Court, tell him some tale and send him packing."

Naganori, nodding that he understood, went out to the carriage entry and stood on the porch, looking down at Mongaku. "Are you not the priest Mongaku? My father is at home, but he has an important visitor. He has seen your protests. Is that not enough?"

"And who are you?"

"The Councilor's third son."

"You must pardon me—but you will not do. Tell the Councilor himself to come."

"Indeed, you lack proper respect for the Councilor by demanding that he come here."

"Not so. I have come here three days in succession, and it surely cannot be any great trouble to show himself. Moreover, it is not private business that brings me here; he can hardly grudge me his time when I come to tell him about my anxieties for the public."

"Visitors such as you are far from rare, and I have no doubt that my father has had enough of such advice."

"Silence! Mongaku does not come to call at grand houses out of any elegant madness. Day and night scores of prisoners are dragged from jail and beheaded by the river!"

"Softly, please! You disturb our guests."

"I do? Then Shinzei can hear me in his apartments. Very well, I shall speak to him from here. If he has visitors, then let them also listen to what I have to say."

Mongaku suddenly came to his feet and drew a deep breath. The voice that had been heard above the thundering of the Nachi Falls for more than ten years now seemed to shake the very rafters of Shinzei's mansion:

"Here, you, master of this house! This is a warning from heaven itself, not the idle gossip of the market-place. By your wanton executions you have created the six rounds of hell on earth. You made a nephew put his uncle to the sword; brother turn against brother; a young father behead his own father. Not even the dumb beasts are so ruthless to each other!"

". . . ."

"Listen further: every day that you speak in the high councils means just so many more are condemned to death. You forced Yoshitomo to bring in his father's head, to behead his brothers, and, still unsatisfied, you saw to it that Tameyoshi's aged wife was drowned and the children and others of his house lined up along the road and stabbed to death in cold blood. Do you think that no one hates you for your malevolence and savagery?"

". . . ."

Naganori and the housemen stood speechless before this fiery torrent of denunciations, which went on:

"Shinzei orders all this done in the name of the throne and by the warriors. What could be more treacherous than this? For three hundred years and more the benevolent rule of our emperors did away with the death penalty. There were no wars in the capital, and the people were regarded as the filial children of the sovereign. Those times are now gone. Oh, sorry state!"

Mongaku's beads rattled angrily as he shook his clenched fist. Despite more than ten years spent in mortifications and spiritual exercises, the essential character of Morito, the youthful, passionate Guard, had changed little. The scars of his ill-fated love affair had well-nigh healed, but the long pursuit of the religious life had not transformed him beyond recognition. New fires burned in him; the laxity and corruption of the clergy drove him to the solitude of the Togano-o Hills, where he dreamed of one day restoring the Tendai sect in all its purity, and he had lately gone to live in the decaying villa that Toba Sojo had once occupied. Stories of the brutalities which followed the end of the Hogen War, however, brought him down to the capital, and what he saw there caused him to admit that the teachers of religion and the enlightenment of Buddhism were powerless against politics and the madness of war. Yet Mongaku was not one to withdraw from the world and remain indifferent to men's inhumanities to one another or the degrading misery of the common folk.

While Mongaku thundered in the courtyard of the inner gate, a pair of ox-carriages drew up at the outer gate and two young courtiers stepped out.

"What's this?"

"A giant of a monk bellowing?"

Tsunemuné of the Fujiwara, the courtier, and another young

nobleman, Nobuyori, stopped for a moment to listen and then entered by the gate. Half-concealed by the hedge near the inner gate, they waited for Mongaku to depart.

Tsunemuné, who had vanished at the outbreak of the fighting, appeared at the Court as soon as the conflict was over, and with disarming tact paid calls on the Regent and on Councilor Shinzei, offering his congratulations on their victory.

Tsunemuné, though unprincipled, possessed a remarkable talent for small talk and gossip, coupled with wit, and charmed and amused all whom he met. He now accompanied the courtier Nobuyori, to whom he had promised an introduction to the Councilor. ("Shinzei is *the* man for you to meet. *The* man just now. He will be controlling state affairs in time. Rather forbidding, but you *must* meet him some time.") Shinzei also had an eye on Nobuyori and had stayed away from Court to receive this young visitor.

Shinzei's son caught sight of the arriving visitors and was about to order his servants to drive out Mongaku, when a noisy scuffling broke out. "Get out! Go home!" he shouted, "You with your filthy abuse! One more word out of you and I'll hand you over to our soldiers."

A loud chuckling greeted Naganori's words. Mongaku was laughing. In the midst of the milling servants and housemen he stood planted, arms flung out wide, glaring at the men who surrounded him.

"Wait, wait! Hands off! I abhor violence more than anything —and it's not you that I fear, but myself when I forget myself! Now, wait! Let me say one more word to your master."

The gleam in Mongaku's eye kept his would-be captors at bay, and he roared:

"Yeh—Councilor Shinzei, listen in earnest to what Mongaku has to say. Leave off those executions and those tortures from today—this very moment, I say! Put an end to this reign of terror! Show mercy to your enemies, or vengeance will be visited on your own head.—Though you become all-powerful, what good will it do you if people come to loathe you? The fires of hell itself will one day consume your house, and you will be forced to listen to the agonized screams of your kin.—Let these abominable executions go on, then I myself will come to bind you to a wheel of fire and escort you to the execution ground at the river's edge. . . . Do you hear me, Shinzei—you?"

"Vile priest! How dare you insult the throne?"

Shinzei's retainers struck out at Mongaku's legs with their spears. Mongaku, taken unawares, reeled. When his attackers saw this, they threw themselves on Mongaku, pinning down his arms and clasping his legs, and by sheer numbers overwhelmed him. Mongaku uttered no sound, but lay breathing heavily under the bodies piled on him. When he saw that they were trying to bind him with ropes, he roared:

"Here, I'll get up," and struggled to his feet, brushing off his opponents as if they were pygmies.

"Don't let him go," shouted some soldiers who blocked Mongaku's path. At the uproar more servants and even the grooms came running to the scene. Instead of making for the gateway, Mongaku leaped to the porch and stood there defiant.

A cry went up: "An assassin—don't let him get in!"

Mongaku reached out and, clutching a man in either hand, slung each over the balustrade. Another he caught by the scruff of his neck and knocked his head against the nearest pillar until the fellow cried out for mercy. A screening-wall gave way and a shutter fell; while the mansion echoed and re-echoed with the commotion, the screams of women increased the bedlam that ensued. Mongaku suddenly appeared again at the entrance porch, his pack on his back, staff in hand, looking about wildly for an avenue of escape.

As he darted toward the inner gate, there was a shout: "You, there!" Mongaku leaped aside nimbly as a javelin was thrust at him. He glared at the mass of unsheathed swords and the flashing halberds between him and the outer gate; some waterlilies growing in a large bronze cistern beside the inner gate caught his eye. Throwing aside his staff, he lifted the unwieldy vessel to him. The water splashed and poured down its side. Amazed by this feat of strength, Mongaku's opponents stood back and watched him. He tottered forward toward the men who blocked the outer gate, and with a great heave sent the vessel crashing to earth with a hollow metallic roar. Mongaku burst into peals of laughter at the sight of the servants and soldiers covered with tangles of waterlilies, and dripping with slime. Then he quickly slipped out by the gate, still laughing heartily, and was soon out of sight.

Tsunemuné and Nobunori, who crouched by the hedge in astonishment, watched Mongaku vanish.

More than a hundred noblemen and warriors were decapitated, but there was no sign that the executions had come to an end. Yorinaga's body was exhumed and identified.

"Were I still Morito of the Guards, I might have been one of those ordered to disinter that corpse, or else I doubtless would have been decapitated on the riverbank. . . . Ah, Kesa-Gozen, beloved one, you were indeed my protecting angel incarnate. . . . Kesa-Gozen!"

Mongaku's love for Kesa-Gozen was undimmed. He had renounced all fleshly love and enshrined her in his heart as a saint. For more than ten years he had tried to atone for his crime by mortifications that few men could endure. He now sat on the bank of the Kamo beside a small fire he had kindled under the August stars. Alone—but not quite alone, for Kesa-Gozen's spirit was beside him. Taking a brush and inkstone from his pack, he began to inscribe prayers on the stones about him, prayers for those who had fallen in battle. He hoped that the casual passer-by who saw these stones—ten thousand, he vowed, would carry his prayers—would stop and piously add other prayers to his own for the dead.

For three days he had gone into hiding when he heard that Councilor Shinzei had ordered his capture. As he rapidly took up stone after stone, he sometimes inscribed the name of a long-dead friend beside a prayer. . . . Ah, life, *karma*—all things visible must undergo change. How escape *karma*?

". . . Still more. The rest must wait until tomorrow night," Mongaku muttered, replacing his writing-materials in his pack. He bathed his face in the river and stood up to go, when he saw a dim figure coming toward him. Mongaku climbed the embankment in the whitening dawn. The silent figure continued to follow. He turned to look at the wraithlike shape. It was a small dirty-looking fellow. A secret agent? Mongaku went on and the shape trailed after him.

"I thank you from my heart. . . . Many a soul that died unwept by this river and elsewhere must now be floating to paradise. . . . I thank you for your pains." Repeating his thanks, the odd little fellow drew near with a friendly air and tripped after Mongaku.

"Are you one of the people who live hereabouts?"

"No. . . ."

"Why do you thank me?"

"You also share my feelings. Nothing makes me happier than to find another being who shares them."

"Oh? Are you, then, one of the condemned?"

"Perhaps. Or someone like that."

"I have something to ask you. Do you have some alms for me?"

"I'm sorry I have nothing with me now. You are welcome to all I have, except my life."

Mongaku began to laugh. "You will give me everything—" and stopped to scrutinize the barefooted fellow in the early light. A beggar, he thought, by his ragged tunic and trousers. He was bareheaded, and his hair matted with filth. "I hesitate to ask you, yet—"

"No, I beg you to tell me. If there is anything I can do for you, I shall consider the day spent worthily."

"It isn't so very much—just one meal. To tell you the truth, I haven't eaten since yesterday morning."

"Ah, food is it?" The little fellow looked puzzled, then with an apologetic air said: "I must admit that I haven't had a roof over my head since the war, and have no idea of where I shall find anything to eat this morning. I keep body and soul together by begging . . . but I shall surely find you something later on.

Will you not wait for me by the well among the ruins of the Willow-Spring Palace until I return?"

Mongaku regretted what he had said and began hastily remonstrating with the little fellow, who, however, cheerfully darted away down an avenue and round a corner.

Mongaku made his way to the site of the Willow-Spring Palace. It seemed a good refuge, for he had not been able to return to his hermitage in the hills and only with difficulty found places to sleep during the day. Arrived at the Willow Spring, he found no trace of its former splendor—broken tiles and scorched trees lay strewn about. Charred boards and dead birds floated on the pond, once famous for its beauty. He found, however, that the ground around the Willow Spring had been swept and cleaned, and boards laid over the well to keep leaves from blowing into it. Fearing to litter the spot, Mongaku withdrew to a clump of trees among which he spied a flimsy shelter of blackened planks. He took off his pack and stretched himself on a rush mat to sleep. He had apparently fallen into a sound slumber, for suddenly he felt someone shaking him.

"Please, sir. Please, sir."

He opened his eyes. It was high noon by the sun. The little fellow was back and had set out some boards for a table and arranged a meal of cooked rice, salted fish, pickles, and some bean paste on oak and paulownia leaves.

"Good, sir. It is ready. Will you not come and eat?" said the fellow, saluting Mongaku with a deep bow.

Mongaku stared at the courteously bowing figure, then at the food laid out on the leaves, and tears sprang to his eyes. "Is this— is this what you got by begging?"

"I will not deceive you. That is exactly what I did—but every bit of this food is clean. The poorest, who have scarcely enough for themselves, have shared their little with this beggar who can hardly recite a sutra. All I did was to beg at each door with folded hands. It is sufficient reward for me that you, a holy man, should eat this, and I am certain that those who gave me this food would feel as I do, did they know. I beg you to eat."

Mongaku sat up silently with his lips tightly closed; finally he took up a pair of chopsticks and said: "I thank you, then. You have not had anything to eat yet. No, I am sure you have not had anything at all today. You must share this with me."

The little man shook his head, but finally consented, and the two slowly tasted the food together.

"Asatori—Asatori, the caretaker!"

A young servant-girl carrying a wooden pail appeared.

"Is it you, Yomogi? Did you want water?"

"Yes, I've come again for some water from your well. People refuse to give water to anyone who is friendly with my mistress, Tokiwa. Some of them even throw stones at our house in passing."

"Wait, now, I'll get you some water myself," Asatori cried, and ran off.

There were tales that soldiers had been throwing all manner of filth into wells, or even the bodies of the dead. The well at the servant-girl's house was one of those which could no longer be used and she was obliged to go elsewhere to draw water. Mongaku heard that Tokiwa was Yoshitomo's mistress, and that the common people were bitterly hostile to him.

From that day on, Mongaku stayed with Asatori in his small shelter, sharing his strange life of beggary. The two often sat on moonlight nights among the desolate Palace ruins contemplating the ebb and flow of life around them in a silence unbroken by the sound of music and gaiety. Asatori went out begging during the day, and Mongaku when darkness fell.

One night Mongaku returned early with a jar of wine and announced that he had decided to leave for the hills in the region of the Nachi Falls, and the wine, which he had got from a temple where they knew him, was to drink to their parting. He thanked Asatori for his great kindness, telling him that this night it was his turn to do the honors of the table.

Asatori became downcast at this news. He protested: "But this is too good for one such as I," but he drained cup after cup of wine, until he was quite intoxicated.

"Ah—I am completely overcome. Good Mongaku, when we next meet, let us hope it will not be in the midst of such ruins, and I shall then listen to one of your religious discourses."

"Ah, Asatori, you have no need for my sermons. The devotion with which you guard the Willow Spring fills me with joy. You have won my admiration by your fidelity in fulfilling your duty to your absent lord. It gladdens my heart to know that there is even one such as you in this world."

"Oh, no, it is all that a dull-witted fellow like me is fit for. In these troubled times I haven't the slightest desire to take up the music my father taught me."

"When all this trouble is over, the aristocrats in their mansions and the noblemen at the Court will resume their nightly banqueting and music, and if you once more become court musician, what a life of elegance and ease you might lead!"

"I have had enough of being kept by the aristocrats. If my playing on the flute and flageolet truly gave them pleasure, then would I enjoy performing for them, and the calling of a musician would not be entirely distasteful to me; but that rarely happens, for in the midst of all that feasting and gaiety I have all too often seen the pitiful rivalries, the jealousies, and the intrigues."

"Yes, I can quite see how the musician remains the outsider who watches the revelers drink themselves to insensibility."

"My father often used to lament being born to the profession of music and having to make a living by dancing attendance on the Court in its orgies and rites."

"You mean that you would rather spend your life among the humble, guarding this spring? I agree with you in that. You should put your skill to better use among the common folk."

"I doubt that the music which is suited to the Court would please them. Yet there must be some way in which I can make those harmonies delightful to them."

"Come, Asatori, will you not play me something on that flute of yours?"

Mongaku's request reminded Asatori of the ex-Emperor's unfulfilled promise and he replied: "Forgive me for refusing you.

There are too many sad memories that my flute would awaken, and I could not play without weeping. The happy mood in which this wine leaves me would vanish and all I shall have left would be my lonely thoughts."

Mongaku did not press him further. There were other sweet sounds to soothe the mind and ear, for far and near in the grass among the ruins myriads of crickets chirred, strummed, and tinkled. A small moon hung high in the night above them.

"Will this, then, be the end of the fighting?"

"I fear not."

"You believe there will be more?" Asatori shuddered.

"Not until men learn to cast out greed and suspicion from their hearts," Mongaku replied. "While sons distrust their fathers, and fathers their children, there is no telling when brothers and kin will become bitter enemies. When master and retainer and friends dare not trust each other, then without even the shedding of blood, life on earth becomes a hell. In this last war the flames of hell itself reached out at us."

"It appears as though the war has ended."

"No, that was only a foretaste of one even more terrible. Councilor Shinzei's ruthlessness is a promise of worse to come. You shall see how this capital becomes the haunt of demons. The thought terrifies me."

"Is this because Shinzei alone is evil?"

"The causes go farther and deeper, and Shinzei alone is not responsible for them. They are in me, too—in you."

"In me—you?"

"Consider, Asatori—man is a most troublesome creature. Supposing someone comes and knocks over this jar of wine that we are enjoying. Do you think we could remain silent? Or what if some person should try to rob you of your precious flute, would you not fight to get it back? We are both solitary souls with no family ties, but if this were not so, we would become victims of blind love, and in our blindness who knows what we might be led to do? Were we free of all such bonds, we would even then find ourselves led astray by our desires and self-love. Do not the teachings of Buddha say that man is a god and a devil by turns, that he is a dangerous creature tossed unceasingly between good and evil? This is true of the prince as well as the pauper, those who are surfeited and those who starve—and the world is made up of both. No wonder, then, that one misstep can lead to the spilling of blood."

"Then are all men evil, and is there no one who is not?"

"It would be safe if each man regarded himself as evil. I must say for myself that I find myself so, and that I easily let my feelings get the better of me."

"Does this mean that force is evil?"

"Undoubtedly. But power is an even more fatal poison. The fascination that power has for men is indeed a mystery. He who once tastes of it cannot avoid creating conflict or is himself drawn into it. Have we not already seen how even the great lords and fair ladies, or even a three-year-old emperor, become mere puppets in this struggle for power?—Even the holy men on their mountains who preach salvation are not free from this greed for power and fame. No, not even among the dancing-girls at Eguchi and the merchants of the market-place, or the hordes of beggars. . . . What troublesome creatures we are!"

Mongaku, preoccupied with his reflections on the follies of mankind, emptied cup after cup of the wine he had brought his friend. Asatori meanwhile sat listening vacantly. These vexing passions of which Mongaku spoke, he could not seem to find in himself. Mongaku's reflections sounded like the confessions of one who wrestled unceasingly with the demons within him.

The two soon lay down to sleep. When the night was half over, Mongaku rose and prepared to depart. Shouldering his pack, and staff in hand, he set out toward the river, fording it where it was shallowest, and vanished into the darkness of the farther shore. Asatori accompanied his friend to the riverbank and watched him disappear before starting back for the ruins. As he turned a corner onto one of the avenues, Asatori saw a long procession of riders approaching in a glare of torches. Shrinking back in fear, he ran to his hut and hid himself, trembling. But sleep would not come because of his anxiety. For many days he had had thought of the ex-Emperor and what might become of him. Whenever he went out begging, he heard gossip that the authorities were preparing to deal with the ex-Emperor; that the Emperor no longer had cause to apprehend and punish his brother Sutoku, who had taken the tonsure and retired to Ninna-ji Temple, and that the sovereign would have his brother taken to a temple farther removed from the capital. There was also a rumor that secret meetings of high officials were being held to decide Sutoku's fate.

Asatori sat up suddenly. Could it be that the procession was going to Ninna-ji Temple? He looked up at the stars in the early dawn, then leaped to his feet, ran out onto an avenue, and, taking a short cut behind the Academy, came out on another avenue where he saw the same lighted procession creeping northward like a glowing centipede in the direction of Ninna-ji Temple, outside the city gates.

On the previous day the Emperor's aide arrived at Ninna-ji Temple and presented himself to the ex-Emperor, Sutoku, saying: "I bring an imperial order. Tomorrow, the 23rd, you are to leave for the land of Sanuki. You have only tonight to arrange your affairs and make your farewells. You are to wait for your escorts."

Banishment! Sutoku heard these words in despair. Banishment across the seas! His thoughts turned to his son. What was to become of him? Sutoku begged for a word with the Abbot. At midnight the Abbot came, and Sutoku told him of his fears for his son and entreated the Abbot to see that the Prince was brought to him and took the tonsure at his hands. Moved by Sutoku's pitiful pleas, the reluctant Abbot consented.

Three gentlewomen, the only attendants Sutoku was allowed to retain, had scarcely completed their preparations for the departure when neighing and the shouts of grooms and soldiers and the rumbling of carriage wheels were heard outside the gate. Smoking pine torches lit up the early hours of the dawn with an unearthly glare. The gates were opened and the scurrying of monks' feet and a bustle filled the temple buildings. One by one pale points of light appeared as candles were lit. Two warriors appeared in Sutoku's chamber, announcing that they were his guards, and led him to the waiting carriage. In the half-light of the dawn monks, menservants, serving-women, and farming folk from the temple estates lined the driveway and crowded the gates sorrowing, and among that throng stood Asatori, craning for a last sight of his master. But Sutoku was not seen, for his carriage was boarded up with wooden shutters. As the procession of warriors and officials moved away, the crowd dispersed, leaving only Asatori staring at the backs of the riders. Asatori then started after them, trudging behind the cavalcade.

The procession avoided the capital by taking the rutted road on the western side, passed the Rashomon Gate, and wound its way south, by Fukumi and the Anrakuju-in Temple, where the Kamo and Katsura rivers meet to form the Yodo River. There the sprawling landscape still lay wrapped in sleep.

Three boats were moored at the landing-stage at Yodo. "They're late. They should have arrived long ago," grumbled some warriors who accompanied the Governor of Sanuki.

"Here they come," cried a sailor.

"Where? I don't see them."

"Can't you see those fishermen in great excitement?"

In a short while two carriages flanked by warriors on horseback arrived. The Governor stepped forward. "You come later than the appointed hour. This inconveniences us who regulate our movements by the tide and winds. See that the exile boards at once."

The sailors and boatmen were now hurriedly setting rudders, loosening ropes and shouting to one another in the morning wind. One of Sutoku's guards seemed to be holding a heated conversation with the Governor.

"About three hundred escorts you say?"

"After all, he's not an ordinary prisoner."

"Even so—so many. There's barely room for him and his three attendants."

"That may be, but we have orders to accompany them. How many vessels do you have ready?"

"As you can see for yourself—one for the exile and his party. Two for the officials and soldiers. It's impossible to take on three hundred. We could take twenty—not more. There's just no room."

Further argument was futile and it was finally settled that twenty warriors would accompany Sutoku; his two guards then took leave of him there. The three gentlewomen entered their vessel and Sutoku followed them. The narrow cabin with its two small windows had only a rough straw mat covering the floor. Inside, the air was dank, and slimy insects crawled about in the crevices. The Governor, whose craft had left the shore, shouted: "Lock the cabin door, and cast off!"

A shouting suddenly arose when a sailor discovered a queer little fellow wedged between a deck-locker and the cabin and dragged him out by the scruff of his neck. The sailor, after carefully looking him over, roared: "You river beggar! What do you mean by crawling in here and hiding? Are you a river imp? You must be —you belong in the river!" And with this he tossed the man overboard. The men on the two vessels watched this scene with guffaws. At the sound of the splash, Sutoku peered from a window and saw Asatori in the foam boiling and bubbling on the surface of the river. Asatori gasped out something, but the swift current caught him and bore him away.

The toilsome sea voyage ended on the 15th of August when the three small fisher-boats arrived on the northeastern coast of Shikoku Island near Sakadé. Sutoku and his three attendants were met by their jailer, a kindly official, who conducted them inland to a temple among the hills, and there Sutoku lived for three years until his removal to his final abode farther south in the fastness of the hills.

Among those in the capital who heard of Sutoku's sudden departure with sorrow was Saigyo, the monk poet (Sato Yoshikiyo), who by devious means succeeded in sending a poem to the lonely exile through his kindly disposed jailer.

One autumn night Sutoku laid down his writing-brush and spoke to one of the gentlewomen:

"I heard it this evening and I seem to hear it again—I can't be imagining it. Don't you hear it, too?"

There it was again—the unmistakable notes of a flute—and it seemed to be coming closer.

"Do you know of anyone who goes about playing his flute in these parts? I wonder who it could be?"

"What a plaintive sound!"

"Go quietly and find out. It must be someone who has seen the light of this candle. . . . It couldn't be one of the guards."

The gentlewoman stole out and ran to the guardhouse, where she knocked softly on the door. A guard appeared, and she told him what she had heard. He listened to her indulgently and was promising that she should speak with the unknown flutist when a young pilgrim appeared, carrying a flute. He replied to the questions that were put to him.

". . . Yes, yes. I came to Shikoku on a pilgrimage in the hope that chance would bring me here, where my music would comfort the royal exile. I have prayed for so long that he would listen to this flute. My name is Asatori. I come of a family of court musicians, but I gave up my calling to serve his majesty for many years as a caretaker of the Willow-Spring Palace."

On learning his name, the gentlewoman, who had often heard her master speak of Asatori, hurried back with the news.

"Asatori? . . . So it was Asatori, after all!" Sutoku exclaimed, as he quickly stepped out on a veranda and seated himself. The veranda jutted out over a lily-pool, and Asatori, who had been forbidden to cross the slender bridge over it, stood on the farther side among the tall grasses. The moon lay trapped in the pool.

As they gazed at each other silently, Sutoku reproached himself bitterly for not keeping the promise he had once made to Asatori—that he would listen to him play the flute on a moonlit night. But Asatori had not forgotten. He had crossed the dangerous seas and faced unnumbered hardships to find him. He had also come to him in the hills during the flight from Shirakawa.

Asatori could not speak for his tears; then, placing his flute against his lips, he began to play, pouring out his heart in infinitely moving strains.

The moon set. Lights were snuffed out, and the music of the flute was heard no more. After bidding his master farewell, Asatori, looking back many times, departed.

As far as it was ever known, Asatori was the only one to visit the ex-Emperor in his exile. In August of the year 1164, when he was forty-six, Sutoku died, broken in body and spirit. In early winter of the following year a pilgrim stood beside a lonely grave in the hills of Shikoku; it was Saigyo, who had left the capital in autumn on a pilgrimage.

CHAPTER XIX

A TEAHOUSE AT EGUCHI

Toward noon of a late November day in 1159, three young warriors were riding rapidly down the left bank of the Yodo River. The withered reeds stretched for miles around like low-hanging smoke, and as far as the eye could see dun-colored clouds came down to meet the ash-gray river. The noon sun was a luminous blot in the bleak sky.

"O-oy—Jiro! Stop pretending you know the way. Are you sure you're turning in the right direction?"

"All right, all right. We just passed the Tenno Hills and must be on the Yamazaki Road. We'll get to Akutagawa by following the foothills."

Tota and Juro, who galloped some distance behind Jiro, jeered: "Jiro seems to know all about this, doesn't he? You say this is your first trip, but you know this road quite well by now, don't you, Jiro?"

"Oh, is that so? So it was you who thought of this and invited us to come along, eh?"

"You liar, Tota! Wasn't it you that's been badgering me all along to go down to Eguchi to spend a night there watching the dancing-girls?"

"No, that was Juro, our man about town, who knows all about dancing-girls!"

"Hey, Tota! Better look out what you say!"

Juro laughed. "Here, here, no telling tales on each other! Jiro doesn't seem to mind in the least!"

"Looks like more snow before night. Let's hope it won't start snowing before we reach Eguchi."

The riders suddenly stopped to listen to the honking of wild geese in the clouds.

Their skillful horsemanship showed that these three, though they came from the capital, were warriors trained in eastern Japan. With the exception of Jiro, the others had come to the capital in answer to Yoshitomo's mustering orders and had taken part in the battle at Shirakawa. Jiro had arrived too late for the fighting, but had remained in Kyoto on General Yoshitomo's orders and been assigned to the Horse Guards.

In the two years since the end of the Hogen War, many changes had taken place in Kyoto. The Emperor's Palace was rebuilt. New ministers headed the various departments of state, and new laws were enacted. Traditional court ceremonials, in abeyance for more than a century, were revived; the Academy of Music and the training school for court dancers once more opened their doors. Wrestling contests were held as before in the Palace park, and a general air of peace prevailed, when without warning or apparent cause the Emperor Goshirakawa was dethroned and the Emperor Nijo ascended the throne.

Toward the end of November, when a lull came in the busy ceremonials of the Court, members of the Guard in turn received several days' leave; now it was the turn of these three warriors who had heard so much about the fabulous beauties at Eguchi. Fearing to be looked down on by their fellow Guards as mere provincials, they made plans to spend a night at Eguchi near the mouth of the Yodo River.

The Kamo and Katsura rivers, merging several miles south of the capital as the Yodo River, formed a delta at Naniwa (Osaka). Vessels loaded with cargo for Kyoto, fishing craft, and other boats from east and west put in at Naniwa, whose inlets were dotted with fishers' settlements among the tall reeds. Eguchi, a short distance above the river mouth, was a village of inns, teahouses, and brothels. The usual mode of travel from Kyoto to Eguchi was the leisurely trip by water, but the three had not time for this.

"So, this is Eguchi and its teahouses!"

"Livelier than the other places we just passed."

"Now for a place to spend the night."

The warriors dismounted and led their horses with some disappointment along the main thoroughfare, peering into each house they passed. Faces pale as moonflowers were pressed against the latticed windows of structures that seemed no larger than birdcages. Now and again they saw dancing-girls in small shelters set up against a board fence, squatting beside clay stoves, cooking or fanning the embers. As they went farther, however, the houses appeared more elegant and prosperous. They saw a few women with winter chrysanthemums in their hair. Some others in wide hats or muffled in their cloaks passed them, accompanying visitors from a landing-place. Somewhere from above them in a second story came the strumming of a harp, and the water running in the ditches carried a faint odor of perfumes.

Toward dusk the warriors tethered their horses outside a house that looked more like an aristocratic villa than a teahouse. There seemed to be several rooms separated from each other by enclosed gardens. A balustraded veranda overlooking the Yodo River extended along one side of the house.

". . . Wine, food—now what about the dancing-girls?"

"You'll have to call for those."

"Doesn't this seem like a warrior's house?"

"There's not much point to staying next to a teahouse and minding our manners."

"No dancing-girls—do we provide our own entertainment?"

"Wait, I'll go and see."

Tota left the room and returned almost immediately.

"They'll be here—very soon."

"Coming? At last—"

"The girls live in that wing with the mistress of the house—a nun."

"A nun, did you say?"

"Seems so. I hear they're quite particular about their guests. They seem to think we're respectable."

"That's bad. We shan't have our fun."

"Too soon to complain. We'll have to see the girls first."

The dancing-girls soon appeared in their flowing multicolored robes. Their bearing, their coiffure, and their elaborate toilette reminded the young men of court ladies, and the ornaments they wore showed that merchants who bartered with smugglers from China were regular guests here.

Juro, the eldest of the three, asked: "Will you tell us your names?"

". . . Senzai."

". . . Kujaku."

". . . Ko-Kannon."

Instead of staying one night as they had planned, they stayed three. Ko-Kannon seemed greatly taken with Jiro's naïveté and his quaint-sounding eastern dialect, and Jiro found Ko-Kannon completely enchanting. While his companions spent their time drinking and playing dice games, or dancing and singing to the music of lutes with the other entertainers in the establishment, Jiro withdrew to a small room with Ko-Kannon. Drowsy with wine, he stared at her pale eyelids and asked: "How long have you lived here in Eguchi?"

"For the last three years."

"Since the Hogen War, then?"

"Yes, my home was destroyed in the fires," Ko-Kannon replied, lowering her gaze. "My father died then, and all my relatives were scattered."

"Oh?"

"I tell you in confidence—my father sided with the ex-Emperor and was beheaded."

"So your father was a courtier? How cruel to take an unfortunate young girl and make her a professional entertainer! If your father were living, you would be a grand lady in your own right."

"Don't say such things, I beg you. . . . I'm not the only one who came here after the war was over. There are other of nobler birth who have—"

"With all those courtiers and generals killed, it's not strange that many guiltless women have had to face misfortunes of every kind. Not all of them, however, seem to have become nuns."

"Not all, to be sure, for here is our Mother, as we call her, who enjoys this kind of life and who chose to come to Eguchi. All the houses here are not what they appear to be, nor all the entertainers mere harlots."

Jiro, who had heard so much of the famous courtesans of Eguchi while he was still in the east, looked at Ko-Kannon with admiration.

"There must be many courtiers and gentlemen who come here. What makes you receive us eastern warriors so hospitably?"

Ko-Kannon smiled at Jiro's query. "We no longer have any respect for those painted, perfumed aristocrats—the ministers and high officials. It vexes us beyond words, after a while, to entertain them. To us those gay, smiling merchants who cross the angry seas and you young warriors seem like real men. I don't know exactly why—and it's not only I that thinks so."

"We'll leave tomorrow," the young men told each other. "Now for our last night of junketing. No jokes about our lady-loves. We'll leave Jiro alone with Ko-Kannon to make his fare-wells."

But Jiro and Ko-Kannon, exchanging pleased smiles at the teasing, joined in the noisy games and dancing, of which neither Juro nor Tota seemed to have had enough. Cup after cup of wine was emptied as the dancing, singing, miming, and joking went on. Toward midnight the entertainers suddenly vanished one by one, until only a sleepy-eyed serving-girl remained to pour the wine.

"What's this all of a sudden?"

"They couldn't be ghosts—and without any explanations. Even Jiro's Ko-Kannon has left us."

"Some important guests just arrived from the capital, I suppose."

"Blossoms before a hurricane—I wonder who they are."

They peered through the branches overhanging the water and saw an elaborately furnished boat touch the shore. Lights streamed down to the water's edge, and presently a gentleman in a hunting cloak, accompanied by attendants, came toward the house.

Ko-Kannon, meanwhile, reappeared; taking Jiro aside, she whispered something to him and then left.

"What did she say, Jiro?"

"She was just explaining things, and apologizing, and crying."

"I was told that that visitor we saw now is not one of the usual travelers, or a wealthy merchant, but some close relative of the proprietress here."

"What's that to us? We're guests, too."

"Losing your temper? It won't do us any good."

"It's all very well to say that when you enjoy having Ko-Kannon crying on your shoulder, but what about us?"

"It doesn't look well for a warrior to appear so irked. Wait until I explain. Those people who just arrived are housemen and servants from Rokuhara. Kiyomori of the Heiké is going on a pilgrimage to Kumano Shrine in Kishu and is to stop here on the way, and these people have arrived to get things in order for his arrival in a day or two."

"From Rokuhara!" gasped Tota and Juro, staring at each other.

"There was talk that he was making this pilgrimage, but the day has actually been set, has it?"

"That means we'll have to leave for the capital at once. We had our instructions from General Yoshitomo of the Genji."

"We mustn't lose a moment getting back."

The three warriors quickly prepared to leave. "Our horses— are they ready?"

"They will be brought around immediately. Unfortunately, we're rather busy. . . . A little patience, please," a manservant replied soothingly.

"No, we're not annoyed. Urgent business takes us back to the capital. . . . Where's the stable? We'll leave from there."

"This way, sirs. Let me take you."

Ko-Kannon waited outside with a lantern and led them through an inner garden, then through a gate. The stable was in a vacant lot between the house and an adjacent building.

"Please don't forget us, and come again," Ko-Kannon said.

"Next time Jiro shall come alone," laughed Tota and Juro as they saddled their horses and prepared to mount. When they looked round for Jiro, they found him peering through a hedge.

"Is that the neighboring house?"

"No, that is where we live with our Mother."

"Jiro! You wretch, peeping! Ko-Kannon, scold him!"

"No, that light over there is in our Mother's room. Ours is on this side of the garden."

Tota immediately thrust his reins into Juro's hands and ran to join Jiro. Despite the cold, a shutter had been left open, and they saw the dignified figure of the woman who sat within. It was difficult to judge her age. The white folds of a nun's coif framed her face becomingly; she seemed to be in her fifties. Her skin gleamed palely in the lamplight and the painted eyebrows gave a youthful comeliness to the face outlined by the headdress. Her nightingale-colored robes lent her distinction as she conversed with someone on the other side of the tall lampstand. Both Tota and Jiro at once recognized this man whom they had seen frequently in the capital, and they gaped at each other in astonishment. It was Kiyomori's younger brother Tsunemori, an officer of the Fifth Rank since the Hogen War.

That night the young warriors hurried toward Kyoto. As they stopped to rest on the way, they discussed what had happened that night. Juro, who had not seen all that Jiro and Tota had, added: "I know that Kiyomori's brother was to arrive earlier than the rest of the party, but who do you suppose the mistress of that house could be? I wonder what her name is."

Then they attempted to recall whether they had said anything indiscreet during the days spent at Eguchi, for they had heard that the mistress of the establishment was in some way related to Kiyomori.

"Now, don't worry about that," Jiro assured the others.

"Jiro, Ko-Kannon surely told you something. It's all very well for you to tell us not to worry, but what makes you say that?"

"I'm inclined to believe what she said, and yet I'm skeptical about it. . . ."

"There, you see! Ko-Kannon must have told you something."

"She did, and this is what she said: that their Mother used to be a dancing-girl in the capital, and that she had once been the Emperor Shirakawa's mistress; she used to be called 'the Lady of Gion.'"

"The Lady of Gion? Seems to me I've heard that name before."

"The Emperor Shirakawa gave her to Tadamori of the Heiké as his wife. They had several sons, and the eldest was Kiyomori. Only a few people know this, and Ko-Kannon made me promise to tell no one."

Juro and Tota slapped their saddles and exclaimed: "Of all things! We shan't be going to Eguchi with Jiro again. We didn't know he was on such friendly terms with Ko-Kannon. But, look here, was she telling the truth? This is serious gossip to be retelling about someone so influential."

"Serious, perhaps, and not quite improbable. Even General

Yoshitomo himself, they say, was the son of a beautiful dancing-girl."

"That's it. I remember—the stories about Kiyomori's real father."

"Anyway, we did have a good time at Eguchi."

"Yes, but what will it be like in the capital?"

"There's no predicting about tomorrow, and not much point in mere warriors like us trying to guess. It's certain, however, that the general has been anxious to know the exact date of Kiyomori's departure for Kumano, and we had strict orders to return when it became known."

"Look, it's hailing! Let's whip up our horses and get warm."

Behind them, road, paddies, and hills were soon a white blur.

CHAPTER XX

A PILGRIMAGE TO KUMANO

Tsunemuné, the courtier, was again spending the day at the Vice-Councilor's suburban villa. Nearly everyone in court circles knew of the close friendship between the two, but for appearance's sake Tsunemuné explained that his frequent visits were to give Fujiwara Nobuyori lessons in football. Those who knew that the courtier was adroit at putting people to his own uses carefully avoided involvement in Tsunemuné's affairs, but he, none the less, never lacked a following. The ex-Emperor Goshirakawa favored him as a partner at football, and the

Emperor Nijo was partial to him, while Nobuyori, the Vice-Councilor, made Tsunemuné his boon companion and confidant.

"Tsunemuné, what could be keeping General Narichika and Councilor Moronaka?"

"They should be here soon. I can't think what would delay them, except they may come late and separately to make themselves inconspicuous. . . . And have you sent word to Korekata?"

"My uncle promises to come tonight, his duties with the Police Commission understandably keep him busy during the day."

"If that's the case, we might as well go on practicing."

"No, I'm tired and have had enough for today. If I'm overtired, my head won't be clear for the discussions later on."

Tsunemuné and Nobuyori were in the football enclosure, where for a time the thwacking of a football resounded with unusual sharpness in the wintry air. They were now resting at the foot of a tree and conversing in low tones. Some of the younger courtiers had been meeting here lately with increasing frequency on the pretext of holding poetry contests and football matches, and the subject for talk at these gatherings was Shinzei.

For almost three years, since the end of the Hogen War, Shinzei's authority had gone unchallenged. He had risen from an obscure court post to one of undisguised absolutism, and this not unnaturally earned him enemies. In power he was bold, as he once had been self-effacing, dispensing policies with a sure hand. There was nevertheless a growing belief among some courtiers that if he were not soon curbed, there would be no telling to what lengths he would go. With the end of the fighting, Shinzei had seen to it that peace was restored without delay. Sweeping reforms were carried out in rapid succession at his direction. New laws governing provincial taxes were enacted, and the carrying of arms in the city precincts prohibited. At his orders the ablest were picked for office, and to him was given the authority to mete out punishment and dispense rewards. His achievements notwithstanding, Shinzei's measures were not acceptable to all, and there were some who questioned his dictatorial powers.

Whether it is the tyrant who creates conflict, or conflict that breeds the tyrant, there was no denying that a despot arrogating extraordinary privileges to himself had appeared overnight and placed himself at the head of the state. Though circumstances were in his favor and his astuteness unquestioned, those who were dissatisfied argued that Shinzei owed his success largely to Kiyomori's military backing; this alone was enough reason for the Genji to take umbrage, and it began to be said that the interests of the state made it imperative to oust Shinzei and his ally eventually.

Out of these frequent meetings and secret talks at Nobuyori's villa there emerged a fantastic plot aimed at Shinzei. It was to be realized within a year or two. Toward the end of November 1159, however, when there were rumors that Kiyomori planned to go on a pilgrimage to Kumano Shrine, a seven-day journey from the capital, the malcontents agreed that the chance to strike had come—an opportunity which might not recur later.

Nobuyori's villa had been the scene of a gathering on the previous day, and the leaders in the plot—Tsunemuné and Nobuyori—had called for another meeting today.

The afternoon sun slanted ruddily across the football enclosure, where five or six men were seated on the ground near the goal post. General Narichika and Councilor Moronaka had now joined the group, which appeared to be engaged in a harmless discussion of football. But they were occupied with something more urgent.

". . . So the 4th of December is the date of Kiyomori's departure for Kumano Shrine?"

"There's no mistake about that, for I got it from one who is to be trusted and who is a frequent visitor at Rokuhara," General Narichika replied.

"The 4th—that means we have little time left. . . ."

The plotters shivered unconsciously at the thought of what lay before them. There was no question now of wavering or withdrawing.

"We had every reason to believe that the pilgrimage would

take place in early spring, but this change in plan means we shall have to hurry with our preparations. In any case, further discussions will have to be carried on indoors."

The company withdrew to the house; the shutters were closed and guards posted along the corridors and galleries to prevent any intrusions. With the appearance of Nobuyori's uncle, Korekata, former Captain of the Bodyguard of the Right, after sundown, the talks took on a more definite character. As an officer of the Police Commission, Korekata was charged with the maintenance of peace and order in the capital. His authority and Yoshitomo's Genji soldiers, the conspirators argued, were an invincible combination.

Master Red-Nose, the owner of an imposing establishment at the entrance to the city markets near the gate to Fifth Avenue, was a parvenu, people said. He employed a large number of assistants —men and women—in his warehouses, which were well stocked with cotton goods, dyestuffs, combs, cosmetics, and perfumes from China. Master Red-Nose was no less than a merchant trader to the ladies of the Court. Bamboku was his real name, but he had come by his nickname because of that feature, the color of an overripe strawberry, which embellished the center of his face. A depression at the side of his nose—the scars left by the pox with which he had been afflicted in childhood—caused his nose to tilt upward, and what might have been a damaging hallmark in any other man in his forties proved to be otherwise for Bamboku, for his nose gave him an air of disarming amiability. Had it been a well-shaped nose with no nonsense about it, it might well have made the beholder wary by allowing his eyes to stray over a face that was decidedly cunning. He was rarely addressed by his real name, but passed as Master Nose among his fellow traders, who even more frequently spoke of him as Red-Nose, or just simply the Nose—so much so, that it was not unusual to find people who were ignorant of his real name.

"Bamboku, you seem to grow more and more prosperous."

"Ah, the honorable Tsunemuné! Have you come for a morning stroll through the markets?"

"Oh, no, I was at the Vice-Councilor's villa last night—the usual poetry contest, you know."

"On your way home, then?"

"You already seem busy at this early hour. Let me speak to you inside—a request to make. . . ."

"No need for apologies. . . . Now, this way, please."

Bamboku led the way through the open shop front to a narrow passage, past a stableyard and a row of warehouses, to an inner court

"You might have come through the gate to the courtyard."

"I found it locked."

"Now, that was very careless of me. . . . Here," Bamboku called in passing his wife's bedchamber, "we have a caller, the honorable Tsunemuné," and continued to lead his guest across the court to a room that received the full light of the winter morning's sun.

"You merchants have fine houses—sunny and cheerful."

"Not at all, sir, nothing like your fine mansions."

"You're mistaken there. Tradition, social position, this keeping up of appearances, complicate our lives, and the less chance we have of seeing the sun. The Emperor and the court ladies spend their days in candlelit rooms. Better not get any richer and build a larger house."

"Ah, no, sir, I can hardly be counted among the wealthy merchants here on Fifth Avenue. I have a few ambitions, though. . . . You need not be concerned for me, sir, and I certainly hope to continue receiving your patronage."

"I heard you made quite a fortune right after the war."

"That's how it seems to people, sir, but far from it."

Tsunemuné laughed. "No fear, Bamboku, I haven't come for a loan."

"But, sir, should you ask for the impossible, I shall be only too glad to try to meet with your wishes."

"Just flattery, I suppose?"

"How could I to my benefactor?"

Just then Bamboku's comely wife, younger than he by some

2 8 3

twenty years, appeared, having completed her morning toilette.

"Welcome, indeed, sir! You come early for a cold morning."

"Well, well, Umeno! How are you—getting on nicely together, I hope?"

Umeno blushed charmingly and Bamboku gazed at his wife with a fatuous, doting look.

"Some nice little cakes or something—and some herb tea?" Bamboku said to his wife, who departed with a demure air.

Bamboku's wife, the granddaughter of a councilor who had come down in the world, had been employed in Tsunemuné's household until the past year, when Tsunemuné had arranged a match for her. Bamboku, at one time a petty clerk at the Court, a post offering at best little advancement beyond a stewardship over the lower order of menials, had resigned from his position ten years before, bought a small shop in the market-place, and turned merchant, and through his former connections did business with the Court and the ladies. Tsunemuné, who first met Bamboku at the Regent's villa, took a fancy to the droll merchant, who always accepted good-naturedly the constant jesting at his expense. Finding him ambitious and energetic like himself, Tsunemuné patronized the shrewd Bamboku and at the end of the war, when there was a demand for numerous commodities, quietly saw to it that Bamboku was commissioned to supply the Court with building-materials for the new palace. These business transactions had resulted in Bamboku's erecting a fine house and a row of warehouses at the gate by Fifth Avenue.

His establishment completed, Bamboku found he needed a wife to manage his household. As he claimed descent from the nobility, Bamboku aspired for the hand of one from the higher circles of society—say, the daughter of a courtier who had seen better days. Moreover, his long years at the Court had kindled in him secret ambitions to live like a gentleman. The desired spouse, as it happened, was provided by Tsunemuné, whom Bamboku in his gratitude declared was his lifelong benefactor. Bamboku, however, anticipated paying dearly for this particular favor, and this morning it came to him instantly that the day of reckoning had come. "You had a request. Now tell me what it is. I'm more than willing to give all I own to accommodate you."

"No, Bamboku, I'm not here for money or anything of that nature. On the contrary, I'm proposing that you make some large profits."

"Well, that sounds too good to be true at this time of the year."

"Not too good to be true. But you will have to promise to agree to this, or refuse before I even disclose the matter."

"Naturally, I cannot refuse. Is it a highly secret matter?"

"Bamboku, will you first see that the shutters are closed so we shan't be interrupted?"

Tsunemuné proceeded to disclose a part of the plot to Bamboku. Detecting the gleam of interest in the Nose, he added, as he fixed him with a searching look, "If you go through with this, I assure you you shall receive whatever you ask for. Bamboku, will you let us have the use of your house? We cannot risk a meeting outside the city gates. I believe this bustling market quarter is the safest place for us. And, furthermore, most of us will come in disguise."

Tsunemuné had a further proposal to make. "In these years since the end of the Hogen War, there has been a strict ban on arms, and we lack the necessary weapons, so you are to get hold of all we require. All very secretly, you understand."

Tsunemuné did not leave until noontime. Bamboku's wife, meanwhile, prepared and served a handsome repast including a flask of flavorsome wine from China, bought in the market from merchants who traded regularly in goods from across the seas. When Tsunemuné was ready to go, he discreetly departed by a rear gate and made his way to the river, where his carriage waited for him. He found the carriage-ox dozing in the winter sun and the ox-boy sprawled asleep in the grass. Tsunemuné gazed across the river to the walls and trees of Rokuhara on the other bank.

Since the end of the Hogen War, Kiyomori had been saying: "It's time I made a pilgrimage to Kumano Shrine to offer thanks. This year I shall go without fail."

His last trip had been in 1154, the year after his father Tadamori's death.

Kiyomori's stepmother, Ariko, was visiting at Rokuhara when Kiyomori remarked half in jest: "I haven't been to Kumano Shrine for so long that I'm sure the gods will punish me."

"Kiyomori, you are too irreverent," Ariko said severely. "If you continue to make such blasphemous remarks, you will some day have reason to regret it. Your good father, Tadamori, was a deeply pious man, but you don't resemble him in the least. You must remember that you are after all the head of the clan and you must for that reason take heed of your conduct in such matters."

Ariko's rebuke silenced Kiyomori. He had never felt at ease with her. Since her husband's death, Ariko had taken the vows of a nun and gone to live in a place north of the capital, and there passed her days in religious devotions. Not infrequently she came to visit at Rokuhara, and at such times Kiyomori felt as though he were a wayward child summoned to receive her kindly meant advice. What chastened him most was his stepmother's habit of saying at every other word "your dear father, the late Tadamori." Not only Kiyomori, but his wife, Tokiko, also stood in awe of Ariko, who reserved her approval and open affection for her eldest grandson, Shigemori. In him she saw an exemplary young man, who, unlike Kiyomori, was not only punctilious but gentler and more attentive to her than anyone else in the household.

"You should before anything else make this pilgrimage to Kumano. Take Shigemori with you. Pray for forgiveness for your past impieties and ask for a blessing for yourself and the rest of the household."

Ariko earnestly begged Kiyomori to go to Kumano Shrine, and in this he was willing to comply. Since he had been detailed to supervise the building of a temple at Shirakawa, he could not leave until the dedication was over. Throughout the autumn Shinzei constantly consulted Kiyomori on matters relating to various civil reforms, and though Kiyomori found little time to attend to his personal affairs, he welcomed the opportunity to get a taste of politics under Shinzei's tutelage and expected a slackening in his duties by the middle of December. When he mentioned his intention of going to Kumano, Shinzei approved of the plan wholeheartedly and even sent Kiyomori a parting gift.

A few days before the date of his departure Kiyomori sent his brother Tsunemori ahead to Eguchi to arrange for lodgings for the party and to hire boats that would take them part of the way to Kumano. On the 4th of December, Kiyomori, accompanied by his eldest son, Shigemori, and Mokunosuké and a company of fifty retainers, left Rokuhara. Their first night's stop was at Eguchi, which they reached by sailing down the Yodo River. There was a choice of a land route or a sea route to Kumano, but with a large party the trip by water was usually preferred, for a large sailing vessel would carry the entire party most of the way.

That same evening Kiyomori arrived at Eguchi, where Tsunemori awaited him. Since a party of more than fifty could not all be lodged in one house, Kiyomori and Shigemori stayed at separate inns. Kiyomori, who had taken a vow of abstinence until the pilgrimage was over, prepared to retire early without the drinking and merrymaking customary at Eguchi. Only a few lights burned in the silent inn.

"Master—my apologies for disturbing you—"

"Ah, Old One, is it you? What is it?"

"Your brother has sent me with a message."

Mokunosuké knelt in the adjoining room and studied Kiyomori's face to see how he might receive the announcement.

"It's a bitterly cold night, Old One; better come in and close the door after you."

Seeing that his master was not out of sorts, Mokunosuké came forward and knelt before Kiyomori and began to relate what Tsunemori had told him.

Mokunosuké was now eighty, the same retainer whom Kiyomori since boyhood had always addressed affectionately as "Old

One." From the old retainer, a spectator of human affairs for so long, who now viewed them as dispassionately as one might the flight of a wasp or a butterfly, or the slow growth of a tree or flower, came a low monotonous recital, uttered as it were by a mask crowned with snowy locks.

But Kiyomori was startled by what he heard. He was told that the proprietress of this house at which they were staying was the widow of a courtier and had become a Buddhist nun. There were many who had known her in days gone by; she had been a famous dancing-girl in the capital and later became the mistress of the Emperor Shirakawa, who gave her to Tadamori of the Heiké as his wife. She, who had had several sons by Tadamori, had been known as the Lady of Gion.

" . . . . "

Kiyomori struggled for a moment with a confusion of emotions that the recital called up in him and then turned a bleak face to Mokunosuké. Tsunemori had played a trick on him, Kiyomori felt. She was his own mother, that lovely mother of his who had forsaken her impoverished husband and sons so long ago. He had long ceased to think of her, and refused to think of her as his mother, but Tsunemori, it seemed, had never forgotten her. He had somehow traced her whereabouts and brought her to Tadamori's deathbed, and even since then had apparently been seeing her, concealing his meetings from both Kiyomori and their stepmother, Ariko.

"Old One, tell Tsunemori this— "

"Yes. . . ."

"Tsunemori may have had such a mother, but she is not mine. I have no desire to see her. There's no reason why I should see her. Tell him so."

"You have no desire to see her?"

"Why should I have feelings one way or the other, Old One? You should know that better than anyone else. Why rake over the ashes of the past?"

"I told you this with all that in mind."

"Then why did you have to come to me at all? You have ruined the first night of my trip."

"I feared that I would, but your brother seemed to feel that as you were on your way to Kumano, it would not be amiss, in memory of your late father, to comfort your aging mother, and it seemed to me that he spoke truly."

"What! Dare you insist on talking? I tell you I have no such mother, you addlepate! Whoever or whatever she is, let Tsunemori go and talk to her if he thinks it will do him good. I'm tired—sleepy. Where is my bedchamber?"

The serving-lad who sat dozing behind Kiyomori suddenly awoke and blinked in astonishment at the sound of his master's voice. Rising quickly, he led the way with a lamp.

All the inn servants long since were abed. About the hour Kiyomori should have been asleep, a figure stealthily crept from his room. Mokunosuké, who was still awake, watched it pass along the corridor, fumble at a shutter, and then unlatch a door. Suspicious, Mokunosuké spoke to the figure. Kiyomori swung round startled and stared intently in the direction from which the voice came; in the darkness he suddenly grinned.

". . . Was it you, Old One?"

"My master, what makes you go out into the garden on a cold night like this?"

"The first night in a strange place leaves me wide-awake. I somehow couldn't get to sleep. To tell you the truth, Old One, I've reconsidered what I said. Do you know where it is?"

"Know what, my master?"

"The apartments of the lady of whom Tsunemori spoke."

"You have decided to see her after all?"

"Umm—yes." Kiyomori scratched the back of his head sheepishly. "After all, when I come to think of it, she must be nearly sixty. Here I am, going on forty-three—and it's ridiculous to let the past keep me from seeing her, particularly when I'm staying under the same roof. I begin to feel that I may regret it if I leave without seeing her."

"Ah, that sounds quite sensible."

"Old One, you do think that it would be better to do so?"

"I had hoped from the very beginning that you would feel as you do now. It would be just what your father would have wanted you to do."

"True. He was no bigoted quibbler like me. Just before he died Tsunemori brought her secretly to my father's bedside and I listened to what he said to her, she who had been so false to him."

"Yes, I know all that happened that morning."

"Old One, I wept as I eavesdropped—at his great love, at what he said to one who had so cruelly injured him."

"In the master's eyes she was one to be deeply pitied. He must have felt so in the long years before they finally parted."

"I can hardly hope to be like him. But I am a man and in my forties. . . . Whatever has happened, there's no denying that she bore me—this Kiyomori. I can at least follow Tsunemori's filial example and meet her this time. Take me to her, Old One."

That night Kiyomori saw his mother, with whom Tsunemori had already been spending the evening.

She was not as Kiyomori had expected to find her. She appeared to be neither sad nor lonely, but on the contrary seemed to enjoy her present life. The furnishings of her room reflected the elegance and comfort in which she had always delighted.

"Lord Harima," she addressed Kiyomori, "Tsunemori is so strait-laced that he came here to Eguchi all fears and qualms, but you've known in your youth of the entertainments to be found in the houses of Sixth Avenue, so you must come here sometimes for a little gaiety. And whenever you come to Eguchi you must stop here and let my young girls entertain you—there are a number of them and all exquisite. If you were not on your way to Kumano Shrine, I would have them come in so you could see for yourself."

This was she—his mother. Kiyomori understood. She had prevailed on Tsunemori to arrange for Kiyomori's stay here that she might meet him. She spoke easily and unaffectedly and with no hint of embarrassment. To his surprise, Kiyomori thought he detected the pride she took in her establishment.

Kiyomori, taken aback, stared at his mother. From her appearance it was impossible to believe that she was nearing sixty; and there was that about her like a lingering fragrance which Kiyomori now recognized as the seductive charm that once led a monarch to woo her, and Tadamori to put up with her infidelities and caprices for so long. And Kiyomori continued to listen to her chatter:

"How delightful to have you staying with us! A pity you are bound by a vow of abstinence. But you must stop here in Eguchi for two or three nights on your way back and give us the honor of your company. Eguchi is a dull place during the winter, when we have few distinguished guests."

While she talked lightly and inconsequentially, she seemed unaware of being the mother of four grown sons. No maternal tenderness prompted her to speak of her joy in seeing her sons grown to manhood; she seemed to have forgotten even Tadamori. That past she appeared to have removed from her memory as casually and easily as she did the cosmetics with which she still adorned herself.

"A most fortunate woman," Kiyomori mused. He began to think himself rather ludicrous. He could hardly be angry with her, she was so utterly naïve. She could not be otherwise. She was the born courtesan. Nature had made her what she was and his mother was not at fault. Kiyomori was glad and relieved that he had consented to meet her, for he no longer felt any resentment toward her. She was not to be blamed, the life of the dancing-girl was natural to her; it was a mistake to want her to be otherwise. Kiyomori studied his mother's face and gestures—this was the life in which she throve and was happiest. He had these many years foolishly eaten out his heart in silence, wanting her to be otherwise.

"Mother—I mean, good hostess, is there to be no wine while we talk? It won't be necessary to forgo that until my return. Some wine—and plenty of it?"

His mother laughed brightly. "Wine? That will be easy enough to get. Here—" she called, clapping to get attention. A serving-girl appeared in answer and was given some instructions in a whisper. Soon after she left, three dancing-girls appeared with lamps and the room was flooded with lights. Wine and food were then carried in.

"Good hostess, are these all the entertainers you have?"

"There are still a few more."

"While we're about it, we might as well have them come, too. Tsunemori—"

"Yes?"

"Have you never come here for some gaiety?"

"I? Never."

Tsunemori seemed sulky. He felt himself alone and an intruder as he watched Kiyomori and his mother.

"This is a house of entertainment. This lady is our hostess. Stop looking so glum now."

Kiyomori kept refilling his own cup and urged his brother to join in.

"Come, you must drink, too."

"I shall drink on our way back from Kumano."

"Are you afraid to drink with your brother, who has broken the fast?" Kiyomori laughed. "Don't be so timid, Tsunemori, there's no need to worry. I'm drinking to the memory of our father before we leave for Kumano."

"But why?"

"Don't you see why? Can't you understand that on his deathbed he was anxious that we should be happy?"

"Was it so?"

"That's why I'm doing this—that his soul may rest in peace. I'm sure that the god of Kumano Shrine will look on this as a filial act and will send no curse upon you, Tsunemori. Come, drink and be gay."

Scarcely had Kiyomori stopped speaking when the room became a dazzling sight as more than ten dancing-girls, each lovelier than the next, entered the room. Kiyomori touched his lips to a large cup and passed it to one of them, and one slender hand after another was held out in turn to receive it.

"Lord Harima is in a genial mood," the dancing-girls chaffed. There was an outburst of light laughter and chatter. Kiyomori, flushed with wine, grew pleasantly lightheaded with the scent of powder and the sight of the glittering hair-ornaments.

"Drums, drums! Someone dance!" he called out in a thick voice.

"Lord Harima orders us to dance. Come, dance, sing!"

There was a buzz of excitement, a bright flutter of long sleeves and skirts as the dancing-girls came to their feet. Screens were pushed back, sliding doors removed, and two rooms thrown into one to make more space. A harp was brought in, large drums were set up on their stands, and flutes removed from their silken cases.

A dancer in a tall headdress, wearing a slender gilt sword at her side, came gliding from the women's living-quarters and across the bridge leading to this room. She held up a fan, which hovered and circled to the rhythm of a popular tune. The liquid movement of her legs, the swaying of her hips, and the curve of her shoulders seemed to blend and become one with the music. Kiyomori put aside his cup and stared at the moving figure, all unconscious of the dance. His eyes were fixed hard on the thickly powdered face under the headdress of gold-colored gauze. Of a sudden he grew restless and kept shifting uneasily in his seat. The dancer's eyes only followed the pattern of the dance and never for an instant strayed his way. Impatience showed in every line of Kiyomori's face. A tedious dance! Away with the drums, the flutes! When were they leaving off, so he could speak alone to this woman?

The dance ended. The music ceased abruptly. As the dancer sank to the floor in a low obeisance, the other entertainers crowded round to replenish Kiyomori's cup.

"Don't bother me! Get back out of my way! Bring that dancer back here!" he snapped, impatiently pushing the women away with his elbows and gesturing before him with his wine-cup. But the dancer had already left the room in quick tripping steps and, crossing the bridge, disappeared into the dancing-girls' apartments.

Kiyomori kept calling for her and sent the others one by one to fetch her, but the dancer refused to appear.

Then one of the women said: "I don't know where she has hidden herself, but she is not to be found anywhere."

Kiyomori was furious. He rarely drank so heavily or behaved so churlishly.

"What, she calls herself a dancing-girl? She used to be called Ruriko, a niece of the nobleman Nakamikado! That's Ruriko, I'm certain! Ho, hostess, what do you mean by hiding her?"

Kiyomori threw down his cup and turned on the proprietress in fury, but she herself appeared fuddled and clung limply to an elbow-rest. Kiyomori's outburst of angry accusations seemed only to amuse her and she broke into peals of laughter.

"So Lord Harima never forgot her? Still remembers her? You so loved her that you could never forget her?"

"This is monstrous! You evil woman!"

"Why? What makes you say that?"

"Your shamelessness is your own affair, but you dragged that —that innocent young girl Ruriko down with you into the slime!"

"She was a ward of the Nakamikado. She practically had no father and I reared her. I myself taught her to dance, to play on various musical instruments, and made her into a woman who could proudly make her way alone in the world. What was wrong in that?"

Kiyomori suddenly sobered and shook his head. "It was wrong; if Ruriko had received the right upbringing, she would have made a good wife for some man, but you poisoned her, trained her to be a whore."

"Lord Harima, you remind me somewhat of your late father. Does it matter if one chooses to become a harlot or anything else that one pleases? If Lord Harima feels so indignant now, why did he not try to become more adept at love-making when Ruriko and I lived with the Nakamikado? Aren't you to be blamed too for being a coward? . . . Still, it's not too late. Come again on your return journey from Kumano. I shall have a good talk with Ruriko and expect to see you again."

Kiyomori and the proprietress were soon laughing once more, weeping maudlinly, exchanging more cups of wine and jests which puzzled the others, until Kiyomori fell into a stupor, with the hostess asleep on his arm.

Tsunemori and Mokunosuké carried Kiyomori to his bed. When Kiyomori awoke the following morning, he found himself in his own room as though nothing unusual had happened.

"Are you awake, my lord? I have your water ready."

A young serving-girl arrived with the customary greeting with which Kiyomori began his day. A basin of water stood ready on a stand by a window. Kiyomori glanced outside as he bathed his face and smoothed down his hair. It was sunny and warm for December. He got a glimpse of the river from the window. A lively plashing of oars and singing reached his ears, the sounds made by the boatmen who were impatiently waiting for him to start. He tried to recapture a feeling of solemnity and inhaled deeply of the crisp morning air. After all, he was on his way to Kumano Shrine and it was only proper that he should be in a serious frame of mind. . . .

As he hurried through his morning meal, various members of his retinue began to appear to greet him. Shigemori, too, arrived and addressed his father ceremoniously. He thought his father looked rather sheepish, but the others busied themselves with restoring Kiyomori's good humor by a rapid exchange of small talk about the journey before them.

Inwardly Kiyomori laughed at himself; no one appeared to know what had taken place the night before, yet something deeply moving was mixed with his self-mockery.

Three large sailing vessels awaited them at a distance. The tide was low, and small boats ferried the party in groups of five or six across to the three craft moored in the estuary; the shore was lined with an unusually gay crowd of sightseers.

"Well, Tsunemori, I leave you in charge of Rokuhara," Kiyomori said, as he prepared to step into one of the boats.

Tsunemori, who was returning straight to the capital, replied: "Very well. A peaceful journey to you."

Kiyomori stood in the boat, shimmering with the light reflected from the water's surface. The entire shoreline was now spread out before him as the craft drew away from the beach, and Kiyomori could see at a glance the rows of people who crowded to the water's edge. There was his mother, standing amid a gaily dressed group of women, some of them wearing wide hats, some veiled in cloaks, and others bareheaded, exposing their sleek jet hair. Fans fluttered in his direction in farewell, but Kiyomori's eyes, narrowed in search of one face, could not discover what they sought. Puzzled, he wondered whether last night he had been dreaming.

The sea journey took several days. Kiyomori's party disembarked in the Bay of Waka. The rest of the trip was to be made in the saddle with a train of pack-horses. The first stop was at noon on the 13th of December, when the party put up at inns in Kiribé. It was here that a courier finally caught up with them. He had ridden furiously for a day and night from Kyoto.

"The worst has happened, my lord! A civil disturbance worse than the last!"

"What! In the capital? Name the leaders!"

Every man turned pale at the monstrous news; they were stupefied and babbled their bewilderment—the distance, no weapons, and this the worst possible time! Kiyomori groaned to himself, wondering whether this was a visitation from the wrathful god of Kumano Shrine.

CHAPTER XXI

RED-NOSE THE MERCHANT

T̲he morning sparkled with frost. The market near the gate of Fifth Avenue was already astir with its usual crowds. The bustle and commotion could be heard across the road in Red-Nose's imposing shop and even in the living-quarters of his home. A notoriously early riser, the Nose even now was returning from one of his usual business transactions. His nose, ruddier than ever, emitted plumes of frozen breath like a horse. Instead of stopping to warm himself at a blazing fire, he made straight for the alley of tenements where the shop clerks lived.

"Oy—oy! Are you all still packing? You're taking too much

297

time getting ready! Come now, hurry—a little more haste, there!"

The Nose turned in another direction toward another block of houses and bellowed for the shop girls.

"This is the last month of the year, mind you! Doesn't anyone realize that today is the 3rd of December? You girls, if you expect to appear in your finery on New Year's, you'll have to hustle and get some things sold."

The Nose then made his way toward his living-quarters and at the veranda overlooking an inner garden, roared: "Umeno, Umeno! Give me my breakfast, my breakfast!" Unfastening his sandals, he entered the house.

His wife busily laid out a meal of steaming gruel, dried fish, and pickles for her industrious husband.

"How cold it must have been for you—and icicles this morning!"

"That's nothing," the Nose replied, blowing noisily on his steaming bowl. "Comes December, and every soul up while it's dark—carts and oxen busily at work, and our shop clerks, who don't know what it is to go hungry, are a sluggish lot. —Ah, is Shika out in the shop? Tell him to come here."

A servant-girl was sent to fetch him. Shika was the chief clerk. After Tsunemuné's visit of the other morning, the Nose had let Shika into the secret and carefully instructed him to keep an eye on every customer entering the shop.

"Shika, you haven't seen any suspicious characters about, have you?"

"Everything's been taken care of as far as the shop is concerned. I put up a sign saying that the shop was closed until the end of the year."

"It's likely that secret agents or someone from Rokuhara will come round here in disguise."

"It's even more important to keep a sharp watch on the eyes and tongues of our clerks."

"That's just why I'm sending them off to peddle their goods, starting today, and they're taking their time about it, too. I've just given them a piece of my mind. You'd better go and give them a talking-to and see that they get on with it, Shika."

"Quite right. I'll see to that at once!"

"Here, wait a moment—just one thing more. Are you sure that the sea-bream I ordered at the fish market will be here? Today's the 3rd, tomorrow's the 4th—tomorrow will be too late."

"The fishing-boats get into Yodo at dawn, and we can't expect the catch to arrive until well toward noon."

"When the order arrives, I'll have to ask you to go along with the mistress."

"Yes, I've kept that in mind, too."

A lively scene was taking place in front of the warehouses where the clerks—men and women—were shouldering their packs and preparing to start out. It was customary for the merchants of Kyoto to send out peddlers at the end of the year to the near-by towns and outlying districts with merchandise. For some unexplained reason, however, the Nose was sending out his goods rather early in the season.

Shika saw the last of the clerks leave, and with a look of utter relief went back to the dying blaze to warm his hands. Just then two men pulling handcarts appeared in the shop. Their caps and their clothes glistened with fish scales.

"Good morning to you. Just look at these large bream—fifty of them, too! The fishermen say they've never had a haul like this before. Look at these fine fellows!"

The two men proudly unloaded twenty-five baskets, each one containing a pair of foot-long bream carefully packed in bamboo leaves.

The Nose soon appeared. "Good work, good work!" he exclaimed, his eyes starting from his head at this magnificent sight. "Here—what's happened to the sea-bass? The most important thing of all—"

"Eh, the bass? Master, you didn't order but one, did you?"

"That's right—the main thing. Without it, the fifty bream wouldn't matter at all."

"Right here, right here, and a most handsome one, sir. Here it is in a special basket all by itself."

As soon as the two men left, the Nose gave Shika instructions for repacking the fish at once as gifts. The fish, resting in baskets lined with fresh bamboo leaves and sprays of evergreen and red berries, were loaded onto a litter.

Bamboku's wife, turned out in her best, proceeded in an easterly direction accompanied by Shika and four domestics bearing two litters—one piled with the baskets of fish and the other with rolls of silk and flasks of Chinese wine tastefully arranged on it—all carefully concealed under coverings of oiled paper. To all appearances, they might have been delivering gifts for a wedding. As they crossed the Gojo Bridge, they found themselves on the outskirts of Rokuhara. Tomorrow being the 4th of December, the date of Kiyomori's departure for Kumano, the streets were choked with more horses, carriages, and people than usual.

The Nose's wife made her way round a corner toward the wing in which the mistress of Rokuhara lived. West of the kitchen gate was the women's entrance, where the guard, with whom Umeno seemed to be on friendly terms, with a smile of recognition, allowed her to pass in. Umeno disappeared beyond the trees round the main entrance of Lady Harima's house.

After some time Umeno reappeared and at the gate stopped for a few words with the guard.

"And how did he take it, Umeno?" the Nose inquired eagerly on his wife's return.

"Ah, you should have seen how pleased he was—and her ladyship!"

"So you *did* get to see the mistress?"

"Not only that—all the things were laid out and admired repeatedly."

"So much for the other things, but did he say nothing of the bass?"

"They were quite curious as to how you knew that the bass was a symbol of good luck to their house, and its arrival on the eve of Lord Harima's departure, they said, was most propitious

—a thoughtful gift for which they had nothing but compliments. I was quite carried away by their pleasure at it."

"You weren't by any chance led to say anything you ought not?"

"Oh, no, not a word about *that* . . . " faltered Umeno, to whom the meaning of her visit and the implications of her husband's risky venture became clear.

The Nose had a sharp eye for profits, an instinct for smelling out the favorable elements of a situation, so when Tsunemuné let him into the secret of the courtiers' plot, the Nose approved of it at once. Was he not after all a man of business, who from a menial post at Court had in a short time become a merchant of considerable means? And if he appeared willing to risk much on his patron's venture, he was, after all, neither such a simpleton nor so disinterested as to risk his life and entire wealth on the scheming of a few aristocrats. As the Nose saw it, another upheaval like the last one was inevitable, and it was to his advantage to place his stakes on both sides. Courtiers or warriors—whatever the outcome for the contending parties, the Nose was a merchant and must look to his gains.

The Nose took both his wife and his chief clerk into his confidence. If he had agreed on the one hand to assist Tsunemuné, neither did he neglect to send Kiyomori an artfully selected farewell gift.

For several years the center of the capital's activities had shifted noticeably toward the gate at Fifth Avenue, and it was commonly said that the increasing prosperity of the Heiké at Rokuhara accounted for this. Rokuhara, on the other side of the river, lay in full view of the gate, and Tsunemuné shrewdly hazarded that the Nose's house would least excite suspicion.

No sooner was it known that Kiyomori would leave the capital for Kumano than the conspirators began to make haste with their preparations. They made Bamboku's house their headquarters, where final plans were drawn up for assembling arms and troops.

A cold drizzle set in on the night of the 7th. Bales of charcoal and empty straw sacks lay heaped round the rear entrance of the Nose's house. Figures in straw mantles and wide hats or disguised in priests' robes hurried after one another into the merchant's house. Some visitors tethered their horses to the willow trees by the entrance, and others, alighting from ox-carriages, were quickly escorted within by attendants with umbrellas.

This was the last of the secret meetings called by the leaders of the conspiracy; in addition to those who met regularly at Nobuyori's villa, Yoshitomo of the Genji and another influential Genji clansman, Yorimasa, also appeared. Yorimasa, yielding to Yoshitomo's persuasions, had finally consented to come.

Yorimasa, a warrior in his early fifties, was considerably older than Yoshitomo, and the oldest by far of any who were present tonight.

"There is not one among us who regrets having you as our ally," Nobuyori said in greeting, to which Korekata added:

"Your coming encourages us immeasurably, so much so that we feel sure of our success."

Yorimasa's presence undoubtedly gave the courtiers much-needed encouragement, for not only was he one of the ten captains named by the late Emperor Toba as guards to the throne, but as the head of the depot for military supplies he could not be lightly ignored, and it was no small matter to have won him over.

Yorimasa, a silent man, remained somewhat aloof, offering little to the heated discussions between Nobuyori and Korekata. The rain had ceased and a sharp wind was blowing when the conspirators finally emerged from Bamboku's house and dispersed one by one into the night.

On the following day, the 8th of December, life in the capital went on as usual. Toward midnight of the 9th, however, a muffled thundering like the sound of galloping horses echoed along the streets between Fourth and Sixth avenues. Before long, shadowy figures on horseback converged on the Cloister Palace on Third Avenue and surrounded it. At each of the Palace gates, weapons clanged and horses neighed. Swords and halberds glinted in the starlight; something dour and savage permeated the frost-laden night.

A group separated itself from the company of six hundred horsemen, drew up before the main gate, and a harsh voice, piercing as a winter blast, cried out:

"Is anyone there? Open the gates—this is the Vice-Councilor, Nobuyori! Urgent business calls me away from the capital! I must have audience with his majesty immediately!"

Hardly had the voice ceased when a tumult broke out as the soldiers began hammering at the gates. There were shouts to break down the doors, but the figure on horseback motioned for silence. Still no answer came from within. Only the wind whining between the white skeleton branches replied.

The ex-Emperor Goshirakawa was still awake, whiling away the night with Shinzei's two sons and other courtiers, with mimes and dances, accompanied by the court musicians. When the noise of hurrying feet and confused sounds were heard along the corridors, the company grew pale. Their first thought was of fire. It was less than a month since one of the palaces on the river-front had burned down and a princess who was to perform at the New Year dances had died in the flames.

Fear immobilized the company when a court official burst into the room announcing, breathlessly: "The Vice-Councilor is here, unaccompanied by torch-bearers and surrounded by armed men! He demands an audience of your majesty. He comes completely armed and to say farewell. He offers no reason for coming like this. There is shouting and a great commotion at the gates. Listen!"

With this the messenger slid back a door. A cold rush of air extinguished the candles and threw the room into blackness.

"Will your majesty grant him an audience?"

"Lights—give me lights!"

On hearing that it was Nobuyori, the ex-Emperor Goshirakawa sprang to his feet and sped down an icy corridor.

Lights were soon kindled and followed the flying figure through the Palace to the South Room. There the doors were thrown open. In the candlelight Goshirakawa made out a figure on horseback, who addressed him, saying:

"Your most gracious majesty, I have just heard a rumor that Councilor Shinzei has brought false charges against me and is sending his troops to arrest me; I have therefore decided to escape east with some of my soldiers and to go into hiding for a time. I have come to take leave of you."

Startled by this announcement from one of his favorites, the ex-Emperor asked: "Who has been spreading these baseless rumors? They are only malicious tales, Nobuyori, and you are being deceived."

"No, there can be no mistake about the rumor."

"But I've not been told anything. . . ."

"Then what does his majesty think of it?"

"I shall see the Emperor himself and make sure that these charges against you are silenced. But, Nobuyori—armed to the teeth?"

"Permit me, then, your majesty, to accompany you to the Court. Here, bring round the carriage."

"What do you mean by these orders, Nobuyori?" Goshirakawa broke in angrily, but before he could utter another word, soldiers hurried up to the carriage porch, seized him, and bore him off to a conveyance. Councilor Moronaka waited beside the vehicle. Dazed and enraged by the rough handling, Goshirakawa refused to enter the carriage and turned on the general.

"You, Moronaka, what do you mean by coming here—and armed?"

The Councilor drew back, faltering. "It is only for the time being, your majesty. Do not be anxious. We shall return with you here shortly."

While he stammered out his excuses, some soldiers hurried forward with a weeping princess, Goshirakawa's younger sister. The ex-Emperor's anger gave way to apprehension when he saw her. Without further protest he let himself be thrust into the carriage after her.

A sharp order was given: "At the signal for the carriage to

start, set fire to all the gates! See that Shinzei's sons don't escape. Spare no one who resists!"

The carriage jerked forward and rolled through one of the Palace gates, which in the next instant burst into flame. Whips cracked across the back of the straining bull as the large wheels bumped and creaked over the frozen road. Yoshitomo and Nobuyori and their mounted soldiers kept pace with the beast, which, crazed by the clanking arms and the sound of galloping hoofs, broke into a wild run until the carriage approached the South Gate of the Imperial Palace.

"North—to the North Gate!"

The disorderly cavalcade thundered along the Palace walls, swung sharply round to the north, and poured into the Palace grounds, coming to a halt between the outer and inner gates near the Palace Archives.

Yoshitomo and Nobuyori conferred briefly:

"We had better keep them in there until the uproar in the city dies down."

Goshirakawa and his sister were led to the Archives and there locked in. Their guards were ordered to keep watch over the prisoners until further orders were issued.

The Emperor Nijo, meanwhile, was rudely awakened by armed soldiers and quickly led off, terrified, to a building on the north side of the Palace and imprisoned there.

Now that the Emperor and the ex-Emperor were out of the way, and the Genji soldiers in complete control of the Guard Office, all that remained for the conspirators to do was to deal with Shinzei and Kiyomori.

As Yoshitomo of the Genji, the Vice-Councilor, and their men rode away from the Archives and rounded the Palace enclosure on the east, they saw the Cloister Palace in flames. The whole sky was on fire. Choking smoke billowed skyward and showered down burning cinders, between which the winter stars trembled, an unearthly blue. Nobuyori's horse reared suddenly as a company of soldiers galloped toward them waving javelins and halberds.

Nobuyori cried out involuntarily: "The enemy!—Genji or Heiké?"

Yoshitomo laughed as he drew up behind.

"They must be our men, but it would not surprise me if they turned out to be Heiké."

The company advanced toward Nobuyori and Yoshitomo with an exultant shout, drew up before them, and related what had taken place at the Cloister Palace. They had captured and beheaded two of the ex-Emperor's advisers, they said, as a soldier held out a sword on which were thrust two heads. Nobuyori averted his eyes with a shudder, but Yoshitomo leaned forward and examined them closely.

"Very well," he ordered, "expose the heads at the East Gate. Proclaim to the public the names of all Genji and Heiké who have been beheaded."

Turning their backs on the cheering soldiers, Nobuyori and Yoshitomo and their mounted soldiers continued on their way, turning sharply west on the avenue running south of the academy. It was two o'clock in the morning. The fire still raged, and a violent wind tossed up burning fragments, whirling them in all directions in a demonic dance.

Korekata and Nobuyori, whose agents told them that Shinzei and his sons were spending the night at the Cloister Palace, ordered it to be burned to the ground. But when it was known that Shinzei was not with his sons, Korekata immediately ordered his soldiers to surround the Councilor's residence and set fire to it, sparing no one who attempted to escape. At daybreak, the soldiers raked in vain among the ashes for traces of Shinzei's body.

When dawn broke on the 10th, the capital still lay in the clutches of fear. Houses and shops remained shuttered, and only straggling groups of soldiers with blackened, bloodstained faces roamed the streets. At the gate of Fifth Avenue, however, the Nose's shop was open as usual for business.

Bamboku had spent the entire night on his rooftop watching the conflagration. At the sight of the buildings going up in flames and smoke, he had groaned: "A shameful waste—those flames are pure gold!"

The merchant's soul sighed at the spectacle of so much wealth reduced to ashes.

"Whatever happens, the Vice-Councilor, it seems, is now in power. Amazing, indeed—indeed! With Shinzei gone, this naturally would happen."

Perched like a vulture on his roof, the Nose watched the fires subside, then turned over in his mind the business for the following day. No fear or misgivings entered his mind. His restless brain churned and revolved.

"How will Lord Kiyomori of Harima receive all this? With him away, Rokuhara is helpless."

Bamboku turned his head in the direction of Rokuhara on the farther bank. He saw no stirring of life there. He pictured to himself what its denizens must feel, and exulted: "After all, I am a merchant—oh, happy fate, that I was born to this!"

Then he clambered down to the ground, calling out in a voice that trembled with emotion: "Woman, wake Shika! . . . You say he's up? Well, then the menservants. Tell them to get out the handcarts and wait by the warehouses."

In his overwrought state the Nose forgot that his spouse was of no mean birth and bawled for her as for any common wife. He was soon busily carrying jug after jug of wine—more than a dozen—from his storehouse, loading them onto three carts.

"See that you deliver these to their excellencies Nobuyori and Yoshitomo. Tell them these are but tokens of my felicitations. Say that I will call in person on the Councilor Tsunemuné this afternoon," the Nose instructed Shika.

The servants hung back. It was still too dangerous to go through the capital with such loaded carts, they protested stubbornly.

The Nose quickly reassured them. "Nonsense! Were you servants to the warriors, you would last night have been dodging swords and arrows to save your skins! Do you think that those warriors and their households ever get enough to fill their bellies?

How do you expect to become merchants in your own right without going through with this?"

After seeing the men safely out on the dim streets, the Nose turned back to his house and a steaming breakfast, then crept to bed and was soon sound asleep.

Nobuyori, the Vice-Councilor, and Korekata of the Police Commission lost no time installing themselves at Court and issuing proclamations in the name of the Emperor.

It was now the 12th of December and nothing had been heard of Shinzei, who had fled from the capital on horseback when his agents gave him warning, shortly before the outbreak on the night of the 10th. There had been no time for him to warn his wife, Lady Kii, or his sons at the Cloister Palace. Shinzei made his way through the dark, along the Uji Road toward one of his manors. Five retainers straggled after him blindly. Toward noon of the 13th, one of Shinzei's retainers who succeeded in escaping from the capital came upon one of his fellow housemen in the hills near Uji.

"Where is our master? Is he safe?" he asked.

The other hesitated and, thinking it wiser to tell him very little, simply assured him that Shinzei was safe, and in his turn eagerly plied him with questions about what had happened in the capital. When he had got as much news as he could, he urged the other retainer to return to Kyoto.

When the retainer finally overtook his master, he recounted all he had heard. Shinzei turned gray with fear and, while they were still speaking, the other retainers, who had gone out to reconnoiter, returned with the news that a company of seventy mounted warriors were approaching.

Shinzei's eyes gleamed like those of a trapped beast. He saw no hope of reaching his own domain now and groaned. Then he turned to his five retainers.

"I have a plan. There's a farmhouse behind this temple. Find some spades and dig a hole there—beyond that bamboo thicket. . . . Hurry!—a hole!"

The housemen feverishly turned up the frozen soil until they had a pit large enough for Shinzei to sit in cross-legged. Shinzei lowered himself into it and ordered the men to pack leaves and branches around him until he was buried up to the neck.

"Now throw in the dirt," he cried, placing a hollow length of bamboo between his lips, "until my shoulders are covered. Cover my head with that bamboo hat and lightly pile on more earth, so that the top of my head is level with the ground. Pull out the wadding from your clothes and gently stop up my ears and nose; then cover up the traces of your work with more leaves. See that nothing chokes this stem through which I shall breathe. Leave me here until tomorrow and come back as soon as it is safe."

Their task completed, Shinzei's retainers fled the spot.

On the following afternoon two of the five retainers stole back and were aghast to find a yawning hole with a corpse in it. Some peasants who came by told them that several soldiers, with a woodcutter as their guide, had come here on the previous evening, unearthed Shinzei, beheaded him then and there, and left after they had thrown the headless corpse back into the pit.

On the day that Shinzei met his death—the 13th of December—a courier from Rokuhara caught up with Kiyomori at Kiribé.

On the 14th, when the news of Shinzei's capture and beheading reached the capital, a proclamation was made, announcing that Shinzei's head would be paraded along the main avenues of the capital and later be displayed in a public place.

High and low alike trooped to see the grisly spectacle. As the head passed before Nobuyori, Korekata, and Yoshitomo in their carriages, a spectator among the crowds was heard to say that he saw the grim emblem nod twice in the direction of the three men. And this strange tale passed swiftly from mouth to mouth among the credulous masses.

Of Shinzei's household, nineteen, including his sons, were captured and beheaded on the banks of the river where so many had died not too long before on Shinzei's orders, and Shinzei's head was set up in a certain tree on the west side of the capital, where all might see the ironic fate of the man who revived the death penalty.

Before the week was over, the usurpers had divided among themselves some of the most envied offices of state, and in self-issued decrees proclaimed themselves the rulers. Nobuyori took to himself the long-coveted title of General of the Imperial Guards and the post of a minister. Korekata, Tsunemuné, and the others each named himself to the post he most coveted, and to Yoshitomo of the Genji was given the province of Harima. Yorimasa of the Genji, however, pleading that his injuries kept him at home, failed to appear at the banquet celebrating the triumph of the conspirators.

All thought of the imprisoned Emperor and Goshirakawa, meanwhile, was forgotten. But while the feasting went on, a court secretary came to Yoshitomo with a message:

"Sir, your son has just arrived from Kamakura. He is waiting in one of the anterooms."

Yoshitomo's face lighted up. "He has?"

Nobuyori had turned red under the powder that covered his face. He had been drinking all evening. Overhearing the secretary, he leaned toward Yoshitomo, who was seated near him. "Master of the Imperial Stables, who is this that has just arrived from Kamakura?"

"My eldest son, Yoshihira. He was sent east as a boy to get his training. He has a bad name for having killed his uncle in a quarrel. A rascal, to be sure, but he seems to have heard of the disturbances here and has come to offer assistance. I am proud of him for that. They say that the more troublesome a child is, the more his parents love him."

"How long is it since you last saw him?"

"I hardly remember how many years it is."

"How old is he?"

"Nineteen."

"He must have ridden day and night without stopping to

get here from Kamakura. You surely want to see each other without losing a moment. Tell him to come here."

Yoshitomo inclined his head. "If it pleases you, sir."

"I'd like to see Yoshihira for myself."

The secretary led in the young man, and the entire company turned expectantly. But a look of disappointment came over their faces, for, his reputation notwithstanding, Yoshihira appeared to be a quite ordinary youth of rather small build. He wore armor suitable for a young warrior. The purple silk cords of his cap were knotted under his chin, enhancing the healthy glow of his young cheeks and lending a certain fineness to his robust looks. His cap was a new one hastily worn for the occasion.

Nobuyori looked down at the young man.

"Yoshihira of the Genji, you bring us good luck. You come on a day of rejoicing," he said. "You, too, must soon prove yourself in battle, and by your prowess win yourself a court post. All these you see around me have distinguished themselves in these last four days and are now being showered with well-deserved praise and honors. Here—wine for Yoshihira."

Yoshihira bowed low in greeting, then sat erect, staring openly at the courtiers ranged in the seats of honor as though he had never before seen such a curious sight. An attendant presented him with a cup of wine. Yoshihira finished it in one draught. His cup was refilled and he again drained it, but said nothing. The glow in his tanned face bespoke a kind of innocence rarely seen in youths in the capital. The clear, straightforward gaze was without guile.

"You drink well, Yoshihira. You enjoy it?"

"I do."

"And—love?"

"Of that I know nothing."

"What brings you to the Capital? To win yourself a name?"

"That is for the future. I came when I heard my father was in need, and what son would not do the same?"

The quick, direct answers seemed to amuse Nobuyori.

"Spoken like an easterner!" He laughed, showing his dyed teeth. Yoshihira frowned slightly with distaste at the sight of the blackened teeth in the painted face.

"You don't boast, yet you act like a man, Yoshihira. Come, you must follow your father's example and win the privilege of taking your place among us. I'll see to it that you do."

A look of scorn hovered under Yoshihira's smile. The courtiers, he thought, still treated the warriors as though they were watchdogs. Here he was being trifled with with a tidbit as though he were a whelp.

"What makes you smile, Yoshihira?" Nobuyori queried. "Are you not interested in coming up in the ranks?"

Yoshihira shook his head. "No. I was thinking of my uncle and what he did during the Hogen War."

"The Hogen War? Your uncle?"

"Tametomo of the Genji is my uncle. He refused a court post from the Minister of the Left when the fighting started, and rode into the thick of battle. . . . I was merely thinking of that."

Nobuyori frowned. He sensed that he had offended this youth. The courtiers glared at Yoshihira; Yoshitomo suppressed an exclamation of approval. The arrival of a dispatch for Nobuyori fortunately broke the uncomfortable silence that fell on the company. A courier had returned with a report of Kiyomori's whereabouts.

With Shinzei dead, only Kiyomori needed to be dealt with, and there was little to fear from Rokuhara, where Kiyomori's brother and brother-in-law were in command. There were rumors that they too had fled with the women and children, and a single order from Nobuyori to his troops would have confirmed this, but Nobuyori and his fellow usurpers were content to wait until they were certain of Kiyomori's next move. They were sure that Kiyomori's fate was sealed; he would not dare strike a blow at them. There was nothing he could do now but surrender. A few, however, ventured to think that Kiyomori might be audacious enough to challenge them in a last desperate fight.

In spite of a few misgivings, the victors were undisturbed by the latest news. "It looks as though Kiyomori has decided to return to the capital. The courier we sent this morning has just arrived back. There is no further news and no way of telling what Kiyomori intends to do next. The next dispatch should tell us that."

The drinking was resumed and Nobuyori turned once more to Yoshihira.

"And by the way, young man, what do you think of all this?"

Yoshihira, who had been listening intently to the fragments of conversation round him, replied eagerly: "Permit me to have a company of soldiers. I will go as far as Abeno and there challenge Kiyomori of the Heiké in single combat and bring back his head."

Yoshihira's self-assurance amused the courtiers, who laughed aloud.

Yoshihira gazed around him blankly, uncomprehending.

CHAPTER XXII

ORANGES FROM THE SOUTH

The winter sea darkened slowly, taking on the indigo iri-
descence of fish scales as the sun dropped toward the
horizon. Far out on the waters the crest of the waves
gleamed white. It was the hour when the vast wheeling of the
earth's orb was almost perceptible to the senses in the swiftly
ebbing light. The long coastline of Kii Peninsula wrinkled away
to the south in a succession of hills, and between them the har-

bor in Kiribé Bay lay sheltered, smooth as a millpond. A few lights dotted the hamlet lying between the river-mouth and the sea.

"There goes the sun—ah, there it goes down," Kiyomori whispered to the darkening sky and the hillside on which Kiribé Shrine stood. Never, never in all his forty-two years, had he watched a sunset with such bitter repining. This was the 13th of December, the day on which he had received news of dire events in Kyoto.

When his party had recovered from their initial bewilderment, Kiyomori obtained the use of a hall in one of the buildings attached to Kiribé Shrine and called a council; with his men gathered round him, Kiyomori began:

"We must not lose heart in this most disastrous moment of our lives. What, then, are we to do? Shigemori, tell us what you think. Mokunosuké—and the rest of you—speak up. Every one of you tell me what you think should be done."

They had none of them ever seen Kiyomori like this. His seriousness changed him beyond recognition. No longer was he the gay and confident leader they had always known. The thick brows, which gave him an obstinate look, were now drawn together into a heavy line, giving his troubled eyes an anxious frown.

A grim look had replaced Shigemori's usually mild expression.

"Tell us first, Father, what you think. We want nothing more than to live or die with you."

Kiyomori immediately outlined two plans. Shigemori was not in favor of them, and Mokunosuké shook his head. And as they deliberated, the short winter's day drew swiftly to its close.

"Every moment is precious, and we must get rest and sleep or else it will go hard with us tomorrow. Why don't we get the shrine-keepers to give us our supper beside a fire? And you, Mokunosuké, tell the men to cook their meals and get some sleep."

The talk ended when the shrine-keepers arrived in a body

to welcome Kiyomori and escorted him to a lodge erected for the use of imperial visitors traveling to Kumano Shrine, several days' journey farther southeast. The open hearth in the guest-house always surprised visitors from the capital by its great size. Kiyomori sat by a blazing fire and listened to the lonely murmuring of the distant sea.

"Father, you must be tired."

"Oh, is it you, Shigemori? Where's the Old One?"

"He will be here very soon."

"I want only the three of us here together."

"Mokunosuké thought so too, and has gone to see that the men are bedded down for the night."

"How did the men appear?"

"They were badly shaken at first, but seem to have recovered their spirits."

"If any try to slip off, let them go. Don't keep too close a watch on them."

Shrine virgins brought in wine and food, and the chief priest arrived soon after to greet Kiyomori. Kiyomori quickly dispensed with the customary salutations.

"They tell me that the climate in these parts is mild, but at night the sea sounds cold and forbidding. We wish to have our meal here beside the fire, undisturbed, for I have private matters to discuss," he said, quickly coming to the point.

Mokunosuké soon joined the pair.

The two plans which Kiyomori had presented to his men that afternoon were: one, to continue on the pilgrimage, since they were powerless to intervene in the struggle even if they turned back. At Kumano he would consult the oracle and act on its advice. The other was to return at once to Naniwa (Osaka) and from there sail to Shikoku Island to watch the course of events, and, in the meantime, try to muster an army.

At best, the plans were little more than expedients. Mokunosuké, however, perceived what was going through Kiyomori's mind. Kiyomori feared the enemy in the capital less than treachery among the soldiers who now formed his party, for a handsome reward awaited any man who brought Kiyomori's head to the authorities. This possibility, in turn, seemed to trouble Kiyomori less than the possible fate of his family at Rokuhara. If Kiyomori were to take up arms against Nobuyori and Korekata, they would not hesitate to put Rokuhara to the torch, slaughter the inhabitants, and then demand Kiyomori's surrender. There was no gainsaying this, and whatever Kiyomori decided, it was necessary that he keep his intentions hidden from friend and foe alike, reach Kyoto without delay, and act quickly.

Mokunosuké, his eighty-year-old frame hunched over, faced father and son across the hearth, mumbling indistinctly.

"What's happened in the capital was bound to come. This Old One can hardly believe what you've just said. I realize too well the difficulties you face in getting back to the capital. But, so far as we are concerned, there are enough bows, arrows, and armor for us all."

"Old One, you don't mean that you brought them along?"

"That is part of the warrior's training; I owe this to your late father, Tadamori."

"Well done!"

Shigemori, who had been quietly studying his father's face in the firelight, said:

"Have you decided to hurry back to the capital after all, Father?"

"That speaks for itself. I have no other choice as a warrior. The gods have granted us this chance. The road to Kumano is beset with hardships and perils—like man's journeying through life, Shigemori. You are of age now, and this will be the supreme test of your manhood."

"That it shall be. But what of those at Rokuhara?"

"Yes, we have every reason to fear for them, and that is the main objection to my going back. We had better send a message to the inn at Tanabé by someone we can trust."

"Hanzo is the man for that. What is the message?"

"The chief priest of Kumano is stopping there. I will write him and ask for assistance along the road."

"Would you rather have me go on a matter of such importance?"

"No, that would make it appear that we are desperate. Hanzo will do."

Kiyomori quickly wrote a letter and sent Hanzo off with it. He then told the chief priest that an unexpected summons from the Court called him back to the capital, and added: "As we start before dawn, I must beg your indulgence and allow us to attend the early morning services."

It was still dark when the blaze of cooking-fires lighted up the shrine yard, and long before the first birds were heard, the shrine resounded to rhythmic clapping and the chanting of prayers.

Clad in full armor, Kiyomori, Shigemori, and their soldiers and retainers wound their way slowly north. Each man wore a twig of yew somewhere in his armor. It was customary for pilgrims to carry a twig of yew, sacred to Kiribé Shrine, as a charm.

The priests, who had not yet heard of the uprising in Kyoto, thought that Kiyomori had been summoned by the usual duties of his office and presented him and the others with large branches, which were secured to their saddles. Kiyomori and his men stared curiously at the fragrant globules of mandarin oranges clustering golden among the dark-green leaves. What an addition they would be, Kiyomori thought, to the New Year's feast at Court, where this strange new fruit would cause the courtiers to marvel. Then he wrenched off one of the fruits, peeled it, and tasted it.

"Here, it's delicious!" he cried, turning suddenly in his saddle. "Shigemori—Old One—taste them. There's little chance we'll get back to the capital with these. Here, men, share your oranges among you."

Kiyomori tore off fruit after fruit and tossed them back to the soldiers, who scrambled for them with eager shouts, fighting over them like excited children. The sun was now well above the horizon, and the chill morning air was broken by the sound of laughter which greeted the shower of golden fruit.

Past hamlet after hamlet they rode until sundown, when

Kiyomori ordered a halt. The following morning they crossed a mountain pass and pressed on until they reached the Kii River. There they were overtaken by twenty armed horsemen dispatched by the chief priest of Kumano Shrine in answer to Kiyomori's letter.

That same day, as the party were on their way through a defile, they were met by a local chieftain and his thirty retainers. In reply to Kiyomori's questions why they had come, the chieftain answered:

"My father was deeply indebted to your late father, Tadamori, who gave us his protection. I heard that you had suddenly decided to return to the capital because of an uprising there and came to give you warning."

The chieftain then went on to say that rumors had reached the capital that Kiyomori had interrupted his pilgrimage to Kumano. Yoshitomo's son, Yoshihira, with three thousand horse, had arrived at Naniwa (Osaka) and was deploying his soldiers in an arc toward the south, in wait for Kiyomori.

A hot surge of blood raced through Kiyomori's veins. Shigemori's eyes grew tense as they swept the sky to the north. Kiyomori's intentions were now clear to all his followers, and Kiyomori realized that the moment had come when they might yet decide to desert him.

"Here, rest your horses. Finish the rest of the oranges. There are not many left. Divide them among you. Let every man have at least a taste," he ordered, and added, laughing: "Perhaps, your last chance."

His eyes searched the faces around him for the effect his words might have had on them.

Kiyomori's men formed a ring round him on the moor.

"I came thus far planning to cross to Shikoku Island, but have changed my mind. There's no safety anywhere, even if I cross to China itself."

Kiyomori spoke without any sign of being troubled.

"If we turn our backs on the unrest in the capital we shall be safe, but warriors elsewhere will despise the Heiké as cowards and refuse us their wholehearted support. It is even more possible that they will rally to the Genji."

The soldiers listened to him intently. From their looks it was plain that no one would follow his suggestion, and Kiyomori suddenly felt shamed by the quizzical glances turned on him. He realized that he was risking his life as much as they, and that they trusted him. Had they intended to desert him, Kiyomori reflected, they had already had ample opportunity to do so.

"I have said enough. This is no time for me to be talking. Though we're only a hundred horse, I am certain that if we are determined, we shall succeed in reaching the capital. And when it becomes known that I am back at Rokuhara, our friends will rally to us. What do you think?"

Loud ayes greeted Kiyomori, for every soldier was anxious about the wife and children he had left in the capital.

Kiyomori continued: "One difficulty still lies before us. I have been told that Yoshihira of the Genji and three thousand horse are lying in wait for us farther north. They are thirty to our one."

It was now the soldiers' turn to persuade Kiyomori of their determination to return to the capital, and they assured him that they were ready to face unnumbered enemies, to follow him wherever he led, and to show how mighty were the arms of the Heiké.

Kiyomori needed no more assurances. Whatever doubts he had had about his soldiers vanished. He then ordered his men to feed and water their horses, cook their evening meal, and look to the cords of their sandals and armor and prepare to charge through enemy territory that same night.

They rested and waited until sundown before starting, and the last rays of the sun slanted golden across the cavalcade as it moved slowly north along the coast.

"We're close now," Kiyomori warned, sending three riders ahead to reconnoiter. When they had gone some distance, they saw the dull glow of fires on the moor and guessed that they had come upon the enemy encampment. Death now lay in their path. Faces grew strained, and the fingers on bows seemed paralyzed.

"Gather round. Draw up close," Kiyomori ordered in a low voice. "Stay together; charge for the thinnest spot in their line and break through. Remember—no hand-to-hand fighting! Our aim is to get to the capital. Shigemori, don't get separated from the rest," Kiyomori warned, turning anxiously to his son.

Shigemori had once heard his uncle Tokitada remark that Kiyomori had not the physique of a warrior. Though Kiyomori sat well in the saddle, Shigemori had lately noticed that his father was beginning to get stout and lacked the lightness and agility for single combat.

"No fear, Father. Take care that you don't lose your stirrups when we start galloping."

"Confound you!" Kiyomori laughed. "How dare you talk to your father like that! Keep quiet and get into line. Don't touch whip to your horse until I give the signal. You're not used to fighting, remember. Those who brag before the battle are most apt to lose their heads when they meet the enemy."

As the horsemen moved forward slowly, they spied figures galloping toward them with flaming torches and brought their bows into position with a shout, but Kiyomori waved them down.

"Hold! Wait! I hear them calling. Let's hear what they have to say."

Several warriors rode up hallooing eagerly: "Are you soldiers of Kiyomori of the Heiké on your way to the capital? Is Lord Harima among you?"

Kiyomori spurred his horse forward. "This is I, Kiyomori of the Heiké. Who are you? Are you not Genji?"

A warrior quickly dismounted and approached Kiyomori.

"We are not Genji, but come from Isé. We heard that your lordship was in great need."

"Heiké of Isé?"

"We are Heiké whom your father once befriended. We have never forgotten his favors to us and have held ourselves in readiness to come to your aid."

"Ah, Isé—the cradle of the Heiké!"

"A thousand have left Isé—two hundred for Rokuhara. Some

five hundred more are on their way there by now. Three hundred horse have come to meet you and give you escort."

"The gods be thanked! Those troops of which we were warned were not the enemy, then? I take no credit for this. I owe all this to my father, who in his lifetime sowed the seeds of this good fortune," Kiyomori cried in his gratitude.

There was great rejoicing that night when Kiyomori rode into the friendly camp. Before dawn they were once more on their way, and Kiyomori, looking back from his saddle, felt his heart swell at the sight of the sun flashing on that host of four hundred—no small company.

The sun was still high when the company reached Fushimi Shrine, several leagues south of the capital, where it was customary for pilgrims returning from Kumano to offer the yew leaves they had brought with them from Kiribé Shrine. Kiyomori called for a halt long enough to offer prayers for victory. As he bowed his head to pray, the vanishing tail of a fox seemed to dart before his closed eyes; he suddenly recalled that hunting trip so many years ago when he had stumbled on three foxes, and Kiyomori, who jeered at superstitions, longed to believe that the gods were on his side.

Kiyomori and his troops reached Rokuhara that night. No lights shone anywhere, and the streets were deserted, though it was nearly the end of the year. Only the sound of dogs howling at the winter moon broke the stillness. With the news of Kiyomori's approach, however, the pent-up feelings of the inhabitants burst forth in cries of relief. The old and young, men and women, soldiers and servants poured from every house into the streets, waving and shouting wildly.

"Tokiko! Tokiko!"

Kiyomori rode up to the two-storied gate, surrounded by a sea of faces. He caught sight of a few members of his household, and called out his wife's name.

Tokiko, who had been waiting outside in the cold with her children, stood holding the hem of her robes up out of the mud. At the sound of her name, she let fall the folds of her skirts, stumbled forward, and clung to the reins of Kiyomori's horse.

"Welcome home! Safe!"

"Ah, here you are," Kiyomori cried, searching her face anxiously.

"The children—our good mother?" he added quickly.

"They have been waiting impatiently for you."

"Are they all well? A miracle this—a miracle indeed!"

Kiyomori rode into the courtyard, where his stepmother and children waited beside the entrance. The darkened space was soon alive with the sound of running feet.

On learning that his stepmother, Tokiko, the children, and all the women in the household had gone that same morning to the hills to hide, but had returned when they heard that he was on his way back, Kiyomori frowned.

"Who ordered you to return? The very opposite of what should have been done. You may stay the night, but at dawn you must all be off to the hills again. I cannot have you look on the horrors to come. The worst is ahead of us, and Rokuhara may soon be a smoking ruin."

On the day that Kiyomori returned to Rokuhara, Nobuyori and Korekata had called a council which all courtiers were ordered to attend on pain of death. Many, none the less, failed to come. Though news had reached Kyoto that warriors from Isé and neighboring provinces were on their way to Rokuhara, and Kiyomori himself was arriving soon, Nobuyori was less concerned with these reports than the sight of the empty seats at the council.

Nobuyori occupied the dais of the Great Hall, staring down uncertainly at the rows of courtiers, when a late-comer appeared, not by the usual way, but by crossing the plaza and mounting the stairs leading up to the hall. His five attendants, in cloaks thrown over their armor and long swords, waited at one of the gates. Nobuyori's cheeks blanched under the powder as the newcomer, his uncle, Mitsuyori, stared grimly at the high dais.

"Alas, an extraordinary sight! Do I see the high seat occupied by dandies and men-about-town, and the rightful occupants cowering below? Is this an entertainment in a teahouse with dancing-girls? Can this be called the Court?" he burst out bitterly.

Nobuyori hung his head in confusion at his uncle's words,

while the others looked on in consternation. Mitsuyori, Korekata's elder brother, who rarely appeared at court councils, was held in awe by the nobles.

A courtier left his seat near Nobuyori and came forward. "Sir, we have been expecting you. Will you not be seated?"

"Then this *is* the Court, after all?"

"Yes—"

"If this is the Court, there is an order of precedence. Who is that painted dandy up there?"

"The new General of the Guards, Minister Nobuyori."

"I have never heard of the man. There is no General Nobuyori of the Guards. Possibly you speak of the Vice-Councilor Nobuyori?"

"He was lately appointed."

"Absurd! Where is his majesty, who alone makes appointments?" Mitsuyori inquired, smiting his thigh angrily with the flat of his wooden mace of office and pointing it at Nobuyori.

"Nobuyori, you are occupying the high seat; where do you propose to seat me, who precede you in rank?"

". . . ."

"As for today's council—what do you intend to discuss? And you, gentlemen, why should those who absent themselves today deserve punishment by death?"

". . . ."

"His majesty alone presides over such councils as this. Where is he? Will no one answer me? Strange and marvelous, indeed!" Mitsuyori exclaimed as he strode from the hall toward a wing of the Palace.

"Korekata, what are you doing here," he exclaimed to his brother, whom he found cowering in an inner apartment.

"Is it you—my brother?"

" 'Brother'? You dare to call me 'brother'?"

"Yes—"

"Then, indeed, am I disgraced, for your guilt is my guilt. This is more than I can bear."

"I have done wrong."

"You acknowledge it, then? What led you to do this?"

". . . ."

"You, an officer of the Police Commission, let yourself be taken to view Shinzei's head? You never stopped to think of what people would say of you? I shrink at the rumors about you. It doesn't seem possible that my own brother could commit such folly. I doubted it all along."

". . . ."

"Our name has never been dishonored until now and you are the first who deserves the name of fool! Think how you have disgraced the name of our dead father—brought shame on our aged mother. What led you to such madness?"

"My own stupidity. I have watched Nobuyori these several days and now regret my folly."

"If you speak the truth, then see that his majesty is released without a moment's delay and taken to safety."

"It shall be done."

"I will not have you abetting these deeds. Do you understand, Korekata? Ah, Korekata," Mitsuyori added pityingly, "why must you risk your life so foolishly?"

With Mitsuyori's unexpected appearance, the council broke up in confusion.

The 19th of December drew to a close. That night news reached the Imperial Guards that Kiyomori had returned to Rokuhara, and the rumor spread that Kiyomori was mustering his fighting men.

That night Nobuyori, who had taken up residence in the Palace, could not sleep for anxiety and sent a gentlewoman to Korekata's apartments, begging him to appear. To his surprise, he was told that Korekata was not there. He next summoned Tsunemuné, but the courtier was not to be found at the Palace.

In the meantime dawn came without the expected attack from Rokuhara. Birds began to call to one another from the frosted treetops in the Palace gardens. Nobuyori, who waited for the sun to rise, fell into a sound sleep.

CHAPTER XXIII

THE EMPEROR KIDNAPPED

he 20th, 21st, and 22nd of December were passed in uncertainty at the Imperial Palace where the coming and going of armed men in the bleak gardens replaced the customary bustle preceding the New Year. There was constant talk
that Kiyomori would attack the Palace. At Rokuhara the strengthening of its defenses continued as word went round that the Genji
would march from the Palace on the Heiké stronghold. Yet neither
side showed any sign of taking the offensive.

But during this lull there was one who bestirred himself. It was the Nose. Korekata and Nobuyori, leaders in the Palace revolt, one night quietly visited Bamboku's house on Fifth Avenue, and soon after they left, Red-Nose made his way to Rokuhara with a letter for Kiyomori.

For almost a week there were rumors that negotiations for a truce were under way, but by the night of the 26th, Nobuyori realized that not even a decree in the name of the throne could stave off conflict, for the Genji captains had grown restive and the Heiké continued with their warlike preparations. The entire situation had now resolved itself into a struggle between the Genji and the Heiké, and if the Heiké were to be crushed, the moment was ripe for it.

The ex-Emperor Goshirakawa, a close prisoner in the Palace Archives since the night of the 9th of December, was visited one night by masked men who said:

"Your majesty, make no outcry and you shall come to no harm. There is talk of fighting before the night is out. A litter awaits you, and we shall accompany you to Ninna-ji Temple."

Goshirakawa made no resistance and allowed himself to be carried through the Northwest Gate. A horse awaited him there and he was quickly made to mount and led away.

At about the same time—three o'clock in the morning—the Emperor, who was imprisoned in another part of the Palace, was suddenly wakened by whispers that he was to leave at once for a place of safety. He was astonished to find that Tsunemuné and Korekata had come for him. They carried swords and wore armor under their cloaks. Too terrified to reply, Nijo let Korekata wrap him in a lady's cloak and lead him away.

Tsunemuné led the trembling Nijo outside and bundled him into a carriage with his sister, the Princess. The carriage quickly got under way. Two ox-tenders and a few attendants hurried the conveyance toward a gate on the west side of the Palace wall, where they were challenged by a Genji guard, Juro.

"Who goes there?"

Soldiers swarmed toward the carriage and brought it to a stop.

"Something suspicious-looking here. Where could this be going at this time of the night?"

"The Princess and her maid are on their way to the temple," came the reply. "Tell Juro to come here."

"This is I, Juro."

"Is that you, Juro?"

"Who speaks?"

"Korekata of the Police Commission."

"You, sir?"

"Open the gates and let us through. I am escorting her highness in person. Need you question us further?"

"Quite unnecessary, sir, but we have our orders from General Yoshitomo and may not allow even you to pass, sir."

"Then call the general."

"I do not know where he is to be found."

"How much longer do you intend to keep her highness waiting here among these rough soldiers? What right have you to question her when I am her escort? Out of the way!"

"A moment, sir. It is our duty to guard this gate and even you cannot force your way through like this. If you insist, however, allow me to inspect the carriage," said Juro stepping forward and pushing aside the curtains with the end of his bow. Guards crowded behind Juro, waving their torches. The glare revealed two frightened young women, huddled motionless in each other's arms. The seventeen-year-old Emperor's eyes were closed and a deathly pallor lay on his delicate, girlish features. Juro, who took him for one of the ladies-in-waiting, ordered the carriage to pass on.

The carriage continued on its way through the throng of warriors and flaming torches, rumbled over the icy ground and into the night.

"Get on, there! Hurry!" Korekata and Tsunemuné cried to the panting ox-tenders as the carriage turned east at the end of the Palace wall.

Both of Kiyomori's daring schemes succeeded. The ex-Emperor escaped to Ninna-ji Temple, and the young Emperor was safely carried off from the Palace. Soon after this a fiery glow and black smoke north of the Imperial Palace caused wild stories to spread; there were rumors that Kiyomori had sent his troops up the river and attacked the imperial residence from the north, and that the monks of Mount Hiei had sided with Kiyomori and were marching on the capital.

Yoshitomo of the Genji sent his son Yoshihira with a small force to the Imperial Palace, while a company on guard there were dispatched north of the city gates to investigate the fire.

Meanwhile, with a sharp cracking of whips and hoarse cries, the ox-tenders strained at the carriage beast, urging it on toward Rokuhara.

"Wait—not so fast! Stop, we're out of danger now . . ." panted Korekata and Tsunemuné as they pursued the Emperor's carriage.

The ox-tenders slowed down and laughed. "Hear them squealing? Shall we wait for them?"

"Seems safe now."

The two men brought the conveyance to a stop and mopped their streaming faces.

The carriage soon reached the tree-lined avenue along the Kamo River, where dark shapes separated themselves from the shadows and came out to meet it. Kiyomori had sent two hundred warriors from Rokuhara to escort Nijo, and as they came to Gojo Bridge the clouds released a flurry of snow.

Rokuhara, which had lain silent and dark for so many nights, shone with countless lights at the Emperor's approach. Candles twinkled everywhere like stars through the falling snow. As soon as the Emperor arrived in Rokuhara, bands of Heiké warriors were sent throughout the avenues of the capital, announcing that the ruler had taken up residence at Rokuhara at the Hour of the Tiger (four a.m.) and that the Cloistered Emperor was now at Ninna-ji Temple. All who were loyal to the Emperor were urged to go to Rokuhara.

By sunrise, courtiers and ministers, led by the Regent, were on their way to Rokuhara.

While all this was happening, Nobuyori, the leader of the revolt, lay in his room at the Imperial Palace in a drunken stupor, attended by ladies-in-waiting. His nightly bouts of drinking had finally alienated Tsunemuné and Korekata, who suspected that Nobuyori was not in his right mind. Mitsuyori's rebuke, moreover, had brought them to their senses and they lost no time in communicating with Kiyomori.

When a councilor arrived panting in Nobuyori's apartment to say that the royal prisoners were gone, Nobuyori sprang from his couch in alarm and then laughed hysterically.

"What impossible tale is this? A hallucination—Korekata and Tsunemuné are seeing to it that their majesties do not escape!"

"Sir, the guards have turned traitor and flown with the prisoners."

"Impossible!" Nobuyori insisted, but misgivings crossed his mind as he spoke; he quickly dressed, buckled on a sword, and ran headlong down the maze of corridors. A stream of oaths and bellows of rage came from Nobuyori when he discovered the truth.

"Let no one hear of this—not even our confederates," he ordered.

It was too late, however, to conceal what had happened. Yoshihira of the Genji already knew that the royal prisoners had escaped and immediately rode back to his father to report it.

"The incredible has already happened tonight! Kiyomori stole a march on us—his majesty has been carried off to Rokuhara and the Cloistered Emperor is now safe at Ninna-ji Temple. Could this possibly be true?"

Yoshitomo did not reply.

"Is this true, Father?" Yoshihira insisted.

Yoshitomo hesitated. "It is so. I also have heard the news, though Nobuyori has said nothing yet."

A look of consternation appeared on the youth's face.

"Yoshihira!"

"Yes—"

"What of the fire at the Palace?"

"That was a trick of the enemy. Kiyomori's troops were not

there, but I found huts and farmhouses outside the city gates in flames."

"Kiyomori's cunning again, or else some crafty agent is advising him. I must admit that our enemy's performance tonight has been masterly. We are in for no easy time."

"But, Father, what use is there in defending the Palace when their majesties are no longer there?"

"No, I pledged the word of a Genji in this pact and cannot withdraw now. A warrior keeps faith even to death. If, however, I keep my word there will be no choice for me except bowing to the Heiké or annihilation."

By his words Yoshitomo confessed what he had dared not until now. He had been mistaken in Nobuyori and bitterly regretted what he had done. Yet, Yoshitomo reflected, had he not linked his fate with the Vice-Councilor's, Shinzei's hostility would in the end have led to an armed clash between the Genji and the Heiké. Shinzei was dead now, but Kiyomori still remained. There was no denying that the Genji had sustained a serious setback with the kidnapping of the Emperor by the Heiké. In the actual conduct of a war, however, Yoshitomo was confident that his experience was far superior to Kiyomori's.

A councilor who had been sent by Yoshitomo to Nobuyori now appeared.

"I have seen the Minister and he denies the reports. He assures me that nothing unusual has happened at the Palace."

The faces gathered around the watch-fires exchanged smiles of pity at Nobuyori's cowardice.

"Then nothing more is to be said," Yoshitomo remarked, "so let those who are assigned to guard the Palace form rank and call the roll."

Nobuyori, the General of the Guards, was about to review his troops from the Great Hall facing the Palace plaza. To either side of him were ranged the splendor of the Court—the ministers and highest-ranking officials, and while the review proceeded, messenger after messenger arrived on horseback through the snow with the latest report on Kiyomori's movements. A company had already assembled, it was said, on the riverbank, awaiting orders to attack. There were also other rumors that Kiyomori's troops were deployed along the flanks of the Eastern Hills, preparing to make a surprise attack on the Palace.

Two thousand Genji waited on horseback in the Palace plaza, as icicles slowly formed on their visors and the blood in their veins foamed with impatience and fear.

Nobuyori wore armor dyed lavender, shading to a deep purple at the hips; under it was a tunic of scarlet cloth; the sword he carried had a sheath inlaid with a fine pattern of chrysanthemums in pure gold; the rivets on his horned helmet glittered and sparkled through the falling snow. His coal-black steed, a famous pedigreed mount from the imperial stables, was hitched to the cherry tree growing at one side of the wide staircase that ascended to the Great Hall.

Yoshitomo was turned out with more than usual care for the details of his accouterment, and his three sons had also put on their finest tunics and the Genji armor. Of the three, the youngest, Yoritomo, a boy of thirteen, drew many glances from the troops. Because of his extreme youth, his father and brothers watched over him with great care; he had just been wakened from a nap in the guardhouse and led, sleepy-eyed and shivering, onto the parade ground in a complete suit of boy's armor. The sight of this pitifully young lad come to take his first lesson in bloodshed moved the soldiers.

By morning the snow had ceased falling and the avenues of the capital were dazzling, but no smoke of cooking-fires rose from the shuttered houses of the common people.

Yoshitomo had prepared to attack Rokuhara instead of taking the defensive. His son Yoshihira, who was sent to reconnoiter, returned soon with the report that he had seen Yorimasa of the Genji riding toward Gojo Bridge. "I fear, Father, that Yorimasa has deceived us by his excuses of being ill; he is on his way to Rokuhara. Let me pursue him and challenge him."

Yoshitomo, stung to the quick, replied: "No, I shall go myself." But as he turned his horse's head, he said with a bitter laugh: "Why should it matter to us what Yorimasa and his kind do? I care nothing for him."

Not long after, Yoshitomo and Yorimasa faced each other across the river near Gojo Bridge, and Yoshitomo spurred his horse forward, crying contemptuously:

"So, Yorimasa, you who are a Genji have sided with the Heiké? A curse on the day that you were born a Genji! Shame on you for coming to challenge the Genji in battle!"

Then Yorimasa appeared and proudly replied: "You speak the truth, Yoshitomo. From times immemorial the Genji have been loyal to the throne, and it is you who have disgraced the Genji by siding with that traitor Nobuyori. I weep at the shame you have brought on the Genji!"

CHAPTER XXIV

DRUMS BEAT

The Emperor Nijo, his entire suite, and the ministers of state occupied the main buildings at Rokuhara, and so crowded were they even then that the outbuildings and cookhouses also were taken over for his attendants.

Kiyomori's son Shigemori crossed the court where the snow had been trampled and turned to mud by innumerable feet, and approached the main building in search of his father.

"Is my father with his majesty?" he asked of an attendant who was leaning over a balustrade.

"No, he is not here," was the reply.

Shigemori wandered from an inner court to the two-storied gate, peered into the guardhouse and then retraced his steps. A search of every building on the estate was impossible. The sun would be up in the meantime, Shigemori thought, looking apprehensively at the sky. He feared seeing the light break along the shoulder of the Eastern Hills. His father, in his present state of elation, might forget that the fateful business of fighting still lay ahead of them. The troops, who had spent the night along the river, were getting restive, waiting for orders to advance.

Shigemori mumbled impatiently to himself. It was unlikely that his father would be in the servants' quarters near the stables. Still, it would be worth while looking there, he thought, and turned his steps in that direction, when he came upon his father crossing the gallery that led from the kitchens.

"Why, Father, here you are!"

"Is that you, Shigemori? What did you want?"

"No wonder I couldn't find you. I never thought to find you here."

"I've been speaking to the cooks myself. I had to see that everything was right for his majesty."

"Why don't you leave that to the cooks and their helpers? The soldiers are tired out with waiting for your orders."

"There's still time until dawn."

"As soon as it's light, the enemy will attack first at the Gojo Bridge, and Rokuhara will be lost if they do."

"Send out some men to reconnoiter."

"That has already been done."

"That will be enough for the time being."

"But we mustn't lose our chance to make the first move at daybreak. That will mean sure victory for us."

"I have no mind to listen to your opinions on strategy. I have my own ideas. Besides, we must have his majesty make a proclamation, and he's in no condition yet to do so after those days of imprisonment in the Palace. He has hardly had any food or sleep in that time. I must see to it that he gets some steaming rice porridge before anything else. I can hardly press him with other matters just now. . . . . Leave the orders until later."

"Yes, Father."

"Tell your brothers and Mokunosuké and the soldiers this."

"As you say."

"Tell them to wait until his majesty has finished his meal. In the meantime, order our men to pile on plenty of logs and thaw out their reins and bowstrings."

Shigemori turned away. He did not doubt that the odds were now against them; his father was clearly distrait. Shigemori, who never questioned his father's judgment, made his way to the riverbank, massed with soldiers, and gave out his father's instructions.

Kiyomori did not need Shigemori to tell him of the seriousness of the situation. He quickly started toward the main house, but was stopped at the turn of the gallery by someone who apparently had been lying in wait for him.

The fellow addressed him with an elaborate bow: "Ah, Lord Harima, allow me to congratulate you on the complete success of your plans."

Kiyomori gave the man a sharp look. It was Red-Nose, the merchant who had carried messages between Korekata, Tsunemuné, and Rokuhara.

"Oh, Bamboku, my thanks for your good offices."

"Not at all, sir, I have done nothing to speak of."

"On the contrary, you've shown considerable ingenuity in all this."

"An exaggeration, sir—a small acknowledgment of your good lady's patronage."

"What of Korekata and Tsunemuné?"

"Quite exhausted, I must say, and getting some sleep in the servants' quarters."

"So. And you came with his majesty last night?"

"Part of the way, in great fear and trembling, I assure you, sir, and not much help at that. . . . I came, however, to see if I might

3 3 6

be of use in the kitchens, washing dishes, and here, quite by acci-
dent, I come on you, sir. . . . A very great privilege, this, I am
sure."

"You will in time hear from me. Wait a few days for your reward."

Kiyomori had no reason for not trusting Bamboku; not only
did Tokiko consider him reliable, but the merchant had proved to
be most useful to him in the secret negotiations of the past week.

Kiyomori made his way to an anteroom, where an official met
him, saying:

"Your son, sir, has been looking for you for some time."

"I saw him a short while ago. But what of his majesty?"

"He has had some hot porridge."

"Does he seem a little more rested?"

"I do not know quite how to tell you—it moved us deeply to
see him weep at the sight of food."

"Good, good!" Kiyomori exclaimed with a warm smile, "and
now we must have him consent to our advancing to the attack."

"That has already been sanctioned and the proclamation will
soon be ready."

"Have my son Shigemori come to me, then," Kiyomori said.

Shigemori, who had been appointed to lead the troops in his
father's stead, soon appeared.

"Shigemori, his majesty consents. Set out at once for the Palace—with all speed!"

When Shigemori appeared before the men to give the command, the warriors roared their applause; gongs sounded and drums
rolled as three thousand horses surged forward through the snow
for the assault on the Palace.

The first rays of the sun now shot over a shoulder of the Eastern Hills, sparkled on the armored ranks, on the horses' harness,
and flashed blindingly in the treetops and on the Palace roofs. All
the gates of the Palace stood open in readiness for Yoshitomo of
the Genji to ride out, but Yoshitomo fumed, realizing that the initial advantage had been thrown away. His plan was to attack Rokuhara before dawn, but Nobuyori's dilatoriness and his conflict-

ing orders to the troops had delayed the start, and the enemy were already on the march.

Quickly ordering the drums to signal a change in the troops' positions, Yoshitomo reassigned his men to the defense of the three gates of the outer wall on the east. Twenty-seven gates there were in all, including those of the inner walls, separated each from the other by wide avenues and parklike stretches. And now two thousand Genji horsemen, flourishing weapons, streamed from all directions into the spacious plaza facing the Great Hall, as the drums and gongs of the Heiké were heard along the eastern wall.

Under a cloudless sky thirty red standards fluttered amid a forest of bows as the Heiké forces came to a standstill before the three eastern gates, which stood open to receive them.

Yoshitomo, bitterness gnawing at his entrails, groaned inwardly as he watched an ashen-faced Nobuyori finally leave the Great Hall, mount his horse awkwardly, and, flanked by armed men, ride reluctantly toward the gate that he was to command. Shigemori and his five hundred horse already waited for him there, and as Nobuyori came into sight Shigemori and his eight liegemen galloped headlong to meet him. Nobuyori looked up with a cry when he saw them, hesitated, then turned and fled with Shigemori in full pursuit. At this, five hundred mounted warriors streamed in through the gate, followed by another five hundred.

From his post at the second gate Yoshitomo saw what was taking place and called loudly to his son Yoshihira, whom he saw ride past.

"The enemy have broken through at the central gate! I cannot leave my post here, but you go assist that coward Nobuyori! Drive back the men of Rokuhara!"

At Yoshitomo's command seventeen horsemen came forward to join Yoshihira. Shigemori rode a chestnut horse, and Yoshihira recognized him by his armor and the red tunic he wore under it. While Shigemori harried the Genji with his arrows, his horsemen kept Yoshihira from approaching and engaging him in hand-to-hand combat. But when Shigemori rested his bow to take breath,

Yoshihira saw his chance. His horse's tail streaming in the wind, he flew toward Shigemori, challenging him loudly:

"This is I, Yoshihira of the Genji, Yoshitomo's son! Your name?"

Shigemori turned his head long enough to stare into Yoshihira's burning eyes; then, splashing mud-streaked snow, he wheeled his horse sharply to reply: "Ah, you, Yoshihira of the Genji! I am Shigemori of the Heiké, Kiyomori's son!"

Thus did a young Genji and a Heiké come face to face in front of the Great Hall. At one side of the wide stairs leading up to the hall grew a cherry tree, on the other a tree of the bitter orange, and here on the plaza the two combatants crossed and recrossed each other's paths, pursuing each other.

With a cry to Yoshihira, who carried no bow, Shigemori suddenly aimed a shaft.

"Coward!" came back the shout. "You stoop to arrows when I carry none? Dare you cross swords with me?"

A second arrow sped on its way, but as Shigemori's hand reached toward his quiver a third time, he found Yoshihira on his heels. The chestnut swerved sharply as the jet horse cut across its path and drew up beside him.

"So you, a Heiké, thought to escape me?"

Another arrow whined; as Yoshihira ducked, Shigemori quickly drew his sword. Steel flashed white against steel; stirrups grated against one another. Whirling, dodging, feinting, and charging in a spectacle of brilliant horsemanship, pursued and pursuing, the two youths rode furiously seven times and then eight round the cherry and orange trees. Their swords grazed, slashed at the air, and seemed to clash in a shower of sparks.

Shigemori's eight liegemen were engaged with Yoshihira's seventeen at other places on the plaza, where the trampled snow was churned with mud and streaked with blood, and Shigemori flew to join the melee, until the arrival of more Genji horsemen forced him to fall back and retreat toward the gate by which he had come.

Mokunosuké, who had been directing the withdrawal, approached Shigemori, whom he found resting at a crossroad.

"Well done!" he cried, "if only your father could have seen you!" adding: "but remember his orders and let the enemy claim the victory now."

"Old One, there's no need to be anxious for me."

With a fresh company of horsemen, Shigemori rode back toward the plaza. There Yoshihira came out to meet them, facing a shower of arrows, and with a welcoming wave.

"Come, you Heiké of Rokuhara! Surely, I am a worthy foe, or is it possible that you fear me?"

Shigemori spurred his horse forward. "Dare you boast? You shall yet have cause to fear me!"

"When did I ever turn my back to you?"

Once more the two charged furiously round the snowy plaza, until Shigemori, spent, turned and fled outside the Palace walls, followed by his wildly shouting soldiers.

Yoshihira, his eyes fixed on the glossy chestnut, continued to gallop after Shigemori, shouting: "Turn back, turn back, coward!"

The snow frothed like smoke under their horses' hoofs as Shigemori fled with Yoshihira in pursuit. Shigemori flattened himself against his horse's shoulder, whipping it forward, while his two liegemen kept pace with him; at a shouted warning, Shigemori's mount vaulted effortlessly across a narrow canal and was followed by the other two. Arrows whistled about them. One struck Shigemori's armor with a dull thud, and a second snapped and hung down as it pierced his shoulder-piece.

"Wait, wait, have you no shame?" cried Yoshihira almost at Shigemori's ear, when his horse shied and stumbled at the canal's edge and threw Yoshihira onto a raft. As he rose to his feet, he called to one of his soldiers who had safely cleared the canal: "Don't wait for me—see that Shigemori doesn't escape."

The rider nodded and set a third arrow on the nock; he aimed it at Shigemori just as the latter's horse reared at a pile of snow-covered lumber in its path. An arrow dug into its belly, a red stain spurted across the snow, and horse and rider crashed sideways to earth. Shigemori's helmet flew from his head; as he sprang to retrieve it, he looked up wildly and saw one of his pursuers bearing down on him. When the soldier's horse also shied at the sight of the lumber beside the canal, the rider leaped down from his saddle and rushed at Shigemori. Shigemori swung his bow sideways with all his strength in his adversary's face, forcing the soldier to fall back a few steps to unsheathe his sword; then one of Shigemori's soldiers leaped between them with outstretched arms to shield Shigemori and closed with the enemy. Like angry bulls with locked horns the two wrestled until both men rolled to the ground.

Yoshihira, who made his way out of the canal, saw his father's favorite retainer fall and ran to his rescue with drawn sword. Meanwhile, Shigemori's other companion arrived at the scene and quickly dismounted; setting Shigemori on his horse, he urged his master to escape and then turned to assist his fallen comrade.

Heavy fighting ensued at the gate that Yoshitomo guarded, as Kiyomori's half-brother Yorimori returned to storm it with a fresh force of mounted bowmen, and when both sides finally exhausted their supply of arrows, the Heiké broke through and poured into the Palace grounds. In the fierce skirmish that followed, only the red and white standards and the strips of cloth in their armor served to distinguish friend from foe. Four times were the Heiké repelled and forced to retire by the gate through which they had entered. Back and forth the tide of fighting rolled until the Heiké were forced to retreat as far as the Gojo Bridge.

As Yoshitomo and his three sons swept the main avenues of straggling Heiké, Yoshitomo chanced to look back toward the Palace and cried out in dismay at the sight of Heiké banners waving over the gate-houses and above the Palace roofs. A hidden force of Heiké had invaded the undefended Palace and taken possession of it.

Yoshitomo was dissatisfied with the course the fighting had assumed. Something told him that all was not well. His troops were not performing with their usual spirit. "There is little chance for victory," he told himself, realizing as he did so that it was unlike him to have such doubts. Reflecting thus, he also admitted to himself that he alone was responsible for this predicament. Kiyomori had again outmaneuvered him in a move that was child's play and cut off his retreat. The odds were now heavily against the Genji; the only course open to him now was to pursue the enemy to Rokuhara, abduct the Emperor, and challenge Kiyomori in single combat, Yoshitomo resolved unhappily. Annihilation—or that one chance in a thousand—this was the last throw of the dice. But Yoshitomo took heart when he saw his captains spiritedly repulsing the enemy and began massing his troops from the Gojo Bridge and northward along the river.

As the Genji closed in along the river, the Heiké began tearing down the bridge on their side. Yoshihira of the Genji rode halfway across the severed bridge, ordering five hundred mounted soldiers to follow him with their arrows pointed at Rokuhara. Meanwhile, from their position on the riverbank, Yoshitomo's soldiers rained down arrows on the Heiké stronghold. Answering volleys came from Kiyomori's forces, and horse and foot from either side began to ford the river.

Yoshihira, impatient at the ineffectual exchange of arrows, turned and led his troops farther downstream for an attack on Rokuhara from the south. As he made his way along the riverbank, he saw in front of him a hundred or more horse drawn up in phalanx, motionless behind a wall of shields, their standards floating in the wind.

"Yorimasa's men!" he burst out bitterly.

A captain who rode beside him said: "Your father intended to cross the river there, but turned back when he saw them."

"What! My father refused to challenge Yorimasa?"

"He denounced him roundly for his treachery, however."

"Was that all?"

"And Yorimasa replied to him."

"But what good does an angry exchange of words do? He, a Genji, dared to desert us for the enemy, and now he waits to see who wins before he makes his choice. I'll give him what he deserves!"

Yoshihira spurred his horse and charged down the embankment straight at the phalanx. The massed horsemen broke ranks in confusion and began making their way across the river toward Rokuhara. Yoshihira's temerity, however, was ill-advised, for it gave Yorimasa an unlooked-for chance to throw in his lot with the Heiké. Pride in the name of Genji had kept him from openly declaring himself against Yoshitomo and the conspirators, and he had chosen to withdraw his troops to a distance to avoid involving himself with either side. But Yoshihira's impetuosity compelled him to abandon his neutral position and side with the Heiké.

Rokuhara seethed with turmoil and consternation. Kiyomori had given strict orders that no fighting should take place inside the walls of the Imperial Palace; the enemy were to be lured outside and there cut to pieces, but the attack had been easier than the withdrawal. Shigemori's flight and Yorimori's repulse by Yoshitomo had ended with the Heiké's disorderly retreat to Rokuhara, and the demolishing of part of the Gojo Bridge.

Their retreat cut off and with nothing more to lose, the Genji fought their way in desperation across the river and over the bodies of their dead until they stood beneath the walls of Rokuhara. From rooftops, walls, and treetops Rokuhara's inhabitants joined with the soldiers to defend what was now the Emperor's residence and hurled down stones and tiles on the invaders.

The moment had arrived for Kiyomori to command his troops in person, for his greatest fear was that the enemy would set fire to Rokuhara. He took his sword from one of his attendants and, fumbling impatiently with the cords of his helmet, started across a covered passageway at a run, when Tokitada, his brother-in-law, who followed him, suddenly called to him in agitation: "Wait—wait!"

Kiyomori, sword thrust under one arm, stopped midway across the gallery and swung round. "What is it, Tokitada? Are you stopping me from going to lead the men?"

"No," Tokitada replied, barely able to contain his laughter, "your helmet is on the wrong way—back to front. We can't have the general go that way!"

343

"My helmet—the wrong way?"

Kiyomori felt at his head, grimaced, and then laughed heartily.

"Wrong, Tokitada! That is as it should be, it faces toward his majesty. Come, lead the way and sweep the enemy before us!"

Tokitada, speechless, left at a run, followed by soldiers, convulsed with laughter.

The fighting which began that morning lasted all day as the Genji fought their way to Rokuhara. By the time Kiyomori went to direct the defense, the besiegers' arrows were thudding thick and fast upon the doors and shutters of his house, and all he could hear were the deafening roars of the enemy as they surged round the walls. Time and again he was certain that Rokuhara was doomed; heedless of danger to himself, he went out to urge forward the terrified soldiers, who were driven back as far as one of the inner gates. Climbing to the turret of the two-storied gate, Kiyomori shouted down encouragement to his soldiers, as he sent shaft after shaft among the enemy.

Had a larger force stormed Rokuhara from the east, it would have fallen, but on this side the attackers were cut to bits or forced to take flight into the snowy hills beyond Kiyomizu Temple.

Yorimasa's horsemen, meanwhile, closed in on the Genji from the rear, and when Yoshitomo saw how badly his men fared, he led his troops in a last desperate charge up to the gates of Rokuhara, shouting: "Lose no time now! That one up in the gatehouse is Kiyomori!"

A supporting flank under Yoshihira suddenly fell back without warning toward the river. Yoshitomo stiffened with rage; casting away his bow, he rode up to the gate, sword in hand, and challenged Kiyomori. Just then a stampeding movement among the horsemen who pressed in on him from every side swept Yoshitomo away toward the river.

Fresh troops of Heiké were now arriving by the highway and bearing down on Yoshitomo's forces from the north. While Yorimasa's horsemen made inroads on Yoshitomo's southern flank, a formidable company of mounted bowmen suddenly appeared on the opposite bank and opened an attack on the Genji. This threat from an unexpected quarter had caused Yoshihira to wheel in the direction of the river. Yoshitomo's main force, which had stormed its way to the very gates of Rokuhara, now saw itself completely surrounded, and in panic began a headlong retreat north along the Kamo River. Though harried by the Heiké on the river front, Yoshihira and his band of soldiers held their ground until they heard Yoshitomo's orders to take flight.

Yoshitomo cast a despairing look round on his trusted liegemen and captains and cried: "The battle is lost! This is the fate of those born to take up arms! My end has come, but fly, each of you, for your lives!"

And when his two younger sons cried they would stay with him even in death, Yoshihira, the eldest of Yoshitomo's sons, came and rebuked them, saying: "I alone shall remain as rear guard. It is what I want above all else. You and our father must fly for your lives."

Then Yoshitomo's captains entreated him to leave with them, saying: "This is not the moment for us Genji to die; if we go into hiding now, a day will come when we shall wipe out this shame."

Guarded by his loyal captains, Yoshitomo and his sons began their retreat through the enemy's line; harassed on every side, they fought their way north toward the hills of the upper Kamo, losing several men at every encounter with the Heiké. And when they reached the safety of a snowbound settlement in the hills, Yoshitomo, looking round, saw how his valiant company of fifty had shrunk to fourteen. Unable to contain his grief and remorse, he wept at the thought of how he had brought ruin on them all, condemning them to a future dark with uncertainty. These hills held out only starvation and wandering. What would become of the loved ones these men had left in the capital? Where were they now? What, indeed, had become of his own—Tokiwa? She had refused to leave Kyoto in order to be near him. Had she after all fled for the country with their three sons as he had entreated her to do? He envisioned her stricken with grief at the news of his defeat.

Their horses stumbled with weariness through the snow; as the party made its way up into the hills, Yoshitomo brought his horse to a stop to gaze back into the distance. Far below in the gathering dusk every pagoda and rooftop in the capital gleamed with silver, and all over the city the glow of fires and dark columns of smoke marked the site of burning buildings.

CHAPTER XXV

SNOWSTORM

Yoshitomo was anxious to reach the other side of Mount Hiei before morning, for in the country of Mino on the farther side of Lake Biwa were Genji who would give him shelter and assistance. So the party redoubled their pace northward, following the course of the Takano River, past Hasé, and east over the pass at Yokokawa, until they found themselves at Katado, near the southern end of the lake.

Scouring winds lashed the lake into an angry sea when two

vessels, bearing the party and a few horses, buffeted their way across the water in the early morning. Sullen clouds hung low over the northern half of the sky, threatening more snow. Some time after midday the fugitives finally beached among the withered reeds on the eastern shore of the lake where the snow lay deeper than in the capital. They stepped ashore silently and stopped to watch the flight of wild geese across a desolate sky. Two of the party then set out for a near-by fishers' settlement to barter some arms for food, while the rest gathered fagots for a fire and waited.

Late that afternoon, warmed and fed, Yoshitomo and his men discussed the next stage of their journey, which they agreed should be resumed after sundown, when there was less danger of pursuit. Then seven of Yoshitomo's captains and retainers proposed to leave Yoshitomo and travel separately, pointing out the safety of journeying in smaller groups. As sundown approached, they each bade Yoshitomo farewell, promising to rejoin him when they reached eastern Japan.

When night came, Yoshitomo, his three sons, and four captains mounted their horses and hurried along a river until they reached a highway over which they continued their flight. The black sky brooded over them, and on every side the mountains rose gaunt and precipitous. Hamlet after hamlet went by, asleep under heavy shrouds of snow; no lights shone to guide the fugitives. No human sounds reached their ears; all life seemed to have been quenched. It was a perfect night for flight, and the small band quickened their pace, until a storm rose and howled around them in blinding swirls of snow.

Meanwhile, on the night that Yoshitomo made his way through the hills to Lake Biwa, Vice-Councilor Nobuyori, prime agent in the plot to snatch power from Kiyomori, escaped to Ninna-ji Temple, north of the city gates, where nearly fifty of his fellow noblemen and courtiers had already taken refuge. There, before the night was out, Nobuyori was carried off under arrest by Kiyomori's soldiers, and on the following day beheaded with other enemies of the throne.

On the 29th of December, the second day after the fighting
had ended, when Kyoto had settled once more to its customary
peaceful pursuits, Kiyomori was ordered to make an inspection of
the imperial residence and other state buildings. Astrologers were
consulted and an auspicious date chosen for the Emperor's return
to the Imperial Palace. For Kiyomori the visit of inspection was
in the nature of a triumphal march and he ordered his brothers
and sons and captains and all who could be spared at Rokuhara
to accompany him in a pageant of magnificently armored warriors
and richly caparisoned horses.

Along the route that stretched from Gojo Bridge and through
the main avenues of the capital, excited crowds jostled one another and goggled at the splendid sight of colorful horsemen in
full battle dress, company after company of bowmen, foot-soldiers
all in armor, and troops of children in their holiday best, who
brought up the rear.

During the fighting the capital's poorest—its hordes of beggars and thieves, its numberless destitute and criminals—had invaded the Palace and made it their home; they rioted through its
halls and state rooms for three days and nights, ransacked the
storehouses for food, mimicked the courtiers in robes and crowns,
and in a travesty of banqueting and merrymaking filled the Palace
with grotesque sights and sounds. When the news of Kiyomori's
approaching visit reached them, there began a panic-stricken exo-
dus. From every cranny of the Palace there streamed a frightened
mob of scarecrows, too numerous for the patrols to deal with or
the city's jails to hold, until at Kiyomori's orders they were herded
back to the Palace grounds and set to cleaning it. There were no
threats of punishment and each man was promised a small por-
tion of rice when his task was accomplished.

"Yes, he knows what it is to starve. He knows," one wretch
remarked to another over his broom. "That's Kiyomori of the
Heiké. I used to know him in the old days when they called him
'Heita.' I'm telling you the truth, too. The penniless son of the
Squint-Eyed One—that's what they called his father—I used to
see him in rags along the Shiokoji, and in the Thieves' Market by

the nettle tree. I'm not saying he was one of us scoundrels, mind you, and I've talked to him, too. And whenever I had wine, I offered him some, didn't I?"

"So he's known hard times, too, has he?"

"That's what I'm telling you. He may look like a lord, but he's one of us, you can be sure."

"And he wasn't above drinking your wine?"

"Well, no, I won't go so far as to say that, but what I mean is that we were friendly, as you might say. That's why he understands our sort."

"There they come!"

"Who—where?"

"The lord of Rokuhara himself—the parade!"

The white road unwound before them in unending monotony, and each rider drowsed fitfully. The numbing cold and the stupor of utter fatigue lulled them deliciously like an opiate. Yoshitomo's shouts, however, roused them from time to time as he called to each member of his party; answering cries continued to assure him that no one was straggling too far behind.

"Don't lose sight of each other," Yoshitomo warned. "See that the snow doesn't freeze on your lashes. Keep calling to one another to stay awake!"

Late that night when they were safely past the sentinel posts along the highway and had crossed the Hino River, they found themselves hoarse and breathless from shouting against the wind and driving snow. It was getting more and more difficult not to lose sight of each other. Suddenly Yoshitomo and Yoshihira, who rode ahead, thought they heard shouts in the distance. They brought their horses to a stop and, blinking away the snow, listened intently.

"Yoritomo—Yoritomo-o! Ho-o!"

Another voice took up the cry: "Ho-o, Yoritomo!"

The sounds appeared to come from their rear.

"Are they calling Yoritomo?"

"He must be straggling far behind. Wait for me here, Father, while I go back."

"No, I'll go with you."

A retainer riding a few steps ahead of Yoshitomo wheeled in his tracks to ask: "Are we all going back?"

Yoshitomo began retracing his steps and counted off his party. They were all there except Yoritomo, his youngest son.

"Yoritomo missing?"

Some time must have elapsed since one of the group made the discovery, for though they hallooed and called in unison, there was no reply.

"You say he's not here," Yoshitomo asked anxiously, addressing no one in particular. "When did you notice this?"

"He was riding between us when we crossed the plain," two captains offered.

"At Hino River?"

"The storm was blowing its worst there and we scattered in order to cross. We might have become separated there. It was our fault. Let us two go back to look for him," the captains said, preparing to turn back.

Then Yoshitomo's voice, hollow with desolation, restrained them. "Wait, wait. That's not necessary. We can't turn back for each straggler.

The party were now huddled together against the storm, and Yoshitomo continued: "It will soon be daybreak and we must change our course to avoid meeting strangers on the road. Unless we take to the hills we are in danger of pursuit, and Yoritomo must be left to his fate if we are to escape. The future of all the Genji depends on our surviving. We can't risk our lives for him alone."

Then the two captains protested: "Sir, he is the youngest of your sons, and beloved of us; how can we abandon him to the storm? You will regret this to the day of your death. Let the future take care of itself. Let us go back now to find him!"

But Yoshitomo was not to be persuaded. "No, though your

words move me deeply. You know well how dear my son is to me, his father, yet all the Genji look to me as their parent and I cannot forsake them for him alone. In defeat they are more than ever my children. . . ."

Yoshitomo's voice died into silence and he suddenly turned his face away and with uplifted hands prayed: "Ah, cruel night! Is this how heaven will try my child? Is it indeed his fate to die in this cold? Merciful heaven, if it is the will of the gods, spare him!"

Nerving himself to a decision from which he saw no escape, Yoshitomo turned once more to the waiting group. "We cannot go back. Hurry on we must, for it will soon be day," he said, and spurred his horse ahead.

Reluctantly the rest took up their positions behind Yoshitomo, all except the youngest captain, who, after exchanging a few meaningful glances with Yoshihira, turned his horse's head in a westerly direction.

White, white all around—an unending white road—around him the white night.

Yoritomo was painfully sleepy, and the even rocking of his horse was as soothing as the motions of a cradle. He could barely keep awake. Nodding . . . nodding, he finally succumbed. Sometimes the sound of someone calling him penetrated his consciousness, and Yoritomo replied, or thought he had. Then sleep engulfed him once more. He was barely fourteen and the rigors of the past few days had been too much for him. All the terrors were forgotten now in sleep. He had only to hold tight to the reins for his horse to move forward, on and on. He recalled passing through the village of Moriyama; then they had crossed a plain, but of the rest he knew nothing, saw nothing of four men following close behind.

A day before Yoshitomo came through Moriyama, a soldier had arrived there from Rokuhara and, summoning the headman and the farming folk, had ordered them to be on the lookout for Yoshitomo. Before the messenger departed, notices were posted in the village and its outskirts offering a reward for Yoshitomo's capture. Gen, a village ne'er-do-well, hearing of this, gathered together a few cronies by promises to share the reward, far more than they could expect for snaring even a dozen boar, he pointed out. Arming himself with a halberd and his companions with bamboo spears, Gen started out in pursuit of Yoshitomo and his small party.

"There he is—and alone too, Gen."

"So he is."

"That's odd."

"Why?"

"I thought I saw hoofprints in the snow near the bridge. Anyway, that's the only one I see. Lucky I fell asleep in the wineshop, or I should never have heard of this. Never can tell when your luck will turn!"

"Not bad this, with the end of the year so close. I never dreamed such luck would be coming my way this year."

"Hey there, get on with you!"

"There's no hurry. Remember, they're armed."

"After all, it's only a boy. It must be Yoshitomo's son."

"Look—look there!"

"He must be asleep. Look, he's nodding!"

"As easy as catching a bear cub. I'll twist his stirrup and throw him from his saddle and when he falls, catch him and pin him down. I'll rope him then."

Gen and his companions charged toward Yoritomo, who suddenly looked up at them.

Gen stopped in his tracks.

"Here, boy, where are you going?" he asked sharply.

Yoritomo did not reply. He suddenly perceived that his father and brothers were no longer with him and gazed about blankly at the falling snow. The pathos of the clear eyes turned on him from under the snow-laden visor, and the delicate lines of Yoritomo's child features gave Gen an uncomfortable feeling under his ribs.

"Get down, get down, there!" Gen shouted as he ran up to Yoritomo's horse and grasped the right stirrup.

Yoritomo twisted himself sideways in his saddle to keep from falling.

"Here, you, get down, I tell you!"

"You blackguard!" Yoritomo cried as he whipped out his sword and swung it with all his might at Gen's head. A curdling scream brought Yoritomo fully awake; a dark stain spread across the snow; bamboo spears grazed him, and he fought off someone who blocked his way with a spear. Something snarled at him and Yoritomo grew afraid, realizing that his father was no longer with him.

"Father! Father! Yoshihira! . . ."

Yoritomo's horse bolted past an assailant and tore forward; on and on he flew.

Yoritomo could not tell which way he was being carried, but he was certain it was not in the direction his father had gone, and when his exhausted horse finally refused to go farther, Yoritomo abandoned him, threw away his heavy helmet, and walked aimlessly over hills and through valleys.

Several days later he dragged himself to a lonely mountain village and threw himself down to sleep under the eaves of a farmer's woodshed. The farm-woman who went out to open a tub of pickles screamed at the sight of a half-frozen child asleep among the piles of firewood and bales of charcoal. She called her husband and together they carried him into their hut, warmed his limbs, and revived him with bowls of steaming potato gruel. And when he was ready to leave, they gave him careful directions for reaching Mino.

"Go round that mountain you see yonder," they said, "and you will find a pass to the south, which you must cross before you are there."

Yoritomo left them, strangely sad at heart. For the first time in his life he had had to share food with such poor folk and they had been kind to him. On the road a pilgrim nun, touched by his extreme youth, gently warned him: "My child, there are Heiké soldiers at a garrison post on this road. Now, don't lose your way," she said at parting.

Day after day he trudged on, sleeping at night in small huts and deserted shrines. There was less and less snow as he went on. He was certain that the New Year had come and gone, and took courage by telling himself that his father and brothers were waiting for him in Mino. Yoritomo had heard that he had a half-sister living there. It was not clear to him just what her relationship was to Ohi, the local chieftain, who was in some way blood kinsman to the Genji, and a man he could trust.

When Yoritomo arrived one day at a river, a fisherman who was washing his boat hailed him. "Are you not one of the Genji —Yoshitomo's son?"

Yoritomo did not attempt to conceal his identity. "Yes, I am Yoshitomo's third son. Yoritomo is my name."

The fisherman seemed pleased and proceeded to relate that his brothers had been servants in Yoshitomo's household. Warning Yoritomo of the dangers of traveling alone, he invited Yoritomo to stop with him.

Yoritomo stayed in the fisherman's hut for several days and then started out once more, accompanied this time by the fisherman's son, who left him only when they reached the chieftain Ohi's house.

The mansion seemed to be deserted, but a servant finally appeared and conducted Yoritomo to a room where the air was heavy with incense.

"And is this Yoritomo?" said a weeping woman. She was Ohi's daugher, Enju, the mother of Yoritomo's half-sister. Enju continued to weep, and her tears puzzled Yoritomo, who concluded that the defeat of the Genji was the cause of her grief. At last she dried her tears and said: "Yoritomo, your father is no longer here. He stayed with us one night and, thinking it safer to go on, went farther east to Owari, to seek out one Tadamuné, the headman there. On the third day of the New Year he was most foully murdered by Tadamuné."

"Eh, my father?"

"Tadamuné sent your father's head back at once to the capital, and it was exposed in a tree near the gates of the East Jail."

"But—can this be true?"

"And that is not all. Your brother Tomonaga died of his wounds. Yoshihira escaped and we have not heard of him since."

"Then my father and brother are dead? I shall never see them again in this world?"

"My poor, poor child. . . . It isn't safe for even you to stay here much longer. The Heiké are hunting for you."

"Father! My father!"

Yoritomo, trembling, turned his face to the ceiling; tears flooded his young cheeks, and he wept aloud, wildly and uncontrollably, as though his heart would break.

Not until Enju's aged father appeared and tried to console Yoritomo did he finally manage to say: "I will not cry any more. . . . I do not want to cry," and, turning to the old chieftain, Yoritomo finally asked: "Where, then, am I to go?"

To this the old warrior replied: "To eastern Japan," naming chieftain after chieftain who would surely befriend Yoritomo. He continued: "I hear there is a lady Tokiwa still in the capital and that she has three sons who are your half-brothers, but they are still mere children. In the east you will undoubtedly find Genji clansmen who will rally to you."

Yoritomo sat quietly thinking.

With every day that he traveled southward, the broad fields on either side of the highway grew greener with the springing barley. Larks sang above him, and Yoritomo walked on, light of heart. Enju had sent him on his way with all the loving care of a mother—in a new suit of clothes, with hunting cloak, sandals, a flint-case, and a sword.

It was nearly February and a new moon floated in the deep blue sky at midday.

"That boy we passed on the road just now—an unusually fine-looking lad. Unusual in these parts," remarked Munekiyo as he turned in his saddle to look back at Yoritomo.

Another warrior too stared after the trudging figure. "An air, too, that would make you think he must be the son of some chieftain in this part of the country."

"Very likely, but rather harsh training for a youngster like that, letting him travel without attendants in these dangerous times."

Without more ado, Munekiyo continued forward, when a sixth sense warned him; he brought his horse to a sudden stop and looked back once more at the vanishing figure.

Munekiyo, retainer to Kiyomori's half-brother, Yorimori, had been dispatched as Yorimori's deputy to confirm the news of Yoshitomo's death, and having completed sundry business connected with commending Tadamuné, was on his way back to the capital. Turning quickly to the soldiers near him, Munekiyo ordered:

"Bring back that boy we just passed on the road. If he tries to escape, I have no doubt who he is. You're to capture him at all costs."

Munekiyo turned and followed after his soldiers at a leisurely pace.

Yoritomo had apparently tried to escape and resisted his captors. He lay on his back now on the bank of the willow-fringed river, staring up at the perspiring soldiers who surrounded him. The soldiers were breathing heavily; large veins stood out like cords on their red faces and necks.

"Come now, get up!"

"Get up, there!"

Yoritomo did not move, but lay quietly blinking up at the sun.

Munekiyo leaned over and peered at him. "What's the matter there? What are you doing?"

"He's little enough, but don't let that deceive you," one of the soldiers said indignantly. "A little fighter he is, too. . . . Look at him there, and ordering us to put him on his feet as though we were his servants!"

A faint smile appeared on Munekiyo's face. "Put him on his feet," he ordered.

Two soldiers stepped forward, grasped Yoritomo's arms, and hauled him to his feet. Yoritomo stood erect, facing Munekiyo. His face was covered with dust. A bruise lay red along a flushed cheek over which a strand of hair straggled.

"Did they hurt you, boy?"

". . . ."

"Where are you going? East?"

". . . ."

"Your father? Who is your father, boy?"

". . . ."

Yoritomo refused to reply, but the last question brought a large tear rolling down his cheek, though he still uttered no word.

"Answer me. If you still refuse, then we'll see if pain will do it," Munekiyo threatened.

Yoritomo straightened his shoulders and with a look of contempt said: "And who are you? Get down from your horse if you must speak to me. I am not one to have mere Heiké soldiers address me from on horseback."

Munekiyo fell silent with astonishment and scrutinized Yoritomo from head to foot. Then, dismounting quickly, he approached Yoritomo and explained that he was a retainer of Yorimori of the Heiké.

Munekiyo had already guessed who Yoritomo was, but he still gently urged: "Who are you? Tell me whose son you are."

CHAPTER XXVI

MERCY

More than a month had gone by since Kiyomori's step-mother, Ariko, had come to Rokuhara for safety, and she had stayed on until the New Year was past, sharing the life of the household and enjoying the fond attentions of her grandchildren. Ariko was little over forty, barely older than Kiyomori himself, too young in appearance yet to be called a grandmother. Kiyomori often felt stabs of jealousy when he saw Aríko and Tokiko together, for he could not help noticing how much comelier his father's widow was than his own wife; there were times when he even pitied himself for his own marriage.

His secret resentment notwithstanding, Kiyomori never was at ease with Ariko. There was something about her that compelled him even against his strongest inclinations to defer to her. He sometimes wondered what it was that made him feel as he did toward her.

One morning as Kiyomori was about to leave for the Court, Ariko's maid appeared with a message that her mistress wished to speak with him. It was his stepmother's habit to spend part of the morning reciting sutras in the oratory attached to her room, and Kiyomori particularly disliked entering this part of the house; not only was his father's name-tablet there, but there was something somber and forbidding about the apartment.

When Kiyomori appeared, Tokiko was already there, sitting quietly near Ariko.

"I wanted to thank you," Ariko began, "and I hope you will pardon me for asking you to come."

Kiyomori sniffed the incense that still rose in slender spirals behind Ariko. He heard a warbler fluting outside the open window through which the sun streamed into the room. The light illumined the white folds of Ariko's nun's robes in a way that gave her profile the lines of a delicate carving. The somber richness of the oratory, its brocade hangings, the deep-coffered ceiling and suspended lamps, all conspired to emphasize the white-garmented figure. And it suddenly occurred to Kiyomori as he paused for an instant at the threshold that Ariko's life, her long widowhood consecrated to prayer and communing with the dead, had in some manner made her part of that spirit world—and there were ways to deal with spirits.

"But why the thanks—and so suddenly? What can I do for you?"

Ariko smiled. "I did not realize how the days have passed. I have been here more than a month, and Yorimori has been sending messages begging me to return, so I have decided to leave to-day. You have all taken such good care of me since the disturb-ances started—"

"Leaving today? I'm afraid I have been so preoccupied with my affairs that I neglected you sadly. Let me tell you, though, that I have been considering a site here in Rokuhara on which to build you a new house."

"It would make me very happy indeed to live here near you."

"Since Shigemori's house in the valley has just been finished, we can start almost immediately on one for you and Yorimori."

"How fortunate I am—in fact, all of us! You must never for a moment forget, Kiyomori, that you are the chief of the Heiké. Continue in the ways of virtue; be firm with yourself; persevere in your duties, for it will not do to take things as lightly as you have until now.—And, Tokiko, never forget your husband's position. Strive to become an even better wife to him, and an even more devoted mother. As the mistress of this household, give him every possible support."

Kiyomori and Tokiko listened to Ariko deferentially, since she was entitled to speak to them as she did.

"And now I leave everything to you two," she ended. With-out more ado she turned to the oratory to meditate a few mo-ments in front of Tadamori's name-tablet before departing.

To Kiyomori it sounded as though his stepmother had charged him with the responsibility of all matters pertaining to the family; he was vaguely troubled by a certain inconsistency in Ariko, but saw no reason for resenting it. He realized that he had not by any means been an exemplary son to Tadamori and had sincerely tried to make amends by deferring to his father's widow, Ariko. And it was only fitting that he, the head of the clan, should set an example of filial obedience.

Several days after Ariko had returned to her home in the northern section of the capital, her son Yorimori appeared at her house. She greeted him eagerly.

"Ah, Yorimori, is it you?"

"At your devotions, Mother?"

"It does not matter. Your new manor at Owari must keep you busy these days."

"Just that. I sent Munekiyo there on some business, and he came back two nights ago, bringing with him a lad that he captured on the road. I was busy all yesterday with that."

"Oh? And who is this lad that Munekiyo brought with him?"

"Yoshitomo's son, Yoritomo, who has just turned fourteen."

"Yoshitomo's son? That is news indeed! Fourteen, you say? Why, a mere child! What could they be thinking of—letting a boy go out to fight! He's too young to understand what it's all about. Poor child! Where is he now?"

"We are waiting for orders from Rokuhara, and in the meantime Munekiyo has charge of him."

"What does Kiyomori propose to do with the child?"

"We should hear about that today."

Nothing more was said of the matter, and Yorimori soon turned to go, when Ariko stopped him. "Stay a little longer," she coaxed, "I'll have your favorite dish cooked. I see so little of you these days; stay and dine with me."

Just as Ariko sent her maid with some instructions to the kitchen, Munekiyo was announced. He had come to speak with his master, the servant said. Ariko took it upon herself to reply that Munekiyo was to wait.

Mother and son enjoyed a quiet meal together, and when they had finished, Yorimori summoned his retainer.

"Munekiyo, was it from Rokuhara?"

"Yes, a messenger."

"What was the message—about Yoritomo?"

"He is to be executed on the 13th of February."

". . . Hmm."

Yorimori's face fell. His gorge rose as the thought of another execution made him recoil inwardly. He had seen too many beheadings after the fighting had ended, and heard enough of the sorrowing crowds that gathered daily to watch boatloads of exiles leave. While the smoke of battle still hung over the capital, he had been less revolted by all these events, but now that peace was restored and the plum trees were in bloom in the garden, everything in him cried out against the savagery of lifting his hand against a mere boy.

Ariko's face, too, clouded; a devout follower of Buddha, mercy was to her the first duty and supreme virtue of the believer.

The effect that his words had on the two seemed to give Munekiyo courage to disclose what lay close to his thoughts, and he turned to Yorimori:

"He is barely fourteen—just the age, if I remember rightly, that your brother would be if he were alive."

"Yes, if only he were—"

"And he looks so much like him. I could almost believe the two were brothers."

"Munekiyo," Ariko interrupted eagerly, "tell me more about this boy."

Munekiyo began to tell her all he knew.

Ariko, profoundly moved by this resemblance to her dead son, was strengthened in her resolve that Yoritomo should be saved. As she fell asleep that night, Munekiyo's account so haunted her that the likeness of her dead son seemed imprinted on her eyelids, and she was overcome by a longing to see him once more.

A few days later Ariko, bearing a spray of rosy plum blossoms, proceeded across the courtyard of her son's house to Munekiyo's modest dwelling on the other side. She had a servant call Munekiyo, and when he appeared, she held out the blossoms:

"Put this in a vase and let the poor child look at it."

The soldier received the spray with a deep bow, and his eyes softened. "A little gift for him?"

"And, Munekiyo—"

Ariko's voice dropped to a whisper. Munekiyo nodded his agreement to whatever it was that she said, and then led the way toward his house. A high bamboo fence surrounded one side. The door was locked and the shutters were closed, except for a small window through which a guard could observe the prisoner.

Munekiyo let himself into the room in which Yoritomo was confined, leaving Ariko to wait outside beside the peephole.

Yoritomo was seated as usual, motionless as a statue of sandalwood, at a small writing-desk; when he turned to look round, his eyes widened with surprise at the sight of the plum blossoms. Although Munekiyo visited him every morning and evening, Yoritomo had not realized that the plums were already in bloom.

"How lovely they are!" he breathed.

"Yes, aren't they?" Munekiyo replied. "There has been so much snow lately that the plums are late this year."

"I do not wish to be reminded of the snow."

"I am sorry. Shall I put these in water for you?"

"Let me do it myself. Thank you."

Yoritomo bent his head to examine the spray, which Munekiyo laid beside the table. A book lay open on it. Munekiyo's glance turned to the spray, which Yoritomo studied intently. This child was dangerous—a threat to the Heiké, Munekiyo reflected; it had become increasingly clear to him that he was growing fond of this boy. In Yoritomo he recognized the highborn warrior, so soon to be cut down—wasted.

"What are you doing today? Writing some verse?"

"No, I was reading."

"What were you reading?"

"I was reading that collection of poems you lent me and an old chronicle."

"Which do you like best?"

"I don't much enjoy the poems."

"Then you prefer the tales of fighting—heroes and battles?"

Yoritomo gave him a long searching look, a look without guile, but it gave Munekiyo an uneasy feeling that the boy was reading his thoughts, and he hastily averted his eyes. Munekiyo's glance traveled to the narrow aperture where Ariko was probably listening, and he felt his heart pounding unaccountably as he waited for the answer.

Yoritomo, in a jacket of pale mauve silk and trousers of the same color, shading to a deep purple at the ankles, sat cross-legged

on a cushion, staring before him. After a long pause he suddenly
replied:

"The sutras—I like those books best which tell about the
Buddha, if you happen to have some."

"I believe I have a few—but what makes you prefer such
melancholy reading?"

"Somehow—I like them. It must be because my mother, who
is dead now, often took me with her on pilgrimages to famous
temples; I once even visited the monk Honen and heard him speak
on the scriptures."

"So—"

"And so, I think when I grow up I would rather become a
monk than a warrior. But now—"

The boy looked down suddenly. It was clear that he had already been schooled to that code which teaches the highborn warrior to expect only death at the hands of his captors.

There had never been such a thronging of carriages across the
Gojo Bridge as was seen this spring when dense crowds, numberless vehicles of every kind, and horses wove their way toward Rokuhara.

Lately Kiyomori had begun to weary of this unending stream
of visitors. Though his court rank still required him to welcome
each titled comer with suitable courtesies, the rest—turncoats and
fawning office-seekers—he turned away without ceremony; Rokuhara it seemed was now a flowering paradise for those gadflies and
wasps who swarmed unceasingly at its gates.

"This is just too much!" Kiyomori exploded. He had changed
impatiently from his court robes one evening and joined the family circle.

"Tokiko, what a large family we've begotten in the meantime! And to think that the years have crept up on me, leaving me
with only an old wife to keep me company and to pour my wine.
What an unromantic moon this is in spite of the plum blossoms!"

Kiyomori rarely drank so heavily, but tonight he was sodden
with wine, determined to find oblivion in sleep.

"Tokiko, come play to me!"

"I? How ridiculous to ask such a thing of me!"

"Woman, you have no refinements at all! Play me something on the harp, or the lute."

"But have you not always said you abhorred imitating the aristocrats?

"It all depends on the time and the place. Music is to please the ear. It soothes the mind. An excellent thing, indeed! Bring me my lute and let me play for my old wife and my children."

Tokiko brought out the lute that Councilor Shinzei had given him long ago, and Kiyomori began awkwardly plucking at a tune, when a servant appeared, announcing hesitantly:

"The honorable Yorimori, my lord, is anxious for a word with you. He has been waiting for some time and wishes to see you at your leisure."

Kiyomori frowned. "Yorimori? What does he want? Ask him to come here."

The servant left, but reappeared almost immediately.

"He begs to see you alone."

"A bad habit of his. . . . I dislike these confidential talks—all this secretiveness—"

Kiyomori pushed aside the lute pettishly. "Very well—I'll be there shortly," he flung at the servant, and strode from the room, bristling with ill humor.

The still waters below the open window in a distant room of the house mirrored the light from a single lamp.

"Yorimori, when you go home try to dissuade our good mother. It is better if she didn't try to interfere in a matter as grave as this. Do you understand me? Women have invariably been behind every instance of misgovernment—and wars."

"But—"

"Yes? Why do you look at me like that? Are you disappointed?"

"I understand."

"Of course you do. It's all as it should be."

". . . but let me speak for myself."

3 6 6

"Did I forbid you to?"

"But all you've done is rant at me without letting me say anything. I am here only to tell you what Mother said and to plead in her behalf. And you—"

"And I have simply been telling you that no argument will induce me to spare Yoritomo. I have nothing more to say."

"That's just it. Those are hard words—saying that Mother is interfering and that it is more in keeping for her to be coddling her grandchildren, or else tending the flowers in her chapel. Am I to tell her that?"

"Yes, repeat me word for word. Hard words they may be, yet what else can I say, when she, a Heiké, talks of saving a Genji."

"I still can't understand what angers you so. Did you not pardon General Narichika merely because Shigemori begged you to?"

"That was done out of gratitude for his kindness to Shigemori when he first entered the Court. What has Yoshitomo's son ever done for our mother or for you?"

"Nothing, but she is a devout follower of Buddha and begs you to show mercy to that child."

"Mercy?—Are you saying that I have no feelings at all?"

"That I did not."

"Fool that you are! Tell our mother just one more thing— that Kiyomori finds it hard enough curbing his heart. By sparing Yoritomo am I to leave our clan exposed to endless threats? Are we to face nothing but wars hereafter?"

"I have had my say and will not bring up this matter again."

"Better not come on another such fool's errand."

Late that night Yorimori rode away with a heavy heart. His mother waited up for him, anxious to hear the answer.

"It was useless. He refused to listen to me. What's more, he was in an ugly mood, as though he bore a grudge, and he was most immoderate in his language."

"Was I the cause of this?"

"No, he seemed to find fault with me as well."

"I'm afraid that is one of his shortcomings."

"Even so, he had no excuse for being quite so abusive."

3 6 7

"And he showed no sign of relenting about Yoritomo?"

"It would be wiser not to bring up this matter again, Mother. You will only rouse needless suspicion and anger him even more."

Only a few days remained until the 13th of February. Munekiyo had not yet told Yoritomo of the fate that awaited him on that day. He saw the boy daily, and every day strengthened his attachment to Yoritomo and increased his feelings of pity.

Yoritomo, who seldom asked for favors, one day begged his guard to bring Munekiyo, who soon appeared.

"Munekiyo, bring me a hundred small pieces of cypress wood and a small knife."

"Cypress wood and a knife? What will you do with them?"

"I have just counted the days and it is almost the forty-ninth since my father died. As my daily task I want to carve prayer tablets for him, and to offer them at some temple for the repose of his soul."

"So many days already?" Munekiyo replied, deeply moved by Yoritomo's request. "Much as I wish to do what you ask, a prisoner is not permitted to have such a thing as a knife. I'm afraid you cannot do more than recite the prayers."

Munekiyo, none the less, returned the next morning with a hundred small pieces of cypress wood, and Yoritomo was engrossed daily in the task of inscribing his father's posthumous Buddhist name on them.

When Ariko heard all this from Munekiyo, her heart was wrung with pity, and she was more determined than ever to save Yoritomo. Virtue, she believed, never went unrewarded, and the Heiké had nothing to lose by an act of mercy; Tadamori's soul too would gain merit. After reasoning thus with herself, she was supremely confident of the duty that lay before her, and called for her carriage and drove straight to Rokuhara.

When he heard that his stepmother had arrived, Kiyomori set his jaw.

Ariko's serving-woman soon brought a message, saying that her mistress wished to see him in her oratory.

Kiyomori assumed a sulky air, not usual with him, and greeted his stepmother morosely.

"Kiyomori, in the name of mercy, will you not listen to me?"

He boldly anticipated her next words. "About Yoritomo—Yoshitomo's son, wasn't it?"

"Yes, the other night—"

"Yorimori already told me, but—"

"Is it not possible?"

"Impossible. This is a matter so serious that I must ask you not to interfere."

Kiyomori was elated by his blunt refusal; this was, in fact, the first time he had defied Ariko. But when he saw her quietly wipe away a tear, Kiyomori's heart suddenly gave way; he averted his eyes in confusion.

A deep sigh escaped her lips. "If it must be so—with your father dead—now that he is gone—"

Ariko's halting speech stung him to impatience, and Kiyomori retorted coldly: "You wrong me—as usual."

"If your father were alive, I doubt that you would speak to me as you do. Kiyomori, when I think of your future, I can only grieve for you."

"You do me an injustice. Have I not always honored you as though you were my own mother? When did I ever give you cause for grief? I only begged you to hold your tongue in this matter."

"And you still refuse to listen to me?"

"But think of it! What difference does it make if scores of men, General Narichika and the like, are given their freedom? With a warrior's son such as Yoritomo, it's an entirely different matter."

"Are you not also a warrior's son?"

"All the more reason to do away with him. I know too well what that means. The leopard's cub does not change its nature. Fondle it and hold him in your arms now; he'll bare his claws and fangs in time."

"He grieves for his dead father and already speaks of becoming a monk—the poor child!"

"Mother, let us not have any more of this. Go to the women's quarters. I would rather have you coddling your granddaughter."

"Surely, you love your children?"

"I do—to foolishness."

"Yoritomo is Yoshitomo's son. And remember, there is a life after death. Do you not fear the world to come?"

"More of your Buddhist preachings?"

"Ah, well, I have said enough." Ariko replied, turning her back on Kiyomori to face her husband's tablet on the altar, and mumbling something under her breath.

Kiyomori's disagreement with his stepmother only served to increase the incompatibility that had always kept them apart. Ariko departed that same day in deep dejection, but she was as sagacious as she was purposeful and would not have spoken to Kiyomori if she had doubts of success. Those who knew her, however, scarcely realized the extent to which her religious convictions had taken possession of her.

Instead of returning home, Ariko drove straight from Rokuhara to the Valley of Little Pines, not far off, where Shigemori lived, and stayed to talk with him until late into the night.

Shigemori, unlike his father, Kiyomori, had always got on well with his grandmother, with whom he had been a favorite even as a child.

"Shigemori, will you also try to persuade your father?"

Shigemori readily agreed to what his grandmother proposed, and on the following night visited Munekiyo in secret, asking him to let him speak with Yoritomo.

Yoritomo was seated at a small writing-desk, inscribing the name-tablets for his father. There was no trace of heat in the room —not even a taper to give light; only a shaft of moonlight slanting in through the small window high up shed some radiance for him to see by. Yoritomo laid down his writing-brush to peer up at the visitor, who stood in the doorway silently.

Shigemori thought he detected a flicker of alarm in the boy's face and, approaching him, said very gently: "What are you doing, Yoritomo?"

"These are for my dead father."

"Do you miss him—your father?"

"No."

"You must have thoughts of avenging him."

"No."

"You don't?"

"No."

"Why is that?"

"When I am writing like this, nothing troubles me."

"Then you only look forward to dying so you can meet your father again? We are told, you know, that we will meet our loved ones in that other world."

"I do not want to die. It frightens me to think of it."

"But did you not take part in the fighting?"

"I was with my father and brothers then, and so excited that I never thought of death."

"Do you sometimes have dreams?"

"No—what kind of dreams?"

"I mean, do you never dream of your father and brothers?"

Yoritomo shook his head. "No—never." A tear glistened and rolled down his cheek, and he looked down quickly.

Shigemori was deeply moved in spite of himself, and when he came to plead with his father, he did so with passionate intensity and an array of carefully marshaled arguments, begging Kiyomori to grant Ariko her wish. But this only caused Kiyomori to turn on his son in fury.

"What, you're nothing but a boy! How dare you argue with me—with the airs of a sage! You're too young yet to be toying with these outrageous religious fantasies! Enough of your grandmother's contentions about 'Buddhahood' and '*karma*' and such profundities—none of which settle the troubles of the world today! See for yourself the rottenness of the priesthood at Nara! Are those ravening wolves on Mount Hiei any holier than the vagrants and beggars in our streets? We are all creatures of flesh and blood, and this world we live in is a den where we devour or are devoured! We give no quarter to our fellow beings; all that matters is whether one wins or loses. . . . If you must meddle with such nonsense—this babbling of 'mercy' and 'good works,' shedding a few easy tears—then take yourself off to some temple or to your grandmother's! I will not have you bring such matters to me when affairs of far greater importance demand my attention."

And though Shigemori reasoned with his father with cool deliberation, Kiyomori raged back at his son in a wild torrent of words. Under the stress of emotion the habits of his reckless younger years asserted themselves, and he stormed at his son in the coarse speech once learned from the ruffians of the marketplace. Yet at times like this when he ranted so scornfully of "easy tears," Kiyomori had great difficulty in concealing his own.

The question of whether Yoritomo should be executed or not was no longer a political issue, but a family dispute in which Kiyomori found his stepmother, his half-brother, and even his own son ranged against him. Though not so intended, he saw himself accused of being a monster of cruelty and heartlessness.

CHAPTER XXVII

A CHAPEL ON THE HILL

It was the 3rd of January and savagely cold. Not a single light was to be seen anywhere. Darkness washed round the bleak, resounding temple buildings and flowed along the maze of open galleries, whose floors had turned to ice. The raw night air found its way through the shutters and even the walls of the Kannon Chapel in the grounds of Kiyomizu Temple.

"Oh, hush, hush, my love. . . . You are safe in Mother's arms. Is it the cold that makes you cry so? What is it, my little one?"

At the base of a wooden pillar near the altar, where some straw matting had been spread, slept two children, huddled under a thin coverlet.

Tokiwa nuzzled the wailing seven-month-old infant in the folds of her robes and whispered through her tears: "My breasts are dry, and it must be hunger that makes you cry so . . . What could be keeping Yomogi? . . . She should be back soon. Hush, hush or you'll break my heart, little one."

The young mother paced the chapel floor in anguish, fearing the wails might wake her sleeping sons. It was like this last night, and tonight toward sundown Ushiwaka had again begun to cry piteously. Tokiwa was beside herself, for her breasts scarcely yielded a trickle sufficient to moisten the baby's lips.

Tokiwa, who worshipped here every month on the Kannon's holy days and was known to the priests, fled to Kiyomizu Temple with her children and servants when fighting broke out in the capital. But rumors soon followed that Kiyomori had sent his soldiers to capture her, and at this her frightened servants left her, all except the nursemaid Yomogi. And the priests, though they pitied her exceedingly, feared Kiyomori and refused to have anything to do with Tokiwa. A young novice, Kogan by name, however, was touched by the sight of her distress and offered to conceal her in the Kannon Chapel, where few worshippers ever came. There she had stayed hidden now these three days. It was Kogan who surreptitiously brought her a pallet and some bedding, and who supplied her with morsels of food, though barely enough to keep her and her children alive.

For the first time in her life Tokiwa tasted the bitterness of man's indifference to man. In the sheltered life of the Court, where she had been a favorite of the former Empress-elect, Lady Shimeko, Tokiwa, whose beauty made her the talk and the envy of the capital's women, had only known happiness. For her Yoshitomo embodied all that was finest in manhood, and his love had encompassed all her needs. Of men Tokiwa knew nothing other than him; of life, only her duties to her mistress and the care of the children she had had by Yoshitomo. Then was she suddenly thrown upon the mercies of a world reeking with vengeance and blood and hunted down as one of the vanquished.

Ushiwaka had been a high-strung infant since birth, and distressed his young mother by his fits of crying. In those terror-haunted days when Tokiwa had had to make her way out of the capital with her children, her breasts had gone dry. She had then fed him with food that disagreed with him, and Ushiwaka showed signs of rapidly sickening. Frantically, she poured out her prayers to Kannon that the child might be spared; and the Tokiwa who prayed was no longer the same mother of happier days. Half-demented by danger and hardships and the fear of capture, all her being had become an anguished will that her three children should live. All consciousness, every desire was now merged into and become one with their being. Distraught, her hair in disorder, Tokiwa paced the chapel by the frail light of a single candle, rocking and soothing her infant. At the cautious creaking of a door, Tokiwa started in alarm, and then asked: ". . . Is that you, Yomogi?"

"Yes, it's Yomogi. I begged the good monk Kogan to cook me a little of the powdered arrowroot, and here it is."

"Oh? Good! Give it to me here. He can scarcely cry any more, he's so starved."

"See how greedily he laps at it!"

". . . He wants to live, you see. He knows it's good for him. See, he won't even wait to take breath as he drinks it down! Just look at him!"

Tokiwa's tears began to flow again as she looked down at the baby in her arms. Why, why, she mused, could not her milk flow as abundantly as her tears? Why could not her flesh and blood and all be changed to milk?

"Lady Tokiwa—he has stopped crying at last, hasn't he?"

Yomogi had forgotten to tell her mistress that the young monk had come with her.

"Oh, good sir, I have put you to much trouble at this late hour."

"I have not done anything at all, really, but something very disturbing has happened."

"What—again?"

"I'm sure you know what it is. There has been so much gossip in the temple, and it is no longer safe for you here."

"Oh, what am I to do if I am forced to leave this place?"

Then Kogan told her that the priests had heard the baby's cries and now knew that Tokiwa was hiding in the chapel. There was talk that Kiyomori's soldiers were arriving next day to make a search of the temple buildings, and that Kogan would be blamed for sheltering fugitives.

"Let me carry one of the children," Kogan urged, "Yomogi can take Imawaka by the hand, and you, my lady, Ushiwaka, and before dawn . . ."

Once the necessity had been impressed upon her, Tokiwa ceased to tremble, and before dawn they were on their way down through the hills around Kiyomizu Temple.

Kogan went with them as far as the river, where a small craft was preparing to sail for E uchi, at the mouth of the Yodo River; and when Tokiwa and her children and the nursemaid were safely aboard, he left them.

Two dancing-girls, who were on their way back to Eguchi, gave the two older children some cakes, exclaiming: "What pretty children! . . . And where are you going at this early hour?"

"Thank you kindly. We have an acquaintance at Mimaki, a short way down the river," Tokiwa replied.

"Then you will be leaving us quite soon. Are you visiting there?"

"No. . . ."

"Then you must be like our parents, whose homes were burned down during the fighting last month. We came up from Eguchi to pay them a visit and are on our way back. Isn't it true that the innocent ones always get the worst of it? . . . What a dreadful time these dear little things must have had!"

"Mmm . . ." Imawaka said, shaking his head with annoyance at the strange woman who stroked his hair. "Look, Mother!

Otowaka is already eating his cake! I want to eat mine, too—Mother!"

"Say 'Thank you' before you do."

The dancing-girls appeared to be fond of children and brought out more cakes from a bamboo hamper; one even removed a pad of silk floss from her shoulders to wrap around the baby.

"Good-by, children!" the women waved as Tokiwa disembarked at Mimata.

Tokiwa's uncle was a dealer in yoke-oxen, which he bred on his farm.

"Well, well, is it you, Tokiwa?" her aunt exclaimed in astonishment, but made no move to invite her in. "I must appear heartless, but you surely know that the soldiers are after you. There's a lot of money coming to whoever hands you over to Kiyomori at Rokuhara—a reward, you know. . . . Come now, you'd better be off while your uncle's asleep; he's not one to let you give him the slip if he finds out you've been here. Now, don't turn down my advice," she said, driving Tokiwa from her door.

Tokiwa could only recall one distant relative to whom she might turn, and he lived in the country of Yamato. Wearily she made her way there, begging where she could for food for her children, sleeping under temple porches, moving on day after day and night after night like a vagrant. Strangers eyed her suspiciously, but they were kind to her and her brood. Those who recognized her for the fugitive that she was, took pity on her and made no attempt to notify the authorities.

This relative whom Tokiwa sought was a priest, and he kept her hidden in the small temple of which he had charge. Along toward early February, when Ushiwaka was well again, Tokiwa's uncle appeared unexpectedly at the priest's house with an old creaking ox-cart. He talked with the priest until late into the night and on the following morning said to Tokiwa:

"You can't hide here much longer, you know. You'd better get back to the capital and think things over, or they may hang or crucify your mother, who's still there."

". . . But why should they?"

"Why? Only natural, isn't it? You clear out with Yoshitomo's children, so they catch your mother instead and throw her into the jail at Rokuhara."

"What—my mother?"

"Who else? Everyone knows about that. And there's some ugly gossip about you too—forgetting your own mother for love of the children you had by Yoshitomo!"

Tomizo's unblinking eyes, the eyes of an uncouth animal, bulged as Tokiwa burst into tears. For long her only thought had been for her children, but now she wept as a child does for her mother.

Tomizo laughed derisively. "Here, enough of that"—when another thought seemed to occur to him, and he continued: "While you're about it, you might as well bawl for that man of yours—Yoshitomo. You think he's gone east and will come back for you soon, but he's dead. Died on the 3rd of January, do you hear?"

". . . ."

Tokiwa stared at her uncle in disbelief; her lips turned waxen and seemed paralyzed.

"That's the truth. You can find out for yourself by going to the capital. His head hung from that tree by the East Jail for seven days. There's not a man in Kyoto who hasn't seen it."

An agonized sigh escaped from Tokiwa's lips: "Then—"

"Tokiwa!"

"But Yoshitomo—"

"Here, Tokiwa, what's come over you? Pull yourself together! Don't stare at me as though you'd gone mad. I had nothing to do with it, do you hear me? It's war that's done this to you and yours, and didn't Yoshitomo have a hand in all this madness? Come now, forget what's past."

But Tokiwa heard nothing; grief threatened to unhinge her mind and she wept as if she would drown in her own tears. Only the child at her breast recalled her to herself, for the wildness of her sorrow frightened him and he cried pitifully.

On the following day, by trickery and cajoling, Tomizo induced Tokiwa to climb into the dilapidated cart with her three children, leaving the tearful nursemaid Yomogi behind. Smacking his lips over the thought of the reward that awaited him, Tomizo whipped up his ox and hurried forward to the capital.

When at last they arrived at the house in which Tokiwa's mother had lived, they found it empty, stripped of its furnishings and everything valuable.

"Well, we might as well spend the night here," Tomizo said, lifting Tokiwa and the children out of the cart, and carrying bedding, cooking utensils, and their few pathetic belongings into the house. "This won't do—the lot of you crying; you must be hungry. I'll see what can be done about some food."

After making some purchases in the market, Tomizo set about cooking, feeding his charges truculently as though they were paupers who had been forced on him. "Get on, now; get done with your eating and then off to sleep," he scolded, with harsh looks for Imawaka and Otowaka. Not long after, Tomizo started off on a visit to one of his cronies in the city.

It was clear to Tokiwa now what her avaricious uncle had in mind. He intended to deliver her over to Kiyomori and collect the reward for himself. She saw no way to escape, for to do so would endanger her mother's life; nor was flight with three helpless children to be thought of. In her despair the thought of doing away with herself and her children recurred to her persistently, but each time the memory of Yoshitomo's last letter held her back.

What is there to say in the bitterness of defeat? I cannot even come to you for a last farewell, for I am on my way—where I do not know. Some day I will surely return for you. Hide in the wilderness, in the hills if need be. Let no harm come to my beloved children, I beseech you. Though many mountains and rivers come between us, remember that I love you forever. And this I implore—that you will not cast away your life in despair.

Those words were inscribed in Tokiwa's memory now like some familiar passage from the Kannon sutras, and whenever death beckoned and whispered to her, she recited them to herself as though they were a prayer against evil.

But all hope had died in her; Yoshitomo was dead, and to-morrow, she believed, would be her last day on earth. Then she suddenly remembered that she had not taken leave of Lady Shimeko, in whose household she had served for nine years. Clasping her youngest in her arms, a child clinging to her on either side, Tokiwa set out into the dusk for the palace on Ninth Avenue, not far off. She was familiar with the entrances to the palace and made her way to the West Gate, where the under-servants knew her. In the gentlewomen's quarters she was soon surrounded by her old friends, who plied her with anxious questions about where she had been, and wept over Tokiwa and her children.

Lady Shimeko soon summoned Tokiwa and greeted her with tears, saying: "Ah, Tokiwa, what sad change is this that has come over you? Why did you not come to me sooner?"

Relief was mingled with rejoicing in Lady Shimeko's household, where there had been great fear that Kiyomori suspected their mistress of having concealed Tokiwa or connived at her escape. And Tokiwa's former companions praised her for having stayed hidden so long and wept because she had returned to her mistress for a last farewell.

"I humbly beg to say that I am Tomizo, the ox-dealer from Mimata—Tokiwa's uncle," said an individual who appeared at Rokuhara toward sundown. Tokitada, Kiyomori's brother-in-law, when told that a man had come with information about Tokiwa, ordered the man to be locked up in the guardhouse.

"This is no joking matter," Tomizo protested to the guard. "I've come a long way to tell you where you'll find this woman you're after, and I want that reward, I say! I don't even get a word of thanks for my pains. . . . What do you mean by throwing me into this hole?"

Tokitada had followed the instructions he had received from Kiyomori, who was disgusted by the number of informers who came to Rokuhara. Many, prompted by greed and desire for self-advancement, were eager to betray former benefactors or the innocent, and Kiyomori had, therefore, ordered Tokitada to open the eyes of such individuals to their own baseness and to send them packing.

Late that night Tokitada related the events of the evening to Kiyomori. "And now what do you wish me to do next?"

"Do next?" Kiyomori replied moodily, and lapsed into silence. The question reminded him unpleasantly of his recent words with his stepmother over Yoritomo's fate. He finally said: "Let Itogo see to Tokiwa."

"You wish him to arrest Tokiwa and bring her and the children here?"

"Yes. He won't need more than a few soldiers for that."

"No, not for a woman with three helpless children."

"If it's true that this uncle of hers found Tokiwa hiding in Yamato and brought her here, then she must have intended in any case to give herself up in order to save her mother."

"Her uncle said nothing of that."

"Naturally not. The rascal's after money and that's why he came to inform against her. He was a hanger-on in Yoshitomo's household and undoubtedly has much to thank his niece for—the ungrateful rascal! See that he gets what he deserves."

"That will be taken care of."

"And tell Itogo when he goes to arrest Tokiwa that he's not to ill-use her or her children."

"I'll tell him that."

"For the time being, he will have charge of the prisoners. He'll hear from me later on when I've had time to think things over."

Tokitada left at once with the orders for Itogo, who started off at dawn with a handful of soldiers for the house on Sixth Avenue. Arrived there, Itogo found the house empty; from house-holders in the neighborhood, he soon learned that Tokiwa had gone the previous evening to the palace on Ninth Avenue. Lest the appearance of armed men provoke disorder, Itogo quickly made himself known to the palace steward, explaining that he had been sent from Rokuhara to arrest Tokiwa. The steward in his turn assured Itogo that no attempt had been made to shelter a fugitive. Tokiwa, he said, was even now preparing to leave for Rokuhara to give herself up.

While Itogo and his men waited in the guard-house of an inner gate, Tokiwa made ready for her departure. This past night, spent in safety among friends who cared for her, had so comforted her that she found the last leave-taking had lost much of its bitterness. Rising early, she bathed and carefully arranged her hair. Opening her dressing-case, she seated herself before a mirror and was surprised by the serenity of the image that looked back at her from its depth. The powder clung smoothly to her skin and she bloomed under the final touches of her toilette.

Tokiwa's eldest son peered at his mother's reflection to ask: "Where are you going, Mother?" and danced with joy when told.

"Somewhere nice—and you are to come with me."

Adorned in the robes that Lady Shimeko and her gentlewomen had given her, Tokiwa reappeared before her mistress and, bowing low, said:

"Though I expect never to return, I cannot forget how good you were to me through the years—nor your kindness to me last night."

Lady Shimeko's voice dropped to a whisper as she leaned toward Tokiwa: "It is best to be resigned to your fate, but do not lose hope entirely. I shall ask my father to speak to Lord Kiyomori."

While the gentlewomen, shedding tears, waited on Imawaka and Otowaka at their morning meal, Tokiwa nursed her youngest for the last time.

Meanwhile, Itogo and his soldiers were growing impatient, and could be heard demanding that Tokiwa start at once. Lady Shimeko quickly sent a message by her steward, asking that Tokiwa be allowed to take her carriage. To this Itogo replied: "It's not customary to let prisoners ride, but because of the children, I see no harm in it."

Shortly after, a lady's carriage, guarded by foot-soldiers, rolled through a rear gate, along the capital's main avenues and down the side-streets.

CHAPTER XXVIII

THE MOTHER

Kiyomori slept poorly that night. There seemed to be no reason for it; if pressed for a reason he would have replied that he was feeling the unaccustomed strain of his official duties—the numerous councils of state, the multitude of court functions. Yet for all his rough and ready ways and his outward contempt for formalities and ritual, Kiyomori was vulnerable. He felt no need for Ariko's or his son's advice for dealing with

Tokiwa and her children, for the news of their capture had disturbed him more than he cared to admit.

"Have you seen them, Tokitada?" Kiyomori inquired toward noon of the following day.

"Yes, I have seen them. Everything has been carried out as you ordered. Itogo now has them in custody and under strict guard."

"Do they seem comfortable?"

"The baby cries from time to time and Tokiwa herself looks worn."

"She whose beauty was once the talk and envy of the court ladies and the common people."

"Only twenty-three and the mother of three. It is hard to believe that all those weeks of flight and starvation have not marred her looks. There is a pathos in her beauty now."

"Hmm?"

"About the trial—do you wish me or Itogo to question her and submit the necessary evidence?"

"No," Kiyomori replied at once with a shake of the head. "Let me cross-examine her myself. She is Yoshitomo's widow and has his three sons with her. This is a matter that I alone should deal with."

Tokitada had heard something of the repercussions from Ariko's appeal in behalf of Yoritomo and concluded that Kiyomori was anxious to settle the matter of Tokiwa's fate before his stepmother took it upon herself to interfere.

"When do you wish to see the prisoner?"

"The sooner the better—before evening."

A visitor was announced just as Tokitada left. It was a courtier, Fujiwara Koremichi, come on behalf of his daughter Lady Shimeko. Kiyomori received him cordially.

"Naturally I would not suspect Lady Shimeko. I'm surprised that you of all people should come to me about this. A pity indeed that there are not more like you at Court to advise us in times like this."

Kiyomori had a secret liking for Koremichi and sensed that the feeling was mutual. By the time his caller was ready to depart, Kiyomori had exchanged far more cups of wine with his guest than was his habit, and while he was still in a genial mood, Tokitada once more appeared to say that the prisoner was ready.

Kiyomori strode down a gallery leading toward the west wing. The mansion was undergoing some extensive repairs and additions, and he picked his way carefully toward a room of an inner court where the garden was being enlarged.

"Where did you say they were?"

"Over there."

"Below—there?"

Kiyomori stepped toward a balustrade and looked down. Tokiwa knelt on a straw mat, head bowed; on either side of her sat a child, tightly clutching her sleeves.

"Itogo, give the woman and the children kneeling-cushions," Kiyomori ordered as he seated himself in the center of the audience room. Itogo looked puzzled and ill at ease. It was not customary to treat prisoners like this.

"Here, bring them up here," Kiyomori said, jerking his head in the direction of the gallery on which the room opened.

Itogo was not the only one who appeared surprised; there was no mistake, however, that Kiyomori meant the gallery.

"Here, my lord?"

Kiyomori nodded as Itogo placed three cushions at the top of the stairs leading up from the courtyard. Tokitada motioned Tokiwa to approach. She looked up trembling and drew her frightened children close. Itogo then spoke to her:

"Go up as you've been ordered to. Take your seats there."

Tokiwa rose, clasping her infant in one arm, and holding Otowaka's small hand, she came forward and slowly ascended the stairs with Imawaka clinging to her robes.

As Tokiwa approached, Kiyomori felt his nerves tingle—expectant. So this was the incomparable beauty whose name had once been on every tongue!

"Are you unhappy, Tokiwa?"

"No, I have no more tears to shed. I implore you to have pity on my mother. Let her go free, I beg you, my lord."

"Hmm—that shall be done," Kiyomori said at once, and then continued: "Where have you been hiding until now? What made you flee with your children?"

"I was in Yamato. As for my children, I can only say that I am no different from other mothers who instinctively cling to their children."

"What brought you back to the capital?"

"Reports of my mother."

"Your uncle came here, you know."

"I did not know that my uncle was here before me. I came here intending to deliver myself up to you."

"As I thought. You are mad to come back as you've done."

Kiyomori fell silent and stared at the young mother and her children; then he suddenly asked: "Are you able to nurse him?"

Tokiwa gazed down at the infant in her arms, but made no reply beyond an almost imperceptible shake of the head.

"Not too well. No, I should think not," Kiyomori said to himself with an abstracted look. "Mothers are such foolish creatures. They pretend there is food where there is none; what little there is they give to their husbands and children while their babies wail for the breast. . . . And you who have fled over hills and plains —it's a miracle that the baby lives at all."

"Tokiwa, you have nothing to fear. The war was between Yoshitomo and me. You are innocent."

"Yes."

"A pity, too, that a man like Yoshitomo should have become discontented and been led astray by those young courtiers to his own undoing. He misjudged me, too."

Tokiwa broke down and wept uncontrollably.

"My lord—my lord—" she began.

Kiyomori's eyes strayed over the face lifted to him and came to rest on the thick lashes, heavy with tears, and his heart was suddenly shot through with pity.

"Tokiwa, you need not weep so. You had nothing to do with this war. Your mother shall be set free, since you have given yourself up to us. Wipe away those tears, Tokiwa, you too shall go free."

Tokiwa suddenly cried out: "No—no, I am not asking you to spare me. But have mercy upon these, my children!"

"What?"

"Spare these children, my lord; let me die in their stead!"

At this, Kiyomori's face suddenly grew hard with anger and he roared:

"Woman, take care what you say! You have that evil habit of all women—of wanting to play on my sympathies. You may not be a Genji, but there's no doubt about those children of yours, in whom the blood of the Genji runs. Them I will not and cannot spare!"

Kiyomori, who had risen to his feet in anger, seated himself once more, but his eyes shifted furtively over the prostrate figure before him.

"So you, too, like Yoshitomo of the Genji, misjudge me. The word 'mercy' is hateful to me. I am utterly merciless. Itogo! Tokitada!"

Itogo and Tokitada came forward.

"Take away this woman and her children. The trial is over."

Without waiting for his attendants, Kiyomori hurriedly left the room and vanished into one of the inner apartments.

Less than a fortnight later Kiyomori relented as he invariably did with his near kin or the weak. Overcome by his stepmother's pleadings, he ordered Yoritomo's death sentence suspended. A messenger was sent to Shigemori, to whom Kiyomori said:

"Shigemori, I've given this matter some thought."

"And what have you decided, Father?"

"After all that your grandmother has said, Shigemori, I've decided to spare Yoritomo."

"Then?"

"He's to be banished. To the most distant spot possible."

"My grandmother will be overjoyed to hear this, and people will praise you for being a dutiful son."

"Nothing of the kind. I make no claim to being filial, but I am a father myself and hesitate to put another man's son to death."

"Yes, Shinzei is one example of a man who ruthlessly killed off his enemies, saw his own sons put to the sword in turn, and then was killed himself."

"Enough of your sermons. I don't pretend to be noble. It's only human to feel as I do about a mere child like Yoritomo. It would be unwise too at this time to have him executed, to earn the hatred of people at large. You go and tell your grandmother what I have decided about Yoritomo."

When the 13th of February drew near, no official orders regarding Yoritomo were issued. Kiyomori preserved a noncommittal silence, and the date went by unnoticed. It was not until a month or so later that a decree was published ordering Yoritomo banished to Izu, in eastern Japan; he was to depart on the 20th of March.

As for Tokiwa and her children, the Capital was astounded several days later by the news that Kiyomori had pardoned them. There were some who even sought out Kiyomori and questioned the wisdom of his doing so, and to such he only replied that he was carrying out the orders of a higher authority. Then it soon began to be said that Kiyomori's assurances were little more than transparent excuses, for gossip reported that Kiyomori's carriage waited night after night outside the house where Tokiwa was still kept a prisoner.

It was the morning of the 2oth of March, the day on which
Yoritomo was to set out for his prison-home in Izu.

Munemori had risen early, and came into Yoritomo's room
for the parting.

"You and Se-no-o went to visit so exalted a personage so
very early this morning—and when even I was still in bed, I
found."

"That, dear Kiyo, he said with a laugh. "You do have to
take care you don't let so important a prisoner escape again."

"Oh, well, if you say so, then I shall do so too dear."

"Why so—"

The guards outside began to call out.

. . . .
face in the pale early sunlight, and his gaze turned toward
far-away places that seemed to tell him that this day would be
. . . .
his face gaunt, and his cheeks growing hollow; but he wore
the new suit of clothing that Ariko had given him.

"Before parting, I should like once more to thank Lady Ariko
and say farewell."

"Yes, Lady Ariko, too, expects you, I'm to take you to her as
soon as you finish your . . . ."

Yoritomo quietly sat down to his meal.

"Munemori, this is my last meal here, isn't it."

"Yes, and I'm sure that I . . . . "

"And I, too, Munemori," Yoritomo said, turning to his tutor.
"I shan't forget how kind you have been."

CHAPTER XXIX

EXILE

The blossoms were still wrapped in darkness when a company of soldiers and a few officials began assembling on
the avenue of cherry trees along the walls of Ariko's residence. In the courtyard, too, the flowering boughs rose overhead
like a blur of clouds. The entire household seemed to be up already, for lights glimmered between the curtain of blossoms as
unseen figures hurried back and forth along the open galleries.

"Did you sleep well last night?"

It was the morning of the 20th of March, the day on which Yoritomo was to set out for his prison-house in Izu.

Munekiyo had risen early and come to help Yoritomo prepare for the journey.

"Yes, I did sleep, but I was so excited and happy that I woke very early this morning; and when I lifted the shutters myself, I found the moon still shining."

"That must have been around midnight. You will have to take care that you don't fall asleep in the saddle again."

"Oh no, Munekiyo, it won't matter if I do so this time."

"Why is that?"

"My guards will see to it that I'm not left behind."

Munekiyo laughed heartily at Yoritomo's high spirits; his rapture was like that of the caged bird set free, and his gaiety so contagious that Munekiyo could not but feel that this day with its festive blossoms was an occasion for joy. A servant soon arrived to conduct Yoritomo to his morning bath. Yoritomo was back soon, his face shining and his cheeks glowing like rosy fruit. He wore the new suit of clothing which Ariko had given him.

"Before starting I should like once more to thank Lady Ariko and say farewell.

"Yes, Lady Ariko, too, expects you. I'm to take you to her as soon as you finish your breakfast."

Yoritomo quickly sat down to his meal.

"Munekiyo, this is my last meal here, isn't it?"

"Yes, and I'm sorry that it is so."

"And I, too, Munekiyo," Yoritomo said, turning to his jailer, "I shan't forget how kind you have been."

Munekiyo made a clucking sound. "I did nothing—only my duty. You must not expect to meet with kindness everywhere. If there is anyone that you particularly wish to have accompany you, I shall ask for you."

"No, there is no one that I can think of. There may be, but he would be afraid to show himself here."

"True enough. Now if you are ready, we shall go to see Lady Ariko."

Yoritomo was led from the small room where he had been confined for a hundred days and taken to Ariko's residence, a small house, exquisitely and richly appointed in the manner of a small chapel. Yoritomo had only the evening before taken supper with her here and been presented with new clothes and all the small necessities for his journey. In addition to the satisfaction she derived from performing what her religion taught was an act of mercy, Ariko had drawn deep comfort from seeing the boy who reminded her so much of her dead son, and on parting had asked Yoritomo if there was some last thing she might give him. Yoritomo had shyly replied: "I should so like to have a dice-game—something to play with if I ever feel lonely when I am in Izu."

Ariko unfortunately did not have one to give him just then, but she had one ready for him by the following morning, and eagerly waited for Yoritomo to appear.

"Madam, I have come to say good-by," said Yoritomo, bowing low to Ariko, whose eyes were brimming. "And when I am in faraway Izu, I shall never forget that it was you who saved my life. I pray morning and night for your happiness, madam."

"So you are leaving. I had nothing to do with saving your life; you owe it all to the blessed Buddha. . . . Remember my words to you last night, Yoritomo, that you are to renounce the way of the warrior, the calling of bloodshed."

"Yes."

"No matter how great the temptation, turn away your ear from the whisperings of evil men. . . . Let your life be consecrated to prayer in memory of your dead mother and father."

"Yes."

"Remember my words even when you are grown to manhood. Let no one draw you into a reckless plot for revenge, lest you be imprisoned again. And never forget that my prayers go with you."

"Yes . . . yes."

"You are a good child. . . . Here is the dice-game I promised you. Does this please you?"

Ariko produced a black lacquer box richly ornamented with a pattern in powdered gold.

"Oh, what a beautiful box! May I open it now?"

Ariko smiled. "I doubt that you have time for that now. Does he, Munekiyo?"

"I'm afraid not. Your boxes are now being loaded on the pack-horses and I'd better put this with the rest, so it won't get broken."

"That is best. . . . It is more important that you go now and meet some people who came to me asking for leave to say farewell. They are waiting in the servants' quarters."

"Oh, for me?"

Yoritomo drew in his breath sharply. Sadness filled him and a nameless ache; he could not guess who these people might be. ". . . Oh!"

The three who waited for Yoritomo turned to him with streaming eyes. One was his maternal uncle, Sukenori, who had refused to take sides in the fighting; the second was Moriyasu of the Genji, whom illness had detained in a distant province until the war was over. The third was Yoritomo's old nurse, who had tended him from his infancy, and she knelt before him weeping.

"My young master, let me today for the last time bind up your hair," she said, and, rising, came and stood behind him. While she combed his hair, she leaned forward long enough to whisper: "This is a sad moment for you, but this is not the last time we shall meet, for your old nurse will not fail to come to you in Izu."

Then the other two also came up close to him while the guard's back was turned and spoke quickly to Yoritomo in low tones: "The gods have saved you by a miracle. Let no man ever persuade you to shave your head and take the vows."

And while his nurse arranged his hair, Yoritomo quietly gazed up at the ceiling, feigning not to hear, but signifying by a slight movement of his brows that he understood and assented.

"It's time to start," an official announced as he left his bench to mount his horse. Beckoning to the attendants, he ordered: "Ready—ready now for the start!"

The pack-horses were led out on the road, while a number of lower officials with bamboo staves motioned back a crowd that was already beginning to gather at the scene. The guards who were accompanying Yoritomo filed out by the gate, leading Yoritomo's horse, and called: "Time to start! Make haste, please!"

Very soon the youthful prisoner appeared at the gate accompanied by members of Ariko's household. This was not the usual exile people were accustomed to see—a gaunt, tear-sodden prisoner—but a gay figure, radiant with youth, who sprang lightly to his saddle.

"Farewell," Yoritomo cried, smiling and inclining his head toward the house.

Ariko and her son Yorimori were among those assembled to see Yoritomo off. "Yoritomo, your health for many a day to come!" "Yoritomo, farewell!" they cried to this boy who already exercised the mysterious power of drawing to himself the devotion of those who came to know him. Yoritomo's eyes, however, were now turned away from them and directed toward a figure beside the gate.

"Munekiyo, farewell." He saluted, inclining his head.

Munekiyo quietly replied: "Farewell," and bowed in return.

The procession began to move off slowly in a flurry of falling petals, and soon nothing remained but a white road, paved with blossoms.

By the time the party began the ascent at Kuritaguchi, the spring sun was high in the heavens. The expanse of roofs in the capital, and all the countryside, stretching from the Northern Hills to the Eastern Hills, seemed to float in a sea of foaming blossoms. Yoritomo looked down many times over his shoulder toward the Kamo River. Who knew that thoughts went through his mind as he recalled that day of blood when he fought on the riverbank with his father and brothers?

Rumors brought a crowd of local people to Otsu on the

shores of Lake Biwa—monks, men and women, travelers, children and their elders—all curious to see Yoritomo depart. When Yoritomo finally arrived and prepared to embark for the other side of the lake, his uncle and Moriyasu of the Genji, who were allowed to accompany Yoritomo this far, took leave of him with tears.

Yoritomo, however, turned to them puzzled. "See, I am not sad. I do not know how other exiles feel at a time like this, but for me this is a moment for rejoicing, a day to celebrate."

As soon as the company had boarded their vessel, Yoritomo at once unpacked the box Lady Ariko had given him and began setting up his dice-game, as he did so calling to the guard in charge of the party: "Will you not come and play with me?"

The guard laughed ruefully. "I must remind you that you are a prisoner and that I am an official. You must observe the rules for prisoners or else you will be punished."

"Is it forbidden to play this game?"

"This is not a pleasure trip, I must once more remind you. When you reach Izu, you will still be treated as a prisoner and put under heavy guard."

Yoritomo frowned with annoyance. "Here, put these away until I reach prison," he ordered one of the attendants, pushing the scattered pieces of the game away from him.

The guard shook his head resignedly. "This child doesn't seem to understand what his position is," he said in an aside.

On the long journey along the Tokaido highway, he and the other attendants had further reason to believe that their young prisoner was perhaps a simpleton, for Yoritomo often tried to engage them in discussions of moves in the dice-game, or else whiled away the time on horseback piping and whistling with blades of grass.

At the time Yoritomo was banished to Izu, Councilor Moronaka, Korekata, the chief of the Police Comission, and Tsunemuné, the courtier, were also sent into exile. Their plot to unseat Kiyomori had ended by placing him even more firmly in power.

Spring had come and the capital was astir with life once more; the busy inhabitants sighed with relief as they breathed the

air of peace and the scent of flowering trees. Kiyomori was unusually occupied with a multitude of official duties. He had, however, disposed of a number of troublesome issues while the hub-
bub subsided. The matter of Tokiwa and her children had been
settled: Imawaka, her eldest son, was sent to a temple near Fushimi, south of the capital, and put in the Abbot's care with the
stipulation that the child was to enter holy orders; the high eccle-
siastic of Tennoji Temple was given charge of Otowaka, also
destined for the priesthood; the youngest, Ushiwaka, despite his
mother's entreaties, was taken from her and sent with a wet-nurse
to the Abbot on Kurama Mountain, where he too was to take
the vows when he came of age.

When all this became known to the public, tongues began to
wag in the capital.

"Now see what a woman's charm can do!"

"That would hardly happen to every one. It takes a woman
with Tokiwa's beauty."

"That's just it. What if Tokiwa had been plain?"

"It's likely that her children would not have been spared."

A bystander remarked irascibly: "Bah, all your foolish gossip!"

"You? You're looking out of sorts!"

"And why not—don't you realize that if she had been ugly
they would never have picked her to serve at the Palace?"

"There's no question of that."

"Lord Yoshitomo would not have become infatuated with
her, and there wouldn't have been those three children."

"As I was saying, all this gossip is nonsense. What makes you
so suspicious?"

"Heh, then tell us what you think. Are you saying that Lord
Kiyomori spared those three children for no reason at all?"

"It wouldn't be unlike him if he had. Don't forget that he's
the lord of Rokuhara. Why should he stoop to dickering or take
unnecessary risks? Why should he make a fool of himself over a
widow with three children, when the world is full of desirable
women?"

"Ah, no, there's only one Tokiwa in all Kyoto."

The speaker laughed. "Ho, ho! So that's what you think, but little you know how a man in his forties—the victor at that—feels when he eyes his ravishing captive."

This was the theme which occupied gossips in the capital— the common folk, the courtiers and their ladies, even the scholars in temple precincts and nuns in their convent retreats; and not least in Rokuhara itself there were whispers of how Kiyomori stood in relation to Tokiwa.

Some of the additions to Kiyomori's mansion were done— complete with their enclosed gardens.

"Red-Nose, this is very fine indeed! This rose court pleases me greatly."

"That's what I expected. I doubt that the Minister of the Left will feel that his garden on the river can match this."

"You're uncommonly proud of this, aren't you, Bamboku?" Kiyomori chaffed.

"For one thing, the plans for the gardens and buildings were mine."

Kiyomori laughed. "Well, Nose, this is your day to brag."

"And if it were not and you disappointed, what a black day this would be for me!"

"Well, well, Nose, your swaggering makes me forget my troubles."

Kiyomori was entertaining the merchant in one of the new rooms looking out on the rose court.

Bamboku was uncanny in the way he guessed what one was thinking, Kiyomori reflected. A slippery fellow. Kiyomori had been wary of him at first, but Tokiko had such a high opinion of him that Kiyomori was persuaded to accept him, and finally began to set more store by Bamboku than even Tokiko did. He was, in fact, getting quite fond of Red-Nose, his droll humor—a character, full of cunning and discernment, which Kiyomori himself lacked. This, Bamboku had proved amply in the ticklish negotiations between Kiyomori and the conspirators in the last Palace intrigue.

Bamboku was worth cultivating, Kiyomori had decided, and began sending for him on one pretext or another. When he felt low in spirits or was in need of a companion to relieve his boredom, he called for the Nose as most people did for those aromatic herbs which act as a tonic to the spirits. This was just another such occasion; the Nose was well in his cups, and the ruddy hues of his nose had spread to the rest of his features.

"Ho, troubles, indeed? And you want to forget them?"

"What are you groaning about?"

"My lord, I can scarcely believe that you would have troubles."

"Blockhead! Am I not human?"

"Let me see—was it you that once told me you were a 'child of the heavens and earth'—a son of nature?"

"That was only a manner of speaking."

"Very stupid of me, to be sure—I see what is troubling you."

"You do?"

"Quite understandable and natural. Besides, spring is here. Isn't that reason enough, my lord?"

"Something of the kind," Kiyomori replied with a wry laugh.

"To tell you the truth, sir, I am disappointed in you this time. I have been mistaken about you."

"About what?"

"You lack courage," the Nose jeered, and continued: "What a spectacle indeed! What fainthearted melancholy is this? I can hardly believe it of you, the hero without peer! The hero, that *man!* Do you call yourself a *man*, spineless creature that you are?"

Under the influence of wine Bamboku often indulged in such plain speaking; only the Nose dared to taunt Kiyomori in this fashion. These gibes pleased Kiyomori, who took the merchant more and more into his confidence.

The Nose was the first to get wind of Kiyomori's visits to Tokiwa—now an open secret—and soon was accompanying him on his calls. Nor did the latest gossip escape the Nose, who carefully trickled it into Kiyomori's ear: "That poor Tokiwa, who has given herself to the lord of Rokuhara for the sake of her children! He is insanely in love with her. How galling for her to submit to the embraces of that libertine! . . ." Thus ran the rumors, embroidered on by everyone to his liking. But the Nose discerned that wishful thinking accounted largely for what the world accepted as fact; if there was some truth in what people were saying, the rest was pure fabrication. The gossip, nevertheless, was unflattering to Kiyomori.

"I find all this annoying—most exasperating. All these rumors—and you so queasy!"

"Come, Red-Nose, stop taunting me. My position is not an easy one, you know."

"Still vacillating, are you? Didn't you make up your mind to it last night?"

"Make up my mind?"

"There now, just as we come to the point, you turn evasive. What makes you hesitate to tell me whether you have or haven't made her your mistress?"

CHAPTER XXX

CHERRY BLOSSOMS

okiwa sat at the window of her boudoir, motionless, gazing out at the misted moon in the spring night. What had become of Imawaka, she wondered. Had Otowaka grown accustomed by now to strangers? Was he thriving—Ushiwaka who had been torn from her arms and carried off to Kurama Mountain? Someone had said to her: "A child can get along very well without its mother."

If only this were true, she prayed, hating those assurances, which were meant to comfort her and which she knew to be cruelly true. What did she have to live for now that her children had been taken from her? What use had she for this poor husk of self? It was almost unbearable, too, that after Ushiwaka was taken from her, her breasts had once more become swollen with milk and grew painful; a fever spread from them throughout all her body, so that she lay sick for many days. Her jailer had finally called a physician lest Kiyomori think he had been neglecting his prisoner. The servants hovered about Tokiwa, but she shrank from them in fear and shame; it was clear what they had in mind, for the elderly woman who had charge of Tokiwa and waited on her had whispered: "My lady, people everywhere praise you for what you have done. She who preserves her chastity is not alone virtuous. They idolize you as the noble mother who sacrificed herself for her children."

And soon after, the jailer's wife also came to Tokiwa's bedside secretly to say: "There are countless women in the capital whose ambition it is to win favor in Lord Kiyomori's eyes, and who deck themselves out for him. You don't seem to realize how fortunate you are. You must have been born under a lucky star. Come, stop fretting and make yourself beautiful, for I can see that you are still young. As a woman the future lies before you, and if his lordship finds you pleasing, then everything will be yours for the asking."

Coloring deeply with shame, Tokiwa could only listen with her face buried in the folds of her robes.

Tokiwa felt that someone was standing behind her, but fear kept her from turning to see who it was.

"Tokiwa, what are you watching?"

It was Kiyomori speaking, and Tokiwa showed that she recognized him, but did not move and only replied: "I am looking at the cherry blossoms."

The room was vaguely luminous with moonlight. Kiyomori finally seated himself, but said nothing more, and Tokiwa continued to sit at the window. It was fortunate for her that the lamp had gone out, for there was no need for her now to shrink away from him to conceal her tear-wet face.

Not long after Tokiwa learned what her children's fate was to be, Kiyomori came to see her from time to time. There was nothing to prevent Tokiwa from forbidding him to come, but she shrank from saying what might wound him, for she was truly grateful to him for his magnanimity toward her; as time went on she no longer hated him, and even as she looked forward to Kiyomori's visits she was horrified by her own faithlessness.

"Oh, the wind is scattering your papers!"

Kiyomori reached out and rescued a slip of paper as it fluttered under a screen. He glanced at it rapidly in the moonlight and was about to restore it to its place on a writing-table when Tokiwa suddenly realized what was happening.

"That—that is—" she exclaimed, startled, and was beside him in an instant, holding out her hand in appeal.

"Do you object to my reading this?"

"No—not particularly."

"This isn't your writing. Who sent you this message?"

". . . ."

"A man apparently."

Tokiwa was at a loss to reply. She could not very well protest that she had written the verse, since the creases in the paper showed that it had been folded into the form of a letter; the handwriting, too, was obviously a man's.

"It is, as you say—a message. An odd-looking monk on the street handed it to Yomogi, telling her to give it to me, and then went away."

"Who is Yomogi?"

"She was my children's nursemaid. I left her in Yamato, where we went to hide, but she followed us and somehow found where we were. She says she met this monk on her way here and it was he that gave her this."

"Then you know who this monk is, don't you, or how else would he know that this girl is your maid?"

"I know him only slightly, for he was the monk who lived like a beggar in the ruins of the Willow-Spring Palace after the Hogen War."

"His name?"

"Mongaku, I believe."

Kiyomori scrutinized the sheet of paper once more. Sure enough, there it was, scrawled almost illegibly—*Mongaku*. The rest was in a large, bold hand.

Mongaku. How long was it since Kiyomori had last seen him—Morito of the Imperial Guards? He occasionally heard about him. Shinzei had once told him about the commotion he had created at Shinzei's mansion. This was the same wandering Mongaku—flitting here and there through the capital, sleeping in the open, without a place to call his own. Kiyomori recalled his old schoolmate with deep pity. To remember Mongaku was to link his name with Kesa-Gozen's and that tragic affair in which he had tossed away a brilliant future, all for love of a woman. They had called him a fool then, but—and Kiyomori suddenly reflected that he was no better than Mongaku had been. What would Mongaku say to him now?—"What difference is there between my folly when I was twenty and yours today, you—now in your forties? Which is worse? Who more culpable? You did right in sparing Tokiwa's three children, but what excuse have you to visit Tokiwa?"

Unquestionably, he was queasy, as timid as the Nose had accused him of being. Kiyomori lacked Mongaku's singleness of purpose, his passion. It was most evident in this affair with Tokiwa. Here he was smoldering to possess her and putting on a fine pretense of being noble!

"Mongaku, as he's called now, was once with the Guards. We were classmates at the academy. . . . Why do you think he sent this poem?"

What made him pursue such irrelevancies, Kiyomori reflected wryly as he continued: "What is he trying to tell you?—'The endless road over the mist-covered waste—'"

"I do not know. I have never met Mongaku."

"Hmm. . . . I believe I know what he means."

"What is he trying to say?"

"The Genji have been defeated. Yoshitomo's seed has been scattered throughout a hostile world, but there will be an end to that, and the Genji will triumph once more. This was meant to encourage you."

"Oh, what a fearful thing to say!"

"No, it isn't surprising. There are many who feel as Mongaku does. He believes I am Shinzei's successor and has a low opinion of me."

"No, no, my lord, you are mistaken. I find another meaning in this poem."

"What is it?"

"That 'mist-covered waste' is my heart. He is speaking of the sorrows of women. He is telling me to take courage."

"One could, if one wished, take it that way."

"I was so grateful to get this. I have been reading it over many times to myself all day. I have made up my mind to go on living, to make my way along that road through the 'mist-covered waste.' "

"Do you still sometimes think of doing away with yourself?"

"Yes, when my loneliness is too much for me, then even the whispering of these blossoms sounds like an invitation to die."

"Is it because you pine for your children?"

"That would be presumptuous—to you, their savior. I am resigned to my loss."

"Do you still grieve for Yoshitomo?"

"Ah, cruel words those!" Tokiwa cried, turning her brimming eyes on Kiyomori.

". . . Tokiwa!"

Kiyomori took Tokiwa in his arms. Tonight as never before he felt her body grow pliant and yielding. Desire swept over him like a flame, and he savagely sought her lips with kisses.

Terrified by the passion she had unloosed, Tokiwa struggled to escape him, but her half-stifled cries went unheard.

Inert, Tokiwa crouched among the silken folds of her robes, softly weeping, and did not even look up when Kiyomori rose to leave. A shower of white petals drifted in through the window and settled on her dark hair and garments, and still she sobbed on through the spring night.

A dark shape stole out from the gateway and began descending the slope.

"How did it come off, my lord?" whispered Bamboku, who soon joined Kiyomori.

". . . ."

"My lord, were you successful? You swore that tonight you would surely—"

Kiyomori stalked on in sullen silence. The Nose had never yet seen him in such a mood. Something unusual had happened. The Nose trailed alongside for some time without speaking, then suddenly began sniggering. Kiyomori glared at Bamboku, but the Nose broke into a noisy laugh.

"My lord, you may deceive others, but there's no fooling me. I'm an old hand at this game."

Kiyomori gave Bamboku a wide grin in the dark. "Stop this chattering of yours, you bother me."

"But haven't I been your friend all along in this affair, and didn't I take it to heart as though it were my own? You might at least tell a fellow whether you've had any success or not. I see nothing wrong in that."

"What a noisy fellow you are! This uproar is enough to drown out any tender feelings I may have. Leave me to walk alone quietly. Keep quiet, you!"

The Nose peered knowingly at Kiyomori's averted face and sighed audibly. He had heard enough to take in what had happened. He also detected the faint, clinging scent of perfume.

"Oy-y-y—!" The Nose suddenly hallooed in the direction of

a pine grove at the foot of the hill where some warriors waited in the dark with Kiyomori's carriage. Some soldiers and the ox-tender brought the vehicle out on the road.

Not even the Nose's voice, however, quite recalled Kiyomori to his senses. He had been like one in a trance, floating in ethereal regions with Tokiwa beside him, and even the present failed to dispel that vision entirely.

"No need to hurry. Let the ox set the pace," Kiyomori ordered through the closed curtains. He intended to enjoy fully the delicious sensation of driving home through the mists of this spring dawn, savoring his honeyed reveries. Did Tokiwa hate him, Kiyomori wondered. How would she greet him when they next met? Physical violence repelled him. He had had his fill of it in the last two wars. He had seen Yoshitomo's head strung up at the gates of the jail and those hundreds of beheadings. . . . The power of life or death over Tokiwa was his, but he had not intended to do violence to her. Her yielding was to take place as naturally as the tender unfolding of a bud, and it had been so. He had only been a suppliant for her love and had not ravished her. He could not have loved her less even if Yoshitomo were alive. . . .

Such thoughts revolved in Kiyomori's mind—exonerating, mitigating, and justifying what he had done that night. There was no denying what Red-Nose had said about him; he lacked daring or else why should he be thinking of Yoshitomo at this moment?

As Kiyomori's carriage left the pine-flanked avenue and swung west, one of the warriors walking behind emitted a hideous yell and fell to the ground with a thud. There was an outcry from the other soldiers, and a shout: "Here, scoundrel!"

A violent scuffling ensued as Kiyomori rose halfway in his seat and reached for a curtain, crying: "Ho, there, what's happened?"

He was about to peer out when a heavy body hurtled against the carriage and an armed figure with wild eyes gazed up at Kiyomori, waving a sword.

"Kiyomori of the Heiké, have you forgotten me?—Yoshihira of the Genji, Yoshitomo's son?"

A hand reached up to seize Kiyomori's sleeve, fumbled, lunged again, and wrenched away the silken blinds as Yoshihira was tossed clear of the carriage shafts. The ox suddenly plunged forward as a sword-cut laid open its haunches.

"Wait, Yoshihira!"

Yoshihira regained his feet and hurried to overtake the carriage, but halberds bristled at him from all sides.

Stunned, Red-Nose retreated among the trees along the highway, crying as he ran: "Yoshitomo's son—Yoshihira of the Genji!" He fled up a lane where the foot-soldiers of Rokuhara had their quarters, shouting all the while: "Help, cutthroats! Help, murderers!"

Figures armed with a variety of weapons appeared almost instantly and began milling about the narrow thoroughfare.

"Off to the crossroads, you there! Someone sound the alarm, sound the alarm!"

An armed band arrived at the crossroads, looked in all directions, and, seeing nothing, stared at one another foolishly.

"What imbecile's been shouting round here and rousing us from a good night's rest?"

But they soon discovered a halberd on the road; farther on, a wounded figure was stretched out, groaning, and a few steps farther a body lay still in the dust. The commotion spread; servants were sent out to inquire what had happened and horses were saddled.

The Nose grew apprehensive. Had he been overhasty in giving the alarm? Kiyomori's carriage, moreover, was nowhere to be seen. Was he safe? He could not possibly have made his way back to the rose court.

The fear-crazed bull tore onward with the carriage, and only stopped when it reached the end of a wall.

"Where are we?" Kiyomori shouted.

His bodyguard and the ox-tender finally came up panting and gasped:

"Lord Hitachi's residence, my lord!"

"Knock on the gates!"

The frenzied note in Kiyomori's voice caused the soldiers to beat on the gates resoundingly. The gates soon opened, and to the gatekeeper's astonishment the carriage was quickly dragged in as far as the main portico without a word of explanation. A servant soon appeared and, on hearing that it was the lord of Rokuhara, ran to tell his master.

Norimori, Kiyomori's younger brother, appeared almost at once. "What's this—at this hour, too?" he asked Kiyomori irritably.

"I was visiting Itogo and was attacked on my way home by some of Yoshitomo's followers."

"Yoshitomo's followers? How many?"

"Actually, just one."

"Just one?"

"Mmm . . ." Kiyomori mumbled in chagrin as he began to take stock of the situation. He had never experienced such panic as he had tonight. Yoshihira alone had terrified him beyond measure and left him completely shaken. What had caused this unreasonable fear, Kiyomori wondered, searching his mind. Yoshitomo's face as it appeared that day when his head hung at the gate to the East Jail kept flickering before his mind's eye as he started on his way home, and at the cry "Yoshitomo's son" the gruesome vision had identified itself with the face that glared between the curtains of the carriage. For an instant Kiyomori believed that he saw Yoshitomo's vengeful ghost. There was still more to explain that harrowing moment: he had come away from Tokiwa gloating lickerishly over his conquest, but under his triumph lurked a deep sense of guilt that had summoned up Yoshitomo's spirit. . . .

Norimori invited his brother to enter the house and soon was questioning him somewhat speculatively.

"Why should Yoshihira alone frighten you? You had an adequate bodyguard, didn't you?" he demanded.

"Something must be the matter with me," Kiyomori admitted.

"Had you been drinking?"

"No, not a drop."

"Where have you been?"

"I was visiting Itogo."

"Visiting Itogo? He's away tonight."

"And so I was turning home when I was attacked."

"Oh—?" Norimori replied, but his mocking eyes added: "You must be lying. I've been hearing of these visits to Tokiwa, you know."

In the meantime the Nose, who had finally traced Kiyomori's whereabouts, arrived.

As soon as he appeared, Kiyomori sprang to meet him, inquiring anxiously: "What's happened to the scoundrel?"

"Got away," the Nose replied. At this news Kiyomori hurriedly prepared to depart, saying that he would ride back in his own carriage. Bamboku at once went off to see that the carriage was made ready. Norimori eyed the departing figure with distaste. He had never liked or trusted Bamboku, and as an added precaution ordered ten of his own retainers to accompany Kiyomori.

The following morning Kiyomori woke later than usual; while he was putting on his court robes and preparing to leave for the Palace, his wife's maid appeared at his dressing-room to say: "My mistress wishes you to breakfast with her and is awaiting you, my lord."

Kiyomori started. "Breakfast?—It's only in the evening that— What does she want with me in the morning?" he replied, and hastily finished dressing as though more urgent matters required his attention.

"I'm late as it is, leaving for the Court. Councils and other business. . . . Tell the mistress I'll be back in the evening."

Ordering his carriage to be brought round to the main portico, Kiyomori quickly drove off. It was true that his days were a round of increasingly onerous duties. His appearance at the Palace was usually the signal for the higher officials and his subordinates to descend on him with demands for advice, confirmation, decisions. There was a certain awe mingled with the eagerness with which the courtiers approached him. Court circles had recently induced Kiyomori to accept a higher rank, one he formerly declined, and it was now generally acknowledged that Kiyomori held preponderating influence with the throne.

New influences had been at work since his father Tadamori's time, when a warrior occupying Kiyomori's post at Court would have scandalized the nobles and created hostility. Kiyomori's confident bearing, too, reflected the change. He was the new era; no decision could be made without him, or regarded as final without his consent. The warrior class, in short, had come into power, and Kiyomori's word was absolute in the conduct of state affairs.

Fujiwara Koremichi, known to be partial to the Heiké, was made Prime Minister at this time, and Kiyomori, who liked him as a man he could trust, insisted on submitting all important decisions to Koremichi. The appointment pleased Kiyomori further because the Prime Minister's daughter was Lady Shimeko, Tokiwa's former mistress.

"I was pleased to learn that you sustained no injuries."

Kiyomori was taken aback by this greeting when he unexpectedly met Koremichi in one of the Palace corridors.

"What's this?" he asked, mystified.

"You appear quite unshaken by it. In fact, that's quite like you. I heard you had an encounter with one of the Genji last night. That's the rumor, at least."

"Ah? Yes, of course, *that*," Kiyomori countered.

"Precisely."

"So it's all over the Court, is it?"

"Yes, it caused quite a sensation when they heard that your assailant was Yoshihira of the Genji. You will have to be more discreet about going out at night," Koremichi added with a meaningful look.

"These spring nights, you know, are—irresistible." Kiyomori laughed, but the warning took effect and Kiyomori returned straight home that night, only to be met by Tokiko's reproaches.

"At your time of life, too! I must ask you not to repeat this again—this stealing out at night by the rear gate of the rose court!"

"When did I ever—"

"Do you think I don't know what has been going on? Aren't Shigemori and our other sons the heads of families, too, with their own households and retainers, and with posts at Court?"

"But what does that have to do with me?"

"I don't see how you can go on pretending to be innocent. With everyone looking up to you as the master of Rokuhara, I really can't understand how you can go off every night with that disreputable Red-Nose to visit your enemy's widow. Don't you realize what a scandalous performance that is? Nor am I saying this out of jealousy."

"Yes, you begin to resemble her more and more."

"Do you think I am joking?"

"No, I'm listening to you quite seriously, and that's why I'm sighing. If you become more like my stepmother, just where am I going to find peace?"

"I have no objections whatever to your keeping a mistress in the rose court, or the other new apartments. There's not much that a wife can do when a man's fancy runs in that direction. But of all women—Yoshitomo's widow!"

"Enough. I understand."

"If only you promise not to behave as you've been doing, I won't say a word more. But how can you expect me not to be upset when I hear that one of the Genji tried to murder you?"

"Ah, so you too are one of those virtuous wives. . . . I begin to find something in favor of such women as the Lady of Gion."

"What are you mumbling to yourself now? If you refuse to take me seriously I shall ask your stepmother to come and speak to you herself. She can decide whether I'm being unreasonable or not."

"No, I humbly beg pardon, but don't for all the world ask her to come here."

"Then you'll give up this disgraceful carrying-on with Tokiwa, I take it? And you'll raise no objections if I speak to Itogo and Bamboku myself?"

4 1 0

"Whatever you wish," Kiyomori replied pettishly.

That night Kiyomori sat at the window of his wife's boudoir, gazing moodily at the misted moon. He had made a surprising discovery: Tokiko, so long preoccupied with the care of their children, who rarely questioned his coming and going, was inordinately jealous.

The following day Tokiko summoned her brother, Tokitada, to her room. It may have been the warm spring weather that caused it, but Tokitada thought his sister appeared rather flushed.

"Tokitada, I wish you to be very firm with Itogo. I have my husband's full consent to this."

"Itogo? What do you wish me to do?"

"Needless to say, it's about Tokiwa. Her three children are taken care of, and there's no reason why she should stay here in Rokuhara any longer."

"But that's hardly a matter for me to decide."

"But you're in charge of the Criminal Department here, and you can't very well say that you're not responsible for her. Tell Itogo to free her, or else send her to a nunnery and see that she takes the vows. See that there is an end to this disgraceful gossip."

"Ah, now I begin to understand. But, Tokiko, you must admit that you're partly to blame for Kiyomori's philandering."

"You think so, do you, Tokitada? You will do me the favor of telling me why you think I'm to blame."

"Well, Tokiko, you have without realizing it become old—let yourself fade, and with never a thought of how you might repair the ravages of the years in order to hold your spouse. What's happened was more or less to be expected."

"When a woman has had several children, it's only natural that she fades. Is it her fault that she is no longer—attractive?"

"No, Tokiko," Tokitada laughed, "you musn't lose your temper like that. I only speak to you with such frankness because you are my sister. I'm simply warning you that a woman must—no, a wife—must learn new graces as she grows older, if she doesn't wish to be cast off by her husband later on."

"Then what do you propose that I do?"

"Despite the years, evoke a subtle aroma of something fresh and exciting."

"I'm no dancing-girl, if that's what you mean!"

"Now that's exactly the kind of thinking common to shrews. What I say is true not only of Kiyomori, but of me. Anyway, when a man reaches his forties, he's ready to make his impression on the world, but suddenly discovers that his wife cuts a poor figure beside him."

"That's probably all you men find to talk about when you're together!"

"As a matter of fact, we do. The complaint seems to be general that, though we love our wives, they do age and stagnate."

"Pure egotism. . . ."

"You're right. We men are a selfish lot, but a man's ego must have a chance to stretch under his own roof before he can face the world and fight its battles. There's an old saying that a man begins to fall prey to doubts when he reaches his forties. We seem to be facing that stage just now, but Kiyomori is about to do great things, take my word for it."

"Do you expect me to believe that? You're another of those who encourage him in such delusions."

"No, you'll find that when he makes a name for himself, you, in spite of yourself, will have to assume those graces and accomplishments which will make you a fit mate, or otherwise fade into a nonentity when his star is rising."

"I've had enough of your talk. You will please leave me now."

"Just one thing more."

"What is it?"

"Wasn't it you who encouraged that merchant Bamboku to come here? It was a great mistake on your part to trust that vulgar fellow. I understand that the Nose has been performing the office of an intermediary in this affair with Tokiwa. As a matter of fact, that night when Yoshihira attacked Kiyomori, Norimori shook his head over the whole affair because that rascal was also there."

Tokitada made the best of his opportunity to tell his sister what he thought of her, and Tokiko retreated into silence, gazing resentfully at the faint smile playing on Tokitada's face. Quarrels between them took place from time to time and Tokiko usually came off the loser, but there was a tightening of her lips now which showed her determination to have the last word this time.

"Yes, I shall deal with Bamboku myself. Meanwhile, I wish you to see Itogo and find out what he intends to do with Tokiwa. You will please see that there is no delay."

"In any case, I understand."

"Not 'in any case'—I want it understood that those are my husband's orders," Tokiko said sharply, recalling as she did so the gossip about Tokiwa's undimmed loveliness. She, the wife, rudely shaken out of her complacency, realized that the world sympathized not with her, but with Tokiwa, whom she now examined with the critical eye of a rival.

That same day Red-Nose also was summoned by Tokiko.

"You may consider yourself unwelcome here. I order you to stop coming from now on."

"Yes—" the usually quick-witted Nose answered lamely, and after a pause added: "Have I done anything to offend you, my lady?"

"Your conscience can best tell you that."

"If I have displeased you, I can only right matters by cutting my throat."

"Do so, then. You know better than anyone else that you have good cause to do so. Here I've let you come and go in my house because I found you amusing, and all you've done is take advantage of me. You've been making a fool of my husband by abetting him in this intrigue with Tokiwa."

"Dear me, that—" the Nose exclaimed, clapping a hand to his head and struggling to remonstrate with Tokiko. But Tokiko had already risen to her feet and swept out of the room with an angry swish of her robes.

CHAPTER XXXI

THE CROW

amboku sent one of his clerks to the western section of the capital where a modest villa, built by some nobleman for his mistress, stood vacant. The clerk had been instructed to purchase the villa without delay. This took place on the day following Red-Nose's dismissal from Rokuhara, and by evening the house was ready for a new occupant. Bamboku had more than enough domestic help to accomplish this quickly, not to mention carriages, ox-carts, and handcarts on which were loaded bedding, kitchen equipment, boudoir furnishings, and the like. The Nose himself spent the entire afternoon arranging the garden to his taste, turning out rooms and even sweeping them, and by dark every screen stood in place in the main rooms; curtains depended where they belonged and even a small oratory and elegant writing-table had been installed in one of the smaller rooms.

"Well, well, this has been a busy day! Come to think of it, we haven't done badly at all. This should certainly please her," the Nose sighed contentedly, looking around at his handiwork by the light from a tall lampstand.

A gentleman alighted from his carriage, leaving it with his attendants in a small grove a discreet distance from the villa. It was Kiyomori.

"Excellent, excellent, indeed! Very quiet here, too. A nice garden, small—and a stream running through it," Kiyomori remarked as he passed down the halls, glancing here and there.

"How do you find this, my lord?"

"Very nicely done indeed, and all in such a short time."

"Those words, my lord, are ample reward for the Nose. I find myself in disgrace with her ladyship, and you do nothing but harry me with orders to get this done quickly and in utmost secrecy. . . . I haven't slept a wink these two nights and days."

"This will do for the present. Now what about Tokiwa?"

"That will have to wait until late tonight when the streets are deserted. I'll see that she's brought here then."

"I see. That's off my mind, then. Now I leave it to you to fix matters with people—explanations and the rest, you know. And you'll be sure that she needs nothing."

"Leaving already?"

"I shan't be around for some time perhaps—difficulties at home," Kiyomori admitted wryly, though he departed with a pleased air.

As he had himself predicted, Kiyomori did not appear at the villa again. It was easy to believe that Tokiko's vigilance would continue for some time to come. More than that, however, he could not see how his duties at the Court would end early enough for an evening's drive to the villa on his way home.

The Nose, however, was punctual in his morning and evening visits to the villa, where he made his regular inquiries after Tokiwa's health and comfort. He was solicitude itself.

"My lady, has Lord Kiyomori not yet paid you a single call? No? Tut-tut, a fickle one indeed!"

Tokiwa had not forgotten Yoshitomo. From her window she could see the outlines of Kurama Mountain and the sky over that distant spot where her children now were. The comfort which now surrounded her daily grew oppressive. No day went by that she did not kneel at her oratory before the image of the Kannon, praying for her children's safety, and commending them to the Kannon's care. It was a small silver image that Yoshitomo had given her in those happy days long ago, and to look on it was to recall not only her children, but Yoshitomo's face and his gentle ways. For Tokiwa the sweetest moments of the day were when she knelt at her prayers.

Yet there were times when she grew hot with shame and was tortured by self-recriminations. What caused her to sit and wait as though she expected someone to come? The villa lay at the edge of a wood by a little-used road on the edge of the capital, and the rare grinding of wheels on the road always startled her into an awareness that made every nerve taut with hope. Her heart would beat wildly, expectant, and then she would sink back once more.

Was she evil to feel as she did, she asked herself. What was this mad thing that possessed her? This aching body, these torturing thoughts from which she could find no escape? And often through the warm spring nights her tears wetted her pillow as her heart ached for her children and for Yoshitomo, while her body waited strangely for Kiyomori, whom she desired and hated.

"Is it true, Shika?"

"I swear to it, and that's why I came back as fast as my legs would carry me."

The Nose groaned, and then said: "Good! I'm glad you told me. I'll go myself to make sure. Now you lead the way."

"But there's no telling whether we'll find anyone in now."

"Well anyway, a little reconnoitering," the Nose said briskly, and with a great show of spirit he started out from his shop on Fifth Avenue.

The cherries were beginning to shed their petals and the leaf-buds to show red on the boughs. The wind smelled of April.

"Down that side-street—there," said Shika, pointing in the direction of an open field on whose farther side a settlement of small houses had lately sprung up.

"How many houses down that side-street?"

"The fifth or the sixth, but you can't tell anything from looking at it as you go by. It has a hedge and small wicket gate, but they're all pretty much alike in that row of Heiké houses."

"Yes, I know . . ." the Nose said, pinching his chin reflectively.

This was what his chief clerk, Shika, had heard while passing through the settlement: a nondescript soldier called Rokuro, living in one of the houses there, had taken in a lodger since early spring. The fellow in question seemed to be a young warrior, short but well-built, from some out-of-the-way place, who went about telling people that he was Rokuro's cousin from Tamba and looking for employment as a servant at Rokuhara. No post, the lodger said, was too menial. There seemed to be nothing wrong with him and people did not question his story until an elderly woman, who washed and mended for Rokuro, a widower, spread a tale of strange doings under Rokuro's roof. It was purely by chance, she claimed, that she saw Rokuro's cousin at breakfast one morning. There was nothing unusual in that, except that she had seen Rokuro waiting respectfully on his cousin; what was more, Rokuro gave his cousin the choicest bits of food, while he consumed cold morsels of whatever remained. An extraordinary performance among the half-starved common people.

When Shika heard this, he recalled that the Nose had several times mentioned his search for a "little fellow." Shika could only conclude that this was he—Yoshihira of the Genji. He had then gone to Rokuro's house, confirmed his suspicions, and flown back to the shop on Fifth Avenue with the news.

"Shika, you wait here in this field. Two of us would make it conspicuous."

"Standing here would be just as bad."

"Stroll around a bit then, while I take a look at that house myself."

Bamboku made off for a side-street. "Fifth—sixth—?" He came to a stop. Warriors were warriors, no matter how poor, and each house had its screening hedge and a small wicket gate, but no name-plate. "Let me see—" The Nose stood in a quandary, until he heard a high-pitched laugh. A tallish soldier accompanied by a rather short companion stepped out from a near-by gate and threw the Nose a searching stare as he passed him.

"Rokuro, did you see that fellow with the disagreeable eyes loitering in front of the house? Is he one of the neighbors?" Yoshihira inquired of his companion as they turned off the lane.

"No, he doesn't appear to be anyone from these poor quarters. He's more like a merchant from one of those large establishments on Fifth or Sixth Avenue."

"What makes you think so?"

"His air and the expensive clothes he wore."

"And did you see that magnificent red nose? A man with an evil eye I could see. You'd better be on your guard, Rokuro."

"I shall. He doesn't seem to be following us, though."

Rokuro kept looking back over his shoulder until the Nose was out of sight. But the pair did not notice Shika, who came strolling toward them at a signal from Bamboku. They kept on, skirting puddles and ruts, past the cluttered craftsmen's settlement of blacksmiths, tanners, makers of bows, dyers, and saddlers.

"Look, Rokuro, these people seem busier than they ever were before the last war."

"True, Rokuhara prospers and the sound of anvils and bellows is heard even at night."

"Arms for the Heiké?"

"Undoubtedly, now that the Genji have been driven out."

Yoshihira suddenly began to study the scene around him with a bitter look. Yes, he thought, what changes had taken place since the Genji had been driven from the capital! All the familiar sights seemed to have vanished; what he now saw and heard made him despair. He himself had been given up for dead when a rumor spread that he had been captured and executed. The truth was that he had escaped north to the country of Echizen and stayed in hiding until it was safe for him to return to Kyoto.

Rokuhara's influence could be seen everywhere—even in matters of fashion and dress Rokuhara was the arbiter. Not only court circles, but merchants and craftsmen sought Kiyomori's patronage. Life itself appeared to revolve around Rokuhara, the life-giving sun! Yoshihira fumed with helpless rage at the fickleness of men and their readiness to take advantage of the new order. This was the first shattering upheaval he had known in his twenty years, and he was convinced that this state of affairs would never end. The world seemed to hold out nothing for him now except the dedicating of his life to revenge—death to Kiyomori for the honor of the Genji.

Shortly after returning to the capital, Yoshihira chanced to meet Rokuro, formerly a soldier in Yoshitomo's employ. As Rokuro later related, he had been one of the many soldiers captured by the Heiké and later hired as a mercenary at Rokuhara. As a result of their unlooked-for meeting, Rokuro, overjoyed, offered to shelter Yoshihira, advising him to wait for a chance to take his revenge. Not long after that Rokuro heard of Kiyomori's nightly visits to Tokiwa, and with Yoshihira planned the attack on Kiyomori. Though the attempt on Kiyomori's life failed, Yoshihira was convinced that Kiyomori was an easy mark.

One other would-be assassin too was in hiding—Konno-maru, the young captain who had turned back in the snowstorm to find Yoritomo. Failing in his search, Konno-maru had returned to the capital and there kept close watch on Kiyomori's movements, seeking a chance to revenge his dead lord, Yoshitomo. In the meantime the gossip about Tokiwa reached his ears, and Konno-maru was filled with rage and contempt at her faithlessness.

Yoshihira and Rokuro were now on their way to meet Konno-maru at a saddler's shop. They had seen him several times before this in different parts of the capital, and their brief impassioned talks had always been of revenge.

"There, Rokuro, there it is. I see the saddler's shop."

"So it is, and he's at work, too. Shall we go and speak to him quietly?"

"Wait, remember what Konno-maru said—to go in as if we had business. He has some understanding with the saddler, but we'll need to be careful of the apprentices. We can't take any risks with them."

"Yes, he told me that repeatedly. Wait somewhere while I go and talk to him."

"I'll go over there, behind that shrine," Yoshihira replied, pointing to a spot on the farther side of a pond.

An ancient shrine stood in a small wood, ravaged and neglected. Yoshihira looked about him, at the tassels of wistaria which hung from the eaves of the shrine, at the branches of the surrounding trees and the golden globeflowers fringing the edge of the water. Konno-maru with Rokuro presently appeared and was about to kneel at Yoshihira's feet, when Yoshihira warned him sharply:

"Careful now, people might see us and suspect. We're no longer master and retainer, but outlaws. Come, sit here beside me."

Yoshihira pointed to a stump as he spoke. "Have you heard anything more, Konno-maru?"

"Nothing about Kiyomori, but did you know that Tokiwa has been moved very quietly to a villa on the edge of the capital?"

"So I hear, but I'm told that Kiyomori hasn't been there even once. I'm waiting for a chance to attack him when he goes there."

"I'm sure he's been on his guard since that night, but our chance is sure to come."

"Yes, sometime."

"Every day drags by filled with regrets. There's no day in which I do not think of my lord."

"The same is true of me when I think of my father."

"And what, sir, do you think of the lady, Tokiwa?"

"She?"

"Should we let her remain alive?"

"We'll not talk about her."

"No, that's not possible. How can we ignore the shame she has brought on the Genji by consenting to become Kiyomori's mistress?"

"Don't forget that because of her the three children have been saved, Konno-maru."

"That's what people say, but how do we know that she sacrificed herself for her children? I doubt it. I'm certain that ambition led her to forget your father and to give herself to Kiyomori."

"What makes you think so?"

"Because she refused to kill herself and follow her lord."

"That's asking too much. You judge her too harshly."

"Harsh, yes, but you must remember, sir, that I grew up in the service of your father," Konno-maru remonstrated. "I was his most trusted retainer and carried his messages to Tokiwa when she was with Lady Shimeko. I was often present when my lord was with his lady. I know how much he loved her. . . . Do you think I can forgive her for what she has done? The war is over, certainly, but what is to keep me from avenging my lord, whom she has betrayed?"

"So, Konno-maru, you intend to kill her?"

"Being a woman, I doubt that she'd have the courage to kill herself. It would be an act of mercy if I did it and wiped out the disgrace she has brought on the Genji."

"No, wait," Yoshihira interposed hastily, "you'll spoil my chances of getting at Kiyomori if you do that."

"No, I'll bide my time. I had no chance when she was living in Itogo's house. When you're through with Kiyomori, I'll deal with Tokiwa," Konno-maru replied bitterly.

In spite of himself, Yoshihira was torn by conflicting emotions. His dead father—this unendurable affront to the Genji, the disgrace.

". . . but not right away. Kiyomori first. Not until you hear that Kiyomori has got what he deserves."

Yoshihira and Konno-maru fell silent, when a sudden crashing overhead brought fragments of bark showering down on them. They looked up, startled. A large crow that had been about to alight on the shrine roof flapped wildly as it flew to a branch higher up. On the roof the two spied a figure—a monk. The ragged shape craned down at them and smiled, showing a row of white teeth through his beard. There was something both friendly and mocking in the quick disinterested look he gave them. Yoshihira, Konno-maru, and Rokuro felt their hair stand on end; they grew pale. Had he overheard them? Their first impulse was to kill the monk, but the figure on the roof seemed to sense this and called down to them:

"I had nothing to do with this. That was the crow. You need not be araid of me."

He had undoubtedly heard every word of what they had been saying, for he sat with his back flattened against the triangular sidewall of the gable; not even the crow had seen the monk in his cramped position on the projecting roof.

Yoshihira at length smiled wryly and motioned to him. "Your reverence, I have something to ask you. Won't you come down here?"

"I'm busy, that's why I'm up here. If you have something to ask me, speak to me from where you are. I can hear you quite well."

"What are you doing up there?"

"Can't you guess? Mending this roof."

"Thatching it?"

"Yes, I'm a traveling monk and I've been living in this old shrine. The sanctuary is always flooded when it rains. That crow must have been scratching around in the thatch, too. A fine day, isn't it?" The monk laughed. "I've been up here all morning, working. What are *you* doing there?"

"..."

"Never mind, you needn't tell me, but since we meet so unexpectedly, let me tell you a few things. You must think I'm only a disreputable monk whose advice means nothing to you, but you're young—so very young that I can't help pitying you. Take better care of your precious lives. Don't forget that the future is still before you."

"What do you take us for?"

"How can I tell? Why should I know?"

"You must have overheard us."

"Was it something that you didn't want me to hear? Very careless of you. A good thing it was I—I'm as harmless as that old crow."

"Here, come down. It was unfortunate that you overheard us. We're not going to let you get off alive."

The monk chuckled with merriment, neither mocking nor admonitory. The narrowed eyes turned down on the youths seemed fondly protective.

"I see him. I recognize him now—that reckless young warrior who pursued Kiyomori's son from the Taikenmon Gate to the canal. And the world has so changed that he hasn't even the spirit to capture the crow on this roof!"

"If you refuse to come down, I'll come up and get you myself."

"Try it—you'll only be wasting your time. I heard you talking, but your secrets are safe with me. I've no more intention of reporting you to Rokuhara than that crow. My sympathies, in fact, are with the defeated and that's why I want to talk to you, young man, who still have the world before you. Your father and brothers are dead and the Genji scattered, but why must you throw away your life? Out of you will come future generations. Guard that priceless life of yours! Forget those foolish plans for revenge. You can't change this world by killing one man. O fool, fool that you are!

Can't you see that that helpless woman, submitting quietly to her agonies for love of her children, is far more courageous than you?"

The three youths under the tree fell silent. The light sifting through the treetops showed that evening was near, and a red glow played over the seated figures.

"See, see how the sun has moved onward while we talked. Nothing can stop it in its course. Prayers cannot halt the revolving of nature. It is the same with human life. Victory and defeat are one in the vast stream of life. Victory is the beginning of defeat, and who can rest safely in victory? Impermanence is the nature of all things of this world. Even you will find that your ill fortunes too will change. It is easy to understand the impatience of the old, whose days are numbered, but why should you young ones fret when the future is yours? Why try to dispel your petty dejection by a rash act that can only hasten death?"

"There's the crow again. It's about time you young men went back. Better still, leave the capital far behind you. And it's time for me to get down from this roof," said the monk, coming to his feet.

The three youths stood up as though spellbound by what they had heard, and Yoshihira ran quickly up to the shrine. "Wait, wait, your words move me. I shall come tomorrow morning to listen to you once more. I shall think on what you just said. But, your reverence, tell me who you are."

"You must pardon me for refusing; my name will only disgrace me."

"You are someone out of the ordinary. What connections do you have with the Genji?"

"None. Nor with the Heiké. I am what you see, only a traveling monk. Let us meet here tomorrow morning."

"But at least tell us who you are."

"No, all I have done is preach to you self-righteously, talked down to you for being so foolish when I at your age made such a fool of myself. I was an even more despicable fool than any of you. I was carried away by an infatuation for another man's wife

4 2 4

and became the laughing-stock of the capital. Only death can wipe away my guilt, but I have spent years at the Nachi Falls, expiating my sin."

"You? Then, you're Mongaku!" Yoshihira exclaimed, craning to see better. But Mongaku had vanished, and he searched in vain. Only a crow stood perched on the gable end, preening his feathers and peering up from time to time at the evening stars.

The three walked away, silent and thoughtful, until Yoshihira shook himself impatiently in self-reproof. Why should the words of that monk cause him to waver? Why had he let himself be carried away for an instant by impractical suggestions? There was no denying, however, that the monk spoke the truth, for men and all earthly things changed from moment to moment.

"He's right—there's no denying it. Even as we walk, the stars keep appearing and the night grows darker. Konno-maru, what do you think? What have you decided?"

"Nothing has changed for me. I was rather taken by what Mongaku said, but those are the teachings of the Jodo Buddhists. I'm a warrior, after all, and a follower of Lord Yoshitomo. Why should the words of a monk change me in an instant?"

"You're right, we were born to the name and calling of the warrior class."

"We cannot deny what we are. Let Mongaku say what he will about the universe and the impermanence of all things. Life is short and the warrior's honor everything."

"Well said! The warrior has his own way of valuing his life," Yoshihira whispered half to himself as he turned his face up to the stars. He felt sure of himself once more. The wind blew on his brows as he remarked cheerfully:

"Well, Konno-maru, until we meet again!"

They stood at the crossroad of the settlement once more. Konno-maru started away and then turned back to ask: "What will you be doing tomorrow morning?"

"Tomorrow morning? What do you mean?"

"Didn't you say you were coming to meet Mongaku?"

"Not that. What is the use of listening to him when we've made up our minds? We'd better be on the lookout for Kiyomori."

"And more reason for me to remember that Tokiwa must not be allowed to live much longer. I'll take care of that. Another time, then," Konno-maru said, and made his way back to the saddler's shop.

Yoshihira and Rokuro also went home, prepared their evening meal by the light of a candle, and when they were through eating, settled down—one to a book, the other to clearing up the remains of their meal. A little later they locked up and soon were asleep.

Toward dawn, when the eaves softly dripped with dew, dark shadows crept up to the house and surrounded it. Warned by Red-Nose, Kiyomori had dispatched three hundred soldiers from Rokuhara. Bamboku was not among them, but his clerk Shika accompanied the captain, guiding the soldiers to this spot. A commotion broke out as the soldiers attacked Rokuro's house and battered down the door. The entire neighborhood awoke with cries of "Earthquake!" "Fire!" There were shouts: "We've got him!" But the soldiers soon discovered that they had the wrong man, for Yoshihira crept out through a privy, cleared a hedge, and made his way to the roof of an adjoining house.

"There he is—my bow!" the captain shouted. "Look, there he goes, there!"

Yoshihira fled, scrambling from roof to roof, and escaped in the ensuing confusion.

Not until ten days later was Yoshihira captured; he was found asleep near a shrine outside the capital and caught only after fighting off his pursuers. Dragged to Rokuhara, he was brought before Kiyomori, whom he refused to acknowledge by more than a nod and a defiant: "Had I been allowed to go out to meet you with three thousand men as I proposed, when you were on your way back from Kumano, I am certain you would have changed positions with my dead father." Then he added with scorn: "Furthermore, had my father been the victor, he would never have done what you have—taken possession of the woman that another loved!"

Kiyomori's attendants and soldiers held their breath, waiting for an angry outburst from Kiyomori, who merely continued to gaze at the youth quietly. Kiyomori could not find it in his heart to hate this boy. Chance only, he reflected, had given him the victory on that day of snow. He also had a son and he could not help comparing Yoshihira with Shigemori.

That night, before Yoshihira was led to the execution ground, Kiyomori ordered wine to be served with the youth's last meal. The story was later repeated that Yoshihira had refused to touch either food or drink given him by his captors, and later when his body was examined, they found that the stomach had shriveled to a small sac, showing that Yoshihira had not eaten for many days before his capture.

CHAPTER XXXII

THE STREET OF THE OX-DEALERS

Yomogi, Yomogi, where are you?"

The road near the gate to Sixth Avenue, known as the Street of the Ox-Dealers, was a thoroughfare lined with the huts of the poor and already buzzing with early summer flies. It was warm enough to cause people to perspire lightly, and the stench of human waste and animal droppings was wafted along on the wind.

"Is it you, good Mongaku?"

Yomogi's sharp eyes picked out a shape moving through the crowds. Mongaku made his way through the throng in his worn sandals. He had neither his hat nor his pilgrim's staff.

"Here we meet again!"

"Yes, a third time."

"Yes, I first met you, crying, on the road from Yamato, as you searched for your mistress, Tokiwa."

"Then again early this month at Kiyomizu Temple on the Kannon's holy day."

"Yes, by the grace of Buddha! And have you been at the chapel again in your mistress's stead?"

"A special prayer to the Kannon, for which I must visit the chapel for one hundred days, and I've only begun."

"Why do you always go in her place? What keeps your mistress from going herself?"

"Because—" Yomogi began, giving Mongaku a reproachful look, "how can you expect me to answer such a question?"

"How?—"

"Of course, she's afraid to stir out of the house, even into her garden. She doesn't want to see people, nor to have people see her."

"She'll make herself ill if she goes on like that. Something is worrying her to death. That poem I once sent her by you—did she see it?"

"Yes, I gave it to her when she was still at Itogo's. Let me see, it went like this—" Yomogi said, repeating the verse.

"That's it. How well you've remembered it!"

"She has it on her writing-table all the time, you see."

"Here, this won't do. There comes a whole string of oxen."

Mongaku swept Yomogi up under one arm and drew to the side of the road. Behind the houses lining the road were fenced-in commons where oxen and horses were left to graze. Dealers were bringing their livestock to market today. Another herd went past, when Yomogi suddenly clutched at Mongaku and tried to hide behind him. A rough-looking man, driving oxen before him, gave

Yomogi a hard, searching look as he passed and then turned to
stare at her once more.

"Who's that man?"

"That's my mistress Tokiwa's uncle. . . ."

"Ho, that rascal, that fellow who tried to get a reward from
Rokuhara after lying to her and bringing her and her three children back to the capital?"

"He's a fiend. Those eyes make me shiver. Do you suppose
he recognized me? What shall I do if he did?"

Mongaku, still a traveling monk, unattached to any monastery
or temple, stayed much of the time in Kumano or at the Nachi
Falls, visiting the temples of other sects when it pleased him, and
when inclination led, returned to the capital. None of his friends
in the capital had seen him for three years, until Mongaku suddenly appeared in Kyoto one day and was astounded to hear that
his old school friend Kiyomori was in power. Kiyomori's rise to
eminence filled Mongaku with misgivings; he found himself taking a proprietary interest in him; people seemed to regard Kiyomori favorably. Would his friend of academy days follow in the
footsteps of his notorious predecessor, Shinzei? This was grotesque, incredible! Was it possible that Kiyomori, that "thick-
skulled fellow" as his former schoolmates called him, had actually
become the man of the hour? What a farce indeed if he over-
reached himself! Yet Mongaku could not suppress his secret satisfaction at seeing how the once despised warriors were now welcomed by the aristocrats as equals.

"Good Mongaku, which way are you going?" Yomogi asked,
still clinging to his arm. Her terrified eyes gazed around fearfully
at the noonday crowd.

Mongaku laughed. "Still frightened by that ox-dealer, are
you?"

"I'm afraid he'll follow me—worried for my mistress."

"You're as loyal as my friend Asatori is to his lord."

"Asatori—the caretaker of the Willow Spring?"

"Yes, don't you remember how you often came to him to get
water?"

"I've often wondered what became of him."

"He lives here in a mean little hut."

"Why, I didn't know that! Are you quite sure?"

"Last year he crossed to Shikoku to visit his lord in his lonely exile. I sometimes meet him on the streets, playing his flute. An odd fellow."

"Oh no, he is the kindest of persons. He was to me, to everybody."

"How old were you at the time?"

"Twelve."

"So you're sixteen now?"

"Yes, sixteen . . ." Yomogi replied, suddenly blushing. "Are you on your way to see him now?"

"No, I was going to pray at the grave of an old woman I once knew."

"Who was this old woman?"

"What a lot of questions you insist on asking!—This old woman was Kesa-Gozen's mother."

"And who was Kesa-Gozen?"

"You would hardly know. You weren't even born when she was alive. Her mother killed herself when Kesa-Gozen died, and I, who did not deserve to live, am still alive. My daily prayers and my monthly visits to her grave are not enough to wash away my guilt. I must do good in this world before I can hope to be forgiven. Yomogi, tell me what I should do."

"I don't know what you're talking about, good Mongaku."

"No, I dare say you don't. I was just muttering to myself. While we're talking like this we may as well call on Asatori. I can't say whether he'll be in or not."

The two made their way along a littered, malodorous lane where flies rose up in clouds at every step they took, and as many children seemed to obstruct their path—children afflicted with running eyes or sores; there was not one but was suffering from boils or maladies of one kind or another, and from filthy hovels came the drunken roars and high-pitched screams of quarreling couples.

"I'm sure this is the right one," Mongaku said, stopping in front of a hut. The roof was weighted with stones, the eaves sagged unevenly and the plaster had fallen from the walls in some places, revealing a framework of bamboo. But a straw mat hung from the lintel in lieu of a door; some bamboo grass and other plants grew under the window. There were signs of someone having swept round the entrance.

"Is Asatori at home?" Mongaku called, lifting the mat as he stepped inside. A man sat by the window reading from a book placed on a wooden crate. He looked round.

"Ah, come in, come in!" he cried, and stared at Yomogi, who stood behind Mongaku. Asatori's eyes widened with astonishment. They had not seen each other since they last met on the ruins of the Willow-Spring Palace. What memories they had of kindliness and warmth when the world was darkened by violence and brutality!

"Why, Asatori, I didn't know you lived here!"

"How you've grown, Yomogi! I hardly recognized you."

"You've changed, too, Asatori. You look older."

"Have I changed much?"

"Not very much. Are you no longer the caretaker of the Willow Spring?"

"No, but at heart I shall remain the caretaker until I die."

"Yes, and that reminds me of what people say about the Willow-Spring Palace. They say you can hear ghostly music on the ruins every night and that the spirit of the exiled Emperor goes wandering about among the trees. People are afraid to go near the place."

"And your mistress's house was not burned down that time; but it must have been in this last war?"

"Yes, not only burned, but we had to escape for our lives."

"You must have had a very hard time."

"It wasn't so much me, but my mistress and the little ones."

"I hear all kinds of gossip from an ox-dealer—a man of some importance round here, called Tomizo."

"Oh, do you know that fiend, Asatori?" Yomogi said with a shudder.

The two continued to talk eagerly, forgetting that Mongaku was even there. Left to his own devices, Mongaku took up the book Asatori had been reading and began leafing through it. Curious—what was Asatori doing with books on medicine? Mongaku slipped out volume after volume from the crate. All medical treatises. A queer fellow and even odder than he had thought him to be. What was Asatori up to now? A court musician turned menial —caretaker of the Willow Spring; he had once surprised Mongaku by telling him that he had joined a company of strolling puppeteers, but here he was, studying these learned tomes. Mongaku could scarcely get over his amazement.

"Have you two at last finished talking?" Mongaku asked, chuckling.

"I'm afraid, Mongaku, I've been very rude."

"Asatori—"

"Yes?"

"Are you studying medicine?"

"Yes, I try to when I find time."

"Then you weren't a puppeteer after all?"

"No, no, let me explain. I can't make a living yet by practicing medicine, so I make ends meet by playing my flute for puppet shows and giving lessons on the bell and drum. In fact, I do a number of things of that kind."

"Hmm—you're a many-sided fellow."

"That's true; there are so many things I want to do that I'm always at my wits' end."

"Why don't you go back to the Court and take up your calling as a musician?"

"If the Court were not what it is, I would."

"Then you think of eventually becoming a physician?"

"I hadn't thought of that exactly, but there are so many around me here, poor and ignorant, that I thought better of becoming a monk like you and decided to practice the art of healing."

433

"Hmm—I see; just like you to think of that. A good thing, and you're the one for it. The aristocrats and the rich can afford physicians and medicines, but the poor just wait for death. I doubt there's one in a hundred here who can pay for a physician."

"Quite so. I visit these hovels and can always be sure of finding someone who's ill. There's no hope for these people. When there's not enough food to feed even the strong, the sick are abandoned in the hills or taken down to the river to die."

"I may be losing to you, Asatori."

"What do you mean?"

"I mean your capacity for love, your love for your fellow beings. You make me feel very humble."

"Nonsense, Mongaku. You must remember that I was born to the profession of music and perform expertly on almost any instrument, but I'm no scholar like you and must wrestle with each of these books."

"I'm afraid you have great difficulty studying by yourself. I'll tell you of a good physician who can teach you."

"How grateful I should be! But do you know someone willing to help me?"

"Yes, there's a famous scholar of the Academy of Physicians. He's quite old now and lives in retirement not far from the capital. You will take a letter from me and find out how he feels about teaching you."

Mongaku without loss of time drew an inkstone to him and wrote a letter of introduction.

While Mongaku and Asatori were absorbed in talk, Yomogi sat by, completely ignored, worried by thoughts of Tomizo. She began to speak anxiously about going home.

"Asatori can take you home," Mongaku said, reassuringly. "I would myself, but I might get into trouble with the soldiers from Rokuhara. Asatori, you'll go with Yomogi, won't you?"

"No trouble at all," Asatori replied, as Yomogi's anxious face suddenly dimpled.

The three started out together and Mongaku parted from them at a crossing near the Street of the Ox-Dealers.

As Yomogi and Asatori approached the deserted suburbs, Yomogi noticed two men following them, but she thought nothing of them, since neither was Tomizo.

"That house over there," she said, pointing, "is my mistress Tokiwa's," and stopped abruptly, disappointed to find that the walk had been so short.

"Good-by until another time," she called, scampering off, and soon vanished inside the gates of the villa.

CHAPTER XXXIII

A WHITE PEONY

An intermittent lowing came from a corner of the pasture where the market had been held at noon. A wakeful bull called to his mate through the dark, and his restless trampling made the surrounding blackness seem even blacker. The only light visible came from a hut where some men were gambling. The narrow space reeked with smoke from the lamp and the fumes of wine, and the chinking of coins could be heard above the guttural voices. A few shopkeepers among the cowherds and professional gamblers there were calling for higher stakes. Sweat rolled down their intent faces and their eyes bulged as they followed each roll of the dice.

Tomizo grunted. "Still at it? What's the use anyway?—Not done with it yet?" Sullen and angry at his losses, he sprawled against the thin boards of the wall, his head propped on a wooden headrest. Pulling himself up from his recumbent position, Tomizo reached for a wine-jar and muttered: "Wonder why everything I've done lately has come to nothing. I just can't understand it. . . ." Gulping down the contents of the flask, he shook his head slowly and writhed, spasmodically slapping his thigh, unable to escape some inner torment. Tokiwa had started his chain of bad luck, he reflected. He'd been a fool, reporting her to Rokuhara. He'd got nothing out of that—not even a penny. Worse than that, they'd jailed him and then let him out after beating him within an inch of his life. He would have fought his tormentors had there been some way of getting back at Kiyomori, but that was not to be thought of. And when he complained to his acquaintances about this, they had jeered at him and only put him in a rage. He had also been hearing that Tokiwa lived somewhere in the capital, enjoying all the luxuries and prestige attached to her position as Kiyomori's mistress.

Wine, women, gambling—he had bit by bit frittered away all that he owned. The last of his herd from his farm had been sold at the market only that morning. He had gambled again after that to recoup his losses and found himself even deeper in debt.

"Lend me some money until next market-day," he demanded, but got no response. "Hey, you'd better not insult me! I have a niece—Tokiwa—and she's worth more to me than all the money you've got there," he snarled, and then lay down once more.

When he woke the next morning, Tomizo found himself alone. Brushing away the flies that crawled on his face, he got up, yawned, and then started out to the sunlit pasture.

"Hey, Kamé, what about yesterday? Didn't I pay you for it, too?"

Kamé, a cowherd whom Tomizo had sent the previous day

to follow Yomogi and Asatori, emerged from a shed, making excuses.

As the next market-day approached, Tomizo needed some money and started off to Mibu villa, where Tokiwa lived. At the servants' entrance he announced himself, saying: "I'm your mistress Tokiwa's uncle. I've come to see how she is. Tell her I'm here."

A servant took the message and went away. As Tomizo waited, Yomogi, carrying a bunch of flowers, walked into the courtyard; on seeing him, she was transfixed with horror.

"Oh, Yomogi, quite a beauty you're getting to be! I've just told them who I am. I also want you to tell your mistress I've come to see her. Hmm—a nice, quiet little place you have here."

"She's not in—she's away just now."

"What?"

"My lady isn't in."

"Think you can fool me, do you?"

"But it's true; she isn't here now!"

"You little hussy! What's this you're trying to tell me? I'm her uncle. Go tell your mistress I'm here!" Tomizo glared at the cringing girl.

The servant who had taken Tomizo's message reappeared just then, accompanied by an elderly woman. "The lady has been ill for some time," the latter said placatingly.

"Sick? All the more reason to see her. I can't leave now without seeing her," Tomizo insisted, seating himself at the entrance and showing no sign of going.

Yomogi in the meanwhile vanished. Her first thought had been to fetch Mongaku, but she could not think where to look for him. "Asatori!" had been her next thought, but she doubted that he would be a match physically for Tomizo. Then it flashed across her mind—Bamboku!

When she arrived at the shop on Fifth Avenue she found Red-Nose there.

"Upon my word, this is terrible! How frightened your mistress must be!" he exclaimed and, calling for his horse, Bamboku galloped off for the villa at Mibu.

At the sound of neighing at the gates, Tomizo came to his feet in alarm. But Bamboku, when he caught sight of Tomizo, stared at him woodenly.

"Here, you, whoever you are—come here a moment." He motioned to the ox-dealer; pressing some money into the quaking Tomizo's palm, Red-Nose slapped him resoundingly on the back. "Leave off this, man! Stop behaving like a fool. If it's money you want, you shall have it. If it's wine, that, too. Come straight to Bamboku's on Fifth Avenue. Yes, I'm very easy to talk to," he said, suddenly cackling with laughter.

Overcome by Bamboku's magnificent gesture, Tomizo stammered: "No harm intended—just came here to see my dear niece. . . . Wasn't going to tell her anything unpleasant, but the lord of Rokuhara is treating her badly, isn't he? Yes, he's doing very badly by her."

Mumbling incoherently, Tomizo carefully tucked away the money and then left. But a moment after he stepped outside the gate, a ghastly shriek went up. The Nose, who had been standing just inside the gate, ran out with a shout and looked up and down the road. Nothing was to be seen but the roofs of the near-by farms enveloped in blue mist under the evening stars.

"Bring torches—a lantern will do! Hurry!" Red-Nose shouted as he stooped to stare at Tomizo's headless corpse. By the light of several torches, he peered at the surrounding ground, where the stones and grass glistened moistly with blood.

Who murdered Tomizo? Very neat work! Bamboku shook his head, puzzled. The servants, however, nodded to one another significantly. A demon—only a demon could have done it.

"No ordinary swordsman could do that, and with no ordinary sword," Bamboku muttered. "What's more, the head's gone. . . . A most unpleasant business, this," he reflected. Unperturbed, he stared fixedly at the light in the lampstand. Then, looking round at the servants gathered in the room, he said: "Yes, we'll keep this very quiet. Your mistress is not to hear about this, you understand?"

Just then Yomogi arrived back with a gruesome tale.

"Just as I got to the stream and was about to cross the bridge, I thought I heard a waterfowl splashing below and looked, and down on the bank I saw a man stooping to wash blood from his sword, and beside him on the ground was a man's head! I was rooted to the spot. Then he looked up and gave me a hideous glare. It may have been the moonlight that made him appear so, but I'm sure I've never seen such a frightful face in all my life. And I ran home as fast as I could. . . . But, oh, I can't forget that look!"

"What was the fellow wearing?"

"A hunting cloak and warrior's cap."

"A warrior? . . . How old did he appear to you?"

"He seemed quite young—barely in his twenties, I should say."

"That makes it even more difficult to guess," Bamboku mumbled, folding his arms.

When told that the youth she had seen was probably Tomizo's murderer, Yomogi's face grew blank with horror and amazement; then her eyes filled and a tear stole down her cheek. At this the other servants stared at her, puzzled. "What are you crying about, Yomogi? He's your mistress's uncle, to be sure, but good riddance. We're better off with that rascal dead. The mistress should be relieved to hear of this. There's no reason for you to cry about him."

But Yomogi shook her head, saying, "I wasn't crying about him. I've been going to the Kannon Chapel every day, and I'm sure the Kannon heard my prayers. It came to me suddenly that that young man was the Kannon in disguise, and for no reason at all that made me cry."

Bamboku, however, continued to sit with arms folded, shaking his head over the affair. To his way of thinking, it took something more than the Kannon's intervention to bring about what had happened. Other matters were also troubling him. For one:

4 4 0

Kiyomori had not shown up since that time he inspected the villa; the Nose was responsible for Tokiwa. What caprice of Kiyomori's was this, anyway, Bamboku reflected, aggrieved. He was also vexed. Not only had Tokiko forbidden him to set foot in Rokuhara, but what did Kiyomori mean by keeping his distance, leaving Red-Nose marooned, so to speak?

Bamboku's calculations had somehow gone amiss. During the last uprising he had staked all his worldly possessions, his reputation, and even his life on Kiyomori's winning. All his efforts now seemed to have been wasted. It was about time he got something in return for all he had risked, yet all his plans seemed to have foundered on this affair with Tokiwa, and with every swift-flying spring day that went by, Red-Nose was increasingly tortured with anxiety. There was no telling when Kiyomori would pay him a visit, and if he, Bamboku, went to call on him—but he had been forbidden Rokuhara, so how was he to see Kiyomori? This posed another question. The Nose looked up suddenly from his contemplation of the lampstand and turned to Yomogi and the servants to ask: "What is your mistress doing this evening?"

"She is probably copying the sutras, as is her custom."

"Well, then, I'll go without disturbing her. See that none of you give her any inkling of what's happened."

Bamboku stepped down from the veranda and shuffled into his sandals, stopping long enough to peer through a screening hedge at the light burning in Tokiwa's room. He could see her through the blinds, sitting at her writing-table. Like a white peony, the Nose mused, wasted on the spring night. He sighed. A pity that such a priceless blossom should thus go to waste. . . . If Kiyomori no longer dared to come because of his wife, then there was no reason why Red-Nose shouldn't have Tokiwa for himself, he thought voluptuously. That at least would be some compensation for all his trouble. . . .

Several days later Red-Nose started out for Rokuhara. At the gate facing on the river he slipped a small bribe to the guard, whom he knew, and waited among the trees in the rose court for Kiyomori's return.

"My lord, a word with you," Bamboku called at last, quaking inwardly.

Kiyomori stopped and looked round. "You, Nose?—I thought you were a huge toad out there. So it's you! What kept you from showing that nose of yours around here lately? You ill-mannered wretch," he grumbled.

"This is more than I ever hoped for. I hardly expected to find you in this frame of mind," Bamboku replied.

Kiyomori began to laugh. "What do you mean by that?"

"This is no laughing matter, sir," Bamboku protested. "You surely know that the mistress ordered me from the house?"

"And what of it?"

"How am I to come here, then? And who was the reason for that, I ask you, sir."

"Imbecile! Her orders have nothing to do with me. If Tokiko forbids you to come here, stop coming by the women's gate, man!"

"But she told me most emphatically that you'd ordered it."

"*I* give such an order? Women always say whatever they please. Only take care that she doesn't see you. Here, you haven't come for over a month, and not a word to me about Tokiwa in the meantime. You good-for-nothing! You lazy, weak-livered scoundrel!"

"Ah, a great oversight on my part. You are more lenient than I deserve, sir!"

"Unusual, too, for one so habitually brazen as you. Tell me, is Tokiwa all right? She hasn't been ill since and is getting on comfortably?"

In spite of his bantering, Kiyomori's inquiries after Tokiwa held more feeling than his words displayed. "There's something else I want to say, but we'd better go in," he said, leading the way to his room. Arrived there, he began questioning the Nose at greater length about Tokiwa, deriving, it seemed, some secret comfort from Bamboku's replies. Bamboku sensed, however, that it was not Tokiko's prohibitions, but something of a highly engrossing nature that kept Kiyomori from visiting Tokiwa, though it was obvious that Kiyomori's duties at Court left him little time for a life of his own. And to illustrate what it was that kept him so occupied, Kiyomori related how one of his captains had recently returned from a successful expedition against some privateers and brought the pirate chief with them. Kiyomori had questioned the pirate at length and had been impressed by his wide knowledge of the outer world, and from him heard tales of the glorious Sung civilization.

Kiyomori was now captured by a dream, no airy fancying, but a scheme for trade. He was convinced of its practicability— a plan for enhancing the arts and literature of the people through commerce with China. The vision had grown, taken hold of him to the exclusion of Tokiko; and even Tokiwa very nearly was put out of mind. The scheme now absorbed him with a consuming fervor, and the sensual passion of a moment shriveled and crumbled away before it.

In his father Tadamori's time, the Heiké had had large feudal holdings in western Japan—Harima, Bingo, Aki, and Higo among them—and Tadamori had traded in secret with ships from China; but such commerce as existed was only on a scale that fitted with Tadamori's plans for insuring the fortunes of his house. Kiyomori now dreamed of the resumption of trade with China on a far more ambitious scale.

". . . As you can see for yourself, Bamboku, the capture of those pirates was priceless to me. Look here, Red-Nose, turn your eyes across the seas and consider the vast prospects of trade there."

"This talk is taking a most unexpected turn. Think what wealth this will mean for the country if we bring in goods from China. As for me—I shall indeed become a merchant prince! No, I don't see how I can go on plodding like this any more," Bamboku ruminated.

"But the point is this—" Kiyomori continued, "we must find a way to bring ships from China directly to the capital. There's not much use in having them put in 'way down there in Kyushu."

"Quite right. If it's known that they're loaded with merchandise, the pirates will lie in wait for them. That's why it hasn't been possible to trade with them from here. With a good port and the Inland Sea cleared of pirates, we should be able to get the ships through to here."

"Well, Bamboku, I'm having the matter looked into and you might in the meantime think it over."

"That I shall. I can see how this is going to be the work of a lifetime. You might, sir, in your leisure also pay some attention to a few manly diversions. This flower you picked by the wayside —a pity to neglect it. You've left me holding it, completely puzzled as to what I'm to do next. What, sir, do you wish me to do?"

"I'll see you about that sometime."

"Not yet?—*Eventually*, did you say?"

"Yes, this matter that I brought up about the trade—that's been going round in my mind; there's the Court, too—some difficulties, you know. I don't see how I can manage right away."

"Well, then, tonight I might casually mention what you said, mightn't I?"

"You've seen to it that she wants nothing?"

"I am seeing to all that myself."

"I might even send her a poem if I had my father's knack for turning out verse. . . . There's not a scrap of the poet in me."

"Ah, no, if I may say so, sir, the lady once showed me a poem of yours. Let me see—how did it go? . . ."

"Come, enough about my verses. . . . With May here the rains will start soon and you'd better take care of your health."

"Is that the message I'm to take her?"

"A vulgar fellow you are! What makes you repeat what's already understood?"

"You will pardon me, sir, if I ask you another question. Do I understand that I'm to come here as before?"

"Come whenever you like," Kiyomori replied, adding: "but don't let Tokiko find you at it."

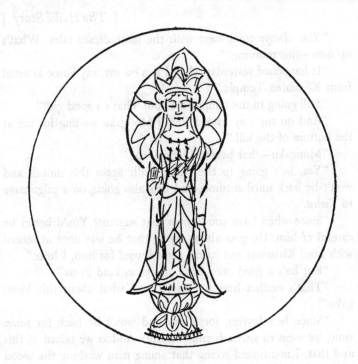

CHAPTER XXXIV

A SILVER IMAGE

One morning early in May when the hills and valleys were still white with haze, Yomogi stood outside the Nose's shuttered house on Fifth Avenue.

"What are you doing here so early," queried Bamboku, still in his night-clothes, and staring bleary-eyed at Yomogi, looking her up and down from her head to her dew-soaked sandals.

"I'm sorry, coming so early, but I've heard something dreadful."

"You always come here with the most dreary tales. What's up now—this morning?"

"It happened yesterday when I was on my way home as usual from Kiyomizu Temple."

"Still going to the temple, are you? That's a good girl!"

"And on my way back I found Mongaku waiting for me at the bottom of the hill."

"Mongaku—that bearded fellow, eh?"

"Yes, he's going to the Nachi Falls again this month and won't be back until autumn, and he's also going on a pilgrimage to Kishu."

"Since when have you known that vagrant? You'd better be careful of him. He goes about saying that he was once at school with Lord Kiyomori and hasn't a good word for him, I hear."

"But he's a good man. He's always so kind to us."

"That's neither here nor there. And what about this Mongaku?"

"Since he's leaving for Kishu and won't be back for some time, we went to visit a friend—Asatori. And as we talked of this and that, I mentioned seeing that young man washing the blood from his sword at the stream, and Tomizo having his head slashed off. . . ."

"Hmm—and then?"

"Then Mongaku exclaimed that this was terrible, that we'd better be careful. Then he said something dreadful would happen to my mistress next—it sounded as if he were prophesying."

"What did he mean exactly by that?"

"He said that the ox-dealer was not the person the young man was really after. That he'd only killed him by chance. That's what Mongaku thinks."

"Let me see—so the murderer must have been hiding inside the grounds there. Isn't that so?"

"Yes, Mongaku thinks that this fellow has been hiding for some time in my mistress's garden or somewhere about the house."

"Ridiculous—absolutely ridiculous!"

"But Mongaku's quite sure that's what happened. He even told me the fellow's name."

"What's the fellow's name?"

"I mustn't tell you."

"What?"

"I promised Mongaku to tell no one. He thinks it would be a pity if the name becomes known, and the Heiké soldiers capture him."

"Are you Mongaku's messenger, or did your mistress send you? What made you come here to me?"

"Now wait until you hear me through. Stop yapping at me like that!"

Yomogi was a fair match for the scornful Nose this morning, and the eager words came tumbling out of her mouth as she went on to tell what Mongaku had said. The youth's name, she insisted, had to be kept a secret; he was a retainer of the Genji who had sworn to avenge his lord by killing Tokiwa; he was lying in wait for her; he had even hidden himself in the garden outside Tokiwa's room, but his courage had deserted him when he finally saw his intended victim. Mongaku had promised Yomogi to drive away the assassin by an incantation which he wrote on a slip of paper. He had given her the paper neatly folded, and had carefully instructed her to suspend it from a hedge in the garden where it could be seen. He assured her that if the paper disappeared during the night, there would no longer be any need to fear him. Until then, Mongaku had repeatedly warned her, everything must be done to shield Tokiwa. Yomogi had then gone home and done exactly as Mongaku told her, tying the paper to a low-hanging branch of a bamboo in a grove on the north side of the house where few people ever went.

". . . And I couldn't sleep a wink last night, wondering whether it would still be there or not by morning."

Yomogi ceased talking, though she still appeared eager to add more, but Bamboku had already guessed who the youth was.

"It must be Konno-maru. He's been hiding in the capital for some time with Yoshihira of the Genji."

"Oh, how did you know?"

"Who wouldn't know? And Mongaku's message—was it still there this morning?"

"It was gone."

"As I thought. . . ."

"But there was another in its place." Yomogi held out a slip of paper and anxiously watched Bamboku's face as he read it.

Bamboku wrinkled his brows and read the message several times over to himself. The writing, blurred by dew, was almost illegible.

"What does it say?"

"Seems to be in answer to Mongaku's note."

"What about the magic Mongaku said he would work?"

"What! You believe that that monk's words would have any effect? Looks more as though he's goaded the killer on."

"Oh, this is dreadful! . . . What are we to do, Bamboku, sir? Tell me, Nose—"

"Hm? What did you call me just now?"

"Nothing, sir, I only—"

"You're only a scatterbrained little fool! This is what comes of being too friendly with Mongaku. This should teach you a lesson!"

"But if it weren't for Mongaku, we wouldn't have known about this terrible person who wants to kill my mistress—or his name. Now if I—"

"Tch, how you chatter! We all know how much you love your mistress, but you might try talking less."

"I can't help it for worrying and worrying. . . . I simply don't know what I'm to do next for worrying."

"How should you know, anyway? You've no more brains than a sparrow! Off with you now to your mistress and put a stop to that twittering and twittering!"

Privy Councilor Kiyomori had spent the night at Court to attend a secret session that lasted until morning. He succeeded in snatching a few hours of sleep, and was on his way through the

Palace halls when a courtier who saw him hurried to him with a message that had come through the Guard Office. One Bamboku from Fifth Avenue, it appeared, wished to speak with the Councilor and was now waiting in the library.

"Bamboku? What could he want?" Kiyomori asked himself, puzzled. It was no ordinary matter that would bring him here, nor would he ordinarily be admitted. Kiyomori sought the library and there found Bamboku and Itogo with him.

Bamboku, fully appreciating the unusual privilege of being where he was, prostrated himself solemnly and, without his usual facetiousness, briefly conveyed his belief that Tokiwa was in immediate danger and begged for Kiyomori's advice.

"That must be Konno-maru, who has sworn to take his revenge on the Heiké. This is very serious," Kiyomori replied, and turned to Itogo. "Take your best soldiers to the Mibu villa, surround it, and get the man. There's only one—a youth."

As he turned to leave, Kiyomori added: "And you, Red-Nose, see that no harm comes to your charge. If anything happens to her, you're responsible."

The Nose bowed profoundly.

That same morning two hundred soldiers under Itogo left for Mibu villa. Scattering his men in a wide arc in the vicinity, Itogo ordered them to close in step by step until the spacious grounds were surrounded.

It was possible for a man to conceal himself for several days, and without too much difficulty, somewhere inside the walls of the villa—containing as it did a miniature lake, about which grew artfully placed groves simulating woods, and even a stretch of rolling ground through which a stream flowed.

Because of the bamboo thickets and woods which grew close outside the villa walls, the soldiers had some difficulty in approaching the house, but step by step the human net tightened and closed. Finally the Nose, accompanied by a few soldiers, entered the gate. "There's no danger of his escaping now," he was saying, "I'll make a search of the house itself. See that the lady is not alarmed."

Half of the soldiers were next sent inside the walls to search the premises; they crawled under the house; some climbed to the roof; others peered down wells or up into the treetops. No trace of the would-be assassin, however, could be found. The whole expedition appeared to have been in vain and the disgruntled soldiers were beginning to complain. The Nose, however, redoubled his efforts. He would be blamed for this uproar, for sounding a false alarm. He turned his spleen on Yomogi. "There's no Konnomaru to be found, is there? What do you mean by your stories! Just look at the commotion you've caused!" he roared as they came face to face in the servants' quarters.

"Here, here, Nose," a soldier who stood near by said in disgust, "what's the use of bawling at the poor girl? Let's call it a day. Besides, our men haven't yet had their supper. . . ."

Itogo retired, leaving twenty soldiers to stand guard around the villa walls.

The Nose turned over the whole affair in his mind once more. He would have to report this sorry business to Kiyomori. He next turned his attention to Yomogi. "Look here, tell your mistress this. Tell her how much we regret having disturbed her and caused such unnecessary excitement. We have set up guards inside as well as outside, so there's no fear of intruders. A thorough search has been made and she can be sure that no strangers are lurking about. You understand, don't you, Yomogi?"

"Yes, I shall tell her so."

"I'm going to Rokuhara now."

"Do be careful, sir."

"Tell her exactly what I said, now, and nothing else. Mind you don't say anything more."

"I really don't chatter so much as you think. Besides, who could have kept quiet this time?"

"There you go again! Twittering and twittering. . . ."

"Well, then, I won't talk any more. I won't say a word even if something does come up!"

"As you please. You wouldn't be of any earthly use anyhow. The soldiers will keep guard from tonight, so you needn't worry a particle. And see here, no more of this chattering when you go out. There's to be no more of this chattering, I warn you!"

"Is that so?" Yomogi pouted, turning her back on the Nose

Two giant oaks spread their branches umbrellawise over a gallery connecting one wing with the main part of Mibu villa, and extended over an inner court. The new leaves and last year's withered foliage made a thick tangle overhead. Konno-maru stirred and sighed with relief as he looked down from his nest. The thick interlacing of branches made it possible for him to stretch or even lie cradled among the leaves. He had hidden up there all day while Itogo's soldiers searched, planning, if discovered, to make his escape by a limb to the roof. It was dark now and he could see several watch-fires spaced out at intervals along the walls.

He recalled the events of the past several days, reproaching himself for his cowardice. Several chances had presented themselves for accomplishing what he had set out to do, but his courage had failed him each time. He found it easier now to consider what he should do next: he would kill Tokiwa tonight without any thought for his own safety. He waited for the hours to go by and the household to settle to sleep. Toward midnight Konno-maru slid down spiderlike from the tree and crept toward a room in which a single light still burned. By now he was familiar with his surroundings, and this he knew was Tokiwa's room. Climbing over a balustrade, he made his way along a gallery and then crouched beside a door. It was locked. It would be simple enough to pry the lock loose with his dagger and throw his weight against the door, though the noise would undoubtedly bring servants and soldiers running; but he could in the meantime stab Tokiwa. What happened to him after that did not matter.

While such thoughts went through his mind, he was startled by a voice.

". . . Who's there?"

It was a woman's voice. A light undulated across a lifted shutter and a silken rustle approached the door; Konno-maru sprang away from it. The door swung open and Tokiwa's pale face appeared, illumined by the lamp she was holding.

"Are you by any chance Konno-maru?" she said.

Konno-maru gave an exclamation of surprise, and stood motionless. Tokiwa, however, showed no surprise or fear. Her next words were in a whisper.

"Konno-maru, I was sure it was you—Lord Yoshitomo's favorite retainer. Come this way—come in—we mustn't let the sentries hear us," she said, motioning to Konno-maru.

As she vanished behind a silken hanging, Konno-maru slipped in after her and crouched in a corner of the room.

Tokiwa went back and softly closed the door. The wick in the lamp burned brightly; on a writing-table were spread the sutras she had been copying.

Tokiwa had heard about Konno-maru from Yomogi and of his designs on her life, but the revelation did not disturb her; she had only quietly expressed surprise at his having been so near for several days. When Yomogi showed her the message Konno-maru had left tied to a tree in the garden, Tokiwa seemed moved and had said: "He was a good and loyal retainer and can hardly be blamed for feeling toward me as he does."

For some time the two sat and watched each other. The light in the lampstand flickered, rose and sank uneasily. Konno-maru could discover nothing repellent in the still figure before him. Tŏkiwa, her dark hair flowing down among the silken folds of her garments, sat in absolute repose. Her head drooped slightly as though she was meditating. Konno-maru felt his limbs grow leaden and powerless, though his thoughts raced on. What kept him from approaching her, stabbing her? With every silent moment that dragged by, his heart began to weaken with overwhelming pity. Nowhere could he see the features of the evil, faithless woman he had expected to find. The smell of incense assailed his nostrils and his eyes turned to the oratory, before which an incense-burner sent up a white thread. Once more he gazed at Tokiwa and winced at the frailness of the thin shoulders under her robes.

". . . Konno-maru, do you remember how long ago you used to come to me with messages from Lord Yoshitomo?"

The quiet voice seemed to bring Konno-maru to his senses, and his eyes hardened as he leaned toward her. "So you haven't forgotten entirely?"

"How could I ever forget?" she replied softly.

"Ah, you faithless woman, how can you say that so shamelessly! You are evil indeed!"

"You are right, Konno-maru. I have wanted someone to tell me that—to accuse me, despise me, shame me."

"Do you mean this?"

"It is the truth, Konno-maru. You can see that for yourself; I'm not trying to escape from you."

"Yes, that is so. But that must be a passing regret."

"I regret nothing I have done. I did only what I chose to do."

"What! you mean that you also choose certain death?"

Konno-maru's hand feverishly felt for his sword; a slight lifting of his hand and he could bury the sharp point in any part of her body that he chose.

Then Tokiwa said musingly: "There is no other choice for a woman. . . . No, at least not for me. I am ashamed—ashamed to have been discovered like this by one who was Lord Yoshitomo's retainer."

As she spoke, she seemed about to faint, but made no sound. "If it would set your mind at rest to take your revenge by killing me, then strike. I am ready. . . . I shall not try to escape, nor cry out in fear," Tokiwa said quietly, holding out some letters that she seemed to have had in readiness. "I have one last request to make. These are letters to each of my children, my last message to my sons. . . . And this—this is my Lord Yoshitomo's. See that this reaches some Genji who can be trusted. That is all I ask of you."

Then she turned away from Konno-maru and clasped her hands before the small Kannon image in the oratory.

Konno-maru was bewildered. He remembered the silver image as one that stood in his master's room, where Yoshitomo prayed to it every morning and night. In his confusion Konno-maru groped for the letter that bore Yoshitomo's familiar writing.

It was his master's last message to Tokiwa. He read it through slowly with tear-blinded eyes and then laid it down. "Forgive me, my lady. How could I have been such a fool? It was true what that monk Mongaku said—that I was mad to have thoughts of revenge, and that you, a helpless woman, are far more courageous than I."

A silence intervened as Konno-maru made an effort to master himself. Then he went on: "Had I killed you, my life would have been darkened even more than Mongaku's. I now realize my folly. I shall start anew, live on with courage. . . . I promise that my lord's letter will reach the Genji in the east, and these letters to your children will be delivered to each one in time by my own hand."

Konno-maru would have thrown himself at Tokiwa's feet, but she rose quickly, opened the door, peered out, and then quickly closed it. "I can see the soldiers' watch-fires. Hadn't you better wait here until dawn?"

But Konno-maru was ready to go. Drawing out a dark scarf, he muffled his face with it, wrapping the long ends round his shoulders.

"There is no need for you to be anxious about me, my lady; they will not be able to see me now."

And with this he stepped to the door, let it swing wide open, and vanished into the dark garden. A few moments later Tokiwa thought she saw a shadow motion to her from the top of a wall as though in farewell, and lifted her lamp in reply.

CHAPTER XXXV

MYRIADS OF CANDLES

The long rains had ended and the droning cicadas, the clouds, and the hot sky announced that it was high summer.

"Let me see—have we been flooded again? . . . Not much damage, I hope," the Nose bellowed. It was his habit to raise his voice at any servant who caught his eye on entering the gates of Mibu villa.

455

Yomogi and several maidservants were washing clothes in the stream running through the grounds. Near by, several paper umbrellas and sunshades had been set out in the sun to dry.

"What a beautiful umbrella this one is, Yomogi! It couldn't possibly be yours?"

"No, it's not mine, but my lady's."

"Your mistress's, eh? And what use would she have for an umbrella like this? She never steps out of the house."

"I bought it only this morning at the West Market. But would you believe it, I found it quite moldy when I opened it, so I've put it out here with the rest."

"Hmm—you got it at the West Market? Does your mistress plan to go out somewhere?"

"I intend to go to the temple with her; the hundredth day of prayer comes the day after tomorrow."

"And where are you accompanying her, may I ask?"

"Where? But, surely, you know—the Kannon Chapel in Kiyomizu Temple."

The Nose passed into the house and spent some time talking with Tokiwa.

There had been no sign or trace of Konno-maru since the day guards had been set up around the house, and the Nose put it down to the soldiers' vigilance. He was, in fact, beginning to forget the whole affair, but was still troubled over Kiyomori's failure to appear. It looked very much as though his little scheme for worming his way into Kiyomori's favor had come to nothing. True enough, Kiyomori had little time to philander, but, with patience, it was not unlikely that he would finally turn up. The Nose was willing to wait, and from time to time visited the villa to make sure that all was running smoothly.

With Konno-maru now a matter of the past, the Nose found himself faced with another problem. Should he or should he not let Kiyomori know that Tokiwa often left the villa? The Nose would of course be held to blame if any mishap overtook her.

"Naturally, I don't want to discourage you from going to the temple, and I'm only too happy to know that you feel so inclined. Still, it may be wise to inquire how Lord Kiyomori feels about this. I shall go there myself today or tomorrow." the Nose said to Tokiwa before departing.

On the following day Tokiwa received a message to the effect that she was permitted to go out, and, accompanied by Yomogi, set out for Kiyomizu Temple. On this last day of Tokiwa's one hundred days of prayer to the Kannon, Tokiwa was astonished to find close to a score of priests at the chapel reciting the sutras in her behalf. Myriads of candles lighted up the chapel's interior, and the air was heavy with incense as she prayed:

"Watch over my three fatherless children, O Holy One. Their mother is all but lost to them. This Tokiwa is only the empty husk, and her spirit wanders through hell. Whatever sorrows and trials come to their mother, spare her children, all-merciful and loving one. Let these pitiful ones not suffer for the sins of the Genji."

And as she recalled that winter night when she prayed in this same chapel with her children beside her, Tokiwa wept.

"My lady, the Mass is at an end, will you not come this way and rest?" a priest whispered.

Tokiwa suddenly came to herself. "Thank you, your reverence," and then exclaimed: "But are you not Kogan?"

"Yes, Kogan—your good health, my lady."

"How can I ever forget your kindness to me that time?" Tokiwa began, raising her clasped hands to him. "I shall never forget how good you were to me who am no longer worthy to speak to you."

"My lady, you must not say that. There's no need for you to feel shame. To me, you are as pure as the Kannon herself."

Another priest appeared. "This way, my lady, this way, please."

Tokiwa declined the invitation. "I thank you, but I have a long way to go and had better leave now."

But the priest detained her. "But, my lady, you have come a great distance and at such an early hour, and he has been waiting for you for some time."

". . . Who—who has been waiting?"

"The gentleman who ordered the Mass."

Tokiwa was mystified. Who could it be? There was no worshipper at this chapel other than she. But the priest must not be kept waiting much longer—so with Kogan to guide her, Tokiwa made her way along the balustraded galleries, until finally conducted to a room. As she entered it, she suddenly drew back, shaken, then slowly sank to her feet.

"Tokiwa—you did not expect to see me, did you?"

The brilliant sunshine sifting through the maple leaves outside illumined Kiyomori's face, investing it with a radiant look.

"I have often thought of you, Tokiwa, but many things prevented my coming—and now summer is here. . . . How swiftly the seasons pass! Has all been well with you, Tokiwa?"

"Yes . . ." Tokiwa replied, and a confusion of emotions welled up in her until she was choked with tears.

As Kiyomori gazed at her, he also struggled with a rush of conflicting feelings—the memory of a spring night and its poignancy filled him. For an instant an awkward, almost boyish shyness overcame him. Mastering himself, he spoke to her once more.

"You could not of course have guessed that it was I who had the Mass said today. Uncalled-for meddling, you may rightly feel. But, Tokiwa, I too have need of prayers. Yes, Kiyomori, this poor blundering fool—this mere fatuous man! Can you, a woman, possibly understand?"

"I think I do—a little."

"Even that little is enough, Tokiwa, and for that I am grateful. I am making an even greater fool of myself now, but I find it difficult to confess to you why. Let Bamboku himself tell you later on."

Kiyomori spoke cheerfully, but as he ended, he abruptly turned his face away, and the light from the dancing leaves was reflected in his tears.

Following this brief meeting, Tokiwa did not see Kiyomori again that summer, nor the next; they were never to meet, for not long after, Kiyomori had the Nose arrange a marriage between Tokiwa and an elderly Fujiwara courtier.

By autumn the gossips had completely forgotten all the talk about Tokiwa.

CHAPTER XXXVI

THE WANDERING POET

Saigyo, the monk poet, had not been back to the capital
for several years, but where he went he heard much
talk of what went on there. He had in the meantime
been staying in a hermitage at Yoshino and made several pilgrimages to Kumano and Ominé. Early in the spring of 1160, he set
out along the Tokaido highway on a pilgrimage that took him to
the northeast, and while he was there the local chieftain, Hidehira, invited Saigyo to stay with him.

Hidehira, who supplied the nobility and warriors in Kyoto
with the famous thoroughbreds of the northeast, had heard much

459

of the monk poet whenever he went to Kyoto on business or appeared there to give the central government an account of his stewardship.

When autumn came, Saigyo took leave of his host and journeyed westward to the province of Echigo; in September he reached the southern end of Lake Biwa, where a vessel was about to set sail for the western shore. Saigyo joined the other passengers on board, and as they waited for the boat to start, Saigyo began to wonder about his companion and disciple, Saiju, from whom he had parted several months before at the Tenryu River.

Saigyo and Saiju had come to the Tenryu River and boarded a ferry that was preparing to sail with a full load, when three warriors, local soldiery, suddenly appeared, waving and shouting to the boatman to stop. The boatman's reluctance to take on any more passengers enraged the warriors, who pushed their way on board with sour looks, blustering: "We're in a great hurry and you've only these peasants and beggar monks on board, haven't you?"

Saigyo knew what to expect of them. Soldiers everywhere were getting to be a belligerent, truculent lot. Ignoring them, he continued to sit quietly gazing out over the river, until one of the soldiers suddenly stood over him and bellowed:

"Here, you beggar—you priest, get up!"

Saigyo made no sign that he heard, but the other soldiers quickly assumed a threatening air and swore at him. "Get off, you! You won't?"

Saigyo did not intend to resist them, but he could feel Saiju beside him trembling with rage, and tightened his grip on his disciple's arm. They had been fellow monks for twenty years, but Saigyo knew that Saiju, his former retainer, was still a hot-blooded warrior at heart. How often he had cautioned Saiju to curb that temper of his!

Saigyo's meekness, however, seemed to enrage the soldiers even more.

"Here, are you deaf?" one shouted. Seizing Saigyo by his collar, he sent him sprawling onto the riverbank. Saigyo's head struck a stone and he groaned softly; blood trickled down over one eye. But as he lay prone, he kept calling to Saiju, who finally came to his assistance.

Saiju was beside himself. "So this is how you, Yoshikiyo, once the bravest of the Imperial Guards, behave when you're insulted!" he raged. "If you expect me to put up with such treatment—cowering like a beaten cur—then I've had enough of the holy life! I took the vows to escape the torments of hell, but this is worse than the fate of the damned! I'm through with this life! Were I not a monk I would give them what they deserve!" Saiju wept with rage.

"Ah, Saiju, are you still not ready for this life that you chose? Have you forgotten that day I sent you to Lady Taikenmon and you got into trouble with the Guards at the Rashomon Gate and were thrown into jail? When I heard you were in trouble, I rode all night back from Toba to rescue you from the terrible Tameyoshi of the Genji. Have you forgotten that, Saiju?"

"That I have not."

"Are you any wiser than you were then?"

"It's all very well for you to say that, but it's not my nature to let ruffians bully harmless people. I can't endure such humiliation, for I've always held my head high before men."

"Saiju, as long as you feel that way, we shall never be able to get along together. Though we travel side by side, our hearts will not be following the same path. It's better that we part here and now, Saiju."

"What makes you say that?"

"For the time being, it would be better for you to do as you please."

"Does this mean I am released from my vows?"

"I have no authority to do that, Saiju. My prayer has always been to find joy in life, and for that one must give up all worldly ambitions and conflict, submit to the influences of nature, and cling to the life of the poet, finding contentment in the precepts of Buddha. That is the vow we took. Who am I to lay down rules? Ah, Saiju, you seem unable to understand me at all."

"No, I am simply a clumsy fool, humbly permitted to follow you. But I dare think that I understand."

"I'm afraid you still don't. You're no better than those who think I retreated from life. It is not so, for I am more than ever of the world. My purpose is to realize myself more completely, to enjoy life even more, and to regret nothing. That is how I wish to make my life worth while, and all that I ask of life. . . . How different that is from your idea of the holy life!"

"No, I agree with you, but—"

"Then why should you so often feel anger, rage over being humiliated, and regret your choice? Had you truly embraced the monk's life, then you'd not repent it, nor regret having taken the vows. You don't seem to have renounced the world, so why go on like this any more? Wouldn't it be better for you to put away all pretense and go back to the world?"

As he spoke, Saigyo realized that the life which should have meant freedom for Saiju had become a burden to him; and out of compassion for him, he insisted that they should part.

At length Saiju said: "I will do as you tell me, and shall think on what you have said—not only think, but act upon it, and when you return to the capital in the autumn I shall be there waiting for you."

Saigyo wondered where Saiju expected to find him after this long separation, for he had no idea of where he himself would be staying. He noticed that the boat was midway across Lake Biwa, and that the peaks of Mount Hiei were beginning to tower above it. He recalled how passengers a year ago seemed to talk of nothing but of Yoshitomo of the Genji and his sons and their flight to East Omi. Then he fell asleep. As he slept one of his fellow passengers glanced at him sharply from time to time, and when Saigyo woke, smiled at him pleasantly, saying:

"Here we meet again!"

"Let me see, who are you?"

"I am Otoami, a carver of Buddhist images—we met some time ago in the northeast."

"Ah, yes, to be sure! . . . Are you on your way back to the capital, too?"

"Yes, though I still have years of work on the temple in the northeast, an urgent call from Rokuhara brought me back, an order for Lady Ariko."

"What an immense distance for you to come!"

"Yes, indeed, and it would also be a pleasure if I were traveling at will like you. As it is, I have orders to fill both in the capital and in the north, and traveling with my men in a limited time. . . ." Otoami smiled, looking round at his companions, who made up more than half the passengers on board. With him were not only apprentices, but lacquer-workers, woodworkers, carvers of metal, and other such artisans. A passenger who sat near Otoami suddenly leaned over and spoke to the latter in undertones and then addressed Saigyo.

"Sir, are you Saigyo, the monk poet? I saw you several times in Koromogawa, where the Chieftain Hidehira himself is one of my patrons," he said, adding: "I am Kichiji, a merchant; I bring placer gold several times a year from the northeast to the capital and exchange it for merchandise from China, which is then sent north. . . . When you next come our way, you must not fail to visit me."

Saigyo nodded amiably, smiling to himself at the thought that rumors about him had reached even those distant parts.

As the boat neared the shore the passengers busied themselves with getting off. Otoami and the merchant were the first to disembark. After loading their pack-horses, they prepared to move off in an impressive procession, when Kichiji turned to Saigyo, saying affably:

"We have enough horses for us all. Would you care to join us tonight at our inn?"

Saigyo declined the invitation and went on his way.

Saigyo spent his time in the hills about Kyoto, visiting tem-

ples and calling on old friends. One day as he walked through the
capital he found himself in the lane where his home had once
stood. Nothing remained of it now except broken tiles and a
waste of tall autumn grasses. He stared at the scene numbly, then
turned away into the dusk, in search of a night's lodging, while the
night winds sighed around his travel-worn figure. He thought of
several friends who would welcome him, but the memory of the
wife and child whom he had abandoned twenty long years ago
haunted him. His wife, he was told, had entered a nunnery; he
wondered about the daughter, who was four when he last saw her.
He had heard she was married. From time to time he paused and
listened to the night, alive with the chirring of crickets. Everything—the trees, the earth itself, the hedgerows, and even the
stars suddenly seemed filled with the sound of weeping, and his
mind ached, and his heart, and he began to wonder why he wandered so aimlessly through the dark streets. What brought him
here like a ghost from the past?

A sudden longing to see Saiju overcame him—not his disciple, but a fellow being of whom he could beg forgiveness and to
whom he could confess his blindness and folly. Twenty years of
the holy life!—and he had only begun to learn tonight that the
human heart could not be denied by an act of will nor by the dis-
ciplines of religion. Where did Saiju expect to find him, after
promising to meet him in the capital? Then Saigyo thought of his
cousin, Lord Tokudaiji, among whose retainers Saiju had several
friends. Saigyo spent the night at a temple in the Eastern Hills
and on the following day went down to the capital. On arriving at
Lord Tokudaiji's mansion, he was surprised to find soldiers, footmen, and servants crowding about the gate, where several grand
carriages waited. He was about to turn away when he heard someone calling him. It was Saiju.

"Ah, Saiju, so you came here after all!"

"Yes, I have been staying here for some time with my friends;
I was sure that you would soon come, and have been waiting impatiently."

"Yes, how good it is to see you again!" Saigyo replied eagerly.

"Ever since we parted at the Tenryu River, I have meditated morning and night upon your reproof. Dunce that I am, I feel I am somewhat the wiser now. Never shall I act so foolishly as I did then. Forgive me for what I said."

"Saiju, you are not the only foolish one. I am even more so. . . . I, too, need to be forgiven. But let us talk of this later."

"No, no, that is not possible. . . . But this is no place for us to talk. Let us go round to the rear gate to my lodgings."

"But my cousin has guests today."

"Not only today. Kiyomori and other state ministers come here frequently to consult with Lord Tokudaiji. We shall not be in the way in my quarters." And so saying, Saiju led Saigyo round to one of the rear gates.

CHAPTER XXXVII

A MERCHANT FROM
THE NORTHEAST

New Year's Day a year ago had hardly been a time for the traditional observances, but this time freshly cut pine trees and pine boughs adorned gateways, giving the entire capital a festive air.

"We mustn't forget that we owe all this to Lord Kiyomori. It would be disrespectful even to sleep with our feet pointing in the direction of Rokuhara," Bamboku was saying to a score or more of his hired men and clerks as they sipped the New Year wine. During the New Year season Bamboku's gate stood open to a stream of guests—relatives, business acquaintances, fellow merchants, and neighbors—whom he entertained sumptuously.

The Nose had every reason for eternal gratitude to the Lord of Rokuhara, though his guests quipped over their wine that Bamboku's hospitality was somewhat on the meager side as compared with the profits he had made in the past year. To the sly remarks that the Nose must be worth his weight in gold, if not more, Bamboku replied airily:

"Joking aside, such profits are mere trifles—nothing like what I shall make when I'm really successful. And when that time comes you shall see what I can really do in the way of entertaining you."

Convivial guffaws greeted Bamboku's remarks, though no one doubted that the Nose would be as good as his word. City merchants never questioned Bamboku's credit or his abilities. Had he not, singlehanded, supplied all the materials for rebuilding the Cloister Palace last year? Kiyomori, moreover, was his patron, and the Nose had a finger in every notable business transaction in the capital. It could not be denied that without Kiyomori's patronage Bamboku could never have achieved his considerable wealth. On the other hand, the Nose had gone to quite some trouble and expense to settle the affair with Tokiwa. But, all told, that had been nothing compared with what he had gained: for one thing, he was in Tokiko's good graces once more. The mistress of Rokuhara had summoned him and condescended to say: "You may come here as you did before, Bamboku." For another, Kiyomori had inclined his ear to Bamboku's long cherished ambition—an appointment at the Court.

There was a time when Red-Nose would have sneered at the idea of a court post, but he was, after all, getting on toward fifty and there was nothing strange in a change of heart after twenty years of making his way in the world. The ludicrous paraphernalia of court life had once disgusted him and made him declare: "All this foolish strutting and groveling! Yes, I'm for myself and myself alone. I'll make my fortune, and gold—yellow gold—shall give me all the pleasures of life." Ironically enough, as his wealth increased Red-Nose began envying what he had once despised. The parvenu once had longed for and acquired a wife of good family; and as the number of his hired men grew, he began to hanker after a little authority. A merchant financier, Red-Nose had numerous occasions to mingle with the aristocrats, whose abilities seemed to him quite insignificant. He could do as well—better he reflected, had he the necessary credentials to that society—a court title. And the more Red-Nose thought of it, the more was he convinced that he was justified in his ambition.

The Nose was the commonest of the common people; but his wife, Umeno, was of noble descent. Kiyomori saw to it that Bamboku was named Warden of the Kamo River—a post with authority over petty officials and workmen in charge of riparian works on the Kamo; the office, moreover, was equivalent to the Fifth Rank and required Bamboku to wear the robes of that rank on all state occasions.

"Yes, a title is all very well, but these clothes are certainly uncomfortable!" Bamboku exclaimed to himself one day while on his way home. "I must find some place to stretch." Then it suddenly occurred to him that Kichiji, the gold-merchant from the northeast, was visiting the capital. He immediately set out for Kichiji's lodgings in the gay quarters at Horikawa, a district lying along a canal lined with willow trees.

"Is Master Kichiji in? I'm the Warden of the Kamo River," Red-Nose announced to a maidservant whom he saw as he entered the gate.

The servant, mumbling indistinctly, disappeared into the house, where Kichiji was in close conversation with a caller. Kichiji was puzzled.

"Warden of the Kamo River—who is it, anyway? I don't know anyone by that name."

His visitor laughed. "That must be Master Red-Nose. He was named Warden of the Kamo River at the awarding of the New Year's honors, you know."

"Ah—the Nose! An important guest—show him to your best room," Kichiji directed, and then continued to talk to his visitor, a familiar figure in this quarter, where he was known as "the Serpent." His business was the buying and selling of women and children.

"That makes it a total of seventeen women we've bought since last autumn—including yesterday's," Kichiji said.

"Yes, and at that I've had great trouble filling your orders, sir, for there aren't too many beauties to be found even in the capital "

"Well, I'll be back in a year or two, but I want you to keep an eye out in the meantime."

"Yes, sir, that I'll do. As a matter of fact I've found one in the slums on the Street of the Ox-Dealers."

"How old is she?"

"Only thirteen."

"That won't matter. I'll keep her as a servant in my house until she's older. I'll take her with me when I leave."

"There's one thing, though—the girl's attached to her parents, who are miserably poor. They love the girl and won't say yes. The father's bedridden and they're heavily in debt. Don't even know where the next meal's coming from—but *what* a beauty!"

"Is she really?"

"I'm not exaggerating if I say she'd compare with the most beautiful at Court."

"A pity—"

"Well, there's no reason why something can't be done about it."

"You mean money would do it, eh?"

"That you know best, sir." The Serpent laughed slyly, a greedy grin twisting his lips.

Kichiji visited the capital every two or three years, and always lodged at the same house in the gay quarters, where he spent lavishly. As many of his transactions were for the Chieftain Hidehira, a name in the northeast, Kichiji was known to every merchant in Kyoto. His business was to acquire every kind of luxury goods for his patron—works of art and even beautiful women—in exchange for the placer gold, horses, lacquerware, and silks he brought from the northeast.

Hidehira's grandfather, the first chieftain, a Fujiwara, had dreamed of building a capital in the barbarous northernmost province of Michinoku, once the territory of the subjugated aborigines, the Ainu. It was to be a metropolis rivaling the grandeur of Kyoto, and the work still went on.

Kichiji, whose mission was completed after several months in the capital, was again disappointed at not having many beautiful young women to take back with him. It was not his practice to kidnap or traffic in women and children, but he offered large sums of money and guarantees of good living-conditions to whoever was willing to go to the northeast. Since Michinoku offered few attractions to those who might otherwise go there, Kichiji was obliged to call on the Serpent to help him in his search for beautiful women.

The maidservant appeared once more to say: "The Warden of the Kamo River says he will call again, if you're busy today, sir."

"Well, Serpent," Kichiji said, pausing on the threshold to dismiss the man, "if you can manage it before I leave, I'll take a look at this girl."

Bamboku was ushered in.

"I must apologize to you for keeping you."

"Not at all, Kichiji, I'm afraid I am interrupting," Bamboku replied.

"No, I'm free now. It was good of you to come. As a matter of fact, I shall be leaving in a day or two and thought of paying you a call. . . . But this is most fortunate."

"Just as I thought," Bamboku interjected. "A little sudden perhaps, but it occurred to me that you might have the time to drink with me this evening before you go."

"Excellent!—though this is hardly the place to invite you."

"Not in the least. But you're to be my guest. A change of scene will do you good, and if you don't object we'll go to one of my favorite houses," Red-Nose insisted, leading the way.

Red-Nose bellowed for the proprietress as he stalked in familiarly. "Taji! Taji! It's I—Bamboku! Is the Violet Room to be had?"

As soon as the two were settled in a room looking out on an elegant inner garden, Red-Nose drew a writing-set to him and quickly wrote a note, addressed it, and then called for a servant, to whom he gave some directions, adding: "Get a runner to take it. Right away—now!"

A sumptuous meal appeared with the wine, but only servants waited on Red-Nose and his guest, for, unlike most establishments of this kind, the proprietress prided herself on her clientele and the excellence of her accomplished entertainers, who appeared only at the request of select guests, and even then only to dance and sing.

It was late and they were well in their cups when Red-Nose insisted on having several dancing-girls sent him; he asked for them by name, and exerted himself to entertain Kichiji.

"When do you expect to be back—next year, perhaps?"

"No, I can't say. . . . But I expect to make another trip in about three years."

"Well, Kichiji, next time you're here, you won't need to stay at Horikawa, since my villa will be at your disposal."

"Your villa—where is it?"

"That's what I'm planning now. And, Master Kichiji, just say where you want it, and it'll be done."

"I'm tempted to accept the offer. Some place with a fine view."

"It shall be done—and you'll bring a little more of your gold with you, eh? This last supply—well, I'm not too happy doing business on such a miserable scale. You may think I'm bragging, but —with overseas trade in mind—you brought me barely enough to meet orders for gold lacquerware alone from my customers in the capital."

Kichiji laughed. "Master Nose, you've had quite a bit to drink, and you talk big."

"No, I'm not lying."

"I don't say you're lying, but you must be exaggerating. I doubt that the amount of gold I bring here can be equaled by what's found elsewhere in Japan. Well, well, being made the

Warden of the Kamo River and an officer of the Fifth Rank may have something to do with your exuberance, but the Heiké aren't the only ones who count, nor Kyoto the only place to live. Pay us a visit just once in the northeast and look around for yourself."

The Nose roared with laughter. "Bragging about your part of the country, eh? I like what you say about the capital—'not the only place to live'!—I'll make a point of visiting you in Michinoku."

"I'll show you around myself."

"Master Kichiji, I'm not convinced that you're only a merchant."

"Hmm—what makes you say that?"

"You think I don't know better? You're a warrior! You're Hidehira's retainer or have a title of some sort, I can see. You don't have to hide it from me. Bamboku of Fifth Avenue is a broad-minded fellow, I assure you. You'll find out for yourself on long acquaintance."

Kichiji gave the Nose a wry smile. "Hmm, that may be so," he replied, adding nothing more, for unlike the loquacious Bamboku, Kichiji was reserved, a taciturn northerner.

"I feel it a compliment to be taken for a warrior in these times. . . . As you know, Master Nose, I travel thousands of miles on horseback carrying untold wealth in gold with me. I may be a merchant at heart, but it takes the courage of a warrior to travel as I do—particularly in dangerous times like these."

"Quite so, quite so. Stands to reason. I was merely joking just now. Come to think of it—I wonder what's happened to my friend. He should be here by now."

"Who's this?"

"He used to be a court secretary—Tokitada—Kiyomori's brother-in-law. I wanted him to meet you."

"Yes, yes, we mentioned that once before, and I'm quite anxious myself to make his acquaintance."

A messenger soon returned to say that Tokitada was not at home and not expected back that night.

Red-Nose and his guest were reeling drunk by now. After

some time, roused from their stupor, they made their way home in the early dawn.

Several days later Tokitada brought his carriage to a stop in front of Red-Nose's shop on Fifth Avenue, but did not alight.

"Bamboku, Bamboku! . . . Is Bamboku there?" he called out at the shop-front.

Some clerks in the shop heard Tokitada, but paid no attention to him.

"Bamboku? Who *is* Bamboku, sir?" a clerk finally asked, approaching the carriage.

"Master Red-Nose—"

"Oh, the master is it, sir?"

Red-Nose came hurrying from his warehouses.

"Ah, it's you, sir! Come round to the house," he greeted him.

"No, I'm on my way to the honorable Yorimori's right now. Can't be bothered getting down, so I'll talk to you here."

"Are you in a hurry? What can I do for you, sir?"

"Nothing—but a message from Rokuhara. I don't know what's wanted, but you're to come to the rose court about sundown when the lamps are lit."

"Hmm . . ." the Nose ruminated. "Something displeasing him?"

"He didn't seem out of sorts, so you needn't worry. . . . And by the way, Bamboku, you sound quite concerned, but he's clay in your hands, isn't he?"

"Dear me, no! I'd never say that of my lord—his terrible temper and all, but clay—never!"

Tokitada laughed until his carriage rocked. "Bamboku—you, I just wanted to see how you'd take it. You're a comical sight, puffing and protesting until that nose of yours turns even redder! But there's a good side to you, too."

"Now, did you come all the way out here to make jokes at my expense?"

"Here, Bamboku, don't take it so hard. Just the sight of your nose is enough to make anyone feel gay. What does your wife say to your nose in her sleep?"

"I'm afraid you've been drinking, sir, even before you arrive at your host's."

"It's still the New Year—no wars—the best New Year in years. . . . Yes, and that reminds me—I'm sorry I was away when your messenger came. Who's this fellow you wanted me to meet?"

"You must have heard of him—Kichiji, the gold-merchant from the northeast."

"Yes, I've heard of him."

"I've noticed some things that make me think he's here for something more than business. I suspect that Hidehira is sending him here to smell out a few things, and I thought it might be worth your while to look the fellow over yourself."

"Ah, that's it, is it? Is this Kichiji staying in the capital much longer?"

"He leaves early tomorrow for the northeast, he says. I thought of seeing him off."

"Good! I'll be there, too. . . . But I'll go in disguise, remember that now." With these words Tokitada drew the carriage blinds.

The following morning Red-Nose accompanied Kichiji as far as one of the city gates, where a large crowd of men and women had gathered to take leave of him.

"Yes, I'll be back before long—in two or three years," Kichiji said affably from his saddle, a courteous word and bow to each of his well-wishers. "You'll make the parting harder for me by coming much farther, so let me say good-by to you all here, and with the best of wishes."

Kichiji finally started away uphill and the crowd gradually dispersed. His servants, grooms, and pack-horses waited for him some distance away. Suddenly Kichiji heard someone behind at the foot of the hill calling to him to stop. The man finally caught up with him on the crest of the hill. He was out of breath and unable to utter a word.

Kichiji turned round. "Was it you that called me?" he asked skeptically, staring at the little fellow who prostrated himself like a beggar in his path. "I don't know who you are. Never seen you before. What do you mean by getting in the way?"

"Yes, yes, you must pardon me for delaying you. . . . I— I'm Asatori, a nobody from the slums on the Street of the Ox-Dealers."

"You must be mistaking me for someone else. What did you say you were?"

"I live on the Street of the Ox-Dealers—in the slums; there's a wheelwright there called Ryozen. . . . And this morning I heard him and his wife crying so loudly that I went to see what was wrong and found that a dealer in women and children, called the Serpent, had carried off their only daughter Asuka. . . . They were in utter despair."

". . . ."

Kichiji turned round in his saddle. A commotion seemed to have started among his train, who were restraining a screaming girl.

"Asatori, save me! Asatori!"

"Is it you, Asuka? Wait. . . . It's all right. I'll take care of you!"

Asatori got to his feet, waved back in reply, and then clung to Kichiji's saddle, beseeching him.

"That's enough nonsense, you puppeteer!" hissed the Serpent, pushing his way through the group of escorts and seizing Asatori by the collar. "What do you mean by saying that I took her away by force? You don't seem to know that her father's been sick for a long time and that I've been lending him money all along. He and his wife begged me to do something for this child because they can't feed her any longer. It doesn't pay, but I begged the master here to take her along with him. . . . What do you mean by interfering?"

Asatori had not the strength or courage to resist the Serpent's knotty arms, which jabbed angrily at his small frame and twisted it. All that Asatori could do was flail helplessly at the air with his legs.

"I'll pay you back," he gasped, "I'll pay you back somehow!"

"You liar, do you think I believe you? Get on home! What do you mean by whining and delaying the master as he starts out?" said the Serpent, threatening to knock his victim down. Kichiji, alarmed, leaned over in his saddle.

"That's enough, Serpent."

"But, master, he'll do it again."

"No, Serpent, let the child go. We don't want to harm anyone. I told you, didn't I, that you were not to force her?"

"The money I lent her sick father isn't much, but they can't even feed the child, so I meant to help them."

"Never mind, let her go. I'm no ogre."

Asatori prostrated himself again before Kichiji, then beckoned to Asuka, who ran to him and threw herself on his breast, sobbing

"Don't cry," Asatori soothed, wiping the tears from her grimy cheeks; "don't cry now, Asuka. You needn't be afraid. Let's go home."

An exquisite little face looked up at him and broke into timid smiles. Kichiji and his train had already vanished.

Hand in hand the two made their way down the hill. No sooner were they out of sight than two horsemen emerged from the woods at the top of the hill and started down toward the capital.

"Bamboku, was that the man?" called Tokitada.

"Yes—"

"Is that the Kichiji you were talking about?"

"Yes, what do you think of him?"

"Nothing specially wrong with him as far as I can see. As merchants go, rather more decent than you, eh?"

"Than me? . . . Very discerning of you, sir!" Bamboku laughed.

"At least more heart than you, Nose. I don't see why he let that rascal buy the girl anyway, but at least he showed some sign of being decent—letting her go."

"And you think I wouldn't, do you?"

Tokitada laughed, but did not reply. "Asuka—Asuka. Pretty name," he said to himself. "No wonder the Serpent had his eye on her. . . . Extraordinary how such blossoms spring up out of the filth in the slums."

CHAPTER XXXVIII

THREE DREAMS

Tokitada was up early the following morning. His carriage and an impressive escort of warriors and grooms awaited him at the door, where he appeared in his court regalia. The equipage soon drew up at a gate in Rokuhara; Tokitada sent in a message to announce his arrival and to inquire whether the mistress was ready. An elegant lady's carriage stood waiting under the portico; purple tassels hung from its blinds; not a speck of dust showed on the gay lacquered body and roof; the gold and silver metalwork with threadlike engravings of ethereal birds and butterflies glittered blindingly. More dazzling, however, than the carriage itself were the two figures who approached the portico by an open gallery, surrounded by a fluttering bevy of waiting-women.

"I'm afraid I kept you waiting, Tokitada," said Tokiko, who was accompanied by her seven-year-old daughter.

"Ah, Tokiko, I hardly recognized you in all your finery!"

"It's not often that I pay a call at the Cloister Palace. . . . And besides, it's spring now."

"You look splendid, indeed! I'm sure no one objects to your turning yourself out so becomingly—no matter how gorgeously. May I suggest that my advice to you has taken effect?"

"Do stop teasing me. The servants are watching us and can hardly keep from laughing."

"Let them laugh. I don't see why you women are afraid to laugh. Serious women like Lady Ariko are too much for me. We can't have you take after her. . . . Isn't that so, Tokuko?" Toki-tada said, stroking his niece's glossy hair. " 'Princess,' come ride with me in my carriage and I'll tell you stories." As Tokitada stooped to pick up his niece, the child hid herself behind her mother's skirts and peeped up at him, shaking her head. The waiting-women who stood about laughed aloud as Tokiko picked up her daughter and stepped into her carriage.

Tokitada's carriage followed Tokiko's, and rolled along the tree-flanked avenue in Rokuhara, with their retinue.

Tokiko scarcely ever went outside Rokuhara; whenever she did, an elaborate escort of warriors always accompanied her. For so many years now she had been occupied with her many children—nine, she often marveled to herself. Her husband was in his prime, Tokiko herself in her early forties. And with a gay, philandering husband, Tokiko had begun to realize that she must keep herself from aging too soon. Kiyomori's affair with Tokiwa a year ago had taught her a bitter lesson and cost her many a heartache. She had often prayed at that time that he would not become more successful, that there would not be another such affair. . . .

To the swaying of her carriage, Tokiko became preoccupied with bitter reflections: forty—her confidence in her physical charms waning. For a man, fortified with experience and wisdom, it was the perfect age for deeds, the accomplishing of great things; the time had come when she must cope with an intractable grown child. . . .

Tokiko's carriage jolted to a stop and she found Tokitada's drawn up beside hers.

"Tokiko, roll up your blinds and take a look round."

"Where—where are we now?"

"West Eighth Avenue—the opposite side of the river from Rokuhara—there's the hamlet of Shimabara, Mibu. There the Kamiya and Omura rivers. . . . Farther south you can see the Yodo River. A magnificent view, isn't it?"

"What made you bring us to this out-of-the-way place? Aren't we going in the opposite direction from the Palace?"

"No, it's not really out of our way. . . . Look, Tokiko, just see for yourself—the thousands of men at work over there!"

"What are they doing?"

"They're building new roads. See those men digging, carrying soil, and getting on with the work? Hear that faint sound off in the distance? That's the stonemasons and carpenters and the others at work. In another six months you won't recognize this place."

"And what are they building here?"

"Mansions and palaces. There'll be a town springing up here in no time—in fact, a city within the city, a great Heiké center!"

"Won't Rokuhara do?"

"Rokuhara's too cramped now. I'm sure Kiyomori is thinking of the future, and there's no telling what a man of his talents will do. He's undoubtedly born to be great and you're his wife. Don't forget that, Tokiko."

"Tokitada, do you really believe that that would make me happy?"

"You're a woman and I should think you have every reason to congratulate yourself on having such a man for your husband."

"Nonsense, Tokitada, Rokuhara suits me perfectly. All this will mean just that much more to worry about. I wish you would discourage him from it."

To Tokitada's surprise, Tokiko drew the blinds of her carriage impatiently. He had taken the trouble to bring her here in the certainty that she would be pleased, and he began to wonder whether he had only brought up another subject for marital discord.

'Tokitada heaved a sigh. ". . . These women, I can't understand them. More grasping than men, more tenacious, and yet they don't seem to enjoy the right things."

The two carriages soon approached the Cloister Palace along the canal at Eighth Avenue.

Tokiko's younger sister, Shigeko, had only last year given birth to the abdicated Goshirakawa's third son, Prince Noribito, and several times begged Tokiko to come and see the infant Prince. Etiquette, however, prevented Tokiko from complying with her sister's wishes until the ex-Emperor himself had sent her an invitation.

"How boring! . . ." Tokitada sighed as he waited. He had come with Tokiko only as her official escort, and was not admitted to the inner apartments, from which voices and the sound of laughter reached his ears. The fretful cries of an infant suddenly startled Tokitada with the realization that he was himself the uncle of the new Prince. It was an astounding thought. One never could tell . . . related to the imperial house. . . . What would his father, an impoverished nobleman, have said if he were alive? Tokitada's thoughts traveled back to his boyhood. They had been so poor that he had taken to cockfighting to see if he couldn't turn a penny by gambling. . . . His thoughts raced ahead into the future: power, glory, splendor outrivaling the Fujiwara! The sound of his sisters' laughter interrupted his reveries once more. Happiness—yes, joy—but how different theirs from his.

The ex-Emperor himself pressed Tokiko to remain for the evening meal, and Tokitada soon joined them. The ex-Emperor drew Tokiko's daughter to him, petting her with the remark: "They say daughters look like their fathers, and that sons take after the mother, and this little one seems to resemble Kiyomori."

Tokiko's joy was unbounded as she watched the ex-Emperor caressing Tokuko and repeating from time to time: "Pretty little thing, such a pretty child! . . ." Nothing, she felt, could equal the honor of these gracious words.

"Tokiko, how many children do you have?" her royal host inquired.

Tokiko replied with a laugh: "So many that I can hardly count them."

"More sons than daughters?"

"More daughters."

"And which is this little one?"

"Our third daughter."

"So many children that you can't remember exactly. Then you surely won't mind if this one comes to live with her aunt, would you?" the ex-Emperor Goshirakawa said, smiling. "Wouldn't you like that, little one?"

The child showed signs of tears; pushing away Goshirakawa's arms she ran to her mother.

"As you can see, your majesty, she is still a baby."

"That's so, but she must come to visit her aunt often to get acquainted. And after that stay here?"

Goshirakawa then turned his attention to Tokiko, courteously inquiring about her and her household and the life at Rokuhara; he talked to her about Kiyomori—his strong points and failings—and encouraged her about her husband's future. So completely charmed was she by the ex-Emperor that Tokiko in spite of herself was soon confiding in him. He coaxed from her by his sympathetic air some of the grievances she nursed against her spouse, and without censuring Kiyomori chose just those tactful replies which most pleased her, by saying:

"No, it's not an easy thing for a woman to be married to such a gifted man. . . . On the other hand you'd be most unhappy with a spineless husband."

"No, I'm sure that an ordinary dull fellow, though poor, who stays at home and pays some attention to his wife would be far more to my liking."

"Yes, he is a most restless individual, driven on forever by his dreams."

"Yes, that's exactly it," Tokiko agreed.

"You might encourage him to be a little more religious. Kiyomori's failing is his habit of belittling people's beliefs—that air of not fearing anything."

The more he touched on her husband's failing, the more did Tokiko come to admire the ex-Emperor. By the time she was ready to leave, Goshirakawa had discovered something about Tokiko's tastes and presented her with a length of fabric, rare and beautiful, and begged her to repeat her visit.

That same evening Bamboku arrived at the rose court and found Kiyomori already there with Michiyoshi, the pirate chief, who a year ago was installed at Rokuhara as Kiyomori's retainer.

"It is finished, my lord," Michiyoshi said, unfolding a large chart and placing it before Kiyomori. Parts of the map—the coastline and ports of China—were purely conjectural; the routes through the Inland Sea were also marked.

Kiyomori bent over the chart eagerly. "This?—Come up closer, Bamboku and examine it for yourself."

"Michiyoshi, which port in China did you trade with?"

"There was no one port. Everything depended on the wind and tide."

"What about the Inland Sea?"

"I've never been there, as it has no good harbors."

Kiyomori indicated four or five points on the map. "What about these?"

"They're barely large enough for fishing-boats and small craft to anchor in."

"Farther out, then?"

"The currents outside the harbors are treacherous. If ships could get into Kumano Bay, there would be good natural harbors among the islands there. In any case, the large sailing vessels of the Chinese wouldn't fit in even there."

"A pity—" Kiyomori sighed, looking up. "Five hundred years ago when our envoys went to the T'ang Court, the treasures of China flowed into our land. Those were glorious days! . . ."

"Better than now?"

"Certainly. You must think it strange if I say so, but I do believe that our country was more flourishing five hundred years ago, our culture more brilliant, our religious teachers wiser, more zealous, and that the people enjoyed more peace. It's strange that we've made no progress. We've stagnated for five hundred years."

"What do you suppose is the reason?"

"We've let ourselves flounder in a mire. The channels for fresh influences are clogged up—have been for centuries, ever since the throne stopped sending embassies to the T'ang Court. What do you think, Red-Nose?" Kiyomori laughed and quickly corrected himself: "Bamboku, I mean. Now, Warden of the Kamo River, don't be content with your title. You're to administer one of the five ports on the Inland Sea and will be sending out ship after ship to China, you know."

"Yes, I'll stake my entire fortune on that."

"When we start—just which port will be the first?" Kiyomori asked.

"What about the port of Kanzaki at the mouth of the river?"

"Not good because of the sandbars."

"Muro?"

"Too narrow."

"Well then, which?"

"Owada (Kobé). I've sailed past it many a time as a boy. My father's fiefs were along the coast there. My own are there, too, and I always pass Owada by ship. . . . And every time we try to land, the high winds and the poor harbor at Owada give us much trouble. Even as a boy I used to wonder what could be done about the harbor there."

Bamboku stared at Kiyomori in surprise. "Eh, *you* had such thoughts since you were a boy?"

"Hmm . . . since my twenties, because, Bamboku, just think—" Kiyomori addressed Red-Nose with unaccustomed seriousness—"it's only now that I can give you a court rank—something I would never have believed possible a few years back. And who was Kiyomori when he was young? A warrior, despised by the aristocrats! A watch-dog and the miserable offspring of a Heiké. . . . How could I have known then what the future held for me? I was young—oppressed, beaten down, though determined to live."

"Yes, I remember those days."

"Yes, you'd remember, Bamboku. You used to be a nobody at Court, too. And there was no chance for youthful hopes or ambitions to grow, except by turning rebel or brigand. . . . That's why, whenever I sailed past Owada with my father, I used to dream of a day when I would slice away part of that hill, and see a whole fleet at anchor in that harbor, and the port a great trading center to which all the ships of China would come. That's what I dreamed of as I stared out at the sea."

Red-Nose, who listened intently, said: "I see I was mistaken. I thought it was a wild plan that you'd hit on lately."

"No, it's been with me for twenty years. Dream dreams while you're young, Bamboku. Mine, as you can see, are beginning to take shape. This is happiness, unbearable happiness for me. . . . I suppose the rest of you also thought it was just a wild scheme?"

Kiyomori rarely reminisced at such length; now he was flushed to the ears, intoxicated by his schemes. Bamboku, recalling the Kiyomori of a year ago—his infatuation with Tokiwa —could hardly believe that he was looking at the same man. Kiyomori folded up the chart as servants began carrying in wine and trays of food; other male members of the household soon joined them for the drinking and the entertainment that followed.

Kiyomori drained cup after cup, watching the dancing-girls through a rosy haze; to him the throbbing hand-drums sounded like the pulsing of the sea.

A carriage meanwhile rolled in noiselessly by the gate, and Tokiko staggered from it with Tokuko fast asleep in her arms.

Kiyomori left the dancers and singing behind him as he made his way along a gallery to Tokiko's room. Her husband was in an unusually amiable mood and not only because he had been drinking, Tokiko noted. More sprightly herself than usual, she was eager to recount every detail of the day's happenings.

Kiyomori's first question was: "How was the young Prince?"

"He is thriving, and looks so much like his father."

"Mm. . . . How did you find Shigeko?"

"*Her highness* was in good health, too." Tokiko corrected, with a disarming smile for Kiyomori.

"Did you speak long with his majesty? Did he say anything?" Kiyomori next asked.

"Yes, he was most gracious and I felt deeply honored by the concern with which he inquired after our family and talked about you."

" . . . ."

Kiyomori studied the expression on Tokiko's face as she talked. He realized that the abdicated monarch was doing his utmost to win over Kiyomori and all the Heiké in the way of military support. Tokiko, however, chattered on endlessly about his majesty's charm, his gentleness, his kindness.

Kiyomori finally suppressed a yawn. "I'm glad you enjoyed your day," he said, "it does you good to get out. A court conference tomorrow, too, so I'll have to leave early," he said, and rose to go.

"Oh, stay and talk a little longer," Tokiko begged.

"Still more to tell me?"

"Yes, I was dozing in the carriage on my way home and had a most extraordinary dream."

"Dream?"

"It may not have been a dream. . . ."

"What nonsense!"

"Dream or not, it was most extraordinary. It happened just as we were coming to Gojo Bridge. Tokuko was asleep in my lap and I must have fallen asleep watching her, for suddenly it seemed as though the carriage were rolling through the clouds; there was no sound whatever of wheels, but instead I heard the pounding of waves. . . . I looked and all about me was the sea, over which I seemed to be flying. I wondered where I was being taken and cried out in my sleep, and what do you think?—instead of oxen, I saw a pair of foxes trotting before the carriage! And then the outlines of an island, beautiful as the peaks of paradise took shape before my eyes; a great rainbow spanned the skies and a voice sounded about me—'Itsuku-shima—Itsuku-shima,' it said. Then the foxes vanished, and the roaring of waves and the strains of a harp woke me."

"You woke up?"

"And even when I was fully awake, I could still hear music and a voice in the clouds saying: 'Itsuku-shima.' I can hear it even now! It was like that in the carriage coming home."

"Can you explain the dream?"

"Do you remember that time—you were thirty then, I think—you needed foxskins for your armor and went hunting? It was that year after the Shrine affair and you had to stay away from Court."

"Oh, yes, I do remember that."

"Remember how you took pity on those foxes and wouldn't shoot them and came home empty-handed?"

"How well you've remembered all that!"

"I never told you this, but ever since that time I've kept the lute Shinzei sent you in our shrine to the Goddess of Music, because her messengers are foxes and the lute her favorite instrument."

"That was an excellent idea of yours. It's not pleasant to remember Shinzei, though I'm sure that his spirit is pleased by your offering to the goddess."

". . . So my dream is, I think, a sign that the foxes you spared are watching over our house. Don't you think that the goddess's messengers came to remind us that we should sometimes pay our respects to the clan god of the Heiké at Itsuku-shima?"

"Is our clan god enshrined at Itsuku-shima?"

"So your stepmother says. Your grandfather as well as your father, whose fiefs were there, went several times in their lifetime to worship at Itsuku-shima."

"Yes, you're quite right. That was so."

"In spite of two wars, we've had no misfortunes to speak of—in fact, not only has everything gone well, but Shigeko is now the mother of a prince, and I can't believe that this is pure chance. I wish you would show some reverence for the gods and, like your father, occasionally make a pilgrimage to our clan shrine."

"Hmm. . . . You mean Itsuku-shima?"

"Yes, Itsuku-shima."

"Yes, I'll try to get down there this year."

Kiyomori, who usually became truculent whenever his stepmother reproved him for his lack of piety, surprised Tokiko by his quick acquiescence.

"You really mean it?" Tokiko asked skeptically.

Kiyomori could not help laughing at the expression on Tokiko's face. He saw through her completely, but he was willing at times to play at being the obtuse husband by agreeing to whatever she said. Yes, he believed her about the dream; he would do whatsoever the ex-Emperor wished; he would try to be a loyal subject and a good husband. Everything was to be as she said.

"No, I won't make fun of religious beliefs, and I promise to go on a pilgrimage to Itsuku-shima this year without fail. I promise it—no, I'll swear to it here."

4 8 8

CHAPTER XXXIX

ASATORI THE PHYSICIAN

Asatori left Momokawa's house and cheerfully made his way down the hill. It was a year since he had taken Mongaku's letter to the physician Momokawa and been accepted as a disciple. There were several others studying under Momokawa, but Asatori's zeal and the experience he gained from tending the many sick he found in the slums had helped him in his studies—dissection, physiology, herbal knowledge, and the other rudiments of medicine introduced from China. Had

489

Asatori gone back to being a court musician, his calling would have given him honor and security, but in the life he had chosen, the life of poverty among the destitute, he found a satisfaction unknown to him at the Court. Half starved most of the time, something in his new life gave color to his thin cheeks.

All over the capital the paulownia trees once more were in bloom, and Asatori sighed as he looked up at them. From the time the paulownias shook down their purple flowers until autumn, epidemics swept through the districts of the poor. In some years they raged more fiercely than in others; he had just been reading of the dreaded dysentery, for which no remedy had yet been found, though its ravages were all too well known. Rich and poor alike were struck down by it, and the afflicted could do nothing but die until the plague spent itself. Thousands in the capital had died of it last year, until the first frosts came. Asatori prayed that the same would not happen again this year, for a third of the dwellers on the Street of the Ox-Dealers had been carried off by the last epidemic.

"Asuka, what are you doing here?" Asatori asked in astonishment as he came to Sixth Avenue. A paulownia was in full bloom by the pasture fence near the Street of the Ox-Dealers. A young girl waited for him under the tree.

"At last, Asatori!" Asuka cried, running up to him and bursting into tears as she seized his outstretched hand.

"What's the matter, Asuka? Were you waiting for me to come home?"

"Yes—"

"Has the Serpent been coming again?"

"He came again today and shouted at us, saying he would take me away this time for sure. That's why I ran away and came here."

"You don't have to be afraid," Asatori assured her. "I'll repay him. Let me talk to him, and I'm sure he won't force you."

At each turning that brought them closer to the Street of the Ox-Dealers, the lanes and alleys grew increasingly squalid. When they came to the wheelwright's clay hut the Serpent was still there, threatening the terrified couple. The Serpent was accompanied by an elderly woman, floridly dressed, who explained with feigned kindness: "You don't want to spend the rest of your life in this miserable slum, do you? I'm here to give you some advice—and you with that ravishing creature for a daughter! Haven't you ever thought of her future?"

Ryozen and his wife showed no sign of yielding, but the Serpent persisted in his threats. "Well, in that case, I'll have you pay me right now for the loan I made you last year. If it weren't for that, Asuka wouldn't be here now—would have been sold to someone up in the northeast. Don't tell me you've forgotten that! Why do you suppose I gave you some money again this spring? Because you said it was too cruel to take her away so young. And here's this woman, promising to set her up as a dancing-girl. What are you complaining about anyway? This is more than you deserve!"

Asatori and Asuka pushed their way through the crowd of inquisitive neighbors who craned in at the door. The Serpent and his companion seemed to grow uneasy at the sight of the mob surrounding the hut.

"We'll be back again. Think it over, you two," the Serpent said menacingly as he left.

"He's a persistent fellow—the Serpent. You'd better look out for Asuka. The devil himself is after you now," remarked Asatori examining the sick Ryozen as usual. "Have you any medicine left? As soon as you run out of it, send someone to me for more," he said kindly, and with a few more words of advice to the invalid, departed.

On the following day Asuka appeared at Asatori's house: "Good Asatori, here's a hair ornament that that man told us to return to you. Is it yours?" she said, handing it to Asatori. The pin, intricately worked of silver and gold, almost too valuable for even a court musician to own, was one that Asatori's mother had given him at his coming-of-age. It had been used to secure the headdress worn by court musicians on formal occasions. His mother had had the pin made for him by selling her few belongings to pay for it, and it was one of Asatori's most treasured possessions. After promising to repay the Serpent for the loan made to Ryozen, Asatori had induced the Serpent to accept the only valuable thing he owned.

". . . Do you really mean that that grasping fellow returned it?"

"Yes," Asuka replied.

"I wonder why."

"I don't know."

"But I can't believe he would do this, unless he intended to come again. You'd better keep this, Asuka, in case he does. . . . I have no use for it any more."

Asuka accepted the pin reluctantly, and it was only after she left that Asatori found it placed carefully on the box holding his books. She had often come to visit him after that day he had rescued her from the Serpent. Lately, however, she was spending more time with him than she did with her parents, and Asatori, who had grown fond of her, helped her with her reading and writing and took pride in her talents, for not only was she a promising calligraphist, but she could already compose verse. Though reared among the poor, Asuka's father, formerly a retainer to a nobleman executed after the Hogen War, had given his daughter some training in the accomplishments of a court lady.

There seemed to be no signs of an epidemic this year, but the unseasonally cool weather rotted and shriveled the rice and wheat seedlings. People talked anxiously of poor crops and of a famine that would follow in the winter.

Asatori was on his way home one day from his lectures in medicine. As he approached his door, he called out to Asuka, expecting to find her there, putting his house in order. There was no reply, however, and as he crossed the threshold he discovered that he had a visitor—Yomogi, staring at him with hostile eyes. He looked around for Asuka and found her sitting defiantly in the small kitchen. Neither of the two girls said anything. A long silence intervened, until Asatori began: "Dear me, what's this?" The sight of the two on the verge of tears puzzled him.

"Ah, Yomogi, here you are! We haven't seen each other for some time, have we?"

"How do you do, Asatori?" Yomogi replied with a stiff nod.

"You may already know that my mistress married last autumn rather suddenly."

"Yes, I did hear of that."

"I haven't been able to get away much since then, because she's surrounded by strange servants and likes to have me with her as much as possible, you know."

"Aren't you fortunate! But this is no place for you to come, though I'd be happy if we could see each other from time to time."

"I'm sure you're quite pleased that I can't come to see you often."

"Oh, that's not so!" Asatori denied, laughing.

"But—I quite understand how it is. I see that for myself."

"What's this? What do you mean?"

"Nothing—nothing at all."

Yomogi turned away and burst into tears. Asuka, who had been quietly watching them, stood up suddenly and ran from the house in her bare feet.

"Asuka! Here, Asuka, where are you off to? What's the matter?"

Asatori leaned from a window and called after her with all his might, but Asuka would not come back. Asatori, still mystified, began to wonder whether Yomogi and Asuka had been quarreling in his absence. One of those little tiffs, he thought, smiling, and went back to Yomogi. He noticed with surprise that she was no longer the child he had known six months or more ago.

Everything about her seemed to have changed—the way in which she wore her hair and bore herself proclaimed her a young woman. Was it possible, Asatori asked himself, that the consciousness of womanhood at seventeen could transform her so completely into this tremulous being? Then he concluded that this was only natural and reproached himself for his blindness. He tried again:

"Yomogi, did Asuka do something to hurt your feelings?"

"No, nothing at all," Yomogi replied curtly, adding: "I even thought she was a mute because she hardly said a word when she first saw me."

493

"She doesn't see many people other than those in this slum. She's poor and I'm sure she felt very shy."

"No, I don't think it was that."

"Then what was it?"

"She glared at me as though she wanted me to leave. I suppose you're going to marry her? Aren't you, Asatori?"

Asatori was startled. Yomogi's eyes searched his with such a determined look that his glance wavered. He grew hot about the ears as it dawned on him that he was the reason for those jealous looks. It startled him, however, to think that one as young as Asuka could also feel jealous. He wondered whether Yomogi had already felt this way about him last autumn when he treated her as though she were still a child.

"Has some errand brought you this way?" Asatori asked, changing the subject.

"No, I wanted your advice about something."

"Oh? . . ." Asatori squirmed; his breath seemed to come in gasps.

"Asatori, I'm thinking of leaving my mistress and coming to live here. What do you say to that?"

"You mean you're leaving Lady Tokiwa?"

"I'm not happy at the thought of leaving her alone there, but—"

"But you were with her ever since her children were born, weren't you? I'm afraid she's going to miss you."

"Yes, I've thought about that a great deal, too."

"What makes you think that you want to come and live here?"

"Haven't you always told me that the life of the grand and the rich is all show? That there's no comparison between them and the poor, among whom you find real goodness and kindness? I've been thinking about that and I believe you're right."

"But, Yomogi, that's no reason for you to choose the miserable life here when people here are trying to get away from all this!"

"I'm sick of the life of luxury. When I found that you gave

4 9 4

up being a court musician because you felt as I do now, I knew that I also wanted to come and live here."

"No, you won't be able to stand this life very long after those years of ease. You must speak to your mistress and ask her how she feels about letting you go."

"Of course she would stop me. To tell you the truth, I don't feel about her as I used to. Not after what happened between her and Lord Kiyomori, and then her marrying again. And though she's beautiful, it's so shameful. . . ."

Yomogi had grown up, Asatori mused; she was a woman standing in judgment over another. She had grown skeptical of her own mistress and was anxious about her own future. It distressed him, however, to realize that Yomogi was asking him to share that future with her. How was he to dissuade her? Asatori's heart sank at the thought of the task before him. But Yomogi seemed content just to be there, chattering to him and ignoring the passing of time. When evening came she helped him prepare his meager supper and stayed to share it with him.

"You had better leave now, Yomogi."

"Yes, but as soon as my mistress can spare me, you'll let me come here, won't you, Asatori?"

But Asatori put her off, saying: "Well, next time Mongaku comes to the capital, you must ask him what he thinks. Don't do anything rash before then."

He went with her as far as the crossroad, then turned back to his house, where he found a smudge fire going. The light from a small lamp fluttered in the night breeze; picking up the lamp, he placed it by his desk and began loosening the cords of his medical books, then he heard a splashing at the rear of the house; a bamboo pole rattled. Craning out across the narrow veranda, he saw a drying-pole slung between the branches of a tree; a small figure was reaching up to hang out some wash. "Is that you, Asuka, out there? Don't try to do any more washing in the dark. Come in here where it's cool."

"But if I do these now, you'll have something clean for tomorrow."

"Oh, you've been so good as to wash out my soiled clothes?"

4 9 5

"I started to do them this afternoon, when that visitor arrived, and so—" Asuka said, approaching the veranda shyly. She finally sat down beside Asatori, tenderly nursing a finger.

"A splinter?"

"From that pole."

"Here, let me look at it." Asatori reached for her hand and drew it close to his eyes. "It's too dark here, come up to the light." He picked up some tweezers and began probing. Asuka surrendered her hand and seemed not to mind the pain.

"Ah, here it is—out! It must hurt, it's bleeding."

"No, not much."

"The bleeding will stop soon," Asatori comforted her, placing the finger in his mouth and sucking it. Asuka suddenly burst into tears. Asatori quickly took her in his arms and cuddled her as though she were a young child.

"What are you crying about, Asuka?" he asked.

"Because I'm happy—so happy," Asuka sniffled.

"Stop crying, then."

"I'm crying because I won't be able to come here any more."

"What makes you say that?"

Asuka, however, refused to reply and Asatori continued to rock her in his arms. Poor child, he thought, so starved for affection, this child of the slums.

"Asuka, why didn't you take this pin I gave you the other day? You're to take it with you tonight . . . you mustn't be shy."

"Is it really for me?"

"You could sell it, you know. Get a dress, perhaps?"

"No—" Asuka shook her head. Clutching the pin to her, she smiled at last. "I shall keep this forever—for the rest of my life."

Her spirits restored, Asuka finally went home and Asatori settled once more to his books. Tonight, however, the difficult text seemed hopelessly confusing and he could make nothing of it.

A week or so later Asatori, who had not seen Asuka for two or three days, was on his way home and stopped at Ryozen's house. He was dumbfounded at finding that a hunchbacked child and a cripple had moved in with their few belongings—a cooking pan and a wooden pail.

The cripple said enviously: "Did you want Ryozen? He moved away the day before yesterday to a fine house off yonder—nothing at all like this clay hut. Someone from the gay quarters came for his daughter, I heard. I've only this hunchback; no one'd want her even if I gave her away. You're a doctor, aren't you? *You* could do something for her, couldn't you?"

That night Asatori applied himself as usual to his books, but he hardly understood what he read, for the Serpent's face and that of an elderly woman kept appearing between him and his open book. He was hurt, too, at Ryozen's not having come to say good-by. Casual acquaintances were a commonplace in the slums, where people arrived in the morning and were gone by night; it happened all the time, he told himself; he had no real reason to feel as he did. He continued to think about Asuka. She was not his child. What could he have done for her anyway? What made him take such an interest in her? Moths and small insects lay scattered on his desk and all over his books, lured to their death by the flame. There were a few fragile, lovely shapes among them—like Asuka; others—horrid creatures—reminded him of the Serpent. What could he do after all but physic the sick? Make Asuka happy? Presumptuous! Why should he believe he could help others? Had he grown so conceited as to think that he was capable of such a superhuman task? He was not able even to heal the sick!

Asatori stepped out to the rear of the house and splashed himself with bucketfuls of water from the well, partly to shake off his drowsiness.

As he dried himself and drew on his cotton robe, he saw people on their roofs, shouting to each other: "Where's the fire?"

"Toward Horikawa."

"In the gay quarters or thereabouts."

Asatori looked up at the red glow in the sky. On hearing that the fire was somewhere near the gay quarters, he was suddenly tempted to follow the sound of clattering feet. But he went back into his house instead, closed the shutters, and fumbled his way to bed. Now and then he heard the thump and roll of an unripe persimmon as it dropped on the thin roof over his head.

CHAPTER XL

THE JEWEL OF THE INLAND SEA

A small fleet of river-boats was preparing to leave for the estuary at Yodo, and a noisy crowd thronged the shore. With summer here and his court duties less pressing, Kiyomori was at last on his way to Itsuku-shima and the ancestral shrine. Vessels of every size and description were there: cabin-boats, boats for carrying horses and arms, craft loaded with food-stuffs, all ruffling the waters and crowding the river.

498

"Hasn't Tokitada come yet?" Kiyomori inquired impatiently.

"He should be here soon," Norimori replied, to pacify his impatient brother.

Norimori and two of his captains as well as Michiyoshi, the former pirate, were accompanying Kiyomori on the trip through the Inland Sea, which he knew well. Carpenters, masons, builders, and other workmen also were in the party of close to thirty men.

Kiyomori turned to Red-Nose, who stood behind. "Bamboku," he said, "Tokitada hasn't come after all. Hadn't we better start?"

"Well, we might wait a little longer. He's late, but he's sure to come."

"What do you think is keeping him?"

"Not anything at the Court, but something about one of his retainers. There was a fire in the gay quarters last night."

"Why should that delay him?"

"I heard that one of his retainers had a falling out with a retainer to some lord, and that that started the fire."

"Another of those clashes between soldiers?"

"There seem to be more and more of them lately. The Guards at the Palace and the Court go about insulting each other and picking quarrels."

"Rivalry at the top filtering down to them? A nuisance—"

"The soldiers don't seem to have cooled down yet since the slaughter of the last two wars. I don't like to say it—but the warriors are growing rather highhanded these days."

"We'll have to overlook that just now. They've been oppressed for so long and are just beginning to hold up their heads. . . . But I wonder what happened last night."

"The retainer had just a little too much to drink and slandered his majesty's second consort. . . . The other fellow overheard him and started an argument. That's how it all began."

"Was that the cause of the fire?"

"Something of the kind."

"We can overlook the swaggering, but fires and turning politics into a private quarrel mustn't be tolerated."

"It looks very much as though these soldiers are turning the enmity between their majesties into a quarrel of their own."

"It's what the soldiers might do that worries me. I wanted Tokitada to keep an eye on them while I was away."

"Oh, there he is—just in time!"

Kiyomori's face cleared as he scanned the shore and perceived Tokitada dismounting among a tangle of vehicles. He seemed to be in great haste; pushing his way through the crowds, he soon boarded Kiyomori's boat.

Behind lowered blinds, Kiyomori and Tokitada were engaged for some time in talk. Kiyomori looked on Tokitada as his right arm and depended on him even more than he did on his own brothers.

". . . Very well, then, I leave you in charge," Kiyomori ended, and Tokitada quickly made his way to the shore to join the throng of men and women from Rokuhara who had come to see Kiyomori off.

In this season of drought the Yodo River was low. Even where it was deepest the boats scraped bottom, forcing the boatmen and soldiers to pull or pole the craft over the shallows. The heat on the windless river was almost intolerable.

Kiyomori's plan was to sail down a tributary of the Kanzaki River to the bay and there board seagoing vessels for the port of Owada (Kobé), but the shallowness of the river obliged the party to take horse the next day and continue the journey across the burning dunes along the sea. From Mikagé they continued westward; behind them was a backdrop of mountains and before them level land that curved to the contours of the coast. Rarely did they come across any signs of human habitation; southwesterly winds unceasingly sprayed the pines on the beach, and from time to time they saw Chinese junks drifting helplessly before the wind and tide. But the weather was fine and the party in good spirits.

This region through which they were passing and which they named Fukuhara—the Plain of Good Fortune—awoke many memories for Kiyomori.

". . . This is where we landed in 1135, when I was with my father. Putting down that revolt in the west, we landed here. . . . Those fishing settlements and the twisted pines haven't changed in the least. Only the times have changed—and I."

All the Heiké lands—Isé, Bingo, Higo, Aki, Harima—bordered on the sea. All his youthful memories of his father, the achievements of the Heiké, were inseparable from the sea, and Fukuhara was the link between that eventful past and Kiyomori's dreams of the future.

For nearly three weeks Kiyomori stayed over at the post-stage in Fukuhara. In that time he often took Bamboku with him to explore the surrounding hills and mountains, or spent whole days crossing the plains under a scorching sun. At other times he had his chief engineer make soundings around Cape Owada and the river mouth. When rain kept them indoors, Kiyomori ordered charts of the surrounding country to be made, then spent the night pouring over them alone, lost in reverie.

Tireless himself, Kiyomori exhausted his men by consulting with them late into the night, and even after everyone was asleep would suddenly sit up in his bed, light a lamp, and continue to study the maps until dawn.

"I wonder if it's quite wise to stay here much longer. How will people in the capital take it when they hear of this, I wonder," Bamboku asked one day.

Kiyomori shook his head. "I can't say. Supposedly, we're on a pilgrimage to Itsuku-shima."

"In that case, sir, let me remain behind to finish the work. I'll follow your plans for surveying the land around here, look into the water-supply and the possibilities of road-building."

Kiyomori fell in with Bamboku's suggestions and, leaving a few of his technicians with him, resumed the journey to Itsuku-shima by water. Day after day he filled his lungs with the air blowing off the endless blue ocean. And as numberless islands floated past them on the Inland Sea, Kiyomori's vision ranged far and free and he exulted: "Ah, how cramped is the capital! What a great to-do people make over that dreary little hollow! My future home will be built in sight of this sea. You shall see what great things I shall accomplish beyond the sea!"

The outlines of Itsuku-shima finally appeared one day, floating on the crest of the waves.

The priests on the island and the shrine virgins soon appeared on the beach to welcome Kiyomori. On landing, he soon found that the shrines and temple were almost in ruins; the winds from the sea had done their worst; the white sands and the wind-twisted pines along the shore alone were beautiful.

Kiyomori and his party lodged in an inn near the beach, and on the following day he began his week's retreat.

During the remainder of his stay, numerous visitors from the mainland rowed to the island to pay their respects to Kiyomori, whose fame had spread to all parts of the country. Aging warriors who had served under Kiyomori's grandfather appeared; others who remembered his father Tadamori also came; while soldiers who had served with Kiyomori in the past flocked to see him once more.

"It's as though I had come home," Kiyomori said to those gathered at a banquet in his honor. "This is so much home to me that I don't want to return to the capital."

Kiyomori's stay lasted two weeks and during that time he unfolded his plans to the chief priest of Itsuku-shima. They were grandiose plans—so incredible that the chief priest could only listen in astonishment. Here was a warrior, in rank but a councilor at the Court, still in his forties—an impossible visionary speaking! For this is what Kiyomori said:

"We cannot leave this beautiful island in such ruins. I want —and I can't tell you how soon this will be done—to see this shoreline and the hills so enhanced in all their natural beauty that this island will outshine Kyoto itself. There will be an archway like no other that has ever been seen, spanning the water as you approach Itsuku-shima from the sea, and those who come to worship here will enter by this great gate. The main shrine and its adjoining buildings will be connected by wide galleries, suspended above the sea, and the ebbing and flowing tide will give the whole variety; at night a hundred stone lanterns will be lit and their brilliance dye the waves, making this island even more enthralling. The main hall of worship will be spacious enough to seat thousands; towers and five-storied pagodas will pierce the pine woods on the flanks of the hills. The shrine and towers, set against the rocks in the hillside, will only increase the beauty of these surroundings. . . ."

Fired by the picture he had painted, Kiyomori continued: "This will not be for my pleasure alone, but all who come from the capital shall see it, and many ships from far countries—from China—will sail past and be told: 'See! this is Japan, where even the smallest and remotest island boasts the noblest in architecture and artistry!' They may say we have aped their buildings, but the pines and the white sands of the shore and their beauty, changing through the seasons, are unique. And when they come ashore, there will be spread before them the essence of our arts through the ages—the Asuka, Nara, and Heian eras. . . . And when their ships put in at Owada, I will welcome them in my own house. Owada? That will take time, but I plan to make it a great seaport, sheltered from winds and tides. And when my villa at Fukuhara is ready, I shall come here to worship every month in ships as stately as those from China. . . ."

To Kiyomori's listeners these were tall tales, the babbling of a madman—an impossible dreamer. Yet there was a breadth to this man that reminded them of the sea, and they were proud to claim him as one of their own.

And when Kiyomori was ready to leave, he was loaded with gifts—priceless treasures from China—incense, sweet-smelling aloes-wood, figured cloths, silk tissues, heavy brocades, paintings, vessels of celadon, dyestuffs and drugs. Not all were from China, for some came from those countries facing the Mediterranean on the east, by caravans from Arabia and the Persian Gulf.

The sight and scent of such exotic merchandise made Kiyomori impatient. "Wait, wait until the port at Owada is completed," he was heard to say. Yet that day came too slowly for him, like the tedious creeping of the shadow across a sundial.

At Owada, Kiyomori once more interrupted his journey back to Kyoto to meet Bamboku, and in September, after an absence of a month and a half, arrived in the capital.

Something was wrong, Kiyomori realized as he entered Rokuhara.

His eldest son, Shigemori, who was among the first to greet him, said: "That troublesome uncle of mine has been up to serious mischief while you were away, but you had better hear the story from Yorimori."

Kiyomori frowned with annoyance at hearing his son speak thus of Tokitada. Undoubtedly, he seemed something of a rowdy to the serious-minded Shigemori, but Kiyomori preferred that touch of wildness and picturesque recklessness, so much a part of Tokitada, to his son's sobriety. His heart, however, stood still at this announcement.

"What's this? Has he dragged Yorimori into one of his usual scrapes?"

"Something more than one of his usual escapades. He's involved in some plot that can shake the government."

"I can't believe he would plot against the throne."

"No, but it would be difficult for his majesty to regard it as anything else."

". . . Well, let us wait. Let me talk with you later on," Kiyomori said, waving Shigemori aside.

After meeting various members of his household and hearing how they had conducted their duties in his absence, Kiyomori made his way to his wife's rooms and there was met by a tearful Tokiko.

"I can't forgive myself for what has happened . . ." she wept, and between her anxious sobs gave him the particulars.

During Kiyomori's long absence from Rokuhara, there had been the usual friction between the Court and the Cloister Palace, he was told. A rumor was heard that Tokitada and Yorimori, both court officers, were plotting to put the Cloistered Emperor's son on the throne. The rumor soon reached the Emperor Nijo, to whom it was clear that not Tokitada, but his own father, the Cloistered Emperor, had inspired this plot. But Tokitada and Yorimori shortly after were deprived of their rank by an imperial decree and banished.

Kiyomori grunted as Tokiko ended her account. She saw a faint smile playing about his lips as he assured her: "There's no reason for you to blame yourself. This was only as the Cloistered Emperor planned it. He's not one to be incited by even Tokitada. . . . That being so, Tokitada is too impetuous for his own good. There is the possibility that he might have been rash enough to attempt something in my absence that would give his majesty an excuse to suspect me, and I would then have had to take sides with the Cloistered Emperor; that is exactly how his majesty wants it to be."

"But what do you think really happened?"

"Don't worry, now that I'm back," Kiyomori assured Tokiko with his usual composure, and said nothing more. Tokiko was disappointed by his refusal to confide in her further, but her own thoughts rushed on. Could it be possible after all that her husband and brother really had schemes to supplant the Heir Apparent with the young Prince, their own nephew? Did the Cloistered Emperor share their secret? Tokiko was distressed by this terrifying possibility. Where would the insatiable ambitions of these men lead them, she wondered. But whatever thoughts he might have, Tokiko knew that her husband, manlike, would keep them to himself.

Upon his return Kiyomori at once presented himself at the Court, where he received a long audience with the young Emperor Nijo. Although Kiyomori was one of the very few whom Nijo trusted, Kiyomori did not broach the subject of the Cloistered Emperor, Nijo's father, nor did Nijo say anything of Tokitada.

A day later Kiyomori set out for the Cloister Palace. To him the ex-Emperor Goshirakawa appeared secretly pleased by the success of his latest intrigue, in which he believed he had Kiyomori's support. But when Kiyomori ended his account of the trip to Itsuku-shima, he bowed gravely and said:

"I must also add that while I was in retreat for seven days and nights, I received a divine message in a dream."

"A dream?" Goshirakawa reiterated, surprised by the seriousness with which the usually skeptical Kiyomori said this.

"Yes, I'm convinced it was a message from the gods. I heard the lapping of the waves and a voice spoke from the purple clouds above me."

"A divine message?"

" 'Kiyomori,' it said 'if you truly deplore the present state of affairs, as a loyal subject let your royal master know this: there is only one sun in the firmament, yet on earth there is a ruler in the Court and in the Cloister Palace, both claiming supreme authority. What discord has followed from this and what untold misery this has brought to men'!"

"Wait, Kiyomori, this was a dream you say?"

"Yes, a dream. I found myself in a lady's carriage, crossing the sea, and, if you can believe it, a pair of foxes preceded me!"

Goshirakawa suddenly laughed aloud. Kiyomori would have laughed even more, but, restraining himself, he continued in serious vein: "That was the dream. No, I must admit that Tokiko is better at interpreting dreams."

"I understand what you mean, Kiyomori. Enough—enough now. . . ."

"I'm glad if the meaning is clear to you," Kiyomori said, "but let me add one word more. Let there be peace between father and son."

Goshirakawa averted his face at these words.

". . . . Yes, Kiyomori, I shall take to heart what you say. You need not be anxious. The Emperor is my son and I have no reason to hate him."

Yet not long after this, in October, the Emperor Nijo ordered two high-ranking courtiers, his father Goshirakawa's favorites, to resign from their posts at the Court, and despite conjectures and rumors of every kind, the reasons for this were never made known. Strangely enough, Goshirakawa, who in the ordinary course would have protested, maintained complete silence.

In March of the following year, the Emperor Nijo recalled from exile the courtier Tsunemuné, whom Goshirakawa had banished after one of the earlier wars.

In 1165, three and a half years after his trip to Itsuku-shima, Kiyomori was still consumed by his fever to make Owada a great seaport and the center of trade with China. He had changed much in the interval—matured. Every moment he could spare was now spent in drawing on Bamboku's worldly experience; he conferred with the merchant constantly, drafted and redrafted plans, applying himself untiringly to the task of reviewing his scheme until he was satisfied that Owada needed only a good harbor. "But I don't see how I can finance this single-handed," he confessed to Bamboku. It was clear that Kiyomori could expect no help from the Cloistered Emperor, for Goshirakawa's ambitions lay elsewhere; he thirsted after undisputed power. No way toward realizing this gigantic scheme seemed possible now except an appeal to the Emperor Nijo himself, and since both sovereigns courted Kiyomori's military backing, Kiyomori seized this as his chance to petition Nijo for two favors. One, the rights to the imperial estates of Fukuhara at Owada, was granted him almost immediately. The other—state funds for completing the harbor at Owada—was ignored. Nijo and his advisers smiled at Kiyomori's fantastic scheme. For a warrior, a Heiké, to dream of foreign trade was nothing short of absurd—a site for a villa at Fukuhara was understandable, but . . . Kiyomori, however, was not discouraged and grew even more determined to succeed in his scheme.

The Cloistered Emperor, however, was disquieted by gossip in some quarters. Kiyomori, he heard, was not seeking trade with China, but a western base for a fleet of warships at Owada, close to the region where many Heiké clansmen were settled.

In this same year, during the torrid heat of July, the young Emperor Nijo, who had been ailing for some time, died suddenly, and the royal funeral was held on the night of the 27th at the Koryuji Temple, north of the capital.

CHAPTER XLI

AN EMPEROR DIES

Thunder had been pealing in the distance for some time and the grass on the plain was limp under the fierce summer sun. Despite the heat great crowds poured from the capital and even from distant Kinugasa to line the route of Emperor Nijo's funeral cortege.

"I'm afraid we're in for a shower, Yomogi."

"Isn't there even a tree under which we can take shelter?—Oh, look, people are beginning to scatter!"

"There's a temple by that grove in the open fields."

Asatori and Yomogi started running in the direction of the temple, where many others had already taken refuge.

Four years had gone by since Yomogi, against Asatori's advice left Tokiwa. Before Asatori fully realized what was happening, Yomogi had come to live with him as his wife, and in due course he accepted the arrangement and soon grew accustomed to his role of husband.

"Oh, I'm so frightened!" Yomogi shuddered, clinging to Asatori's arm with each peal of thunder.

It was said that the imperial cortege would arrive at the temple on Funaoka Hill that same night.

Late in the afternoon an ominous radiance began to fill the sky as dazzling shafts of light broke through the angry clouds over Funaoka Hill, and the awed multitudes stared at the fearsome spectacle as though they saw a portent.

"Here, you, clear out now! We'll need this place at sunset," came an order as twenty horsemen rode into the temple compound and began herding people before them. As soon as they heard that these were Heiké warriors from Rokuhara, the crowd melted away down the slope on which the small temple stood.

Toward the west the clouds darkened suddenly as with oncoming night and heavy drops of rain pelted down on the surrounding trees.

"Here, there are still a few more of them inside the gate. Drive them out!" a young soldier ordered, turning in his saddle. Some men and women were crouched behind a hurriedly improvised cloth screen at the base of a pillar. Several soldiers came forward and impatiently wrenched away the screen with repeated orders to the huddled group to leave.

Four or five gaily dressed women and a manservant quickly sprang from their position around an elderly woman stretched inert on a straw pallet.

". . . someone ill?" inquired a young warrior kindly as he dismounted. He warned away the impatient soldiers as he approached the group.

A frightened manservant replied: "Yes, the heat was too

much for our mistress and she fainted on the road. We brought her here and are trying to revive her. We'll carry her away if you'll give us a little time."

"No, wait, she seems to be in pain. Stay here a little longer until she's better."

"Sir, do you mean it?"

"Certainly, she mustn't get wet. . . . Let me see if I have some medicine for her. Here," the young warrior said, fumbling in his sleeve with a disappointed look, "does anyone happen to have some? Where are you women from?" he finally asked.

"We're from the gay quarters at Horikawa."

"Dancing-girls?" the officer asked, glancing at the young women once more. "Did you come all that way just for the funeral?"

"Yes . . ." replied one of the older women, "our mistress, Toji, insisted on coming to pay her last respects, and this is what happened. I don't know what we're to do now."

"I'll get you an ox-cart. You'd better take the sick woman home."

The officer sent off a soldier to round up a cart. In the meantime the figure on the pallet was seized with a fit that left her moaning with pain.

Asatori, who had been watching all this at a distance, could no longer restrain himself at the sight of the woman's suffering and went back to the gate. He took one look at the sick woman, then ran to Yomogi.

"Yomogi—"

"What is it?"

"I'd like to do something for that poor woman."

"No, not with the Heiké soldiers there."

"Why should that matter? I must help her."

"Yes, but have you noticed that young manservant standing to the right of those dancing-girls?" Yomogi asked.

"Yes, he came with the woman who's sick."

"I know," Yomogi continued, "but don't you recognize him?"

"Why?"

"Well, he's the reason for my not wanting you to go back there. I could hardly believe my eyes. I'm sure if he sees me he'd be surprised, so I'd rather stay here under this tree."

"That manservant? Why, he's only an ordinary servant."

"He used to be one of Lord Yoshitomo's retainers—Konno-maru."

Asatori started. "What! Konno-maru—*he*?"

"You do know him, then, don't you? He's the retainer that the Heiké soldiers tried to capture after the Heiji War."

"I'm sure you're mistaken, Yomogi."

"No, I'd never mistake him. I often saw him when he visited my mistress Tokiwa in secret at the Mibu villa."

"How odd of him to hire himself out as a manservant in the gay quarters!"

"Nor can I understand why he should, but the Heiké soldiers would never guess that he's Konno-maru. What a fuss there'll be if they ever find out!"

"That doesn't interest me in the least. I'm neither a Genji nor a Heiké, so nothing worries me now, but I'm a physician and my conscience would trouble me if I didn't do something for her."

"Must you see her?"

"It's nothing serious, just the heat that's affected her. I could make her more comfortable in no time. No one over there would recognize me. There'd be no harm in it if I went alone. You'd better stay right here, Yomogi."

Asatori started off once more for the temple gate. At the sound of his cautious approach, the group around the sick woman glanced at him suspiciously, but his kindly looks and his assurances that he was a physician soon dispelled their fears. The young officer, too, welcomed him. After silently scrutinizing the woman's features, Asatori finally took her pulse, felt her all over, and then began his treatment; deftly he administered acupuncture at various points in her body; then he rolled a few pills into the palm of his hand and turned to the dancing-girls who were looking on: "One of you take these, chew them, and force them

between her lips," he said. The manservant motioned to the
dancing-girls, who drew back. Then one of them pushed a
younger one toward Asatori, saying: "Giwo, you should do it.
You've always been like a daughter to Toji, and you're her favorite."

". . . . If that's you all want me to do," the young girl,
Giwo, replied, quickly untying the cords of her wide hat and
laying it down to one side. She took her place beside Asatori,
extending a delicate, translucent hand; the palm was turned up
to receive some minute pearl-colored pellets, when Giwo suddenly
exclaimed:

"You!"

"Asuka! Can it really be you?"

The small globes melted away between her fingers.

"Dear me, this won't do!" Asatori cried. Fearing that
the others had heard him, he quickly poured out a few more pills
from his medicine pouch, saying: "Now give these to her at
once. . . . Open her mouth—now some water."

An ox-cart arrived in the meantime, and the young officer went off to mount his horse, directing a soldier to take
charge.

"Now get her onto the cart. It may be rather uncomfortable,
and the rest of you, except this man, ride with her. Let me look
at the patient once more. From her color, she seems to be much
better."

The dancing-girls then turned to the soldier who was to accompany them, saying: "We were most fortunate in meeting
that kind officer. Can you tell us who he is?"

The warrior replied: "It's only a short time since he came to
the capital from Kumano. He's Tadanori, Lord Kiyomori's half-
brother, and an officer of the Police Commission."

The dancing-girls gazed after the disappearing figure, remarking: "Lord Kiyomori's half-brother—Tadanori?"

As they turned to climb into the cart, the young women
stopped to thank Asatori, but found him gone.

The heavy downpour soon abated and Tadanori, his armor soaked and his horse steaming, arrived at Funaoka Hill. As he neared the hill, an officer commanding the Guards on the eastern side called to him sharply:

"Tadanori, where were you?"

"I was clearing the route as you ordered."

"Very well, but what about your men?"

"We found a sick woman on the road and I had them fetch her an ox-cart. They should arrive shortly, sir."

"I hear the route is crowded with people, but it's not your business to be caring for the sick. Let these people look after themselves."

"Yes, sir."

Tadanori took the rebuke quietly, abashed at the thought of his inexperience and rustic upbringing. It was only a few weeks since he had accompanied Kiyomori, his half-brother, from Kumano. Shortly after arriving in the capital, Tadanori had been assigned to the lowest rank in the Police Commission. The officer who had just spoken to him was Norimori, Kiyomori's youngest brother. The funeral was Tadanori's first chance to take part in an important public function, and it was only natural that he should find his duties bewildering, though he had only a few warriors to command.

The sky soon cleared and a rainbow appeared, causing a flurry of excitement among the functionaries, who hurried to complete the final arrangements while there was light.

The imperial tomb was on Funaoka Hill, where a stone vault lay ready to receive the coffin. Palings enclosed the foot of the hill and the Koryuji Temple at its base; within were curtained pavilions for the titled mourners, the temple dignitaries, and the performers of sacred music; everywhere were funeral banners and the clustered branches of the "sacred tree."

Here the representatives of the greater and lesser monasteries of Nara and Mount Hiei would soon arrive to take up their positions in the strictly prescribed order of rank fixed by custom. From times immemorial the Todaiji monastery, under court patronage, ranked first among the seven main temple groups; after them came the Kofukuji bishops of Nara. The Enryakuji monastery of Mount Hiei ranked third, with the other monasteries following in diminishing order of importance.

Darkness fell; the stars blazed down blue and clear and a primeval silence filled the night as the long funeral cortege slowly crept toward Funaoka. Watch-fires lighted up the hill where streaming banners, crested with emblems of the sun and moon, writhed like dragons against the sky. But a sudden turmoil broke the spell when the ecclesiastics of Kofukuji found that the Enryakuji priests had occupied their position on the hill. Angry roars filled the air and torches waved menacingly as the Kofukuji monks prepared to fall on their rivals with broadswords and halberds. Then their anguished Abbot appeared, exhorting his followers to desist from violence. Two deputies were sent off at once to demand apologies from Enryakuji.

Reports of the disturbance soon reached Norimori at the main gate; quickly ordering the captains of the Guards to follow him, he made his way to the scene of the dispute. Tadanori, who accompanied his half-brother, found he could make nothing of the situation and stood in blank amazement among the raging monks.

"Tadanori, why aren't you in there putting down the rioters!" Norimori cried, pointing at some of the Kofukuji monks.

"These or the others over there?" Tadanori called back.

"Yes, those—don't let them come any farther!"

"By any means?"

"Short of drawing your sword," was the answer as Tadanori plunged fearlessly into the angry mob at which Norimori had pointed.

Deliberate in temper, naturally courageous, and hardened by the rigorous training he had received from childhood in Kumano, Tadanori swept up the first monk who attacked him and flung him bodily at another. Assailant after assailant went down as Tadanori, nimbly wrenched away halberds and struck at his attackers.

Someone cried out: "Who's that fellow there?"

"Not one of the monks. . . ."

"If he's not one of us, then he's one of the police or a Heiké!"

The raging monks wavered and fell back as Tadanori laid about him singlehanded until Norimori rode in among the struggling monks shouting:

"Back, back! The imperial carriage has arrived!"

At the bottom of the hill, marching flames marked the progress of the approaching cortege, and the clamoring mob suddenly grew silent; the wounded were carried off swiftly, and disordered robes hurriedly rearranged to conceal armor and the long swords under them. The monks of Enryakuji discovered too late that their rivals had ousted them from their position, for the funeral carriage had reached the foot of Funaoka Hill in a blaze of torches, and silence enveloped the mourning crowds.

Flanked by white-robed mourners and high-ranking officials, the funeral carriage rolled by. Countless candles burned; blazing watch-fires and thousands of torches illumined Funaoka Hill, where the gates finally swung open to receive the imperial coffin.

The requiem ended, the lustration rites over, a new day dawned. Watch-fires paled and the vast crowds melted away to the last strains of a dirge. Mounted warriors, litters, carriages, and common folk on foot streamed back toward the capital.

Last night's dispute between the monks, however, provided the departing people with speculations and gossip, and uppermost in their minds was the question of how soon fighting would break out between Enryakuji and Kofukuji. Already there were rumors that the ex-Emperor and his advisers had caused the disturbance to stir up further enmity between the rival monasteries, and even as the earliest arrivals set foot in Kyoto, new reports were heard that the Cloistered Emperor had sent his deputies to confer with the Enryakuji monks, who were rallying, fully armed, at West Sakamoto.

Late that summer Kiyomori's family and numerous servants and retainers moved to the new mansion on the opposite bank of the Kamo from Rokuhara, though Kiyomori himself remained at Rokuhara. He had not, in fact, returned to his home for more than ten days after the imperial funeral, but stayed at Court attending to the innumerable arrangements that opened a new reign.

The new ruler was barely two years old, and everything relating to state affairs was necessarily in the hands of a few senior court officers. Since his old and trusted friend, the Prime Minister, Koremichi, was now dead, Kiyomori felt it his duty to preside over the state councils. A new array of faces, inexperienced and absurdly youthful, surrounded him, and Kiyomori could only shake his head as he looked round at them. The late Prime Minister's several sons filled various key posts—the youngest, only sixteen, was Lord Keeper of the Privy Seal. Tsunemuné, still the suave courtier after all the changes of his fortunes, had been made Minister of the Right. Nothing, Kiyomori thought, had changed at Court. The Regent, the Lord High Chancellor, and the state ministers—all were Fujiwara. And nothing could please the Cloistered Emperor Goshirakawa more or suit his purposes better than this, Kiyomori reflected with misgivings.

Though appointed only a State Councilor and General of the Guards of the Left, authority was thrust upon Kiyomori and objections to his exercising powers to which his rank did not entitle him soon subsided. The Court, the seat of government, however, was empty, and Kiyomori found himself presiding over state councils whose principal members were absent. The Regent and the ministers were occupied elsewhere—at the Cloister Palace, currying favor with the ex-Emperor Goshirakawa.

"There's no end to this waiting," Kiyomori told himself at length. "If I stay here much longer I shall have to act for the Regent himself. . . ." For the first time in many days Kiyomori recalled Rokuhara and prepared to go home. As he drove away from the Office of Court Affairs, he looked up at the sky. Autumn already! Shut in for so long, he was invigorated by the freshness of the air. As he drew up at the Guard Office, several captains saluted him.

"On your way home, sir?" they asked with looks of relief.

"But what's this—you're all armed?" Kiyomori replied, looking round suspiciously at the several hundreds of armed warriors from Rokuhara.

Just then Kiyomori's brother, Tsunemori, appeared beside the carriage. He gave one look at Kiyomori's tired face and then whispered: "Then you haven't heard yet? The rumor is all over the Court and I was sure that you knew."

"Knew what? What's all this about? Has something gone wrong at Rokuhara?"

"Nothing to worry about yet and Rokuhara's well guarded."

"What's happened," Kiyomori persisted. "Why are you fully armed?"

"The monks of Mount Hiei—"

"What of them?"

"It's still a rumor, but we hear that the Cloistered Emperor is inciting them. We can't afford to take risks."

"What? Are you trying to tell me that he's stirred up the monks against me?" Kiyomori laughed aloud. "Nonsense! What utter nonsense!" he cried, and without listening further to Tsunemori ordered the ox-tender to drive on.

As with rumors of this kind, no one knew where they started. Their causes remained wrapped in obscurity. But it was common knowledge now that the Imperial Guards were chosen only from among the Heiké; that the swaggering of the lowest Heiké soldier was creating resentment everywhere; that Kiyomori had vast building projects on foot, and that his brothers and sons occupied influential posts at the Court. From this it was natural to conclude that the ex-Emperor Goshirakawa was anxious to nip Kiyomori's growing influence. Goshirakawa himself, moreover, had lately hinted at a need for changing the system of selecting Guards, and the climate of the Cloister Palace itself had suddenly altered. Goshirakawa was attracting ambitious followers, daring men, eager to share his predilection for personal intrigue and politics.

New rumors spread, adding fuel to earlier ones; it was said that the monks of Mount Hiei had armed—two thousand strong —at West Sakamoto, hundreds at other points, preparing for an attack on Rokuhara. Each fresh report added credence to the popular belief that fighting was imminent. The movements of the Heiké soldiers further confirmed it, for Heiké troops had been called out and a defense line drawn around Rokuhara and west of Gojo Bridge to include West Eighth Avenue.

In the meantime Kiyomori arrived at Rokuhara. Every step of the way he was met by troops drawn up behind a wall of bows and shields. From his carriage Kiyomori stared out at this scene with looks of displeasure.

Summoning his sons and captains for a council, Kiyomori turned to each and demanded:

"Who ordered this?"

No one replied and he once more insisted: "Will no one answer me? Who ordered the mobilizing of the troops? You— Munemori?"

"Sir—"

"Motomori, do you also refuse to answer me?"

Motomori replied surlily: "No one in particular, but as you were so busy at the Court, we did not have the time to come to you for orders. My brothers and I and our uncle Tokitada decided that we had better be prepared to strike the first blow."

Kiyomori nodded thoughtfully. "I don't see Norimori," he said suddenly.

"He's taken his stand on the main highway. Do you wish to see him?" one of his sons offered.

"Yes, call him," Kiyomori replied. While he waited for his brother to appear, Kiyomori questioned his sons in turn.

"Was your brother Shigemori consulted in all this?"

"He was."

"What did he have to say?"

"He advised us to speak to you first. He seemed to think that the troops should be called out only if the situation demanded it."

"As I thought. He's not one to lose his head like this. . . ."

Norimori arrived just then, and Kiyomori turned to him:

"Norimori, I understand there was some misunderstanding between the monks of Enryakuji and Kofukuji during the imperial funeral at Funaoka. You were commanding the Guards at the time. Just how did you settle that affair? I heard something of the disturbance, but I want you to give me the particulars."

His eyes narrowed to slits, Kiyomori listened closely to his brother's account.

"There's nothing much to tell in any detail. Tadanori was there at the time and I had him restore order among the Kofukuji monks while I looked after the others."

"Before this happened, however, did you by any chance receive any orders from two counselors sent by the Cloistered Emperor?"

"There was talk that I did, but do you think I would listen to them?"

"So it *did* happen."

"Yes. It's a fact that Mount Hiei has no love for the Heiké, and I know that on two or three occasions they slandered us to the Cloistered Emperor. His two counselors, however, have been saying that the Enryakuji monks of Mount Hiei were at fault that night and they urged me at the time to take strong measures against them as well as Kofukuji—to wound and kill if need be— saying that they would set matters right with his majesty."

"And what did you do then?"

"I heard them out, but ignored the orders. Tadanori gave the Kofukuji monks a good trouncing, but I did nothing more than get between the two sides and somehow made them calm down."

"Then Mount Hiei has nothing against us, I take it?"

"There's no reason why they should."

"Then what's at the bottom of these disturbing rumors of the last few days?"

"I suspect the Cloistered Emperor's advisers are stirring up the monks of Mount Hiei as they tried to stir up me."

"Good! That explains it," Kiyomori exclaimed, looking relieved. Calling for writing-materials, he quickly inscribed a short letter, then called to his half-brother, who sat at the farther end of the room:

"Tadanori, your face isn't too well known here in the capital, so you're best suited for this. Leave your armor behind—carry this to Mount Hiei and make sure that one of the three abbots there gets it. An answer? . . . I think not. You'd better take care, though—agents from the Cloister Palace may be on the lookout for you."

When Tadanori left with the letter, the others stared at Kiyomori, curious as to when and how he had come to be on corresponding terms with the leaders on Mount Hiei.

"We're in trouble now," Kiyomori remarked half to himself. "Get me my armor. I might as well be prepared for the worst," adding as he rose reluctantly: "The truth is I'm tired and more ready for some sleep than anything else."

While he drew on his black corselet and fastened the cords of his greaves, he muttered between his teeth: ". . . too fond of meddling. The worst sort of men around him. Too headstrong for his own good. . . . If only he'd stop meddling!"

Toward evening of that same day there were reports that the monks of Mount Hiei were pouring into the capital. Kiyomori groaned. Had his letter reached Mount Hiei too late? Without further delay he ordered his sons to ride to the Court with reinforcements, assuring them that he would remain to defend Rokuhara.

In the meantime, remnants of Heiké soldiers and the Police Commission, who had gone to West Sakamoto and north along the Kamo to repulse the monks, arrived back in the twilit capital with the news that the monks had put the Heiké troops to rout. The entire capital was now in turmoil as though an earthquake had struck it. Panic seized the populace as they waited for the outbreak of fighting between Kiyomori and the ex-Emperor. But in the midst of this uproar an imperial carriage rolled along Fifth Avenue, rumbled across Gojo Bridge and into Rokuhara.

"His majesty—the Cloistered Emperor—here?" Kiyomori received the announcement in a daze, then hurried out to meet his visitor.

"Is that you, Kiyomori?" Goshirakawa called, rolling up the blinds of his carriage and smiling. "Your hand. . . . Help me down," he said in his usual friendly manner.

Kiyomori stared at the disarming smile on Goshirakawa's lips, then moved forward like a sleepwalker to assist him and led him indoors.

"But, your majesty, what is this? What is meant by this honor, a visit so late at night?" Kiyomori exclaimed in astonishment.

Kiyomori, who felt equal to any situation, was completely taken aback by this fantastic turn of affairs. But the ex-Emperor continued to smile imperturbably. Though considerably younger than Kiyomori, he wore a triumphant look that said he was not one to be taken in by Kiyomori.

"Did I take you by surprise, Kiyomori?"

"Indeed you did, your majesty."

"What else was there for me to do? Had I let these rumors continue, they would undoubtedly have led to bloodshed."

"Is it true that all these reports were nothing more than rumors?"

"Do you still doubt me, Kiyomori? Did I not come here—to you?"

"Yes, truly," Kiyomori replied lamely. Here he was, fully armed. Had his faulty judgment been the sole cause of this terrible blunder? The ex-Emperor regarded him after all as ungenerous, untrustworthy. Kiyomori writhed inwardly at the thought of the false situation into which he was being forced. Then his savage warrior's pride asserted itself and tears sprang to his eyes.

"Kiyomori—tears?"

"Tears of gratitude, your majesty."

"How comic, Kiyomori! You armed and your soldiers armed —and then you in tears!"

"True, a comic performance. I laugh at myself for a fool."

"All is well, then. Let us be glad that we no longer misunderstand each other. Don't be deceived by mere rumors Kiyomori. Believe in me, trust me." And with these words Goshirakawa departed, escorted by troops from Rokuhara.

Soon after his departure, Kiyomori's eldest son arrived. "Has his majesty left?" he asked. "I just heard of his visit from my brothers."

"Shigemori, not in armor?"

"No, it was exactly as I thought and had been telling the others—that his majesty had no intention of turning against the Heiké."

"You think so, do you? I'm still puzzled," Kiyomori replied.

"Why is that?"

"All this could not have happened without his majesty himself intending that it should. He has a dangerous smile. I have no doubt that he has secret designs upon the Heike."

"Father! . . ."

"Why that look?" Kiyomori said sharply.

"That's unlikely, Father, but to say it! You must take care not to do anything that will turn him against us. I pray that you will serve him with even greater loyalty."

"Of all that I need no reminding. But, Shigemori, I doubt that you understand what's behind that charming manner. I know, and that makes it all the harder for me."

"No, I'm sure that if you serve him with all your heart the gods will watch over you."

"Take care," Kiyomori exclaimed with a laugh, "don't preach to your father—it's not quite that simple, Shigemori. You, your mother and the rest of you are completely deceived by his charm. I alone see through him. . . . Yes, and it really matters little that the rest of you don't."

But while they were talking, a glare filled the sky over Kiyomizu Temple; flames soon swept through the temple buildings, raining sparks and burning fragments on Rokuhara. There, the excited inhabitants told each other that the monks of Mount Hiei were revenging themselves on Kofukuji by setting fire to their rivals' temple.

In the midst of this uproar Tadanori arrived back with a letter from the Abbot Jisso—a cryptic message intended for Kiyomori alone.

All that night of August 9, while flames lapped at one side of the Eastern Hills, several thousand fighting monks made their way back to Mount Hiei.

CHAPTER XLII

THE LIGHT OF TRUTH

All that remained of Kiyomizu Temple, its pagoda and other buildings of the temple group, was a waste of ashes. Days went by, but no priest returned to view the ruins or repent the awful desecration; only the common folk—men and women—came and prostrated themselves with streaming eyes among the ashes and prayed. Yet among that crowd of dazed penitents a young monk—still in his early thirties—knelt in prayer. His robes, severely plain, proclaimed him a seminarian; the figure in all its humility eloquently conveyed the impression of one bowed down with sorrow. At length, when he reached for his pilgrim hat and rose, the people about him suddenly pressed toward him hungrily.

"Your reverence, are you not one of the priests of Kiyomizu Temple?"

"No, I come from Mount Hiei," the priest replied.

Every eye was now suddenly fixed on him. "Mount Hiei? . . . But aren't you afraid to be found here?—From a temple on Mount Hiei, you say?"

"From Kurodani on the west. It is true that I belong on Mount Hiei, yet we are not all ruffians. The man whose disciple I am—and there are others too—seeks after the truth in solitude. There are many like him, seeking enlightenment of the Buddha in order to share the light with suffering man."

"Is this true? Is it possible that such men live on Mount Hiei today?" exclaimed the people incredulously, gathering about him eagerly.

"They do, but how can I expect you to believe me when you see those armed thousands? It is true that in the hidden valleys and in the depths of the forests on Mount Hiei the well-spring of light is not quenched. How can we, the priesthood, let the flame die when you who have lived through the sufferings of the Hogen and Heiji wars have not forgotten to love and comfort each other?"

"Your words give us hope, but if there are others like you, why do they not come down among us and teach us how to live?"

"But—" The monk's brows contracted in an expression of deep distress. "But do you, who have come here to pray among the ashes, not listen to the teachings of your priests here?"

"Liars, liars all of them! We believe nothing they say! Who will believe them when he sees this ruin? Better swallow offal than their words! They give us nothing but fine words when they're no better than thieves and make it their business to deceive us! Can we trust them? Do you wonder that we hate them?"

"Then you no longer believe them and despair?"

"Yes, and that is why we sit here lost, praying to these ashes."

"Ah, then the Buddha has at last come down among you! Believe me!"

"Enough of that! We want no such empty comfort!"

"You are right. You speak the truth. . . . But even though the holy image is gone from the sanctuary—reduced to ashes, the Kannon is still here."

"Where—where do you see the Kannon?"

"In the ashes themselves, about it."

"Aren't ashes only ashes?"

"Yes."

"What is there to see?"

"The divine presence cannot be seen."

"Show it to us. . . . No, you're still too young for that. Is there no true priest who can show us the unseen while we still live?"

"There is. There's no reason to think that he does not exist."

"Where is he? Where is this priest?" clamored the people eagerly as they closed in about the monk.

"Ah—let me go, please," the monk pleaded, waving his hat and pushing his way through the crowd. "I have said too much. I cannot tell you that yet, but I am sure that there is such a man. He will come among you soon. If he does not, then indeed are the teachings of the Buddha false, and paradise a lie— man's true destiny and all the precepts of Buddha but empty mouthing. Then, and then alone, will you have reason to despair. No, the vision and the light of truth have not vanished altogether from Mount Hiei."

His face hidden under his wide hat, the monk fled, crying out as he went: "Do not despair or lose faith in each other! Live on in courage until he comes!"

The crowd dispersed rapidly as many tried to pursue the monk; some followed him with yells of derision. Then the cloud of ashes settled down once more on the ruins.

A lay priest who appeared just then turned to stare at the **flying figure.**

"Who was that, Yasunori? I'm sure I've seen him before," remarked Saiko, a Fujiwara courtier and current favorite at the Cloister Palace, turning to a member of the Police Commission who accompanied him. "Do you recognize him?"

The officer, Yasunori, quickly replied: "Did you not meet him, sir, through the Abbot of Ninna-ji Temple?"

"Ah, that's it. I hear that the Tendai sect has none more learned than he. I do recall the Abbot telling me about him. A monk—what's his name?—who lives in Kurodani on Mount Hiei."

"That must be Honen."

"Honen—that's it, I was sure it was he. He never leaves his hermitage in Kurodani. . . . I wonder what brought him down here."

"The destruction of the temple caused so much talk that curiosity probably got the better of him and he couldn't resist coming to see the ruins for himself."

"It must have been that," Saiko said, looking round him cautiously to make sure that no one had recognized him.

After viewing the ruins carefully, Saiko motioned to a retainer to bring him his horse, and shortly after was riding back to the Cloister Palace.

The Cloister Palace blazed with lights every night, for it was now Goshirakawa's custom to invite four or five of his favorites to dine with him in the evening. Saiko had just finished speaking. Goshirakawa, who listened closely to the priest's account of his visit to Kiyomizu Temple that afternoon, turned to Saiko, saying:

"So people are coming in great numbers to the ruins and praying to the ashes, you say? Comic and yet touching—something will have to be done soon to placate the Kofukuji monks so we can rebuild the temple. . . . Isn't that so, Toshitsuné?"

"Yes, your majesty," the courtier Toshitsuné replied, looking down, at a loss how he should continue, for he had returned in great distress a few days before from Nara. The Kofukuji monks had been obdurate, spurned all his overtures for a truce, and demanded that there should be no delay in punishing the authorities of Mount Hiei. Goshirakawa had received the news with a bare nod and gave no indication of what he thought. Toshitsuné, however, had seen that the monks of Kofukuji were preparing for a war. It also stood to reason that Goshirakawa knew that the monks would soon enter the capital with their sacred emblems to plunder and burn the temples in Mount Hiei's jurisdiction, and that Mount Hiei would retaliate in kind. Nor was there anything, short of a powerful army, to keep the monks from marching on the Cloister Palace and intimidating Goshirakawa himself. Until now it would have been a matter of course to call upon the Heiké for support. Yet no one knew how Goshirakawa stood in relation to Kiyomori, for though the ex-Emperor's visit to Rokuhara had apparently dispelled Kiyomori's distrust of Goshirakawa, there was still some doubt as to what went on in Kiyomori's mind. Without him, however, there was no way to send the warriors out to repulse the monks.

Goshirakawa then turned to the priest: "Saiko, what are people in the capital saying nowadays about that recent affair?"

A shrewd look of comprehension entered Saiko's eyes as he inclined his head. "What is it that your majesty wishes to know?"

Goshirakawa turned his eyes full on Saiko. "There was a rumor all over the capital on the night Kiyomizu Temple burned down that I gave out secret orders to attack the Heiké."

"It was so."

"But that is preposterous, Saiko; what do you think of this?"

The other guests listened intently for Saiko's reply. What they had just heard was a complete reversal of all that Goshirakawa had been urging until now. But the answer came without a moment's hesitation:

"Your majesty, the gods speak through the lips of men. Though your majesty may hesitate to say it, the people see how arrogant the Heiké have grown and they have spoken for the gods, have they not?"

Goshirakawa nodded his agreement, then suddenly laughed aloud. "Enough, Saiko! You have said enough!"

No sooner did he realize that he could not dispense with Kiyomori, than Goshirakawa lost no time in courting his good will; his brother, Yorimori, and his brother-in-law, Tokitada, who had been banished from Kyoto, were quickly recalled. Goshirakawa soon saw Kiyomori's popularity increase at the Court and all over the capital.

Kiyomori, at the head of his warriors, went out to parley with the Kofukuji monks as they marched on Kyoto. In a day or two he succeeded in arranging a meeting between the heads of Mount Hiei and Kofukuji, with the result that the latter withdrew their forces to Nara. The swiftness of the amicable settlement that followed astounded the frightened populace and mystified Goshirakawa's followers. And even when Saiko learned the names of the three powerful leaders of Mount Hiei, proverbially hostile to the Heiké, with whom Kiyomori had exchanged letters on several occasions, there was nothing to explain how Kiyomori had come to know them. Long since forgotten was that summer's day, eighteen years before, when Kiyomori defied the monks of Mount Hiei at Gion, and no one knew that he won a few friends among them by his daring.

In the following year, 1166, State Councilor Fujiwara Motozané, to whom Kiyomori's second daughter was married, died suddenly at the early age of twenty-four. A year later Kiyomori was appointed a State Minister, with all the authority and prestige attached to this high post. He had just turned fifty; the new mansion at West Eighth Avenue had been completed; his labors, it seemed, had received their final reward. But new vistas continued to unfold before him, peak after challenging peak, for the triumph of the Heiké was only beginning. His brothers and sons, still in their thirties or forties, all were high-ranking officials at the Court and in the government. Yet power and renown had come to Kiyomori without resort to force or to intrigues; his connections with the aristocracy had come without his seeking: both his daughter and his wife's sister Shigeko, had been sought after in marriage, the one by the former Regent for his son, the latter by the ex-Emperor Goshirakawa.

CHAPTER XLIII

TWO DANCING-GIRLS

The Heiké had now entered into a period of great influence, and in the popular mind nothing counted so much as even the slightest connection with the Heiké. And it was about this time that the gossips of the capital delighted to tell the story of Giwo.

Giwo, from the gay quarters of Kyoto, was one of the dancing-girls who accompanied their mistress to the Emperor Nijo's funeral at Funaoka Hill. That day when Toji fell ill, prostrated by the heat, a young Heiké warrior had taken pity on her and lent Toji an ox-cart to carry her back to her home in the capital. Toji recovered within a day or two, and one hot afternoon as she ate chilled melons she chatted about the events of that day with the girls in her establishment.

"Yes, he was most kind. I don't know what we would have done if he had driven us from that temple gate."

"Yes, Mother, we **were** frantic. There you were, stretched out in pain, and the rain coming down, when the soldiers came to drive us away."

"If that young warrior hadn't been there and taken pity on me, it would have gone badly for us all."

"We should have had to carry you all that way home. I'm sure you would never have been sitting up so soon like this. . . . And to have lent us an ox-cart to bring us all the way home! . . . We really must do something about calling on the gentleman and thanking him, Mother."

Toji had been turning this over in her mind for some time. The young warrior, she soon found out, was Kiyomori's younger brother, Tadanori. Had he not been a Heiké, she would not have hesitated so long, but her good sense told her that whatever form her gratitude took, it must also serve to establish some connection with the Heiké. She waited until autumn and then called her favorite pupil, Giwo, to her and said: "You are most suited to go to Rokuhara as my messenger to thank the honorable Tadanori for me."

Giwo suddenly colored, and complied willingly, but the anxious look in her face led Toji to add: "You needn't be afraid; I've talked to Master Bamboku about this, and he's promised to meet you inside the main gate at Rokuhara. He'll see to it that you meet the honorable Tadanori. . . . All you need do is take a carriage and go there."

Giwo was ready to leave at once, but Toji called her back: "No, no, it won't do for you to go like that! Remember, you're going to Rokuhara. This may be the first and the last time and you're to go in your best. . . . Now I'll help you get dressed."

Toji herself attended to Giwo's toilette, applying cosmetics
with great care, until she was satisfied with her handiwork. Arrayed
in a pale-blue costume, a headdress of gold-colored gauze and a
silver sword at her waist, Giwo quickly stepped into the lady's carriage that awaited her. Kowaka, the manservant, in a new suit of
clothes suitable to the occasion, accompanied her, walking beside
the carriage.

As her carriage crossed Gojo Bridge and entered Rokuhara,
Giwo's heart fluttered wildly with her joy; she was like one in a
trance. From the day she had met the young warrior she had never
ceased to dream of him. That figure, his voice, and his face had
been with her constantly. At the thought that she would be seeing him soon, her cheeks flushed and grew feverish. What was she
to say? How would she reply?

Giwo's carriage soon drew up at one of several gates.

"Please—" Kowaka asked of the soldier at the entrance, "has
Master Bamboku come?"

"Ah, you mean Red-Nose, don't you?" the soldier corrected.
"If it's Red-Nose, go in by the gate over there and ask at the lodge
on your right. I saw him there just awhile ago."

Kowaka bowed his thanks and started away, when a shout
made him turn.

"No, no! Not that way! Bring your carriage this way!" Bamboku directed, waving.

The carriage finally drew up at a portico and Giwo stepped
down. She approached a footman uncertainly to say:

"I am called Giwo and was sent by my mistress Toji at Horikawa to thank the honorable Tadanori."

Other footmen soon collected at the entrance and stared at
Giwo for some moments in silent amazement, until one came to
himself and started away with her message.

"Here, you, wait!" Bamboku suddenly called after the footman. "Your master is expecting us. You needn't go. I'll take the
lady in myself." Bamboku was already ascending the stairs. "Come,
Giwo, this way," he said.

Giwo rustled past the staring menials. She followed Red-Nose through long hallways, past several inner gardens. As they came to a connecting bridge between two apartments, she heard rapid footsteps approaching them. Two or three attendants appeared and quickly warned them back: "Lord Kiyomori—step back, please."

Bamboku and Giwo instantly withdrew to one side and waited deferentially. The sound of a clear laugh reached their ears from beyond; then Kiyomori appeared, engrossed in conversation with some courtiers. He cast an interested glance at Giwo as he went past and looked back at her over his shoulder once more, with a whispered question to one of his companions.

"I hope we're not disturbing you, sir," Red-Nose called as he and Giwo paused at the entrance to Tadanori's apartments.

"Is that you, Bamboku?"

"You are busy reading, I see. I apologize. . . ."

"No need for that. I was looking through this collection of poems which I'm told were written by my father, Tadamori, and was pleasantly surprised to find that he had quite a gift for writing verse."

"So I understand," Bamboku remarked, showing no particular interest in the subject.

"You're sure I'm not intruding? As a matter of fact, I've come about that matter I mentioned this morning. Toji at Horikawa sent you a message by one of her pupils, whom I've left waiting in the next room."

"Oh? Yes, to be sure, bring her here," said Tadanori, putting aside his book and turning away from his writing-table. He glanced toward the next room.

Giwo, who had been drinking in the sound of Tadanori's voice, bemused, looked up in confusion as Red-Nose drew aside the screening-curtain.

Tadanori stared at the exquisite vision before him, then turned to say: "But, Bamboku, who is this?"

"This is Giwo, the dancing-girl, a pupil of Toji, to whom you were so kind."

"But her costume is like a man's."

"That is what the dancing-girls in the capital wear when they entertain at banquets."

Tadanori laughed. "I'm only an ignorant bumpkin, I'm afraid."

"Giwo, you want to thank him, don't you?" Bamboku said encouragingly.

"Yes. . . . I—my mistress Toji sent you her respectful greetings and her very deep thanks."

"Is she better now?"

"Thanks to you, she has recovered completely."

Someone was heard calling for Bamboku, then a footman appeared. "Lord Kiyomori wishes to see you at once," he announced.

Bamboku, who knew how impatient Kiyomori could be, began excusing himself immediately. "Sir, if you will allow me—I shall be back as soon as possible," he said, wondering at the same time whether urgent business regarding the construction work at Fukuhara had come up, for Bamboku lately had been spending the greater part of each month there.

Giwo, too, prepared to take leave of Tadanori, who made no attempt to detain her, when Red-Nose, ignoring Tadanori, waved her back. "Come, stay a little longer and chat with the gentleman, who seems to find this something of a treat. I'm sure I shan't be long."

Red-Nose listened to Kiyomori with some impatience. It looked as though he would be kept here much longer than he had expected. Kiyomori rambled on tediously and seemed unconscionably long about coming to a point. He could not very well ask why he had been sent for without giving offense, Bamboku thought.

But finally Kiyomori suggested: "Wine?" and gave orders to the servant to prepare the table.

"I thank you, my lord, I—"

Red-Nose could no longer conceal his impatience. "To tell you the truth, my lord . . ." he began, tapping his forehead.

"What's this, Bamboku, something else you have in mind?"

"Exactly, my lord."

"Fool! Do you expect me to guess what it is? . . . . What's preventing you from staying?"

"Not quite that, but I left someone waiting with the honorable Tadanori."

"Someone?"

"Yes."

"What exactly do you mean by 'someone'?"

"To tell you the truth, a dancing-girl from Horikawa."

Kiyomori chuckled and then grinned. "A dancing-girl, did you say?"

Red-Nose slapped his forehead. Dense, he was! He should have known that this was why he had been called.

"You may have noticed her, sir, as you passed us?"

"Yes, I saw her," Kiyomori said. "Someone I've never seen before. What's her name?"

"Giwo, sir."

"Why did you bring her to see Tadanori? Has that countrified brother of mine already taken to going out at night?"

"On the contrary—" Bamboku denied it with exaggerated zeal, and then carefully recounted the happenings that led to Giwo's appearance at Rokuhara. He added significantly that she was Toji's most cherished pupil, only seventeen and so precious that she had not yet been presented in public.

By the time wine and trays of food appeared, Bamboku was his usual loquacious self again.

"Red-Nose," Kiyomori began expansively before even touching the wine, "She'll do very well. Bring her here."

"Eh, sir, you mean Giwo?"

"Hmm—" Kiyomori nodded.

One by one lamps were lit under the dark eaves and along the galleries, while Giwo watched them as in a dream. This was fairyland, she thought. The evening sky deepened to indigo and insects began to chirr softly among the grasses of the inner garden. If only this could go on forever, she sighed to herself, until the lamps suddenly reminded her that it was time for her to go back. What had she and Tadanori talked of?—Just a few words in answer to

5 3 4

his—nothing of all that she might have said. She sat all the while motionless, staring out at the garden. Never had she known such bliss! No, that was not quite true—there had been another such time long ago, when she lived on the Street of the Ox-Dealers.

She was called Asuka—a mere child then—and she had loved Asatori. She was only thirteen or fourteen at the time, scarcely able to pin up her hair for herself, and she had worshipped him. But another woman had come to live with him and be his wife, and Asuka not long after was sold into bondage in the gay quarters. Even the memory of that love was fast fading from mind, and then she had come upon Asatori quite by chance near Funaoka Hill. She had seen his wife with him, and when Giwo reached home she had wept all that night into her pillow. Then, gradually, Tadanori had crowded out the memories of Asatori, until she knew that she was in love with the handsome young warrior. She never dreamed that she would see him so soon again, like this, and she asked nothing more than to be near him.

Giwo in the midst of her musings looked up and found a lighted lampstand beside her. Tadanori was seated once more at his writing-table, poring over the collection of poems by the fast receding light, oblivious of Giwo.

"You must find it difficult to see," she said, pushing the lamp toward him.

"Oh, are you still here?"

"I'm afraid I'm in the way. . . . I wonder what is keeping Master Bamboku."

"Yes, he did say something about coming to fetch you."

"My mistress will be worried, so I had better leave now."

"Going? You might lose your way; let me see you to the carriage porch."

Tadanori was leading the way down the corridors when the two suddenly came on Bamboku. With a look of relief, Tadanori left Giwo to Bamboku and made his way back to his rooms.

"This way, Giwo, come this way."

"It's growing dark, so I had really better be leaving."

"Lord Kiyomori wishes to see you. Come in here."

Giwo suddenly drew back. "But—" she protested, clinging to a pillar and refusing to go farther. A light was burning at the far end of the room, and as footmen hurried by, she suddenly saw that this was not the way by which she had come from the carriage entry.

"You needn't be so anxious. If you're late, the soldiers will escort you home. If you think Toji will be worried, a runner can be sent right off to tell her where you are. In any case, you must not offend Lord Kiyomori by refusing."

Coaxing, scolding, and reproving her in turn, Red-Nose finally led her to Kiyomori.

Kiyomori began pouring himself some wine. From where he sat, the headdress of gauze and the pale-blue tunic gleamed unreal in the lamplight. "Red-Nose, remove the headdress and sword; they look uncomfortable," he said.

"Giwo—is that your name? Come up closer—here. . . . Come and talk to me for a while. What is the latest gossip in the capital?"

Red-Nose sniggered to himself at Kiyomori's clumsiness, his foolish speech and the sheepish look that came over his face— the awkwardness that always characterized his encounters with women. Kiyomori, susceptible to beauty, and vulnerable, had never learned to conceal his feelings. This was not new to Bamboku, for he had seen Kiyomori with Tokiwa and after that with a number of other women, and it had always been the same. But it still puzzled the Nose, as he thought of himself, that this powerful patron of his, so magnificently placed, should be so meek when faced with a woman.

Kiyomori had once confessed, while in his cups, that no matter how old he grew, he could not get over the agitation and shyness of a woman who had captured his fancy. He had said of himself scornfully that the virginal shrinking of a young girl only made him shy and awkward himself. Bamboku had finally arrived at the conclusion that this was only Kiyomori's way of boasting, for what else explained Kiyomori's behavior toward Tokiwa? Wounded already, what reason had Kiyomori to wound her further? If it were true, as Kiyomori had said, that he was timid with a young woman, then it followed that he shrank equally from doing her injury, though his actions belied his words. As Bamboku explained it to himself, there was a strain of cruelty in Kiyomori which he sought to conceal even from himself in his relations with women.

"Red-Nose, you know where Giwo lives, don't you? You know her mistress, too?"

"I do, but—"

"One of your favorite haunts?"

"Not altogether that."

"There's no need to conceal anything. You'll go there for me?"

"Where, sir?"

"To Toji and tell her that Giwo is to stay here. Assure Toji that she shall have whatever compensation she wants in gold or silver."

To this Bamboku replied dubiously: "You wish me tell her that, sir?"

"Yes, go now," Kiyomori ordered, his eyes turned in fascination upon the frightened Giwo. Without her headdress she seemed even more pathetically young and frightened, and she wept softly, murmuring incoherently, into the folds of her pale-blue tunic.

Bamboku hesitated. "It's quite late now, so what do you wish me to do about the answer?"

"Tomorrow will do—any time," Kiyomori replied.

Bamboku bowed and withdrew, carefully closing the double doors after him. He took the lady's carriage, which still waited, and had Kowaka, the manservant, drive him to Toji's address.

The story of Giwo soon became the sensation of the capital. To have gone to Rokuhara uninvited, to have twisted Kiyomori around her little finger, and then to have been installed in state in the rose court! And the gossips speculated interestedly in all that this must mean to her parents, who were so badly off.

Giwo, on her first short visit to her parents, who now had a new home, arrived in a splendid lacquered coach, shining with trimmings of silver and gold, and with an impressive escort of warriors. Never had such a dazzling sight been seen on Juzenji Road, where a great crowd soon gathered to gape at Giwo and to wait patiently until she departed. When Giwo reappeared, accompanied to the gate by her father and mother, the inquisitive spectators surged toward her to examine her carefully from head to foot. Lifting a sleeve to conceal her face, Giwo quickly entered her coach, but the few who stood close to her caught a glimpse of her pale, mournful face and wondered why one so successful should be so sad.

Ryozen, Giwo's father, his health restored, fat and sleek in his fine clothes, soon had a stream of visitors making for his door. They made much of him and his wife, admiring the rich furnishings and costly clothes they saw everywhere, and speculated among themselves how much this was costing Kiyomori every month. Among these visitors was the Serpent, who came often to drink with Ryozen.

"Well, Ryozen," the Serpent unfailingly said, "don't you find that I've brought you good luck?"

Ryozen enjoyed the Serpent's flatteries and in an expansive mood was heard to say: "No, this is not bad at all. And if Giwo has a child by Lord Kiyomori, even I will be counted among his relatives. I am sure to get a post of some kind at Rokuhara then."

Good-natured Ryozen, however, was no match for the sly Serpent, or his bullying.

"Yes, Ryozen," the Serpent said, "if it weren't for me, where would you be? Wasn't it I that got you out of the Street of the Ox-Dealers, when you were starving, looked out for your daughter, saw that she became a dancing-girl? We're so well acquainted that we might consider each other relatives, eh? Yes, I might lose my temper with you now and then, but that's because I always have your good in mind."

Ryozen was rarely to be found at home now; he went about constantly in the company of the Serpent, who took him off to gamble, to drinking bouts, and to the gay quarters. The once peaceful home became the scene of violent domestic quarrels, for Ryozen's wife soon found that her husband kept a woman somewhere on Sixth Avenue and reproached him. "Remember," she said, almost in tears, "this fine life of ours isn't because of you, and if you go in for loose living, we'll be the laughing-stock of our neighbors. What's more, how do you think that loving child, Giwo, is going to take it?"

About this time people began to talk about another bewitching dancing-girl called Hotoké in another house in the gay quarters. She was only sixteen, and had come to Kyoto as a child from the province of Kaga, her birthplace. Trained from childhood to her profession, her dancing and singing were reputed to be superior to that of even the most polished performers at the Court, and the dandies of Kyoto who saw her swore that she was the equal of Giwo. As Giwo's fame spread, Hotoké's mistress began to feel that she had cause to be proud of her protégée despite all that was said about Giwo, and one day called Hotoké to her.

"There's no doubt that you're the finest dancer in the capital, but only the gay blades of Kyoto have seen you. If you should attract the attention of Lord Kiyomori, your fortunes will be made. Even Giwo was admitted to Rokuhara, and there's no reason why you shouldn't be. Adorn yourself as Giwo did and see whether you can do as well as she."

Hotoké complied eagerly, for she was innocent and proud of her dancing. The thought of what she might gain by it never entered her mind.

Early in the autumn a gay lady's coach drew up at the gate to West Eighth Avenue, where Kiyomori, a State Minister since February, had come to live in his palatial mansion. Many stately residences stood along the wide avenues—here Lady Ariko's, there Tokiko's—and beyond were side-streets and lanes where the warriors lived. All over one saw a blending of the ancient and new styles in architecture, the outward reflection of the changing times.

Hotoké, arrayed in her loveliest, leaned out from her carriage as a guard challenged her at the gate. "I am Hotoké, a dancing-girl

—from birth, alas, the plaything of men. I have been sent by my mistress and make so bold as to come without being summoned. Allow me to dance and sing before my lord Kiyomori."

The guard hesitated, curious; then, fearing Kiyomori's displeasure, he burst out in anger:

"What's this? Coming here without being summoned? Get out—go back!"

"No, it is the custom among dancing-girls to pay visits like this, and I do this with all respect to his lordship. I am young and I cannot bear the disgrace of being refused."

Hotoké, dejected, turned to go, when a footman called her back.

"Since you insist, I shall see what can be done," he said, leading the way to the mansion.

To Hotoké's startled eyes, halls and splendid rooms stretched endlessly before her, and then she saw one who appeared to be Kiyomori. He was surrounded by attendants, one of whom approached her and said:

"Are you Hotoké? Count yourself fortunate, for not everyone can expect to be presented to his lordship. You are here only because Giwo begged his lordship to make an exception. . . . You might sing for us in return for this great favor."

Hotoké bowed, then turned to Giwo with a look of deep gratitude, to which Giwo replied with a steady gaze of encouragement, and Hotoké began to sing. It was a simple song repeated thrice. From her artless lips there flowed a clear stream of sound, moving the hearts of her listeners and lingering there in melodious echoes.

Kiyomori suddenly stirred. "Indeed, you sing well. Now you shall dance. Here—bring drums!"

Hotoké inclined her head and rose. Slowly she glided into stately motion, clothed in a dignity that belied her youth.

Kiyomori watched her intently with an ecstatic look, but as his eyes followed her, drinking in her grave beauty, he was seized by a savage impulse to claw at this loveliness and to destroy it.

"Very fine. Better than I thought," he finally said. "A toast to this—Hotoké? We'll finish our wine in the Spring Pavilion and watch Hotoké dance once more."

Hotoké was ordered to remain at Kiyomori's mansion on West Eighth Avenue, and all over the capital, wherever people met, there was talk that Lord Kiyomori had acquired a new mistress. But it was not so, for Hotoké, out of gratitude to Giwo, would not bend to Kiyomori's wishes, and begged piteously day after day for leave to go home.

"Tell Giwo she is to go," Kiyomori ordered. "I have done everything to make her happy. She has all that she needs to spend the rest of her days in ease."

Giwo received the news of her dismissal with relief, though she wept when she thought of Tadanori, Kiyomori's half-brother; for she was a woman who had been made the pawn and plaything of one man when her heart was secretly given to another.

No sooner was it known in the capital that Giwo had received her dismissal than the men about town importuned her with messages to appear at their banquets and sent her gifts daily, but Giwo hid herself at home and refused to see anyone.

Yet Giwo grew heartsick when she found how her father, Ryozen, had changed completely. He was now a quarrelsome, household tyrant, a drunkard and loaded with debts. Her mother, whom Giwo believed she had made happy through her own unhappiness, was in despair. Not long after that, Ryozen vanished with the Serpent and was heard of no more.

In late spring of the following year, 1168, Giwo, her sister, and her mother cut off their long hair and went to live as recluses in the hills at Saga, near a temple north of the city gates. They had not been long there when the dancing-girl Hotoké escaped from the mansion on West Eighth Avenue and came to Saga, begging to be taken into their midst. She too, like them, had seen enough of the evils of wealth and rank and grown weary of the life of pleasure.

CHAPTER XLIV

A FRACAS

Kiyomori's trips to Fukuhara became more and more frequent, and travelers between the capital and western Japan were astonished by the changes they saw there in the space of five or six years, for the fishermen's settlements and the open country had become a flourishing colony of villas with Kiyomori's palatial residence as its center. Not only were the roads good, but the many shops strung along the shoreline already lent Owada the aspects of a port.

Although Kiyomori's mansion was completed and a host of

similar Heiké dwellings had sprung up round it, Kiyomori made little progress on the vast harbor of which he still dreamed. Though boats specially constructed to carry stones emptied load after load into the sea for the breakwater, it was as steadily demolished by the strong southwesterly wind and heavy seas. And whenever the mole began to take shape, the autumn typhoons destroyed every trace of it. But Kiyomori refused to abandon the work. Undaunted, he appealed:

"Is there no one with the skill and the confidence to accomplish this? I would give much to secure such a man. Find me such a one, send him to me."

After searching far and wide, a man was found to continue with the construction, and thousands of men and boats labored at it. Day after day the work went on, week after week went by, and then months, with Kiyomori financing the work singlehanded. And whenever Kiyomori visited Fukuhara, it was not to beguile his leisure with the elegant pastimes of courtly life in a villa, but to follow the progress of the harbor, giving himself body and soul over to considering its many problems.

During one of his visits to Fukuhara, Kiyomori ignored the symptoms of a cold, and not until the night he was on his way back to the capital did he finally succumb to a high fever. There was consternation in the capital when the news of Kiyomori's illness leaked out from the mansion on West Eighth Avenue. The Emperor sent his chief physician to Kiyomori's bedside. All day long the carriages of courtiers and high officials drew up at the gates of the mansion to inquire after his condition. No one—not even Kiyomori's relatives—was admitted to the sickroom, and all anyone knew was what Kiyomori's physician told them. But Kiyomori grew worse. He had taken no nourishment for several days. The fever did not leave him, and even his own physician seemed unable to put a finger on what ailed him.

Very soon the news went round that Kiyomori was sinking fast. A Heiké official in northern Kyushu, hearing of this, set out at once for Kyoto with a Chinese physician who had recently come from China.

Kiyomori's stepmother, Lady Ariko, and his eldest son, Shigemori, visited the chief temples and shrines in the Eastern Hills and on Mount Hiei to offer prayers for his recovery.

It was only inevitable that people should speculate on what would happen if Kiyomori died. The Heiké were not strong enough yet to keep power from passing into the hands of the ex-Emperor Goshirakawa, and no one doubted that his first step would be to crush the Heiké—and with them the warrior class. The Cloister Palace, in the meantime, was daily besieged with visitors from the Court, and on one such day Goshirakawa ordered his carriage and drove to Kiyomori's mansion.

On hearing that the ex-Emperor had arrived, Kiyomori appeared terrified. He ordered his room to be swept and incense burned. As he prostrated himself before the royal visitor, Goshirakawa noticed how emaciated Kiyomori had become, and said gently:

"It is better for you to lie down."

"No, your majesty, I can still sit up."

Erect in his night-clothes of white silk, and looking more punctilious than he had ever appeared, Kiyomori replied to the ex-Emperor's solicitous questions.

There were some other matters of a deeply important nature which Goshirakawa discussed at Kiyomori's bedside. As it later became known, they concerned the dethroning of the boy-Emperor Rokujo in favor of Goshirakawa's own son, Takakura. It was apparent that the ex-Emperor had for some time had this in mind as a means of ultimately securing the reins of power. He believed that Kiyomori would fall in with his plans, since Takakura was Kiyomori's nephew. He had no assurance, however, that he would succeed in coaxing Kiyomori to agree with him, and there was the possibility that Kiyomori might even turn the tables on him.

On the day after his visit the ex-Emperor dispatched his own physician to the mansion on West Eighth Avenue, and upon his return drew him aside to question him.

"How did you find him? Is there any hope that Kiyomori will live?"

To this the physician replied: "Your majesty, I find it difficult to say. There was no way in which I could tell what was ailing him. The peculiar symptoms of his feigned illness make it difficult for me to name his malady."

Feigned illness? Goshirakawa listened thoughtfully. Whether Kiyomori lived or not made little difference to him; his own schemes would in any case go through.

Kiyomori, ill, was helpless. His robust health had always made him contemptuous of physical weakness, though it was quite another matter when Kiyomori had something wrong with him. His wife, Tokiko, often used to laugh and say: "I've never seen anyone quite so timid and fussy as you when you're ill!"

This time the sick man, strangely enough, did not fuss or fume; he took no interest in food; the fever showed no sign of abating. From time to time there were moans from the sickroom and the incoherent mutterings of delirium. Kiyomori's physician grew alarmed. Tokiko, Lady Ariko, and Kiyomori's eldest son, Shigemori, spent many hours in their private chapel. Soothsayers were called in, and messengers, sent to the great centers of worship, ordered special services to be said for Kiyomori's recovery. It looked altogether as though the angry deities were taking their revenge on the unbeliever who had blasphemed and defied them too long.

But Kiyomori's delirium held no terrors for him. Whenever the fever left him, he was aware only of the pain in his distended abdomen; attacks of strangling nausea returned and made him long for the fever to dissolve the nightmare of pain once more into that blissful state in which he floated disembodied on a rosy cloud. In his semiconscious state he was aware of himself saying: "So this is the boundary between life and death. . . ." Then he would see angels and cherubs weaving between the clouds to the sound of music, and among that host spy a child—himself at the age of eight. He was on the dancing-stage at Gion, and what seemed to be clouds were cherry blossoms. There she stood under the trees, his exquisite mother, smiling as she watched him dance. There was his father beside her.—Mother! Father! Watch me dance!—

And Kiyomori danced on and on until he fell exhausted. Suddenly his father was gone, and his mother. Then the wailing of children pierced his ears. Listen! that was the *Old Ono*, singing lullabies. There was the stable at home and the horses staring at him out of their lean, hungry faces. And beneath the moon in an indigo sky was Imadegawa—the decaying house where he had once lived—rising before his eyes. The sound of his young brothers crying with hunger drove him to wander about as if crazed. His mother had abandoned these children. . . . His father—where was he? And Kiyomori would come upon the Squint-Eyed One leaning against a post and staring up silently at the eaves. . . . I am no man's son, but you are my real father—and in his delirium Kiyomori called over and over again: "Father!—my father!"

Then a voice—Shigemori's—saying: "Father, what is it?"

Kiyomori's other sons had gathered round him and were shaking him awake.

"Was I saying anything strange in my dreams?" Kiyomori asked.

"You were delirious, Father."

"They were beautiful dreams. It pains me to be awake once more."

"The Chinese physician from Kyushu has just arrived, Father. You want him to come here, don't you?"

"What! From the country of Sung? Yes, bring him."

The physician soon appeared in his traveling robes, his white hair flowing about his shoulders, ascetic-looking, and lean as a crane. He carefully examined Kiyomori; inclined his head to one side from time to time, muttering, and then withdrew to one side of Kiyomori's bed.

Kiyomori turned toward the physician to ask: "Will I recover?"

A smile accompanied the reply: "I believe you will be over this in two or three days."

Kiyomori could hardly believe his ears, but after the physician left, took the powders that had been left him. On the following morning Kiyomori felt much improved and continued to drink the potions as he had been directed, and that night he fell into a deep and invigorating sleep.

Kiyomori's illness had been caused by intestinal parasites. Once they were removed with drugs and purgatives, Kiyomori began to recover rapidly, and the news spread about the capital that his life had been saved by a miracle. Medicine, still in its elementary stages, linked the presence of parasites in the human body with supernatural causes, and necromancers and astrologists were usually called in to effect a cure.

At the mansion on West Eighth Avenue and in Rokuhara, life resumed its customary briskness; there was feasting and rejoicing everywhere, and music was heard once more in the great houses of the Heiké.

Soon after his recovery Kiyomori, to the amazement of those who knew him, took the tonsure and withdrew from public life. For Kiyomori there was nothing more he could desire; his position was secure, his reputation established; the highest he could seek in the way of government honors was also his. Despite all this, two ambitions were unfulfilled—the harbor at Owada, and trade with China. He still clung to his dream of making Fukuhara a great center of commerce, and Itsuku-shima the jewel of the Inland Sea, linking Japan with the land of the Sung. To what strange and glorious flowering might this yet lead!

Shortly after handing back his portfolio, Kiyomori settled at Fukuhara to devote all his time to the last stages of the work on the harbor, and it happened while he was there that the Emperor Rokujo was dethroned in favor of Goshirakawa's nine-year-old son. It was asserted and believed everywhere that this was the work of Kiyomori. The most damaging accusations came from the Fujiwara courtiers, the emperor-makers for centuries, without whose knowledge this change was made. This unheard-of usurping of their prerogatives struck at the roots of their authority. A warrior had done this—Kiyomori of the Heiké. Nevertheless, though the gravest of charges were leveled against Kiyomori, it was pointed out that Tokitada, Kiyomori's brother-in-law, was the prepotent figure behind the scenes. Kyoto suddenly found itself under the shadow of fear as the wildest of rumors spread. It was said that Tokitada had agents planted everywhere to report those who criticized the Heiké.

In July 1170 a fracas, long remembered, took place between the retainers of the Fujiwara Regent and those of Shigemori of the Heiké.

By all accounts it was a momentous month. An eclipse of the sun had been predicted and seven platforms were erected at the Imperial Palace for viewing the phenomenon, though toward noon the sky clouded, and the rain soon after fell in a deluge. The summer, to begin with, had started out unpropitiously. There were great fears of a drought, and special prayers for rain were offered at the Great Shrine as well as all the lesser shrines; then followed a downpour whose like had not been seen in a decade. Rivers flooded their banks, and the capital itself was inundated. On the 3rd of July, the day after the eclipse, many members of the Court—the princes and princesses and the Regent—attended High Mass at the temple near Shirakawa, north of Rokuhara.

It was a day of torrid heat. The Regent, in his heavy court robes, was driving away from the service. He was tempted to turn home and rid himself of his cumbersome garments. But no, the sun was still high, he decided. He would return to the Court, attend to some business, and then drive home in the cool of the evening. Ordering his driver to take him back to the Imperial Palace, the young Regent settled himself once more to the slow swaying of his carriage.

The fierce sun beating against the blinds lighted up the white-robed figure. The Regent was still in his mid-twenties. Elegant and correct in his court robes, he sat erect, with streams of perspiration pouring down his cheeks from under the ponderous headdress that he wore. But his retinue of runners, ox-drivers, and grooms suffered even more from the merciless sun. Bathed in dust, they switched at the flies with gestures of complete exhaustion.

The oxen were left to set the pace, and the long procession crept along the highway. As they neared a crossroad, they saw far away and coming toward them another carriage, surrounded by numerous attendants. As it drew nearer, it resolved itself into a gay lady's coach. The Regent's carriage, distinguishable by the insignia emblazoned on it, proceeded up the center of the highway. Etiquette demanded that even a court lady give the Regent precedence, but the oncoming coach showed no sign of turning aside. Nearer it came: forty yards—fifteen, ten, then seven. It was almost on top of the Regent, and still came on boldly. The lady's runners were gesticulating wildly to the Regent's carriage to pull to the side, when the Regent's attendants darted forward, waving the coach to stop. But the lady's coach continued to approach. Wild cries, shouts, and imprecations failed to stop it.

"Are you deaf? Can't you see whose carriage this is?"

"Use your eyes! This is the Regent himself!"

"Who are you, anyway?"

The coach came on steadily, cutting a swathe through the Regent's attendants, and scattering the men to either side of the road.

"Pull up, there! Pull up!"

An attendant suddenly ran forward with a shout. "Insolent fellows!" he yelled, knocking down the ox-driver and snatching the reins from his hands as he dragged the coach to one side.

"Dare you lay hands on our master's coach?"

The guards and soldiers to the rear of the coach ran forward in a body, threateningly. "You've insulted us, have you? What's meant by this?"

The Regent's attendants replied in kind.

"Shut up! Anyone but country oafs would know that this is the Regent himself!—Get back, there! Out of the way, you ruffians!"

" 'Country oafs,' did you say?"

"No more sense than cats or dogs! 'Country oafs' is too good for you!"

"Ready for a fight, are you!"

"You started this and we're ready!"

Four or five of the Regent's armed guards stalked forward.

"What are you up to?"

A wild battle ensued as the Regent's men threw themselves at the lady's attendants.

"Give it to them!"

"You dogs of Rokuhara!"

A tumult of angry shouts arose. Sticks and stones rattled on the Regent's carriage. The dust rose in yellow clouds, enveloping the combatants until friend and foe were indistinguishable in the savage fighting that followed. The Regent's retinue consisted of some eighty men, including the warriors, while the other numbered barely forty. But the Rokuhara soldiers were muscular, hard-bitten fighters, coarse of speech and rude of manner.

The occupant of the coach seemed to have been entirely forgotten. It was not a lady, but Kiyomori's grandchild, Shigemori's ten-year-old son, on his way home from his flute lessons. The coach swayed wildly from side to side and then spun round. Pandemonium reigned, while the terrified child cowered inside, trembling at the sight of bleeding faces, gashed heads, and bloody figures grappling with one another. A stray missile ripped through a blind, and suddenly he broke into a piercing wail.

In spite of their mettle, the Heiké attendants were forced to take to their heels with their wounded and a badly damaged coach. But they had given as good as they had taken, and retreated vowing revenge.

Dusk deepened and even the cicadas of the tree-flanked avenue in Rokuhara were silent. News of the brawl had already reached Rokuhara, and a procession of lighted torches came out to meet the coach. There were cautious calls:

"Is that you, Shiro? Is the young master safe?"

"All's well, but the Regent's men shamed us outrageously. . . . They outnumbered us."

"Tell that to the master, but what of the young master—no injuries?"

"Safe and sound, though he cried a little."

"Hurry up, there! Don't you realize how worried they are at the house?"

No sooner did the coach draw up at a carriage porch than Shigemori appeared, calling anxiously to his son.

Shigemori listened to an account of the skirmish by one of his captains. The fault had not been theirs but the Regent's, the captain insisted. The Regent's attendants had not only challenged them, but laid violent hands on the coach. No, they would have given way respectfully to the Regent had his men not been the first to insult them. There was no choice but to defend the honor of the Heiké. . . .

As the captain ended his story, the usually dispassionate Shigemori was flushed with anger. "Had it been dark, I could understand their not recognizing my son, but there's no reason why they should not have known in broad daylight. Clearly, the Regent is at fault, and I shall see that we get redress."

On the following day, July 5, Shigemori started for the Court with a larger retinue of armed warriors than usual, determined to slight the Regent if they met.

The Regent, in the meantime, learned that it was Shigemori's son whom his attendants had insulted and for several days did not dare to appear at the Court. In private the Regent raged at his captains and attendants.

"Couldn't you see who it was before you attacked them? Of all persons to insult—Kiyomori's grandson! Blockheads—fools! See what you've brought on me!"

But, for all his outbursts, the Regent felt helpless to mend matters, until one of his friends, a councilor, suggested that the Regent send his guilty attendants as hostages to Rokuhara. This, he assured the Regent, would without doubt soften Shigemori's anger. Two captains, and several soldiers and ox-tenders forthwith were led bound to Rokuhara. The Councilor, acting as the Regent's deputy, soon returned with the men, saying that he had not been able to talk with Shigemori.

"I was told that Lord Shigemori was indisposed and would see no one. I gathered, however, that he is unwilling to discuss the matter with anyone but you."

On the 16th of July, when the Regent was to appear at the

temple at Shirakawa, he sent out his men to reconnoiter, and on being told that Heiké warriors were posted along the route he was to take, canceled all his plans for going out that day.

Several months later, on the 21st of October, the day on which the Regent was to preside over a state council at which the final arrangements for the child-Emperor's coming-of-age were to be made, a message reached the Imperial Palace saying that the Regent had been ambushed on his way to the Court and was unable to attend the Council. The entire Court overflowed with alarm. A new date was set for the State Council, and the ministers and court officials dispersed in confusion. People soon learned that the attack had taken place not far from one of the Palace gates; the Regent had escaped without harm; some two hundred warriors had suddenly appeared on the highway and surrounded his carriage; the six mounted guards who preceded it had been dragged from their horses and badly mauled, and as the crowning insult had their topknots shorn off by their unknown assailants. Other members of the retinue, less than a score, who failed to escape, met a like fate.

People looked round for an explanation, and it was soon whispered that Kiyomori had revenged himself on the Regent for the insult to his favorite grandson. Actually, however, Kiyomori all the while was in Fukuhara, where news of the incident in which his grandson had been involved did not reach him until very much later.

As public excitement subsided, the truth emerged out of the wild tangle of rumors and denials that prevailed in the capital: Shigemori himself had ordered the assault on the Regent.

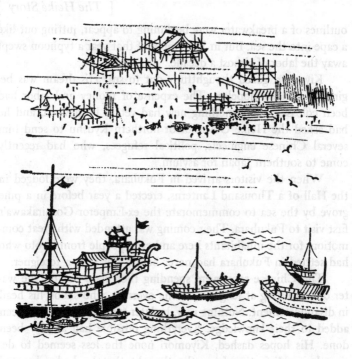

CHAPTER XLV

THE BUILDING OF A HARBOR

The year 1170 was a year of floods and natural calamities, which robbed thousands of peasants of homes and crops, and the saying was: "No one starves at Fukuhara. There is work there for all," as the destitute poured into Fukuhara to work on the construction of the harbor. Nine years had already gone by since Kiyomori embarked on the gigantic task, and the outlines of a breakwater were beginning to appear, jutting out like a cape into the sea. But in September of that year a typhoon swept away the labor of almost a decade.

Kiyomori gazed thoughtfully out to sea. His dream was beginning to look hopeless. The expense of money and labor had been colossal, but something new had yet to be devised, and he had asked the Heiké Governor of northern Kyushu to send him several Chinese engineers, political refugees, who had recently come to southern Japan for asylum.

When the visitors arrived in Fukuhara, they were lodged in the Hall of a Thousand Lanterns, erected a year before in a pine grove by the sea to commemorate the ex-Emperor Goshirakawa's first visit to Fukuhara. Their coming was attended with great commotion, for the inhabitants here and even people from Kyoto who had settled in Fukuhara had never before this seen a foreigner.

The Chinese soon were spending their days out on the water or consulting at length with the overseer, who shook his head in disappointment. Nothing new, he later told Kiyomori, had been added to their knowledge. Everything possible had already been done. His hopes dashed, Kiyomori none the less seemed to derive deep satisfaction from the thought that he had exhausted every known device, and that his men had not been lacking in skill or industry. He then ordered that the work on the harbor should continue as before, adding, to the overseer:

"We have failed to withstand these autumn storms because the work has never progressed far enough before the season of typhoons. Nine tenths of the breakwater must be completed between the autumn and summer of the following year. If we can accomplish that, I am certain of success. We need more men, more materials—and money, but you need not be anxious because of that."

Kiyomori appeared confident. Until now he had drawn solely on the wealth of the Heiké; there was a limit, however, to even that source, but he was certain that the government would now shoulder the undertaking. Two years had already passed since the ex-Emperor had promised Kiyomori to allot state funds for completing the harbor, and though nothing was done, Kiyomori did not doubt that Goshirakawa would give him support.

Formal representations had long since been made to the ex-Emperor Goshirakawa by Kiyomori for the promised state funds, and Goshirakawa had replied each time that Kiyomori should wait a little longer, and Kyomori had waited. But he now realized that he could wait no longer. The harbor must be completed soon or forever abandoned, and he made up his mind to appeal to Goshirakawa once more in person for aid.

When reports of the altercation between the Regent's retainers and Shigemori's first reached Kiyomori, he did not explode in anger as he was fully expected to do, but merely shook his head saying: "My grandchildren and nephews only grow more idle as they get older. Undoubtedly, my grandson is guilty of a breach of etiquette, and the Regent too young and conceited." Then he added, sadly: "Their life has been too easy for them and there's the danger."

Not long after, the ex-Emperor visited Fukuhara at Kiyomori's invitation. His first visit a year before had been to see the progress made on the harbor of Owada and to attend the dedication of a new temple. This time Kiyomori had arranged that Goshirakawa should see the eight Chinese who were staying at Fukuhara. Two young women, daughters of one of the engineers, were to dance before the ex-Emperor and to impress him with some of the exquisite refinements of the Sung civilization. But Kiyomori's real reason was to remind Goshirakawa once more of his promise of aid.

After the ex-Emperor's departure, Kiyomori perceived that no help was to be expected from Goshirakawa. The ex-Emperor had skillfully parried and eluded Kiyomori's reminders.

But Kiyomori still refused to accept defeat. He was now fifty-three; his mental vigor was undiminished; his outlook youthful, and to his contemporaries at the Court he was a man possessed whose actions needed watching, for he applied himself once more to the task of completing the harbor.

That autumn every able-bodied man to be found in his western feudatories was brought to Fukuhara and every kind of material was collected in this last effort to prove that Kiyomori's dream had not been vain. Day and night, month after month the unstinting labor of thousands of men was poured with pitiless purpose into this task which must end before next year's season of storms. The near-by cape and surrounding hills were scraped clean of rocks and stones, which were piled along the beach. Giant tree-trunks, lashed together to form rafts and weighted with stones in wooden crates, were towed seaward and submerged. Massive rocks, piled on boat after boat, sank beneath the sea; beams laid across beams, and boat upon boat.

Through the lengthening nights of late autumn, squadrons of small craft with blazing torches were strung out along the bay like mysterious sea-lights, and Kiyomori looked on content. He had done his utmost; the rest lay with the gods. As he gazed at the Milky Way one night, it occurred to him that many months had passed since he left the capital, and he wondered what was taking place there. Who of all his sons and brothers, he reflected, was able enough to replace him as the chief of the Heiké? Tsunemori, his younger brother, was frail; Norimori, the next younger, only meek. Tokitada, his brother-in-law, was apt to go to extremes; obviously gifted, but too headstrong. Though promising, Tadanori, his half-brother, was still too young.

As for his eldest son and successor, Shigemori—Kiyomori knew that he was respected by all the Heiké, but not really loved. There was something forbidding about him; beneath that quiet exterior was hidden a meanness of soul. Kiyomori did not much like the cool, astute eyes, whose shrewdness, he often regretted, made Shigemori seem petty rather than wise. Shigemori had changed, too. Much of the freshness and vigor he had had as a youth had vanished. Was he ill? Kiyomori wondered. He would have a good physician examine him as soon as he got back to Kyoto. Whatever the case, he had been hearing that Shigemori now had a private chapel where he spent much of his time. . . . That was most likely at the bottom of it. There was entirely too much of this nonsense going on, he often mused. His brothers and children were beginning to ape the aristocrats: they had grown to love luxurious living; were immersed in all manner of elegant refinement; made an ornamental pastime of their religion, kneeling at their prayers with painted faces and eyebrows, and their teeth dyed black.

Kiyomori had no objections to elegance and refinement. They were thoroughly desirable. Life was richer for them. As for religion—even he had taken the vows. Not by any means did he approve of the disbeliever, but this aping of the aristocrats and this travesty of religion—he would have none of it. At Rokuhara he had tried to encourage certain ideals for the warrior class. He had seen to it that Buddhism received the respect it deserved in their way of life, but from early youth he had refused to tolerate the superstitions that grew up around it. The mysterious universe alone deserved to be worshipped. He would have Tokiko speak seriously to Shigemori about all this. It was more likely that he would listen to his mother in such matters. . . .

Late in the autumn, Kiyomori returned to Kyoto, where there was talk that he would remain in the capital for the winter.

One tranquil day when the maples were just beginning to crimson, the Regent's carriage drew up at the mansion on West Eighth Avenue where Kiyomori waited to receive his illustrious visitor. Despite assurances on every side that Kiyomori was amiably disposed, the Regent had set out in a state of apprehension, but found on arriving that his fears were quite unjustified.

"It is most gratifying, sir, to find you in good health. I have wanted for some time to call on you at Fukuhara to see the progress on the harbor and to admire your villa, but with his majesty's coming-of-age so near, various duties have kept me from paying my respects to you, sir."

"On the contrary, such trifles must not interfere with the responsibilities of your high office. When the coming-of-age rites are over, you must give yourself a leisurely trip to Fukuhara. And that reminds me to ask whether a date for the rites has been set."

"The last State Council decided on the third day of the New Year."

"That will be a day of great rejoicing for us all," Kiyomori said fervently.

The Regent's brows contracted in a troubled frown. "To tell you the truth—" he began. "You have probably already heard that there was a serious altercation between my men and your son's on the day that the State Council met."

"Hmm—that I did. I was told that it was quite a gaudy affair."

"I have no wish to apportion blame when our men have been at each other's throats, but people have let their imaginations and tongues run away with them and say that there is discord between our two houses."

"We have no way of bridling their tongues. Let who will talk . . . but I have reproved my son, Shigemori. It was a most childish performance." . . .

"On the contrary, sir—and my reason for calling on you today was to offer my apologies. I equally deserve your censure. Neither your son nor I knew what was happening. I also understand that your grandson has been sent to Isé in disgrace and beg you to recall him as well as accept my very humble apologies."

"It is not for you to apologize," Kiyomori said with a deprecating smile. "This whole affair seems to have troubled you more than it should. Shigemori only dealt with his son as he should. I took Shigemori to task because I love him. He is my heir and it ill becomes one in his position to fly into a passion as his retainers did over a trifle. It is not at all like him to do so and I lay it to his illness. The Chinese physician who cured me has examined Shigemori and found that he is suffering from some disorder of the stomach, and has ordered him to rest. Difficult as it may be for you, I beg you to overlook this affair."

"This is more than I deserve, sir."

"Shigemori will soon be here and I shall have my other sons

as well as Tokitada join us and drink with us in token of our reconciliation."

On January 3, 1173, the eleven-year-old boy-Emperor celebrated his coming-of-age with great pomp and solemnity, and in October the ex-Emperor, in his son's name, asked for the hand of Kiyomori's daughter, Tokuko, who was seventeen, and who subsequently became Takakura's Empress.

The current of events moved on relentlessly and the Heiké willy-nilly were swept to eminence and power. Kiyomori's name was on every tongue and no one dared to repeat anything derogatory to the Heiké. Fear also was in the air.

Kiyomori, however, seemed indifferent to all that was taking place, even scornful of the position that the Heiké occupied, for his heart's wish had been granted: the harbor at Owada was almost completed. This at last was the year in which a fleet of vessels lay cradled in the smooth waters of the bay, waiting for the ships of Sung to sail in.

CHAPTER XLVI

A MONK IS BANISHED

hat was that? It was a mild afternoon in spring when an extraordinary strident voice reciting sutras interrupted the musicians at their playing.

"Impossible! You shall not pass—where are you off to?" a guard challenged.

A noisy argument ensued.

An astonished courtier laid his lute aside as another discordant shout reverberated through the screening-wall.

560

The ex-Emperor motioned to one of the courtiers. "Go and see what it's all about."

The courtier stepped out on the gallery just as a powerfully built priest flung aside a guard and pushed his way through a gate of the inner court. His hair hung to his shoulders and his hairy legs protruded from his tattered robes like massive pine logs.

"His majesty can hear me now. He must be tired with listening to music all day. Let him listen for a change to what Mongaku preaches to the common people in the streets of the capital!" he said, looking about the narrow inner court and unrolling a sutra scroll.

"Mongaku from the hills of Takao!" a courtier exclaimed, recognizing the odd figure that he often saw at street corners appealing for alms and donations.

Mongaku read off an appeal for donations for a new temple; it sounded, however, like a peroration against maladministration and the extravagance of the aristocrats.

"See that the man is arrested," the ex-Emperor ordered. One of his attendants leaped upon a balustrade and swooped down on Mongaku, pinning his arms to his sides.

"Are you mad! Don't you realize that this is the Palace?"

Mongaku stood motionless as the body hurtled against him.

"I do," Mongaku replied fiercely to the attendant who clung to him. "I have spent years in the hills of Takao praying for the erection of a temple from which enlightenment will come to the world, and in the streets of the capital have begged for donations from the common people. I have come to beg for a gift from his majesty—even a pittance willingly given is enough. Let me present my humble petition."

"What's meant by all this violence when you've come to beg?"

"I know where respect is due. I have knocked several times on the gates, but the sound of music has drowned out everything and the guards have pretended not to hear me. There was nothing left for me but to force my way in. Don't trifle with me or you'll pay for it!"

"Here, you mad monk!"

Mongaku freed one hand and with a twist of his wrist sent his opponent flying over one shoulder and crashing to the ground. The attendant quickly came to his feet and lunged at Mongaku, who struck him on the cheek with the sutra scroll. As he returned once more to the attack, Mongaku gave him another blow on the chest. The attendant staggered back and fell and did not rise again.

"Will you still interfere with me?"

Mongaku glared at the dozen or more soldiers closing in on him.

"Don't flinch! At his legs!" the soldiers yelled, throwing themselves on Mongaku.

Mongaku still held the scroll, but a dagger suddenly flashed in his right hand. "Get back," he threatened; the soldiers fell back as he made his way rapidly toward some stairs. An officer of the Guards threw himself on Mongaku as Mongaku struck out at him with his dagger; the officer, his arm bleeding, clung to him until more soldiers arrived, overpowered Mongaku, and led him off to the jail.

Mongaku was ordered banished to Izu in eastern Japan. There had been considerable disagreement among Goshirakawa's advisers whether Mongaku should be pardoned or not, for not only was he a priest, but the common people had only good to say of him and even loved him.

Mongaku, astride a barebacked horse, was smiling, his teeth showing white through his beard.

"I hear our good Mongaku had been banished."

"That amusing fellow?"

"Why is that? Banished—and where to?"

"Izu. To Izu, people say."

Sympathetic crowds flocked to meet Mongaku as he rode through the streets of the capital. At crossroads he stopped to make odd speeches to the people until his guards prodded him on impatiently. A little man stood on tiptoe, staring intently over people's shoulders at the hulking figure as it moved off into the distance.

Head high and smiling, Mongaku rode out by the city gate, from which unnumbered exiles had departed in grief and tears. But there was laughter and even gaiety among the crowd as they took leave of Mongaku. Once outside the city walls only a few odd stragglers followed the cavalcade down the tree-lined highway.

Mongaku suddenly turned to halloo to the captain of his guards, who pretended not to hear him. Mongaku next leaned toward the soldier who was leading his horse. "Stop. Let me get down," he said, explaining that an intimate matter needed to be attended to. The soldier stopped and waited for the captain to ride up alongside and give an order. Mongaku, who was marched off into the near-by woods, was soon back, but instead of mounting, he ambled up a small mound and seated himself on a stone, saying: "Bring me some water. I'm thirsty."

The captain shook his head and frowned. It was exactly as he had predicted. He fully expected to have trouble with his prisoner and had taken the precaution of selecting toughened, well-built soldiers for guards—and several more than was thought necessary.

". . . There's not much we can do. Give him water," he said. "Don't annoy him and coax him back on his horse as quickly as possible."

When Mongaku had relieved his thirst, he turned to the captain and began: "While we're here, I want to talk to you. Get down and come here. Rest awhile."

"What's this? You're a prisoner on your way into exile and we're your guards. What do you mean by this? We sail from Otsu and you can talk to me when we're on board."

"It will be too late then."

"We're barely out of the capital and can't waste time like this. Get back on your horse. We can't keep the boat at Otsu waiting."

Mongaku did not move. "You don't want to talk?" he said, and broke into a mocking laugh. "Ah, my poor captain—the last of the Genji in the capital! When I heard that Yorimasa's son was to accompany me, I was pleased at the thought of having someone to talk to. Alas, you're no different from the rest of these!"

The captain flushed self-consciously, then dismounted. Handing the reins to a soldier, he approached Mongaku with a placating air.

"Your reverence, my father often spoke of you. My men have orders not to treat you like a common prisoner, but I cannot have you behave in this extraordinary fashion if I am to carry out my duties."

"No, captain, I don't intend to cause trouble, but surely you won't keep an exile from saying farewell to his friends?"

"There's no regulation that says you may not. The least we can do is look the other way while you talk to a few."

"That's it! I want you to do just that. I'm rather tender-hearted, and when I see how some have followed me all the way from jail, I feel that I must try to console them and send them on home. Give me a little time to talk to them."

The captain frowned his reluctance. "Well then, be quick about it," he said, ordering the guards to the side of the road.

Mongaku stood up and waved to some figures in the distance. The soldiers soon saw several persons approach at a run—four or five young monks, a couple, and a nondescript fellow. The monks were Mongaku's disciples from Takao, to whom he gave a few words of advice. Mongaku's eyes next sought the couple—Asatori and his wife, Yomogi, who had anxiously mingled with the crowd in the hope of having a last word with him. They gazed at Mongaku with brimming eyes.

"So it was you, after all," Mongaku said. "How have things gone with you? Do you still live on the Street of the Ox-dealers? Everything all right? It's time there were children—do you have any?"

"We had one, who died soon after he was born, and there have been none since," Asatori said. "Yomogi and I have known you for a long time, but we never dreamed that we would part like this."

"True, many strange chances brought us together. After the

Hogen War, Asatori and I shared food and shelter on the ruins of the Willow-Spring Palace. And you, Yomogi, you were Lady Tokiwa's little nursemaid then and used to come with your pail to the Willow Spring. Yes, how you've changed, and the world too!"

"Of course, that's to be expected. It's seventeen years since that happened," Yomogi said, pressing a small parcel into Mongaku's hand. "Here is some medicine, in case you are taken sick. There are seven kinds there. The other things are rice dumplings steamed with mugwort, which I cooked early this morning. Something to eat when you cross the lake."

"How well you've remembered my favorite sweet! I'm most grateful to you for that and the medicine."

Mongaku turned to Asatori again. "And your studies?"

"That's another thing I wanted to tell you—and you'll be pleased to hear this. Quite recently I was licensed to practice and invited to join the Academy of Physicians. But I have no desire whatever to serve the Court, for I hope to spend the rest of my life humbly in the Street of the Ox-Dealers, helping the poor."

Mongaku nodded his approval. "What different paths our lives have taken, though we want the same thing—a paradise on earth! You're by nature humble, and I—stormy!"

"Good Mongaku, how right you are, and you do well to denounce the countless evils in the world. Still, I can't understand what made you behave as you did at the Cloister Palace, where they thought you insane."

"Unfortunately, Asatori, my deeds and my heart are not in harmony with each other.—Yes, I spent years at the Nachi Falls, hoping to be sanctified by its waters, but I now realize that salvation does not lie in that direction for me. I was not meant for the life of contemplation, for I cannot ignore the evils and corruption in the world. I can only act as I think right for me, and I have thought of finding a way by which to rid the entire face of this capital of its rottenness—the corruption of the Cloister Government and the arrogance of the Heiké. How this will be done I cannot yet tell you, but, Asatori, you shall see that for yourself in a few years' time."

Mongaku ended abruptly as he glanced warily at his guards and the captain, who stood not far off.

Fearing another outburst, Asatori motioned to Yomogi with his eyes, but the captain had already turned to Mongaku and was urging him to make haste.

Mongaku mounted his horse. "Go on," he said and then turned once more to say good-by to Asatori and Yomogi.

A young man who stood half-hidden in the grove behind the mound, waiting for a chance to speak to Mongaku, emerged just as the procession moved off. He stood still, gazing after Mongaku. When the latter turned to look back once more, a swift look of recognition passed between them. Then Mongaku turned coolly and stared before him at the sunlight piercing the tunnel of leaves.

As Yomogi and Asatori turned to go, they heard someone calling them by name.

"Oh? When did we last meet?"

"Perhaps you remember seeing me at Funaoka Hill several years ago—at the funeral, when my mistress Toji fell ill. You were very kind to her."

"Yes, to be sure, you were with the dancing-girls who were looking after the sick woman."

"Yes—and my mistress called on you later at your home in the Street of the Ox-Dealers to thank you."

"Now I remember. . . . Are you on your way somewhere?"

"I came to say good-by to the prisoner."

"You knew him, too?"

"A long time ago. He gave me some advice when I needed it most and I have always been grateful to him for it. But that is about all," said the young man. He seemed anxious to say more and continued: "If it were not for him I shouldn't be alive today, nor this good woman's mistress. Two lives were spared that day I met him."

Yomogi started, then stared at the stranger whose eyes were fixed on hers. The stranger looked cautiously down the road and, seeing no one, whispered:

"Yomogi—you and I served Lord Yoshitomo of the Genji almost twenty years ago. Don't you remember?"

"Yes, his lady—"

"Lord Yoshitomo was your mistress's lover, you know."

"I can't help weeping when I think of the past—"

"I was Lord Yoshitomo's favorite retainer. Surely you haven't forgotten that it was I who tried to avenge my dead lord when your mistress took Kiyomori for her lover. It was I who left that note in the garden at Mibu villa."

"Why, you must be Konno-maru!"

"I am."

Yomogi's eyes widened with amazement. Her legs shook with fear, and she clung to Asatori's arm for support.

"You needn't be afraid," Konno-maru said, "I gave up all my evil plans long ago. I became a servant in the gay quarters and have watched over Lady Tokiwa at a distance."

Yomogi suddenly seemed to be ashamed of her fears. "Konno-maru, do you sometimes see my lady?" she asked.

"Yes, for almost ten years I have stolen into her garden and seen her for moments at a time. I am the only one left of those who knew her in happier days, and she is always glad to see me."

"Oh, what have I done!" Yomogi said half to herself in distress. "I haven't been back to see her even once since I left to be married. How is my lady these days?"

"She has been unwell for almost a year."

"Ill?"

"She has kept to her bed these last six months. I haven't seen her once in all that time, though I still go to her garden secretly."

"I had not dreamed that she was so ill. . . ."

"But for the good monk, I would not have come here today I wanted to speak to you. It's rather sudden, but—" Konno-maru turned to Asatori. "Could you take a message to her for me?"

Asatori opened his mouth for the first time.

"Why do you ask me?"

"You are a physician and Yomogi was once her maid, so it won't be difficult for you to see the lady. I want you to give her something for me."

Asatori looked at his wife hesitantly and did not reply. But

Yomogi, pleased at having an excuse to call on her former mistress, agreed at once.

"It would be no trouble at all, and if my husband comes with me he can find out why she is unwell. She would be quite pleased to see us I'm sure. What did you want us to take her?"

"I don't have it with me now, but tomorrow night I will bring it to your home. Remember that this must be kept a secret."

"Naturally, we shan't tell anyone."

"I don't know whether to believe this or not, but I've been told that agents of the Heiké are everywhere, listening and looking."

"But you're not asking us to do something that's difficult, are you?"

"Not at all. Just see that a very small packet is put into my lady's hands. Don't let it fall into the hands of any of the Heiké, or she may get into trouble. This must be kept an absolute secret. I'll come to the Street of the Ox-Dealers tomorrow night," Konno-maru ended, and slipped away down a footpath.

Konno-maru was as good as his word and appeared at Asatori's house on the following night. After repeating his warnings of secrecy, he left a small sealed packet and went away.

"What do you suppose is in it?" Asatori asked anxiously.

"Just a letter, I'm sure," Yomogi replied assuringly, full of anticipations of the coming visit. "Not one, but a number of them. And when do you think you can come with me?"

"Any day. Aren't you afraid people will suspect us?"

"Why should they?"

"People still remember that Lady Tokiwa once had connections with the Genji, and if we go—"

"After all, I was only a servant and was with my lady even after she married again. I can't see why people would suspect me. Besides, you haven't yet paid your respects to her and it's about time that you did, now that we're married. Don't you agree with me?"

CHAPTER XLVII

"THE GENJI WILL RISE AGAIN . . ."

A few days later Asatori, turned out in a fresh suit of clothes that Yomogi had laid out for him, and Yomogi in her holiday best set out for the mansion on First Avenue where Tokiwa now lived.

Tokiwa was now past her middle thirties. She had had one child by her second marriage to an elderly Fujiwara courtier, but because of her delicate health lived alone like a recluse in a distant wing of the large, shabby mansion. Few visitors ever came to call on her, and her solitude was only interrupted by priests who came to say Mass on certain holy days.

Konno-maru alone visited her regularly, and in secret, bringing her news of her three sons. And whenever Konno-maru came to see her he talked of the future with passion, saying:

"The Heiké would never dream of what is happening in the east, but their triumph will not last forever. They are drunk with power and cannot realize that the Genji will some day take their revenge. Yoritomo in Izu is now a man, and your youngest son, Ushiwaka, on Kurama Mountain, too, will soon reach manhood."

Tokiwa, who was all too familiar with the horrors of war, shuddered each time Konno-maru talked in this strain. Nor was she convinced that a few surviving Genji could ever supplant the Heiké, and she pleaded with Konno-maru over and over again, saying: "Do not let my sons be drawn into that fearful abyss, Konno-maru. Never speak to them of such things."

She yearned most for Ushiwaka. He was fifteen—high-spirited and headstrong, she had heard, for he alone of her three sons kept insisting that Konno-maru should bring him to see her. He had even threatened to come alone. And Tokiwa was tempted beyond reason to agree to his coming when Konno-maru said:

"My lady, I beg you to come as far as the thickets along the upper part of the river where he can see you at a distance."

But she knew what risks Ushiwaka would be taking, and most of all she was certain that once he gained his freedom, he would never consent to return to the monastery on Kurama Mountain. She finally refused to see Konno-maru any more and sent him word by her maid that she was ill.

All the doors and windows of Tokiwa's room were closed excepting those facing on an inner court. Tokiwa was engrossed in her daily task of copying the sutras, when her maid appeared and announced that two visitors had come to call. Tokiwa's surprise turned to joy when she heard who they were, and she hurriedly pushed aside her writing-table to receive them.

Yomogi forgot her carefully rehearsed greetings and burst into tears on seeing her former mistress.

"How good of you to come, Yomogi!" Tokiwa said. "It's so many years since we last saw each other. And how you've changed since you married!"

As the two eagerly greeted each other, Asatori studied Tokiwa's appearance with the practiced eye of a physician. He saw nothing wrong with her. The talk meanwhile drifted to Konnomaru, and Asatori was forgotten until Yomogi suddenly recalled her reason for coming.

"Konno-maru was telling us that you were ill, but fortunately my husband, who is a physician, has come with me today. This is Asatori," Yomogi said, introducing her husband for the first time. With great pride she explained that Asatori had once been a court musician, who had given up his profession to study medicine.

Asatori sat across from his talkative wife and listened with an occasional nod of agreement. Then Tokiwa turned to him, gently smiling.

"I am sorry that you were so anxious about me. To tell you the truth, I am not at all ill. I was afraid that people might otherwise gossip, and I thought it would discourage Ushiwaka from coming if Konno-maru told him I was unwell. If Ushiwaka should escape from Kurama Mountain and come here, I know that it will be the end of him."

A few tears rolled down Tokiwa's cheek as she spoke. Yomogi tactfully produced a small packet and placed it before Tokiwa.

"This is something Konno-maru sent you, my lady."

Tokiwa stared at the small object, overcome by a wild longing. Then she rapidly opened it. It could only have come from Ushiwaka, her instinct told her—Ushiwaka, of whom she heard nothing but tales of wrongdoing. He was wild and mischievous, the terror of all the monasteries on Kurama Mountain and detested by all the monks. The Abbot had finally washed his hands of the boy and sent him to a brother abbot, who also found him incorrigible. And the yearly reports on his conduct which reached

Kiyomori grew so alarming that an officer finally arrived from Rokuhara to look into this deplorable state of affairs. And the last that Tokiwa heard was that the civil authorities had redoubled their vigilance over Ushiwaka.

Next year he would be sixteen, old enough to take holy orders, Tokiwa reflected, old enough to mourn his father's death through treachery and his mother's unhappy fate. And her only prayer had been that he would cease to rebel against captivity, bow to his fate, and live out the rest of his days in peace.

From the packet Tokiwa drew forth a bright-colored sleeve, the sleeve from an acolyte's robe, wrapped around a letter.

"My mother," the letter ran:

> Are you well again? After Konno-maru told me you were ill, I have dreamed of you every night. From the top of this mountain I can see the lights of the capital and I look in the direction of your home, praying that you will soon be well.
>
> They tell me that I am to take the tonsure this year, but I do not want to become like these monks.
>
> This sleeve is from the robe that I wore when I was seven and first took part in the sacred dramas. Of course, I have grown since then.
>
> The Great Festival of Kurama Mountain falls on the 20th of June. I may take part in the sacred dramas then, but I cannot tell what will happen to me next year.
>
> My mother, send me by Konno-maru some little thing you have worn.
>
> It is still cold this spring, so you must take your medicines and recover quickly.
>
> Your son,
> Ushiwaka

Tokiwa's tears fell on the small sheet of paper, from which she seemed unable to tear her eyes. Then she held it out to Yomogi, saying "Yomogi—read it," and fell to weeping again over the sleeve Ushiwaka had sent.

Yomogi and Asatori exchanged looks of pity and prepared

to cut short a visit that had only saddened Tokiwa instead of cheering her, but Tokiwa pressed them to stay until the lamps were lit.

When they finally took their leave, she brought out a small case, saying: "There is a letter inside this for Ushiwaka. Will you see that he gets it?"

The case, small enough to rest in the palm of a hand, held a silver image of the Kannon and a folded sheet of paper.

As soon as Asatori and Yomogi reached their home, they placed the image on a table.

"How can we be sure that Ushiwaka gets this without anyone seeing us? There will be too many people watching us on Kurama Mountain. We shall get into trouble if the authorities at Rokuhara find out," Asatori ruminated.

Yomogi gave a deep sigh. "I wonder why she does it."

"What do you mean?"

"What I mean is—if my lady is so worried about Ushiwaka, why does she refuse to see Konno-maru?"

Asatori leaned toward his wife. "It's not quite so simple as you think. Konno-maru's idea of loyalty is quite different from my lady's."

"In what way?"

"I'd better not tell you."

"Not even me—your wife?"

"Now, Yomogi, you're too easily offended."

"After all, she was my beloved mistress, and I used to carry Ushiwaka on my back and look after him, begging for milk for him. I did all sorts of things for him, and there isn't much that I wouldn't do for him now. Why shouldn't I? It's only natural, isn't it?"

"Well, Yomogi, I'm not saying you mustn't. What Konno-maru wants for Ushiwaka is quite the opposite of what Lady Tokiwa wants for him."

"The *opposite?*"

"Yes, that's the point. We'll have to think very carefully before we do anything."

"Yes, but what do you mean by *anything*? What do you mean by *opposite*? You'll have to explain all that to me first."

Asatori's voice dropped to a whisper as he cautiously peered out of the window. "Look here, Yomogi, you *are* rather talkative, so you'll have to take very great care that no one hears about this."

"I'm just a chatterbox, anyway, so there!"

"No, Yomogi, don't get into a huff like that! First listen to what I'm going to tell you. Why do you suppose Lady Tokiwa has gone on living and enduring all that humiliation?"

"It's because of Lord Yoshitomo's last words to her, of course. After all, he loved her and she had three children by him. . . . And even when her heart was broken and her children taken from her, my lady's only thought has been for them. I'd do the same if I were in her place."

"With Konno-maru it's quite another matter, though. He's a warrior and he never forgets it. Loyalty, as he understands it, means that he must make sure that one of the children succeeds his father, Lord Yoshitomo, as chief of the Genji. That is to say, the Genji must one day become powerful enough to overthrow the Heiké."

"That should make my lady happy."

"Ah, Yomogi, have you already forgotten what it was like during the Hogen and Heiji wars? You still tell me about the terrible hardships you went through with Lady Tokiwa and the children. Don't you remember all the sad things that happened to you? Of course, it wasn't as if Ushiwaka was your own flesh and blood."

"What makes you say that?"

"If you'd been Lady Tokiwa, trying to escape from the capital with her young children, you'd never want another war."

"But I never said that I'd like to see another war."

"It comes to the same thing though, if you believe Konno-maru is right."

"Are you saying that Konno-maru is wicked for thinking as he does?"

"No. He thinks he is doing his duty as a warrior, but I believe that Tokiwa is right in wanting her children never to take part in bloodshed, and preferring that they should live peacefully as monks."

"Well then, what are we going to do with that image?"

"It's going to be more difficult than ever to get it to him, now that they've set up guards round the mountain. Still, I'd never be happy in my mind unless I tried to see Ushiwaka myself and gave him his mother's letter. Nor would it be right if I didn't talk to him about how his mother feels and convince him of his duty to her."

"What a difficult task we have before us!"

"That's exactly what I thought when we were talking with Lady Tokiwa. It will be difficult enough getting to see Ushiwaka alone, but it's going to be even more difficult to get him to understand what his mother wants for him."

"Difficult? I believe you're only making it seem so!"

"No, you're mistaken about that, Yomogi. There's more to this than you think, and if something should go wrong, there'll be another war," Asatori said with a sigh that was also a prayer. Then he began to tell Yomogi of how he would reach Kurama Mountain.

Yomogi, who had never suspected her husband of being quite so courageous, listened amazed to his daring plan.

"I'd better go alone, Yomogi. It would be better that way."

"Will you be safe going alone?"

"I'm not too sure myself, but I've made up my mind to it."

Asatori prepared himself for his task as though he were going on a long journey. After putting together some dried grain and some other provisions, he armed himself with a dagger and then brought out his loved flute, which he had not played for many a year, and secured it to the belt of his close-fitting trousers. And one night in May he started out for Kurama Mountain. Instead of the usual route, which would bring him to the foot of the mountain by dawn, he chose a little-used and difficult path to avoid meeting strangers. The start of his journey took him across a dark and lonely moor. The season of rains was near and there were no stars to guide him. As he entered hilly country where the mountains loomed up before him, tales of brigands who once infested these parts began to haunt him. He grew afraid and decided to get shelter at the first house he saw. Suddenly a light wavered between the tall grass-tops; Asatori sighed with relief as he made his way toward a dilapidated hut in a clearing. Around it he could make out rows of ripening wheat. The bubbling of a spring broke the stillness. Then he heard voices.

"A horse? A horse would no doubt be convenient for sending messages."

"By all means a horse! Not only would it come in handy—but to be riding one again!"

"Grown flabby, have you, from hiding so long?"

"That's it. Fretting with idleness."

"But we'll need money for that."

"Nothing to worry about there. You'll find bays, chestnuts, and grays in the best stables down in the capital."

"No, not that."

Smoke escaped through a small window in one of the rough, plastered walls. Asatori raised himself on his toes and peered through the vent; seven or eight hunters, charcoal-burners, and woodcutters were gathered round the blazing hearth, drinking. He was struck by their appearance and drew back. These were not ordinary mountain-folk!

"What's wrong with that?" said one of the men thickly, grasping a flask by its neck and pouring some wine for a companion to whom he addressed the question.

"I hardly need explain. If it's a horse, it has to be a pack-horse."

"A pack-horse wouldn't be of any use."

"Yes, but a thoroughbred is bound to attract attention and make people suspect us."

"True—quite true. We've talked enough. There's no point in discussing the impossible."

"Why not some songs that we sing on horseback?"

"Just the thing! When you're sick for the east, sing!"

The two who had been arguing heatedly joined the rest, who were already clapping time to a tune. It was a wild song whose words made little sense to Asatori. The men sang it over and over again, and the musician in Asatori recognized the sturdy rhythms as springing from the soil, chanting of wide moors, the morning winds, and the stars at night. There was no resemblance between it and the music heard at the Court, and Asatori listened rapt.

A cloud of smoke suddenly belched through the window at which Asatori watched; he choked, coughed several times in spite of himself, and then ducked.

"What's that?"

There was silence. Asatori, doubled over, ran off swiftly into the dark. At the sound of his steps, turmoil broke out in the hut. A piercing shout rang out. There were more shouts and cries as footsteps thudded after him. Arrows began to whistle about him and whiz past his ears. Asatori felt his legs begin to give way as he stumbled forward blindly.

Two days later Asatori sat on a rock ledge, munching his first meal—a paste of fermented beans and some dried vegetables. A handful of cooked, dried rice soaked in a near-by mountain stream. The clouds were beautiful in the setting sun, and fish flashed to the surface of the stream. Wondering where he was, Asatori clambered to a ridge and gazed down over the surrounding country. Only mountaintops met his eyes.

He had slept soundly all that afternoon in the woods and wakened refreshed, though still unable to guess where he was. All the previous day he had climbed through hilly country where he sometimes came upon woodcutters' and charcoal-burners' huts. Unseen himself, he had watched men, strangely resembling those he had seen the other night, hard at work, and had been startled by the sight of bows and spears hanging on the rude plaster walls of their huts.

Asatori gazed about him. All the landscape seemed to swim in a deep liquid blue. Stars soon swarmed into the sky, and across the valley on a peak opposite him shone forth three lights. It suddenly came to him then that he was not very far from Kurama Mountain, and the lights were from one of the monasteries. At once he decided to reach Kurama Mountain before dawn and hide there until he could see Ushiwaka alone.

The trail dwindled and disappeared for stretches at a time, but the stars were unusually brilliant for May. The moon rose later as Asatori made his way through valleys and over ridges. He came finally to a decayed log slung across a stream and crossed it, groping about in the undergrowth for a trail, when the sound of deep, muffled voices startled him. He turned to look back and saw several figures crossing the stream. They were in dark, close-fitting suits and wore long swords. Their faces were masked. They slipped past close to where he stood and vanished noiselessly like swirls of night mist.

CHAPTER XLVIII

THE DEMONS OF KURAMA
MOUNTAIN

A dozen or more small inns and public-houses straggled along the road leading up to Kurama Mountain and its eighteen monasteries. A traveler dismounted in front of a public-house and began tethering his horse to a hitching post as he gazed up at the eaves of the house.

"These wistaria are magnificent!" he cried over his shoulder. "The landlord in good health? I'm back again this year, as you see!" There were a few benches and tables at one side of the house where several monks were talking loudly among themselves and laughing. An old man, the landlord, separated himself from the group and came running.

"Good day, sir! From the northeast again, sir? You seem in the best of health, I'm sure!" The landlord greeted the newcomer effusively and then called for some hot water and a cushion for his guest.

"No, my good man, you haven't changed in the least. I don't often make pilgrimages like this. When was I here last?"

"Last year—toward midsummer I recall, and quite a thunderstorm there was at the time."

"Sure enough! The lightning split a great cedar tree apart and nearly killed me. I remember now. I shall never forget how frightened I was as I burst into your house here."

"And how's that young fellow, Kowaka, that you brought with you then? Not traveling alone this year, are you?"

"No, Kowaka should be arriving with my baggage soon. He seems to be taking his time, but he'll be here shortly, no doubt."

The monks left off drinking, threw a few stealthy glances in the direction of the traveler, and whispered among themselves. Then one of their number got up and approached him:

"You will pardon me, I hope, for asking, sir, but are you not Master Kichiji from the northeast?"

"Yes, I'm Kichiji."

"Then I was right after all. My companions thought they recognized you. Greetings, sir!"

"And you?"

"I am a seminarian from Abbot Toko's monastery."

"Oh?—To tell you the truth, I always stay at the neighboring monastery whenever I come here and haven't ever missed the seven-day retreat for years, so I know your Abbot slightly. He's well, I hope?"

"I regret to say that he died a few months ago. Are you here for the retreat?"

"Yes, I find that these retreats are good for business. I seem to prosper. In fact, I'm sure I owe my good fortune to the gods here."

A tinkling of bells at the bottom of the hill announced the arrival of the pack-horse. A young man, his sleeves pulled back out of the way, his face red and drenched with sweat, approached with the groom, panting.

"Well, Kowaka, you were slow in coming. I've waited so long that I'm ready to yawn."

Kowaka, a short, muscular fellow, cast an inquiring look round at the faces near him, then burst into a loud laugh.

"You must be joking, master! It's easy for you, coming as you did on horseback. It's almost three leagues from the capital, and with a heavy load like this—see, even the horse is lathering."

The monks and a crowd of men and women had collected in front of the public-house; they paid no attention to Kowaka, but examined the great load of votive offerings curiously. Rolls of silk were piled high on the pack-horse; large drum-shaped containers, finely lacquered, hung at either side of the saddle, and a cask of placer gold, carefully wrapped in layers of paper and straw, was lashed on top.

Kichiji and his assistant, who had changed from his dusty suit into a fresh one, had their noon meal as they rested outside. Presently they rose and took leave of the landlord with promises to see him on their return.

The most arduous part of the climb lay ahead of them, and the road soon grew too steep for the horse, which was quickly relieved of its burden by a number of carriers on their way back to the summit. Even the monks assisted in carrying part of the load, and the antlike procession crawled slowly up the tortuous path. As they came in sight of the monastery where Kichiji was to stay, the Abbot and his monks trooped out to welcome him.

On the following day Kichiji entered the temple for the seven days' retreat. Kowaka, meanwhile, was lodged in one of the hostels set aside for the servants who accompanied pilgrims, and there occupied himself as best he could until Kichiji appeared.

Kowaka quietly stole from his lodgings toward midnight and made his way to a shrine north of the monastery gate. A path on the farther side of the shrine led down to another monastery. He squatted in the shadows and waited, seeing no one and hearing only the soughing of the pines overhead. Suddenly a door in the monastery below slid open, and a small figure appeared on the long, open gallery, poised itself for an instant on the balustrade, then swooped to the ground noiselessly and glided off with the swiftness of a swallow.

"Is it you, my young master, Ushiwaka?"

"Konno-maru!"

The two shadows merged into one and then hurried off into the darkness of the valley below.

"There's no need to hurry now, sir. No one can find us."

"But the others must be waiting."

"Yes, but by the moon I can tell that we're earlier than we were last night."

"You meet the others from time to time, but I only see them once a year."

"It's lonely for you, I know, and after tonight we shall have to scatter and go into hiding."

Ushiwaka slowed his steps and looked down, biting his nail. He was barefooted and wore a novice's short, close-fitting tunic. Kowaka dropped to his knees anxiously, thinking that Ushiwaka had cut his foot on the sharp-edged scrub bamboo.

"What is it, my young master?"

Ushiwaka merely shook his head. "Nothing—nothing at all," he replied after a pause, and moved forward again.

To Konno-maru the small figure walking ahead appeared more thoughtful than he had seen it these past several nights. He was sure that he alone knew Ushiwaka well—his strong points and weaknesses, his wildness and his moods. It was not for nothing that Konno-maru had contrived to spend ten years and more as the servant, Kowaka, in Toji's establishment at Horikawa. Not only did he find a safe hiding-place in the gay quarters, but the fact that it was frequented by those closely connected with the Court and those in high places in the government gave him opportunities to observe the fluctuations in politics, and in particular the movements of the Heiké. And often, on the pretext of visiting his mother in Tamba, Konno-maru made his way to Kurama Mountain to see Ushiwaka in secret, or met with other Genji in the hills thereabouts to confer with them, or even traveled to eastern Japan, bringing back messages to Tokiwa.

And it was during his employment by Toji that Konno-maru came to know Kichiji, who on his protracted visits to the capital stayed invariably at Toji's. It was not long before they saw through each other and concluded a pact benefiting them mutually, for Kichiji, the merchant, was ambitious. He dreamed of wielding as much influence with his overlord, Chieftain Hidehira, who ruled the northeast, as Bamboku did with Kiyomori of the Heiké. From Kichiji himself it was impossible to guess whether Hidehira approved his plan to kidnap Ushiwaka, but with characteristic tenacity and patience Kichiji from year to year made pilgrimages to Kurama Mountain, taking Konno-maru with him each time.

People said that a race of winged demons—the Tengu—lived in a certain valley of Kurama Mountain, and on nights when lightning flashes played through the clouds over this valley, they warned one another that the Tengu were holding their revels. And no man dared venture into that valley to spy on them, for the beak-nosed Tengu would scent out the stranger and set him swinging from the tallest treetop or else tear him to pieces. In all the villages around Kurama Mountain, where people had heard stories of the Tengu for generations, no one doubted that the demons still lived in the valley, for the Tengu still performed the most incredible feats: they hurled boulders down mountainsides, unleashed torrents which washed away rice-paddies, and rained down stones on near-by hamlets. Lately, however, more tales of their mischief had created a state of terror among the simple villagers.

For the seventh night in succession a strange meeting took place in a valley of Kurama Mountain. Tengu they might well have been.

"Has he come yet?"

"Not yet."

"He's late."

"No, we're earlier than usual. The moon is still over there," replied one, pointing up at the sky. Several pairs of eyes followed the pointed finger.

"Well then, we might as well go on talking."

The floor of the valley was strewn with boulders, and the roaring of a torrent through a gorge sounded all round this singular gathering.

"Tonight will be the last time we meet."

"Not exactly—we can meet here whenever we like, but it will be another year before we hear from Chieftain Hidehira in the northeast."

"Kichiji says we shall have to wait another year. He keeps insisting that it's still too soon, but if we wait another year, the Heiké may discover what's happening and the work of ten years come to nothing."

"I don't quite trust Kichiji. He's put us off from one year to the next with one excuse or another. I wonder if he really has an understanding with Chieftain Hidehira."

"True. We can't be sure of that."

"The Genji have had many allies in the northeast for generations, but Hidehira isn't hostile to the Heiké. One might even say that he and Kiyomori have ambitions in common."

"Is that possible? . . . Who can tell?"

A thoughtful silence ensued.

Another Tengu resumed: "It might be well for us to think that over. It's two years now since Hidehira was made a general of the army in the northeast. People say that he owed it to Kiyomori. That alone is enough to show us what the Heiké think of the chieftain."

"No, that's too simple a conclusion. You're assuming too much. That was only a sop to Hidehira and proves nothing about how Kiyomori feels toward him. The harbor at Owada and the buildings at Itsuku-shima are costing Kiyomori a great deal, and Kiyomori needs all the gold he can get from Hidehira. There's no doubt that Hidehira knows it. They're rivals and they know it."

"Good! that's more like the truth. Anyway, Konno-maru should soon be here, and he'll tell us about his talk with Kichiji last night. We'll soon know what they've decided. We can't risk anything now, nor can we delay much longer. No matter what Kichiji says, we'd better take matters into our own hands."

A scout who had been peering down into the ravine suddenly shouted down to the Tengu: "I see them now! They're coming!"

A shape approached down the precipitous valley wall, swinging from branch to branch, slithering nimbly from boulder to boulder. It stood out clearly in the moonlight which flooded the surface of the rocks and the trees. The Tengu below stared up at it in silence, with absorbed, adoring eyes.

"Konno-maru, we've come out in a different spot tonight."

"I can hear a roaring below; we must have come out above the falls."

"The falls, eh?"

"It's dangerous there; we'd better find another way down."

"Look, they're waiting down there. Let's go down this way."

"Impossible!"

"You go round the other way, I'm going to jump."

Konno-maru knew from experience that it was useless to remonstrate with Ushiwaka, and clung to some shrubs as his eyes searched the steep rock-face. More than twenty feet below him yawned a chasm of rocks, and at the bottom lay a pool into which a cataract leaped in sprays of mist.

Konno-maru gave a warning cry, but Ushiwaka had already leaped into space and now swung from the branch of a large tree below, fumbling for a foothold in another tree lower down.

"This is how to do it, Konno-maru!" Ushiwaka shouted as the branch bent under his weight. He wound his feet around another branch and released his hold.

Konno-maru had difficulty following him.

"You're not much good at this, Konno-maru," Ushiwaka jeered mischievously.

He was small for his age; there was a wizened look about his cheeks; his arms and legs were overly slender. Scantily fed and thinly clad since the time he arrived at the monastery, Ushiwaka seemed to have survived by a miracle. He was the smallest and least prepossessing of all the novices at the monastery, the butt of innumerable cruel jokes. High-strung and obstinate, Ushiwaka often went off by himself to relieve his feelings in wild fits of crying that became the talk of all the monasteries around. By the time he was ten, he received, in addition to his religious training, training in arms, for the monasteries on Kurama Mountain were under the jurisdiction of Mount Hiei and not only trained their monks to fight, but maintained a modest-sized army of mercenaries.

As Ushiwaka grew older, his eyes took on a keen hawklike look; the lines of the intelligent mouth hardened early and he bore himself with a haughty air. He cared nothing, however, about his appearance. His hair grew long and unkempt, his legs bore scars of old wounds and were always marked with fresh ones, and in spite of reminders that he should mend the tears in his tunic and trousers, he went about with large rents in his clothes. But a startling change had come over him in the past few years. He suddenly became amenable, eager to obey and please his superiors, who put it down to the training they gave him. But the truth was that Ushiwaka had been stealing out of the novices' dormitory at night to meet the Tengu in the valley below, and there learned what had been kept from him: that he was their chieftain, the son of Yoshitomo of the Genji, and a prisoner of Kiyomori of the Heiké. From the Tengu he also heard of his father's sudden end and his mother's fate. And from that time on he needed no promptings from the Tengu as to what his future should be, nor was he ignorant of the dangers before him.

"All right, Konno-maru, can you follow me?"

"Yes, but you must be careful of yourself."

"No need to worry about me. Here, I'm going to jump," Ushiwaka said over his shoulder; then, crossing from tree limb to tree limb, he measured the distance between him and the pool below and leaped to a boulder.

"Neatly done!" the Tengu cried, running forward and surrounding Ushiwaka.

Konno-maru, however, drew back, and the Tengu shouted with scorn until all the valley echoed. But Konno-maru suddenly called to the Tengu below:

"I see someone hiding beyond that rock. Catch him!"

The Tengu scattered in consternation and scrambled over rocks and boulders. From his superior position Konno-maru saw a shape in the moonlight slipping away among the shadows of the rock-strewn valley.

It was easy to escape and lie hidden among the large boulders heaped along the riverbank, among the massive tree-trunks felled by the weather and rot, or in the thick undergrowth. Asatori fled, stumbling and darting among the shelter of rocks. He finally crawled between two boulders and crouched there breathless, listening to the shouts overhead.

"Did you get him?"

"No, have you searched over there?"

"Yes, but I can't find him."

From a distance came a shout, borne on the wind: "Oy-y-y, have you caught him?"

"Nothing at all. Any luck over there?"

"Can't see a thing over here."

"I wonder what caused Konno-maru to make such a commotion."

"He must have seen a monkey or a deer."

The voices soon faded away. The Tengu seemed to have abandoned the search, and only the sound of the wind filled the valley.

Asatori sighed. It was painful lying still in his cramped position, so he crawled out of his hole. His eyes on the hollow where the Tengu had gathered, he once more stealthily made his way toward them. They were sitting cross-legged in a ring, absorbed in talk. Seated above them on some object was Ushiwaka, with Konno-maru beside him. There were close to a score of them, calling each other by names which Asatori recognized were those of illustrious Genji warriors in the east.

"Well, Konno-maru, does Kichiji insist that it's too soon?"

One of the Tengu, who seemed to be the acknowledged leader of the group, replied: "It is so. We told him very definitely what we think of the matter, but Kichiji refuses to change his plans. He insists that it's far too soon yet."

"Exactly when does he think it will be time to act?"

"He was vague about that, but implied that we are to wait until some upheaval takes place."

"What did he mean by that?"

"For instance, there are signs that all is not well between the ex-Emperor Goshirakawa and Kiyomori of the Heiké. Whatever comes of that, there'll be no mistaking the signs when the rupture comes."

"What if this present state of affairs goes on for years?"

"Yes, we'll have to take that into account, too."

"Are you men prepared for that? Are you willing to wait indefinitely?"

The leader saw that none of his comrades were willing to wait further. Yet Kichiji was their only hope now. Everything depended on following his orders. Without him and Hidehira's help there was no way to insure Ushiwaka's safety or the future of the Genji.

The men fell silent, dejected

Suddenly Ushiwaka spoke. "Enough—let's not talk of this any more. Let's not even think of it."

The men stared at Ushiwaka in astonishment, and one of them addressed him with tears in his eyes, saying:

"My young master, what makes you say that? Think of all we have gone through until now, and of our oath to you."

"I only meant that all this arguing is useless."

"Why useless?"

"Why should we wait and hope for something that may never happen? The time is near when I shall have to take the vows, and I want nothing of that."

"Yes, that is what makes us so anxious. We want Kichiji to come to an understanding with the Chieftain Hidehira soon."

"Kichiji—that trader? Depend on him?"

The men listened incredulously. Ushiwaka had said what none of them had dared to put into words.

Ushiwaka looked round him. "Very well, I expect nothing of him. What's to become of me if we have to depend on Kichiji? No matter what anyone says, nothing will keep me from escaping from Kurama Mountain this year. You shall see!"

The men heard him in consternation, and then broke into protests, warning him not to be rash.

Asatori, who caught only snatches of what was being said, crept up closer, determined that he would risk being caught in order to give Ushiwaka what his mother, Tokiwa, had sent him. But before this happened, Ushiwaka broke into loud and prolonged weeping.

Asatori wakened to the sound of birds singing. He went over the curious events of the past night, piecing together what he had heard and shaping them into coherence.

The sun was high, and the whole valley was flooded with the May sunlight. He crept cautiously from his hiding-place and looked about him. For two days he stayed where he was, catching fish in the mountain stream near by and bringing down a bird or two with his sling. Then he had made up his mind to stay here and wait until a chance came to find Ushiwaka alone.

Days went by and then weeks, until one day Asatori saw some travelers approaching along a ridge. Even at a distance he could see that they were not priests. He watched the procession wistfully, for he had not seen or talked to anyone in several weeks. He was sure that these were pilgrims on their way from the region of Lake Biwa, or from Tamba, so he set out to meet them. As they drew closer, his heart beat wildly, for he could tell by the color of their cloaks and the shapes of their head-dresses that they were court musicians. He wondered if he would find some of his old friends among them, and impulsively ran down the road over which the procession of eighteen or more men were approaching. As the men caught sight of Asatori they halted, then huddled together.

Asatori realized that they took him for a brigand. Bowing low, he called to them: "Do not be afraid. I also am a musician. Which way are you going?"

The musicians hurriedly whispered to one another, then one of them approached Asatori and said:

"We are musicians from Shuzan and have come again this year to perform at the festival on Kurama Mountain. You say that you also are a musician, but what brings you here?"

Asatori hesitated for a reply, and then asked: "The festival? When does that take place?"

"It will not be for another two weeks or so, but we are here for the rehearsals."

"From Shuzan?"

"Yes, but there are groups of other musicians coming as well."

"Are you not musicians of the Abé family?"

"You actually recognize us!"

"I, too, am one of the Abé of Kyoto."

"You too?"

The musicians suddenly hurried forward in a body and surrounded Asatori with eager questions.

That night Asatori went with the musicians to their inn, not far from Kurama Mountain, and talked with them late into the night.

"You are no ordinary musician," they said, curious and admiring; "tell us something about yourself."

"I have given up music to become a physician."

"What made you give up your post at the Court?"

"I was not happy there."

"You didn't like the narrow life it imposed on you?"

"Yes, that is more or less what it was," Asatori replied, and added: "I was in the hills collecting herbs, and when I saw you I could not help wanting to talk to you. How would it be if I went with you and saw something of the festival? If you can think of something I can do, I shall only be too glad to be of use."

A few welcomed the idea of including Asatori in their party, but some hesitated, and it was not until the following morning that they agreed to take Asatori with them.

On Kurama Mountain they were lodged in one of the dormitories where other groups of musicians were also staying. Rehearsals were going on in all the monasteries, where novices were practicing their parts in the sacred dramas. Asatori went each day to the rehearsals, certain that he would find Ushiwaka.

As the day of the festival drew near, the monasteries echoed from dawn until dark with the sound of drums, bells, flutes and flageolets. One night Asatori stole away to a shrine near the dormitory in which he now knew Ushiwaka lived, and, drawing out his flute from its case, began to play. He had succeeded several days ago in slipping a message into Ushiwaka's sleeve, and for two nights in succession had come here to play his flute, expecting Ushiwaka to appear. This was the last night he dared to come, lest his playing cause the monks to suspect him.

Ushiwaka hid in the shadows not far from the shrine and listened to Asatori play. As Asatori began to put away his flute, Ushiwaka stole up and stood beside him silently.

"Who are you?" Asatori asked, startled.

"Is it you that have been playing his flute these several nights?"

"Are you Ushiwaka?"

"And you—who are you?"

"It was I that put that note into your sleeve."

"Yes, but tell me who you are. Who are you? Are you trying to play a trick on me?"

"No, that I am not. I am a physician, and Asatori is my name," Asatori said, prostrating himself.

"A physician who plays the flute—and so beautifully?"

"Let me tell you of that later. Since you are afraid to trust me, take this. Your mother asked me to give this to you. There is a letter to you in the case."

Ushiwaka stooped and picked up the object that Asatori laid at his feet, said nothing, and disappeared into the shrine. There by the light of the sanctuary lamp he read his mother's letter. "I pray for your happiness morning and night," the letter began. "Obey your superior in all things. It makes me happy to think that you are diligent in your studies. This image which I send you by a messenger belonged to your father, Yoshitomo of the Genji. It was his last gift to me. . . ."

The rest of the letter spoke of Tokiwa's prayers and hopes for him—that he would put away all thought of a warrior's life and follow the ways of peace and holiness as a priest.

Asatori waited for Ushiwaka to appear, then finally rose and peered into the sanctuary; there he saw Ushiwaka staring thoughtfully at the letter before him. He quickly slipped in and knelt before Ushiwaka and began to speak to him of his mother, imploring Ushiwaka to heed all that she had written.

Ushiwaka said nothing for a time; then he finally looked up. "Yes, Asatori, I know what my mother wants of me."

"You do?" Asatori replied eagerly.

"But—" Ushiwaka went on, "my mother is a woman and cannot understand. From her letter I can tell how truly womanly she is. If only I could meet her! Is she at all like the mother of whom I dream all the time?"

"Do you really want so much to see her?"

"What stupid things you keep saying!"

"There's no reason why you shouldn't see her after you've taken the vows. When people recognize you as a great sage and a holy man, I am sure that you will be allowed to return to the capital to see her. Even the Heiké may some day welcome you among them."

"I can't wait so long. I *must* see her now. . . ."

"If you make the wrong choice, you may never see her."

"Is it unnatural for me to want to see my mother?"

"You must remember the Heiké."

"Who are they, and what are they to me? Are they gods? Are they supernatural beings?"

"It is war that brought all this unhappiness on you, and you must turn away from those things which bring about war."

"Is this to go on forever? Am I to stay as I am, a prisoner here from the time I was born?"

Asatori went on: "It is for us to find a way of life which will not bring conflict or create a hell on earth. Only by following the path which leads to peace will you show how much you love your mother. The world cannot be changed overnight, nor can we escape *karma*."

"Was that all you came to tell me, Asatori?" Ushiwaka asked, wrapping the letter round the image and thrusting them into the folds of his tunic. Suddenly he stamped his foot at Asatori, who knelt before him.

"Now I know who you are," he said. "You're the one who spied on us that night in the valley. Off with you! I'll see that my answer reaches my mother. Don't stay here any longer—go at once —now!"

As he spoke, Ushiwaka ran from the shrine and disappeared into the surrounding woods. Asatori tried to follow him, but Ushiwaka had already vanished.

CHAPTER XLIX

USHIWAKA ESCAPES

The morning haze rose like steam from the mountain. It was the last day of the three-day festival. Thousands of lamps glimmered in the early dawn and the chanting of sutras and the sound of music were everywhere. It promised to be another sweltering day.

"Ushiwaka's looking quite elegant, isn't he?"

"Not a bit like him, when he's all dressed up!"

"You must be Ushiwaka. Come, let's see if you really are."

The novices were gathered in a room behind the dance stage and teasing Ushiwaka, who wore a poppy-colored tunic and trousers of a deep purple. His hair was arranged in an elaborate knot on his head. While the other novices laughed and shouted and leaped about in their excitement, Ushiwaka alone sat apart, quietly waiting.

"You're worried, aren't you," one of his companions asked.

Ushiwaka shook his head. "No, I couldn't sleep at all last night."

"You're lying! What kept you awake, then?"

"I was too excited."

"Excited? About what?"

"Today, of course."

"Queer, aren't you?" Another novice snorted and then ran off to join his companions who were leaning over the balustrades of a gallery.

A great shout went up: "Just look at the crowds today!"

"There are still more coming up! Like ants in a procession!"

"Where, where? Let me take a look!"

The novices climbed onto the balustrades and swarmed up pillars in their excitement. While their backs were turned, Ushiwaka sprang to his feet and disappeared down a hall into his room. From behind the books on his small writing-table he snatched a small case, took out the silver image, threw the case away, and carefully placed the image in the inner folds of his tunic; he patted it to see that it was safe, then tightened the sash around his waist.

"Ushiwaka! Ushiwaka, where are you?"

The sound of voices startled Ushiwaka, who ran back, replying as he ran.

A score of novices were already lined up, and a monk who saw Ushiwaka shouted at him angrily:

"Where were you anyway?"

"I went to the privy."

"You're lying! I saw you coming from your room."

"I was tightening the sash of my trousers."

A monk led the procession, cutting a path through the crowds. Musicians followed him, sounding bells and gongs; after them marched high priests and the many novices who were taking part in the sacred dramas.

Hotter and hotter it grew, and not a cloud was to be seen as the procession made its way round the mountain, from shrine to shrine, from temple to temple. The novices panted and perspired, straggled, broke rank as their high spirits got the better of them, and dodged and darted about. Ushiwaka, the smallest of them, marched at the end, orderly and sedate. His eyes, however, were busy, darting to left and right among the watching pilgrims, and sometimes a gleam of recognition came into his eyes as he tramped on after the rest.

When the four-hour march round the mountain ended, the novices scattered for their noonday meal and then prepared themselves for the dances in which they were to take part. All afternoon and into the night the dancing and music went on. Bonfires were lighted all over the mountain. Multitudes of pilgrims pushed and jostled one another, moving from one performance to the next. Novices wriggled their way through the crowds, anxious not to miss anything. Ushiwaka alone wandered about aimlessly on the fringes of sightseers, until without warning a man approached him from behind, threw a thin, summer cloak about him, and whispered:

"Now, sir!"

"Is that you, Masachika?"

"I will go with you as far as the road leading down to the valley."

"That road has been fenced in."

"No matter—hurry!"

Ushiwaka started running. No sooner was he out of sight than Masachika put his fingers to his lips and gave two shrill whistles. Several men quietly slipped through the crowd, absorbed in watching the bamboo-splitting rites, and disappeared into the night. Not long after, priest after priest, taking part in the rites, quickly left the scene.

Someone was heard to say: "A monk was killed at the barriers to one of the valleys."

People were soon talking among themselves excitedly. A novice had broken through a barrier and escaped. He had killed two guards as he got away. No, a Tengu had done it, people claimed.

The rumor soon reached the musicians, who were resting and drinking in their quarters. Asatori, who had been drinking with the rest, sat up.

"A novice escaped? Who was it? What was his name? Is this true?" he asked his companions, and then stealthily left his seat to slip away outside.

The Tengu were now gathered in the hut where Asatori had first seen them.

"The first step has now been safely taken and we congratulate you," said one, turning to Ushiwaka, who huddled among the dark bodies that surrounded him, still dazed by his narrow escape.

One of the men, who seemed to be older and more experienced than the rest, interposed: "It's a little too early to congratulate ourselves. Remember, we still have to reckon with the Chieftain Hidehira and, furthermore, we've done this without Kichiji's consent. It's easy enough to get away from Kurama Mountain, but how are we going to manage the rest? If luck is with us, Kichiji will be told of this; otherwise it will be practically impossible for us to elude Kiyomori's soldiers and escape east."

Another broke in: "But this was our last chance. In any case, Ushiwaka took matters into his own hands."

"We won't depend on Kichiji. If he refuses help, then we'll manage the rest ourselves. Remember, we expected this to happen when Ushiwaka said that he would escape on his own. There was nothing else we could do, and it would have been cowardly to do otherwise."

"Hardly cowardly. It's only proper to take every precaution in a matter as serious as this."

"There's not much use in arguing about this. I carefully warned Konno-maru of what would happen tonight. It worries me that he hasn't appeared yet."

The futility of trying to escape east was apparent, for the Heiké would give the alarm and block every road leading east. Kichiji alone could assist them. They waited then for Konno-maru, who finally appeared a little before dawn.

"Yes, it took me by surprise. I hadn't expected this to happen until midnight, and I had great difficulty following you."

"We're sorry about that. It couldn't be helped. We said midnight, but our plans changed suddenly because a better chance came. . . . We're lucky to be here, though. What of Kichiji? What did he have to say?"

"He laughed at our impatience and seemed to think that there was nothing he could do but fall in with our plans."

"So he agrees with us?"

"Did Kichiji then offer some ideas, or did he insist that it was still too soon to tell you what they were? What did he say, Konno-maru?"

Dawn was beginning to fill the sky, and a faint radiance filtered in through a small window of the hut.

The Tengu hung on Konno-maru's words.

"Kichiji is more than ever with us, but he has some conditions. He says he will not answer for Ushiwaka's life if we don't accept his terms."

"What are they?"

"He will answer only for Ushiwaka's safety. The rest of you, he says, must look after yourselves."

"What! He's going to leave us out of this entirely?"

"Yes, he says that Ushiwaka's safety depends on that."

"How is that possible?"

"No one in this region knows who you are. People take you for Tengu demons, but if you come with Ushiwaka, Kichiji believes that that will be enough to put his life in danger."

"Konno-maru, do *you* believe he's right?"

"I do. We have played our part. Now that Ushiwaka has left

5 9 8

Kurama Mountain, there is nothing more for us to do but leave him and disappear."

"And what will Ushiwaka do without us?"

"Kichiji will take care of the rest."

"Do we dare trust him?"

"If *he* was not to be trusted, he would never in the first place have trusted us—so he says."

"What if you're mistaken?"

"If anything goes wrong, then Kichiji will be the first to pay for it—and with his life. There's not much use in saying more. All we can do is trust him," Konno-maru said.

The rest now turned to Ushiwaka expectantly, and Masachika asked:

"You have just heard how matters are. What is your will?"

Faced now with the fulfillment of his greatest hope, Ushiwaka replied without hesitation: "I do not wish to go east at once. If I go, there's no telling whether I shall ever see my mother again. I must go to the capital—alone, or with all of you. I must see my mother. . . . Take me this once to see her."

News of Ushiwaka's escape reached Rokuhara toward dawn. Soldiers and agents set out immediately for Kurama Mountain, where the monks most familiar with the mountain terrain had already begun the hunt for Ushiwaka. By noon, when several hundred warriors from Rokuhara arrived on Kurama Mountain, Ushiwaka and his followers were on their way to Sajiki Peak. When they reached it, Konno-maru said: "From here the roads lead to the provinces of Shiga, Tamba, and Sanjo, and we shall leave you now. I alone will stay with our young master until he reaches the capital." Then he turned to Ushiwaka. "I will stay with you until you are ready to leave for the northeast with Kichiji. After that you will be entirely alone. You're quite sure you want to go, aren't you, Ushiwaka?"

Ushiwaka hesitated; then he again asked: "Konno-maru, will you really take me to see my mother? When will you do this?"

"I must first talk to Kichiji," Konno-maru replied. "Kichiji will think of a way to do it."

"Can't you manage alone, Konno-maru? Why must you first speak to Kichiji?"

"I promised that nothing would be done without his consent."

"Now—for the future!"

"Which way are you going, Goro?"

"First to Tamba, where I'll stay in hiding for a time."

"And you, Adachi?"

"I'm thinking of going to North Shiga. And you, Kamata?"

"I'll cross to Omi and then to Owari, where my father was assassinated together with Lord Yoshitomo."

One by one the men took leave of Ushiwaka, with promises to rally to him in the east. At sunset Ushiwaka and Konno-maru were alone on Sajiki Peak, towering above Kurama Mountain; the sun was setting and the mist eddied about them.

"Ushiwaka, will you be able to walk much farther?"

"Of course!"

"We shall see the lights of the capital tomorrow at this time. A carriage will be waiting for us at a certain spot."

"A carriage? . . . And where shall we be going?"

"That I don't know, but you need not worry about it. Kichiji will see to everything. You need only trust him. If I have reason to doubt him, he'll not get off alive."

The two started down the peak. They saw no one until dusk, when they met a stranger of whom they asked the way. They went on for several leagues, until they passed a small settlement, then far below them they saw some lights dotting the darkness.

"Konno-maru, are those the lights of the capital?"

"No, that is Mount Atago over there—the lights of the Atago Shrine and the monastery."

"We've come a good way, but are we any nearer the capital?"

"Not yet. We've been doubling on our tracks to escape pursuit, but we're getting closer and closer to the capital."

"Ushiwaka—" Konno-maru said suddenly, "when we reach the capital you must never call me Konno-maru, but Kowaka."

"Call you Kowaka?"

"That's what people there call me."

"Oh? . . . I'm hungry, Konno-maru," he said.

"That's natural. I'll see if I can find you something to eat. Wait in that shrine over there."

After what seemed a long time, Konno-maru returned and found that Ushiwaka had flung himself down to sleep on the shrine porch. He could hear his even breathing as he lay there under the stars. Konno-maru shook him awake, and together they devoured the food that Konno-maru had brought from a farmhouse; then they lay down to sleep until the short summer's night whitened into dawn.

They walked on for half the day. From time to time they met strangers from whose appearance they could tell that they were nearing Kyoto.

"We're not far from Saga now," Konno-maru told Ushiwaka as they came in sight of a hill against whose side nestled a thatched cottage, enclosed by a brushwood hedge. "Look, he's come as he promised! There's the ox-carriage on the road below the cottage," Konno-maru exclaimed.

Ushiwaka was unmoved by what he saw, but the look of relief on Konno-maru's face caused him to look up expectantly. Konno-maru cautiously approached a gate in the hedge and peered over it into the cottage.

Finally he called softly:

"Good-day, is this where the recluse Giwo lives?"

A sound of chanting ceased. "Yes?—" came a fresh voice from within; then a face, surprisingly young and lovely for a nun's, appeared over the hedge. "Who is it, please?"

"Are you not Giwo?"

"No, I am her younger sister."

Konno-maru smiled as he recognized her. "Don't you remember me—Kowaka, Toji's servant?"

"Is it really you, Kowaka? Come inside and wait. I'll call Giwo."

Giwo appeared almost immediately, and Konno-maru greeted her, saying:

"Ah, Giwo! How long is it since I last saw you? I've thought of you often, but—"

"Has all gone well with you, Kowaka? Are you still with Toji?"

"Yes, it's lively there. The work's pleasant, and the years slip by before I know it. Yes, it must be at least eight years since I went with you to Rokuhara."

"It's like a dream, isn't it? Five or six years have gone by since I came to live here with my mother, sister, and Hotoké."

"Yes indeed, all those years since you went to Rokuhara. You never came back to us after that."

Giwo's face clouded. "Please, Kowaka, don't talk of the past. Now that I have taken the vows of a nun, I blush when I think of it."

"Forgive me; it was stupid of me to go on like that—and that reminds me of why I'm here."

"You promised to meet Master Kichiji here, didn't you?"

"Yes, he's Toji's most respected and generous patron."

"He often asked me to perform for him. I was quite amazed when he arrived here yesterday."

"Yesterday?"

"Yes, we talked for some time, then he left, saying that he had hired a boat on the Hozu River and was taking several of Toji's girls to spend the evening on the water."

"Has he come back yet?"

"He was back again early this morning to admire the morning-glories about the house, and told me that you might be coming to fetch him. He ordered his carriage to be left in the shade where you would see it. I was to tell you that he was staying at that temple you can see from here."

Konno-maru thanked Giwo and said good-by. Then he motioned to Ushiwaka, and together they walked over to the carriage. Konno-maru lifted a blind and looked inside. The interior smelled of incense, perfume, and scented oils.

"Ushiwaka, will you wait inside here? I shall be back right away."

From the back of the carriage Konno-maru pulled out a white tunic such as ox-tenders wear and threw it on over his clothes before setting out for the temple.

Ushiwaka examined the carriage's interior curiously. The mustiness and the cloying odors stifled him. They reminded him of his mother—her letters about which clung the same fragrance, the smell that he had come to think of as the smell of women. He lifted the blinds, which Konno-maru had carefully drawn, and looked out from time to time.

Kichiji lay napping in a room in the temple when a priest appeared and wakened him, saying that a manservant had arrived to fetch him. Kichiji quickly got up and went to a door at the back of the temple.

"Kowaka! So you've come—my thanks!"

"I was afraid that I wouldn't get here in time," Konno-maru replied. "Shall we leave at once?"

After thanking the priest, the two left the temple for Giwo's cottage, near by.

"I shall be back again," Kichiji smiled. "I'm afraid, though, that I've put you to some trouble," he said apologetically as he stepped into his carriage.

His sudden appearance took Ushiwaka by surprise; he stared at Kichiji without saying a word. As the carriage jolted into motion, Kichiji leaned toward him and whispered:

"You need not fear anything now that I'm here."

After a moment's silence Kichiji once more whispered: "But —if you're not a Heiké, you're a nobody. That's how the world is today. If you're depending on me to help you escape to the northeast, then you must be ready to put up with a number of things and to do exactly as I tell you."

The carriage drew to a stop as they arrived in front of a villa by a river. The sound of wheels brought two dancing-girls running from among the willow trees. Kichiji alighted and greeted them.

"Where are the others? Gone on ahead, did you say? Never mind, then, I can hire a horse or litter for myself."

After chattering somewhat inconsequentially, the two dancing-girls squeezed themselves into the carriage beside Ushiwaka.

"Well, you might as well start on ahead." Kichiji waved to Kowaka, who nodded and laid his whip to the ox.

Ushiwaka guessed from their conversation that the dancing-girls were sisters—one, Kichiji's mistress. They stared frankly at Ushiwaka, whispered to each other, and then smiled at him.

"Charming, isn't he?"

"Rather small for his age, though, don't you think?"

With sidelong glances the two women remarked on Ushiwaka's appearance from time to time as though they had acquired a household pet. Ushiwaka felt suffocated by the rich scent of the women's garments; his heart thumped, and he kept his face glued to the small window as he stared out at the scenery.

"He seems to find the sights of the city quite absorbing. Isn't that so—sir?"

Ushiwaka ignored the questions addressed to him. He was entranced by everything he saw as they passed through the capital.

"Look!—there's Master Kichiji himself, ahead of us," exclaimed one of the dancing-girls, pointing to one side of the road. As Kichiji rode past them, he glanced over his shoulder at the carriage and flung a few words at Kowaka, who was leading the ox.

Soon the willow-lined street at Horikawa came into view. Lights from the houses along the canal danced on the waters, and the sound of flutes and drums and the scents of a warm summer's night penetrated the carriage blinds. They soon turned down a lane and drew up in front of a neat-looking house where Kichiji was already waiting.

"Sir," he said to Ushiwaka, "won't you come in? This is my house, and you are to make this your home."

Ushiwaka was unable to sleep that night. All the sights and sounds of his new surroundings disquieted him. Even the food tasted strangely.

He was not allowed to go out and grew restless. It was two weeks later when Kichiji, who had not come again since the night he first arrived here, appeared.

"How are you getting on?" he asked Ushiwaka. "Not lonely, are you? The Heiké are keeping a close watch on everyone, so I purposely avoided coming. Don't think I've forgotten you."

Ushiwaka said nothing to this, and Kichiji went on: "Fortunately, I don't think they will be coming around much longer. All the roads, ports, and city gates are closely watched. Those who have had any connections with the Genji until now are suspect, but I foxed them," he laughed. "Who would ever think of searching the gay quarters?"

Ushiwaka still said nothing.

Kichiji remarked: "Of course, sir, I need not remind you of how precious your life is to the Genji. If it were not for you and your half-brother Yoritomo in Izu, the Genji would have nothing to live for. All their hopes are in you."

"Kichiji—when do I start for the northeast?" Ushiwaka suddenly broke in.

"Well, I have to be very careful. I can't take any risks. I'll wait until the Heiké are off their guard. Perhaps spring will be the time for me to accompany you north."

"Spring?"

"Early next year, I should say."

"And before then?"

"It will be safe enough for you here in the capital. To make sure, however, you are to dress up like a girl, and when you're quite used to your disguise, you can go about safely without fear of being recognized. You will stay here until I come back for you."

Kichiji soon after set out for the northeast, promising to return in either February or March. Konno-maru received careful instructions as to what he was to do while Kichiji was away, and Ushiwaka was left in the care of the two sisters.

"I don't want to dress up like a girl," Ushiwaka kept insisting to the two sisters and to Konno-maru, who appeared daily; it was only after much persuading that Ushiwaka finally agreed to having his hair pinned up and knotted as though he were a girl. He wore the bright-colored dress that young dancing-girls wore. His face was carefully powdered and rouged until he could be taken only for a girl. As he grew accustomed to his disguise and the name Rindo (gentian), he began to harass Konno-maru with reproaches.

"Kowaka, you lied to me," he kept repeating. "You haven't yet told me when I am to see my mother. You once said that she was ill, but that isn't so. Asatori told me that she too wants to see me."

Since his flight from Kurama Mountain, Ushiwaka seemed obsessed by the thought of his mother. But Konno-maru tried his best to point out the risks he would be taking. "You must understand that I'm not trying to prevent your seeing her, but the Heiké are guarding the mansion day and night. They are sure you will try to go there, and are on the watch for you."

But Ushiwaka persisted.

"You're going to the northeast, aren't you?"

"No. I must see my mother first."

"I have told you all along that for your mother's sake as well as your own you must not try to see her now."

"First Avenue where she lives is not far from here, is it, Kowaka? Then what is wrong about my wanting to see her?"

"If the Heiké soldiers were not on guard there, there would be nothing to prevent your seeing her."

"You are cruel, Kowaka, not to let me see my mother. I only wish I were a man, and then I would punish the Heiké."

"Well said! If you wish to see your mother, don't forget that that is what you must do first."

"How I hate them—the Heiké!" Ushiwaka often exclaimed with a harsh, intent look.

Ushiwaka, disguised as pretty Rindo, soon became a familiar sight to people living along the willow-fringed canal at Horikawa, where he often walked alone. The two sisters with whom he lived sometimes took him to the markets on Fourth and Fifth avenues. Very soon they were giving him lessons on the drum and flute, and by winter he went regularly to his dancing lessons.

Daijo, a maker of hand-drums who lived close by, had a ten-year-old daughter who came daily to the two sisters for lessons. She was called Shizuka and could perform more skillfully on the drum and flute than Ushiwaka, whom she looked up to as if he were an elder sister.

"Rindo, why don't you become a dancing-girl?" she asked Ushiwaka one day.

"I don't know about that," Ushiwaka replied. "I'm still very clumsy at playing the drum and flute."

"Why not next year, then?"

"Yes, but what about you, Shizuka?"

"I—" Shizuka hesitated, thoughtfully.

"Don't you like dancing-girls?"

"I'm not quite sure."

They were tumbling in the snow one day, forgetting that they must be on their way home, when Ushiwaka suddenly asked:

"Don't you want to come with me to First Avenue?"

"Where is First Avenue?"

"A little way up the river."

Ushiwaka was familiar by now with the shabby mansion on the river; he had gone past it many a time with a beating heart, haunted by the fear that the Heiké guards there would recognize him.

"Rindo! Where are you off to?" Konno-maru exclaimed when he came upon the truants. He knew that Ushiwaka often wandered about First Avenue and he had brought a carriage with him to fetch Ushiwaka home. Ushiwaka's clothes were draggled; he was cold and miserable, and sobbed with disappointment as Konno-maru bundled him and his little companion into the carriage and started for Horikawa. Inside, the two huddled against each other, Shizuka warming Ushiwaka's frozen hands against her cheeks, and Ushiwaka holding her close in his arms, until they soon fell fast asleep.

CHAPTER L

JOURNEY TO THE EAST

ew Year's Day of 1174 was clear and serene; the entire
capital wore a tranquil air. The elaborate ceremonials
at Court were over, and without mishaps. No man
died of hunger on the streets of Kyoto. And never had there been
such peace under the Fujiwara as had lasted now for ten or more
years under the Heiké. There had been no bloody upheavals in all
that time, and the common people believed that they owed this to
Kiyomori.

Such peace notwithstanding, there were sporadic outbursts of vituperation against the Heiké, coming not from the common people, but the aristocrats. The Heiké were slandered for their power, their arrogance, and even their noble lineage. Lately, however, persistent gossip of another kind occupied tongues in the capital. There was talk that the Genji were not completely crushed, and that they were preparing to challenge the Heiké once more. These rumors seemed to have been spread by the monks of Kurama Mountain whenever they came to the capital, and Ushiwaka's disappearance and stories of the Tengu went far to justify these rumors.

The Heiké redoubled their vigilance. Even the gay quarters became suspect, until in February officers arrived from Rokuhara periodically to make a house-to-house search of Horikawa, and agents of the Police Commission were often seen there.

Two or three blossoms had unfolded on the plum tree by Daijo's shop toward noon of a day in February, and the drum-maker called to a passer-by from his workshop:

"Hullo, hullo there! Isn't that you, Kowaka?"

Kowaka retraced his steps and peered in at the threshold.

"You seem busy as usual, Daijo. You're sure I won't be in the way?"

"Sit down for a moment. You can't go by without looking in."

"I was afraid I might be in the way."

". . . By the way, I had something to tell you. I couldn't very well go to Toji's to see you about this, and I was just telling my wife this morning that I hoped you'd come by."

"Eh? Has anything unusual happened?"

"Look here, do you know a man by the name of Serpent?"

"I do."

"You'd better be careful of him."

"Of the Serpent, you say?"

"To tell you the truth, he was here yesterday and told me that there's something unusual about the girl Rindo."

"What! He said that to you?"

"Now listen—you know how Rindo and my daughter Shizuka

are always playing together. Well, the Serpent has been coming here for no reason I can see. He seems to be after something. I made Shizuka promise not to say a thing to him."

"Has this Serpent been putting some odd questions to your little daughter?"

"He's been taking Shizuka aside and telling her that Rindo isn't a girl. He threatened Shizuka, saying that if she didn't tell the truth he'd send the Heiké soldiers after her."

"Hmm? . . . A disagreeable fellow . . . putting ideas into people's heads."

"Kowaka—"

"Yes."

"That's all I wanted to tell you, but I warn you to be careful. Other people as well as the Serpent are apt to notice things."

"Well, Daijo, I'm grateful to you and wouldn't like to get you into trouble. You won't repeat this, I know."

"No fear of it. If I was one to go about gossiping, I wouldn't tell you this."

"Thank you, Daijo. . . . I won't try to tell you anything now. You can guess for yourself," Kowaka said with a deep bow and a proud look that belied his menial position.

Daijo, reaching for his chisel, suddenly smiled. "That's enough now! Such formality won't be popular in the gay quarters, you know," he said lightly, sweeping together some shavings and throwing them onto the fire.

The moon was rising over the Eastern Hills, and the waters of the Kamo River took on the sheen of pearls. The crowds thronging across Gojo Bridge suddenly melted away as the bleakness of a February night set in along the river front. Oblivious of the gathering twilight, however, a small figure continued to lean over the balustrade as though absorbed in watching the waterfowl on the river.

It was Ushiwaka, wrapped in a cloak and wearing black lacquered clogs with high supports, the kind ladies were accustomed to wear. He was carrying a flute in its case and looked for all the world like a young dancing-girl. Only that afternoon the two sisters with whom he stayed had taken him to the market on Fifth Avenue to make some purchases for the Festival of Dolls. It was only a few days now until the 3rd of March, and they had lingered long, looking at the many displays in the stalls. While they were thus strolling, the two sisters met some gentlemen whom they seemed to know rather well, and they soon accepted an invitation to visit their mansions, and had told Ushiwaka to go on home alone. His curiosity got the better of him, however, and he crossed the bridge to Rokuhara, which he had long wanted to see. He wandered about Rokuhara until almost sundown, amazed by its size, the grand houses along the wide avenues, the numberless side-streets lined with tiled houses, the carriages and richly clothed courtiers, and the innumerable warriors who brushed past him as he stood in front of Kiyomori's mansion. This was the flourishing town where his father's enemies lived!

Miserable and lonely, Ushiwaka made his way back, until halfway across the Gojo Bridge, he collapsed weeping against the balustrade. Was this the spot where his father, Yoshitomo, and his brothers met their defeat? How often Konno-maru had told him the story of that fateful day! And as he stood there, staring down into the water, he was aware as he had never been before that he was the son of Yoshitomo of the Genji. Between clenched teeth he murmured: "Father, I am a man now. I am sixteen and your son. I shall never forget to avenge you. That day is not far off."

As Ushiwaka turned away from his musings to resume his walk home, a stranger planted himself in Ushiwaka's path. Ushiwaka tried to slip by, but the man suddenly threw out his arms and ran toward him.

"Wait! Don't move, Rindo!"

"What do you want? Who are you?"

"I?" the man grimaced. "There's not one dancing-girl in the Capital who doesn't know me. I'm called the Serpent—and don't you forget it!"

"That means nothing to me. I'm in a hurry, let me go!"

"Here—" the Serpent clutched at Ushiwaka's cloak convulsively. "I have business with you. You're a boy, aren't you?"

"Of course not. . . . Let me go!"

"Come, I know enough about dancing-girls to see through all your finery!"

"Let me go, I say! I'll scream if you don't!"

"So you think I'm trying to kidnap you, you imp? *I'll* tell you who you are—Ushiwaka!"

" . . . ."

"You've nothing to say to that, eh?"

"I'm no such person, but Rindo—a dancing-girl!"

"A dancing-girl, eh? From Kurama Mountain?—You're Tokiwa's son, or else why should I see you wandering about in the neighborhood of First Avenue!"

The Serpent grasped Ushiwaka by the shoulders in an attempt to march him off in the direction of Rokuhara.

"The Serpent's right, isn't he? Come along with me, now. What are you afraid of, anyway? We're going to my house," the Serpent said and then staggered forward with the cloak in his hands as Ushiwaka suddenly ducked and threw himself flat on the bridge.

"Confound you!" the Serpent exclaimed when Ushiwaka's legs lunged out at his own. In a flash Ushiwaka was on his feet and off.

"Now I know you're Ushiwaka and I'm going to get you!" cried the Serpent, regaining his feet and pursuing him. His footsteps thudded across the bridge as he gained on the small flying figure. There was a yell as he came to the end of the bridge. Something flashed in the moonlight. Everything grew still. The Serpent's headless body tottered forward a few steps and then fell heavily to the ground.

Ushiwaka woke from a sound sleep and stared about him. A huge statue loomed up beside him—up to the rafters. He suddenly remembered the Serpent and their encounter last night.

Ushiwaka's eyes slowly traveled round the barnlike room in which statues, large and small, surrounded him. He recognized Asura, the God of War; the scowling Devas; the Wind and Thunder gods, and even a Kannon, smiling contemplatively.

For an instant he thought he was in a temple treasure-house; then he recalled being brought here and falling asleep. A sound brought him fully awake and he looked up and saw Kowaka getting up from a corner piled with various tools and painting equipment.

"Are you awake, Ushiwaka?" Konno-maru asked.

"You're not calling me 'Rindo' this morning, are you?"

"There's no need for that any more. And you're to call me 'Konno-maru' again."

"What's happened?"

"We're not going back to the gay quarters any more."

"Where are we now?"

"We're in the workroom of a maker of Buddhist images."

"Oh?"

"You might be worried if I don't tell you exactly. Otoami, a disciple of the famous Unkei, lives here. He spent many years in the northeast making images for Hidehira, and that is why Otoami knows Kichiji so well. So you see why you needn't feel anxious about being here."

"Whereabouts is this house?"

"Not far from Shirakawa."

"Then it isn't very far from First Avenue, is it?"

"Ushiwaka—"

"Yes?"

"You had a narrow escape last night, didn't you?"

"Yes, if it hadn't been for you and your sword—"

"I wasn't trying to remind you of that, but I think the Serpent has warned the Heiké about you. It will be dangerous for you to show yourself outside."

"How did you ever get to Gojo Bridge in the nick of time?"

"The two sisters got home and said that they'd left you at the corner of the market on Fifth Avenue. The minute I heard that, I knew you'd be in trouble, for it was only that morning that the drum-maker warned me about you."

Ushiwaka said nothing to this, and Konno-maru went on: "I flew off at once to the neighborhood of First Avenue, and you weren't there. I thought you might by chance still be at Fifth Avenue, and Providence must have guided me to Gojo Bridge at the time that I did."

"And sometime very late last night we came here to hide, didn't we?"

"Yes, and did you sleep well?"

"I did, but I'm afraid of what may happen to the two sisters."

"Kichiji has told them what they are to do if there's trouble. I warned them last night, so they may already have left Horikawa."

"Where have they gone?"

"They probably will hide in the country and later go to the northeast. Kichiji will see to that. In the meantime, however, you are in great danger—at least until we reach the east."

"Am I to go to the northeast soon?"

"As things are now, it would be better for you not to stay in the capital much longer. Kichiji has also written that he will be here for you very soon."

"And before that?"

"You are to hide here for several days. You will have to be quite patient, until Kichiji arrives for you, but it won't be for very long now."

On waking each morning Ushiwaka's eyes sought the high window of the workshop, through which he could only see the sky. Then he would sigh to himself. "Oh, to be off! How much longer am I to wait here?"

He fretted with impatience at the monotony of each day spent among the grotesque images. Then one night in March, when the plum trees were in full bloom, a furious storm arose and beat upon the roof. He woke to the sound of a roaring wind. His pillow was wet and he heard a steady dripping from the statues around him. He sat up and listened. All the furies of nature seemed to have been unloosed. Konno-maru, who had left the workshop that evening with Otoami, had not returned yet, and Ushiwaka was alone. The thought then came to him that this was the night for him to do what he had planned for so long. He sprang from his bed and felt for the door. It was locked. Konno-maru or Otoami had secured it from outside, leaving him a prisoner here! All his instincts rebelled against the idea of being a prisoner. Konno-maru, the Tengu—all of them—kept telling him that everything depended on Kichiji. What did he care for Kichiji anyway! Who was Kichiji to tell him what he should or should not do? Now was the time to show Kichiji what he thought of him, but he would see his mother first. . . .

Ushiwaka climbed up on a statue and reached toward the window. The wind and rain lashed at his face. He took a deep breath and leaped into space. It was completely dark everywhere as he started running in the direction of First Avenue.

The wind tore at the eaves and shook the shutters as it shrieked about the old mansion. Tokiwa longed for it to become light, for the roaring of the river set her nerves on edge and kept her awake. She pulled the bedclothes up over her ears to shut out the wind's howling. This time she was sure she heard a grating sound at the end of the hall. It was repeated again and again; Tokiwa finally pushed back the coverlets and turned over in bed toward Yomogi.

Yesterday was the 3rd of March—the Festival of Dolls—and Tokiwa had arranged some paper and clay dolls in her room. Yomogi had come to call on her, bringing a spray of peach blossoms and some sweetmeats she had prepared herself. They had talked until evening, when the storm forced Yomogi to stay the night.

Yomogi was awake, too, squirming restlessly.

"Yomogi—what can that sound be?"

"It's an odd sound. It couldn't be the wind. I've been bothered by it, too. I'll go and see," Yomogi replied, getting out of bed and lighting a lamp. The flame flickered wildly. "It's strange how the wind keeps rushing through the house."

Her shadow undulated crazily as Yomogi stepped out into the hall, holding up the light.

Tokiwa sat up in bed. Yomogi, meanwhile, made her way down the long passage; she stopped at each turning, where the darkness seemed to rush at her eerily; the sound of rain dripping suddenly made her turn; a door facing on the river was open and a figure stood in the dim square of the doorway.

"Are you one of the servants?" the figure asked.

"Yes," Yomogi replied. "I was spending the night with my former mistress."

As she went toward the open door, the lamp flickered and went out.

Yomogi realized that it was one of the Heiké soldiers who stood guard here every night.

"Did you see anyone?" he asked.

"No, no one," Yomogi replied.

"It must have been the wind after all, but it's strange how the door has been lifted off its hinges."

"Yes, everything about here seems to be falling to pieces."

"That's true. What are you doing up at this hour?"

"I couldn't sleep because of all this racket—the wind blowing through the house."

"But the storm's almost over."

"This is a bad night for you out there, isn't it?"

"Not an easy life, I can tell you. Besides there have been strange goings-on at Fifth Avenue and Horikawa lately, and we have to keep our eyes open."

"What happened at Fifth Avenue and Horikawa?"

"All this talk about Tengu demons and the mischief they're up to. . . . Housebreakers more likely, but I'm not supposed to be gossiping like this. Better lock the door and get to bed. It'll be day soon."

Yomogi listened to the soldier's departing footsteps; then, setting the door in its place, she groped her way back to her room. Suddenly her blood ran cold as something warm and soft brushed against her. She was about to scream, but steadied herself. "Who —who's there?" she asked.

Something stirring by the wall startled her and caused her to draw back.

"Please—" it said, and threw its arms about Yomogi.

She felt a cheek against her own and then the grip tightened. "Are you my mother?" came a hoarse whisper.

Yomogi gasped. "Who—who is it?"

"Ushiwaka—it's Ushiwaka, Mother!"

"No, no! I'm not your mother. Not your mother," Yomogi repeated, struggling to free herself. Then something struck her shoulder, and she reeled. Wrenching herself free, she ran down the hall.

"My lady, my lady—Ushiwaka!" she exclaimed breathlessly into Tokiwa's ear.

"Yes?" Tokiwa replied quietly.

"Wait, my lady, until I bring a light."

"No, Yomogi, not now. It will only bring the guards."

"That's true, but—a very small light?"

"Not even that. . . . I wonder what it will be like to see my son again. No—the thought frightens me. It wasn't a dream after all, and he's actually here!"

". . . ."

"Ushiwaka, where are you?"

"Here, here I am! Here, Mother!"

There was a sound of sobbing in the dark.

"Ushiwaka, how you've grown!"

"Yes—"

"My letters and messages reached you on Kurama Mountain, didn't they?"

"They did."

"What can I say to you, now that you are sixteen this spring, a man? If you were still at the monastery, there would be some things I would want to tell you as your mother. They are my prayers for my son. . . . Yet no matter how fervent one's prayers, they rarely are answered. You call me *Mother*, but I did so little for you."

"No, no—" Ushiwaka protested, clinging to Tokiwa and burying his face in her lap. "It was not your fault that it was so. The Heiké—Kiyomori is the guilty one!"

Tokiwa caught her breath sharply; her pale face drooped forward against Ushiwaka's shoulder, and he lifted his face to hers in the dark, saying:

"Mother, that's true, isn't it? I tricked them by escaping. I'm glad that I did it. You hoped that I would become a monk, but I am Yoshitomo's son and a warrior. How is it possible for me to be anything else? There is no refuge anywhere from the fret of existence. Where indeed is there such a life? What difference is there between the life here and that in the remotest temple where men fawn on the Heiké, fear and obey them?"

". . . ."

"Forgive me, Mother. I may be going against your wishes. But I am Yoshitomo's son and cannot be anything else than a warrior. I must see that the name of Genji is honored once more. I shall soon be a man. Kiyomori's triumph will not last long."

Tokiwa listened to Ushiwaka in great agony of mind. He had heard only of how the Genji had been wronged, but she alone knew that Ushiwaka owed his life to Kiyomori of the Heiké. Nor had she the right to tell him this. It would remain her secret.

Yomogi could not sit still because of her anxiety and kept stealing out to the hall to make sure that no one was about. The storm had spent itself, and a faint light was filling the sky. The far-off crowing of a cock increased her agitation.

"Isn't it about time to go? It's almost dawn," she whispered to Tokiwa from the hallway. There was only a silence. In the faint light that filtered through the narrow slits over the shutters Yomogi saw Ushiwaka lying still in his mother's arms, as though asleep. She hesitated to disturb them and turned away for a while. Then she whispered once more, insistently:

"My lady—the dawn."

Ushiwaka sprang away from his mother and shook himself.

"It is time for me to go. . . . When I return I shall not fail to come with a retinue of Genji warriors to fetch you."

"No, better than that—"

"What did you say, Mother?"

"Only take good care of yourself. That is all I ask."

"That I shall. Keep well, Mother, until that day we meet again."

"That is all I now have to live for, Ushiwaka. Be warned that in righting wrong and putting down the arrogant, you too may follow the example of those you most deplore; others then will rise to humble you, and the fearful and foolish history of bloodshed will go on repeating itself forever. As a warrior, remember to love and protect the oppressed and weak, that your name may be honored ever more."

"I understand, Mother. I shall never forget what you say."

"How more can you honor your father, Yoshitomo, than by being a noble and chivalrous warrior? . . . Look, Yomogi—the dawn!"

"My young master," Yomogi said, wringing her hands, "how will you leave?"

"Don't be alarmed. I'll go the way I came last night."

"But you're wet to the skin! How can you go that way?"

"I never had anything as good as this to wear when I was at the monastery. I don't mind the wind or rain, but—" Ushiwaka suddenly turned to Tokiwa with a pleading air—"give me one of your dolls as a keepsake," he said, pointing to a doll, which his mother quickly handed him. Ushiwaka smiled, then quickly sped down the hall, leaped from the balustrade of the open gallery to the ground, and disappeared among the trees. A moment later he appeared on top of the wall overlooking the Kamo River. There he stood to look back at his mother for an instant, and then was gone.

Ushiwaka picked his way up the turgid shallows of the river, splashing through the water where it was deep. He was free now. He depended on no one now. Konno-maru, Kichiji, the Chieftain Hidehira—none of them mattered any more to him. He had only himself to rely on. He stood still in the middle of the river and looked about him; the sun was just rising behind the Eastern Hills. He looked back once more toward the mansion on First Avenue, when he heard a shout. There it was again, somewhere from the riverbank. He looked up and smiled as he saw a figure running toward him. It was Konno-maru, straining and panting as he ran.

"My young master, what happened to you?" he managed to say as he staggered up to Ushiwaka and gripped his arm until Ushiwaka winced. "You don't realize how worried we were about you. I brought Kichiji back with me and found you gone."

"Has Kichiji come back?"

"Even Kichiji is quite a state. Where in the world have you been?"

"I went to see my mother."

"What!—your mother?"

"Was there anything wrong in that?"

"It was very risky."

"That's because you didn't keep your promise."

"You should not have been so thoughtless. What if something had happened to you then?"

"Yes, that's all you keep saying to me—that my safety matters more than anything else—more than my seeing my mother. Do you think I'd feel that my life was worth anything if I couldn't see her?"

"I'll say nothing more about that. In any case, Kichiji is frantic about you. We'd better hurry back to Otoami's house."

As they came in sight of Otoami's house, they saw Kichiji leading a pack-horse out by a rear gate. He was unaccompanied by his usual retinue of servants and appeared as though he were starting on a journey.

"We're leaving immediately, sir," he said to Ushiwaka in a peremptory tone. "You'll ride the horse, since you're a child." Then he turned to Konno-maru. "Konno-maru, we part here as you promised. I'll be responsible for Ushiwaka. You can be sure he's quite safe with me."

"I'm sure you'll be very careful, but it's a long trip, and Ushiwaka is inexperienced, so you'll have to see that nothing happens to him."

"You need not worry in the least. My life depends on seeing him safely to his destination. There won't be much to fear when we get past Mount Ashigara. The rest will be easy."

Ushiwaka turned in his saddle to Konno-maru. "Konno-maru, where are *you* going?" he asked dejectedly.

"I will go back to the hills and tell my comrades that you have left safely. We promised Kichiji that we would stay behind when you left the capital with him. The Chieftain Fujiwara Hidehira will look after you. Some day when you are grown and the Heiké are humbled, we shall all meet once more in the east."

Ushiwaka's head was bent as he blinked back his tears. "Yes, Konno-maru, we shall surely see each other again. Some day you will be rewarded for your loyalty. Tell this to the others too."

Kichiji drew the horse round by its reins. "Well, Konno-maru, we'll meet again soon. Good-by, good-by!"

As they made their way toward the hills beyond Shirakawa, the horse broke into a trot as though eager to cross Shiga Pass, which led east.

Historical Background of The Heiké Story *and Its Author*

The capital of Japan until a short time ago was not Tokyo but Kyoto, the seat of the Imperial Court from A.D. 794 to 1868, and the flourishing center of Japanese civilization. Hemmed in on the north and east by mountains, the Kamo River flowing along its eastern boundary, Kyoto was the setting for a government by aristocrats from the time it was settled until the beginning of the twelfth century. Countless temples, pagodas, and shrines grew up on the thickly wooded hills and mountaintops or in their many valleys; a number of imposing gates, among them the Rashomon Gate on the south, gave access to the rectangular-shaped capital and its principal avenues, intersecting at regular intervals. Beyond the city was the pleasant countryside, with its many scenic spots, favored by the Court for its outings, and several racecourses in sight of the Kamo River.

At about the time the capital was moved from Nara to Kyoto, the central government had won control over western Japan as well as the eastern provinces as far as the modern Tokyo, and the aristocratic Fujiwara clan were beginning to assume a dominant role in state affairs. By evolving a system of rule that centered in the emperor, and by filling all the important positions of state, the Fujiwara soon made themselves the rulers. To seal their bond with the imperial family they gave their fairest daughters in marriage to the emperors and princes, and none but the offspring of these alliances ascended the throne. The Fujiwara, furthermore, kept power in their hands by forcing the abdication of an emperor whenever they saw fit and replaced him by a Fujiwara grandson. We even have at one time an example of a child-emperor ruling while two abdicated sovereigns—an ex-emperor and a cloistered emperor—were also holding imperial state.

As the authority of the central government spread to the farthest provinces, so did the wealth of the Fujiwara increase, and the life of the aristocrats took on a luxury and profusion unknown before. The arts flourished and the Fujiwara were the patrons of the literate and highly literary society that developed round the Court. And it was during their ascendancy early in the eleventh century that the *Tale of Genji*, a novel by a court lady, was written, revealing the curiously elegant and urbane life of an aristocracy that had reached the extremes of decadence.

Less than a century after the *Tale of Genji* appeared, the end of Fujiwara supremacy was in sight. As their influence waned, there developed among them a struggle for power in which the question of imperial succession created a state of conflict that became felt in every stratum of society, and in the growing disorder some emperors even attempted to restore authority to the throne.

Meanwhile, the Buddhist church, which had flourished under Fujiwara patronage and acquired great wealth in the form of tax-free estates, had grown corrupt. The great temples and monasteries trained their priests and monks to fight, maintained armies of mercenaries to protect their acquisitions, and flouted the orders of the government. Most powerful of these temples was Enryakuji on Mount Hiei, northeast of the capital.

Crime, disorder, and discontent were rampant in the capital by the beginning of the twelfth century. The Fujiwara, who now had no authority beyond that which they could back with force, were compelled to range the Heiké or the Genji clans on their sides. These two military families, offshoots of the imperial house, had until then managed the great Fujiwara estates in the far provinces or were employed as guards at the Court; they were called in now to play off one Fujiwara faction against another, to quell civil disturbances, to repulse the warlike monks who entered Kyoto and threatened the authorities, or to intervene in the armed clashes between the great temples and monasteries.

By the middle of the century a distinct military class had appeared, and the Heiké, under their young chieftain, Kiyomori, put an end to Fujiwara dominance as well as gained ascendancy over their rivals, the Genji. Though the Heiké had replaced the Fujiwara, Kiyomori failed to evolve a new system of government and ruled as did his predecessors. This in time led to a struggle for power between the Heiké and the Genji, and in the last quarter of the century the Heiké were overborne by the Genji.

But even the triumph of the Genji did not last long, nor did it end the clashes that went on in various parts of Japan, for by the early 1300's the Genji in their turn were brought low by disaffected elements in their midst. And while this went on, the emperor and the aristocrats attempted to regain power from the warring military clans.

All Japan was in conflict when the sixteenth century opened. Local war-lords in every part of the land were fighting each other until the entire country was in the throes of a devastating civil war. Not until the close of the century when a general, Ieyasu of the Tokugawa, appeared was there peace. He was the first of a line of military dictators who administered Japan with an iron rule that lasted for two hundred and fifty years—until 1868, when a successful combination between the Emperor, some aristocrats, and several military clans once more restored authority to the throne. This did not, however, put an end to the unequal balance of power between the elements that had made the Restoration possible, and the disequilibrium persisted until 1945 when Japan was defeated in the Pacific War.

As we look back over the history of Japan we discover how closely linked the modern era is with the twelfth century. The outlook of the Japanese today is still deeply permeated by the teachings of *Bushido*, the warrior's code of ethics, which originated among the military caste. The stories of medieval heroes and heroines, which delight Japanese children even now, are those which grew up around the historical figures of that period. The lyric drama, Noh, the popular Kabuki, and the many legends handed down by word of mouth, all have been inspired by twelfth-century men and women and become the literary heritage of the Japanese people. It can almost be said that without some knowledge of that century our understanding of Japan and the many branches of her art is incomplete.

Of the many sources that throw light on that period, the *Heiké Monogatari* (the *Tale of the Heiké*), an epic composed early in the thirteenth century, not long after the defeat of the Heiké, survives as a document of historical importance and as one of the great literary achievements of its time. It cannot be doubted that the fall of the Heiké made a deep impression upon the people, since this long poem recounting the tragic end of the Heiké was carried to every corner of Japan by itinerant ballad-singers, who chanted it to the accompaniment of the lute, and for centuries after it was first sung remained one of the best-loved romances of the Japanese, who made its heroes their idols.

Mr. Yoshikawa began writing *The Heiké Story* soon after the end of the Pacific War, when the tragic aftermath was a powerful reminder of what the *Heiké Monogatari* had related seven centuries before, and his theme is the futility and degradation of war, the fatuity of the lust for power. The author makes Kiyomori one of the principal actors, but *The Heiké Story*, unlike its prototype, is more than a chronicle of the deeds of warriors and princes, for the story is carried beyond the events recorded in the medieval epic, and the defeat of the Heiké is made to take place after Kiyomori's death, when a Genji chieftain, Yoritomo, appears on the stage to play an important role as he once did in history.

The author introduces a host of historical figures as well as imaginary ones in his novel, but none of them is the hero in the ordinary sense. History, or the irresistible cycle of events, is the real protagonist of *The Heiké Story*, sweeping everything before it, and the greatest men are but figures rescued for a short space from the vast stream of time, and Mr. Yoshikawa writes in the strain of those lines with which the ancient epic begins: "The temple bell echoes the impermanence of all things. The colors of the flowers testify to the truth that those who flourish must decay. Pride lasts but a little while, like a dream on a spring night. Before long the mighty are cast down, and they are as dust before the wind."

For his particular interpretation of history in *The Heiké Story*, Mr. Yoshikawa studied not only the literature of the twelfth and thirteenth centuries but diaries, letters, chronicles, and picture scrolls, which provided him with a rich source of material and authentic detail in the telling of his story.

The author occupies a unique position among Japanese novelists writing today. Where most, if not all, have at some time in their careers come under the influence of European literature, particularly of Russian and French writers, Mr. Yoshikawa, because of the circumstances of his early life, had no opportunity for becoming acquainted with the literature of the West even in translations. His reading in youth—and he read voluminously—was confined to the classics of Japan, ancient and medieval, which he found in lending libraries. Consequently his background and technique as a writer have been shaped exclusively by the traditions of Japanese classical literature on which he draws entirely for his models and sources.

The Heiké Story, which Mr. Yoshikawa began writing in 1951, is not yet finished, but more than two thirds of this monumental work has been completed and has appeared in book form. It is now a best-seller, with an ever-widening circle of readers, and is acclaimed by critics as a landmark in modern Japanese literature.

A few words need to be added here regarding the translation. It would be more accurate to call it an English version, since with the author's generous consent *The Heiké Story* has been modified considerably for Western readers. Much that is significant and of great interest to a Japanese audience familiar with the historical setting has been omitted in translation; entire chapters have been condensed and a large number of sub-plots and subsidiary characters entirely left out. This translation is therefore only a partial one and fails to do justice to the complexity and diversity of the original. None the less, it is the translator's fervent wish that *The Heiké Story* will give Western readers an opportunity to share some of the delight that it gives readers here and also provide a diverting introduction to Japan and the Japanese.

Other Titles in the Tuttle Library

Philosophy and Religion

THREE AGES OF ZEN: Samurai, Feudal, and Modern *by Trevor Leggett*

A FIRST ZEN READER *compiled and translated by Trevor Leggett*

A FLOWER DOES NOT TALK: Zen Essays *by Abbot Zenkei Shibayama of the Nanzenji Monastery*

A SECOND ZEN READER: The Tiger's Cave & Translations of Other Zen Writings *by Trevor Leggett*

AN INVITATION TO PRACTICE ZEN *by Albert Low*

BUSHIDO: The Soul of Japan *by Inazo Nitobe*

SHINTO: The Kami Way *by Sokyo Ono in collaboration with William P. Woodard*

SQUARE SUN SQUARE MOON: A Collection of Sweet Sour Essays *by Paul Reps*

THE IRON COW OF ZEN *by Albert Low*

ZEN AND JAPANESE CULTURE *by Daisetz T. Suzuki*

ZEN AND THE WAYS *by Trevor Leggett*

ZEN ART FOR MEDITATION *by Stewart W. Holmes and Chimyo Horioka*

ZEN COMICS: Books One, Two *by Ioanna Salajan*

ZEN DICTIONARY *by Ernest Wood*

ZEN FLESH, ZEN BONES: A Collection of Zen and Pre-Zen Writings *by Paul Reps*

ZEN MUNCHKINS: Little Wisdoms *by D. T. Munda*

ZEN TELEGRAMS: 79 Picture Poems *by Paul Reps*

ZEN WAY—JESUS WAY *by Tucker N. Callaway*

Language Books

CONCISE ENGLISH-TAGALOG DICTIONARY *by Jose Villa Panganiban*

A HANDBOOK OF JAPANESE USAGE *by Francis G. Drohan*

A REFERENCE GRAMMAR OF KOREAN *by Samuel E. Martin*

BEGINNING KOREAN *by Samuel E. Martin and Young-Sook C. Lee*

EASY THAI *by Gordon H. Allison*

JAPANESE MADE EASY *by Tazuko Ajiro Monane*

JAPANESE WORD-AND-PHRASE BOOK FOR TOURISTS *compiled by Eldora S. Thorlin*

KANSAI JAPANESE: The Language of Osaka, Kyoto, and Western Japan *by Peter Tse*

KOREAN IN A HURRY *by Samuel E. Martin*

LAO FOR BEGINNERS *by Tatsuo Hoshino and Russell Marcus*

NIHONGO PERAPERA: A User's Guide to Japanese Onomatopoeia *by Susan Millington*

READING AND WRITING CHINESE by *William McNaughton*

READING JAPANESE by *Eleanor Harz Jorden and Hamako Ito Chaplin*

THE CHINESE LANGUAGE FOR BEGINNERS by *Lee Cooper*

TUTTLE'S CONCISE INDONESIAN DICTIONARY by *A.L.N. Kramer, Sr.*

Literature

A CHIME OF WINDBELLS: A Year of Japanese Haiku in English Verse *translated by Harold Stewart*

A HUNDRED VERSES OF OLD JAPAN: Being a Translation of the Hyaku-nin-isshu *translated by William Porter*

A LATE CHRYSANTHEMUM: Twenty-one Stories from the Japanese *selected and translated by Lane Dunlop*

A NET OF FIREFLIES: Japanese Haiku and Haiku Paintings *translated by Harold Stewart*

ANTHOLOGY OF MODERN JAPANESE POETRY *translated and compiled by Edith M. Shiffert and Yuki Sawa*

BOTCHAN by *Soseki Natsume, translated by Umeji Sasaki*

CLASSIC HAIKU: A Master's Selection by *Yuzuru Miura*

CRACKLING MOUNTAIN AND OTHER STORIES by *Osamu Dazai, translated by James O'Brien*

EVERYDAY LIFE IN TRADITIONAL JAPAN by *Charles J. Dunn*

FIRES ON THE PLAIN by *Shohei Ooka, translated by Ivan Morris*

FIVE WOMEN WHO LOVED LOVE *by Saikaku Ihara, translated by William Theodore de Bary*

GENJI MONOGATARI *by Murasaki Shikibu, translated by Kencho Suematsu*

HAIKU IN ENGLISH *by Harold G. Henderson*

HARP OF BURMA *by Michio Takeyama, translated by Howard Hibbett*

I AM A CAT: Volumes 1, 2, 3 *by Soseki Natsume, translated by Aiko Ito and Graeme Wilson*

JAPANESE TALES OF MYSTERY AND IMAGINATION *by Edogawa Rampo, translated by James B. Harris*

MAX DANGER: The Adventures of an Expat in Tokyo *by Robert J. Collins*

RASHOMON AND OTHER STORIES *by Ryunosuke Akutagawa, translated by Takashi Kojima*

ROMAJI DIARIES AND SAD TOYS *by Takuboku Ishikawa, translated by Sanford Goldstein and Seishi Shinoda*

SHANK'S MARE: Japan's Great Comic Novel of Travel and Ribaldry *by Ikku Jippensha, translated by Thomas Satchell*

SENRYU: Poems of the People *compiled and illustrated by J. C. Brown*

SHIOKARI PASS *by Ayako Miura, translated by Bill and Sheila Fearnehough*

THE FLOATING WORLD OF JAPANESE FICTION *by Howard Hibbett*

THE GOSSAMER YEARS : The Diary of a Noblewoman of Heian Japan *translated by Edward Seidensticker*

THE HEIKE STORY *by Eiji Yoshikawa, translated by Uenaka Uramatsu*

Martial Arts

With little more than a primary-school education, **Eiji Yoshikawa** wrote a number of best-selling novels, of which *The Heiké Story* is the most famous. Credited with greatly elevating popular fiction, he was the first writer of such work to be awarded the Order of Culture.